West's

ANNOTATED

INDIANA CODE

Under Arrangement of the Official

Indiana Code

Title 6

Taxation

6–3–3 to 6–6–4.1

 **WEST GROUP**

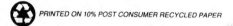 PRINTED ON 10% POST CONSUMER RECYCLED PAPER

PREFACE

Indiana Code, Title 6, Taxation, contains basic revenue measures of the state of Indiana and includes provisions pertaining to property taxes; gross income tax, gross retail and use taxes, local taxation, and tax administration.

All acts through the 1999 First Regular Session of the 111th Indiana General Assembly are included in this volume.

OFFICIAL CLASSIFICATION AND NUMBERING OF LAWS

The classification and arrangement of the law in West's Annotated Indiana Code, Title 6, is that of the Official Indiana Code as amended through 1999. A citation to West's Annotated Indiana Code is equivalent to a citation to the other. The section headings, however, have generally been editorially supplied.

MULTIPLE AMENDMENTS

In those instances in which the same section is amended more than once and there is uncertainty as to the effective law, until remedial legislation is enacted, the text of the section is set forth reflecting the effect of each amendment separately with appropriate notes.

DUPLICATE CITATIONS

Where different new sections have been assigned the same Indiana Code citation by separate acts, the text of such sections are set forth with each accompanied by a note alerting the reader to the existence of the other. Citations to such sections include a reference to the Public Law number to avoid ambiguity.

HISTORICAL AND STATUTORY NOTES

Editorially prepared historical and statutory notes explain alterations in and additions to the text of the law. In addition, unclassified sections of a law are set out under the section or sections of Title 6 affected.

COMPARATIVE LAWS

Citations to corresponding or similar laws in other states dealing with the same subject matter appear under various sections where they will be of aid to the busy practitioner in obtaining comparative statutory material and authorities from other jurisdictions.

PREFACE

CONSTITUTIONAL PROVISIONS

Select provisions of the Constitution of the State of Indiana have been set out as a separate feature following the text of various sections of the Indiana Code where appropriate.

CROSS REFERENCES

There is an obvious relationship among the various sections of Title 6 and Title 6 is interrelated with the Indiana Code as a whole. To enable full research, time-saving cross references to related or qualifying constitutional and statutory provisions are provided.

ADMINISTRATIVE CODE REFERENCES

References have been made, where appropriate, to pertinent administrative rules and regulations published in the official Indiana Administrative Code.

LAW REVIEW AND JOURNAL COMMENTARIES

Informative articles and discussions in various Indiana Law Reviews and other Indiana legal periodicals are brought to the attention of the user by references under the sections to which they are pertinent. As legal articles and commentaries develop in the future they will be noted in the supplement to this volume.

LIBRARY REFERENCES

An important feature is the library references providing citations to the Key Numbers (☞) of the Indiana Digest and the other digests in the American Digest System, to Corpus Juris Secundum (C.J.S.), to Indiana Law Encyclopedia (I.L.E.) and to pertinent Indiana Practice volumes. These references afford quick access to the total law of Indiana on a given subject as well as to that of all other jurisdictions.

UNITED STATES CODE ANNOTATED

Editorial references to U.S.C.A. are included to alert the user to applicable federal law.

UNITED STATES SUPREME COURT REFERENCES

This feature specially annotates, in alphabetical order by subject, pertinent references to leading decisions of the United States Supreme Court, regardless of the geographical origins of the cases.

PREFACE

JUDICIAL CONSTRUCTIONS OR NOTES OF DECISIONS

The annotations or judicial constructions of Title 6 contained in this volume cover and include reported decisions in the following:

North Eastern Reporter, Second Series ----------------------- 721 N.E.2d 158
Indiana Reports --- 275 Ind.*
Indiana Appellate Decisions --- 182 Ind.App.*
Supreme Court Reporter -- 120 S.Ct. 630
United States Reports --- 521 U.S. (part)
Lawyers' Edition, Second Series ---------------------------- 146 L.Ed.2d (part)
Federal Reporter, Third Series --- 197 F.3d 511
Federal Supplement, Second Series ------------------------ 70 F.Supp.2d 1368
Federal Rules Decisions --- 189 F.R.D. 499
Bankruptcy Reporter -- 242 B.R. 113
Federal Claims Reporter --- 45 Fed.Cl. 339
Opinions of the Attorney General ---------------------- Op.Atty.Gen. No. 98–08
Other Standard Reports
* Discontinued.

The judicial constructions and opinions of the attorney general relevant to each provision are grouped thereunder by subject matter under descriptive headings or catchlines. These catchlines are numbered and alphabetically indexed. Since the same numbers under the same arrangement will be used in supplementary Pocket Parts and Pamphlets, the user will be able to locate readily the later decisions construing a particular point of law.

All citations of these constructions give the full name of each case, all standard reporters in which the case may be found, and a complete case history.

INDEX

A complete and exhaustive alphabetical descriptive-word Index to Title 6 covers the text in detail with precise as well as comprehensive references.

ANCILLARY RESEARCH AIDS

Other research aids of value include tables of contents, tables of comparable or uniform laws and analyses of articles, chapters and sections.

Disposition tables and references in the notes of the repealed sections of Title 6 indicate the new sections of Title 6 where the parallel subject matter may now be found.

PAMPHLETS AND POCKET PARTS

West's Annotated Indiana Code includes, along with its many dependable features, a supplementary system of current Pamphlets and annual cumulative Pocket Parts. This system assures the fastest possible availability of the laws and judicial constructions.

THE PUBLISHER

April, 2000

*

V

WESTLAW ELECTRONIC
RESEARCH GUIDE

WESTLAW, Computer Assisted Legal Research

WESTLAW is part of the research system provided by West Group. With WESTLAW, you find the same quality and integrity that you have come to expect from West books. For the most current and comprehensive legal research, combine the strengths of West books and WESTLAW.

WESTLAW Adds to Your Library

Whether you wish to expand or update your research, WESTLAW can help. For instance, WESTLAW is the most current source for case law, including slip opinions and unreported decisions. In addition to case law, the online availability of statutes, statutory indexes, legislation, court rules and orders, administrative materials, looseleaf publications, texts, periodicals, news and business information makes WESTLAW an important asset to any library. Check the online WESTLAW Directory or the print *WESTLAW Database Directory* for a list of available databases and services. Following is a brief description of some of the capabilities that WESTLAW offers.

Natural Language Searching

You can now search most WESTLAW databases using WIN®, the revolutionary Natural Language search method. As an alternative to formulating a query using terms and connectors, WIN allows you to simply enter a description of your research issue in plain English:

> What is the government's obligation to warn military
> personnel of the danger of past exposure to radiation?

WESTLAW then retrieves the set of documents that have the highest statistical likelihood of matching your description.

Retrieving a Specific Document

When you know the citation to a case or statute that is not in your library, use the Find service to retrieve the document on WESTLAW. Access Find and type a citation like the following:

> find 181 ne2d 520
> find in st 25–1–9–15

WESTLAW GUIDE

Updating Your Research

You can use WESTLAW to update your research in many ways:

- Retrieve cases citing a particular statute.

- Update a state statute by accessing the Update service from the displayed statute using the jump marker.

- Retrieve newly enacted legislation by searching in the appropriate legislative service database.

- Retrieve cases not yet reported by searching in case law databases.

- Read the latest U.S. Supreme Court opinions within an hour of their release.

- Update West digests by searching with topic and key numbers.

Determining Case History and Retrieving Citing Cases

KeyCite^{TM}: Cases and other legal materials listed in KeyCite Scope can be researched through West Group's KeyCite service on WESTLAW. Use KeyCite to check citations for form, parallel references, prior and later history, and comprehensive citator information, including citations to other decisions and secondary materials.

Additional Information

For more detailed information or assistance, contact your WESTLAW Account Representative or call 1–800–REF–ATTY (1–800–733–2889).

TABLE OF CONTENTS

TITLE 6
TAXATION

Section Analysis, see beginning of each Chapter

TABLE OF CONTENTS

TABLE OF CONTENTS

TABLE OF CONTENTS

Index, see volume containing end of Title 6,
Taxation

TABLE OF TITLES
INDIANA CODE

*

ABBREVIATIONS

A.B.A.J. ------------------- American Bar Association Journal
Art. ------------------------ Article
Banking L.J. ------------ Banking Law Journal
Black ---------------------- Black's Reports, U.S.
Blackf. -------------------- Blackford Reports
c. ---------------------------- Chapter of Act
C.A. ----------------------- United States Court of Appeals Reports
C.C.A. --------------------- United States Circuit Courts of Appeals
                                    Reports
C.J.S. ---------------------- Corpus Juris Secundum
Ch. ------------------------- Chapter
Cl. -------------------------- Clause
Com.L.J. ------------------ Commercial Law Journal
Const. --------------------- Constitution
D.C. ----------------------- United States District Court
Eff. ------------------------- Effective
Emerg. eff. --------------- Emergency effective
F. ---------------------------- Federal Reporter
Fed.Cas.No. ------------- Federal Cases
Fed.Cl. -------------------- Federal Claims Reporter
F.2d ----------------------- Federal Reporter, Second Series
F.3d ----------------------- Federal Reporter, Third Series
F.R.D. --------------------- Federal Rules Decisions
F.Supp. ------------------- Federal Supplement
Gav. & H.Rev.St. ----- Gavin and Hord's Revised Statutes
How. ---------------------- Howard's Reports, U.S.
IC -------------------------- Indiana Code
I.L.E. ---------------------- Indiana Law Encyclopedia
Ind. ----------------------- Indiana Reports
Ind.App. ----------------- Indiana Appellate Court Reports
Ind.L.J. ------------------- Indiana Law Journal
Ind.L.Rev. --------------- Indiana Law Review
☞ (Key Number) ----- Indiana Digest and other units of the American
                                    Digest System
L.Ed. ---------------------- United States Reports, Lawyers' Edition
L.Ed.2d ------------------- United States Reports, Lawyers' Edition,
                                    Second Series
N.E. ----------------------- North Eastern Reporter
N.E.2d -------------------- North Eastern Reporter, Second Series
No. ------------------------ Number
Notre Dame L.Rev. -- Notre Dame Law Review
Op.Atty.Gen. ----------- Opinions Attorney General

ABBREVIATIONS

Par.	Paragraph
PEB	Permanent Editorial Board for the Uniform Commercial Code
Pet.	Peters Reports, U.S.
P.L.	Public Law
Res Gestae	Res Gestae, Indiana State Bar Association Journal
s.	Section of Act
Sec.	Section of Act
SEC.	Section of Act
Section	Section of Code
Smith	Smith's Reports
S.Ct.	Supreme Court Reporter
(ss)	Special Session
Subsec.	Subsection
Subd.	Subdivision
U.C.C.L.J.	Uniform Commercial Code Law Journal
U.L.A.	Uniform Laws Annotated
U.S.	United States Reports
U.S.C.A.	United States Code Annotated
Val.U.L.Rev.	Valparaiso University Law Review
Wall.	Wallace's Reports, U.S.
Wheat.	Wheaton's Reports, U.S.
Wils.	Wilson Superior Court Reports

EFFECTIVE DATES OF ACTS

CONSTITUTIONAL PROVISIONS

Const. Art. 1, § 25, provides:

"No law shall be passed, the taking effect of which shall be made to depend upon any authority, except as provided in this Constitution."

Const. Art. 4, § 28, provides:

"No act shall take effect, until the same shall have been published and circulated in the several counties of the State, by authority, except in cases of emergency, which emergency shall be declared in the preamble, or in the body, of the law."

STATUTORY PROVISIONS

IC 1–1–1–9 provides:

"Because an emergency exists, the Indiana Code takes effect January 21, 1976." *As amended by P.L.1–1991, SEC.2, emerg. eff. April 23, 1991.*

IC 1–1–3–1 provides:

"It shall be the duty of the several clerks of circuit courts in this state, immediately on the receipt of the laws of any session as provided for by IC 2–6–1.5–5, to transmit to the governor a certificate stating the day when such laws were so received." *As amended by Acts 1978, P.L.3, SEC.1, eff. Jan. 1, 1979.*

IC 1–1–3–2 provides:

"So soon as certificates from all the counties have been received, the governor shall issue and publish his proclamation, announcing the date at which the latest filing took place; of the facts contained in which proclamation, all courts shall take notice."

IC 1–1–3–3 provides:

"(a) As used in this section, 'regular session' includes a regular technical session.

"(b) Except as otherwise provided in subsection (d), each provision of each act passed at a regular session of the general assembly takes effect on July 1 next following its enactment, unless a different time is specified in the act.

"(c) Except as otherwise provided in subsection (d), each provision of each act passed at a special session of the general assembly takes effect on the first day of the third calendar month after the calendar month of sine die adjournment, unless a different time is specified in the act.

EFFECTIVE DATES OF ACTS

"(d) If an act contains a SECTION that specifies an effective date or dates for one (1) or more other provisions of the act or declares that an emergency exists for the act, then the SECTION takes effect at the same time as the earliest date that any other provision of the act takes effect.

"(e) This section does not apply to acts that are vetoed by the governor." *As added by Acts 1978, P.L.3, SEC.2, eff. Jan.1, 1979. Amended by P.L.1–1983, SEC.1, emerg. eff. Jan. 1, 1983; P.L.1–1987, SEC.1, eff. Jan. 1, 1988; P.L.1–1993, SEC.1, emerg. eff. retroactive to Jan. 1, 1993; P.L.4–1995, SEC.1, emerg. eff. Feb. 8, 1995.*

IC 2–6–1.5–5 provides:

"Sec. 5. Not more than fourteen (14) days (including Saturdays, Sundays, and legal holidays) after the last day the governor must take action on enrolled acts passed during any session of the general assembly, the legislative services agency shall distribute to the clerk of the circuit court of each county one (1) copy of each enrolled act of that session which became law. This distribution shall be delivered by certified mail, or by any other means of delivery that includes a return receipt, to each of the clerks of the counties of the state, and shall fulfill the publication and circulation requirements of Art. 4, Sec. 28 of the Constitution of the State of Indiana." *As amended by Acts 1978, P.L.3, SEC.3, eff. Jan. 1, 1979; P.L.8–1997, SEC.2, emerg. eff. May 1, 1997.*

PRIOR SESSION LAWS—PROMULGATION DATE

Prior to January 1, 1979, acts not containing an emergency clause or a specific effective date provision took effect upon promulgation, i.e., completion of official distribution of session laws to the clerks of all circuit courts.

TABLE

The table below lists, for each edition of session laws from 1852 to 1978, the designation of the promulgation date. Although the Indiana Code replaces the session laws for sessions before 1976, information on those session laws is useful in construing certain Code provisions. This table is compiled from a listing certified by the Secretary of State for sessions from 1852 to 1969 and from proclamations of the Governor for sessions after 1969.

Volume of Acts	Session of General Assembly	Date of Promulgation
1852 Special Acts	36th Assembly; Regular	November 6, 1852
1852 Revised Statutes	36th Assembly; Regular	May 6, 1853 [1]
1853 Acts	37th Assembly; Regular	July 24, 1853
1855 Acts	38th Assembly; Regular	August 17, 1855 [2]
1857 Acts	39th Assembly; Regular	August 24, 1857
1858 (ss) Acts	39th Assembly; Special	August 6, 1859
1859 Acts	40th Assembly; Regular	August 6, 1859
1861 Acts	41st Assembly; Regular	July 5, 1861
1861 (ss) Acts	41st Assembly; Special	September 7, 1861
1863 Acts	42nd Assembly; Regular	October 10, 1863
1865 Acts	43rd Assembly; Regular	September 2, 1865
1865 (ss) Acts	43rd Assembly; Special	April 13, 1866
1867 Acts	45th Assembly; Regular [3]	June 6, 1867
1869 (Reg. and ss) Acts	46th Assembly; Regular and Special	August 16, 1869
1871 Acts	47th Assembly; Regular	July 10, 1871

TABLE

Volume of Acts	Session of General Assembly	Date of Promulgation
1872 (ss) Act	47th Assembly; Special	July 7, 1873
1873 Acts	48th Assembly; Regular	July 7, 1873
1875 (Reg. and ss) Acts	49th Assembly; Regular and Special	August 24, 1875
1877 (Reg. and ss) Acts	50th Assembly; Regular and Special	July 2, 1877
1879 (Reg. and ss) Acts	51st Assembly; Regular and Special	May 31, 1879
1881 (Reg. and ss) Acts	52nd Assembly; Regular and Special	September 19, 1881
1883 Acts	53rd Assembly; Regular	June 5, 1883
1885 (Reg. and ss) Acts	54th Assembly; Regular and Special	July 18, 1885
1887 Acts	55th Assembly; Regular	May 21, 1887
1889 Acts	56th Assembly; Regular	May 10, 1889
1891 Acts	57th Assembly; Regular	June 3, 1891
1893 Acts	58th Assembly; Regular	May 18, 1893
1895 Acts	59th Assembly; Regular	June 28, 1895
1897 Acts	60th Assembly; Regular	April 14, 1897
1899 Acts	61st Assembly; Regular	April 27, 1899
1901 Acts	62nd Assembly; Regular	May 15, 1901
1903 Acts	63rd Assembly; Regular	April 23, 1903
1905 Acts	64th Assembly; Regular	April 15, 1905
1907 Acts	65th Assembly; Regular	April 9, 1907 [4]
1908 (ss) Acts	65th Assembly; Special	November 20, 1908
1909 Acts	66th Assembly; Regular	April 5, 1909

TABLE

Volume of Acts	Session of General Assembly	Date of Promulgation
1911 Acts	67th Assembly; Regular	April 21, 1911
1913 Acts	68th Assembly; Regular	April 30, 1913
1915 Acts	69th Assembly; Regular	April 26, 1915
1917 Acts	70th Assembly; Regular	May 31, 1917
1919 Acts	71st Assembly; Regular	May 15, 1919
1920 (ss) Acts	71st Assembly; Special	No promulgation date [5]
1920 (2 ss) Acts	71st Assembly; 2nd Special	November 13, 1920
1921 Acts	72nd Assembly; Regular	May 31, 1921
1921 (ss) Acts	72nd Assembly; Special	No promulgation date [5]
1923 Acts	73rd Assembly; Regular	April 30, 1923
1925 Acts	74th Assembly; Regular	April 25, 1925
1927 Acts	75th Assembly; Regular	May 16, 1927
1929 Acts	76th Assembly; Regular	May 21, 1929
1931 Acts	77th Assembly; Regular	June 30, 1931
1932 (ss) Acts	77th Assembly; Special	September 30, 1932
1933 Acts	78th Assembly; Regular	May 22, 1933
1935 Acts	79th Assembly; Regular	June 10, 1935
1936 (ss) Acts	79th Assembly; Special	May 11, 1936
1937 Acts	80th Assembly; Regular	June 7, 1937
1938 (ss) Acts	80th Assembly; Special	No promulgation date [5]

TABLE

Volume of Acts	Session of General Assembly	Date of Promulgation
1939 Acts	81st Assembly; Regular	June 14, 1939
1941 Acts	82nd Assembly; Regular	July 8, 1941
1943 Acts	83rd Assembly; Regular	November 3, 1943
1944 (ss) Acts	83rd Assembly; Special	No promulgation date [5]
1944 (2 ss) Acts	83rd Assembly; 2nd Special	No promulgation date [5]
1945 Acts	84th Assembly; Regular	December 12, 1945
1947 Acts	85th Assembly; Regular	August 20, 1947
1949 Acts	86th Assembly; Regular	September 10, 1949
1951 Acts	87th Assembly; Regular	July 20, 1951
1951 (ss) Acts	87th Assembly; Special	No promulgation date [5]
1953 Acts	88th Assembly; Regular	August 18, 1953
1955 Acts	89th Assembly; Regular	June 30, 1955
1957 Acts	90th Assembly; Regular	June 25, 1957
1959 Acts	91st Assembly; Regular	July 20, 1959
1961 Acts	92nd Assembly; Regular	July 6, 1961
1963 Acts	93rd Assembly; Regular	August 12, 1963
1963 Acts, Chs. 430–433	93rd Assembly; Regular	February 24, 1964 [6]
1963 (ss) Acts	93rd Assembly; Special	August 12, 1963
1965 Acts	94th Assembly; Regular	July 8, 1965
1965 (ss) Acts	94th Assembly; Special	July 16, 1965

TABLE

Volume of Acts	Session of General Assembly	Date of Promulgation
1965 (2 ss) Acts	94th Assembly; 2nd Special	December 29, 1965
1967 Acts	95th Assembly; Regular	July 26, 1967
1969 Acts	96th Assembly; Regular	August 18, 1969
1971 Acts	97th Assembly; 1st Regular	September 2, 1971
1972 Acts	97 Assembly; 2nd Regular	July 28, 1972
1973 Acts	98th Assembly; 1st Regular	July 26, 1973
1974 Acts	98th Assembly; 2nd Regular	June 11, 1974
1975 Acts	99th Assembly; 1st Regular	July 29, 1975
1976 Acts	99th Assembly; 2nd Regular	June 1, 1976
1977 (Reg. and ss) Acts	100th Assembly; 1st Regular and Special	August 29, 1977
1978 Acts	100th Assembly; 2nd Regular	June 28, 1978

Since January 1, 1979, the promulgation date is no longer necessary in the determination of the effective date for current provisions, see Effective Dates of Acts, supra.

[1] See *Jones v. Cavins*, 4 Ind. 305 (1853).

[2] First promulgation date declared by Governor in accordance with Acts 1855, ch. 100.

[3] A misnumbering of the legislative sessions occurred following the regular and special sessions of the 43rd General Assembly in 1865. The General Assembly of 1867 was known as the 45th instead of the 44th, and the error was continued in subsequent legislatures.

[4] Governor's proclamation specified April 9 as date of distribution but proclaimed Acts in effect April 10.

[5] No Governor's proclamation; each Act contained emergency clause and took effect on passage.

[6] These Acts, Governor's veto invalidated by Indiana Supreme Court decision, were promulgated in pamphlet form on the date specified. *See* Acts 1965, p. iii.

*

CITE THIS BOOK

By Title, Article, Chapter and Section
Thus: West's A.I.C. _____

*

West's
ANNOTATED
INDIANA CODE

TITLE 6

TAXATION

Sections 6–3–3 to 6–6–4.1–27 appear in this volume

1

ARTICLE 3

OTHER STATE INCOME TAXES

WESTLAW Computer Assisted Legal Research

WESTLAW supplements your legal research in many ways. WESTLAW allows you to

- update your research with the most current information
- expand your library with additional resources
- retrieve current, comprehensive history and citing references to a case with KeyCite

For more information on using WESTLAW to supplement your research, see the WESTLAW Electronic Research Guide, which follows the Preface.

Chapter 3

Credits

6–3–3–1   Amounts deducted and withheld

Sec. 1.   The amount deducted and withheld as tax under IC 6–3–4–8, IC 6–3–4–12, and IC 6–3–4–13 during any taxable year shall be allowed as a credit to the taxpayer against the tax imposed on him by IC 6–3–2.

As amended by P.L.2–1988, SEC.8.

Historical and Statutory Notes

P.L. 2–1988, Sec.8, emerg. eff. Feb. 16, 1988, corrected internal references.

Acts 1965, c. 233, s. 15.

Formerly:
  Acts 1963 (ss), c. 32, s. 301.

Cross References

Community revitalization enhancement district tax credit, state and local tax liability, see IC 6–3.1–19–1.
Incremental tax financing fund, revenues, see IC 36–7–13–15.
Industrial development fund, state and local income taxes, see IC 36–7–13–3.8.
Military base recovery tax credit,
    Against other taxes owed, priority of application, see IC 6–3.1–11.5–24.
    State tax liability, see IC 6–3.1–11.5–14.

Library References

Taxation ☞1073.
WESTLAW Topic No. 371.

C.J.S. Taxation § 1103.
I.L.E. Taxation §§ 207, 208, 213, 222.

Notes of Decisions

Credit for federal taxes   1

1. Credit for federal taxes
  Indiana does not provide credit against state income tax liability for federal income taxes

paid.   Thomas v. Indiana Dept. of State Revenue, 1997, 675 N.E.2d 362.

6–3–3–2   Corporations

Sec. 2.   Corporations shall be entitled to a credit, not to exceed the amount of the tax imposed by IC 6–3–2, against the tax imposed by IC 6–3–2 for any taxable year in an amount equal to any tax imposed on gross income by IC 6–2.1–2 for the same taxable year.

As amended by P.L.2–1988, SEC.9.

Historical and Statutory Notes

P.L. 2–1988, Sec.9, emerg. eff. Feb. 16, 1988, corrected internal references.

Formerly:
  Acts 1963 (ss), c. 32, s. 302.

6–3–3–3   Taxes paid to other states

Sec. 3.   (a) Whenever a resident person has become liable for tax to another state upon all or any part of his income for a taxable year derived from sources without this state and subject to taxation under IC 6–3–2, the amount of tax paid by him to the other state shall be credited against the amount of the tax payable by him.   Such credit shall be allowed upon the production to the department of satisfactory evidence of the fact of such payment, except that such application for credit shall not operate to reduce the tax payable under IC 6–3–2 to an amount less than would have been payable were the income from the other state ignored.   The credit provided for by this subsection shall not be granted to a taxpayer when the laws of the other state, under which the adjusted gross income in question is subject to taxation, provides for a credit to the taxpayer substantially similar to that granted by subsection (b).

(b) Whenever a nonresident person has become liable for tax to the state where he resides upon his income for the taxable year derived from sources within this state and subject to taxation under IC 6–3–2, the proportion of tax paid by him to the state where he resides that his income subject to taxation under IC 6–3–2 bears to his income upon which the tax so payable to the other state was imposed shall be credited against the tax payable by him under IC 6–3–2, but only if the laws of the other state grant a substantially similar credit to residents of this state subject to income tax under the laws of such other state, or impose a tax upon the income of its residents derived from sources in this state and exempt from taxation the income of residents of this state.   No credit shall be allowed against the amount of the tax on any adjusted gross income taxable under IC 6–3–2 that is exempt from taxation under the laws of the other state.

As amended by P.L.2–1988, SEC.10.

Historical and Statutory Notes

P.L. 2–1988, Sec.10, emerg. eff. Feb. 16,   **Formerly:**
1988, corrected internal references.   Acts 1963 (ss), c. 32, s. 303.

Notes of Decisions

In general   1

---

1. In general

Taxpayer was not due credit against his state income tax liability for federal income tax paid. Thomas v. Indiana Dept. of State Revenue, 1997, 675 N.E.2d 362.

Department of State Revenue erred in issuing tax warrant for taxpayer's unpaid state income taxes without responding to taxpayer's written protests and without holding hearing, where taxpayer filed written protest on proposed assessment, and Department issued tax warrant on proposed assessment without formally ruling on protest and without holding hearing according to statutory procedures. Thomas v. Indiana Dept. of State Revenue, 1997, 675 N.E.2d 362.

6–3–3–4   Repealed

(Repealed by Acts 1977, P.L.78, SEC.6.)

Historical and Statutory Notes

Acts 1977, P.L. 78, provided in § 8(b), containing emergency clause, that § 6 takes effect retroactively to January 1, 1977; however, the act also provided in § 7 that the retirement income credit provided by § 6–3–3–4 was not applicable for taxable years beginning after Dec. 31, 1975.

The former section related to credits for retirement income and to exemptions for military pay.

Provisions pertaining to a deduction for military pay, including retirement and survivors' benefits are now contained in § 6–3–2–4, and provisions pertaining to a unified tax credit for the elderly are now contained in § 6–3–3–9.

Formerly:

Acts 1963 (ss), c. 32, s. 304.
Acts 1965, c. 279, s. 1.
Acts 1967, c. 355, s. 1.

6–3–3–4.1   Repealed

(Repealed by Acts 1981, P.L.25, SEC.9.)

Historical and Statutory Notes

Acts 1981, P.L. 25, provided in § 10(c), containing emergency clause, that § 9 takes effect retroactively to January 1, 1981, and affects taxable years beginning after December 31, 1980.

The former section related to a tax credit for the elderly.

Provisions pertaining to a unified tax credit for the elderly are now contained in § 6–3–3–9.

Formerly:

Acts 1977, P.L.78, SEC.4.
Acts 1979, P.L.68, SEC.2.

6–3–3–5   Charitable contributions to institutions of higher education within state

Sec. 5.   (a) At the election of the taxpayer, there shall be allowed, as a credit against the adjusted gross income tax imposed by IC 6–3–1 through IC 6–3–7 for the taxable year, an amount (subject to the applicable limitations provided by this section) equal to fifty percent (50%) of the aggregate amount of charitable contributions made by such taxpayer during such year to institutions of higher education located within Indiana, to any corporation or foundation organized and operated solely for the benefit of any such institution of higher education, or to the associated colleges of Indiana.

(b) In the case of a taxpayer other than a corporation, the amount allowable as a credit under this section for any taxable year shall not exceed one hundred dollars ($100) in the case of a single return or two hundred dollars ($200) in the case of a joint return.

(c) In the case of a corporation, the amount allowable as a credit under this section for any taxable year shall not exceed:

(1) ten percent (10%) of such corporation's total adjusted gross income tax under IC 6–3–1 through IC 6–3–7 for such year (as determined without regard to any credits against that tax); or

(2) one thousand dollars ($1,000);

whichever is less.

(d) For purposes of this section, the term "institution of higher education" means any educational institution located within Indiana:

(1) which normally maintains a regular faculty and curriculum and normally has a regularly organized body of students in attendance at the place where its educational activities are carried on;

(2) which regularly offers education at a level above the twelfth grade;

(3) which regularly awards either associate, bachelors, masters, or doctoral degrees, or any combination thereof; and

(4) which is duly accredited by the North Central Association of Colleges and Schools, the Indiana state board of education, or the American Association of Theological Schools.

(e) The credit allowed by this section shall not exceed the amount of the adjusted gross income tax imposed by IC 6–3–1 through IC 6–3–7 for the taxable year, reduced by the sum of all credits (as determined without regard to this section) allowed by IC 6–3–1 through IC 6–3–7.

(f) Any taxpayer subject to an income tax under the provisions of IC 6–2.1 as well as under the provisions of IC 6–3–1 through IC 6–3–7 may elect to claim the credit allowed by this section against the income tax imposed by IC 6–2.1, but in no event shall a credit be claimed against both such taxes.

As amended by Acts 1978, P.L.45, SEC.1; Acts 1981, P.L.77, SEC.10; P.L.20–1984, SEC.4; P.L.66–1988, SEC.1; P.L.5–1995, SEC.6.

Historical and Statutory Notes

Acts 1978, P.L. 45, § 1, emerg. eff. retroactively to Jan. 1, 1978, in Subsec. (a), substituted "or to the associated colleges of Indiana" for "and/or to the associated colleges of Indiana"; in Subsec. (b), increased the credit for a single return from $50 to $100 and for a joint return from $100 to $200; in Subsec. (c)(1), increased the credit rate from 5% to 10%; in Subsec. (c)(2), increased the dollar amount from $500 to $1,000; in Subsec. (d), in the introductory clause, substituted "means" for "shall include" and "and any educational institution" for "or educational institutions", in Cl. (3), deleted "or" preceding "bachelors" and "masters", and in

Cl. (4), substituted "is duly accredited" for "are duly accredited"; in Subsec. (f), twice substituted "IC 6–2–1" for "Gross Income Tax Act of 1933 as amended", substituted "subject to an income tax" for "subject to tax" and "against the income tax imposed" for "against tax imposed"; substituted "IC 6–3–1 through IC 6–3–7" for "this chapter" throughout the section; and deleted Subsec. (g) which read: "This section shall apply only with respect to taxable years beginning on or after December 31, 1977."

Acts 1978, P.L. 45, provided in § 2:

"Because an emergency exists, this act takes effect retroactively to January 1, 1978, and applies to taxable years which begin after December 31, 1977."

Acts 1981, P.L. 77, § 10, emerg. eff. April 29, 1981, in Subsec. (f), twice substituted "IC 6–2.1" for "IC 6–2–1."

Acts 1981, P.L. 77 was a part of a codification of the laws relating to gross income tax.

P.L. 20–1984, Sec.4, eff. June 30, 1984, in Subsec. (d), substituted "state board of education" for "department of public instruction" in Cl. (4); and made nonsubstantive corrective changes.

P.L. 66–1988, Sec.1, emerg. eff. February 29, 1988, substituted in Subsec. (c)(1) "any credits against that tax" for "this section".

P.L.5–1995, Sec.6, eff. June 1, 1995, amended this section by removing Indiana Vocational Technical College from the definition of "institution of higher learning" in Subsec. (d) and by adding "and Schools" in Subsec. (d)(4).

Formerly:

Acts 1963 (ss), c. 32, s. 305.
Acts 1967, c. 201, s. 1.
Acts 1969, c. 326, s. 4.
Acts 1971, P.L.64, SEC.8.

Cross References

Commercial vehicle excise tax, see IC 6–6–5.5–1.

Library References

Taxation ⊕1073.
WESTLAW Topic No. 371.

C.J.S. Taxation § 1103.
I.L.E. Taxation § 217.

United States Supreme Court

Charitable tax deduction, payments for religious auditing and training services, see Hernandez v. C.I.R., 1989, 109 S.Ct. 2136, 490 U.S. 680, 104 L.Ed.2d 766, rehearing denied 110 S.Ct. 16, 492 U.S. 933, 106 L.Ed.2d 630.

Notes of Decisions

College or university foundations 1

_____

1. College or university foundations
Gifts to "college or university foundations," such as Indiana University Foundation or Pur-

due Research Foundation, do not qualify for the credit allowed in Act 1963, c. 32, s. 305 [now this section]. 1968 Op.Atty.Gen. No. 41.

6–3–3–5.1 Contributions to twenty-first century scholars program; tax credits; amount

Sec. 5.1. (a) At the election of the taxpayer, a credit against the adjusted gross income tax imposed by IC 6–3–1 through IC 6–3–7 for the taxable year, is permitted in an amount (subject to the applicable limitations provided by this section) equal to fifty percent (50%) of the aggregate amount of contributions made by the taxpayer during the taxable year to the twenty-first century scholars program support fund established under IC 20–12–70.1–5.

(b) In the case of a taxpayer other than a corporation, the amount allowable as a credit under this section for any taxable year may not exceed:

(1) one hundred dollars ($100) in the case of a single return; or

(2) two hundred dollars ($200) in the case of a joint return.

(c) In the case of a taxpayer that is a corporation, the amount allowable as a credit under this section for any taxable year may not exceed the lesser of the following amounts:

(1) Ten percent (10%) of the corporation's total adjusted gross income tax under IC 6–3–1 through IC 6–3–7 for the taxable year (as determined without regard to any credits against that tax).

(2) One thousand dollars ($1,000).

(d) The credit permitted under this section may not exceed the amount of the adjusted gross income tax imposed by IC 6–3–1 through IC 6–3–7 for the taxable year, reduced by the sum of all credits (as determined without regard to this section) allowed by IC 6–3–1 through IC 6–3–7.

(e) Any taxpayer subject to an income tax under IC 6–2.1 as well as under IC 6–3–1 through IC 6–3–7 may elect to claim the credit allowed by this section against the income tax imposed by IC 6–2.1, but may not claim a credit against both of these taxes.

As added by P.L.56–1990, SEC.1.

6–3–3–6   Repealed

(Repealed by Acts 1981, P.L.25, SEC.9.)

Historical and Statutory Notes

Acts 1981, P.L. 25, provided in § 10(c), containing emergency clause, that § 9 takes effect retroactively to Jan. 1, 1981.

The former section related to tax credits and refunds for the elderly and for the disabled.

Provisions pertaining to a unified tax credit for the elderly are now contained in § 6–3–3–9.

Formerly:
Acts 1973, P.L.50, SEC.2.
Acts 1980, P.L.54, SEC.3.

6–3–3–7   Repealed

(Repealed by P.L.96–1989, SEC.25.)

Historical and Statutory Notes

P.L.96–1989, Sec.25, eff. Jan. 1, 1990.

Former IC 6–3–3–7 related to tax credit or refund for certain gasoline taxes paid.

Formerly:
Acts 1975, P.L.352, SEC.1.

Acts 1979, P.L.71, SEC.1.
Acts 1980, P.L.51, SEC.3.
Acts 1981, P.L.77, SEC.11.
P.L.82–1983, SEC.6.

6–3–3–8   Repealed

(Repealed by Acts 1981, P.L.25, SEC.9.)

Historical and Statutory Notes

Acts 1981, P.L. 25, provided in § 10(c), containing emergency clause, that § 9 takes effect retroactively to Jan. 1, 1981.

The former section related to a credit for the elderly which was intended to provide relief for state gross retail and use taxes paid on utilities.

Formerly:
Acts 1978, P.L.43, SEC.2.
Acts 1980, P.L.54, SEC.4.

6–3–3–9   Unified tax credit for the elderly

Sec. 9.   (a) The credit provided by this section shall be known as the unified tax credit for the elderly.

(b) As used in this section, unless the context clearly indicates otherwise:

(1) "Household federal adjusted gross income" means the total adjusted gross income, as defined in Section 62 of the Internal Revenue Code,[1] of an individual, or of an individual and his spouse if they reside together for the taxable year for which the credit provided by this section is claimed.

(2) "Household" means a claimant or, if applicable, a claimant and his or her spouse if the spouse resides with the claimant and "household income" means the income of the claimant or, if applicable, the combined income of the claimant and his or her spouse if the spouse resides with the claimant.

(3) "Claimant" means an individual, other than an individual described in subsection (c) of this section, who:

(A) has filed a claim under this section;

(B) was a resident of this state for at least six (6) months during the taxable year for which he or she has filed a claim under this section; and

(C) was sixty-five (65) years of age during some portion of the taxable year for which he has filed a claim under this section or whose spouse was either sixty-five (65) years of age or over during the taxable year.

(c) The credit provided under this section shall not apply to an individual who, for a period of at least one hundred eighty (180) days during the taxable year for which he has filed a claim under this section, was incarcerated in a local, state, or federal correctional institution.

(d) The right to file a claim under this section shall be personal to the claimant and shall not survive his death, except that a surviving spouse of a claimant is entitled to claim the credit provided by this section. For purposes of determining the amount of the credit a surviving spouse is entitled to claim under this section, the deceased spouse shall be treated as having been alive on the last day of the taxable year in which the deceased spouse died. When a claimant dies after having filed a timely claim, the amount thereof shall be disbursed to another member of the household as determined by the commissioner. If the claimant was the only member of his household, the claim may be paid to his executor or administrator, but if neither is appointed and qualified within two (2) years of the filing of the claim, the amount of the claim shall escheat to the state.

(e) For each taxable year, subject to the limitations provided in this section, one (1) claimant per household may claim, as a credit against Indiana adjusted gross income taxes otherwise due, the credit provided by this section. If the allowable amount of the claim exceeds the income taxes otherwise due on the claimant's household income or if there are no Indiana income taxes due on such income, the amount of the claim not used as an offset against income taxes after audit by the department, at the taxpayer's option, shall be refunded to the claimant or taken as a credit against such taxpayer's income tax liability subsequently due.

(f) No claim filed pursuant to this section shall be allowed unless filed within six (6) months following the close of claimant's taxable year or within the extension period if an extension of time for filing the return has been granted under IC 6–8.1–6–1, whichever is later.

(g) The amount of any claim otherwise payable under this section may be applied by the department against any liability outstanding on the books of the department against the claimant, or against any other individual who was a member of his household in the taxable year to which the claim relates.

(h) The amount of a claim filed pursuant to this section by a claimant that either (i) does not reside with his spouse during the taxable year, or (ii) resides with his spouse during the taxable year and only one (1) of them is sixty-five (65) years of age or older at the end of the taxable year, shall be determined in accordance with the following schedule:

HOUSEHOLD FEDERAL ADJUSTED GROSS INCOME FOR TAXABLE YEAR	CREDIT
less than $1,000	$100
at least $1,000, but less than $3,000	$ 50
at least $3,000, but less than $10,000	$ 40

(i) The amount of a claim filed pursuant to this section by a claimant that resides with his spouse during his taxable year shall be determined in accordance with the following schedule if both the claimant and spouse are sixty-five (65) years of age or older at the end of the taxable year:

HOUSEHOLD FEDERAL ADJUSTED GROSS INCOME FOR TAXABLE YEAR	CREDIT
less than $1,000	$140
at least $1,000, but less than $3,000	$ 90
at least $3,000, but less than $10,000	$ 80

(j) The department may promulgate reasonable rules under IC 4–22–2 for the administration of this section.

(k) Every claimant under this section shall supply to the department on forms provided under IC 6–8.1–3–4, in support of his claim, reasonable proof of household income and age.

(l) Whenever on the audit of any claim filed under this section the department finds that the amount of the claim has been incorrectly determined, the department shall redetermine the claim and notify the claimant of the redetermination and the reasons therefor. The redetermination shall be final.

(m) In any case in which it is determined that a claim is or was excessive and was filed with fraudulent intent, the claim shall be disallowed in full, and, if the claim has been paid or a credit has been allowed against income taxes otherwise payable, the credit shall be canceled and the amount paid shall be recovered by assessment as income taxes are assessed and such assessment shall bear interest from the date of payment or credit of the claim, until refunded or paid at the rate determined under IC 6–8.1–10–1. The claimant in such a case commits a Class A misdemeanor. In any case in which it is determined that a claim is or was excessive and was negligently prepared, ten percent (10%) of the corrected claim shall be disallowed and, if the claim has been paid or credited against income taxes otherwise payable, the credit shall be reduced or canceled, and the proper portion of any amount paid shall be similarly recovered by assessment as income taxes are assessed, and such assessment shall bear interest at the rate determined under IC 6–8.1–10–1 from the date of payment until refunded or paid.

As added by Acts 1982, P.L.6, SEC.5. Amended by P.L.83–1983, SEC.1; P.L.73–1985, SEC.2.

1. 26 U.S.C.A. § 62.

Historical and Statutory Notes

Acts 1981, P.L. 25, § 6, emerg. eff. retroactively to Jan. 1, 1981, purportedly added this text as IC 6–6–3–9; however, an examination of the text indicates an intent to add this text as IC 6–3–3–9.

Acts 1981, P.L. 25, provided in § 10(c):

"Because an emergency exists for the retroactive taking effect of Sections 6, 7, and 9 of this act, those sections take effect retroactively January 1, 1981, and affect taxable years beginning after December 31, 1980."

Acts 1982, P.L.6, Sec.5, emerg. eff. Feb. 15, 1982, correctively added the text of this section, which was added as IC 6–6–3–9 in error by Acts 1981, P.L.25, Sec.6.

P.L. 83–1983, Sec.1, emerg. eff. Jan. 1, 1983, substituted "subsection (c)" for "subsection (b)" in the introductory clause of Subsec. (b)(3); rewrote Subsec. (d) which is set forth below; and substituted "age" for "of age or disability" at the end of Subsec. (k).

Prior to the 1983 amendment, Subsec. (d) read:

"(d) The right to file a claim under this section shall be personal to the claimant and shall not survive his death. When a claimant dies after having filed a timely claim, the amount thereof shall be disbursed to another member of the household as determined by the commissioner. If the claimant was the only member of his household, the claim may be paid to his executor or administrator, but if neither is appointed and qualified within two (2) years of the filing of the claim, the amount of the claim shall escheat to the state".

Section 2 of P.L. 83–1983 provided that this act affects taxable years that begin after Dec. 31, 1982.

P.L.73–1985, Sec.2, emerg. eff. retroactive to Jan. 1, 1985, in Subsec. (h) increased the amount of the credits in the schedule from $65 to $100, from $35 to $50, and from $25 to $40; and in Subsec. (i) increased the amount of the credits from $90 to $140, from $60 to $90, and from $50 to $80.

Section 3 of P.L.73–1985 provided that this act applies to taxable years beginning after Dec. 31, 1984.

Cross References

Class A misdemeanor, punishment, see IC 35–50–3–2.

Administrative Code References

Adjudged gross income tax, credits, elderly and disabled persons, see 45 IAC 3.1–1–78 et seq.

Library References

Taxation ☞1047, 1073.
WESTLAW Topic No. 371.
C.J.S. Taxation §§ 1098, 1103.

Notes of Decisions

Medicaid payments   1

_____

1. Medicaid payments
Under provisions of § 6–3–3–6 [repealed; see, now, this section], Medicaid payments should not have been included in determining the eligibility for a credit or refund of a portion of Indiana real property taxes paid by persons age sixty-five years and over and for disabled persons. 1980 Op.Atty.Gen. No. 21.

6–3–3–10   Enterprise zone credit against qualified state tax liability

Sec. 10. (a) As used in this section:

"Base period wages" means the following:

(1) In the case of a taxpayer other than a pass through entity, wages paid or payable by a taxpayer to its employees during the year that ends on the last day of the month that immediately precedes the month in which an enterprise zone is established, to the extent that the wages would have been qualified wages if the enterprise zone had been in effect for that year. If the taxpayer did not engage in an active trade or business during that year in the area that is later designated as an enterprise zone, then the base period wages equal zero (0). If the taxpayer engaged in an active trade or business during only part of that year in an area that is later designated as an enterprise zone, then the department shall determine the amount of base period wages.

(2) In the case of a taxpayer that is a pass through entity, base period wages equal zero (0).

"Enterprise zone" means an enterprise zone created under IC 4–4–6.1.

"Enterprise zone adjusted gross income" means adjusted gross income of a taxpayer that is derived from sources within an enterprise zone. Sources of adjusted gross income shall be determined with respect to an enterprise zone, to the extent possible, in the same manner that sources of adjusted gross income are determined with respect to the state of Indiana under IC 6–3–2–2.

"Enterprise zone gross income" means gross income of a taxpayer that is derived from sources within an enterprise zone.

"Enterprise zone insurance premiums" means insurance premiums derived from sources within an enterprise zone.

"Monthly base period wages" means base period wages divided by twelve (12).

"Pass through entity" means a:

(1) corporation that is exempt from the adjusted gross income tax under IC 6–3–2–2.8(2);

(2) partnership;

(3) trust;

(4) limited liability company; or

(5) limited liability partnership.

"Qualified employee" means an individual who is employed by a taxpayer and who:

(1) has his principal place of residence in the enterprise zone in which he is employed;

(2) performs services for the taxpayer, ninety percent (90%) of which are directly related to the conduct of the taxpayer's trade or business that is located in an enterprise zone;

(3) performs at least fifty percent (50%) of his services for the taxpayer during the taxable year in the enterprise zone; and

(4) in the case of an individual who is employed by a taxpayer that is a pass through entity, the individual was first employed by the taxpayer after December 31, 1998.

"Qualified increased employment expenditures" means the following:

(1) For a taxpayer's taxable year other than his taxable year in which the enterprise zone is established, the amount by which qualified wages paid or payable by the taxpayer during the taxable year to qualified employees exceeds the taxpayer's base period wages.

(2) For the taxpayer's taxable year in which the enterprise zone is established, the amount by which qualified wages paid or payable by the taxpayer during all of the full calendar months in the taxpayer's taxable year that succeed the date on which the enterprise zone was established exceed the taxpayer's monthly base period wages multiplied by that same number of full calendar months.

"Qualified state tax liability" means a taxpayer's total income tax liability incurred under:

(1) IC 6–2.1 (gross income tax) with respect to enterprise zone gross income;

(2) IC 6–3–1 through IC 6–3–7 (adjusted gross income tax) with respect to enterprise zone adjusted gross income;

(3) IC 27–1–18–2 (insurance premiums tax) with respect to enterprise zone insurance premiums; and

(4) IC 6–5.5 (the financial institutions tax);

as computed after the application of the credits that, under IC 6–3.1–1–2, are to be applied before the credit provided by this section.

"Qualified wages" means the wages paid or payable to qualified employees during a taxable year.

"Taxpayer" includes a pass through entity.

(b) A taxpayer is entitled to a credit against the taxpayer's qualified state tax liability for a taxable year in the amount of the lesser of:

(1) the product of ten percent (10%) multiplied by the qualified increased employment expenditures of the taxpayer for the taxable year; or

(2) one thousand five hundred dollars ($1,500) multiplied by the number of qualified employees employed by the taxpayer during the taxable year.

(c) The amount of the credit provided by this section that a taxpayer uses during a particular taxable year may not exceed the taxpayer's qualified state tax liability for the taxable year. If the credit provided by this section exceeds the amount of that tax liability for the taxable year it is first claimed, then the excess may be carried back to preceding taxable years or carried over to succeeding taxable years and used as a credit against the taxpayer's qualified state tax liability for those taxable years. Each time that the credit is carried back to a preceding taxable year or carried over to a succeeding taxable year, the amount of the carryover is reduced by the amount used as a credit for that taxable year. Except as provided in subsection (e), the credit provided by this section may be carried forward and applied in the ten (10) taxable years that succeed the taxable year in which the credit accrues. The credit provided by this section may be carried back and applied in the three (3) taxable years that precede the taxable year in which the credit accrues.

(d) A credit earned by a taxpayer in a particular taxable year shall be applied against the taxpayer's qualified state tax liability for that taxable year before any credit carryover or carryback is applied against that liability under subsection (c).

(e) Notwithstanding subsection (c), if a credit under this section results from wages paid in a particular enterprise zone, and if that enterprise zone terminates in a taxable year that succeeds the last taxable year in which a taxpayer is entitled to use the credit carryover that results from those wages under subsection (c), then the taxpayer may use the credit carryover for any taxable year up to and including the taxable year in which the enterprise zone terminates.

(f) A taxpayer is not entitled to a refund of any unused credit.

(g) A taxpayer that:

(1) does not own, rent, or lease real property outside of an enterprise zone that is an integral part of its trade or business; and

(2) is not owned or controlled directly or indirectly by a taxpayer that owns, rents, or leases real property outside of an enterprise zone;

is exempt from the allocation and apportionment provisions of this section.

(h) If a pass through entity is entitled to a credit under subsection (b) but does not have state tax liability against which the tax credit may be applied, an

14

individual who is a shareholder, partner, beneficiary, or member of the pass through entity is entitled to a tax credit equal to:

(1) the tax credit determined for the pass through entity for the taxable year; multiplied by

(2) the percentage of the pass through entity's distributive income to which the shareholder, partner, beneficiary, or member is entitled.

The credit provided under this subsection is in addition to a tax credit to which a shareholder, partner, beneficiary, or member of a pass through entity is entitled. However, a pass through entity and an individual who is a shareholder, partner, beneficiary, or member of a pass through entity may not claim more than one (1) credit for the qualified expenditure.

As added by P.L.23–1983, SEC.12. Amended by P.L.9–1986, SEC.6; P.L.347–1989(ss), SEC.9; P.L.120–1999, SEC.3.

Historical and Statutory Notes

P.L.9–1986, Sec.6, emerg. eff. April 1, 1986, inserted the definitions of enterprise zone gross income and enterprise zone insurance premiums, inserted the definition of qualified state tax liability, in Subsec. (a); in Subsecs. (b) and (c), substituted "taxpayer's qualified state tax liability" for "tax imposed under IC 6–3–1 through IC 6–3–7, on his enterprise zone adjusted gross income"; in Subsec. (c), deleted "after the application of all credits except the credit provided by this section" following "taxable year" in the first sentence, substituted "taxpayer's qualified state tax liability" for "tax otherwise due and payable under IC 6–3–1 through IC 6–3–7" in the second sentence; inserted "qualified state" preceding "tax liability" in Subsec. (d); added Subsec. (g); and made nonsubstantive changes.

P.L.347–1989(ss), Sec.9, eff. Jan. 1, 1990.

P.L.347–1989(ss), Sec.9, in Subsec. (a), in definition of "Qualified state tax liability" added Subsec. (4).

P.L.120–1999, Sec.3, eff. Jan. 1, 2000, in Subsec. (a), designated Subsec. (1) and inserted "In the case of a taxpayer other than a pass through entity" and added Subsec. (2) in the definition of "base period wages", added the definition of "pass through entity", added Subsec. (4) in the definition of "qualified employee", and added the definition of "taxpayer"; added Subsec. (h); and made other nonsubstantive changes.

P.L.120–1999, Sec.7, eff. Jan. 1, 2000, provides:

"IC 6–3–3–10 and IC 6–3.1–7–1, both as amended by this act, apply only to taxable years beginning after December 31, 1999."

Library References

Taxation ⬠1047, 1073.
WESTLAW Topic No. 371.

C.J.S. Taxation §§ 1098, 1103.
Words and Phrases (Perm.Ed.)

Chapter 3.1

Neighborhood Assistance Credits

6–3–3.1–1 to 6–3–3.1–7   Repealed

(Repealed by P.L.51–1984, SEC.3.)

Historical and Statutory Notes

P.L. 51–1984 provided in Section 5(a), containing emergency clause, that Section 3 of this act takes effect Jan. 1, 1984.

Section 5(a) of P.L. 51–1984 provided that Section 3 of this act affects taxable years that begin after Dec. 31, 1983.

The repealed chapter pertained to tax credits for neighborhood assistance or community services.

For provisions relating to carry back or carry forward of credits earned before Jan. 1, 1984, see Historical Note under section 6–3.1–1–1.

Formerly:

IC 6–3–3.1–2.
Acts 1976, P.L.16, SEC.1.
Acts 1977, P.L.80, SEC.2.
Acts 1981, P.L.72, SEC.7.

DISPOSITION TABLE

Showing where the subject matter of the repealed sections of Title 6 is now covered in new sections of Title 6, West's Annotated Indiana Code.

Repealed Sections	New Sections	Repealed Sections	New Sections
6–3–3.1–1	6–3.1–9–1	6–3–3.1–4	6–3.1–9–3
6–3–3.1–2	None	6–3–3.1–5	6–3.1–9–4
6–3–3.1–3	6–3.1–9–2	6–3–3.1–6	6–3.1–9–5
		6–3–3.1–7	6–3.1–9–6

Chapter 3.2

Prison Investment Credits

6–3–3.2–1 to 6–3–3.2–7   Repealed

(Repealed by P.L.51–1984, SEC.3.)

Historical and Statutory Notes

P.L. 51–1984 provided in Section 5(a), containing emergency clause, that Section 3 of this act takes effect Jan. 1, 1984.

Section 5(a) of P.L. 51–1984 provided that Section 3 of this act affects taxable years that begin after Dec. 31, 1983.

The repealed chapter related to income tax credits for prison investments.

For provisions relating to carry back or carry forward of credits earned before Jan. 1, 1984, see Historical Note under section 6–3.1–1–1.

Formerly:

IC 6–3–3.2–3.
IC 6–3–3.2–7.
Acts 1981, P.L.83, SEC.1.

DISPOSITION TABLE

Showing where the subject matter of the repealed sections of Title 6 is now covered in new sections of Title 6, West's Annotated Indiana Code.

Repealed Sections	New Sections	Repealed Sections	New Sections
6–3–3.2–1	6–3.1–6–1	6–3–3.2–4	6–3.1–6–5
6–3–3.2–2	6–3.1–6–2	6–3–3.2–5	6–3.1–6–3
6–3–3.2–3	None	6–3–3.2–6	6–3.1–6–4
		6–3–3.2–7	None

Chapter 3.3

Energy System Credits

6–3–3.3–1 to 6–3–3.3–11   Repealed

(Repealed by P.L.51–1984, SEC.3.)

Historical and Statutory Notes

P.L. 51–1984 provided in Section 5(a), containing emergency clause, that Section 3 of this act takes effect Jan. 1, 1984.

Section 5(a) of P.L. 51–1984 provided that Section 3 of this act affects taxable years that begin after Dec. 31, 1983.

The repealed chapter related to income tax credits for the installation of qualified energy systems in dwellings and other buildings.

For provisions relating to carry back or carry forward of credits earned before Jan. 1, 1984, see Historical Note under section 6–3.1–1–1.

Former sections 6–3–3.3–1 to 6–3–3.3–11 were reenacted and renumbered as sections 6–3.1–8–1 to 6–3.1–8–12, respectively.

Chapter 3.4

Investment Credits

6–3–3.4–1 to 6–3–3.4–16   Repealed

(Repealed by P.L.51–1984, SEC.3.)

Historical and Statutory Notes

P.L. 51–1984 provided in Section 5(a), containing emergency clause, that Section 3 of this act takes effect Jan. 1, 1984.

Section 5(a) of P.L. 51–1984 provided that Section 3 of this act affects taxable years that begin after Dec. 31, 1983.

The repealed chapter related to tax credits for qualified investments.

For provisions relating to carry back or carry forward of credits earned before Jan. 1, 1984, see Historical Note under section 6–3.1–1–1.

Former sections 6–3–3.4–1 to 6–3–3.4–16 were reenacted as sections 6–3.1–5–1 to 6–3.1–5–16, respectively.

Chapter 3.5

Railroad Station Donation Credit

6–3–3.5–1 to 6–3–3.5–6   Repealed

(Repealed by P.L.51–1984, SEC.4.)

Historical and Statutory Notes

P.L.51–1984 provided in Section 5(b) that Section 4 of this act takes effect Jan. 1, 1985.

The repealed chapter related to income tax credits for railroad companies for transfers of

railway stations and renovation funds to governmental units.

Chapter 3.6

Teacher Summer Employment Credits

6–3–3.6–1 to 6–3–3.6–7   Repealed

(Repealed by P.L.51–1984, SEC.3.)

Historical and Statutory Notes

P.L. 51–1984 provided in Section 5(a), containing emergency clause, that Section 3 of this act takes effect Jan. 1, 1984.

Section 5(a) of P.L. 51–1984 provided that Section 3 of this act affects taxable years that begin after Dec. 31, 1983.

The repealed chapter related to teacher summer employment credits.

For provisions relating to carry back or carry forward of credits earned before Jan. 1, 1984, see Historical Note under section 6–3.1–1–1.

Former sections 6–3–3.6–1 to 6–3–3.6–7 were reenacted as sections 6–3.1–2–1 to 6–3.1–2–7, respectively.

Chapter 3.7

Credit For Donations Of High Technology Equipment To Schools

6–3–3.7–1 to 6–3–3.7–10   Repealed

(Repealed by P.L.51–1984, SEC.3.)

Historical and Statutory Notes

P.L. 51–1984 provided in Section 5(a), containing emergency clause, that Section 3 of this act takes effect Jan. 1, 1984.

Section 5(a) of P.L. 51–1984 provided that Section 3 of this act affects taxable years that begin after Dec. 31, 1983.

The repealed chapter related to credits for donations of high technology equipment to schools.

For provisions relating to carry back or carry forward of credits earned before Jan. 1, 1984, see Historical Note under section 6–3.1–1–1.

Former sections 6–3–3.7–1 to 6–3–3.7–10 were reenacted as sections 6–3.1–3–1 to 6–3.1–3–10, respectively.

Chapter 3.8

Research Expense Credits

6–3–3.8–1 to 6–3–3.8–6   Repealed

(Repealed by P.L.51–1984, SEC.3.)

Historical and Statutory Notes

P.L. 51–1984 provided in Section 5(a), containing emergency clause, that Section 3 of this act takes effect Jan. 1, 1984.

Section 5(a) of P.L. 51–1984 provided that Section 3 of this act affects taxable years that begin after Dec. 31, 1983.

The repealed chapter related to research expense credits.

For provisions relating to carry back or carry forward of credits earned before Jan. 1, 1984, see Historical Note under section 6–3.1–1–1.

Former sections 6–3–3.8–1 to 6–3–3.8–6 were reenacted as sections 6–3.1–4–1 to 6–3.1–4–6, respectively.

Chapter 3.9

Enterprise Zone Loan Interest Credit

6–3–3.9–1 to 6–3–3.9–6   Repealed

(Repealed by P.L.51–1984, SEC.3.)

Historical and Statutory Notes

P.L. 51–1984 provided in Section 5(a), containing emergency clause, that Section 3 of this act takes effect Jan. 1, 1984.

Section 5(a) of P.L. 51–1984 provided that Section 3 of this act affects taxable years that begin after Dec. 31, 1983.

The repealed chapter related to enterprise zone loan interest credits.

For provisions relating to carry back or carry forward of credits earned before Jan. 1, 1984, see Historical Note under section 6–3.1–1–1.

Former sections 6–3–3.9–1 to 6–3–3.9–6 were reenacted as sections 6–3.1–7–1 to 6–3.1–7–6, respectively.

Chapter 4

Returns and Remittances

Section
6–3–4–15.7   Annuity, pension, retirement, or other deferred compensation plans; withholding; requests; payor responsibility

6–3–4–1   Who must make returns

Sec. 1.   Returns with respect to taxes imposed by this act [1] shall be made by
the following:

(1) Every resident individual having for the taxable year gross income in
an amount greater than the modifications provided under IC 6–3–1–
3.5(a)(3) and IC 6–3–1–3.5(a)(4).

(2) Every nonresident individual having for the taxable year any gross
income from sources within the state of Indiana, except for a team member
(as defined in IC 6–3–2–2.7) who is covered by a composite return filed
under IC 6–3–2–2.7.

(3) Every corporation having for the taxable year any gross income from
sources within the state of Indiana.

(4) Every resident estate having for the taxable year any gross income from
sources within the state of Indiana.

(5) Every resident trust having for the taxable year any gross income from
sources within the state of Indiana.

(6) Every nonresident estate having for the taxable year any gross income
from sources within the state of Indiana.

(7) Every nonresident trust having for the taxable year any gross income
from sources within the state of Indiana.

As amended by Acts 1981, P.L.25, SEC.7; P.L.63–1997, SEC.3.

[1] Section 6–3–1–1 et seq.

Historical and Statutory Notes

Acts 1981, P.L. 25, § 7, emerg. eff. retroactively to Jan. 1, 1981, in Cl. (1), substituted
"income in an amount greater than the modifications provided under IC 6–3–1–3.5(a)(3) and
IC 6–3–1–3.5(a)(4)" for "income of one thousand dollars ($1,000) or more."

Acts 1981, P.L. 25, provided in § 10(c):

"Because an emergency exists for the retroactive taking effect of Sections 6, 7, and 9 of this
act, those sections take effect retroactively to
January 1, 1981, and affect taxable years beginning after December 31, 1980."

P.L.63–1997, Sec.3, eff. Jan. 1, 1998, amended the section by inserting "except for a team
member (as defined in IC 6–3–2–2.7) who is
covered by a composite return filed under IC 6–
3–2–2.7" in Subsec. (2).

P.L.63–1997, Sec.4, eff. Jan. 1, 1998, provides:

"This act applies to taxable years that begin
after December 31, 1997."

Formerly:
    Acts 1963 (ss), c. 32, s. 401.
    Acts 1965, c. 233, s. 16.

Cross References

Adjusted gross income defined, see IC 6–3–1–3.5.
Community revitalization enhancement district tax credit, state and local tax liability, see IC 6–3.1–
19–1.
Incremental tax financing fund, revenues, see IC 36–7–13–15.
Industrial development fund, state and local income taxes, see IC 36–7–13–3.8.

Military base recovery tax credit,
    Against other taxes owed, priority of application, see IC 6–3.1–11.5–24.
    State tax liability, see IC 6–3.1–11.5–14.
Rounding to nearest whole dollar, see IC 6–8.1–6–4.5.

Library References

Taxation ☞1079.
WESTLAW Topic No. 371.

C.J.S. Taxation § 1102.
I.L.E. Taxation §§ 220, 221.

6–3–4–2   Returns; fiduciaries; husband and wife

Sec. 2.   (a) If an individual is deceased, the return of such individual shall be made by the individual's executor, administrator, or other person charged with the property of such decedent.

(b) If an individual is unable to make a return, the return of such individual shall be made by a duly authorized agent, the individual's committee, guardian, fiduciary, or other person charged with the care of the person or property of such individual.

(c) Returns of an estate or a trust shall be made by the fiduciary thereof.

(d) Where a joint return is made by husband and wife pursuant to the Internal Revenue Code, a joint return shall be made pursuant to this article. Where a joint return is filed by a husband and wife hereunder, one spouse shall have no liability for the tax imposed by this article upon the income of the other spouse.

(e) Where separate returns are made by husband and wife pursuant to the Internal Revenue Code, separate returns shall be made pursuant to this article.
As amended by Acts 1977(ss), P.L.4, SEC.9; P.L.3–1989, SEC.39.

Historical and Statutory Notes

Acts 1977 (ss), P.L. 4, § 9, eff. Jan. 1, 1978, substituted "article" for "act" in the first and second sentences of Subsec. (d), and added Subsec. (e).

P.L.3–1989, Sec.39, emerg. eff. May 5, 1989, made corrective changes.

Formerly:

Acts 1963 (ss), c. 32, s. 402.
Acts 1965, c. 233, s. 17.

Cross References

Returns by fiduciaries, gross income tax, see IC 6–2.1–5–7.

Library References

Taxation ☞1079.
WESTLAW Topic No. 371.

C.J.S. Taxation § 1102.
I.L.E. Taxation §§ 220, 221.

6–3–4–3   Filing date

Sec. 3.   Returns required to be made pursuant to section 1 of this chapter shall be filed with the department on or before the 15th day of the fourth month following the close of the taxable year.
As amended by Acts 1980, P.L.61, SEC.4.

Historical and Statutory Notes

Acts 1980, P.L. 61, § 4, eff. Jan. 1, 1981, substituted "section 1 of this chapter" for "section 401 of this act"; and deleted a proviso at the end of the section which read: "Provided, however, the department may grant a reason-able extension of time for filing any return required by this act."

Formerly:

Acts 1963 (ss), c. 32, s. 403.

Library References

Taxation ⟋1079.
WESTLAW Topic No. 371.
C.J.S. Taxation § 1102.

6–3–4–4   Repealed

(Repealed by P.L.260–1997(ss), SEC.95.)

Historical and Statutory Notes

Former IC 6–3–4–4 related to declarations of estimated tax.

Formerly:

Acts 1963 (ss), c. 32, s. 404.
Acts 1965, c. 233, s. 18.
Acts 1969, c. 326, s. 5.
Acts 1973, P.L.49, SEC.6.
Acts 1977 (ss), P.L.4, SEC.10.

Acts 1980, P.L.61, SEC.5.
Acts 1981, P.L.77, SEC.13.
P.L.82–1983, SEC.8.
P.L.92–1987, SEC.3.
P.L.63–1988, SEC.7.
P.L.1–1991, SEC.52.
P.L.8–1996, SEC.4.
P.L.28–1997, SEC.13.

6–3–4–4.1   Estimated tax; declarations and payments; filing; corporations; failure to file; penalty; electronic funds transfer

Sec. 4.1. (a) This section applies to taxable years beginning after December 31, 1993.

(b) Any individual required by the Internal Revenue Code [1] to file estimated tax returns and to make payments on account of such estimated tax shall file estimated tax returns and make payments of the tax imposed by this article to the department at the time or times and in the installments as provided by Section 6654 of the Internal Revenue Code. [2] However, in applying Section 6654 of the Internal Revenue Code for the purposes of this article, "estimated tax" means the amount which the individual estimates as the amount of the adjusted gross income tax imposed by this article for the taxable year, minus the amount which the individual estimates as the sum of any credits against the tax provided by IC 6–3–3.

(c) Every individual who has gross income subject to the tax imposed by this article and from which tax is not withheld under the requirements of section 8 of this chapter shall make a declaration of estimated tax for the taxable year. However, no such declaration shall be required if the estimated tax can reasonably be expected to be less than four hundred dollars ($400). In the case of an underpayment of the estimated tax as provided in Section 6654 of the Internal Revenue Code, there shall be added to the tax a penalty in an amount prescribed by IC 6–8.1–10–2.1(b).

(d) Every corporation subject to the adjusted gross income tax liability imposed by IC 6–3 shall be required to report and pay an estimated tax equal to twenty-five percent (25%) of such corporation's estimated adjusted gross income tax liability for the taxable year, less the credit allowed by IC 6–3–3–2 for the tax imposed on gross income. Such estimated payment shall be made at the same time and in conjunction with the reporting of gross income tax as provided for in IC 6–2.1–5. The department shall prescribe the manner and forms for such reporting and payment.

(e) The penalty prescribed by IC 6–8.1–10–2.1(b) shall be assessed by the department on corporations failing to make payments as required in subsection (d) or (g). However, no penalty shall be assessed as to any estimated payments of adjusted gross income tax plus supplemental net income tax plus gross income tax which equal or exceed:

(1) twenty percent (20%) of the final tax liability for such taxable year; or

(2) twenty-five percent (25%) of the final tax liability for the taxpayer's previous taxable year.

In addition, the penalty as to any underpayment of tax on an estimated return shall only be assessed on the difference between the actual amount paid by the corporation on such estimated return and twenty-five percent (25%) of the sum of the corporation's final adjusted gross income tax plus supplemental net income tax liability for such taxable year.

(f) The provisions of subsection (d) requiring the reporting and estimated payment of adjusted gross income tax shall be applicable only to corporations having an adjusted gross income tax liability which, after application of the credit allowed by IC 6–3–3–2, shall exceed one thousand dollars ($1,000) for its taxable year.

(g) If the department determines that a corporation's:

(1) estimated quarterly adjusted gross income tax liability for the current year; or

(2) average estimated quarterly adjusted gross income tax liability for the preceding year;

exceeds, before January 1, 1998, twenty thousand dollars ($20,000), and, after December 31, 1997, ten thousand dollars ($10,000), after the credit allowed by IC 6–3–3–2, the corporation shall pay the estimated adjusted gross income taxes due by electronic funds transfer (as defined in IC 4–8.1–2–7) or by delivering in person or overnight by courier a payment by cashier's check, certified check, or money order to the department. The transfer or payment shall be made on or before the date the tax is due.

(h) If a corporation's adjusted gross income tax payment is made by electronic funds transfer, the corporation is not required to file an estimated adjusted gross income tax return.

As added by P.L.278–1993(ss), SEC.23. Amended by P.L.18–1994, SEC.9; P.L.19–1994, SEC.8; P.L.85–1995, SEC.10; P.L.8–1996, SEC.5; P.L.260–1997(ss), SECS.51, 95; P.L.28–1997, SEC.14; P.L.2–1998, SEC.32.

[1] 26 U.S.C.A. § 1 et seq.
[2] 26 U.S.C.A. § 6654.

Historical and Statutory Notes

P.L.278–1993(ss), Sec.23, eff. Jan. 1, 1994.

P.L.278–1993(ss), Sec.24, eff. July 1, 1993, provides:

"Sections 19 through 23 of this act apply to taxable years that begin after December 31, 1993 and end before January 1, 1998, and do not affect income tax payments due on the last day of January, 1994."

Section 32 of P.L.278–1993(ss), emerg. eff. retroactive to June 28, 1993, provides:

"(a) Notwithstanding the passage of HEA 1001ss–1993, the provisions of this act supersede the provisions of any conflicting provisions in HEA 1001ss–1993.

"(b) IC 1–1–3.1 does not apply to this act or to HEA 1001ss–1993.

"(c) Notwithstanding IC 1–1–3.1, the effective date of the Sections in this act and HEA 1001ss–1993 are as specified in this act and HEA 1001ss–1993, respectively, regardless of a veto of either act by the governor and the subsequent veto override of either or both acts."

P.L.18–1994, Sec.9, and P.L.19–1994, Sec.8, both emerg. eff. March 18, 1994 and amending this section by identical language, substituted "returns" for "declarations" and "Section 6654" for "Section 6015 and Section 6153" in Subsec. (b), deleted "In addition to the requirements in Section 6015(a) of the Internal Revenue Code," from the beginning of Subsec. (c), and inserted "quarterly" throughout Subsec. (g).

P.L.85–1995, Sec.10, eff. Jan. 1, 1996, amended the section by substituting "payments of adjusted gross income tax plus supplemental net income tax plus gross income tax which equal or exceed" for "payment which equals or exceeds" in Subsec. (e); designating Subsecs. (e)(1) and (2); deleting "as to any estimated payment which shall equal or exceed" from Subsec. (e)(1); adding "sum of the" and "plus supplemental net income tax" to Subsec. (e), and by substituting "funds" for "fund" in Subsecs. (g) and (h).

P.L.85–1995, Sec.44, emerg. eff. May 10, 1995, provides:

"IC 6–2.1–1–4.5, as added by this act, IC 6–2.1–2–5, as amended by this act, IC 6–3–1–11, as amended by this act, and IC 6–3–1–3.5, as amended by this act, apply to taxable years that begin after December 31, 1994. IC 6–3–4–4.1, as amended by this act, applies only to taxable years that begin after December 31, 1995."

P.L.8–1996, Sec.5, eff. Jan. 1, 1997, amended the section by substituting "four hundred dollars ($400)." for "one hundred dollars ($100)." in Subsec. (c).

P.L.260–1997(ss), Sec.51, amended the section by deleting "Notwithstanding section 1 of this chapter," from the beginning of, and deleting "and ending before January 1, 1998" from the end of, Subsec. (a); and inserting "before January 1, 1998," and "and, after December 31, 1997, ten thousand [sic] dollars ($10,000)," in Subsec. (g).

P.L.2–1998, Sec.32, emerg. eff. retroactive to Jan. 1, 1998, made corrective changes.

6–3–4–5   Payment of tax

Sec. 5.   When a return of tax is required pursuant to sections 1 and 3 of this chapter,[1] the taxpayer required to make such return shall, without assessment or notice and demand from the department, pay such tax to the department at the time fixed for filing the return without regard to any extension of time for filing the return.   Herff Jones, Inc. v. State Bd. of Tax Com'rs, Ind.Tax, No. 49T05–8610–TA–00030., 1987, 512 N.E.2d 485.

As amended by P.L.2–1988, SEC.11.

[1] Sections 6–3–4–1 and 6–3–4–3.

Historical and Statutory Notes

P.L. 2–1988, Sec.11, emerg. eff. Feb. 16, 1988, corrected internal references.

Formerly:

Acts 1963 (ss), c. 32, s. 405.

United States Supreme Court

Income taxation, utility deposits as advance payments, complete dominion test, see C.I.R. v. Indianapolis Power & Light Co., U.S.Ind.1990, 110 S.Ct. 589, 493 U.S. 203, 107 L.Ed.2d 591.

6–3–4–6   Copies of federal return; notice of modification

Sec. 6.   (a) Any taxpayer, upon request by the department, shall furnish to the department a true and correct copy of any tax return which he has filed with the United States Internal Revenue Service which copy shall be certified to by the taxpayer under penalties of perjury.

(b) Each taxpayer shall notify the department of any modification of:

(1) a federal income tax return filed by the taxpayer after January 1, 1978; or

(2) the taxpayer's federal income tax liability for a taxable year which begins after December 31, 1977.

The taxpayer shall file the notice, on the form prescribed by the department, within one hundred twenty (120) days after the modification is made.

As amended by Acts 1977(ss), P.L.4, SEC.11; P.L.119–1998, SEC.5.

Historical and Statutory Notes

Acts 1977 (ss), P.L. 4, § 11, eff. Jan. 1, 1978, designated Subsec. (a), and added Subsec. (b).

P.L.119–1998, Sec.5, emerg. eff. retroactive to Jan. 1, 1998, amended the section by deleting "except a resident individual," after "taxpayer"

in Subsec. (b); and making other nonsubstantive changes.

Formerly:

Acts 1963 (ss), c. 32, s. 406.
Acts 1965, c. 233, s. 19.

Administrative Code References

Federal returns,
Notice of modification, see 45 IAC 3.1–1–94.

6–3–4–7   Repealed

(Repealed by Acts 1980, P.L.61, SEC.15.)

Historical and Statutory Notes

Acts 1980, P.L. 61, provided in § 16 that the act takes effect Jan. 1, 1981.

The former section related to filing returns on prescribed forms, and certifying returns under penalty of perjury.

Provisions pertaining to tax forms and to the certification of returns and forms are now contained in §§ 6–8.1–3–4 and 6–8.1–6–4.

Formerly:
   Acts 1963 (ss), c. 32, s. 407.

6-3-4-8 Withholding rate; liability of employer; wages of precinct election officer; payment of taxes withheld to department; declarations of withholding; penalties; domestic service employees

Sec. 8. (a) Except as provided in subsection (d), every employer making payments of wages subject to tax under IC 6-3, regardless of the place where such payment is made, who is required under the provisions of the Internal Revenue Code[1] to withhold, collect, and pay over income tax on wages paid by such employer to such employee, shall, at the time of payment of such wages, deduct and retain therefrom the amount prescribed in withholding instructions issued by the department. The department shall base its withholding instructions on the adjusted gross income tax rate for persons, on the total rates of any income taxes that the taxpayer is subject to under IC 6-3.5, and on the total amount of exclusions the taxpayer is entitled to under IC 6-3-1-3.5(a)(3) and IC 6-3-1-3.5(a)(4). Such employer making payments of any wages:

(1) shall be liable to the state of Indiana for the payment of the tax required to be deducted and withheld under this section and shall not be liable to any individual for the amount deducted from his wages and paid over in compliance or intended compliance with this section; and

(2) shall make return of and payment to the department monthly of the amount of tax which under IC 6-3 and IC 6-3.5 he is required to withhold.

(b) An employer shall pay taxes withheld under subsection (a) during a particular month to the department no later than thirty (30) days after the end of that month. However, in place of monthly reporting periods, the department may permit an employer to report and pay the tax for:

(1) a calendar year reporting period, if the average monthly amount of all tax required to be withheld by the employer in the previous calendar year does not exceed ten dollars ($10);

(2) a six (6) month reporting period, if the average monthly amount of all tax required to be withheld by the employer in the previous calendar year does not exceed twenty-five dollars ($25); or

(3) a three (3) month reporting period, if the average monthly amount of all tax required to be withheld by the employer in the previous calendar year does not exceed seventy-five dollars ($75).

An employer using a reporting period (other than a monthly reporting period) must file the employer's return and pay the tax for a reporting period no later than the last day of the month immediately following the close of the reporting period. If an employer files a combined sales and withholding tax report, the reporting period for the combined report is the shortest period required under this section, section 8.1 of this chapter, or IC 6-2.5-6-1.

(c) For purposes of determining whether an employee is subject to taxation under IC 6-3.5, an employer is entitled to rely on the statement of his employee as to his county of residence as represented by the statement of address in forms claiming exemptions for purposes of withholding, regardless of when the employee supplied the forms. Every employee shall notify his employer within five (5) days after any change in his county of residence.

(d) A county that makes payments of wages subject to tax under IC 6–3:

(1) to a precinct election officer (as defined in IC 3–5–2–40.1); and

(2) for the performance of the duties of the precinct election officer imposed by IC 3 that are performed on election day;

is not required, at the time of payment of the wages, to deduct and retain from the wages the amount prescribed in withholding instructions issued by the department.

(e) Every employer shall, at the time of each payment made by him to the department, deliver to the department a return upon the form prescribed by the department showing:

(1) the total amount of wages paid to his employees;

(2) the amount deducted therefrom in accordance with the provisions of the Internal Revenue Code;

(3) the amount of adjusted gross income tax deducted therefrom in accordance with the provisions of this section;

(4) the amount of income tax, if any, imposed under IC 6–3.5 and deducted therefrom in accordance with this section; and

(5) any other information the department may require.

Every employer making a declaration of withholding as provided in this section shall furnish his employees annually, but not later than thirty (30) days after the end of the calendar year, a record of the total amount of adjusted gross income tax and the amount of each income tax, if any, imposed under IC 6–3.5, withheld from the employees, on the forms prescribed by the department.

(f) All money deducted and withheld by an employer shall immediately upon such deduction be the money of the state, and every employer who deducts and retains any amount of money under the provisions of IC 6–3 shall hold the same in trust for the state of Indiana and for payment thereof to the department in the manner and at the times provided in IC 6–3. Any employer may be required to post a surety bond in the sum the department determines to be appropriate to protect the state with respect to money withheld pursuant to this section.

(g) The provisions of IC 6–8.1 relating to additions to tax in case of delinquency and penalties shall apply to employers subject to the provisions of this section, and for these purposes any amount deducted or required to be deducted and remitted to the department under this section shall be considered to be the tax of the employer, and with respect to such amount the employer shall be considered the taxpayer. In the case of a corporate or partnership employer, every officer, employee, or member of such employer, who, as such officer, employee, or member is under a duty to deduct and remit such taxes shall be personally liable for such taxes, penalties, and interest.

(h) Amounts deducted from wages of an employee during any calendar year in accordance with the provisions of this section shall be considered to be in part payment of the tax imposed on such employee for his taxable year which begins in such calendar year, and a return made by the employer under subsection (b) shall be accepted by the department as evidence in favor of the employee of the amount so deducted from his wages. Where the total amount so deducted exceeds the amount of tax on the employee as computed under IC 6–3 and IC 6–3.5, the department shall, after examining the return or returns filed by the employee in accordance with IC 6–3 and IC 6–3.5, refund the amount of the excess deduction. However, under rules promulgated by the department, the excess or any part thereof may be applied to any taxes or other claim due from the taxpayer to the state of Indiana or any subdivision thereof. No refund shall be made to an employee who fails to file his return or returns as required under IC 6–3 and IC 6–3.5 within two (2) years from the due date of the return or returns. In the event that the excess tax deducted is less than one dollar ($1), no refund shall be made.

(i) This section shall in no way relieve any taxpayer from his obligation of filing a return or returns at the time required under IC 6–3 and IC 6–3.5, and, should the amount withheld under the provisions of this section be insufficient to pay the total tax of such taxpayer, such unpaid tax shall be paid at the time prescribed by section 5 of this chapter.

(j) Notwithstanding subsection (b), an employer of a domestic service employee that enters into an agreement with the domestic service employee to withhold federal income tax under Section 3402 of the Internal Revenue Code may withhold Indiana income tax on the domestic service employee's wages on the employer's Indiana individual income tax return in the same manner as allowed by Section 3510 of the Internal Revenue Code.

(k) To the extent allowed by Section 1137 of the Social Security Act, an employer of a domestic service employee may report and remit state unemployment insurance contributions on the employee's wages on the employer's Indiana individual income tax return in the same manner as allowed by Section 3510 of the Internal Revenue Code.

(*l*) A person who knowingly fails to remit trust fund money as set forth in this section commits a Class D felony.

As amended by Acts 1979, P.L.68, SEC.3; Acts 1980, P.L.61, SEC.6; Acts 1982, P.L.49, SEC.2; P.L.2–1982(ss), SEC.9; P.L.26–1985, SEC.10; P.L.70–1986, SEC.2; P.L.94–1995, SEC.1; P.L.8–1996, SEC.6.

[1] 26 U.S.C.A. § 3401 et seq.

Historical and Statutory Notes

Acts 1979, P.L. 68, § 3, eff. Jan. 1, 1980, substituted "IC 6–3" for "this article" and for "the provisions of this article" throughout the section; in the introductory clause of Subsec. (a), substituted "IC 6–3–1–3.5(a)(3) and (4)" for "IC1971, 6–3–1–3(a)(2) and (a)(3)", and deleted "After June 30, 1963" at the beginning of the clause; in Subsec. (a)(1), inserted "IC 6–3.5–1," and reduced the percentage from 2% to 1.9%; in Subsec. (a)(ii), substituted "IC 6–3.5–1" for "such Law", and reduced the first stated percentage from 2% to 1.9%; in Subsec. (a)(iii), substituted "IC 6–3.5–1" for "such Law" at the beginning of the subsection, inserted "For purposes of determining whether or not an employee is subject to taxation under IC 6–3.5–1," at the beginning of the fourth complete sentence, and substituted "regardless of when the employee supplied the forms" for "whether such form is supplied to the employer before or after the effective date of the County Adjusted Gross Income Tax Law" at the end of that sentence, and inserted "(5)" following "five" in the fifth complete sentence; in Subsec. (b), substituted "the amount of adjusted gross income tax deducted therefrom" for "the amount deducted therefrom" in the first sentence; in Subsec. (f), added "of this chapter"; and rewrote Subsec. (g) to read:

"A person who recklessly violates this section commits a Class B misdemeanor. The attorney general shall have concurrent jurisdiction with the prosecuting attorney in instituting and prosecuting an action under this section."

Prior to the 1979 act, Subsec. (g) read:

"Any employer, and the officers and partners thereof, violating any of the provisions of this section shall be guilty of a misdemeanor, and on conviction thereof shall be fined not less than one hundred dollars ($100) nor more than one thousand dollars ($1,000), to which may be added imprisonment in the county jail not to exceed six (6) months. In addition to the foregoing penalties, any person who shall knowingly swear to or verify any false or fraudulent statement with the intent to defraud the state or to evade the payment of the tax imposed hereunder shall be guilty of the offense of perjury and on conviction thereof, shall be punished in the manner provided by law. The criminal prosecution of any person or persons guilty of having violated any of the provisions of this section may be instituted by filing an affidavit or indictment in the same manner as other criminal cases are commenced, and the attorney general shall have concurrent jurisdiction with the prosecuting attorney in instituting and prosecuting such action. The attorney general and/or the prosecuting attorney shall be allowed at all times to appear before the grand jury for the purpose of reporting any violation of this section, or for the purpose of rendering legal advice with respect thereto when required, or for the purpose of interrogating witnesses before the grand jury. When any affidavit charging any person with a violation of any of the provisions of this section has been made as provided for by law, either the attorney general or the prosecuting attorney shall approve the same by indorsement, using the words "approved by me" and by signing the same as attorney general or prosecuting attorney."

Acts 1980, P.L. 61, § 6, eff. Jan. 1, 1981, deleted the second sentence of Subsec. (g), as rewritten by the 1979 act.

Acts 1982, P.L.49, Sec.2, emerg. eff. April 1, 1982, in Cl. (2) of the present third sentence of Subsec. (a), added "unless an earlier date is specified by section 8.1 of this chapter."

Section 8 of Acts 1982, P.L.49, provided that this act affects returns and payments due to the department after March 31, 1982.

P.L. 2–1982(ss), Sec.9, emerg. eff. Jan. 1, 1983, rewrote Subsec. (a), which prior thereto read:

"(a) Every employer making payments of wages subject to tax under IC 6–3 regardless of the place where such payment is made who is required under the provisions of the Internal Revenue Code to withhold, collect and pay over income tax on wages paid by such employer to such employee, shall, at the time of payment of such wages deduct and retain therefrom an amount equal to the following percentages of the amount by which gross wages exceed a proportionate part of the exclusions provided for in IC 6–3–1–3.5(a)(3) and (4) attributable to the pay period for which such wages are payable:

"(i) in the case of an individual who is liable for the adjusted gross income tax imposed by IC 6–3 and who is not a county taxpayer subject to a county adjusted gross income tax as imposed pursuant to the County Adjusted Gross Income Tax Law, IC 6–3.5–1, an amount equal to one and nine-tenths percent (1.9%);

"(ii) in the case of an individual who is liable for the adjusted gross income tax imposed by IC 6–3 and who is a county taxpayer subject to a county adjusted gross income tax as defined in IC 6–3.5–1, an amount equal to the sum of one and nine-tenths percent (1.9%) plus either the county rate in the county of residence of a resident county taxpayer or one-fourth of one percent (1/4%) in the case of any other county taxpayer; or

"(iii) in the case of an individual who is a county taxpayer subject to a county adjusted gross income tax as defined in IC 6–3.5–1 but who is not liable for the adjusted gross income tax imposed by IC 6–3, an amount equal to the rate of one-quarter percent (1/4%) of the taxpayer's adjusted gross income. Provided, however, That the department may modify the foregoing formula in order to approximate the actual amount of tax that will be due. Such employer making payments of any wages: (1) shall be liable to the state of Indiana for the payment of the tax required to be deducted and withheld under this section and shall not be liable to any individual for the amount deducted from his wages and paid over in compliance or intended compliance with this section; and (2) shall make return of and payment to the department monthly whenever the amount of tax due under IC 6–3 exceeds an aggregate amount of fifty dollars ($50.00) per month with such payment due on the thirtieth (30th) day of the following month, unless an earlier date is specified by section 8.1 of this chapter. Where the aggregate amount due under IC 6–3 does not exceed fifty dollars ($50.00) per month, then such employer shall make return of and payment to the department quarterly on such dates and in such manner as the department shall prescribe, the amount of tax which, under IC 6–3, he is required to withhold. For purposes of determining whether or not an employee is subject to taxation under IC 6–3.5–1, an employer shall be entitled to rely on the statement of his employee as to his county of residence as represented by the statement of address in forms claiming exemptions for purposes of withholding, regardless of when the employee supplied the forms. Every employee shall advise his employer of his county of residence on or before May 30, 1973, if such address is not that of his residence or does not permit identification of his county of residence and thereafter shall notify his employer within five (5) days after any change in his county of residence."

P.L. 2–1982(ss), Sec.9, also, in Subsec. (b), deleted "county adjusted gross" preceding "income tax" where secondly appearing in the first sentence and substituted "the amount of each" for "county adjusted gross" in the last sentence; in Subsec. (d), substituted "IC 6–8.1" for "IC 6–3" in the first sentence; and inserted "or returns" and references to IC 6–3.5 where appearing throughout.

P.L.26–1985, Sec.10, eff. July 1, 1986, redesignated the first four sentences of former Subsec. (a) as Subsec. (a) and the fifth and sixth sentences of former Subsec. (a) as Subsec. (c); in the third sentence of Subsec. (a), deleted "whenever the amount of tax due under IC 6–3 and IC 6–3.5 exceeds an aggregate amount of fifty dollars ($50.00) per month with such payment due on the thirtieth (30th) day of the following month, unless an earlier date is specified by section 8.1 of this chapter. Where the aggregate amount due under IC 6–3 does not exceed fifty dollars ($50.00) per month, then such employer shall make return and payment to the department quarterly on such dates and in such manner as the department shall prescribe," following "(2) shall make return of and payment to the department monthly"; inserted Subsec. (b); in the first sentence of Subsec. (c), substituted "is entitled" for "shall be entitled";

redesignated former Subsecs. (b) to (g) as Subsecs. (d) to (i); in Subsec. (d), in the first sentence, substituted "the form prescribed" for "such form as shall be prescribed", inserted the subdivision numbering, and substituted "any other information" for "other information as" in Subd. (5), and in the second sentence, substituted "in this section" for "herein" and "the employees, on the forms" for "such employees, on forms to be"; in Subsec. (e), substituted "money" for "moneys" twice, and in the second sentence, substituted "the sum the department determines" for "such sum as the department shall determine"; in Subsec. (f), in the first sentence, substituted "the employer" for "he"; in Subsec. (g), in the first sentence, deleted "of this section" following "subsection (b)", and in the third sentence, substituted "rules promulgated by the department, the excess" for "regulations promulgated by the department, such excess"; and rewrote Subsec. (i) [former Subsec. (g)], which had read:

"(g) A person who recklessly violates this section commits a Class B misdemeanor."

P.L.70–1986, Sec.2, eff. July 1, 1986, inserted the last sentence in Subsec. (b).

P.L.94–1995, Sec.1, emerg. eff. March 28, 1995, amended the section by adding "Except as provided in subsection (d)," in subsection (a); adding subsection (d); redesignating former subsections (d) through (i) as (e) through (j); and by substituting "money" for "monies" in subsection (j).

P.L.94–1995, Sec.2, emerg. eff. March 28, 1995, provides:

"This act applies to taxable years that begin after December 31, 1994."

P.L.8–1996, Sec.6, emerg. eff. retroactive to Jan. 1, 1996, amended the section by substituting "IC 6–3–1–3.5(a)(4)" for "(a)(4)" at the end of Subsec. (a); adding Subsecs. (j) and (k); and by redesignating Subsec. (j) as (*l*).

P.L.8–1996, Sec.14, emerg. eff. retroactive to Jan. 1, 1996, provides:

"IC 6–3–4–8, as amended by this act, applies to taxable years beginning after December 31, 1995."

Formerly:

Acts 1963 (ss), c. 32, s. 408.
Acts 1965, c. 233, s. 20.
Acts 1969, c. 326, s. 6.
Acts 1971, P.L.65, SEC.1.
Acts 1973, P.L.50, SEC.3.

Cross References

Gross income tax, withholding provisions, see IC 6–2.1–6–1 et seq.

Penalty for class B misdemeanors, see IC 35–50–3–3.
Tax refunds, generally, see IC 6–8.1–9–1 et seq.

Administrative Code References

Adjusted gross income tax,
    Refunds, see 45 IAC 3.1–1–103.
    Withholding, see 45 IAC 3.1–1–97 et seq.

Law Review and Journal Commentaries

Responsible officer tax liabilities. Kathleen
Madinger Angelone, 23 Res Gestae 68 (1979).

Library References

Taxation ⊕1100, 1103.
WESTLAW Topic No. 371.

C.J.S. Taxation § 1107.
I.L.E. Taxation §§ 207, 220, 221.

Notes of Decisions

In general   1
Employer's liability   2
Presumptions   3

-----

1.   In general

Method for determining whether given individual is responsible person, personally liable for nonpayment of taxes, is the same under gross retail tax and withholding tax; individual is personally liable if she is officer, employee, or member of employer who had duty to remit taxes to Department of Revenue. Indiana Dept. of State Revenue v. Safayan, 1995, 654 N.E.2d 270.

Party may be responsible person liable for trust taxes without having exclusive control over corporation's funds. Indiana Dept. of State Revenue v. Safayan, 1995, 654 N.E.2d 270.

Income tax scheme provides that individuals make payments on their adjusted gross income throughout year; this is done through withholding process, in which employer withholds federal, state, and local income tax, as well as Federal Insurance Contributions Act (FICA) payments, from each employee's wage payment. Longmire v. Indiana Dept. of State Revenue, 1994, 638 N.E.2d 894.

Prerequisite to employer's obligation to withhold is employer-employee relationship. Longmire v. Indiana Dept. of State Revenue, 1994, 638 N.E.2d 894.

2.   Employer's liability

Statutory duty to remit trust taxes falls on any officer or employee of corporation who has authority to see that taxes are paid. Indiana Dept. of State Revenue v. Safayan, 1995, 654 N.E.2d 270.

In determining whether officer or employee has duty to remit trust taxes, court considers person's position within power structure of corporation, authority of officer or employee as established by articles of incorporation, bylaws, or employment contract, and whether officer or employee actually exercised control over finances of business. Indiana Dept. of State Revenue v. Safayan, 1995, 654 N.E.2d 270.

Corporate president who was also member of board of directors and major shareholder of closely held corporation was responsible person personally liable for nonpayment of gross retail, and withholding trust taxes; delegation of responsibility to pay taxes to another or lack of participation in day to day operations of corporation did not relinquish position of authority, and president's actions in firing employees and starting bankruptcy proceedings after finding out about corporation's financial difficulties was proof of actual control over corporate finances. Indiana Dept. of State Revenue v. Safayan, 1995, 654 N.E.2d 270.

Evidence supported conclusion that corporation, and not general partnership composed of corporate officers, owned and operated restaurant, and was liable for restaurant's sales and withholding taxes; partnership agreement did not show that partnership owned and operated restaurant during years in issue, while restaurant used corporation's tax identification number, corporation was assessed for restaurant's delinquent taxes, and parties believed corporation was the owner and operator of restaurant. Safayan v. Indiana Dept. of State Revenue, 1994, 631 N.E.2d 25, reversed 654 N.E.2d 270.

President of corporation which owned and operated restaurant was not personally liable for delinquent sales and withholding taxes of corporation, where president did not participate

31

in management of corporation or have specific authority under bylaws, or with bank to disburse funds of corporation, and where president's interests and involvement in corporation was more as investor and not as manager of restaurant. Safayan v. Indiana Dept. of State Revenue, 1994, 631 N.E.2d 25, reversed 654 N.E.2d 270.

President of corporation, who was a majority shareholder and member of board of directors, was presumed to have the responsibility and authority to control funds of the corporation and failed to overcome presumption by merely indicating that another person may have been involved in decisions concerning sales/use and withholding taxes, and hence, president of corporation was personally liable for the taxes; president made decisions on all bills for supplies, utilities, repair, and payroll. State, Dept. of Revenue v. Hogo, Inc., App. 4 Dist.1990, 550 N.E.2d 1320, transfer denied.

Under version of tax statute in force during period of assessment, responsible officer for taxpayer was liable for payment of gross retail and use taxes only, and not for penalties and interest. Wechter v. Indiana Dept. of State Revenue, 1989, 544 N.E.2d 221, affirmed 553 N.E.2d 844.

3. Presumptions

Although responsible person liable for nonpayment of taxes need not be a corporate officer, if individual were high ranking officer, court presumes that he had sufficient control over company's finances to give rise to duty to remit trust taxes. Indiana Dept. of State Revenue v. Safayan, 1995, 654 N.E.2d 270.

In determining responsible person liability for nonpayment of taxes, presumption that high ranking officer had sufficient control over company's finances to give rise to duty to remit trust taxes is especially strong where officer is high ranking officer and member of board of directors and major shareholder in closely held corporation. Indiana Dept. of State Revenue v. Safayan, 1995, 654 N.E.2d 270.

For purposes of responsible person liability for nonpayment of taxes, presumption that high ranking officer had sufficient control over company's finances to give rise to duty to remit trust taxes may be rebutted by showing that officer did not in fact have that authority. Indiana Dept. of State Revenue v. Safayan, 1995, 654 N.E.2d 270.

6–3–4–8.1 Monthly return and remittance of taxes

Sec. 8.1. (a) Any entity that is required to file a monthly return and make a monthly remittance of taxes under sections 8, 12, 13, and 15 of this chapter shall file those returns and make those remittances twenty (20) days (rather than thirty (30) days) after the end of each month for which those returns and remittances are filed, if that entity's average monthly remittance for the immediately preceding calendar year exceeds one thousand dollars ($1,000).

(b) The department may require any entity to make the entity's monthly remittance and file the entity's monthly return twenty (20) days (rather than thirty (30) days) after the end of each month for which a return and payment are made if the department estimates that the entity's average monthly payment for the current calendar year will exceed one thousand dollars ($1,000).

(c) If a person files a combined sales and withholding tax report and either this section or IC 6–2.5–6–1 requires the sales or withholding tax report to be filed and remittances to be made within twenty (20) days after the end of each month, then the person shall file the combined report and remit the sales and withholding taxes due within twenty (20) days after the end of each month.

(d) If the department determines that an entity's:

(1) estimated monthly withholding tax remittance for the current year; or

(2) average monthly withholding tax remittance for the preceding year;

exceeds ten thousand dollars ($10,000), the entity shall remit the monthly withholding taxes due by electronic fund transfer (as defined in IC 4–8.1–2–7) or by delivering in person or by overnight courier a payment by cashier's check, certified check, or money order to the department. The transfer or payment shall be made on or before the date the remittance is due.

(e) If an entity's withholding tax remittance is made by electronic fund transfer, the entity is not required to file a monthly withholding tax return. However, the entity shall file a quarterly withholding tax return before the twentieth day following the end of each calendar quarter.

As added by Acts 1982, P.L.49, SEC.3. Amended by P.L.70–1986, SEC.3; P.L.92–1987, SEC.4; P.L.63–1988, SEC.8; P.L.28–1997, SEC.15.

Historical and Statutory Notes

Acts 1982, P.L.49, Sec.3, emerg. eff. April 1, 1982, added this section.

Section 8 of Acts 1982, P.L.49, provided:

"Because an emergency exists, this act takes effect April 1, 1982, and affects returns and payments due to the department after March 31, 1982."

P.L. 70–1986, Sec.3, eff. July 1, 1986, added Subsec. (c).

P.L.92–1987, Sec.4, eff. July 1, 1987, added Subsecs. (d) and (e).

P.L. 63–1988, Sec.8, emerg. eff. March 5, 1988, substituted $20,000 for $10,000 and modified payment and delivery provisions which formerly were "in person or by courier a cash payment", and substituted in Subsec. (e) "by electronic fund transfer" for "under subsection (d)", and made other nonsubstantive changes.

P.L.28–1997, Sec.15, eff. Jan. 1, 1998, amended the section by substituting "ten thousand dollars ($10,000)" for "twenty thousand dollars ($20,000)" in Subsec. (d).

Library References

Taxation ⟨⟩1079.
WESTLAW Topic No. 371.
C.J.S. Taxation § 1102.

6–3–4–8.2   Withholdings from winnings

Sec. 8.2. Each person in Indiana who is required under the Internal Revenue Code [1] to withhold federal tax from winnings shall deduct and retain adjusted gross income tax at the time and in the amount described in withholding instructions issued by the department.

As added by P.L.28–1997, SEC.16.

[1] 26 U.S.C.A. § 1 et seq.

Historical and Statutory Notes

P.L.28–1997, Sec.16, eff. Jan. 1, 1998.

6–3–4–8.5   Liability of transferee of property

Sec. 8.5. In the case of a transferee of the property of a transferor, liability for any accrued tax liability of the transferor is transferred to the transferee as provided in section 6901 of the Internal Revenue Code.[1]

As added by Acts 1977(ss), P.L.4, SEC.12.

[1.] 26 U.S.C.A. § 6901.

Historical and Statutory Notes

Acts 1977 (ss), P.L. 4, § 12, eff. Jan. 1, 1978, added this section.

United States Code Annotated

Federal taxes, liability of transferees and fiduciaries, see 26 U.S.C.A. § 6901 et seq.

Notes of Decisions

Partnerships 1

———

1. Partnerships

Under prior law, income received by an affiliated group of corporations from corporate partnerships in which group members were partners should not have been included in the group's adjusted gross income, even though none of the corporate partnerships filed state income tax returns or paid adjusted gross income tax; the prior law taxed corporate partnership income at the partnership level, whereas current law taxes it at the partner level. Hunt Corp. v. Department of State Revenue, 1999, 709 N.E.2d 766.

6–3–4–9 Reports of payment to recipients

Sec. 9. All individuals, corporations, limited liability companies, partnerships, fiduciaries, or associations, in whatever capacity acting, including but without being limited to, lessees or mortgagors of real or personal property, fiduciaries, and employers making payment to other persons of interest, rent, wages, salaries, premiums, annuities, compensation, remunerations, emoluments, other fixed or determinable means, profits and income, or corporate liquidation distributions shall make returns to the department setting forth the amount of such payments and the name and address of the recipient of such payment at such time or times in such manner, and on such forms as prescribed by the department.

As amended by P.L.8–1993, SEC.84.

Historical and Statutory Notes

P.L.8–1993, Sec.84, inserted "limited liability companies".

Formerly:
Acts 1963 (ss), c. 32, s. 409.

Administrative Code References

Information returns, see 45 IAC 15–11–6.

Library References

Taxation ⊂∋1100.
WESTLAW Topic No. 371.

C.J.S. Taxation § 1107.
I.L.E. Taxation §§ 220, 221.

6–3–4–10 Partnership returns

Sec. 10. (a) Except as provided in subsection (b), every partnership doing business in this state, every partnership any partner of which is a resident, and every partnership which has gross income derived from sources within this state, shall make a return for each taxable year on a form to be prescribed by the department, which return shall correspond with the returns required by Section 6031 of the Internal Revenue Code,[1] insofar as consistent with the provisions of this article.   However, this section shall not be construed to render any partnership a taxpayer under this article.

(b) A partnership or a corporation that is exempt from income tax under Section 1363 of the Internal Revenue Code[2] is not required to file:

(1) federal income tax Schedule K–1 (Form 1065) Partner's Share of Income, Credits, Deductions, Etc.; or

(2) federal income tax Schedule K–1 (Form 1120S) Shareholder's Share of Income, Credits, Deductions, Etc.;

with an annual return filed with the department.   However, a federal income tax schedule described in this subsection must be available for inspection upon request by the department.

As amended by P.L.2–1987, SEC.20; P.L.18–1994, SEC.10.

[1] 26 U.S.C.A. § 6031.
[2] 26 U.S.C.A. § 1363.

Historical and Statutory Notes

P.L.2–1987, Sec.20, amended this section emergency effective retroactive to Jan. 1, 1987.

P.L.2–1987 provides in Section 54 that this act applies to taxable years beginning after Dec. 31, 1986.

P.L.18–1994, Sec.10, designated the former section as Subsec. (a), and added the exception for Subsec. (b) at the beginning; and added Subsec. (b).

Formerly:

Acts 1963 (ss), c. 32, s. 410.

Cross References

Partnership defined, see IC 6–3–1–19.

Administrative Code References

Partnership annual returns, see 45 IAC 3.1–1–105.

Library References

Taxation ⬩1079.
WESTLAW Topic No. 371.

C.J.S. Taxation § 1102.
I.L.E. Taxation §§ 220, 221.

United States Code Annotated

Federal income tax, partnership returns, see 26 U.S.C.A. § 6031.

Notes of Decisions

In general   1

___

1. In general

Under prior law, income received by an affiliated group of corporations from corporate partnerships in which group members were partners should not have been included in the group's adjusted gross income, even though none of the corporate partnerships filed state income tax returns or paid adjusted gross income; the prior law taxed corporate partnership income at the partnership level, whereas current law taxes it at the partner level. Hunt Corp. v. Department of State Revenue, 1999, 709 N.E.2d 766.

Partnerships do not file state and federal income tax returns per se but, rather, informational returns in which they report items of gross income and deduction and names and distributive shares of their partners. Longmire

v. Indiana Dept. of State Revenue, •1994, 638 N.E.2d 894.

6–3–4–11   Partnerships not subject to tax

Sec. 11.   (a) A partnership as such shall not be subject to the adjusted gross income tax imposed by IC 6–3–1 through IC 6–3–7.   Persons or corporations carrying on business as partners shall be liable for the adjusted gross income tax only in their separate or individual capacities.   In determining each partner's adjusted gross income, such partner shall take into account his or its distributive share of the adjustments provided for in IC 6–3–1–3.5.

(b) The adjustments provided for in IC 6–3–1–3.5 shall be allowed for the taxable year of the partner within or with which the partnership's taxable year ends.

As amended by Acts 1980, P.L.54, SEC.5.

Historical and Statutory Notes

Acts 1980, P.L. 54, § 5, eff. May 1, 1980, in Subsec. (a), substituted "IC 6–3–1 through IC 6–3–7" for "this act" in the first sentence; and substituted "IC 6–3–1–3.5" for "section 103 of this act" in the third sentence of Subsec. (a) and in Subsec. (b).

Formerly:

Acts 1963 (ss), c. 32, s. 411.
Acts 1965, c. 233, s. 21.

Cross References

Gross income tax, certain partnerships exempt, see IC 6–2.1–3–25.

Administrative Code References

Reporting of partners' distributive shares, see 45 IAC 3.1–1–106.

Library References

Taxation ☞1017.
WESTLAW Topic No. 371.
C.J.S. Taxation § 1093.

Notes of Decisions

In general   1
Burden of proof   4
Partnership income   3
Separate or individual tax liability   2

1. In general

Partnerships are unique entities and are not subject to income tax. Longmire v. Indiana Dept. of State Revenue, 1994, 638 N.E.2d 894.

2. Separate or individual tax liability

Individual partners of partnership are individually liable for their respective distributive shares of partnership's taxable income. Longmire v. Indiana Dept. of State Revenue, 1994, 638 N.E.2d 894.

Each partner reports his distributive share of partnership income on his individual adjusted gross income tax return. Longmire v. Indiana Dept. of State Revenue, 1994, 638 N.E.2d 894.

3. Partnership income

Mere issuance of W–2 forms is not dispositive of question whether persons were hired as individuals rather than as partnership for purpose of determining whether income earned was individual income or partnership income. Longmire v. Indiana Dept. of State Revenue, 1994, 638 N.E.2d 894.

Income was partnership income and not subject to taxation, even though individual partners had been issued W–2 forms by government agency which employed them, where testimony indicated that employer knew it was hiring partnership because partnership had no employees and no intent to delegate responsibility to anyone other than partners, bids and applications were submitted prior to each project, and employer placed no restrictions on partners as to where to work, when to work, or how to work. Longmire v. Indiana Dept. of State Revenue, 1994, 638 N.E.2d 894.

4. Burden of proof

Although statutes that impose tax are to be strictly construed against state, it is well settled in Indiana that taxpayer who claims he is not within ambit of taxation bears burden of proof.

Longmire v. Indiana Dept. of State Revenue, 1994, 638 N.E.2d 894.

To meet burden of proof that he is not within ambit of taxation, taxpayer must present "prima facie case," or one in which evidence is sufficient to establish given fact and which if not contradicted will remain sufficient. Longmire v. Indiana Dept. of State Revenue, 1994, 638 N.E.2d 894.

Once taxpayer has presented prima facie case, that he is not within ambit of taxation, duty to go forward with that evidence may shift several times. Longmire v. Indiana Dept. of State Revenue, 1994, 638 N.E.2d 894.

6–3–4–12 Nonresident partners; withholding rate; returns; credits for tax withheld

Sec. 12. (a) Every partnership shall, at the time that the partnership pays or credits amounts to any of its nonresident partners on account of their distributive shares of partnership income, for a taxable year of the partnership, deduct and retain therefrom the amount prescribed in the withholding instructions referred to in section 8 of this chapter. Such partnership so paying or crediting any nonresident partner:

(1) shall be liable to the state of Indiana for the payment of the tax required to be deducted and retained under this section and shall not be liable to such partner for the amount deducted from such payment or credit and paid over in compliance or intended compliance with this section; and

(2) shall make return of and payment to the department monthly whenever the amount of tax due under IC 6–3 and IC 6–3.5 exceeds an aggregate amount of fifty dollars ($50) per month with such payment due on the thirtieth day of the following month, unless an earlier date is specified by section 8.1 of this chapter.

Where the aggregate amount due under IC 6–3 and IC 6–3.5 does not exceed fifty dollars ($50) per month, then such partnership shall make return and payment to the department quarterly, on such dates and in such manner as the department shall prescribe, of the amount of tax which, under IC 6–3 and IC 6–3.5, it is required to withhold.

(b) Every partnership shall, at the time of each payment made by it to the department pursuant to this section, deliver to the department a return upon such form as shall be prescribed by the department showing the total amounts paid or credited to its nonresident partners, the amount deducted therefrom in accordance with the provisions of this section, and such other information as the department may require. Every partnership making the deduction and retention provided in this section shall furnish to its nonresident partners annually, but not later than thirty (30) days after the end of its taxable year, a record of the amount of tax deducted and retained from such partners on forms to be prescribed by the department.

(c) All money deducted and retained by the partnership, as provided in this section, shall immediately upon such deduction be the money of the state of Indiana and every partnership which deducts and retains any amount of money under the provisions of IC 6–3 shall hold the same in trust for the state of Indiana and for payment thereof to the department in the manner and at the times provided in IC 6–3. Any partnership may be required to post a surety bond in such sum as the department shall determine to be appropriate to protect the state of Indiana with respect to money deducted and retained pursuant to this section.

(d) The provisions of IC 6–8.1 relating to additions to tax in case of delinquency and penalties shall apply to partnerships subject to the provisions of this section, and for these purposes any amount deducted, or required to be deducted and remitted to the department under this section, shall be considered to be the tax of the partnership, and with respect to such amount it shall be considered the taxpayer.

(e) Amounts deducted from payments or credits to a nonresident partner during any taxable year of the partnership in accordance with the provisions of this section shall be considered to be in part payment of the tax imposed on such nonresident partner for his taxable year within or with which the partnership's taxable year ends. A return made by the partnership under subsection (b) shall be accepted by the department as evidence in favor of the nonresident partner of the amount so deducted for his distributive share.

(f) This section shall in no way relieve any nonresident partner from his obligations of filing a return or returns at the time required under IC 6–3 or IC 6–3.5, and any unpaid tax shall be paid at the time prescribed by section 5 of this chapter.

(g) Instead of the reporting periods required under subsection (a), the department may permit a partnership to file one (1) return and payment each year if the partnership pays or credits amounts to its nonresident partners only one (1) time each year. The return and payment are due not more than thirty (30) days after the end of the year.

As amended by Acts 1979, P.L.68, SEC.4; Acts 1982, P.L.49, SEC.4; P.L.2–1982(ss), SEC.10; P.L.23–1986, SEC.3.

Historical and Statutory Notes

Acts 1979, P.L. 68, § 4, eff. Jan. 1, 1980, substituted "IC 6–3" for "this article" or "the provisions of this article" throughout the section; inserted "as defined in IC 6–3.5–1" in Subsec. (a)(i); reduced the first stated percentage from 2% to 1.9% in Subsecs. (a)(i) and (a)(ii); substituted "IC 6–3.5–1" for "such Law" in Subsecs. (a)(ii) and (a)(iii); and added "of this chapter" to Subsec. (f).

Acts 1982, P.L.49, Sec.4, emerg. eff. April 1, 1982, in Cl. (2) of the present second sentence of Subsec. (a), added "unless an earlier date is specified by section 8.1 of this chapter" to the second sentence.

Section 8 of Acts 1982, P.L.49, provided:

"Because an emergency exists, this act takes effect April 1, 1982, and affects returns and payments due to the department after March 31, 1982."

P.L. 2–1982(ss), Sec.10, emerg. eff. Jan. 1, 1983, in Subsec. (a), substituted "the amount prescribed in the withholding instructions referred to in section 8 of this chapter" in lieu of the provisions of former Cls. (i) thru (iii); substituted "IC 6–8.1" for "IC 6–3" in Subsec. (d); inserted "or returns" in Subsec. (f); and inserted references to IC 6–3.5 where appearing throughout.

P.L. 23–1986, Sec.3, eff. Jan. 1, 1987, substituted "money" for "moneys" twice in Subsec. (c); and added Subsec. (g).

Section 23(b) of P.L.23–1986 provides that Section 3 of this act applies to taxable years that begin after Dec. 31, 1986.

Formerly:
Acts 1963 (ss), c. 32, s. 412.
Acts 1965, c. 233, s. 22.
Acts 1969, c. 326, s. 7.
Acts 1971, P.L.65, SEC.2.
Acts 1973, P.L.50, SEC.4.

Administrative Code References

Partnership withholding,
Requirements, see 45 IAC 3.1–1–107.
Returns, see 45 IAC 3.1–1–108.

Library References

Taxation ☞1100.
WESTLAW Topic No. 371.

C.J.S. Taxation § 1107.
I.L.E. Taxation §§ 207, 220, 221.

6–3–4–13 Corporations; withholding from dividends to nonresident shareholders

Sec. 13. (a) Every corporation which is exempt from tax under IC 6–3 pursuant to IC 6–3–2–2.8(2) shall, at the time that it pays or credits amounts to any of its nonresident shareholders as dividends or as their share of the corporation's undistributed taxable income, withhold the amount prescribed by the department. Such corporation so paying or crediting any nonresident shareholder:

(1) shall be liable to the state of Indiana for the payment of the tax required to be withheld under this section and shall not be liable to such shareholder for the amount withheld and paid over in compliance or intended compliance with this section; and

(2) when the aggregate amount due under IC 6–3 and IC 6–3.5 exceeds one hundred fifty dollars ($150) per quarter, then such corporation shall make return and payment to the department quarterly, on such dates and in such manner as the department shall prescribe, of the amount of tax which, under IC 6–3 and IC 6–3.5, it is required to withhold.

(b) Every corporation shall, at the time of each payment made by it to the department pursuant to this section, deliver to the department a return upon such form as shall be prescribed by the department showing the total amounts paid or credited to its nonresident shareholders, the amount withheld in accordance with the provisions of this section, and such other information as the department may require. Every corporation withholding as provided in this section shall furnish to its nonresident shareholders annually, but not later than the fifteenth day of the third month after the end of its taxable year, a record of the amount of tax withheld on behalf of such shareholders on forms to be prescribed by the department.

(c) All money withheld by a corporation, pursuant to this section, shall immediately upon being withheld be the money of the state of Indiana and every corporation which withholds any amount of money under the provisions of this section shall hold the same in trust for the state of Indiana and for payment thereof to the department in the manner and at the times provided in IC 6–3. Any corporation may be required to post a surety bond in such sum as the department shall determine to be appropriate to protect the state of Indiana with respect to money withheld pursuant to this section.

(d) The provisions of IC 6–8.1 relating to additions to tax in case of delinquency and penalties shall apply to corporations subject to the provisions of this section, and for these purposes any amount withheld, or required to be withheld and remitted to the department under this section, shall be considered to be the tax of the corporation, and with respect to such amount it shall be considered the taxpayer.

(e) Amounts withheld from payments or credits to a nonresident shareholder during any taxable year of the corporation in accordance with the provisions of this section shall be considered to be a part payment of the tax imposed on such nonresident shareholder for his taxable year within or with which the corporation's taxable year ends. A return made by the corporation under subsection (b) shall be accepted by the department as evidence in favor of the nonresident shareholder of the amount so withheld from the shareholder's distributive share.

(f) This section shall in no way relieve any nonresident shareholder from the shareholder's obligation of filing a return or returns at the time required under IC 6–3 or IC 6–3.5, and any unpaid tax shall be paid at the time prescribed by section 5 of this chapter.

(g) Instead of the reporting periods required under subsection (a), the department may permit a corporation to file one (1) return and payment each year if the corporation pays or credits amounts to its nonresident shareholders only one (1) time each year. The withholding return and payment are due on or before the fifteenth day of the third month after the end of the taxable year of the corporation.

(h) If a distribution will be made with property other than money or a gain is realized without the payment of money, the corporation shall not release the property or credit the gain until it has funds sufficient to enable it to pay the tax required to be withheld under this section. If necessary, the corporation shall obtain such funds from the shareholders.

(i) If a corporation fails to withhold and pay any amount of tax required to be withheld under this section and thereafter the tax is paid by the shareholders, such amount of tax as paid by the shareholders shall not be collected from the corporation but it shall not be relieved from liability for interest or penalty otherwise due in respect to such failure to withhold under IC 6–8.1–10.

(j) A corporation described in subsection (a) may file a composite adjusted gross income tax return on behalf of some or all nonresident shareholders if it complies with the requirements prescribed by the department for filing a composite return.

As amended by Acts 1979, P.L.68, SEC.5; Acts 1982, P.L.49, SEC.5; P.L.2–1982(ss), SEC.11; P.L.23–1986, SEC.4; P.L.18–1994, SEC.11; P.L.2–1995, SEC.32.

Historical and Statutory Notes

Acts 1979, P.L. 68, § 5, eff. Jan. 1, 1980, substituted "IC 6–3" for "this article" or "the provisions of this article" throughout the section; in the introductory clause of Subsec. (a), deleted "1971" following "IC"; in Subsec. (a)(1), inserted "as defined in IC 6–3.5–1"; in Subsecs. (a)(i) and (a)(ii), reduced the percentage from 2% to 1.9%; in Subsecs. (a)(ii) and (a)(iii), substituted "IC 6–3.5–1" for "such law"; in the last sentence of Subsec. (a)(iii), substituted "manner" for "maner"; and added "of this chapter" to Subsec. (f).

Acts 1982, P.L.49, Sec.5, emerg. eff. April 1, 1982, in Subsec. (a), added "unless an earlier date is specified by section 8.1 of this chapter" to Cl. (2) of the present second sentence.

Section 8 of Acts 1982, P.L.49, provided:

"Because an emergency exists, this act takes effect April 1, 1982, and affects returns and payments due to the department after March 31, 1982."

P.L. 2–1982(ss), Sec.11, emerg. eff. Jan. 1, 1983, in Subsec. (a), substituted "the amount prescribed in the withholding instructions referred to in section 8 of this chapter" in lieu of the provisions of former Cls. (i) thru (iii) of the first sentence; substituted "IC 6–8.1" for "IC 6–3" in Subsec. (d); inserted "or returns" in Subsec. (f); and inserted references to IC 6–3.5 where appearing throughout.

P.L.23–1986, Sec.4, eff. Jan. 1, 1987, substituted "IC 6–3–2–2.8(2)" for "IC 6–3–2–3(b)" in the first sentence of the introductory paragraph of Subsec. (a); substituted "money" for "moneys" in the second sentence of Subsec. (c); and added Subsec. (g).

Section 23(b) of P.L.23–1986 provides that Section 4 of this act applies to taxable years that begin after Dec. 31, 1986.

P.L.18–1994, Sec.11, substituted references to withholding for references to deducting and retaining throughout; in Subsec. (a), provided that the amount withheld would be prescribed by the department, in lieu of prescribed in the withholding instructions referred to in section 8 of this chapter, in the introductory paragraph, deleted a requirement that corporations make return of and payment to the department monthly whenever the amount of tax due under Articles 6–3 and 6–3.5 exceeded an aggregate amount of $50 per month, with such payment due on the 30th day of the following month, unless an earlier date was specified by section 8.1 of this chapter, and required quarterly returns and payments when the aggregate amount exceeded $150 per quarter, in lieu of when the aggregate amount did not exceed $50 per month, in Subd. (2); in Subsec. (b), required records to be furnished to nonresident shareholders not later than the 15th day of the third month after the end of its taxable year, in lieu of not later that 30 days after the end of its taxable year; in Subsec. (g), provided that the return and payment were due on or before the 15th day of the third month after the end of the taxable year of the corporation, in lieu of not more than 30 days after the end of the year; added Subsecs. (h) though (j); and made nonsubstantive language and punctuation changes throughout.

P.L.2–1995, Sec.32, emerg. eff. May 5, 1995, which was part of the correction bill, made nonsubstantive changes.

Formerly:

Acts 1963 (ss), c. 32, s. 413.
Acts 1965, c. 233, s. 23.
Acts 1969, c. 326, s. 8.
Acts 1971, P.L.65, SEC.3.
Acts 1973, P.L.50, SEC.5.

Administrative Code References

S corporation, see 45 IAC 1.1-3-10.
Subchapter S corporations; withholding requirements, see 45 IAC 3.1–1–109.

Law Review and Journal Commentaries

Taxatiori of Ohio limited liability company under Revenue Procedure 95–10. 21 Dayton L.Rev. 119 (1995).

Library References

Taxation ☞1100.
WESTLAW Topic No. 371.

C.J.S. Taxation § 1107.
I.L.E. Taxation §§ 207, 220, 221.

6–3–4–14 Affiliated group of corporations; consolidated returns

Sec. 14. (a) An affiliated group of corporations shall have the privilege of making a consolidated return with respect to the taxes imposed by IC 6–3. The making of a consolidated return shall be upon the condition that all corporations which at any time during the taxable year have been members of the affiliated group consent to all of the provisions of this section including all provisions of the consolidated return regulations prescribed pursuant to Section 1502 of the Internal Revenue Code [1] and incorporated herein by reference and all regulations promulgated by the department implementing this section prior to the last day prescribed by law for the filing of such return. The making of a consolidated return shall be considered as such consent. In the case of a corporation which is a member of the affiliated group for a fractional part of the year, the consolidated return shall include the income of such corporation for such part of the year as it is a member of the affiliated group.

(b) For the purposes of this section the term "affiliated group" shall mean an "affiliated group" as defined in Section 1504 of the Internal Revenue Code [2] with the exception that the affiliated group shall not include any corporation which does not have adjusted gross income derived from sources within the state of Indiana.

(c) For purposes of IC 6–3–1–3.5(b), the determination of "taxable income," as defined in Section 63 of the Internal Revenue Code,[3] of any affiliated group of corporations making a consolidated return and of each corporation in the group, both during and after the period of affiliation, shall be determined pursuant to the regulations prescribed under Section 1502 of the Internal Revenue Code.

(d) Any credit against the taxes imposed by IC 6–3 which is available to any corporation which is a member of an affiliated group of corporations making a consolidated return shall be applied against the tax liability of the affiliated group.

As amended by Acts 1980, P.L.54, SEC.6.

[1] 26 U.S.C.A. § 1502.
[2] 26 U.S.C.A. § 1504.
[3] 26 U.S.C.A. § 63.

Historical and Statutory Notes

Acts 1980, P.L. 54, § 6, eff. May 1, 1980, substituted "Taxes imposed by IC 6–3" for "tax imposed by this act" in the first sentences of Subsecs. (a) and (d); and in Subsec. (c), substituted "IC 6–3–1–3.5(b)" for "section 103(b) of this act" and deleted "and in effect on January 1, 1965" following "Internal Revenue Code" at the end of the subsection.

Formerly:

Acts 1963 (ss), c. 32, s. 414.
Acts 1965, c. 233, s. 24.

Cross References

Corporations, adjusted gross income defined, see IC 6–3–1–3.5(b).
Gross income tax, consolidated returns by affiliated corporations, see IC 6–2.1–5–5.

Administrative Code References

Affiliated groups, see 45 IAC 3.1–1–111.
Consolidated returns, see 45 IAC 3.1–1–110, 45 IAC 3.1–1–112.

Library References

Taxation ☜1080.
WESTLAW Topic No. 371.

C.J.S. Taxation § 1102.
I.L.E. Taxation §§ 220, 221.

United States Code Annotated

Federal income tax, consolidated returns by affiliated corporations, see 26 U.S.C.A. § 1501 et seq.

Notes of Decisions

Taxable income   1

_____

1. Taxable income

Income received by an affiliated group of corporations from corporate partnerships in which group members are partners is not subject to an apportionment calculation at the partnership level; although the regulations require each member of an affiliated group to calculate its taxable income separately, apportionment occurs only after such income is aggregated into adjusted gross income for the whole group and then segregated into business and non-business income, again for the whole group. Hunt Corp. v. Department of State Revenue, 1999, 709 N.E.2d 766.

Three members of an affiliated group of corporations lacked adjusted gross income derived from sources within the state, and thus could not participate in the group's consolidated state income tax return, where they had no sales, payroll, or property within the state, even though they received interest income from commercial paper issued by a bank in the state. Hunt Corp. v. Department of State Revenue, 1999, 709 N.E.2d 766.

6–3–4–15   Trusts or estates; distribution of income to nonresident beneficiaries; deduction, retention and pay over of tax due; returns required

Sec. 15.   (a) A trust or estate shall, at the time that it distributes income (except income attributable to interest or dividends) to a nonresident beneficiary, deduct and retain therefrom the amount prescribed in the withholding instructions referred to in section 8 of this chapter.   The trust or estate so distributing income to a nonresident beneficiary:

(1) is liable to this state for the tax which it is required to deduct and retain under this section and is not liable to the beneficiary for the amount deducted from the distribution and paid to the department in compliance, or intended compliance, with this section; and

(2) shall pay the amount deducted to the department before the thirtieth day of the month following the distribution, unless an earlier date is specified by section 8.1 of this chapter.

(b) A trust or estate shall, at the time that it makes a payment to the department under this section, deliver to the department a return which shows the total amounts distributed to the trust's or estate's nonresident beneficiaries, the amount deducted from the distributions under this section, and any other information required by the department. The trust or estate shall file the return on the form prescribed by the department. A trust or estate which makes the deduction and retention required by this section shall furnish to its nonresident beneficiaries annually, but not later than thirty (30) days after the end of the trust's or estate's taxable year, a record of the amount of tax deducted and retained from the beneficiaries. The trust or estate shall furnish the information on the form prescribed by the department.

(c) The money deducted and retained by a trust or estate under this section is money of this state. Every trust or estate which deducts and retains any money under this section shall hold the money in trust for this state until it pays the money to the department in the manner and at the time provided in this section. The department may require a trust or estate to post a surety bond to protect this state with respect to money deducted and retained by the trust or estate under this section. The department shall determine the amount of the surety bond.

(d) The provisions of IC 6–8.1 relating to penalties or to additions to tax in case of a delinquency apply to trusts and estates which are subject to this section. For purposes of this subsection, any amount deducted, or required to be deducted and remitted to the department, under this section is considered the tax of the trust or estate, and with respect to that amount, it is considered the taxpayer.

(e) Amounts deducted from distributions to nonresident beneficiaries under this section during a taxable year of the trust or estate are considered a partial payment of the tax imposed on the nonresident beneficiary for his taxable year within or with which the trust's or estate's taxable year ends. The department shall accept a return made by the trust or estate under subsection (b) as evidence of the amount of tax deducted from the income distributed to a nonresident beneficiary.

(f) This section does not relieve a nonresident beneficiary of his duty to file a return at the time required under IC 6–3. The nonresident beneficiary shall pay any unpaid tax at the time prescribed by section 5 of this chapter.
As added by Acts 1977(ss), P.L.4, SEC.13. Amended by Acts 1979, P.L.68, SEC.6; Acts 1982, P.L.49, SEC.6; P.L.2–1982(ss), SEC.12.

Historical and Statutory Notes

Acts 1977 (ss), P.L. 4, § 13, eff. Jan. 1, 1978, added this section.

Acts 1979, P.L. 68, § 6, eff. Jan. 1, 1980, reduced the percentage from 2% to 1.9% in Subsec. (a); and substituted "IC 6–3" for "this article" in Subsecs. (d) and (f).

Acts 1982, P.L.49, Sec.6, emerg. eff. April 1, 1982, in Subsec. (a)(2), added "unless an earlier date is specified by section 8.1 of this chapter."

Section 8 of Acts 1982, P.L.49, provided:

"Because an emergency exists, this act takes effect April 1, 1982, and affects returns and payments due to the department after March 31, 1982."

P.L.2–1982(ss), Sec.12, emerg. eff. Jan. 1, 1983, in Subsec. (a), substituted "therefrom the amount prescribed in the withholding instructions referred to in section 8 of this chapter" for "one and nine-tenths percent (1.9%) of the income" in the first sentence; and substituted "IC 6–8.1" for "IC 6–3" in Subsec. (d).

Administrative Code References

Distributions to nonresident beneficiaries of Indiana trusts and estates, withholding, see 45 IAC 3.1–1–113, 45 IAC 3.1–1–114.

Library References

Taxation ⚯1034, 1079.
WESTLAW Topic No. 371.

C.J.S. Taxation §§ 1099, 1102.
I.L.E. Taxation §§ 207, 208, 213, 220 to 222.

6–3–4–15.7 Annuity, pension, retirement, or other deferred compensation plans; withholding; requests; payor responsibility

Sec. 15.7. (a) The payor of a periodic or nonperiodic distribution under an annuity, a pension, a retirement, or other deferred compensation plan, as described in Section 3405 of the Internal Revenue Code, that is paid to a resident of this state shall, upon receipt from the payee of a written request for state income tax withholding, withhold the requested amount from each payment. The request must be dated and signed by the payee and specify the flat whole dollar amount to be withheld from each payment. The request must also specify the payee's name, current address, taxpayer identification number, and the contract, policy, or account number to which the request applies. The request shall remain in effect until the payor receives in writing from the payee a change in or revocation of the request.

(b) The payor is not required to withhold state income tax from a payment if the amount to be withheld is less than ten dollars ($10) or if the amount to be withheld would reduce the affected payment to less than ten dollars ($10).

(c) The payor is responsible for custody of withheld funds, for reporting withheld funds to the state and to the payee, and for remitting withheld funds to the state in the same manner as is done for wage withholding, including utilization of federal forms and participation by Indiana in the combined Federal/State Filing Program on magnetic media.

As added by P.L.91–1989, SEC.1.

Historical and Statutory Notes

P.L.91–1989, Sec.1, emerg. eff. Jan. 1, 1990.

Chapter 5

Reciprocity

Section
6–3–5–3   Indiana residents working in Illinois

6–3–5–1   Nonresidents; Indiana income

Sec. 1.   The tax imposed by IC 6–3–2 on the adjusted gross income derived from sources within the state of Indiana by persons who are nonresidents of this state, shall not be payable if the laws of the state or territory of residence of such persons, at the time such adjusted gross income was earned in this state, contained a reciprocal provision by which residents of this state were exempted from taxes imposed by such state on income earned in such state.

As amended by P.L.2–1988, SEC.12.

Historical and Statutory Notes

P.L. 2–1988, Sec.12, emerg. eff. Feb. 16, 1988, corrected internal references.

Formerly:
Acts 1963 (ss), c. 32, s. 501.

Cross References

Community revitalization enhancement district tax credit, state and local tax liability, see IC 6–3.1–19–1.
Incremental tax financing fund, revenues, see IC 36–7–13–15.
Industrial development fund, state and local income taxes, see IC 36–7–13–3.8.
Military base recovery tax credit,
   Against other taxes owed, priority of application, see IC 6–3.1–11.5–24.
   State tax liability, see IC 6–3.1–11.5–14.

Administrative Code References

Reciprocity agreements, see 45 IAC 3.1–1–115.

Library References

Taxation ☞1012.
WESTLAW Topic No. 371.

C.J.S. Taxation § 1092.
I.L.E. Taxation § 210.

6–3–5–2   Repealed

(Repealed by P.L.28–1997, SEC.31.)

Historical and Statutory Notes

Former IC 6–3–5–2 related to effective date of chapter.

P.L.2–1988, SEC.13.

Formerly:
Acts 1963 (ss), c. 32, s. 502.

6–3–5–3   Indiana residents working in Illinois

Sec. 3.   The department of state revenue, with the approval of the governor and the budget agency after the review of the state budget committee, may enter into an agreement with the state of Illinois that establishes a methodology for determining individual income taxes paid by residents of each state to the other state and an obligation, in exchange for a like obligation on the part of

Illinois, to make a payment to Illinois. The payment obligation by Indiana may not be greater than the difference between the amount of Indiana individual adjusted gross income taxes for the previous taxable year that would be collected from:

(1) Indiana residents working in Illinois if there were a reciprocity agreement between Indiana and Illinois; and

(2) Indiana residents working in Illinois and from Illinois residents working in Indiana without a reciprocity agreement between Indiana and Illinois. The amount needed to make the payment is appropriated from the state general fund.

As added by P.L.7–1999, SEC.1.

Chapter 6

Penalties and Administration

6–3–6–1 to 6–3–6–9   Repealed

(Repealed by Acts 1980, P.L.61, SEC.15.)

Historical and Statutory Notes

Acts 1980, P.L. 61, provided in § 16 that the act takes effect Jan. 1, 1981.

Former IC 6–3–6–1 related to the audit of returns, to tax credits and refunds, to interest and penalties for tax deficiencies and failure to file returns, and to procedures for demand for payment under jeopardy circumstances or failure to file returns.

Former IC 6–3–6–2 related to corrective assessments by the department of revenue.

Former IC 6–3–6–3 related to remedies, including levy upon property, for the collection of unpaid taxes, penalties and interest.

Former IC 6–3–6–4 related to taxpayers' petitions and civil actions to recover refunds.

Former IC 6–3–6–5 related to tax remittances.

Former IC 6–3–6–6 related to annual audits of department of revenue books and records.

Former IC 6–3–6–7 related to records to be kept by the department of revenue.

Former IC 6–3–6–8 related to the confidentiality of tax information and provided penalties for violations by department personnel.

Former IC 6–3–6–9 related to withholding certificates of voluntary corporate dissolution or withdrawal until notice from the department declaring all corporate taxes paid.

Provisions pertaining to issuance of certificates of voluntary dissolution or withdrawal are now contained in IC 6–8.1–10–8.

Provisions pertaining to the administration, collection, and enforcement of taxes are now contained in IC 6–8.1–1–1 et seq.

Formerly:
Acts 1963 (ss), c. 32, ss. 601 to 609.
Acts 1965, c. 233, ss. 25 to 27.
Acts 1969, c. 326, ss. 9 to 11.
Acts 1971, P.L.64, SECS.5, 6.
Acts 1977 (ss), P.L.4, SECS.14 to 16.
Acts 1978, P.L.2, SECS.619, 620.
Acts 1979, P.L.72, SEC.1.
Acts 1979, P.L.321, SEC.3.

6–3–6–10   Taxpayers' recordkeeping requirements; false entries; offenses

Sec. 10.   (a) A taxpayer subject to taxation under this article shall keep and preserve records and any other books or accounts as required by IC 6–8.1–5–4. All the records shall be kept open for examination at any time by the department or its authorized agents. A taxpayer who violates this subsection or fails to comply with the request of the department pursuant to IC 6–3–4–6 commits a Class A misdemeanor.

(b) It is a Class D felony for a taxpayer to make false entries in his books, or to keep more than one (1) set of books, with intent to defraud the state or evade the payment of the tax, or any part thereof, imposed by this article.

As amended by Acts 1978, P.L.2, SEC.621; P.L.6–1987, SEC.8.

Historical and Statutory Notes

Acts 1978, P.L. 2, § 621, emerg. eff. July 1, 1978, rewrote the section which prior thereto read:

"(a) It shall be the duty of every taxpayer subject to taxation hereunder to keep and preserve records of his adjusted gross income and such other books or accounts as may be necessary to determine the amount of tax for which he is liable under the provisions of this act. All such records shall be open for examination at any time by the department or it duly authorized agents. Any taxpayer violating any of the provisions of this subsection (a) or failing to comply with the request of the department pursuant to section 406 of this act shall be guilty of a misdemeanor, and on conviction thereof shall be fined not less than one hundred ($100) nor more than five hundred dollars ($500).

"(b) it shall be unlawful for any taxpayer to make false entries in his books with intent to defraud the state or evade the payment of the tax, or any part thereof, imposed by this act or to keep more than one set of books with like intent. It shall also be unlawful for the president, vice-president, secretary, treasurer or other officer or employee of any corporation, company or association, or for any partner or employee of any partnership or for the employee of any person to make, cause to be made, or permit to be made any false entries in the books of such person, corporation, company, association, or partnership with the intent to avoid the payment of any tax imposed hereunder, or to keep or permit to be kept more than one (1) set of books for such person, corporation, company, association or partnership with like intent. Any person violating any of the provisions of this subsection (b) shall be guilty of a felony, and on conviction thereof shall be fined not more than five thousand dollars ($5,000), or imprisoned not exceeding five (5) years in a state penitentiary or punished by both such fine and imprisonment."

P.L.6–1987, Sec.8, provided that taxpayers should keep records required by IC 6–8.1–5–4 instead of records necessary to determine the amount of tax liability, and increased the penalty for failure to keep records from a Class C infraction to a Class A misdemeanor.

Formerly:

Acts 1963 (ss), c. 32, s. 610.

Cross References

Community revitalization enhancement district tax credit, state and local tax liability, see IC 6–3.1–19–1.

Copies of federal tax returns, provision to department of revenue, see IC 6–3–4–6.

Incremental tax financing fund, revenues, see IC 36–7–13–15.

Industrial development fund, state and local income taxes, see IC 36–7–13–3.8.

Military base recovery tax credit,

    Against other taxes owed, priority of application, see IC 6–3.1–11.5–24.

    State tax liability, see IC 6–3.1–11.5–14.

Penalties,

    Class D felonies, see IC 35–50–2–7.

    Infractions, see IC 34–28–5–4.

Library References

Taxation ⬤1103.
WESTLAW Topic No. 371.

C.J.S. Taxation § 1107.
I.L.E Taxation § 325.

Notes of Decisions

Discovery 1

_____

1. Discovery

Under the "required records" exception to the Fifth Amendment, the government can de-mand production of records which are required to be kept by statute. Smith v. State, App. 4 Dist.1992, 588 N.E.2d 1303, rehearing denied, transfer denied, certiorari denied 113 S.Ct. 659, 506 U.S. 1022, 121 L.Ed.2d 584, denial of habe-as corpus reversed 35 F.3d 300.

6–3–6–11 Evasion of tax; offenses; prosecution

Sec. 11. (a) It is a Class D felony for a taxpayer to fail to make any return required to be made under this article, or to make any false return or false statement in any return, with intent to defraud the state or to evade the payment of the tax, or any part thereof, imposed by this article. It is a Class D felony for a person to knowingly fail to permit the examination of any book, paper, account, record, or other data by the department or its authorized agents, as required by this article, to knowingly fail to permit the inspection or appraisal of any property by the department or its authorized agents, or to knowingly refuse to offer testimony or produce any record as required in this article.

(b) The attorney-general has concurrent jurisdiction with the prosecuting attorney in instituting and prosecuting actions under this section.

As amended by Acts 1978, P.L.2, SEC.622.

Historical and Statutory Notes

Acts 1978, P.L. 2, § 622, eff. July 1, 1978, rewrote the section which prior thereto read:

"(a) It shall be unlawful for any taxpayer to fail or refuse to make any return required to be made under the provisions of this act, or to make any false or fraudulent return or false statement in any return, with intent to defraud the state or to evade the payment of the tax, or any part thereof, imposed by this act; or for the president, vice-president, secretary, treasurer, or other officer or employee of any firm, corporation, company or association or any partner or employee of any partnership to make or cause to be made or permit to be made for any person, corporation, company, association or partnership, as the case may be, any false return or any false statement in any return with the intent to evade the payment of any tax hereunder; or for any person to fail or refuse to permit the examination of any book, paper, account, record or other data by the department or its duly authorized agents, as required by this act; or to fail or refuse to permit the inspection or appraisal of any property by the department or its duly authorized agents, or to refuse to offer testimony or produce any record as required in this act. Any taxpayer violating any of the provisions of this section shall be guilty of a felony, and on conviction thereof shall be fined not more than five thousand dollars ($5,000), or imprisoned not exceeding five (5) years in a state penitentiary, or punished by both such fine and imprisonment. In addition to the foregoing penalties, any taxpayer who shall knowingly swear to or verify any false or fraudulent statement, with the intent to defraud the state or to evade the payment of the tax imposed hereunder shall be guilty of the offense of perjury and, on conviction thereof, shall be punished in the manner provided by law. Any corporation, company or association for which a false return or a return containing a false statement shall be made shall be guilty of a misdemeanor, and shall be subject to a fine of not more than five thousand dollars ($5,000). No officer or employee of the department shall be civilly or criminally liable for instituting any criminal or civil prosecution provided for under the provisions of this act.

"(b) The prosecution of any corporation, person or persons guilty of having violated any of the penal provisions hereof may be instituted by the filing of an affidavit or indictment in the same manner as other criminal cases are commenced, and the attorney-general shall have concurrent jurisdiction with the prosecuting attorney in instituting and prosecuting such actions. The attorney-general, the prosecuting attorney and the department shall be allowed at all times to appear before the grand jury for the purpose of reporting any violations of this act, or for the purpose of rendering legal advice with respect thereto when required, or for the purpose of interrogating witnesses before the grand jury. When any affidavit charging any person or corporation with a violation of any of the penal provisions of this act has been made as provided for by law, either the attorney-general or the prosecuting attorney shall approve the same by indorsement using the words 'approved by me' and by signing the same as attorney-general or prosecuting attorney."

Formerly:

Acts 1963 (ss), c. 32, s. 611.

Cross References

Penalty for class D felonies, see IC 35–50–2–7.

Law Review and Journal Commentaries

Income taxation: Survey of recent tax law. Thomas B. Allington, 10 Ind.L.Rev. 345 (1976).

Library References

Taxation ☞1103.
WESTLAW Topic No. 371.

C.J.S. Taxation § 1107.
I.L.E. Taxation § 126.

Notes of Decisions

Filing of return   1
Notice to taxpayer   2

return is filed.   State v. Moles, App. 3 Dist.1975, 337 N.E.2d 543, 166 Ind.App. 632.

1. Filing of return

For purpose of IC1971, 6–3–6–11, making it an offense to make a false and fraudulent income tax return, to make a false statement in a tax return, and to swear to or verify a false and fraudulent statement in a tax return, a taxpayer does not "make" a tax return until the return is filed with the department of revenue, and the offense is committed in the county in which the

2. Notice to taxpayer

A recommendation to the attorney general for prosecution in a criminal tax case, or the initiation of such an action, serves as notice to taxpayer that investigatory process has become criminal.   Green v. State ex rel. Dept. of State Revenue, App. 1 Dist.1979, 390 N.E.2d 1087, 181 Ind.App. 163, certiorari denied 101 S.Ct. 134, 449 U.S. 848, 66 L.Ed.2d 58.

6–3–6–12 to 6–3–6–14   Repealed

(Repealed by Acts 1980, P.L.61, SEC.15.)

Historical and Statutory Notes

Acts 1980, P.L. 61, provided in § 16 that the act takes effect Jan. 1, 1981.

Former IC 6–3–6–12 related to the duties of the commissioner of revenue, selection of department personnel, funding and fixing of salaries, and appropriation for legal services for the department.

Former IC 6–3–6–13 related to the promulgation of rules and regulations by the department, the preparation of forms, and subsequent employment by department employees.

Former IC 6–3–6–14 related to the appraisal of property by the department of revenue and to the department's investigatory powers.

Provisions pertaining to the powers and duties of the department of revenue are now contained in IC 6–8.1–3–1 et seq.

Formerly:

Acts 1963 (ss), c. 32, ss. 612 to 614.

Chapter 7

Miscellaneous

6–3–7–1   Tax on persons or shareholders exempt from adjusted gross income tax

Sec. 1.   In the event the tax imposed by IC 6–3–1 through IC 6–3–7 is held inapplicable or invalid with respect to any person, or the shareholders of any corporation described in IC 6–3–2–2.8(2), or the partners of any such partnership, then notwithstanding IC 6–2.1–3–23 or IC 6–2.1–3–24 such person or such corporation or such partnership shall be liable for the tax on gross income as imposed by IC 6–2.1 for the taxable periods with respect to which the tax imposed by IC 6–3–1 through IC 6–3–7 is held inapplicable or invalid.

As amended by Acts 1977(ss), P.L.4, SEC.17; Acts 1981, P.L.77, SEC.14; P.L.67–1986, SEC.2.

Historical and Statutory Notes

Acts 1977 (ss), P.L. 4, § 17, eff. Jan. 1, 1978, rewrote the section which prior thereto read:

"(a) Except as otherwise provided in Subsection (b) of this section, any person subject to this act, any corporation which is exempt from Adjusted Gross Income Tax under IC1971, 6–3–2–3(b), and any partnership shall not be liable for any tax on gross income received subsequent to June 30, 1963, as imposed by Sections 2 and 3 of the Gross Income Tax Act of 1933, as amended (IC1971, 6–2–1, Secs. 2 and 3): Provided, however, In the event the tax imposed by this article is held inapplicable or invalid with respect to any person, or the shareholders of any such corporation, or the partners of any such partnership, then such person or such corporation or such partnership shall be liable for the tax on gross income as imposed by said Sections 2 and 3 of the Gross Income Tax Act of 1933, as amended (IC1971, 6–2–1, Sec.2 and Sec.3) for the taxable periods with respect to which the tax under this article is held inapplicable or invalid.

"(b) Every partnership of which one or more of the partners is a corporation shall be liable for the tax imposed by Sections 2 and 3 of the Gross Income Tax Act of 1933 as amended (IC1971, 6–2–1, 2 and 3) and by the Adjusted Gross Income Tax Act of 1963 as amended (IC1971, 6–3–1 through 6–3–7). No partner of such partnership shall be liable for the tax imposed on the partner's distributive share of partnership income by the Gross Income Tax Act of 1933 as amended or the Adjusted Gross Income Tax Act of 1963 as amended."

Acts 1981, P.L. 77, § 14, emerg. eff. April 29, 1981, rewrote the section which prior thereto read:

"(a) Except as otherwise provided in subsection (b) of this section, any person subject to this article, any corporation which is exempt from adjusted gross income tax under IC 6–3–2–3(b), and any partnership shall not be liable for any tax on gross income received subsequent to June 30, 1963, as imposed by sections 2 and 3 of IC 6–2–1. However, in the event the tax imposed by this article is held inapplicable or invalid with respect to any person, or the shareholders of any such corporation, or the partners of any such partnership, then such person or such corporation or such partnership shall be liable for the tax on gross income as imposed by said sections 2 and 3 of IC 6–2–1 for the taxable periods with respect to which the tax under this article is held inapplicable or invalid.

"(b) Every partnership of which one or more of the partners is a corporation shall be liable for the tax imposed by sections 2 and 3 of IC 6–2–1 and by this article. No partner of such partnership shall be liable for the tax imposed on the partner's distributive share of the partnership income by IC 6–2–1 or this article."

Acts 1981, P.L. 77, was part of a codification of the laws relating to gross income tax.

P.L.67–1986, Sec.2, emerg. eff. March 10, 1986, substituted "IC 6–3–2–2.8(2)" for "IC 6–3–2–3(b)" and "imposed by" for "under".

Formerly:

Acts 1963 (ss), c. 32, s. 701.
Acts 1965, c. 233, s. 28.
Acts 1969, c. 326, s. 12.
Acts 1971, P.L.64, SEC.7.

Cross References

Certain corporations exempt from adjusted gross income tax also exempt from gross income tax, see IC 6–2.1–3–24.
Community revitalization enhancement district tax credit, state and local tax liability, see IC 6–3.1–19–1.
Exemptions, adjusted gross income tax, see IC 6–3–2–2.8.
Income derived by certain exempt organizations from unrelated trade or business not exempt from gross income tax, see IC 6–2.1–3–23.
Incremental tax financing fund, revenues, see IC 36–7–13–15.
Industrial development fund, state and local income taxes, see IC 36–7–13–3.8.
Military base recovery tax credit,
    Against other taxes owed, priority of application, see IC 6–3.1–11.5–24.
    State tax liability, see IC 6–3.1–11.5–14.

Administrative Code References

Corporate partnerships, tax liability, see 45 IAC 3.1–2–1, 45 IAC 3.1–1–66, 45 IAC 3.1–1–67.
Revocation of exemption, see 45 IAC 1.1-3-15.
Taxation of shareholders, see 45 IAC 3.1–1–67.

Law Review and Journal Commentaries

Survey of recent developments in Indiana law: Taxation. John W. Boyd, 16 Ind.L.Rev. 355 (1983).

Library References

Taxation ⚲979.
WESTLAW Topic No. 371.

C.J.S. Taxation § 1096.
I.L.E. Taxation §§ 207, 208, 213, 222.

Notes of Decisions

Partnerships subject to tax 2
Purpose 1

1. Purpose

Intent of legislature in passing 1969 amendment to Adjusted Gross Income Tax [section 6–3–1–1 et seq.] providing that every partnership of which one or more of the partners is a corporation is liable for the tax imposed by the Act was to plug a tax loophole whereby one corporation which was paying gross income tax might join with another to form a partnership in order to circumvent the tax and such intent should not be frustrated by allowing two or more corporations to marshal their assets in a partnership whose purpose is to enter into a second partnership and thereby avoid corporate

taxation treatment of the second partnership. Park 100 Development Co. v. Indiana Dept. of State Revenue, 1981, 429 N.E.2d 220.

2. Partnerships subject to tax

Under pre-1981 law, corporation tax liability was properly assessed against development company where ultimate beneficial enjoyment of 45 percent ownership resided in the two corporate parents of one of the three partners. Park 100 Development Co. v. Indiana Dept. of State Revenue, 1981, 429 N.E.2d 220.

Where the department of revenue originally found that partnership, a member of which was a corporation, was not liable for payment of a gross income tax under this section providing that every partnership of which one or more of the partners is a corporation is liable for a gross income tax, and where no payments were assessed to partnership for a seven-year period, doctrine of legislative acquiescence prevented a subsequent finding of tax liability. Indiana Dept. of Revenue, Indiana Gross Income Tax Division v. Glendale-Glenbrook Associates, 1981, 429 N.E.2d 217.

Corporation exempt from gross income tax liability under section 6–3–2–3 because it was an insurance company was not made subject to tax liability under this section providing that every partnership of which one or more of the partners is a corporation shall be liable for gross income tax, by becoming a member of the partnership which itself would not otherwise have been subject to tax liability. Indiana Dept. of Revenue, Indiana Gross Income Tax Division v. Glendale-Glenbrook Associates, 1981, 429 N.E.2d 217.

Partnership consisting of individuals and one corporate partner was not exempt from gross income tax even though corporate partner, by itself, was exempted from liability for gross income taxes. Indiana Dept. of Revenue v. Glendale-Glenbrook Associates, App. 1 Dist.1980, 404 N.E.2d 1178, vacated 429 N.E.2d 217.

6–3–7–2   Repealed

(Repealed by Acts 1980, P.L.61, SEC.15.)

Historical and Statutory Notes

Acts 1980, P.L. 61, provided in § 16, that the act takes effect Jan. 1, 1981.

The former section related to the exchange of information with other state or U.S. officials under reciprocal agreements.

Provisions pertaining to reciprocal information agreements are now contained in § 6–8.1–3–7.

Formerly:
Acts 1963 (ss), c. 32, s. 702.

6–3–7–2.5   Allocation and deposit of revenues

Sec. 2.5.   (a) Revenues derived from the imposition and collection of the adjusted gross income tax (IC 6–3–1 through IC 6–3–7) shall be allocated between and deposited in the state general fund and the property tax replacement fund (IC 6–1.1–21) in the manner prescribed by this section and section 3 of this chapter.

(b) With respect to each adjusted gross income tax payment received from a corporation, the amount determined in STEP FOUR of the following STEPS shall be allocated to and deposited in the state general fund:

STEP ONE: Enter the adjusted gross income tax rate in effect for the taxable year for which the payment is made.

STEP TWO: Subtract three percent (3%) from the rate entered under STEP ONE.

STEP THREE: Divide the remainder determined under STEP TWO by three percent (3%).

STEP FOUR: Multiply the amount of the adjusted gross income tax payment by the quotient determined under STEP THREE.

As added by P.L.390–1987(ss), SEC.38.

Historical and Statutory Notes

P.L.390–1987(ss), Sec.38, adding this section, was made effective July 1, 1987.

6–3–7–3   Corporate taxes; taxes on persons; disposition

Sec. 3.   (a) All revenues derived from collection of the adjusted gross income tax imposed on corporations (except the tax revenues allocated under section 2.5 of this chapter to the state general fund) shall be deposited as follows:

(1) Ten million dollars ($10,000,000) shall for each state fiscal year be deposited in the state general fund.

(2) The balance of such revenues shall be deposited into the property tax replacement fund.

(b) All revenues derived from collection of the adjusted gross income tax imposed on persons shall be deposited in the state general fund.

As amended by Acts 1977(ss), P.L.4, SEC.18; P.L.390–1987(ss), SEC.39.

Historical and Statutory Notes

Acts 1977 (ss), P.L. 4, § 18, eff. Jan. 1, 1978, deleted "Commencing for the fiscal year July 1, 1973, and for each fiscal year thereafter" at the beginning of the introductory clause; deleted "1971" following "IC" where it appears throughout the section; deleted "to become an addition to the appropriation for general aid to local schools distributed as part of the regular school aid distribution program" at the end of Cl. (i); and substituted "6–1–21" for "6–1–68" in Cl. (ii).

P.L. 390–1987 (ss), Sec.39, eff. July 1, 1987, rewrote the section, which formerly read:

"All revenues derived from the imposition and collection of the tax on corporations imposed by chapters 1 through 7 of this article in excess of the credit against tax allowed by IC 6–3–3–2, shall be deposited as follows:

"(i) Ten Million Dollars ($10,000,000) shall for each such fiscal year be deposited in the general fund of the state.

"(ii) The balance of such revenues shall be specially deposited into the general fund of the state, which special deposits shall be held in the special fund created by IC 6–1.1–21 known as the 'Property Tax Replacement Fund.'"

Formerly:

Acts 1963 (ss), c.32, s.704.
Acts 1965, c.233, s.29.
Acts 1969, c.425, s.1.
Acts 1973, P.L.50, SEC.6.

Notes of Decisions

Source of revenue   1

------

1. Source of revenue

The only revenue that could be "derived from the imposition and collection of the tax on corporations imposed" by the "Adjusted Gross Income Tax Act of 1963" [now § 6–3–1–1 et seq.] must necessarily be the amount by which the adjusted gross income tax exceeds the amount of gross income tax. 1964 Op.Atty.Gen. No. 38.

6–3–7–4   Repealed

(Repealed by Acts 1980, P.L.54, SEC.9.)

Historical and Statutory Notes

Acts 1980, P.L. 54, provided in § 10 that the act takes effect May 1, 1980.

The former section related to county property tax relief.

Formerly:

Acts 1963 (ss), c. 32, s. 705.
Acts 1967, c. 345, s. 1.

6–3–7–5 Independent contractor; worker's compensation election for exemption; notification of tax treatment

Sec. 5. (a) As used in this section, "independent contractor" refers to a person described in IC 22–3–6–1(b)(7).

(b) Not more than thirty (30) days after the department receives a copy of an independent contractor's statement and validated affidavit from the worker's compensation board under IC 22–3–2–14.5 or IC 22–3–7–34.5, the department shall provide the independent contractor with an explanation of the department's tax treatment of independent contractors and the duty of the independent contractor to remit any taxes owed.

(c) The information received from an independent contractor's statement and validated affidavit is to be treated as confidential by the department and is to be used solely for the purposes of this section.

As added by P.L.75–1993, SEC.1.

Chapter 8

Supplemental Corporate Net Income Tax

Cross References

Taxation, individual development account tax credit, state tax liability defined, see IC 6–3.1–18–5.

6–3–8–1 Imposition of tax

Sec. 1. A tax to be called the "supplemental net income tax" is hereby imposed on the net income of every corporation, except corporations subject to taxation under the financial institutions tax (IC 6–5.5).

As amended by P.L.21–1990, SEC.10.

Historical and Statutory Notes

P.L.21–1990, Sec.10, emerg. eff. retroactive to Jan. 1, 1990.

P.L.21–1990, Sec.10, inserted "except corporations subject to taxation under the financial institutions tax (IC 6–5.5)".

Formerly:

Acts 1973, P.L.50, SEC.8.

Constitutional Provisions

Article 10, § 8, provides:

"The general assembly may levy and collect a tax upon income, from whatever source derived, at such rates, in such manner, and with such exemptions as may be prescribed by law."

Cross References

Administration, enforcement, and collection of tax, department of state revenue, see IC 6–8.1–1–1 et seq.

Community revitalization enhancement district tax credit, state and local tax liability, see IC 6–3.1–19–1.

Corporation for innovation development, exemption from supplemental net income tax, see IC 6–3.1–5–9.

Gross income tax, see IC 6–2.1–1–1 et seq.

Incremental tax financing fund, revenues, see IC 36–7–13–15.

Industrial development fund, state and local income taxes, see IC 36–7–13–3.8.

Life and health insurance guaranty association assessments, insurer's tax credit, see IC 27–8–8–16.

Military base recovery tax credit,
    Against other taxes owed, priority of application, see IC 6–3.1–11.5–24.
    State tax liability, see IC 6–3.1–11.5–14.

Purchases qualifying for investment credit, exemption from supplemental net income tax, see IC 6–3.1–5–10.

Tax credits against supplemental net income tax,
    Energy system credits, see IC 6–3.1–8–1 et seq.
    Neighborhood assistance credits, see IC 6–3.1–9–1 et seq.
    Prison investment credits, see IC 6–3.1–6–1 et seq.

Administrative Code References

Corporation credit for certain taxes paid, see 45 IAC 3.1–1–72.

Corporations taxable for supplemental corporate net income tax, see 45 IAC 3.1–2–1.

Law Review and Journal Commentaries

Constitutional considerations of state taxation of multinational corporate income. William W. Stuart and Michael K. Williams, 16 Ind.L.Rev. 783 (1983).

Income taxes. Thomas B. Allington, 10 Ind. L.Rev. 345 (1976).

Taxation; department of revenue: Survey of recent law. Marc S. Weinstein, 13 Ind.L.Rev. 1 (1980).

Library References

Taxation ☞980, 1015.
WESTLAW Topic No. 371.

C.J.S. Taxation §§ 1093, 1096.
I.L.E. Taxation § 31.

United States Supreme Court

Preemption, outer continental shelf oil and gas, inclusion in state apportionment formula for corporate income tax, see Shell Oil Co. v. Iowa Dept. of Revenue, U.S.Iowa1988, 109 S.Ct. 278, 488 U.S. 19, 102 L.Ed.2d 186.

Notes of Decisions

In general 1
Net operating losses 2

Indiana Dept. of State Revenue, 1992, 586 N.E.2d 953.

1. In general

Indiana imposes three different income taxes: gross income tax, adjusted gross income tax, and supplemental corporate net income tax. Longmire v. Indiana Dept. of State Revenue, 1994, 638 N.E.2d 894.

Indiana corporations pay greater of gross income tax or adjusted gross income tax, plus supplemental net income tax. Longmire v. Indiana Dept. of State Revenue, 1994, 638 N.E.2d 894.

Term "adjusted gross income" does not include subchapter S corporation's "built-in gains," and thus, they are not subject to taxation by State. F.A. Wilhelm Const. Co., Inc. v.

2. Net operating losses

Net operating losses which could be carried over and deducted in arriving at taxable income for federal income tax purposes of corporate taxpayer could be reflected in computation of Indiana adjusted gross income and supplemental net income taxes. Indiana Dept. of State Revenue v. Endress & Hauser, Inc., App. 1 Dist.1980, 404 N.E.2d 1173.

Former Massachusetts corporation which effected an "F reorganization" and reincorporated in Indiana was entitled to deduct net operating losses suffered in Massachusetts in computing Indiana adjusted gross income and supplemental net income taxes. Indiana Dept. of State Revenue v. Endress & Hauser, Inc., App. 1 Dist.1980, 404 N.E.2d 1173.

6–3–8–2   Definitions

Sec. 2.   (a) As used in this chapter, the term "corporation" shall mean and apply to corporations and shall also mean and apply to banks and trust companies, national banking associations, mutual savings banks, and savings and loan associations not subject to taxation under the financial institutions tax (IC 6–5.5) and domestic insurance companies organized under the laws of the state of Indiana notwithstanding that such organizations are exempt from the tax imposed on adjusted gross income pursuant to IC 6–3–2–1 whether such exemption is accorded under the provisions of IC 6–3–2–2.8(3) or IC 6–3–2–2.8(4), or under the provisions of IC 27–1–18–2, as such section pertains to domestic insurance companies, or under the provisions of any other law of the state of Indiana.

(b) The term "net income" shall mean adjusted gross income derived from sources within the state of Indiana, as determined in accordance with the provisions of IC 6–3–2–2, adjusted as follows: Subtract an amount equal to the greater of:

(1) the amount of tax imposed by IC 6–3–2 on the taxpayer's adjusted gross income for the same taxable year (before the allowance of credits provided for in IC 6–3);

(2) the amount of tax imposed on the gross income of the taxpayer for such taxable year by IC 6–2.1; or

(3) the amount of tax imposed on premiums received on policies of insurance by IC 27–1–18–2.

(c) However, in the case of domestic insurance companies organized under the laws of the state of Indiana, the term "net income" shall mean:

(1) either:

(A) for life insurance companies (as defined in Section 816(a) of the Internal Revenue Code), life insurance company taxable income (as defined in Section 801 of the Internal Revenue Code); or

(B) for insurance companies subjected to the imposition of tax under Section 831 of the Internal Revenue Code, taxable income (as defined in Section 832 of the Internal Revenue Code); multiplied by

(2) a fraction:

(A) the numerator of which is the direct premiums and annuity considerations received during the taxable year for insurance upon property or risks in this state; and

(B) the denominator of which is the direct premiums and annuity considerations received during the taxable year for insurance upon property or risks everywhere; and

(3) the product of such multiplication shall be adjusted as follows: Subtract an amount equal to the greater of either:

(A) the amount of tax imposed on the gross income of the taxpayer by IC 6–2.1 and paid by the taxpayer for the same taxable year; or

(B) the amount of tax imposed on the gross premiums of the taxpayer and paid by the taxpayer pursuant to IC 27–1–18–2 for the same taxable year.

(d) For the purpose of subsection (c), the term "direct premiums and annuity considerations" shall be defined as gross premiums received from direct business, as reported in the company's annual statement filed with the insurance department of this state on the form prescribed.

As amended by Acts 1980, P.L.54, SEC.7; Acts 1981, P.L.84, SEC.6; Acts 1981, P.L.77, SEC.15; P.L.76–1985, SEC.4; P.L.67–1986, SEC.3; P.L.2–1987, SEC.21; P.L.21–1990, SEC.11; P.L.42–1993, SEC.4.

Historical and Statutory Notes

Acts 1980, P.L. 54, § 7, eff. May 1, 1980, deleted "1971" following "IC" throughout the section; in Subsec. (b), in the first paragraph, substituted "IC 6–3–1–3.5(b)" for "IC 1971, 6–3–1–3(b)," and in Cl. (i), in that paragraph substituted "on the taxpayer's adjusted gross income" for "from the taxpayer's adjusted gross income" and "IC 6–3–3" for "chapter 3" following "provided for in", in the second paragraph, in Cl. (ii), added "of the Internal Revenue Code," and in cl. (i) of the third paragraph, substituted "the amount of tax imposed on the gross income of the taxpayer by sections 2 and 3 of IC 6–2–1" for "the amount of tax imposed on the gross income of the taxpayer by IC1971, 6–2–2 and 3."

Acts 1981, P.L. 84, § 6, emerg. eff. retroactively to Jan. 1, 1981, in Subsec. (b), substituted

"IC 6–3" for "IC 6–3–3" in Cl. (i) in the first paragraph.

Acts 1981, P.L. 84, provided in § 7:

"Because an emergency exists for the retroactive taking effect of this act, this act takes effect January 1, 1981, and applies to taxable years that begin after December 31, 1980."

Acts 1981, P.L.77, § 15, emerg.eff. April 29, 1981, in Subsec. (b), in Cl. (ii) of the first paragraph and in the third paragraph, substituted "IC 6–2.1" for "sections 2 and 3 of IC 6–2–1."

Acts 1981, P.L. 77, was part of a codification of the laws relating to gross income tax.

Acts 1982, P.L.52, which related to income taxation, provided in Section 6:

"Any amendment to the Internal Revenue Code made by the Economic Recovery Tax Act of 1981, or any other act passed by the first session of the 97th Congress, which is effective for any taxable year that began before January 1, 1982, and which affects:

"(1) individual adjusted gross income, as defined in Section 62 of the Internal Revenue Code;

"(2) corporate taxable income, as defined in Section 63 of the Internal Revenue Code; or

"(3) trust and estate taxable income, as defined in Section 641(b) of the Internal Revenue Code;

"is also effective for that same taxable year for purposes of determining 'adjusted gross income' under IC 6–3–1–3.5 and 'net income' under IC 6–3–8–2(b). However, the Accelerated Cost Recovery System (ACRS) provided for under the Economic Recovery Tax Act of 1981 iš first applicable in this state for taxable years that begin after December 31, 1981. In addition, the All-Savers Interest Exclusion provided by Section 128 of the Internal Revenue Code is not available for any taxable year that began before January 1, 1982."

P.L. 82–1983, provided in Section 12, emerg. eff. Jan. 1, 1983:

"(a) Except as provided in subsection (b), any amendment to the Internal Revenue Code:

"(1) made by:

"(A) the Subchapter S Revision Act of 1982;

"(B) the Highway Revenue Act of 1982;

"(C) the Technical Corrections Act of 1982;

"(D) the Miscellaneous Revenue Act of 1982;

"(E) the Tax Equity and Fiscal Responsibility Act of 1982; or

"(F) any other act passed by the second session of the 97th Congress;

"(2) that is effective for any taxable year that began before January 1, 1983; and

"(3) that affects:

"(A) individual adjusted gross income, as defined in Section 62 of the Internal Revenue Code;

"(B) corporate taxable income, as defined in Section 63 of the Internal Revenue Code;

"(C) trust and estate taxable income, as defined in Section 641(b) of the Internal Revenue Code;

"(D) life insurance company taxable income, as defined in Section 802(b) of the Internal Revenue Code;

"(E) mutual insurance company taxable income, as defined in Section 821(b) of the Internal Revenue Code; or

"(F) taxable income, as defined in Section 832 of the Internal Revenue Code;

"is also effective for that same taxable year for purposes of determining 'adjusted gross income' under IC 6–3–1–3.5 and 'net income' under IC 6–3–8–2(b). Notwithstanding any other law, the temporary provisions relating to the taxation of life insurance companies under subtitle D of the Tax Equity and Fiscal Responsibility Act of 1982 shall only be effective for purposes of determining adjusted gross income under IC 6–3–1–3.5 and net income under IC 6–3–8–2(b) for taxable years that begin before January 1, 1984.

"(b) The amendments made to Section 85 of the Internal Revenue Code by the Tax Equity and Fiscal Responsibility Act of 1982 are first applicable in this state for taxable years that begin after December 31, 1983."

P.L.49–1984 provided in Section 4, emerg. eff. Jan. 1, 1984:

"Any amendment to the Internal Revenue Code made by an act passed by the first session of the 98th Congress that is effective for any taxable year that began before January 1, 1984, and that affects:

"(1) individual adjusted gross income, as defined in Section 62 of the Internal Revenue Code;

"(2) corporate taxable income, as defined in Section 63 of the Internal Revenue Code;

"(3) trust and estate taxable income, as defined in Section 641(b) of the Internal Revenue Code;

"(4) life insurance company taxable income, as defined in Section 802(b) of the Internal Revenue Code;

"(5) mutual insurance company taxable income, as defined in Section 821(b) of the Internal Revenue Code; or

"(6) taxable income, as defined in Section 832 of the Internal Revenue Code;

"is also effective for that same taxable year for purposes of determining 'adjusted gross income' under IC 6–3–1–3.5 and 'net income' under IC 6–3–8–2(b)."

P.L.76–1985, Sec.4, emerg. eff. retroactive to Jan. 1, 1985, substituted, in Subsec. (b)(i), "Section 816(a)" for "Section 801(a)" and "Section 801" for "Section 802(b)".

Section 10 of P.L.76–1985 provided that Section 4 of this act applies to taxable years that begin after Dec. 31, 1984.

Section 3 of P.L.74–1985, as amended by Section 7 of P.L.76–1985, emerg. eff. retroactive to Jan. 1, 1985, provided:

"Section 3. Any amendment to the Internal Revenue Code made by an act passed by the second session of the 98th Congress that is effective for any taxable year that began before January 1, 1985, and that affects:

"(1) individual adjusted gross income, as defined in Section 62 of the Internal Revenue Code;

"(2) corporate taxable income, as defined in Section 63 of the Internal Revenue Code;

"(3) trust and estate taxable income, as defined in Section 641(b) of the Internal Revenue Code;

"(4) life insurance company taxable income, as defined in Section 801(b) of the Internal Revenue Code;

"(5) mutual insurance company taxable income, as defined in Section 821(b) of the Internal Revenue Code; or

"(6) taxable income, as defined in Section 832 of the Internal Revenue Code;

"is also effective for that same taxable year for purposes of determining 'adjusted gross income' under IC 6–3–1–3.5 and 'net income' under IC 6–3–8–2(b)."

P.L.67–1986, Sec.3, emerg. eff. March 10, 1986, in Subsec. (a), substituted "IC 6–3–2–2.8(3) or (4)" for "IC 6–3–2–3(c) or (d)".

P.L.2–1987, Sec.21, amended this section emergency effective retroactive to Jan. 1, 1987.

P.L.2–1987 provides in Section 54 that this act applies to taxable years beginning after Dec. 31, 1986.

P.L.21–1990, Sec.11, emerg. eff. retroactive to Jan. 1, 1990.

P.L.21–1990, Sec.11, in Subsec. (a), in the first sentence, inserted "and" preceding "savings and loan", and inserted "not subject to taxation under the financial institutions tax (IC 6–5.5)"; redesignated Subsec. (b)(i), (ii) and (iii) as Subsec. (b)(1), (2) and (3); redesignated Subsec. (c)(1)(i) and (ii) as Subsec. (c)(1)(A) and (B); redesignated Subsec. (c)(3)(i) and (ii) as Subsec. (c)(3)(A) and (B).

P.L.42–1993, Sec.4, emerg. eff. May 13, 1993, in Subsec. (a), deleted a reference to private banks.

Formerly:

Acts 1973, P.L.50, SEC.8.

Cross References

Exemptions, adjusted gross income tax, see IC 6–3–2–2.8.
Insurance companies, gross premium privilege tax, see IC 27–1–18–2.

Library References

Taxation ☞980, 1015.
WESTLAW Topic No. 371.

C.J.S. Taxation §§ 1093, 1096.
Words and Phrases (Perm. Ed.)

6–3–8–3   Repealed

(Repealed by P.L.28–1997, SEC.31.)

Historical and Statutory Notes

Former IC 6–3–8–3 related to effective date.

Formerly:

Acts 1973, P.L.50, SEC.8.

6–3–8–4   Repealed

(Repealed by Acts 1982, P.L.52, SEC.8.)

Historical and Statutory Notes

Acts 1982, P.L.52, provided in Section 9(a), containing emergency clause, that the act takes effect retroactive to Jan. 1, 1982.

The repealed section provided for the rate of the supplemental net income tax.

See, now, IC 6–3–8–4.1.

6–3–8–4.1 Rate of tax

Sec. 4.1. The rate of the supplemental net income tax is four and five-tenths percent (4.5%).

As added by Acts 1982, P.L.52, SEC.5. Amended by P.L.390–1987(ss), SEC.40.

Historical and Statutory Notes

Acts 1982, P.L.52, Sec.5, emerg. eff. Jan. 1, 1982, added this section.

P.L.390–1987(ss), Sec.40, emerg. eff. retroactive to Jan. 1, 1987, increased the tax rate from four to four and five-tenths percent.

P.L.390–1987(ss) provides in Section 58(b) that Section 40 of this act applies to taxable years that begin after Dec. 31, 1986.

Formerly:

IC 6–3–8–4.
Acts 1973, P.L.50, SEC.8.
Acts 1975, P.L.61, SEC.1.

Library References

Taxation ⚖1001.
WESTLAW Topic No. 371.

C.J.S. Taxation § 1096.
I.L.E. Taxation §§ 31, 61.

6–3–8–5 Adjusted gross income tax provisions; applicability

Sec. 5. All of the provisions of IC 6–3–1 through IC 6–3–7 apply to the imposition, collection, payment, and administration of the supplemental net income tax in the same manner as such provisions apply to the imposition, collection, payment and administration of the tax imposed by IC 6–3–2, and any reference to "tax" or "adjusted gross income tax" shall also mean and include the supplemental net income tax to the extent necessary to harmonize and coordinate the imposition of the adjusted gross income tax and the supplemental net income tax, except that the provisions of IC 6–3–3–2, and IC 6–3–3–5, providing for certain credits shall not be applicable to the supplemental net income tax imposed by this section, and the provisions of IC IC [1] 6–3–2–2.8(3) and (4) shall not apply to any organization included in the definition of "corporation" as set forth in section 2(a) of this chapter, and the provisions of IC 6–3–2–2 shall not apply to the allocation or apportionment of the net income of domestic insurance companies.

As amended by P.L.67–1986, SEC.4.

[1] So in enrolled act.

Historical and Statutory Notes

P.L.67–1986, Sec.4, emerg. eff. March 10, 1986, changed references throughout by substituting "IC 6–3–1 through IC 6–3–7" for "IC 1971, 6–3, shall", "IC 6–3–2" for "(IC 1971, 6–3–2)", "IC 6–3–2–2.8(3) and (4)" for "IC 1971, 6–3–2–3(c) and (d)" and "2(a)" for "1(b)".

Formerly:

Acts 1973, P.L.50, SEC.8.

Library References

Taxation ⚖979.
WESTLAW Topic No. 371.

C.J.S. Taxation § 1096.
I.L.E. Taxation §§ 31, 201, 202.

6–3–8–6   Deposit of revenues in general fund

Sec. 6.   All of the revenues collected from the imposition of the supplemental net income tax shall be deposited in the general fund of the state.

Historical and Statutory Notes

Formerly:

Acts 1973, P.L.50, SEC.8.

Library References

States ☞126.
WESTLAW Topic No. 360.
C.J.S. States § 228.

ARTICLE 3.1

STATE TAX LIABILITY CREDITS

WESTLAW Computer Assisted Legal Research

WESTLAW supplements your legal research in many ways. WESTLAW allows you to
- update your research with the most current information
- expand your library with additional resources
- retrieve current, comprehensive history and citing references to a case with KeyCite

For more information on using WESTLAW to supplement your research, see the WESTLAW Electronic Research Guide, which follows the Preface.

Chapter 1

Definitions; Priority of Credits

6–3.1–1–1   Definitions; application

Sec. 1. Except as otherwise provided in this article, the definitions contained in IC 6–3–1 apply throughout this article.
As added by P.L.51–1984, SEC.1.

Historical and Statutory Notes

P.L. 51–1984, Sec.1, emerg. eff. Jan. 1, 1984, added this article.

Section 5(a) of P.L. 51–1984 provided that Section 1 of this act affects taxable years that begin after Dec. 31, 1983.

Section 2 of P.L. 51–1984 provided:

"Notwithstanding the repeal of tax credits by section 3 of this act, any credit a taxpayer earned before January 1, 1984, under any of those repealed code citations may be carried back or carried forward and utilized in the same manner they could have been had those credits not been repealed."

Library References

Taxation ⬯1047.
WESTLAW Topic No. 371.
C.J.S. Taxation § 1098.

6–3.1–1–2   Order of application

Sec. 2. (a) The tax credits a taxpayer is entitled to shall be applied against the taxpayer's tax liabilities in the following order:

(1) First, credits which may not be refunded to a taxpayer nor carried over and applied against any tax liability for any succeeding taxable year.

(2) Second, credits which may not be refunded to a taxpayer, but which may be carried over and applied against any tax liability for any succeeding taxable year.

(3) Third, credits which will be refunded to a taxpayer to the extent the credit exceeds the tax liability it is to be applied against.

(b) Credits described in subsection (a)(2) shall be applied against a taxpayer's tax liabilities so that the credits which may be applied to the fewest succeeding taxable years are utilized first.
As added by P.L.51–1984, SEC.1.

Cross References

Community revitalization enhancement district tax credit, state and local tax liability, see IC 6–3.1–19–1.
Military base recovery tax credit, state tax liability, see IC 6–3.1–11.5–14.
Taxation,
    Individual development account income tax credit, see IC 6–3.1–18–6.
    Individual development account tax credit, state tax liability defined, see IC 6–3.1–18–5.

Library References

Taxation ⬯1047.
WESTLAW Topic No. 371.
C.J.S. Taxation § 1098.

Notes of Decisions

Credits   1

_____

1. Credits

Current year bank tax credits offset national bank's current year state gross income tax lia-

bility; any excess credits are carried back three years if needed and then forward three years if needed.   Horizon Bancorp v. Indiana Dept. of State Revenue, 1993, 626 N.E.2d 603, affirmed in part, reversed in part 644 N.E.2d 870.

Chapter 2

Teacher Summer Employment Credits

6–3.1–2–1   Definitions

Sec. 1.   As used in this chapter, the following terms have the following meanings:

(1) "Eligible teacher" means a teacher:

(A) certified in a shortage area by the professional standards board established by IC 20–1–1.4; and

(B) employed under contract during the regular school term by a school corporation in a shortage area.

(2) "Qualified position" means a position that:

(A) is relevant to the teacher's academic training in a shortage area; and

(B) has been approved by the Indiana state board of education under section 6 of this chapter.

(3) "Regular school term" means the period, other than the school summer recess, during which a teacher is required to perform duties assigned to him under a teaching contract.

(4) "School corporation" means any corporation authorized by law to establish public schools and levy taxes for their maintenance.

(5) "Shortage area" means the subject areas of mathematics and science and any other subject area designated as a shortage area by the Indiana state board of education.

(6) "State income tax liability" means a taxpayer's total income tax liability incurred under IC 6–2.1 and IC 6–3, as computed after application of

credits that under IC 6–3.1–1–2 are to be applied before the credit provided by this chapter.

As added by P.L.51–1984, SEC.1. Amended by P.L.20–1984, SEC.5; P.L.46–1992, SEC.1.

Historical and Statutory Notes

P.L. 51–1984, Sec.1, emerg. eff. Jan. 1, 1984, added this article.

Section 5(a) of P.L. 51–1984 provided that Section 1 of this act affects taxable years that begin after Dec. 31, 1983.

For provisions relating to carry back or carry forward of credits earned before Jan. 1, 1984, see note under section 6–3.1–1–1.

P.L. 20–1984, Sec.5, eff. June 30, 1984, substituted "state board of education" for "commission on teacher training and licensing" where first and thirdly appearing, and for "commission on general education" where secondly appearing.

P.L.46–1992, Sec.1, in the definition of "eligible teacher", substituted "professional standards board established by IC 20–1–1.4"for "state board of education".

Formerly:

IC 6–3–3.6–1.
P.L.82–1984, SEC.7.

Library References

Taxation ☞1047.
WESTLAW Topic No. 371.
C.J.S. Taxation § 1098.

6–3.1–2–2   Credit for employment of eligible teacher

Sec. 2.   Subject to the limitation established in sections 4 and 5 of this chapter, a taxpayer that employs an eligible teacher in a qualified position during a school summer recess is entitled to a tax credit against his state income tax liability as provided for under section 3 of this chapter.

As added by P.L.51–1984, SEC.1.

Historical and Statutory Notes

Formerly:
IC 6–3–3.6–2.
P.L.82–1983, SEC.7.

Library References

Taxation ☞1047.
WESTLAW Topic No. 371.
C.J.S. Taxation § 1098.

6–3.1–2–3   Amount of credit

Sec. 3.   A taxpayer is entitled to a credit for a taxable year for each eligible teacher employed under section 2 of this chapter in an amount equal to the lesser of:

(1) two thousand five hundred dollars ($2,500); or

(2) fifty percent (50%) of the amount of compensation paid to the eligible teacher by the taxpayer during the taxable year.

However, the aggregate credits that a taxpayer may receive for a particular taxable year under this chapter may not exceed the taxpayer's state income tax liability for that taxable year.

As added by P.L.51–1984, SEC.1.

Historical and Statutory Notes

Formerly:
  IC 6–3–3.6–3.
  P.L.82–1983, SEC.7.

Library References

Taxation ☞1047.
WESTLAW Topic No. 371.
C.J.S. Taxation § 1098.

6–3.1–2–4 Disallowance of credit; employer's duty

Sec. 4. (a) The department shall disallow a credit provided under this chapter with respect to employment of an eligible teacher during a school summer recess if the teacher discontinues his teaching duties for the purpose of becoming employed by the taxpayer during the regular school term that immediately follows the recess. The taxpayer shall, within thirty (30) days after the eligible teacher had discontinued his teaching duties, notify the department of that fact and pay to the department the amount of the credit previously allowed.

(b) A taxpayer that fails to notify and pay the department as prescribed in subsection (a) is liable for interest and a penalty on the amount of the credit in the amounts established in IC 6–8.1–10–1 and IC 6–8.1–10–2.1.

As added by P.L.51–1984, SEC.1. Amended by P.L.1–1991, SEC.53.

Historical and Statutory Notes

P.L.1–1991, Sec.53, emerg. eff. April 23, 1991.

P.L.1–1991, Sec.53, substituted "IC 6–8.1–10–2.1" for "IC 6–8.1–10–2" in Subsec. (b).

Formerly:

IC 6–3–3.6–4.
P.L.82–1983, SEC.7.

Library References

Taxation ☞1047.
WESTLAW Topic No. 371.
C.J.S. Taxation § 1098.

6–3.1–2–5 Application of credit

Sec. 5. (a) A credit to which a taxpayer is entitled under this chapter shall be applied in the following manner:

(1) First, against the taxpayer's gross income tax liability for the taxable year.

(2) Second, against the taxpayer's adjusted gross income tax liability for the taxable year.

(3) Third, against the taxpayer's supplemental net income tax liability for the taxable year.

(b) A taxpayer that is subject to the financial institutions tax may apply the credit provided by this chapter against the taxpayer's financial institutions tax liability for the taxable year.

As added by P.L.51–1984, SEC.1.   Amended by P.L.347–1989(ss), SEC.10.

Historical and Statutory Notes

P.L.347–1989(ss), Sec.10, eff. Jan. 1, 1990.

P.L.347–1989(ss), Sec.10, designated the section as Subsec. (a) and added Subsec. (b).

Formerly:

IC 6–3–3.6–5.
P.L.82–1983, SEC.7.

Library References

Taxation ⚘1047.
WESTLAW Topic No. 371.
C.J.S. Taxation § 1098.

6–3.1–2–6   Qualified position certificate; applications; determination of qualified position; issuance; maximum amount of credit; aggregate amount of credits

Sec. 6.   (a) A taxpayer who seeks to obtain the credit provided by this chapter must file an application for a qualified position certificate for that year with the state board of education.   The board shall prescribe the form and contents of the application.

(b) Upon receipt of an application filed under subsection (a), the state board of education shall determine whether the position in question is a qualified position.   The board shall also determine the amount of compensation that the taxpayer intends to pay to the eligible teacher in the qualified position during the school summer recess, or the parts of the school summer recesses that fall within the taxable year with respect to which the taxpayer is applying for a certificate.   If the board approves the application, it shall issue a qualified position certificate to the taxpayer for the taxable year.   The certificate shall indicate the maximum amount of credit to which the taxpayer is entitled for the taxable year under this chapter with respect to the eligible teacher.   That amount is the lesser of:

(1) two thousand five hundred dollars ($2,500); or

(2) fifty percent (50%) of the amount of compensation that the taxpayer intends to pay to the eligible teacher in the qualified position during the school summer recess, or the parts of the school summer recesses that fall within the taxable year.

The taxpayer shall attach the certificate to the income tax return that is filed for the taxable year for which the credit is claimed.

(c) The state board of education shall record the time of filing of each application for a qualified position certificate, and shall approve the applications, if they otherwise qualify, in the chronological order in which they are filed. However, the board may not approve any application in a state fiscal year if the aggregate amount of allowable credits indicated on qualified position certificates issued in the fiscal year exceeds five hundred thousand dollars ($500,000).

As added by P.L.51–1984, SEC.1. Amended by P.L.20–1984, SEC.6.

Historical and Statutory Notes

P.L. 20–1984, Sec.6, eff. June 30, 1984, in Subsec. (a), substituted "state board of education" for "commission on general education" in the first sentence; and made corrective changes in conformity therewith throughout.

Formerly:

IC 6–3–3.6–6.

P.L.82–1983, SEC.7.

Library References

Taxation ☞1047.
WESTLAW Topic No. 371.
C.J.S. Taxation § 1098.

6–3.1–2–7   Rules; qualified positions

Sec. 7. Notwithstanding IC 6–8.1–3–3, the state board of education shall adopt rules under IC 4–22–2 for determining which positions are qualified positions.

As added by P.L.51–1984, SEC.1. Amended by P.L.20–1984, SEC.7.

Historical and Statutory Notes

P.L.20–1984, Sec.7, eff. June 30, 1984, substituted "state board of education" for "commission on general education".

Formerly:

IC 6–3–3.6–7.

P.L.82–1983, SEC.7.

Library References

Taxation ☞1047.
WESTLAW Topic No. 371.
C.J.S. Taxation § 1098.

Chapter 3

Credit for Donations of High Technology Equipment to Schools

6–3.1–3–1 to 6–3.1–3–10   Repealed

(Repealed by P.L.28–1997, SEC.31.)

Historical and Statutory Notes

Former IC 6–3.1–3–1 to 6–3.1–3–10 related to credit for donations of high technology equipment to schools.

Formerly:

IC 6–3–3.7–1 to 6–3–3.7–10.

P.L.84–1983, SEC.1.

P.L.20–1984, SEC.8.

P.L.47–1984, SEC.6.

P.L.51–1984, SEC.1.

P.L.52–1984, SEC.2.

P.L.217–1987, SEC.25.
P.L.80–1989, SECS.2, 3.

P.L.92–1989, SEC.1.
P.L.347–1989(ss), SECS.11, 12.

Chapter 4

Research Expense Credits

6–3.1–4–1 Definitions

Sec. 1. As used in this chapter:

"Base amount" means base amount (as defined in Section 41(c) of the Internal Revenue Code).

"Base period Indiana qualified research expense" means base period research expense that is incurred for research conducted in Indiana.

"Base period research expense" means base period research expense (as defined in Section 41(c) of the Internal Revenue Code before January 1, 1990).

"Indiana qualified research expense" means qualified research expense that is incurred for research conducted in Indiana.

"Qualified research expense" means qualified research expense (as defined in Section 41(b) of the Internal Revenue Code).

"Pass through entity" means:

(1) a corporation that is exempt from the adjusted gross income tax under IC 6–3–2–2.8(2);

(2) a partnership;

(3) a limited liability company; or

(4) a limited liability partnership.

"Research expense tax credit" means a credit provided under this chapter against any tax otherwise due and payable under IC 6–2.1 or IC 6–3.

"Taxpayer" means an individual, a corporation, a limited liability company, a limited liability partnership, a trust, or a partnership.

As added by P.L.51–1984, SEC.1. Amended by P.L.57–1990, SEC.1; P.L.8–1993, SEC.85; P.L.8–1996, SEC.7.

70

Historical and Statutory Notes

P.L. 51–1984, Sec.1, emerg. eff. Jan. 1, 1984, added this article.

Section 5(a) of P.L. 51–1984 provided that Section 1 of this act affects taxable years that begin after Dec. 31, 1983.

For provisions relating to carry back or carry forward of credits earned before Jan. 1, 1984, see note under section 6–3.1–1–1.

P.L.57–1990, Sec.1, emerg. eff. retroactive to Jan. 1, 1989.

P.L.57–1990, Sec.1, added the definitions of base amount, pass through entity and taxpayer; in the definition of base period research expense substituted "41(c)" for "44F(c)" and added "before January 1, 1990"; and in the definition of qualified research expense substituted "41(b)" for "44F(b)".

P.L.57–1990, Secs. 7 and 8 provide:

"Sec. 7. This act applies to taxable years that begin after December 31, 1988.

"Sec. 8. Because an emergency exists, this act takes effect January 1, 1989 (retroactive)."

P.L.8–1993, Sec.85, inserted "a limited liability company" in the definitions of "pass through entity" and "taxpayer".

P.L.8–1996, Sec.7, emerg. eff. retroactive to Jan. 1, 1996, amended the section by adding Subsec. (4) under the definition of "Pass through entity"; adding "a limited liability partnership," under the definition of "Taxpayer"; and by making other nonsubstantive changes.

P.L.8–1996, Sec.13, emerg. eff. retroactive to Jan. 1, 1996, provides:

"IC 6–3.1–4–1, as amended by this act, applies only to taxable years beginning after December 31, 1995."

Formerly:

IC 6–3–3.8–1.
Acts 1982, P.L.52, SEC.4.

Cross References

Gross income tax, see IC 6–2.1–1–1 et seq.

Library References

Taxation ⊘1047.
WESTLAW Topic No. 371.
C.J.S. Taxation § 1098.

6–3.1–4–2   Research expense tax credit

Sec. 2.   (a) A taxpayer who incurs Indiana qualified research expense in a particular taxable year is entitled to a research expense tax credit for the taxable year.

(b) A taxpayer who does not have income apportioned to this state for a taxable year under IC 6–3–2–2 is entitled to a research expense tax credit for the taxable year in the amount of the product of:

(1) five percent (5%); multiplied by

(2) the remainder of the taxpayer's Indiana qualified research expenses for the taxable year, minus:

(A) the taxpayer's base period Indiana qualified research expenses, for taxable years beginning before January 1, 1990; or

(B) the taxpayer's base amount, for taxable years beginning after December 31, 1989.

(c) A taxpayer who has income apportioned to this state for a taxable year under IC 6–3–2–2 is entitled to a research expense tax credit for the taxable year in the amount of the lesser of:

(1) the amount determined under subsection (b); or

(2) five percent (5%) multiplied by the remainder of the taxpayer's total qualified research expenses for the taxable year, minus:

    (A) the taxpayer's base period research expenses, for taxable years beginning before January 1, 1990; or

    (B) the taxpayer's base amount, for taxable years beginning after December 31, 1989;

further multiplied by the percentage determined under IC 6–3–2–2 for the apportionment of the taxpayer's income for the taxable year to this state.

As added by P.L.51–1984, SEC.1. Amended by P.L.53–1984, SEC.1; P.L.57–1990, SEC.2.

Historical and Statutory Notes

P.L. 53–1984, Sec.1, eff. Jan. 1, 1985, deleted "who is entitled to an income tax credit under Section 44F of the Internal Revenue Code" following "A taxpayer" in Subsec. (a); and inserted "1986, 1987, or 1988" in Subsec. (d)(2).

P.L.57–1990, Sec.2, emerg. eff. retroactive to Jan. 1, 1989.

P.L.57–1990, Sec.2, rewrote the section.

For application and effective date of P.L.57–1990, see Historical Note under § 6–3.1–4–1.

Formerly:

IC 6–3–3.8–2.

Acts 1982, P.L.52, SEC.4.

Library References

Taxation ☞1047.
WESTLAW Topic No. 371.
C.J.S. Taxation § 1098.

6–3.1–4–3   Limits on credit; carryover of excess and application; carryback or refund

Sec. 3. (a) The amount of the credit provided by this chapter that a taxpayer uses during a particular taxable year may not exceed the sum of the taxes imposed by IC 6–2.1 and IC 6–3 for the taxable year after the application of all credits that under IC 6–3.1–1–2 are to be applied before the credit provided by this chapter. If the credit provided by this chapter exceeds that sum for the taxable year for which the credit is first claimed, then the excess may be carried over to succeeding taxable years and used as a credit against the tax otherwise due and payable by the taxpayer under IC 6–2.1 or IC 6–3 during those taxable years. Each time that the credit is carried over to a succeeding taxable year, it is to be reduced by the amount which was used as a credit during the immediately preceding taxable year. The credit provided by this chapter may be carried forward and applied to succeeding taxable years for fifteen (15) taxable years following the unused credit year.

(b) A credit earned by a taxpayer in a particular taxable year shall be applied against the taxpayer's tax liability for that taxable year before any credit carryover is applied against that liability under subsection (a).

(c) A taxpayer is not entitled to any carryback or refund of any unused credit.

As added by P.L.51–1984, SEC.1. Amended by P.L.57–1990, SEC.3.

Historical and Statutory Notes

P.L.57–1990, Sec.3, emerg. eff. retroactive to Jan. 1, 1989.

P.L.57–1990, Sec.3, in the last sentence of Subsec. (a), substituted "fifteen (15) taxable years following the unused credit year" for "the period provided in Section 44F(g)(2)(A)(ii) of the Internal Revenue Code".

For application and effective date of P.L.57–1990, see Historical Note under § 6–3.1–4–1.

Formerly:

IC 6–3–3.8–3.
Acts 1982, P.L.52, SEC.4.

Library References

Taxation ⚲1047.
WESTLAW Topic No. 371.
C.J.S. Taxation § 1098.

6–3.1–4–4 Interpretation and administration of credit provided by this chapter

Sec. 4. The provisions of Section 41 of the Internal Revenue Code and the regulations promulgated in respect to those provisions are applicable to the interpretation and administration by the department of the credit provided by this chapter, including the allocation and pass through of the credit to various taxpayers and the transitional rules for determination of the base period.
As added by P.L.51–1984, SEC.1. Amended by P.L.57–1990, SEC.4.

Historical and Statutory Notes

P.L.57–1990, Sec.4, emerg. eff. retroactive to Jan. 1, 1989.

P.L.57–1990, Sec.4, substituted "41" for "44F".

For application and effective date of P.L.57–1990 see Historical Note under § 6–3.1–4–1.

Formerly:

IC 6–3–3.8–4.
Acts 1982, P.L.52, SEC.4.

Library References

Taxation ⚲1047.
WESTLAW Topic No. 371.
C.J.S. Taxation § 1098.

6–3.1–4–5 Qualified research expenses; determination

Sec. 5. In prescribing standards for determining which qualified research expenses are considered Indiana qualified research expenses for purposes of computing the credit provided by this chapter, the department may consider:

(1) the place where the services are performed;

(2) the residence or business location of the person or persons performing the services;

(3) the place where qualified research supplies are consumed; and

(4) other factors that the department determines are relevant for the determination.

As added by P.L.51–1984, SEC.1.

Historical and Statutory Notes

Formerly:
　IC 6–3–3.8–5.
　Acts 1982, P.L.52, SEC.4.

Library References

Taxation ⚮1047.
WESTLAW Topic No. 371.
C.J.S. Taxation § 1098.

6–3.1–4–6　No credit; date

Sec. 6.　Notwithstanding the other provisions of this chapter, a taxpayer is not entitled to a credit for Indiana qualified research expense incurred after December 31, 1999.　Notwithstanding Section 41 of the Internal Revenue Code, the termination date in Section 41(h) of the Internal Revenue Code does not apply to a taxpayer who is eligible for the credit under this chapter for the taxable year in which the Indiana qualified research expense is incurred.
As added by P.L.51–1984, SEC.1.　Amended by P.L.53–1984, SEC.2; P.L.57–1990, SEC.5; P.L.43–1992, SEC.10; P.L.76–1993, SEC.1; P.L.19–1994, SEC.9; P.L.8–1996, SEC.8.

Historical and Statutory Notes

P.L. 53–1984, Sec.2, eff. Jan. 1, 1985, designated Subsec. (a), and substituted "1988" for "1985" at the end thereof; and added Subsec. (b).

P.L.57–1990, Sec.5, emerg. eff. retroactive to Jan. 1, 1989, rewrote this section.

For application and effective date of P.L.57–1990, see Historical Note under § 6–3.1–4–1.

P.L.43–1992, Sec.10, emerg. eff. retroactive to Jan. 1, 1992, rewrote the section, which formerly read:

"(a) Notwithstanding the other provisions of this chapter, a taxpayer is not entitled to a credit for Indiana qualified research expense incurred after:

　"(1) December 31 of the year following the last year in which Section 41 of the Internal Revenue Code is effective; or

　"(2) December 31, 1991;

"whichever is earlier.

"(b) If Section 41 of the Internal Revenue Code is repealed or expires before January 1, 1992, the credit provided by this chapter remains available to Indiana taxpayers for expenses incurred through December 31 of the year following the last year in which Section 41 of the Internal Revenue Code is effective, using the language of Section 41 of the Internal Revenue Code as it existed immediately before its repeal or expiration.

"(c) If Section 41 of the Internal Revenue Code is not repealed or does not expire before January 1, 1992, the credit provided by this chapter remains available to Indiana taxpayers for expenses incurred through December 31, 1991."

P.L.76–1993, Sec.1, emerg. eff. retroactive to July 1, 1992, rewrote the section, which formerly read:

"Notwithstanding the other provisions of this chapter, a taxpayer is not entitled to a credit for Indiana qualified research expense incurred after the last date that an expense may be incurred with regard to the credit allowed under Section 41 of the Internal Revenue Code."

P.L.76–1993, Sec.2, provides:

"This act applies to taxable years that begin after December 31, 1991."

P.L.19–1994, Sec.9, emerg. eff. retroactive to January 1, 1992, rewrote this section.

P.L.19–1994, Sec.20, emerg. eff. retroactive to January 1, 1992, provides:

"IC 6–3.1–4–6, as amended by this act, applies to taxable years after December 31, 1991."

P.L.8–1996, Sec.8, amended the section by substituting "1999" for "1996" following "December 31,".

INVESTMENT CREDITS

Formerly:
IC 6–3–3.8–6.
Acts 1982, P.L.52, SEC.4.

Library References

Taxation ⚭1047.
WESTLAW Topic No. 371.
C.J.S. Taxation § 1098.

6–3.1–4–7 Pass through entity; shareholder or partner

Sec. 7. (a) If a pass through entity does not have state income tax liability against which the research expense tax credit may be applied, a shareholder or partner of the pass through entity is entitled to a research expense tax credit equal to:

(1) the research expense tax credit determined for the pass through entity for the taxable year; multiplied by

(2) the percentage of the pass through entity's distributive income to which the shareholder or partner is entitled.

(b) The credit provided under subsection (a) is in addition to a research expense tax credit to which a shareholder or partner of a pass through entity is otherwise entitled under this chapter. However, a pass through entity and a shareholder or partner of the pass through entity may not claim a credit under this chapter for the same qualified research expenses.

As added by P.L.57–1990, SEC.6.

Historical and Statutory Notes

P.L.57–1990, Sec.6, emerg. eff. retroactive to Jan. 1, 1989.

For application and effective date of P.L.57–1990, see Historical Note under § 6–3.1–4–1.

Chapter 5

Investment Credits

6–3.1–5–1 Purposes of chapter

Sec. 1. The purposes of this chapter are:

(1) to encourage capital investment in Indiana;

(2) to encourage the establishment or expansion of business and industry;

(3) to provide additional jobs within Indiana; and

(4) to encourage research and development activities within Indiana.

As added by P.L.51–1984, SEC.1.

Historical and Statutory Notes

P.L. 51–1984, Sec.1, emerg., eff. Jan. 1, 1984, added this article.

Section 5(a) of P.L. 51–1984 provided that Section 1 of this act affects taxable years that begin after Dec. 31, 1983.

For provisions relating to carry back or carry forward of credits earned before Jan. 1, 1984, see Historical Note under section 6–3.1–1–1.

Formerly:

IC 6–3–3.4–1.

Acts 1981, P.L.86, SEC.1.

Library References

Taxation ☞1047.
WESTLAW Topic No. 371.

C.J.S. Taxation § 1098.
I.L.E. Taxation §§ 207, 208, 213, 222.

6–3.1–5–2 Definitions

Sec. 2. As used in this chapter:

"New partnership interest" means a general or a limited partnership interest in a limited partnership if the interest is acquired by the taxpayer from the limited partnership.

"New stock" means a share of stock of a corporation if the stock, when purchased by the taxpayer, is authorized but unissued.

"Qualified entity" means the state corporation or other corporation or limited partnership in which the state corporation purchases, before January 1, 1984, new stock or a new partnership interest under section 7(d) of this chapter.

"Qualified investment" means new stock or a new partnership interest in a qualified entity, if the new stock or the new partnership interest is purchased by the taxpayer solely for cash.

"State corporation" means the corporation organized under sections 7 and 8 of this chapter.

"State tax liability" means a taxpayer's total tax liability that is incurred under:

(1) IC 6–2.1 (the gross income tax);

(2) IC 6–3–1 through IC 6–3–7 (the adjusted gross income tax);

(3) IC 6–3–8 (the supplemental net income tax);

(4) IC 6–5–10 (the bank tax);

(5) IC 6–5–11 (the savings and loan association tax);

(6) IC 27–1–18–2 (the insurance premiums tax); and

(7) IC 6–5.5 (the financial institutions tax);

as computed after the application of the credits that under IC 6–3.1–1–2 are to be applied before the credit provided by this chapter.

"Taxpayer" means any person, corporation, partnership, or other entity that has any state tax liability.

As added by P.L.51–1984, SEC.1.   Amended by P.L.80–1989, SEC.4; P.L.347–1989(ss), SEC.13.

Historical and Statutory Notes

P.L.80–1989, Sec.4, emerg. eff. retroactive to Nov. 10, 1988, in the definition of "qualified investment", substituted "if the new" for "which" following "entity" and inserted "the new partnership"; and made other nonsubstantive changes.

P.L.347–1989(ss), Sec.13, eff. Jan. 1, 1990, in definition of "State tax liability" added Subsec. (7).

Formerly:

IC 6–3–3.4–2.

Acts 1981, P.L.86, SEC.1.

P.L.23–1983, SEC.6.

Cross References

Adjusted gross income tax, amounts withheld, credits, see IC 6–3–3–1.

Library References

Taxation ⚖1047.
WESTLAW Topic No. 371.
C.J.S. Taxation § 1098.

6–3.1–5–3 Purchase of qualified investment in qualified entity; entitlement years

Sec. 3.   Subject to section 6 of this chapter, a taxpayer is entitled to a credit against any state tax liability which may be imposed on the taxpayer for a particular taxable year that begins after December 31, 1981, if the taxpayer purchases a qualified investment in a qualified entity.   However, a taxpayer may only receive a credit for qualified investments purchased during calendar years 1981, 1982, and 1983.

As added by P.L.51–1984, SEC.1.

Historical and Statutory Notes

Formerly:
  IC 6–3–3.4–3.
  Acts 1981, P.L.86, SEC.1.

Library References

Taxation ⊗1047.
WESTLAW Topic No. 371.
C.J.S. Taxation § 1098.

6–3.1–5–4   Amount of credit; determination steps

Sec. 4.   Subject to section 6 of this chapter, the amount of the credit that a taxpayer may receive under this chapter for a particular taxable year is equal to the lesser of the taxpayer's state tax liability for that taxable year, or the amount determined in STEP THREE of the following steps:

     STEP ONE: Add the consideration paid for all qualified investments the taxpayer purchased during that taxable year.

     STEP TWO: Multiply the amount determined in STEP ONE by three-tenths (0.3).

     STEP THREE: Add the product determined in STEP TWO to the credit carryover, if any, to which the taxpayer is entitled for the taxable year under section 5 of this chapter.

As added by P.L.51–1984, SEC.1.

Historical and Statutory Notes

Formerly:
  IC 6–3–3.4–4.
  Acts 1981, P.L.86, SEC.1.

Library References

Taxation ⊗1047.
WESTLAW Topic No. 371.
C.J.S. Taxation § 1098.

6–3.1–5–5   Carryover of excess credit

Sec. 5.   (a) If the amount determined under STEPS ONE through THREE of section 4 of this chapter for a particular taxpayer and a particular taxable year exceeds the taxpayer's state tax liability for that taxable year, then the taxpayer may carry the excess over to the immediately succeeding taxable years. However, the credit carryover may not be used for any taxable year that begins on or after January 1, 1987. The amount of the credit carryover from a taxable year shall be reduced to the extent that the carryover is used by the taxpayer to obtain a credit under this chapter for any subsequent taxable year.

  (b) A credit based on a qualified investment purchased during 1981 shall be a credit carryover to taxable years that begin after December 31, 1981.

As added by P.L.51–1984, SEC.1.

Historical and Statutory Notes

Formerly:
IC 6–3–3.4–5.
Acts 1981, P.L.86, SEC.1.

Library References

Taxation ☞1047.
WESTLAW Topic No. 371.
C.J.S. Taxation § 1098.

6–3.1–5–6   Total amount of credits allowed; limitation

Sec. 6.   (a) The total amount of credits allowed under this chapter may not exceed in the aggregate five million dollars ($5,000,000) for all taxpayers and all taxable years.

(b) The aggregate amount of consideration paid by all taxpayers for qualified investments in a particular qualified entity, other than the state corporation, which may be used by all those taxpayers as a basis for credits under this chapter, may not exceed an amount equal to five (5) times the amount of consideration paid by the state corporation for new stock or a new partnership interest in the qualified entity.

(c) The state corporation shall administer the provisions of this section and shall issue the forms required by section 15 of this chapter only to the extent consistent with the limits in this section.

(d) If aggregate consideration paid for qualified investments which would otherwise qualify for the credit provided by this chapter exceeds the limits imposed by this section, the credit shall be allowed to taxpayers in the order of the time of the purchase of the qualified investments.

As added by P.L.51–1984, SEC.1.

Historical and Statutory Notes

Formerly:
IC 6–3–3.4–6.
Acts 1981, P.L.86, SEC.1.

Library References

Taxation ☞1047.
WESTLAW Topic No. 371.
C.J.S. Taxation § 1098.

6–3.1–5–7   Corporation for Innovation Development; incorporation; purpose; directors; authority; transaction of business; contribution to state universities; name

Sec. 7.   (a) To carry out the purposes of this chapter, the state corporation shall be formed under IC 23–1.   The articles of incorporation of the state corporation shall comply with the provisions set forth in subsections (b) through (i).

(b) The purpose of the state corporation shall be solely to raise funds which shall be used to make investments in qualified entities described in subsection (d) and to:

(1) provide financing to Indiana business firms described in subsection (e) in a manner that will encourage capital investment in Indiana;

(2) encourage the establishment or expansion of business and industry in Indiana;

(3) provide additional jobs within Indiana; and

(4) encourage research and development activities.

(c) The directors need not be shareholders in the state corporation, and there shall be not less than three (3) nor more than seven (7) directors, three (3) of whom shall be persons who have been nominated to be directors by the lieutenant governor.

(d) The state corporation may purchase new stock in a corporation organized under IC 23–1, a new partnership interest in a limited partnership, or a membership interest in a limited liability company organized under IC 23–18 that has its principal office located in Indiana if the corporation, partnership, or limited liability company:

(1) has received a license or a statement of intent to license as a small business investment company from the Small Business Administration of the United States under the Small Business Investment Act of 1958, as amended;[1] and

(2) is organized and operated solely for the purpose of performing the functions and conducting the activities contemplated by the Small Business Investment Act of 1958, as amended.

(e) The state corporation may provide financing to entities doing business primarily in Indiana, including but not limited to minority businesses, corporations, limited liability companies, and partnerships, to be used solely for the purpose of enhancing the production capacity of the entity or the ability of the entity to do business in Indiana. The financing may include any combination of equity investments, loans, guarantees, and commitments for financing, and the amount of financing is unlimited.

(f) The state corporation may borrow from the industrial development fund created by IC 4–4–8–2.

(g) No business shall be transacted or indebtedness incurred, except such as shall be incidental to the state corporation's organization or to obtaining subscriptions to or payment for its shares, until consideration for such shares equal to at least two million dollars ($2,000,000) shall have been paid in, which amount paid in shall be the initial stated capital of the state corporation.

(h) Not less than five percent (5%) of the net income of the state corporation for federal income tax purposes shall be contributed to state universities to be used by the universities for research for the purpose of developing business and industry in the state of Indiana. The allocation of funds among the universities shall be directed by the commission for higher education, which shall determine the universities and the amounts in its discretion.

(i) The name of the state corporation shall be "Corporation for Innovation Development".

As added by P.L.51–1984, SEC.1.   Amended by P.L.149–1986, SEC.40;   P.L.8–1993, SEC.86.

[1] 15 U.S.C.A. § 661 et seq.

Historical and Statutory Notes

P.L.149–1986, Sec.40, emerg. eff. April 1, 1986, in Subsecs. (a) and (d), substituted "IC 23–1" for "IC 23–1–1 through IC 23–1–12 (the Indiana general corporation act)".

P.L.8–1993, Sec.86, inserted references to limited liability companies in Subsecs. (d) and (e).

Formerly:

IC 6–3–3.4–7.
Acts 1981, P.L.86, SEC.1.
P.L.23–1983, SEC.15.

Library References

Taxation ⟐1047.
WESTLAW Topic No. 371.
C.J.S. Taxation § 1098.

6–3.1–5–8   State corporation; duties and powers of lieutenant governor

Sec. 8.   (a) The lieutenant governor shall cause the state corporation to be formed, and he shall designate the incorporators and the first three (3) members of the first board of directors, no more than two (2) of which may be members of the same political party.

(b) The lieutenant governor may expend such funds as he deems appropriate for the purpose of organizing the state corporation and marketing the securities thereof.

As added by P.L.51–1984, SEC.1.

Historical and Statutory Notes

Formerly:
IC 6–3–3.4–8.
Acts 1981, P.L.86, SEC.1.

Library References

States ⟐42, 45.
WESTLAW Topic No. 360.
C.J.S. States §§ 79, 80, 88 to 90, 131, 136.

6–3.1–5–9   State corporation; tax exemption

Sec. 9.   The state corporation is exempt from all state tax levies, including but not limited to the gross income tax (IC 6–2.1), state gross retail tax (IC 6–2.5), use tax (IC 6–2.5–3), adjusted gross income tax (IC 6–3–1 through IC 6–3–7), and the supplemental net income tax (IC 6–3–8).   However, the state corporation is not exempt from employment taxes or taxes imposed by a county or by a municipal corporation.

As added by P.L.51–1984, SEC.1. Amended by P.L.80–1989, SEC.5.

Historical and Statutory Notes

P.L.80–1989, Sec.5, deleted a reference to the intangibles tax (IC 6–5.1) in the first sentence and made other nonsubstantive changes.

P.L.80–1989, Sec.19, containing an emergency clause, provides that section 5 of the act amending this section takes effect retroactive to Nov. 10, 1988.

Formerly:
IC 6–3–3.4–9.
Acts 1981, P.L.86, SEC.1.

Library References

Taxation ☞213.
WESTLAW Topic No. 371.
C.J.S. Taxation §§ 251, 253, 259, 260.

6–3.1–5–10 Tax exemption; income received by reason of ownership of qualified investment

Sec. 10. (a) Except as provided in subsection (b), income that is received by a taxpayer by reason of ownership of a qualified investment is exempt from gross income tax (IC 6–2.1), adjusted gross income tax (IC 6–3–1 through IC 6–3–7), and supplemental net income tax (IC 6–3–8).

(b) The exemption provided under subsection (a) shall not apply to any income realized by reason of the sale or other disposition of the qualified investment.

As added by P.L.51–1984, SEC.1.

Historical and Statutory Notes

Formerly:
IC 6–3–3.4–10.
Acts 1981, P.L.86, SEC.1.

Library References

Taxation ☞1048.
WESTLAW Topic No. 371.
C.J.S. Taxation § 1098.

6–3.1–5–11 Exempt taxpayer

Sec. 11. A taxpayer is exempt from a tax to the extent that the tax is based on or measured by a qualified investment, including but not limited to a tax which might otherwise be imposed with respect to the qualified investment under the bank tax (IC 6–5–10) or the savings and loan association tax (IC 6–5–11).

As added by P.L.51–1984, SEC.1. Amended by P.L.80–1989, SEC.6; P.L.2–1995, SEC.33.

Historical and Statutory Notes

P.L.80–1989, Sec.6, deleted a reference to the intangibles tax (IC 6–5.1) and made certain other nonsubstantive changes.

P.L.80–1989, Sec.19, containing an emergency clause, provides that section 6 of the act amending this section takes effect retroactive to Nov. 10, 1988.

P.L.2–1995, Sec.33, emerg. eff. May 5, 1995, which was part of the correction bill, made nonsubstantive changes.

Formerly:
IC 6–3–3.4–11.
Acts 1981, P.L.86, SEC.1.
P.L.88–1983, SEC.7.

Library References

Taxation ⬥1048.
WESTLAW Topic No. 371.
C.J.S. Taxation § 1098.

6–3.1–5–12 Redemption of qualified investment by qualified entity; disallowance of credit

Sec. 12. (a) If a qualified investment which is the basis for a credit under this chapter is redeemed by the qualified entity within five (5) years of the date it is purchased, the credit provided by this chapter for the qualified investment shall be disallowed, and any credit previously claimed and allowed with respect to the qualified investment so redeemed shall be paid to the department of revenue with the appropriate return of the taxpayer covering the period in which the redemption occurred.

(b) When payments are made to the department under this section, the amount collected shall be handled in exactly the same manner as if no credit had been allowed.

As added by P.L.51–1984, SEC.1.

Historical and Statutory Notes

Formerly:
IC 6–3–3.4–12.
Acts 1981, P.L.86, SEC.1.

Library References

Taxation ⬥1047.
WESTLAW Topic No. 371.
C.J.S. Taxation § 1098.

6–3.1–5–13 Order of application of credit

Sec. 13. (a) A credit to which a taxpayer is entitled under this chapter shall be applied against taxes owed by the taxpayer in the following order:

(1) First, against the taxpayer's gross income tax liability (IC 6–2.1) for the taxable year.

(2) Second, against the taxpayer's adjusted gross income tax liability (IC 6–3–1 through IC 6–3–7) for the taxable year.

(3) Third, against the taxpayer's supplemental net income tax liability (IC 6–3–8) for the taxable year.

(4) Fourth, against the taxpayer's bank tax liability (IC 6–5–10) or savings and loan association tax liability (IC 6–5–11) for the taxable year.

(5) Fifth, against the taxpayer's insurance premiums tax liability (IC 27–1–18–2) for the taxable year.

(b) If the tax paid by the taxpayer under a tax provision listed in subsection (a) is a credit against the liability or a deduction in determining the tax base under another Indiana tax provision, the credit or deduction shall be computed without regard to the credit to which a taxpayer is entitled under this chapter.

(c) A taxpayer that is subject to the financial institutions tax may apply the credit provided by this chapter against the taxpayer's financial institutions tax liability for the taxable year.

As added by P.L.51–1984, SEC.1. Amended by P.L.80–1989, SEC.7; P.L.347–1989(ss), SEC.14.

Historical and Statutory Notes

P.L.80–1989, Sec.7, emerg. eff. retroactive to Nov. 10, 1988, deleted a Subd. (4) relating to the intangibles tax (IC 6–5.1) in Subsec. (a); and made certain nonsubstantive changes in Subsec. (b).

P.L.347–1989(ss), Sec.14, eff. Jan. 1, 1990.

P.L.347–1989(ss), Sec.14, added Subsec. (c).

Formerly:

IC 6–3–3.4–13.
Acts 1981, P.L.86, SEC.1.
P.L.88–1983, SEC.8.

Library References

Taxation ☞1047.
WESTLAW Topic No. 371.
C.J.S. Taxation § 1098.

6–3.1–5–14   Claiming of credit; filing of form with annual state tax return

Sec. 14.   To receive the credit provided by this chapter, a taxpayer must:

(1) claim the credit on the taxpayer's annual state tax return or returns in the manner prescribed by the department of state revenue; and

(2) file with the department and with the taxpayer's annual state tax return or returns a copy of the form issued by the state corporation as to the qualified investment by the taxpayer, which shall include an undertaking by the taxpayer to report to the department of revenue any redemption of the qualified investment, if the redemption is covered by section 12 of this chapter.

As added by P.L.51–1984, SEC.1.

Historical and Statutory Notes

Formerly:

IC 6–3–3.4–14.
Acts 1981, P.L.86, SEC.1.

6–3.1–5–15 Forms; contents; filing; copies

Sec. 15. (a) The state corporation shall complete forms prescribed by the department which shall show as to each qualified investment in any qualified entity the following:

(1) The name, address, and employer identification number of the qualified entity.

(2) The name, address, and identification number of the taxpayer who purchased the qualified investment.

(3) The extent of the qualified investment purchased by the taxpayer and the amount paid for it.

(b) The forms required to be filed with the department shall be filed by the state corporation on or before the fifteenth day of the second month following the month in which the qualified investment is purchased.

(c) Copies of the forms shall be mailed to the taxpayer and, where the qualified entity is not the state corporation, the qualified entity on or before that same date.

As added by P.L.51–1984, SEC.1.

Historical and Statutory Notes

Formerly:

IC 6–3–3.4–15.
Acts 1981, P.L.86, SEC.1.

6–3.1–5–16 Exemptions of IC 6–3.1–5–9, IC 6–3.1–5–10 and IC 6–3.1–5–11; modification

Sec. 16. The tax exemptions contained in sections 9, 10, and 11 of this chapter may be repealed or modified by the general assembly of the state of Indiana.

As added by P.L.51–1984, SEC.1.

Historical and Statutory Notes

Formerly:

IC 6–3–3.4–16.
Acts 1981, P.L.86, SEC.1.

Library References

Taxation ⊕1047, 1048.
WESTLAW Topic No. 371.
C.J.S. Taxation § 1098.

Chapter 6

Prison Investment Credits

Library References

Taxation ⊕1047.   C.J.S. Taxation § 1098.
WESTLAW Topic No. 371.   I.L.E. Taxation § 313.

6–3.1–6–1 Definitions

Sec. 1.   For the purposes of this chapter:

"Agreement" means any agreement entered into with the commissioner of the department of correction under IC 11–10–7–2 that has been approved by a majority of the members of the state board of correction.

"Qualified property" means any machinery, tools, equipment, building, structure, or other tangible property considered qualified property under Section 38 of the Internal Revenue Code [1] that is used as an integral part of the operation contemplated by an agreement and that is installed, used, or operated exclusively on property managed by the department of correction.

"State income tax liability" means a taxpayer's total income tax liability incurred under IC 6–2.1 and IC 6–3, as computed after application of credits that, under IC 6–3.1–1–2, are to be applied before the credit provided by this chapter.

"Wages paid" includes all earnings surrendered to the department of correction under IC 11–10–7–5.

As added by P.L.51–1984, SEC.1.

1.   26 U.S.C.A. § 38.

Historical and Statutory Notes

P.L.51–1984, Sec.1, emerg. eff. Jan. 1, 1984, added this article.

Section 5(a) of P.L.51–1984 provided that Section 1 of this act affects taxable years that begin after Dec. 31, 1983.

For provisions relating to carry back or carry forward of credits earned before Jan. 1, 1984, see Historical Note under section 6–3.1–1–1.

Formerly:
IC 6–3–3.2–1.

86

Acts 1981, P.L.83, SEC.1.

6–3.1–6–2 Income tax credit; amount; creditable year

Sec. 2.   (a) A taxpayer who enters into an agreement is entitled to receive an income tax credit for a taxable year equal to:

(1) the taxpayer's state income tax liability for the taxable year;

(2) an amount equal to the sum of:

(A) fifty percent (50%) of any investment in qualified property made by the taxpayer during the taxable year as part of the agreement; plus

(B) twenty-five percent (25%) of the wages paid to inmates during the taxable year as part of the agreement; or

(3) one hundred thousand dollars ($100,000);

whichever is least.

(b) A tax credit shall be allowed under this chapter only for the taxable year of the taxpayer during which:

(1) the investment in qualified property is made in accordance with Section 38 of the Internal Revenue Code;[1] or

(2) the wages are paid to inmates;

as part of an agreement.
As added by P.L.51–1984, SEC.1.

[1]. 26 U.S.C.A. § 38.

Historical and Statutory Notes

Formerly:
  IC 6–3–3.2–2.
  Acts 1981, P.L.83, SEC.1.

Cross References

Programs for employment of offenders by private persons, agreements to construct facilities, see IC 11–10–7–2.

6–3.1–6–3 Application; procedure

Sec. 3.   The department shall apply a credit to which a taxpayer is entitled under this chapter in the following manner:

(1) First, against the taxpayer's gross income tax liability for the taxable year.

(2) Second, against the taxpayer's adjusted gross income tax liability for the taxable year.

(3) Third, against the taxpayer's supplemental net income tax liability for the taxable year.

As added by P.L.51–1984, SEC.1.

Historical and Statutory Notes

Formerly:
IC 6–3–3.2–5.
Acts 1981, P.L.83, SEC.1.

Cross References

Adjusted gross income tax, see IC 6–3–1–1 et seq.
Gross income tax, see IC 6–2.1–1–1 et seq.
Supplemental net income tax, see IC 6–3–8–1 et seq.

6–3.1–6–4 Recapture tax; amount; reports, tax liability, change in use of property

Sec. 4. (a) A taxpayer is liable for a recapture tax if qualified property is converted to any use, other than the use contemplated in the agreement, within three (3) years after the end of the taxable year in which a tax credit was allowed for investment in that qualified property. The recapture tax equals:

(1) seventy-five percent (75%) of the tax credit if the use is converted not later than one (1) year after the end of the taxable year in which the tax credit was allowed;

(2) fifty percent (50%) of the tax credit if the use is converted after one (1) year and not later than two (2) years after the end of the taxable year in which the tax credit was allowed; or

(3) twenty-five percent (25%) of the tax credit if the use is converted after two (2) years and not later than three (3) years after the end of the taxable year in which the tax credit was allowed.

(b) Any recapture tax liability must be reported by the taxpayer on his annual state income tax return for the taxable year during which the use was converted.

(c) The commissioner of the department of correction shall report any change in the use of qualified property to the department.
As added by P.L.51–1984, SEC.1.

Historical and Statutory Notes

Formerly:
IC 6–3–3.2–6.
Acts 1981, P.L.83, SEC.1.

6–3.1–6–5 Effect of agreements; considerations; verification of information related to credit

Sec. 5. (a) Before entering into an agreement, the commissioner of the department of correction shall thoroughly consider the effect of the agreement upon the workforce in the community where the correctional institution is located and shall not enter into any agreement if it will cause increased unemployment in the community. The taxpayer shall have the burden of proving by a preponderance of the evidence that the agreement shall not increase unemployment in the community where the correctional institution is located.

(b) The commissioner shall verify any information related to the credit provided by this chapter when requested to do so by the department of state revenue.

As added by P.L.51–1984, SEC.1. Amended by P.L.21–1995, SEC.11.

Historical and Statutory Notes

P.L.21–1995, Sec.11, emerg. eff. May 10, 1995, amended the section by substituting "workforce" for "work force" in Subsec. (a), and adding "state" to Subsec. (b).

Formerly:

IC 6–3–3.2–4.

Acts 1981, P.L.83, SEC.1.

Cross References

Programs for employment of offenders by private persons, agreements to construct facilities, see IC 11–10–7–2.

Chapter 7

Enterprise Zone Loan Interest Credit

Section

Library References

Taxation ⚷1047.
WESTLAW Topic No. 371.
C.J.S. Taxation § 1098.

6–3.1–7–1 Definitions

Sec. 1. As used in this chapter:

"Enterprise zone" means an enterprise zone created under IC 4–4–6.1.

"Pass through entity" means a:

(1) corporation that is exempt from the adjusted gross income tax under IC 6–3–2–2.8(2);

(2) partnership;

(3) trust;

(4) limited liability company; or

(5) limited liability partnership.

"Qualified loan" means a loan made to an entity that uses the loan proceeds for:

(1) a purpose that is directly related to a business located in an enterprise zone;

(2) an improvement that increases the assessed value of real property located in an enterprise zone; or

(3) rehabilitation, repair, or improvement of a residence.

"State tax liability" means a taxpayer's total tax liability that is incurred under:

(1) IC 6–2.1 (the gross income tax);

(2) IC 6–3–1 through IC 6–3–7 (the adjusted gross income tax);

(3) IC 6–3–8 (the supplemental net income tax);

(4) IC 6–5–10 (the bank tax);

(5) IC 6–5–11 (the savings and loan association tax);

(6) IC 27–1–18–2 (the insurance premiums tax); and

(7) IC 6–5.5 (the financial institutions tax);

as computed after the application of the credits that, under IC 6–3.1–1–2, are to be applied before the credit provided by this chapter.

"Taxpayer" means any person, corporation, limited liability company, partnership, or other entity that has any state tax liability. The term includes a pass through entity.

As added by P.L.51–1984, SEC.1. Amended by P.L.9–1986, SEC.7; P.L.80–1989, SEC.8; P.L.347–1989(ss), SEC.15; P.L.8–1993, SEC.87; P.L.120–1999, SEC.4.

Historical and Statutory Notes

P.L.51–1984, Sec.1, emerg., eff. Jan. 1, 1984, added this article.

Section 5(a) of P.L.51–1984 provided that Section 1 of this act affects taxable years that begin after Dec. 31, 1983.

For provisions relating to carry back or carry forward of credits earned before Jan. 1, 1984, see Historical Note under section 6–3.1–1–1.

P.L.9–1986, Sec.7, emerg. eff. April 1, 1986, inserted Subd. (3) in the definition of "qualified loan"; and made nonsubstantive changes.

P.L.80–1989, Sec.8, emerg. eff. retroactive to Nov. 10, 1988, deleted a reference to the intangibles tax (IC 6–5.1) in the definition of "State tax liability".

P.L.347–1989(ss), Sec.15, eff. Jan. 1, 1990.

P.L.347–1989(ss), Sec.15, in definition of "State tax liability" added Subsec. (7).

P.L.8–1993, Sec.87, inserted "limited liability company" in the definition of "taxpayer".

P.L.120–1999, Sec.4, eff. Jan. 1, 2000, added the definition of "pass through entity" and added the final sentence in the definition of "taxpayer".

P.L.120–1999, Sec.7, eff. Jan. 1, 2000, provides:

"IC 6–3–3–10 and IC 6–3.1–7–1, both as amended by this act, apply only to taxable years beginning after December 31, 1999."

Formerly:

IC 6–3–3.9–1.

P.L.23–1983, SEC.16.

Library References

Words and Phrases (Perm.Ed.)

6–3.1–7–2   Eligible taxpayers; amount of credit; pass through entities

Sec. 2.   (a) A taxpayer is entitled to a credit against his state tax liability for a taxable year if he receives interest on a qualified loan in that taxable year.

(b) The amount of the credit to which a taxpayer is entitled under this section is five percent (5%) multiplied by the amount of interest received by the taxpayer during the taxable year from qualified loans.

(c) If a pass through entity is entitled to a credit under subsection (a) but does not have state tax liability against which the tax credit may be applied, an individual who is a shareholder, partner, beneficiary, or member of the pass through entity is entitled to a tax credit equal to:

(1) the tax credit determined for the pass through entity for the taxable year; multiplied by

(2) the percentage of the pass through entity's distributive income to which the shareholder, partner, beneficiary, or member is entitled.

The credit provided under this subsection is in addition to a tax credit to which a shareholder, partner, beneficiary, or member of a pass through entity is entitled.   However, a pass through entity and an individual who is a shareholder, partner, beneficiary, or member of a pass through entity may not claim more than one (1) credit for the qualified expenditure.

As added by P.L.51–1984, SEC.1.   Amended by P.L.120–1999, SEC.5.

Historical and Statutory Notes

P.L.120–1999, Sec.5, eff. Jan. 1, 2000, added Subsec. (c).

P.L.23–1983, SEC.16.

Formerly:
  IC 6–3–3.9–2.

Notes of Decisions

Carryover   1
Interest receipt   2

1.   Carryover

Enterprise loan interest credits are applied against current state income tax liability and any excess credits may be carried forward ten years from time of underlying loan, but loan credits may not be carried back or refunded. Horizon Bancorp v. Indiana Dept. of State Revenue, 1993, 626 N.E.2d 603, affirmed in part, reversed in part 644 N.E.2d 870.

National bank's enterprise zone loan interest credit were to be applied against state gross income tax liability before bank tax credits were applied.   Horizon Bancorp v. Indiana Dept. of State Revenue, 1993, 626 N.E.2d 603, affirmed in part, reversed in part 644 N.E.2d 870.

2.   Interest receipt

Bank holding company which had made loans to businesses located within enterprise zone (EZ), for which it received interest, was entitled to loan interest tax credit, even though holding company had not registered as an EZ business, or reinvested in EZ the amount of money its financial institutions tax (FIT) had been reduced by the credit.   CNB Bancshares, Inc. v. Department of State Revenue, 1999, 706 N.E.2d 616.

In order to qualify for loan interest credit for loans made to businesses located in enterprise zone (EZ), taxpayer need only receive interest from a qualified loan, and is not required to comply with statute requiring zone businesses to pay annual registration fee and reinvest in EZ any credits they receive.   CNB Bancshares, Inc. v. Department of State Revenue, 1999, 706 N.E.2d 616.

6–3.1–7–3 Credit carryover

Sec. 3. (a) If the amount determined under section 2(b) of this chapter for a particular taxpayer and a particular taxable year exceeds the taxpayer's state tax liability for that taxable year, then the taxpayer may carry the excess over to the immediately succeeding taxable years. Except as provided in subsection (b), the credit carryover may not be used for any taxable year that begins more than ten (10) years after the date on which the qualified loan from which the credit results is made. The amount of the credit carryover from a taxable year shall be reduced to the extent that the carryover is used by the taxpayer to obtain a credit under this chapter for any subsequent taxable year.

(b) Notwithstanding subsection (a), if a loan is a qualified loan as the result of the use of the loan proceeds in a particular enterprise zone, and if the phase-out period of that enterprise zone terminates in a taxable year that succeeds the last taxable year in which a taxpayer is entitled to use credit carryover that results from that loan under subsection (a), then the taxpayer may use the credit carryover for any taxable year up to and including the taxable year in which the phase-out period of the enterprise zone terminates.

As added by P.L.51–1984, SEC.1.

Historical and Statutory Notes

Formerly:
  IC 6–3–3.9–3.
  P.L.23–1983, SEC.16.

Notes of Decisions

In general 1

_____

1. In general
  Enterprise loan interest credits are applied against current state income tax liability and any excess credits may be carried forward ten years from time of underlying loan, but loan credits may not be carried back or refunded. Horizon Bancorp v. Indiana Dept. of State Revenue, 1993, 626 N.E.2d 603, affirmed in part, reversed in part 644 N.E.2d 870.

6–3.1–7–4 Application of credit; order

Sec. 4. (a) A credit to which a taxpayer is entitled under this chapter shall be applied against taxes owed by the taxpayer in the following order:

(1) First, against the taxpayer's gross income tax liability (IC 6–2.1) for the taxable year.

(2) Second, against the taxpayer's adjusted gross income tax liability (IC 6–3–1 through IC 6–3–7) for the taxable year.

(3) Third, against the taxpayer's supplemental net income tax liability (IC 6–3–8) for the taxable year.

(4) Fourth, against the taxpayer's bank tax liability (IC 6–5–10) or savings and loan association tax liability (IC 6–5–11) for the taxable year.

(5) Fifth, against the taxpayer's insurance premiums tax liability (IC 27–1–18–2) for the taxable year.

(b) If the tax paid by the taxpayer under a tax provision listed in subsection (a) is a credit against the liability or a deduction in determining the tax base under another Indiana tax provision, the credit or deduction shall be computed without regard to the credit to which a taxpayer is entitled under this chapter.

As added by P.L.51–1984, SEC.1.   Amended by P.L.80–1989, SEC.9.

Historical and Statutory Notes

P.L.80–1989, Sec.9, deleted a Subd. (4) relating to the intangibles tax (IC 6–5.1) in Subsec. (a); and made certain nonsubstantive changes in Subsec. (b).

P.L.80–1989, Sec.19, containing an emergency clause, provides that section 9 of the act amending this section takes effect retroactive to Nov. 10, 1988.

Formerly:
   IC 6–3–3.9–4.
   P.L.23–1983, SEC.16.

Notes of Decisions

Gross income tax liability   1

———

1. Gross income tax liability
   National bank's enterprise zone loan interest credit were to be applied against state gross income tax liability before bank tax credits were applied. Horizon Bancorp v. Indiana Dept. of State Revenue, 1993, 626 N.E.2d 603, affirmed in part, reversed in part 644 N.E.2d 870.

6–3.1–7–5   Claiming of credit on annual state tax return

Sec. 5. To receive the credit provided by this chapter, a taxpayer must claim the credit on his annual state tax return or returns in the manner prescribed by the department. The taxpayer shall submit to the department all information that the department determines is necessary for the calculation of the credit provided by this chapter and for the determination of whether a loan is a qualified loan.

As added by P.L.51–1984, SEC.1.

Historical and Statutory Notes

Formerly:
   IC 6–3–3.9–5.
   P.L.23–1983, SEC.16.

6–3.1–7–6   Disallowance of credit

Sec. 6. (a) If the department determines that the proceeds from a loan are used for a purpose other than the purpose stated at the time a credit was claimed under this chapter for interest on that loan, and if that stated purpose caused the department to designate the loan as a qualified loan, then the department shall disallow the credit allowed under this chapter for interest on that loan.

(b) A taxpayer shall pay to the department the amount of any credit disallowed under this section.

As added by P.L.51–1984, SEC.1.

Historical and Statutory Notes

Formerly:
IC 6–3–3.9–6.
P.L.23–1983, SEC.16.

Chapter 8

Energy Systems Credit

6–3.1–8–1 to 6–3.1–8–12   Repealed

(Repealed by P.L.1–1993, SEC.39.)

Historical and Statutory Notes

P.L.1–1993, Sec.39, emerg. eff. May 4, 1993.

Former IC 6–3.1–8–1 to 6–3.1–8–2 related to
energy systems credit.

Formerly:
IC 6–3–3.3–1 to 6–3–3.3–11.

Acts 1980, P.L.20, SEC.3.
Acts 1981, P.L.84, SECS.1 to 5.
Acts 1981, P.L.85, SECS.1 to 4.
P.L.51–1984, SEC.1.
P.L.43–1984, SECS.5 to 8.
P.L.72–1986, SECS. 1, 2.
P.L.68–1986, SECS.2, 3.

Chapter 9

Neighborhood Assistance Credits

Library References

Taxation ☞1047.
C.J.S. Taxation § 1098.

WESTLAW Topic No. 371.
I.L.E. Taxation § 313.

6–3.1–9–1   Definitions

Sec. 1.   As used in this chapter:

"Business firm" means any business entity authorized to do business in the
state of Indiana that is:

(1) subject to the gross, adjusted gross, supplemental net income, or
financial institutions tax;

(2) an employer exempt from adjusted gross income tax (IC 6–3–1 through
IC 6–3–7) under IC 6–3–2–2.8(2); or

(3) a partnership.

"Community services" means any type of counseling and advice, emergency assistance, medical care, recreational facilities, housing facilities, or economic development assistance to individuals, groups, or neighborhood organizations in an economically disadvantaged area.

"Crime prevention" means any activity which aids in the reduction of crime in an economically disadvantaged area.

"Economically disadvantaged area" means an enterprise zone, or any area in Indiana that is certified as an economically disadvantaged area by the department of commerce after consultation with the community services agency. The certification shall be made on the basis of current indices of social and economic conditions, which shall include but not be limited to the median per capita income of the area in relation to the median per capita income of the state or standard metropolitan statistical area in which the area is located.

"Education" means any type of scholastic instruction or scholarship assistance to an individual who resides in an economically disadvantaged area that enables him to prepare himself for better life opportunities.

"Enterprise zone" means an enterprise zone created under IC 4–4–6.1.

"Job training" means any type of instruction to an individual who resides in an economically disadvantaged area that enables him to acquire vocational skills so that he can become employable or be able to seek a higher grade of employment.

"Neighborhood assistance" means either:

(1) furnishing financial assistance, labor, material, and technical advice to aid in the physical or economic improvement of any part or all of an economically disadvantaged area; or

(2) furnishing technical advice to promote higher employment in any neighborhood in Indiana.

"Neighborhood organization" means any organization, including but not limited to a nonprofit development corporation:

(1) performing community services in an economically disadvantaged area; and

(2) holding a ruling:

(A) from the Internal Revenue Service of the United States Department of the Treasury that the organization is exempt from income taxation under the provisions of the Internal Revenue Code; and

(B) from the department of state revenue that the organization is exempt from income taxation under IC 6–2.1–3–20.

"Person" means any individual subject to Indiana gross or adjusted gross income tax.

"State fiscal year" means a twelve (12) month period beginning on July 1 and ending on June 30.

"Tax credit" means a deduction from any tax otherwise due and payable under IC 6–2.1, IC 6–3, or IC 6–5.5.

As added by P.L.51–1984, SEC.1. Amended by P.L.21–1990, SEC.12; P.L.25–1993, SEC.10.

Historical and Statutory Notes

P.L.51–1984, Sec.1, emerg. eff. Jan. 1, 1984, added this article.

Section 5(a) of P.L.51–1984 provided that Section 1 of this act affects taxable years that begin after Dec. 31, 1983.

For provisions relating to carry back or carry forward of credits earned before Jan. 1, 1984, see Historical Note under section 6–3.1–1–1.

P.L.21–1990, Sec.12, emerg. eff. retroactive to Jan. 1, 1990.

P.L.21–1990, Sec.12, in the first paragraph, inserted "or financial institutions"; and in the last paragraph inserted "or IC 6–5.5"; and made a nonsubstantive change.

P.L.25–1993, in the definition of "Business firm", added Subds. (2) and (3); in the definition of "Neighborhood organization", substituted "nonprofit" for "not-for-profit"; and made other nonsubstantive changes.

Formerly:
IC 6–3–3.1–1.
Acts 1976, P.L.16, SEC.1.
Acts 1977, P.L.80, SEC.1.
Acts 1981, P.L.77, SEC.12.
Acts 1981, P.L.72, SEC.6.
P.L.23–1983, SEC.13.

Cross References

Religious, charitable, scientific, literary, educational and civic organizations, exemption from gross income tax, see IC 6–2.1–3–20.

Administrative Code References

Adjusted gross income tax, neighborhood assistance credits, see 45 IAC 3.1–1–86.
Neighborhood assistance credit program, contributions, see 45 IAC 3.1–1–87 et seq.

Law Review and Journal Commentaries

Income taxation: Survey of recent tax law. Thomas B. Allington, 10 Ind.L.Rev. 345 (1976).

6–3.1–9–2 Eligible persons; proposals; approval

Sec. 2. (a) A business firm or a person who contributes to a neighborhood organization or who engages in the activities of providing neighborhood assistance, job training or education for individuals not employed by the business firm or person, or for community services or crime prevention in an economically disadvantaged area shall receive a tax credit as provided in section 3 of this chapter if the director of the department of commerce approves the proposal of the business firm or person, setting forth the program to be conducted, the area selected, the estimated amount to be invested in the program, and the plans for implementing the program.

(b) The director of the department of commerce, after consultation with the community services agency and the commissioner of revenue, may adopt rules for the approval or disapproval of these proposals.

As added by P.L.51–1984, SEC.1.

Historical and Statutory Notes

Formerly:
IC 6–3–3.1–3.
Acts 1976, P.L.16, SEC.1.

Acts 1977, P.L.80, SEC.3.
Acts 1981, P.L.72, SEC.8.

Administrative Code References

Neighborhood assistance credit program, regulations, see 45 IAC 3.1–1–87 et seq.

Law Review and Journal Commentaries

Income taxation: Survey of recent tax law.
Thomas B. Allington, 10 Ind.L.Rev. 345 (1976).

6–3.1–9–3   Amount of credit; application; shareholders or partners of firms without tax liability

Sec. 3. (a) Subject to the limitations provided in subsection (b) and sections 4, 5, and 6 of this chapter, the department shall grant a tax credit against any gross, adjusted gross, or supplemental net income tax due equal to fifty percent (50%) of the amount invested by a business firm or person in a program the proposal for which was approved under section 2 of this chapter.

(b) The credit provided by this chapter shall only be applied against any income tax liability owed by the taxpayer after the application of any credits which under IC 6–3.1–1–2 must be applied before the credit provided by this chapter. In addition, the tax credit which a taxpayer receives under this chapter may not exceed twenty-five thousand dollars ($25,000) for any taxable year of the taxpayer.

(c) If a business firm that is:

(1) exempt from adjusted gross income tax (IC 6–3–1 through IC 6–3–7) under IC 6–3–2–2.8(2); or

(2) a partnership;

does not have any tax liability against which the credit provided by this section may be applied, a shareholder or a partner of the business firm is entitled to a credit against the shareholder's or the partner's liability under the adjusted gross income tax.

(d) The amount of the credit provided by this section is equal to:

(1) the tax credit determined for the business firm for the taxable year under subsection (a); multiplied by

(2) the percentage of the business firm's distributive income to which the shareholder or the partner is entitled.

The credit provided by this section is in addition to any credit to which a shareholder or partner is otherwise entitled under this chapter. However, a business firm and a shareholder or partner of that business firm may not claim a credit under this chapter for the same investment.

As added by P.L.51–1984, SEC.1. Amended by P.L.25–1993, SEC.11; P.L.1–1994, SEC.29.

Historical and Statutory Notes

P.L.25–1993, Sec.11, added Subsec. (c).

P.L.1–1994, Sec.29, emerg. eff. March 18, 1994, part of the correction bill, made nonsubstantive changes.

Formerly:

IC 6–3–3.1–4.
Acts 1976, P.L.16, SEC.1.
Acts 1977, P.L.80, SEC.4.

Administrative Code References

Adjusted gross income tax, limitations on neighborhood assistance credits, see 45 IAC 3.1–1–87.
Neighborhood assistance credit program, amount of tax credit,
    Limits, see 45 IAC 3.1–1–87, 45 IAC 3.1–1–89.

6–3.1–9–4 Application for credit; form, contents; priority; notification of credit allowable, filing of statement; disallowance

Sec. 4. (a) Any business firm or person which desires to claim a tax credit as provided in this chapter shall file with the department, in the form that the department may prescribe, an application stating the amount of the contribution or investment which it proposes to make which would qualify for a tax credit, and the amount sought to be claimed as a credit. The application shall include a certificate evidencing approval of the contribution or program by the director of the department of commerce.

(b) The director of the department of commerce shall give priority in issuing certificates to applicants whose contributions or programs directly benefit enterprise zones.

(c) The department shall promptly notify an applicant whether, or the extent to which, the tax credit is allowable in the state fiscal year in which the application is filed, as provided in section 5 of this chapter. If the credit is allowable in that state fiscal year, the applicant shall within thirty (30) days after receipt of the notice file with the department of revenue a statement, in the form and accompanied by the proof of payment as the department may prescribe, setting forth that the amount to be claimed as a credit under this chapter has been paid to an organization for an approved program or purpose, or permanently set aside in a special account to be used solely for an approved program or purpose.

(d) The department may disallow any credit claimed under this chapter for which the statement or proof of payment is not filed within the thirty (30) day period.

As added by P.L.51–1984, SEC.1.

Historical and Statutory Notes

Formerly:
IC 6–3–3.1–5.
Acts 1976, P.L.16, SEC.1.

Acts 1977, P.L.80, SEC.5.
P.L.23–1983, SEC.14.

Administrative Code References

Adjusted gross income tax, procedure for claiming neighborhood assistance credit, see 45 IAC 3.1–1–88.
Neighborhood assistance credit program,
    Application procedures and requirements, see 45 IAC 3.1–1–88.
    Eligibility, see 45 IAC 3.1–1–86.

6–3.1–9–5   Limitation on tax credits; approval of applications; failure to file statement of proof of payment

Sec. 5. (a) The amount of tax credits allowed under this chapter may not exceed two million five hundred thousand dollars ($2,500,000) in the state fiscal year beginning July 1, 1997, and ending June 30, 1998, and each state fiscal year thereafter.

(b) The department shall record the time of filing of each application for allowance of a credit required under section 4 of this chapter and shall approve the applications, if they otherwise qualify for a tax credit under this chapter, in the chronological order in which the applications are filed in the state fiscal year.

(c) When the total credits approved under this section equal the maximum amount allowable in any state fiscal year, no application thereafter filed for that same fiscal year shall be approved. However, if any applicant for whom a credit has been approved fails to file the statement of proof of payment required under section 4 of this chapter, an amount equal to the credit previously allowed or set aside for the applicant may be allowed to any subsequent applicant in the year. In addition, the department may, if the applicant so requests, approve a credit application, in whole or in part, with respect to the next succeeding state fiscal year.

As added by P.L.51–1984, SEC.1. Amended by P.L.95–1995, SEC.1; P.L.64–1997, SEC.1.

Historical and Statutory Notes

P.L.95–1995, Sec.1, amended the section by substituting "one million five hundred thousand dollars ($1,500,000)" for "one million dollars ($1,000,000)" in Subsec. (a).

P.L.95–1995, Sec.2, emerg. eff. Jan. 1, 1995, provides:

"This act applies to taxable years that begin after December 31, 1994."

P.L.64–1997, Sec.1, amended the section by substituting "two million five hundred thousand dollars ($2,500,000)" for "one million five hundred thousand dollars ($1,500,000)", and inserting "beginning July 1, 1997, and ending June 30, 1998, and each state fiscal year thereafter", in Subsec. (a); and making other nonsubstantive changes.

Formerly:

IC 6–3–3.1–6.
Acts 1976, P.L.16, SEC.1.

Administrative Code References

Adjusted gross income tax, maximum amount of neighborhood assistance credit, see 45 IAC 3.1–1–89.
Neighborhood assistance credit program, amount, limitations, see 45 IAC 3.1–1–87.

Law Review and Journal Commentaries

Income taxation: Survey of recent tax law. Thomas B. Allington, 10 Ind.L.Rev. 345 (1976).

6–3.1–9–6   Allowable years of credit

Sec. 6. A tax credit shall be allowable under this chapter only for the taxable year of the taxpayer in which the contribution qualifying for the credit is paid or permanently set aside in a special account for the approved program or purpose.

As added by P.L.51–1984, SEC.1.

Historical and Statutory Notes

Formerly:
  IC 6–3–3.1–7.
  Acts 1976, P.L.16, SEC.1.

Administrative Code References

Neighborhood assistance credit program, computation procedures and restrictions, see 45 IAC 3.1–1–87, 45 IAC 3.1–1–89.

Chapter 10

Enterprise Zone Investment Cost Credit

Library References

Taxation ⟐1047.
WESTLAW Topic No. 371.
C.J.S. Taxation § 1098.

6–3.1–10–1   Enterprise zone defined

Sec. 1. As used in this chapter, "enterprise zone" means an enterprise zone created under IC 4–4–6.1.

As added by P.L.9–1986, SEC.8.

Historical and Statutory Notes

P.L. 9–1986, Sec.8, emerg. eff. retroactive to Jan. 1, 1986, added this chapter.

Section 11(b) of P.L.9–1986 provides that Sections 8 and 10 of this act apply to taxable years that begin after Dec. 31, 1986.

6–3.1–10–1.7   "Pass through entity" defined

Sec. 1.7. As used in this chapter, "pass through entity" means:

(1) a corporation that is exempt from the adjusted gross income tax under IC 6–3–2–2.8(2);

(2) a partnership;

(3) a limited liability company; or

(4) a limited liability partnership.

As added by P.L.57–1996, SEC.1.

Historical and Statutory Notes

P.L.57–1996, Sec.1, emerg. eff. retroactive to Jan. 1, 1995.

6–3.1–10–2   Qualified investment defined

Sec. 2.   As used in this chapter, "qualified investment" means the purchase of an ownership interest in a business located in an enterprise zone if the purchase is approved by the department of commerce under section 8 of this chapter.

As added by P.L.9–1986, SEC.8.   Amended by P.L.379–1987(ss), SEC.8.

Historical and Statutory Notes

P.L.379–1987(ss), Sec.8, emerg. eff. May 6, 1987, substituted "an ownership interest in" for "the stock of".

Section 15 of P.L.379–1987(ss) provides that this act applies to taxable years that begin after Jan. 1, 1987.

6–3.1–10–2.5   "SIC Manual" defined

Sec. 2.5.   As used in this chapter, "SIC Manual" refers to the current edition of the Standard Industrial Classification Manual of the United States Office of Management and Budget.

As added by P.L.379–1987(ss), SEC.9.   Amended by P.L.24–1995, SEC.23.

Historical and Statutory Notes

P.L.379–1987(ss), Sec.9, added this section emergency effective upon passage May 6, 1987.

Section 15 of P.L.379–1987(ss) provides that this act applies to taxable years that begin after Jan. 1, 1987.

P.L.24–1995, Sec.23, amended the section by substituting "current edition" for "1972 Edition."

6–3.1–10–3   State tax liability defined

Sec. 3.   As used in this chapter, "state tax liability" means a taxpayer's total tax liability that is incurred under IC 6–3–1 through IC 6–3–7 (the adjusted gross income tax), as computed after the application of the credits that, under IC 6–3.1–1–2, are to be applied before the credit provided by this chapter.

As added by P.L.9–1986, SEC.8.

6–3.1–10–4   Taxpayer defined

Sec. 4.   (a) As used in this chapter, "taxpayer" means any individual that has any state tax liability.

(b) Notwithstanding subsection (a), for a credit for a qualified investment in a business located in an enterprise zone in a county having a population of more than one hundred thousand (100,000) but less than one hundred seven thousand (107,000), "taxpayer" includes a pass through entity.

As added by P.L.9–1986, SEC.8.   Amended by P.L.24–1995, SEC.24;   P.L.57–1996, SEC.2.

Historical and Statutory Notes

P.L.24–1995, Sec.24, amended the section by deleting "or trust" after "individual."

P.L.57–1996, Sec.2, emerg. eff. retroactive to Jan. 1, 1995, amended the section by designating Subsec.(a); and by adding Subsec. (b).

6–3.1–10–5   Transfer ownership defined

Sec. 5.   As used in this chapter, "transfer ownership" means to purchase existing investment in a business, including real property, improvements to real property, or equipment.

As added by P.L.9–1986, SEC.8.

6–3.1–10–6   Credit for qualified investment; amount

Sec. 6.   (a) A taxpayer is entitled to a credit against the taxpayer's state tax liability for a taxable year if the taxpayer makes a qualified investment in that taxable year.

(b) The amount of the credit to which a taxpayer is entitled is the percentage determined under section 8 of this chapter multiplied by the price of the qualified investment made by the taxpayer during the taxable year.

As added by P.L.9–1986, SEC.8.

6–3.1–10–6.5   Pass through entity; credit

Sec. 6.5.   (a) If a pass through entity is entitled to a credit under section 6 of this chapter but does not have state tax liability against which the tax credit may be applied, an individual who is a shareholder, partner, or member of the pass through entity is entitled to a tax credit equal to:

(1) the tax credit determined for the pass through entity for the taxable year; multiplied by

(2) the percentage of the pass through entity's distributive income to which the shareholder, partner, or member is entitled.

(b) The credit provided under subsection (a) is in addition to a tax credit to which a shareholder, partner, or member of a pass through entity is otherwise entitled under this chapter.   However, a pass through entity and an individual

who is a shareholder, partner, or member of the pass through entity may not claim more than one (1) credit for the same investment.
As added by P.L.57–1996, SEC.3.

Historical and Statutory Notes

P.L.57–1996, Sec.3, emerg. eff. retroactive to Jan. 1, 1995.

P.L.57–1996, Sec.6, emerg. eff. retroactive to Jan. 1, 1995, provides:

"IC 6–3.1–10–6.5 and IC 6–3.1–16–7.5, both as added by this act, apply only to taxable years beginning after December 31, 1994."

6–3.1–10–7 Carryover of excess credit

Sec. 7. (a) If the amount determined under section 6(b) of this chapter for a taxpayer in a taxable year exceeds the taxpayer's state tax liability for that taxable year, the taxpayer may carry the excess over to the following taxable years. The amount of the credit carryover from a taxable year shall be reduced to the extent that the carryover is used by the taxpayer to obtain a credit under this chapter for any subsequent taxable year.

(b) A taxpayer is not entitled to a carryback or refund of any unused credit.
As added by P.L.9–1986, SEC.8.

6–3.1–10–8 Qualifying for credit; request for determination; findings; certification of credit percentage; application of credit on transfer of ownership

Sec. 8. (a) To be entitled to a credit, a taxpayer must request the department of commerce to determine:

(1) whether a purchase of an ownership interest in a business located in an enterprise zone is a qualified investment; and

(2) the percentage credit to be allowed.

The request must be made before a purchase is made.

(b) The department of commerce shall find that a purchase is a qualified investment if:

(1) the business is viable;

(2) the business has not been disqualified from enterprise zone incentives or benefits under IC 4–4–6.1;

(3) the taxpayer has a legitimate purpose for purchase of the ownership interest;

(4) the purchase would not be made unless a credit is allowed under this chapter; and

(5) the purchase is critical to the commencement, enhancement, or expansion of business operations in the zone and will not merely transfer ownership, and the purchase proceeds will be used only in business operations in the enterprise zone.

The department may delay making a finding under this subsection if, at the time the request is filed under subsection (a), an urban enterprise zone association has made a recommendation that the business be disqualified from enterprise zone incentives or benefits under IC 4–4–6.1 and the enterprise zone board has not acted on that request. The delay by the department may not last for more than sixty (60) days.

(c) If the department of commerce finds that a purchase is a qualified investment, the department shall certify the percentage credit to be allowed under this chapter based upon the following:

(1) A percentage credit of ten percent (10%) may be allowed based upon the need of the business for equity financing, as demonstrated by the inability of the business to obtain debt financing.

(2) A percentage credit of two percent (2%) may be allowed for business operations in the retail, professional, or warehouse/distribution codes of the SIC Manual.

(3) A percentage credit of five percent (5%) may be allowed for business operations in the manufacturing codes of the SIC Manual.

(4) A percentage credit may be allowed for jobs created during the twelve (12) month period following the purchase of an ownership interest in the zone business, as determined under the following table:

JOBS CREATED	PERCENTAGE
Less than 11 jobs	1%
11 to 25 jobs	2%
26 to 40 jobs	3%
41 to 75 jobs	4%
More than 75 jobs	5%

(5) A percentage credit of five percent (5%) may be allowed if fifty percent (50%) or more of the jobs created in the twelve (12) month period following the purchase of an ownership interest in the zone business will be reserved for zone residents.

(6) A percentage credit may be allowed for investments made in real or depreciable personal property, as determined under the following table:

AMOUNT OF INVESTMENT	PERCENTAGE
Less than $25,001	1%
$25,001 to $50,000	2%
$50,001 to $100,000	3%
$100,001 to $200,000	4%
More than $200,000	5%

The total percentage credit may not exceed thirty percent (30%).

(d) If all or a part of a purchaser's intent is to transfer ownership, the tax credit shall be applied only to that part of the investment that relates directly to the enhancement or expansion of business operations at the zone location. *As added by P.L.9–1986, SEC.8. Amended by P.L.379–1987(ss), SEC.10.*

Historical and Statutory Notes

P.L.379–1987(ss), Sec.10, emerg. eff. May 6, 1987, rewrote Subsec. (c), which read as added in 1986:

"(c) If the department of commerce finds that a purchase is a qualified investment, the department shall certify the percentage credit to be allowed under this chapter based upon criteria developed by rule of the enterprise zone board that consider the following:

"(1) The need of the business for equity financing.

"(2) The employment impact on the zone.

"(3) The total investment impact on the zone.

"The percentage credit may not exceed thirty percent (30%)."

Section 15 of P.L.379–1987(ss) provides that this act applies to taxable years that begin after Jan. 1, 1987.

6–3.1–10–9 Claiming credit

Sec. 9. To receive the credit provided by this chapter, a taxpayer must claim the credit on the taxpayer's annual state tax return or returns in the manner prescribed by the department of state revenue. The taxpayer shall submit to the department of state revenue the certification of the percentage credit by the department of commerce and all information that the department of state revenue determines is necessary for the calculation of the credit provided by this chapter and for the determination of whether an investment cost is a qualified investment cost.

As added by P.L.9–1986, SEC.8.

Chapter 11

Industrial Recovery Tax Credit

Library References

Taxation ☞1047.
WESTLAW Topic No. 371.
C.J.S. Taxation § 1098.

6–3.1–11–1 "Applicable percentage" defined

Sec. 1. As used in this chapter, "applicable percentage" means the percentage determined as follows:

(1) If a plant that is located on an industrial recovery site was placed in service at least twenty (20) years ago but less than thirty (30) years ago, the applicable percentage is fifteen percent (15%).

(2) If a plant that is located on an industrial recovery site was placed in service at least thirty (30) years ago but less than forty (40) years ago, the applicable percentage is twenty percent (20%).

(3) If a plant that is located on an industrial recovery site was placed in service at least forty (40) years ago, the applicable percentage is twenty-five percent (25%).

The time that has expired since a plant was placed in service shall be determined as of the date that an application is filed with the board for designation of the location as an industrial recovery site under this chapter.

As added by P.L.379–1987(ss), SEC.11.

Historical and Statutory Notes

P.L.379–1987(ss), Sec.11, added this chapter emergency effective upon passage May 6, 1987.

Section 15 of P.L.379–1987(ss) provides that this act applies to taxable years that begin after Jan. 1, 1987.

6–3.1–11–2 "Board" defined

Sec. 2. As used in this chapter, "board" means the enterprise zone board created under IC 4–4–6.1.

As added by P.L.379–1987(ss), SEC.11.

6–3.1–11–3 "Executive" defined

Sec. 3. As used in this chapter, "executive" has the meaning set forth in IC 36–1–2–5.

As added by P.L.379–1987(ss), SEC.11.

6–3.1–11–4 "Floor space" defined

Sec. 4. As used in this chapter, "floor space" means the usable interior floor space of a building.
As added by P.L.379–1987(ss), SEC.11.

6–3.1–11–5 "Industrial recovery site" defined

Sec. 5. As used in this chapter, "industrial recovery site" means an industrial recovery site designated under this chapter.
As added by P.L.379–1987(ss), SEC.11.

6–3.1–11–6 "Legislative body" defined

Sec. 6. As used in this chapter, "legislative body" has the meaning set forth in IC 36–1–2–9.
As added by P.L.379–1987(ss), SEC.11.

6–3.1–11–7 "Municipality" defined

Sec. 7. As used in this chapter, "municipality" has the meaning set forth in IC 36–1–2–11.
As added by P.L.379–1987(ss), SEC.11.

6–3.1–11–8 "Placed in service" defined

Sec. 8. As used in this chapter, "placed in service" means that property is placed in a condition or state of readiness and availability for a specifically assigned function. In the case of a plant comprised of a complex of buildings, the entire plant shall be considered to have been placed in service as of the date that a building was placed in service if the building has floor space that, when aggregated with the floor space of all buildings in the complex placed in service on earlier dates, exceeds fifty percent (50%) of the total floor space of all buildings in the complex.
As added by P.L.379–1987(ss), SEC.11.

6–3.1–11–9 "Plant" defined

Sec. 9. As used in this chapter, "plant" means a building or complex of buildings used, or designed and constructed for use, in production, manufacturing, fabrication, assembly, processing, refining, finishing, or warehousing of tangible personal property, whether the tangible personal property is or was for sale to third parties or for use by the owner in the owner's business.
As added by P.L.379–1987(ss), SEC.11.

6–3.1–11–10 "Qualified investment" defined

Sec. 10. As used in this chapter, "qualified investment" means the amount of the taxpayer's expenditures for rehabilitation of property located within an industrial recovery site under a plan contained in an application approved by the board under section 18 of this chapter. An expenditure for purposes or by persons not covered by such a plan may not be a qualified investment.

As added by P.L.379–1987(ss), SEC.11.

6–3.1–11–11   "Rehabilitation" defined

Sec. 11. As used in this chapter, "rehabilitation" means the remodeling, repair, or betterment of real property in any manner or any enlargement or extension of real property.

As added by P.L.379–1987(ss), SEC.11.

6–3.1–11–12   "State tax liability" defined

Sec. 12. As used in this chapter, "state tax liability" means the taxpayer's total tax liability that is incurred under:

(1) IC 6–2.1 (the gross income tax);

(2) IC 6–3–1 through IC 6–3–7 (the adjusted gross income tax);

(3) IC 6–3–8 (the supplemental net income tax);

(4) IC 6–5–10 (the bank tax);

(5) IC 6–5–11 (the savings and loan association tax);

(6) IC 27–1–18–2 (the insurance premiums tax); and

(7) IC 6–5.5 (the financial institutions tax);

as computed after the application of the credits that, under IC 6–3.1–1–2, are to be applied before the credit provided by this chapter.

As added by P.L.379–1987(ss), SEC.11.   Amended by P.L.80–1989, SEC.10; P.L. 347–1989(ss), SEC.16.

Historical and Statutory Notes

P.L.80–1989, Sec.10, emerg. eff. retroactive to Nov. 10, 1988, deleted Subd. (6) relating to IC 6–5.1 (the intangibles tax).

P.L.347–1989(ss), Sec.16, eff. Jan. 1, 1990.

P.L.347–1989(ss), Sec.16, added Subsec. (7).

6–3.1–11–13   "Taxpayer" defined

Sec. 13. As used in this chapter, "taxpayer" means any person, corporation, limited liability company, partnership, or other entity that has any state tax liability and that is the owner or developer of an industrial recovery site. The term includes a lessee that is assigned some part of a credit under section 16(c) of this chapter.

As added by P.L.379–1987(ss), SEC.11.   Amended by P.L.8–1993, SEC.89; P.L.8– 1996, SEC.9.

Historical and Statutory Notes

P.L.8–1993, Sec.89, inserted "limited liability company".

P.L.8–1996, Sec.9, emerg. eff. March 21, 1996, amended the section by adding the last sentence.

6–3.1–11–14 "Vacant" defined

Sec. 14. As used in this chapter, "vacant" means with respect to a plant that at least seventy-five percent (75%) of the plant placed in service is not used to carry on production, manufacturing, assembly, processing, refining, finishing, or warehousing of tangible personal property.

As added by P.L.379–1987(ss), SEC.11.

6–3.1–11–15 "Vacant industrial facility" defined

Sec. 15. As used in this chapter, "vacant industrial facility" means a tract of land on which there is located a plant that:

(1) has at least three hundred thousand (300,000) square feet of floor space;

(2) was placed in service at least twenty (20) years ago; and

(3) has been vacant for two (2) or more years unless the tract and the plant are owned by a municipality or a county, in which case the two (2) year requirement does not apply.

As added by P.L.379–1987(ss), SEC.11.

6–3.1–11–16 Credit for qualified investment; computation of amount; assignment of credit

Sec. 16. (a) Subject to section 21 of this chapter, a taxpayer is entitled to a credit against the taxpayer's state tax liability for a taxable year if the taxpayer makes a qualified investment in that year.

(b) The amount of the credit to which a taxpayer is entitled is the qualified investment made by the taxpayer during the taxable year multiplied by the applicable percentage.

(c) A taxpayer may assign any part of the credit to which the taxpayer is entitled under this chapter to a lessee of the industrial recovery site. A credit that is assigned under this subsection remains subject to this chapter.

(d) An assignment under subsection (c) must be in writing and both the taxpayer and the lessee must report the assignment on their state tax return for the year in which the assignment is made, in the manner prescribed by the department of revenue. The taxpayer shall not receive value in connection with the assignment under subsection (c) that exceeds the value of the part of the credit assigned.

As added by P.L.379–1987(ss), SEC.11. Amended by P.L.8–1996, SEC.10.

Historical and Statutory Notes

P.L.8–1996, Sec.10, emerg. eff. March 21, 1996, amended the section by adding Subsecs. (c) and (d).

6–3.1–11–17 Carryover of excess credit; carryback or refund of unused credit barred

Sec. 17. (a) If the amount determined under section 16(b) of this chapter for a taxable year exceeds the taxpayer's state tax liability for that taxable year, the taxpayer may carry the excess over to the immediately following taxable years. The amount of the credit carryover from a taxable year shall be reduced to the extent that the carryover is used by the taxpayer to obtain a credit under this chapter for any subsequent taxable year.

(b) A taxpayer is not entitled to a carryback or refund of any unused credit. *As added by P.L.379–1987(ss), SEC.11.*

6–3.1–11–18 Designation of vacant industrial facility as an industrial recovery site; application; requisites; procedures

Sec. 18. (a) After approval by ordinance or resolution of the legislative body, the executive of any municipality may submit an application to the board requesting that a vacant industrial facility within the municipality be designated as an industrial recovery site. After approval by resolution of the legislative body, the executive of any county may submit an application to the board requesting that a vacant industrial facility within the county, but not within any municipality, be designated as an industrial recovery site. In addition to any other information required by the board, the application shall include a description of the plan proposed by the municipality or county for development and use of the vacant industrial facility.

(b) If the property described in the application submitted to the board meets the definition of a vacant industrial facility as of the date of filing of the application, the board shall:

(1) evaluate the application;

(2) arrive at a decision based on the factors set forth in section 19 of this chapter; and

(3) either designate the property as an industrial recovery site or reject the application.

(c) If the board determines that:

(1) a substantial reduction or cessation of operations at a facility in Indiana after January 1, 1987, has created a vacant industrial facility; and

(2) the operations formerly located at that facility have been relocated to a specific site or sites outside the United States;

the facility may be designated as an industrial recovery site only if it has been donated or sold to the municipality. Such a facility may be designated as an industrial recovery site whether it is owned by the municipality or by a taxpayer who acquired it from the municipality after the donation or sale.

As added by P.L.379–1987(ss), SEC.11.

6–3.1–11–19 Evaluation of applications; factors considered

Sec. 19. The board shall consider the following factors in evaluating applications filed under this chapter:

(1) The level of distress in the surrounding community caused by the loss of jobs at the vacant industrial facility.

(2) The desirability of the intended use of the vacant industrial facility under the plan proposed by the municipality or county and the likelihood that the implementation of the plan will improve the economic and employment conditions in the surrounding community.

(3) Evidence of support for the designation by residents, businesses, and private organizations in the surrounding community.

(4) Evidence of a commitment by private or governmental entities to provide financial assistance in implementing the plan proposed by the municipality or county, including the application of IC 36–7–12, IC 36–7–13, IC 36–7–14, or IC 36–7–15.1 to assist in the financing of improvements or redevelopment activities benefiting the vacant industrial facility.

(5) Evidence of efforts by the municipality or county to implement the proposed plan without additional financial assistance from the state.

(6) Whether the industrial recovery site is within an economic revitalization area designated under IC 6–1.1–12.1.

(7) Whether action has been taken by the metropolitan development commission or the legislative body of the municipality or county having jurisdiction over the proposed industrial recovery site to make the property tax credit under IC 6–1.1–20.7 available to persons owning inventory located within the industrial recovery site and meeting the other conditions established by IC 6–1.1–20.7.

As added by P.L.379–1987(ss), SEC.11.

6–3.1–11–20 Contingent conditions upon designation; revocation of approval for failure to comply

Sec. 20. The board may provide that the industrial recovery site designation is contingent on the development and use of the vacant industrial facility in substantial compliance with the plan described in the application submitted under section 18 of this chapter. The board may revoke its approval of an industrial recovery site designation for failure to comply with these conditions.

As added by P.L.379–1987(ss), SEC.11.

6–3.1–11–21   Disqualification to claim credit due to substantial reduction or cessation of operations in Indiana; determination

Sec. 21. A taxpayer is not entitled to claim the credit provided by this chapter to the extent that it substantially reduces or ceases its operations in Indiana in order to relocate them within the industrial recovery site. A determination that a taxpayer is not entitled to the credit provided by this chapter as a result of a substantial reduction or cessation of operations shall apply to credits that would otherwise arise in the taxable year in which the substantial reduction or cessation occurs and in all subsequent years. Determinations under this section shall be made by the board.

As added by P.L.379–1987(ss), SEC.11.

6–3.1–11–22   Application of credit against taxes owed; order; computation

Sec. 22. (a) A credit to which a taxpayer is entitled under this chapter shall be applied against taxes owed by the taxpayer in the following order:

(1) Against the taxpayer's gross income tax liability (IC 6–2.1) for the taxable year.

(2) Against the taxpayer's adjusted gross income tax liability (IC 6–3–1 through IC 6–3–7) for the taxable year.

(3) Against the taxpayer's supplemental net income tax liability (IC 6–3–8) for the taxable year.

(4) Against the taxpayer's bank tax liability (IC 6–5–10) or savings and loan association tax liability (IC 6–5–11) for the taxable year.

(5) Against the taxpayer's insurance premiums tax liability (IC 27–1–18–2) for the taxable year.

(6) Against the taxpayer's financial institutions tax (IC 6–5.5) for the taxable year.

(b) Whenever the tax paid by the taxpayer under any of the tax provisions listed in subsection (a) is a credit against the liability or a deduction in determining the tax base under another Indiana tax provision, the credit or deduction shall be computed without regard to the credit to which a taxpayer is entitled under this chapter.

As added by P.L.379–1987(ss), SEC.11. Amended by P.L.80–1989, SEC.11; P.L. 347–1989(ss), SEC.17; P.L.1–1990, SEC.79.

Historical and Statutory Notes

P.L.80–1989, Sec.11, emerg. eff. retroactive to Nov. 10, 1988, deleted Subd. (4) relating to the intangibles tax (IC 6–5.1) in Subsec. (a); and made certain nonsubstantive changes in Subsec. (b).

P.L.347–1989(ss), Sec.17, eff. Jan. 1, 1990.

P.L.347–1989(ss), Sec.17, added Subsec. (a)(6).

P.L.1–1990, Sec.79, emerg. eff. upon passage March 20, 1990, made corrective changes in Subsec. (a)(6).

6–3.1–11–23 Claiming of credit on annual tax return; certification; required information

Sec. 23. To receive the credit provided by this chapter, a taxpayer must claim the credit on the taxpayer's annual state tax return or returns in the manner prescribed by the department of state revenue. The taxpayer shall submit to the department of state revenue the certification of the board stating the percentage of credit allowable under this chapter and all other information that the department determines is necessary for the calculation of the credit provided by this chapter and for the determination of whether an expenditure was for a qualified investment.

As added by P.L.379–1987(ss), SEC.11.

Chapter 11.5

Military Base Recovery Tax Credit

6–3.1–11.5–1 "Applicable percentage" defined

Sec. 1. As used in this chapter, "applicable percentage" means the percentage determined as follows:

(1) If a building that is located on a military base recovery site was placed in service at least twenty (20) years ago but less than thirty (30) years ago, the applicable percentage is fifteen percent (15%).

(2) If a building that is located on a military base recovery site was placed in service at least thirty (30) years ago but less than forty (40) years ago, the applicable percentage is twenty percent (20%).

(3) If a building that is located on a military base recovery site was placed in service at least forty (40) years ago, the applicable percentage is twenty-five percent (25%).

The time that has expired since a building was placed in service shall be determined as of the date that an application is filed with the board for designation of the location as a military base recovery site under this chapter.
As added by P.L.125–1998, SEC.2.

Historical and Statutory Notes

P.L.125–1998, Sec.2, emerg. eff. March 13, 1998.

P.L.125–1998, Sec.26, emerg. eff. March 13, 1998, provides:

"IC 6–3.1–11.5, as added by this act, applies only to taxable years beginning after December 31, 1997."

Cross References

Enterprise zone board, powers of, see IC 4–4–6.1–2.

6–3.1–11.5–2   "Board" defined

Sec. 2.   As used in this chapter, "board" refers to the enterprise zone board created under IC 4–4–6.1.
As added by P.L.125–1998, SEC.2.

6–3.1–11.5–3   "Executive" defined

Sec. 3.   As used in this chapter, "executive" has the meaning set forth in IC 36–1–2–5.
As added by P.L.125–1998, SEC.2.

6–3.1–11.5–4   "Facility" defined

Sec. 4.   As used in this chapter, "facility" means a building that:

(1) is used, or designed and constructed for use, for training, housing, supplying, military readiness or other military activities, or for the support of military activities, military personnel and their dependents, including retired or reserve military personnel; and

(2) has a minimum floor space of:

(A) twenty thousand (20,000) square feet, if the facility is located in an economic development area established under IC 36–7–14.5–12.5; or

(B) one hundred thousand (100,000) square feet, if the facility is located in a military base reuse area established under IC 36–7–30.

As added by P.L.125–1998, SEC.2.

6–3.1–11.5–5   "Floor space" defined

Sec. 5. As used in this chapter, "floor space" means the usable interior floor space of a building.

As added by P.L.125–1998, SEC.2.

6–3.1–11.5–6   "Legislative body" defined

Sec. 6. As used in this chapter, "legislative body" has the meaning set forth in IC 36–1–2–9.

As added by P.L.125–1998, SEC.2.

6–3.1–11.5–7   "Military base recovery site" defined

Sec. 7. As used in this chapter, "military base recovery site" means a military base recovery site designated under this chapter.

As added by P.L.125–1998, SEC.2.

6–3.1–11.5–8   "Municipality" defined

Sec. 8. As used in this chapter, "municipality" has the meaning set forth in IC 36–1–2–11.

As added by P.L.125–1998, SEC.2.

6–3.1–11.5–8.5   "Pass through entity" defined

Sec. 8.5. As used in this chapter, "pass through entity" means:

(1) a corporation that is exempt from the adjusted gross income tax under IC 6–3–2–2.8(2);

(2) a partnership;

(3) a limited liability company; or

(4) a limited liability partnership.

As added by P.L.125–1998, SEC.2.

6–3.1–11.5–9   "Placed in service" defined

Sec. 9. As used in this chapter, "placed in service" means that property is placed in a condition or state of readiness and availability for a specifically assigned function.

As added by P.L.125–1998, SEC.2.

6–3.1–11.5–10   "Qualified investment" defined

Sec. 10.   As used in this chapter, "qualified investment" means the amount of the taxpayer's expenditures after December 31, 1997, for rehabilitation of property located within a military base recovery site under a plan contained in an application approved by the board under section 20 of this chapter.   An expenditure for purposes or by persons not covered by such a plan is not a qualified investment.

As added by P.L.125–1998, SEC.2.

6–3.1–11.5–11   "Redevelopment authority" defined

Sec. 11.   As used in this chapter, "redevelopment authority" means a redevelopment authority established under IC 36–7–14.5–12.5.

As added by P.L.125–1998, SEC.2.

6–3.1–11.5–12   "Rehabilitation" defined

Sec. 12.   As used in this chapter, "rehabilitation" means the remodeling, repair, or betterment of real property in any manner or any enlargement or extension of real property.

As added by P.L.125–1998, SEC.2.

6–3.1–11.5–13   "Reuse authority" defined

Sec. 13.   As used in this chapter, "reuse authority" refers to a military base reuse authority established under IC 36–7–30.

As added by P.L.125–1998, SEC.2.

6–3.1–11.5–14   "State tax liability" defined

Sec. 14.   As used in this chapter, "state tax liability" means the taxpayer's total tax liability that is incurred under:

(1) IC 6–2.1 (the gross income tax);

(2) IC 6–3–1 through IC 6–3–7 (the adjusted gross income tax);

(3) IC 6–3–8 (the supplemental net income tax);

(4) IC 6–5–10 (the bank tax);

(5) IC 6–5–11 (the savings and loan association tax);

(6) IC 27–1–18–2 (the insurance premiums tax); and

(7) IC 6–5.5 (the financial institutions tax);

as computed after the application of the credits that, under IC 6–3.1–1–2, are to be applied before the credit provided by this chapter.

As added by P.L.125–1998, SEC.2.

6–3.1–11.5–15   "Taxpayer" defined

Sec. 15.   As used in this chapter, "taxpayer" means an individual, corporation, limited liability company, partnership, or other entity that has any state tax liability and that is the owner or developer of a military base recovery site. The term includes a lessee that is assigned some part of a credit under section 18(c) of this chapter.

As added by P.L.125–1998, SEC.2.

6–3.1–11.5–16   "Vacant" defined

Sec. 16.   As used in this chapter, "vacant" means, with respect to a building, that at least seventy-five percent (75%) of the building placed in service is not used for training, housing, supplying, military readiness, or other military activities, or for the support of military activities, military personnel, and their dependents, including retired or reserve military personnel.

As added by P.L.125–1998, SEC.2.

6–3.1–11.5–17   "Vacant military base facility" defined

Sec. 17.   As used in this chapter, "vacant military base facility" means a facility that:

    (1) is located in:

        (A) an economic development area established under IC 36–7–14.5–12.5; or

        (B) a military base reuse area established under IC 36–7–30;

    (2) was placed in service at least twenty (20) years ago; and

    (3) has been vacant for two (2) or more years.

However, subdivision (3) does not apply to a facility that is owned by a municipality, a county, a military base reuse authority, or a redevelopment authority.

As added by P.L.125–1998, SEC.2.

6–3.1–11.5–18   Entitlement to credit; amount; assignment

Sec. 18.   (a) Subject to section 23 of this chapter, a taxpayer is entitled to a credit against the taxpayer's state tax liability for a taxable year if the taxpayer makes a qualified investment in that year.

(b) The amount of the credit to which a taxpayer is entitled is the qualified investment made by the taxpayer during the taxable year multiplied by the applicable percentage.

(c) A taxpayer may assign any part of the credit to which the taxpayer is entitled under this chapter to a lessee of the military base recovery site.   A credit that is assigned under this subsection remains subject to this chapter.

(d) An assignment under subsection (c) must be in writing and both the taxpayer and the lessee must report the assignment on their state tax return for

the year in which the assignment is made, in the manner prescribed by the department of state revenue. The taxpayer shall not receive value in connection with the assignment under subsection (c) that exceeds the value of the part of the credit assigned.
As added by P.L.125–1998, SEC.2.

Library References

Taxation ⊙1047, 1073.
WESTLAW Topic No. 371.
C.J.S. Taxation §§ 1098, 1103.

6–3.1–11.5–19   Credit carryover; carryback or refund unavailable

Sec. 19.   (a) If the amount determined under section 18(b) of this chapter for a taxable year exceeds the taxpayer's state tax liability for that taxable year, the taxpayer may carry the excess over to the immediately following taxable years. The amount of the credit carryover from a taxable year shall be reduced to the extent that the carryover is used by the taxpayer to obtain a credit under this chapter for any subsequent taxable year.

(b) A taxpayer is not entitled to a carryback or refund of any unused credit.
As added by P.L.125–1998, SEC.2.

Library References

Taxation ⊙1047.
WESTLAW Topic No. 371.
C.J.S. Taxation § 1098.

6–3.1–11.5–20   Application requesting designation as military base recovery site

Sec. 20.   (a) After approval by ordinance or resolution of the legislative body, the executive of a municipality may submit an application to the board requesting that a vacant military base facility within the municipality be designated as a military base recovery site.

(b) After approval by resolution of the legislative body, the executive of a county may submit an application to the board requesting that a vacant military base facility within the county, but not within any municipality, be designated as a military base recovery site.

(c) In addition to any other information required by the board, an application submitted under this section must include:

(1) a description of the plan proposed for development and use of the vacant military base facility; and

(2) the maximum amount of qualified investment for which a credit will be available under this chapter.

(d) If the property described in the application submitted to the board meets the definition of a vacant military base facility as of the date of filing of the application, the board shall:

(1) evaluate the application;

(2) arrive at a decision based on the factors set forth in section 21 of this chapter; and

(3) either designate the property as a military base recovery site or reject the application.

(e) If the board determines that a substantial reduction or cessation of operations at a military base in Indiana after January 1, 1987, has created a vacant military base facility, the facility may be designated as a military base recovery site only if it has been donated or sold to a municipality, a county, a reuse authority, or a redevelopment authority. Such a facility may be designated as a military base recovery site, whether it is owned by the municipality, a county, a reuse authority, or a redevelopment authority or by a taxpayer who acquired it from the municipality, a county, a reuse authority, or a redevelopment authority after the donation or sale.

As added by P.L.125–1998, SEC.2.

6–3.1–11.5–21   Factors in evaluating applications

Sec. 21.   The board shall consider the following factors in evaluating applications filed under this chapter:

(1) The level of distress in the surrounding community caused by the loss of jobs at the vacant military base facility.

(2) The desirability of the intended use of the vacant military base facility under the plan proposed for the development and use of the vacant military base facility and the likelihood that the implementation of the plan will improve the economic and employment conditions in the surrounding community.

(3) Evidence of support for the designation by residents, businesses, and private organizations in the surrounding community.

(4) Evidence of a commitment by private or governmental entities to provide financial assistance in implementing the plan for the development and use of the vacant military base facility, including the application of IC 36–7–12, IC 36–7–13, IC 36–7–14, IC 36–7–14.5, IC 36–7–15.1, or IC 36–7–30 to assist in the financing of improvements or redevelopment activities benefiting the vacant military base facility.

(5) Evidence of efforts to implement the proposed plan without additional financial assistance from the state.

(6) Whether the proposed military base recovery site is within an economic revitalization area designated under IC 6–1.1–12.1.

(7) Whether action has been taken by the legislative body of the municipality or county having jurisdiction over the proposed military base recovery site to establish an enterprise zone under IC 4–4–6.1–3(g).

As added by P.L.125–1998, SEC.2.

6–3.1–11.5–22 Designation may be made contingent on development and use in compliance with plan

Sec. 22.   The board may provide that the military base recovery site designation is contingent on the development and use of the vacant military base facility in substantial compliance with the plan described in the application submitted under section 20 of this chapter.   The board may revoke its approval of a military base recovery site designation for failure to comply with these conditions.

As added by P.L.125–1998, SEC.2.

6–3.1–11.5–23 Ineligibility for credit to extent of reduction or cessation of operations in Indiana

Sec. 23.   A taxpayer is not entitled to claim the credit provided by this chapter to the extent that the taxpayer substantially reduces or ceases its operations in Indiana in order to relocate its operations within the military base recovery site.   A determination that a taxpayer is not entitled to the credit provided by this chapter as a result of a substantial reduction or cessation of operations applies to credits that would otherwise arise in the taxable year in which the substantial reduction or cessation occurs and in all subsequent years. Determinations under this section shall be made by the board.

As added by P.L.125–1998, SEC.2.

6–3.1–11.5–24 Priority of application of credit against other taxes owed

Sec. 24.   (a) A credit to which a taxpayer is entitled under this chapter shall be applied against taxes owed by the taxpayer in the following order:

(1) Against the taxpayer's gross income tax liability (IC 6–2.1) for the taxable year.

(2) Against the taxpayer's adjusted gross income tax liability (IC 6–3–1 through IC 6–3–7) for the taxable year.

(3) Against the taxpayer's supplemental net income tax liability (IC 6–3–8) for the taxable year.

(4) Against the taxpayer's bank tax liability (IC 6–5–10) or savings and loan association tax liability (IC 6–5–11) for the taxable year.

(5) Against the taxpayer's insurance premiums tax liability (IC 27–1–18–2) for the taxable year.

(6) Against the taxpayer's financial institutions tax (IC 6–5.5) for the taxable year.

(b) Whenever the tax paid by the taxpayer under any of the tax provisions listed in subsection (a) is a credit against the liability or a deduction in determining the tax base under another Indiana tax provision, the credit or deduction shall be computed without regard to the credit to which a taxpayer is entitled under this chapter.

As added by P.L.125–1998, SEC.2.

Library References

Taxation ⊕1047, 1073.
WESTLAW Topic No. 371.
C.J.S. Taxation §§ 1098, 1103.

6–3.1–11.5–25   Method of claiming credit; submission of information

Sec. 25. To receive the credit provided by this chapter, a taxpayer must claim the credit on the taxpayer's annual state tax return or returns in the manner prescribed by the department of state revenue. The taxpayer shall submit to the department of state revenue the certification of the board stating the percentage of credit allowable under this chapter and all other information that the department determines is necessary for the calculation of the credit provided by this chapter and for the determination of whether an expenditure was for a qualified investment.

As added by P.L.125–1998, SEC.2.

6–3.1–11.5–26   Pass through entities entitled to credit; use by shareholder, partner, or member

Sec. 26. (a) If a pass through entity is entitled to a credit under this chapter but does not have state tax liability against which the credit may be applied, an individual who is a shareholder, partner, or member of the pass through entity is entitled to a credit equal to:

(1) the credit determined for the pass through entity for the taxable year; multiplied by

(2) the percentage of the pass through entity's distributable income to which the individual is entitled.

(b) The credit provided under subsection (a) is in addition to a tax credit to which a shareholder, partner, or member of a pass through entity is in addition to a tax credit to which a shareholder, partner, or member of a pass through entity is otherwise entitled under this chapter. However, a pass through entity and an individual who is a shareholder, partner, or member of the pass through entity may not claim more than one (1) credit for the same investment.

As added by P.L.125–1998, SEC.2.

Library References

Taxation ⊗ 1047.
WESTLAW Topic No. 371.
C.J.S. Taxation § 1098.

Chapter 12

Drug and Alcohol Abuse Prevention Credits

6–3.1–12–1 to 6–3.1–12–11   Repealed

(Repealed by P.L.2–1995, SEC.140.)

Historical and Statutory Notes

P.L.2–1995, Sec.140, emerg. eff. May 5, 1995.

The repealed sections related to drug and alcohol abuse prevention credits.

P.L.21–1990, SEC.13, 14
P.L.2–1992, SEC.69
P.L.40–1994, SEC.1

Formerly:
P.L.93–1989, SEC.1

Chapter 13

Economic Development for a Growing Economy Tax Credit

Cross References

Property taxes, economic development incentive accountability, see IC 6–1.1–43–1.

6–3.1–13–1 "Board" defined

Sec. 1. As used in this chapter, "board" means the economic development for a growing economy board established by this chapter.
As added by P.L.41–1994, SEC.1.

Historical and Statutory Notes

P.L.41–1994, Sec.1, emerg. eff. Feb. 28, 1994.

P.L.41–1994, Sec.3, emerg. eff. Feb. 28, 1994, provides:

"A credit provided under IC 6–3.1–13, as added by this act, may be claimed only for taxes owed for taxable years that begin after December 31, 1993. However, the incremental income tax withholdings on which a credit is based may include withholdings from wages paid after December 31, 1993."

6–3.1–13–2 "Credit amount" defined

Sec. 2. As used in this chapter, "credit amount" means the amount agreed to between the board and applicant under this chapter, but not to exceed the incremental income tax withholdings attributable to the applicant's project.
As added by P.L.41–1994, SEC.1.

6–3.1–13–3 "Director" defined

Sec. 3. As used in this chapter, "director" means the director of the department of commerce.
As added by P.L.41–1994, SEC.1.

6–3.1–13–4 "Full-time employee" defined

Sec. 4. As used in this chapter, "full-time employee" means an individual who is employed for consideration for at least thirty-five (35) hours each week or who renders any other standard of service generally accepted by custom or specified by contract as full-time employment.
As added by P.L.41–1994, SEC.1.

6–3.1–13–5 "Incremental income tax withholdings" defined

Sec. 5. As used in this chapter, "incremental income tax withholdings" means the total amount withheld under IC 6–3–4–8 by the taxpayer during the taxable year from the compensation of new employees.
As added by P.L.41–1994, SEC.1.

6–3.1–13–6   "New employee" defined

Sec. 6.   (a) As used in this chapter, "new employee" means a full-time employee first employed by a taxpayer in the project that is the subject of a tax credit agreement and who is employed after the taxpayer enters into the tax credit agreement.

(b) The term "new employee" does not include:

(1) an employee of the taxpayer who performs a job that was previously performed by another employee, if that job existed for at least six (6) months before hiring the new employee;

(2) an employee of the taxpayer who was previously employed in Indiana by a related member of the taxpayer and whose employment was shifted to the taxpayer after the taxpayer entered into the tax credit agreement; or

(3) a child, grandchild, parent, or spouse, other than a spouse who is legally separated from the individual, of any individual who is an employee of the taxpayer and who has a direct or an indirect ownership interest of at least five percent (5%) in the profits, capital, or value of the taxpayer (an ownership interest shall be determined in accordance with Section 1563 of the Internal Revenue Code [1] and regulations prescribed under that Section).

(c) Notwithstanding subsection (b)(1), if a new employee performs a job that was previously performed by an employee who was:

(1) treated under the agreement as a new employee; and

(2) promoted by the taxpayer to another job;

the employee may be considered a new employee under the agreement.

(d) Notwithstanding subsection (a), the board may credit awards to an applicant that met the conditions of this chapter at the time of the applicant's location or expansion decision, if:

(1) the applicant is in receipt of a letter from the department of commerce stating an intent to enter into a credit agreement; and

(2) the letter described in subdivision (1) is issued by the department of commerce not later than March 15, 1994.

As added by P.L.41–1994, SEC.1.

[1] 26 U.S.C.A. § 1563.

6–3.1–13–7   "Pass through entity" defined

Sec. 7.   As used in this chapter, "pass through entity" means:

(1) a corporation that is exempt from the adjusted gross income tax under IC 6–3–2–2.8(2); or

(2) a partnership.

As added by P.L.41–1994, SEC.1.

6–3.1–13–8 "Related member" defined

Sec. 8. As used in this chapter, "related member" means a person that, with respect to the taxpayer during all or any portion of the taxable year, is any one (1) of the following:

(1) An individual stockholder, or a member of the stockholder's family enumerated in Section 318 of the Internal Revenue Code, [1] if the stockholder and the member of the stockholder's family own directly, indirectly, beneficially, or constructively, in the aggregate, at least fifty percent (50%) of the value of the taxpayer's outstanding stock.

(2) A stockholder, or a stockholder's partnership, estate, trust, or corporation, if the stockholder and the stockholder's partnership, estate, trust, or corporation owns directly, indirectly, beneficially, or constructively, in the aggregate, at least fifty percent (50%) of the value of the taxpayer's outstanding stock.

(3) A corporation, or a party related to the corporation in a manner that would require an attribution of stock from the corporation to the party or from the party to the corporation under the attribution rules of Section 318 of the Internal Revenue Code, if the taxpayer owns directly, indirectly, beneficially, or constructively at least fifty percent (50%) of the value of the corporation's outstanding stock.

(4) A component member (as defined in Section 1563(b) of the Internal Revenue Code) [2].

(5) A person to or from whom there is attribution of stock ownership in accordance with Section 1563(e) of the Internal Revenue Code except, for purposes of determining whether a person is a related member under this subdivision, twenty percent (20%) shall be substituted for five percent (5%) wherever five percent (5%) appears in Section 1563(e) of the Internal Revenue Code.

As added by P.L.41–1994, SEC.1.

[1] 26 U.S.C.A. § 318.
[2] 26 U.S.C.A. § 1563(b).

6–3.1–13–9 "State tax liability" defined

Sec. 9. As used in this chapter, "state tax liability" means a taxpayer's total tax liability that is incurred under:

(1) IC 6–2.1 (the gross income tax);

(2) IC 6–3–1 through IC 6–3–7 (the adjusted gross income tax);

(3) IC 6–3–8 (the supplemental net income tax);

(4) IC 6–5–10 (the bank tax);

(5) IC 6–5–11 (the savings and loan association tax);

(6) IC 27–1–18–2 (the insurance premiums tax); and

(7) IC 6–5.5 (the financial institutions tax);

as computed after the application of the credits that under IC 6–3.1–1–2 are to be applied before the credit provided by this chapter.

As added by P.L.41–1994, SEC.1.

6–3.1–13–10 "Taxpayer" defined

Sec. 10. As used in this chapter, "taxpayer" means a person, corporation, partnership, or other entity that has any state tax liability.

As added by P.L.41–1994, SEC.1.

6–3.1–13–11 Credit against state tax liability

Sec. 11. Subject to the conditions set forth in this chapter, a taxpayer is entitled to a credit against any state tax liability that may be imposed on the taxpayer for a taxable year after December 31, 1993, if the taxpayer is awarded a credit by the board under this chapter for that taxable year.

As added by P.L.41–1994, SEC.1.

Library References

Taxation ☞1047.
WESTLAW Topic No. 371.
C.J.S. Taxation § 1098.

6–3.1–13–12 Economic development for a growing economy board; establishment; members

Sec. 12. (a) The economic development for a growing economy board is established. The board consists of the following seven (7) members:

(1) The director or, upon the director's designation, the executive director of the department of commerce.

(2) The director of the budget agency.

(3) The commissioner of the department of state revenue.

(4) Four (4) members appointed by the governor, not more than two (2) of whom may be members of the same political party.

(b) The director shall serve as chairperson of the board. Four (4) members of the board constitute a quorum to transact and vote on the business of the board.

(c) The department of commerce shall assist the board in carrying out the board's duties under this chapter.

As added by P.L.41–1994, SEC.1.

Law Review and Journal Commentaries

Selling the city without selling out: New legislation on development incentives emphasized accountability. Jennifer L. Gilbert, 27 Urb. Law. 427 (1995).

6–3.1–13–13   Foster job creation; credit awards

Sec. 13.   (a) The board may make credit awards under this chapter to foster job creation in Indiana.

(b) The credit shall be claimed for the taxable years specified in the taxpayer's tax credit agreement.

As added by P.L.41–1994, SEC.1.

Law Review and Journal Commentaries

Selling the city without selling out: New legislation on development incentives emphasizes accountability.   Jennifer L. Gilbert, 27 Urb. Law. 427 (1995).

Library References

Taxation ⟐1047.
WESTLAW Topic No. 371.
C.J.S. Taxation § 1098.

6–3.1–13–14   Agreement for tax credit; job creation; application form

Sec. 14.   A person that proposes a project to create new jobs in Indiana may apply to the board to enter into an agreement for a tax credit under this chapter. The director shall prescribe the form of the application.

As added by P.L.41–1994, SEC.1.

6–3.1–13–15   Agreement for tax credit; conditions

Sec. 15.   After receipt of an application, the board may enter into an agreement with the applicant for a credit under this chapter if the board determines that all of the following conditions exist:

(1) The applicant's project will create new jobs that were not jobs previously performed by employees of the applicant in Indiana.

(2) The applicant's project is economically sound and will benefit the people of Indiana by increasing opportunities for employment and strengthening the economy of Indiana.

(3) There is at least one (1) other state that the applicant verifies is being considered for the project.

(4) A significant disparity is identified, using best available data, in the projected costs for the applicant's project compared to the costs in the competing state, including the impact of the competing state's incentive programs. The competing state's incentive programs shall include state, local, private, and federal funds available.

(5) The political subdivisions affected by the project have committed significant local incentives with respect to the project.

(6) Receiving the tax credit is a major factor in the applicant's decision to go forward with the project and not receiving the tax credit will result in the applicant not creating new jobs in Indiana.

(7) Awarding the tax credit will result in an overall positive fiscal impact to the state, as certified by the budget agency using the best available data.

(8) The credit is not prohibited by section 16 of this chapter.

As added by P.L.41–1994, SEC.1.

Law Review and Journal Commentaries

Selling the city without selling out: New legislation on development incentives emphasizes accountability. Jennifer L. Gilbert, 27 Urb. Law. 427 (1995).

Library References

Taxation ☞1047.
WESTLAW Topic No. 371.
C.J.S. Taxation § 1098.

6–3.1–13–16 Relocation of jobs from one site to another within state; credit prohibited

Sec. 16. A person is not entitled to claim the credit provided by this chapter for any jobs that the person relocates from one (1) site in Indiana to another site in Indiana. Determinations under this section shall be made by the board.

As added by P.L.41–1994, SEC.1.

Library References

Taxation ☞1047.
WESTLAW Topic No. 371.
C.J.S. Taxation § 1098.

6–3.1–13–17 Amount of credit awarded; factors

Sec. 17. In determining the credit amount that should be awarded, the board shall take into consideration the following factors:

(1) The economy of the county where the projected investment is to occur.

(2) The potential impact on the economy of Indiana.

(3) The magnitude of the cost differential between Indiana and the competing state.

(4) The incremental payroll attributable to the project.

(5) The capital investment attributable to the project.

(6) The amount the average wage paid by the applicant exceeds the average wage paid within the county in which the project will be located.

(7) The costs to Indiana and the affected political subdivisions with respect to the project.

(8) The financial assistance that is otherwise provided by Indiana and the affected political subdivisions.

As added by P.L.41–1994, SEC.1.

Library References

Taxation ⬤1047, 1073.
WESTLAW Topic No. 371.
C.J.S. Taxation §§ 1098, 1103.

6–3.1–13–18   Duration of tax credit; maximum credit

Sec. 18.   The board shall determine the amount and duration of a tax credit awarded under this chapter.   The duration of the credit may not exceed ten (10) taxable years.   The credit may be stated as a percentage of the incremental income tax withholdings attributable to the applicant's project and may include a fixed dollar limitation.   The credit amount may not exceed the incremental income tax withholdings.   However, the credit amount claimed for a taxable year may exceed the taxpayer's state tax liability for the taxable year, in which case the excess shall be refunded to the taxpayer.

As added by P.L.41–1994, SEC.1.

Library References

Taxation ⬤1047, 1073.
WESTLAW Topic No. 371.
C.J.S. Taxation §§ 1098, 1103.

6–3.1–13–19   Agreement for tax credit; requirements

Sec. 19.   The board shall enter into an agreement with an applicant that is awarded a credit under this chapter.   The agreement must include all of the following:

(1) A detailed description of the project that is the subject of the agreement.

(2) The duration of the tax credit and the first taxable year for which the credit may be claimed.

(3) The credit amount that will be allowed for each taxable year.

(4) A requirement that the taxpayer shall maintain operations at the project location for at least two (2) times the number of years as the term of the tax credit.

(5) A specific method for determining the number of new employees employed during a taxable year who are performing jobs not previously performed by an employee.

(6) A requirement that the taxpayer shall annually report to the board the number of new employees who are performing jobs not previously performed by an employee, the new income tax revenue withheld in connection with the new employees, and any other information the director needs to perform the director's duties under this chapter.

(7) A requirement that the director is authorized to verify with the appropriate state agencies the amounts reported under subdivision (6), and after

doing so shall issue a certificate to the taxpayer stating that the amounts have been verified.

(8) A requirement that the taxpayer shall provide written notification to the director and the board not more than thirty (30) days after the taxpayer makes or receives a proposal that would transfer the taxpayer's state tax liability obligations to a successor taxpayer.

(9) Any other performance conditions that the board determines are appropriate.

As added by P.L.41–1994, SEC.1.

6–3.1–13–20 Certificate of verification; submission to department of state revenue; failure to submit copy

Sec. 20.   A taxpayer claiming a credit under this chapter shall submit to the department of state revenue a copy of the director's certificate of verification under this chapter for the taxable year.   However, failure to submit a copy of the certificate does not invalidate a claim for a credit.

As added by P.L.41–1994, SEC.1.

6–3.1–13–21 Pass through entity; calculation of tax credit; shareholder or partner claiming credit

Sec. 21.   (a) If a pass through entity does not have state income tax liability against which the tax credit may be applied, a shareholder or partner of the pass through entity is entitled to a tax credit equal to:

(1) the tax credit determined for the pass through entity for the taxable year; multiplied by

(2) the percentage of the pass through entity's distributive income to which the shareholder or partner is entitled.

(b) The credit provided under subsection (a) is in addition to a tax credit to which a shareholder or partner of a pass through entity is otherwise entitled under a separate agreement under this chapter.   A pass through entity and a shareholder or partner of the pass through entity may not claim more than one (1) credit under the same agreement.

As added by P.L.41–1994, SEC.1.

Library References

Taxation ☞1047.
WESTLAW Topic No. 371.
C.J.S. Taxation § 1098.

6–3.1–13–22 Noncompliance with agreement; assessments

Sec. 22.   If the director determines that a taxpayer who has received a credit under this chapter is not complying with the requirements of the tax credit agreement or all of the provisions of this chapter the director shall, after giving the taxpayer an opportunity to explain the noncompliance, notify the department of commerce of the noncompliance and request an assessment. The director shall state the amount of the assessment, which may not exceed the sum of any previously allowed credits under this chapter. After receiving such a notice, the department of commerce shall make an assessment against the taxpayer under IC 6–8.1 for the amount stated in the director's notice.

As added by P.L.41–1994, SEC.1.

Library References

Taxation ☞1047.
WESTLAW Topic No. 371.
C.J.S. Taxation § 1098.

6–3.1–13–23 Annual report by director

Sec. 23. On or before March 31 each year, the director shall submit a report to the board on the tax credit program under this chapter. The report shall include information on the number of agreements that were entered into under this chapter during the preceding calendar year, a description of the project that is the subject of each agreement, an update on the status of projects under agreements entered into before the preceding calendar year, and the sum of the credits awarded under this chapter. A copy of the report shall be delivered to the executive director of the legislative services agency for distribution to the members of the general assembly.

As added by P.L.41–1994, SEC.1.

6–3.1–13–24 Biennial evaluation by board

Sec. 24. On a biennial basis, the board shall provide for an evaluation of the tax credit program, giving first priority to using the Indiana economic development council, established under IC 4–3–14–4. The evaluation shall include an assessment of the effectiveness of the program in creating new jobs in Indiana and of the revenue impact of the program, and may include a review of the practices and experiences of other states with similar programs. The director shall submit a report on the evaluation to the governor, the president pro tempore of the senate, and the speaker of the house of representatives after June 30 and before November 1 in each odd-numbered year.

As added by P.L.41–1994, SEC.1.

6–3.1–13–25 Rules adoption; fees

Sec. 25. The department of commerce may adopt rules under IC 4–22–2 necessary to implement this chapter. The rules may provide for recipients of tax credits under this chapter to be charged fees to cover administrative costs of the tax credit program. Fees collected shall be deposited in the economic development for a growing economy fund.

As added by P.L.41–1994, SEC.1.

6–3.1–13–26   Economic development for a growing economy fund; use; investments; appropriations

Sec. 26. (a) The economic development for a growing economy fund is established to be used exclusively for the purposes of this chapter, including paying for the costs of administering this chapter. The fund shall be administered by the department of commerce.

(b) The fund consists of collected fees, appropriations from the general assembly, and gifts and grants to the fund.

(c) The treasurer of state shall invest the money in the fund not currently needed to meet the obligations of the fund in the same manner as other public funds may be invested. Interest that accrues from these investments shall be deposited in the fund.

(d) The money in the fund at the end of a state fiscal year does not revert to the state general fund but remains in the fund to be used exclusively for the purposes of this chapter. Expenditures from the fund are subject to appropriation by the general assembly and approval by the budget agency.

As added by P.L.41–1994, SEC.1.

Chapter 14

Maternity Home Tax Credit

6–3.1–14–1   Definitions

Sec. 1. (a) The definitions in IC 16–18–2–219, IC 16–18–2–220, IC 16–18–2–290, and IC 16–18–2–349 apply throughout this chapter.

(b) As used in this chapter, "department" refers to the state department of health.

As added by P.L.117–1990, SEC.2. Amended by P.L.2–1993, SEC.56.

Historical and Statutory Notes

P.L.2–1993, Sec.56, rewrote the section which prior thereto read: "The definitions in IC 16–2.5–1 apply throughout this chapter."

6–3.1–14–2   Entitlement to credit; amount

Sec. 2. Each taxable year a person that owns and operates a registered maternity home located in Indiana under IC 16–26–1 and provides a temporary residence to at least one (1) pregnant woman for at least sixty (60) consecutive days during the pregnancy is entitled to a maternity home tax credit. The amount of the credit for a taxable year equals the lesser of the following:

(1) An amount equal to the sum of two hundred dollars ($200) for each pregnant woman who resided in the maternity home during the taxable year multiplied by a fraction equal to:

(A) the number of days that each pregnant woman resided in the maternity home during the taxable year; divided by

(B) thirty (30);

minus the amounts collected or owed from each pregnant woman.

(2) Three thousand dollars ($3,000).

As added by P.L.117–1990, SEC.2. Amended by P.L.2–1993, SEC.57.

Historical and Statutory Notes

P.L.2–1993, Sec.57, in the introductory clause, substituted "IC 16–26–1" for "16–2.5–2".

Library References

Taxation ☞1047, 1073.
WESTLAW Topic No. 371.
C.J.S. Taxation §§ 1098, 1103.

6–3.1–14–3   Utilization of tax credit

Sec. 3. With the exception of a husband and wife, if there is more than one (1) taxpayer that owns and operates a registered maternity home, then each taxpayer may utilize the credit in proportion to the taxpayer's ownership interest in the registered maternity home. In the case of a husband and wife who own and operate a registered maternity home jointly and who file separate tax returns, they may take the credit in equal shares or one (1) of them may utilize the whole credit.

As added by P.L.117–1990, SEC.2.

Library References

Taxation ☞1047.
WESTLAW Topic No. 371.
C.J.S. Taxation § 1098.

6–3.1–14–4   Application of tax credit

Sec. 4. The department of state revenue shall apply a credit to which a taxpayer is entitled under this chapter in the following manner:

(1) First, against the taxpayer's gross income tax liability (IC 6–2.1–1) for the taxable year.

(2) Second, against the taxpayer's supplemental net income tax liability (IC 6–3–8) for the taxable year.

(3) Third, against the taxpayer's adjusted gross income liability (IC 6-3-1 through IC 6-3-7) for the taxable year.

As added by P.L.117-1990, SEC.2.

6-3.1-14-5   Carryover of tax credit; no carryback or refund of unused credit

Sec. 5.   (a) If the amount determined under section 2 of this chapter for a taxpayer in a taxable year exceeds the taxpayer's state tax liability (IC 6-3-1 through IC 6-3-7) for that taxable year, the taxpayer may carry the excess over to the following taxable years.   The amount of the credit carryover from a taxable year shall be reduced to the extent that the carryover is used by the taxpayer to obtain a credit under this chapter for any subsequent taxable year.

(b) A taxpayer is not entitled to a carryback or refund of an unused credit.

As added by P.L.117-1990, SEC.2.

Library References

Taxation ☞1047.
WESTLAW Topic No. 371.
C.J.S. Taxation § 1098.

6-3.1-14-6   Adoption of rules for determining eligibility and compliance

Sec. 6.   Notwithstanding IC 6-8.1-3-3, the board shall adopt rules for determining eligibility and compliance of maternity home operators that apply for maternity home tax credits.

As added by P.L.117-1990, SEC.2.

6-3.1-14-7   Procedures to obtain tax credit

Sec. 7.   To obtain a maternity home tax credit provided by this chapter, a taxpayer must:

(1) file an application with the board on a form prescribed by the board;

(2) claim the credit in the manner prescribed by the department of state revenue; and

(3) file with the department a copy of the application completed and approved by the board stating the credit allowed.

As added by P.L.117-1990, SEC.2.

6-3.1-14-8   Maximum annual tax credit

Sec. 8.   The amount of tax credits allowed under this chapter may not exceed five hundred thousand dollars ($500,000) in a state fiscal year.

As added by P.L.117-1990, SEC.2.

Library References

Taxation ☞1047, 1073.
WESTLAW Topic No. 371.
C.J.S. Taxation §§ 1098, 1103.

Chapter 15

Tax Credit for Computer Equipment Donations

6–3.1–15–1   "Buddy system project" defined

Sec. 1.   As used in this chapter, "buddy system project" has the meaning set forth in IC 20–10.1–25.1–4(1)(A).

As added by P.L.43–1992, SEC.11.

Historical and Statutory Notes

P.L.43–1992, Sec.11, added this chapter effective Jan. 1, 1993.

P.L.43–1992, Sec.18(c), provides:

"Section 11 of this act applies to taxable years beginning after December 31, 1992."

P.L.70–1993, Sec.8, emerg. eff. retroactive to Jan. 1, 1993, provides:

"Notwithstanding P.L. 43–1992, Section 18(c), the tax credit under IC 6–3.1–15, as amended by this act, applies to taxable years that either end or begin after December 31, 1992. However, the tax credit is available only for qualified computer equipment (as defined in IC 6–3.1–15–2) that is donated after January 1, 1993."

Library References

Words and Phrases (Perm. Ed.)

6–3.1–15–2   "Qualified computer equipment" defined

Sec. 2.   As used in this chapter, "qualified computer equipment" means computer equipment, including hardware and software, specified by the state board under section 11 of this chapter.

As added by P.L.43–1992, SEC.11.

Library References

Words and Phrases (Perm. Ed.)

6–3.1–15–3 "Service center" defined

Sec. 3. As used in this chapter, "service center" means an educational service center established under IC 20–1–11.3.

As added by P.L.43–1992, SEC.11.

Library References

Words and Phrases (Perm. Ed.)

6–3.1–15–4 "State board"

Sec. 4. As used in this chapter, "state board" refers to the Indiana state board of education.

As added by P.L.43–1992, SEC.11.

6–3.1–15–5 "State tax liability" defined

Sec. 5. As used in this chapter, "state tax liability" means a taxpayer's total tax liability incurred under:

(1) IC 6–2.1 (the gross income tax);

(2) IC 6–3–1 through IC 6–3–7 (the adjusted gross income tax);

(3) IC 6–3–8 (the supplemental net income tax);

(4) IC 6–5–10 (the bank tax);

(5) IC 6–5–11 (the savings and loan association tax);

(6) IC 6–5.5 (the financial institutions tax); and

(7) IC 27–1–18–2 (the insurance premiums tax);

as computed after the application of the credits that under IC 6–3.1–1–2 are to be applied before the credit provided by this chapter.

As added by P.L.43–1992, SEC.11. Amended by P.L.70–1993, SEC.7.

Historical and Statutory Notes

P.L.70–1993, Sec.7, emerg. eff. retroactive to Jan. 1, 1993, added Subds. (4) to (7).

Library References

Words and Phrases (Perm. Ed.)

6–3.1–15–6 "Taxpayer" defined

Sec. 6. As used in this chapter, "taxpayer" means any person, corporation, limited liability company, partnership, or entity that has any state tax liability.

As added by P.L.43–1992, SEC.11. Amended by P.L.8–1993, SEC.90.

Historical and Statutory Notes

P.L.8–1993, Sec.90, inserted "limited liability company".

Library References

Words and Phrases (Perm. Ed.)

6–3.1–15–7 Taxpayers entitled to credit

Sec. 7. A taxpayer that has donated during the taxable year qualified computer equipment to a service center is entitled to a tax credit as provided in section 8 of this chapter.

As added by P.L.43–1992, SEC.11.

Library References

Taxation ☞1047.
WESTLAW Topic No. 371.
C.J.S. Taxation § 1098.

6–3.1–15–8 Amount of credit

Sec. 8. The department shall grant a tax credit of one hundred dollars ($100) against the state tax liability of a taxpayer who qualifies for the tax credit under this chapter for each unit of qualified computer equipment that is donated under section 7 of this chapter.

As added by P.L.43–1992, SEC.11. Amended by P.L.62–1997, SEC.2.

Historical and Statutory Notes

P.L.62–1997, Sec.2, amended the section by substituting "one hundred dollars ($100)" for "one hundred twenty-five dollars ($125)".

Library References

Taxation ☞1047, 1073.
WESTLAW Topic No. 371.
C.J.S. Taxation §§ 1098, 1103.

6–3.1–15–9 Applications for credit

Sec. 9. A taxpayer that desires to claim a tax credit under this chapter shall file with the department, in the form that the department prescribes, a tax credit application that includes a certification from:

(1) the applicant stating that the applicant is a taxpayer; and

(2) a service center, that is issued under section 11 of this chapter, stating that the applicant donated qualified computer equipment in accordance with this chapter.

As added by P.L.43–1992, SEC.11.

6–3.1–15–10   Minimum standards for equipment; certification

Sec. 10. The state board shall, in consultation with the corporation for educational technology if the corporation is established under IC 20–10.1–25.1–3, establish minimum standards for qualified computer equipment. Upon receipt of computer equipment, a service center shall promptly inspect the equipment. If the computer equipment meets the minimum standards established by the state board, the service center shall accept the computer equipment as qualified computer equipment and shall, subject to section 11(b) of this chapter, promptly send a certification to the computer equipment owner for the tax credit available under this chapter.

As added by P.L.43–1992, SEC.11.

Library References

Taxation ☞1047.
WESTLAW Topic No. 371.
C.J.S. Taxation § 1098.

6–3.1–15–11   Remittance of tax credits; defective equipment

Sec. 11. (a) Before September 1 of each year, the department shall send to the state board a statement of the aggregate tax credits approved by the department for the preceding state fiscal year, listing the amount of credits approved from each service center. Within thirty (30) days following receipt of the department's notice, the state board shall direct each service center to remit to the department the entire amount of credits specified in the department's notice and attributable to the service center. Each service center shall remit the payment required under this section to the department within thirty (30) days after receipt of the state board notice.

(b) If a service center determines within thirty (30) days of receipt of a unit of computer equipment that the equipment is defective or otherwise fails to meet the minimum standards for qualified computer equipment, the service center may refuse to issue a tax credit certification under section 10 of this chapter. If the service center elects not to issue a tax credit certification for a particular unit of computer equipment, the service center shall promptly notify the donor of the equipment and allow the donor thirty (30) days to retrieve the equipment. Upon the expiration of the thirty (30) day period, the service center may retain the equipment for any purpose.

As added by P.L.43–1992, SEC.11.

Library References

Taxation ☞1047.
WESTLAW Topic No. 371.
C.J.S. Taxation § 1098.

6–3.1–15–12   Sale of equipment

Sec. 12. (a) A service center may sell qualified computer equipment received by taxpayers under this chapter only to the following:

(1) Public or private elementary or secondary schools.

(2) The parent or guardian of a student enrolled in grade 1 through 12 that is a participant in a buddy system project or enrolled in a school's computer education program.

(b) A service center may sell qualified computer equipment under this chapter to schools, parents, or guardians located outside the service center's normal service area, but not outside Indiana.

(c) Before a public or private elementary school may purchase qualified computer equipment from a service center, the school must submit a statement to the service center detailing the following:

(1) The school's computer education program or planned computer education program.

(2) The school's planned use of the qualified computer equipment, including the goals of the plan, the implementation of the plan, and the number of students that will be served with the qualified computer equipment.

(d) A school that purchases qualified computer equipment from a service center may sell the qualified computer equipment to a parent or guardian of a child who is enrolled in the school's computer education program, including a buddy system project.

(e) Before a parent or guardian of a student may purchase qualified computer equipment from a service center, the parent or guardian must present proof, in the form approved by the service center, that:

(1) the child of the parent or guardian is a participant in a buddy system project or enrolled in a school's computer education program; and

(2) the qualified computer equipment will be used by the child for an educational purpose.

As added by P.L.43–1992, SEC.11. Amended by P.L.62–1997, SEC.3.

Historical and Statutory Notes

P.L.62–1997, Sec.3, amended the section by inserting "the following" in Subsec. (a); designating Subsec. (a)(1); adding Subsec. (a)(2); inserting "parents, or guardians" in Subsec. (b); inserting "including a buddy system project" in Subsec. (d); and adding Subsec. (e).

Cross References

Taxation, computer equipment sales which qualify for exemptions, see IC 6–2.5–5–38.1.

6–3.1–15–13   Price for resale of equipment

Sec. 13. A service center shall establish a price for the resale of qualified computer equipment that equals:

(1) the amount of the service center's payment to the department under section 11 of this chapter in the preceding year and as anticipated for the current year; and

(2) the service center's actual operating expenses in purchasing, inspecting, testing, refurbishing, and reselling qualified computer equipment under this chapter, including a reasonable allowance for operating overhead.

As added by P.L.43–1992, SEC.11. Amended by P.L.1–1993, SEC.40; P.L.62–1997, SEC.4.

Historical and Statutory Notes

P.L.1–1993, Sec.40, emerg. eff. May 4, 1993, substituted "computer" for "computers" in the first sentence of Subd. (2).

P.L.62–1997, Sec.4, amended the section by substituting "that equals:" for "based upon" in

the first paragraph; and substituting "including a reasonable allowance for operating overhead" for "However, a service center may not resell a unit of qualified computer equipment under this chapter for more than five hundred dollars ($500)" in Subsec. (2).

6–3.1–15–14 Projections of anticipated demand for equipment; refusal to issue credit

Sec. 14. (a) Each service center shall develop a two (2) year projection of the anticipated demand for the purchase of qualified computer equipment. Each service center shall submit the service center's projection to the state board by January 10 of each calendar year.

(b) A service center may refuse to issue tax credit certification under section 10 of this chapter when the demand for qualified computer equipment, determined under subsection (a), is equal to or less than the anticipated supply of qualified computer equipment.

As added by P.L.43–1992, SEC.11.

Library References

Taxation ⊜1047.
WESTLAW Topic No. 371.
C.J.S. Taxation § 1098.

6–3.1–15–15 Notification of schools

Sec. 15. Before July 1 of each year, the state department of education shall notify each school that complies with the minimum instructional days required by IC 20–10.1–2–1 for the preceding school year that the program created by this chapter exists, including how the school may participate in the program.
As added by P.L.43–1992, SEC.11.

6–3.1–15–16 Rules

Sec. 16. The state board shall adopt rules under IC 4–22–2 to implement this chapter, including rules that:

(1) assure equitable allocation and nondiscrimination in the distribution of qualified computer equipment to authorized purchasers under section 12(a) of this chapter;

(2) require inter-regional cooperation among the service centers in complying with this chapter; and

(3) provide for annual audits of the service centers by the state board to determine compliance with this chapter.

As added by P.L.43–1992, SEC.11.

6–3.1–15–17 Annual reports

Sec. 17. The state board shall perform an annual review of the program implemented by this chapter and before September 1 of each year file an annual report with the budget committee for review by the budget committee and approval of the budget agency. The report must include the following:

(1) A listing of the schools that participated in the program including the school's location, whether the school is a private or public school, whether the school participates in a buddy system project, and a description of the demographics of the students of each school.

(2) The board's opinion regarding the success of the program.

(3) The amount of tax credits granted to donors.

As added by P.L.43–1992, SEC.11. Amended by P.L.62–1997, SEC.5.

Historical and Statutory Notes

P.L.62–1997, Sec.5, amended the section by deleting former Subsec. (4), which prior thereto read:

"(4) The board's recommendation regarding the continuation of the program and tax credits."

Chapter 16

Historic Rehabilitation Credit

6–3.1–16–1 Definitions

Sec. 1. The definitions set forth in:

(1) IC 14–8–2 that apply to IC 14–21–1; and

(2) IC 14–21–1;

apply throughout this chapter.

As added by P.L.77–1993, SEC.1. Amended by P.L.1–1995, SEC.49.

Historical and Statutory Notes

P.L.77–1993, Sec.1, eff. Jan. 1, 1994.

P.L.1–1995, Sec.49, amended the section by substituting Subsecs. (1) and (2) for "IC 14–3–3.4–1".

6–3.1–16–2   "Division"

Sec. 2. As used in this chapter, "division" means the division of historic preservation and archaeology of the department of natural resources.

As added by P.L.77–1993, SEC.1.

6–3.1–16–2.7   "Pass through entity" defined

Sec. 2.7. As used in this chapter, "pass through entity" means:

(1) a corporation that is exempt from the adjusted gross income tax under IC 6–3–2–2.8(2);

(2) a partnership;

(3) a limited liability company; or

(4) a limited liability partnership.

As added by P.L.57–1996, SEC.4.

Historical and Statutory Notes

P.L.57–1996, Sec.4, emerg. eff. retroactive to Jan. 1, 1995.

6–3.1–16–3   "Preservation"

Sec. 3. (a) As used in this chapter, "preservation" means the application of measures to sustain the form, integrity, and material of:

(1) a building or structure; or

(2) the form and vegetative cover of property.

(b) The term includes stabilization work and the maintenance of historic building materials.

As added by P.L.77–1993, SEC.1.

Library References

Taxation ☞1047.
WESTLAW Topic No. 371.
C.J.S. Taxation § 1098.

6–3.1–16–4 "Qualified expenditures"

Sec. 4. (a) As used in this chapter, "qualified expenditures" means expenditures for preservation or rehabilitation that are chargeable to a capital account.

(b) The term does not include costs that are incurred to do the following:

(1) Acquire a property or an interest in a property.

(2) Pay taxes due on a property.

(3) Enlarge an existing structure.

(4) Pay realtor's fees associated with a structure or property.

(5) Pay paving and landscaping costs.

(6) Pay sales and marketing costs.

As added by P.L.77–1993, SEC.1.

Library References

Taxation ☜1047.
WESTLAW Topic No. 371.
C.J.S. Taxation § 1098.

6–3.1–16–5 "Rehabilitation"

Sec. 5. As used in this chapter, "rehabilitation" means the process of returning a property to a state of utility through repair or alteration that makes possible an efficient contemporary use while preserving the parts or features of the property that are significant to the historical, architectural, or archeological values of the property.

As added by P.L.77–1993, SEC.1.

Library References

Taxation ☜1047.
WESTLAW Topic No. 371.
C.J.S. Taxation § 1098.

6–3.1–16–6 "State tax liability"

Sec. 6. As used in this chapter, "state tax liability" means a taxpayer's total tax liability incurred under:

(1) IC 6–2.1 (the gross income tax);

(2) IC 6–3–1 through IC 6–3–7 (the adjusted gross income tax); and

(3) IC 6–3–8 (the supplemental net income tax);

as computed after the application of all credits that under IC 6–3.1–1–2 are to be applied before the credit provided by this chapter.

As added by P.L.77–1993, SEC.1.

6–3.1–16–6.1   "Taxpayer"

Sec. 6.1.   As used in this chapter, "taxpayer" means an individual, a corporation, an S corporation, a partnership, a limited liability company, a limited liability partnership, a nonprofit organization, or a joint venture.
As added by P.L.54–1997, SEC.2.

6–3.1–16–7   Credit; amount; married couple filing separate returns

Sec. 7.   (a) Subject to section 14 of this chapter, a taxpayer is entitled to a credit against the taxpayer's state tax liability in the taxable year in which the taxpayer completes the preservation or rehabilitation of historic property and obtains the certifications required under section 8 of this chapter.

(b) The amount of the credit is equal to twenty percent (20%) of the qualified expenditures that:

(1) the taxpayer makes for the preservation or rehabilitation of historic property; and

(2) are approved by the division.

(c) In the case of a husband and wife who:

(1) own and rehabilitate a historic property jointly; and

(2) file separate tax returns;

the husband and wife may take the credit in equal shares or one (1) spouse may take the whole credit.
As added by P.L.77–1993, SEC.1.

Historical and Statutory Notes

P.L.54–1997, Sec.11, emerg. eff. May 13, 1997, provides:

"(a) IC 6–3.1–16, as amended by this act, applies only to taxable years beginning after December 31, 1996.

"(b) For purposes of IC 6–3.1–16, for taxable years beginning after December 31, 1993, 'taxpayer' includes an S corporation, a partnership, a limited liability company, a limited liability partnership, a nonprofit organization, or a joint venture. A taxpayer is allowed to file a claim for a credit under IC 6–3.1–16 for taxable years beginning after December 31, 1993.

"(c) Notwithstanding IC 6–3.1–16–8(7), as amended by this act, a taxpayer:

"(1) whose qualified expenditures for preservation or rehabilitation of the historic property exceed five thousand dollars ($5,000);

"(2) whose project was approved by the division of historic preservation and archeology before December 31, 1996; and

"(3) who meets the conditions contained in subdivisions (1) through (6) of IC 6–3.1–16–8, as amended by this act;

"qualifies for a credit under IC 6–3.1–16–7."

Library References

Taxation ⟀1047, 1073.
WESTLAW Topic No. 371.
C.J.S. Taxation §§ 1098, 1103.

6–3.1–16–7.5   Credit; pass through entity

Sec. 7.5.   (a) If a pass through entity is entitled to a credit under section 7 of this chapter but does not have state tax liability against which the tax credit may be applied, a shareholder, partner, or member of the pass through entity is entitled to a tax credit equal to:

(1) the tax credit determined for the pass through entity for the taxable year; multiplied by

(2) the percentage of the pass through entity's distributive income to which the shareholder, partner, or member is entitled.

(b) The credit provided under subsection (a) is in addition to a tax credit to which a shareholder, partner, or member of a pass through entity is otherwise entitled under this chapter. However, a pass through entity and a shareholder, partner, or member of the pass through entity may not claim more than one (1) credit for the same qualified expenditure.

As added by P.L.57–1996, SEC.5. Amended by P.L.54–1997, SEC.3.

Historical and Statutory Notes

P.L.57–1996, Sec.5, emerg. eff. retroactive to Jan. 1, 1995.

P.L.57–1996, Sec.6, emerg. eff. retroactive to Jan. 1, 1995, provides:

"IC 6–3.1–10–6.5 and IC 6–3.1–16–7.5, both as added by this act, apply only to taxable years beginning after December 31, 1994."

P.L.54–1997, Sec.3, amended the section by deleting former Subsec. (a); and redesignating former Subsecs. (b) and (c) as Subsecs. (a) and (b). Prior to deletion, former Subsec. (a) read:

"(a) This section applies to a credit for a qualified expenditure for the preservation or rehabilitation of historic property located in a county having a population of more than one hundred thousand (100,000) but less than one hundred seven thousand (107,000)."

Library References

Taxation ☞1047.
WESTLAW Topic No. 371.
C.J.S. Taxation § 1098.

6–3.1–16–8 Qualifying conditions

Sec. 8. A taxpayer qualifies for a credit under section 7 of this chapter if all of the following conditions are met:

(1) The historic property is:

(A) located in Indiana;

(B) at least fifty (50) years old; and

(C) except as provided in section 7(c) of this chapter, owned by the taxpayer.

(2) The division certifies that the historic property is listed in the register of Indiana historic sites and historic structures.

(3) The division certifies that the taxpayer submitted a proposed preservation or rehabilitation plan to the division that complies with the standards of the division.

(4) The division certifies that the preservation or rehabilitation work that is the subject of the credit substantially complies with the proposed plan referred to in subdivision (3).

(5) The preservation or rehabilitation work is completed in not more than:

    (A) two (2) years; or

    (B) five (5) years if the preservation or rehabilitation plan indicates that the preservation or rehabilitation is initially planned for completion in phases.

The time in which work must be completed begins when the physical work of construction or destruction in preparation for construction begins.

(6) The historic property is:

    (A) actively used in a trade or business;

    (B) held for the production of income; or

    (C) held for the rental or other use in the ordinary course of the taxpayer's trade or business.

(7) The qualified expenditures for preservation or rehabilitation of the historic property exceed ten thousand dollars ($10,000).

As added by P.L.77–1993, SEC.1. Amended by P.L.54–1997, SEC.4.

Historical and Statutory Notes

P.L.54–1997, Sec.4, amended the section by deleting former Subsec. (1)(A); redesignating former Subsecs. (1)(B) through (1)(D) as Subsecs. (1)(A) through (1)(C); deleting "before commencing preservation or rehabilitation work" from the end of Subsec. (3); and substituting "ten thousand dollars ($10,000)" for "five

thousand dollars ($5,000)" in Subsec. (7). Prior to deletion, former Subsec. (1)(A) read:

"(A) at least two thousand (2,000) square feet on the ground floor;"

For related provisions of P.L.54–1997, see Historical and Statutory Note under IC 6–3.1–16–7.

Library References

Taxation ⏣1047.
WESTLAW Topic No. 371.
C.J.S. Taxation § 1098.

6–3.1–16–9 Certifications; conditions; appeal

Sec. 9.   (a) The division shall provide the certifications referred to in section 8(3) and 8(4) of this chapter if a taxpayer's proposed preservation or rehabilitation plan complies with the standards of the division and the taxpayer's preservation or rehabilitation work complies with the plan.

(b) The taxpayer may appeal a decision by the division under this chapter to the review board.

As added by P.L.77–1993, SEC.1.

6–3.1–16–10 Claim procedure

Sec. 10.   To obtain a credit under this chapter, a taxpayer must claim the credit on the taxpayer's annual state tax return or returns in the manner prescribed by the department of state revenue. The taxpayer shall submit to the department of state revenue the certifications by the division required under section 8 of this chapter and all information that the department of state revenue determines is necessary for the calculation of the credit provided by this chapter.

As added by P.L.77–1993, SEC.1.

Library References

Taxation ⚏1079.1.
WESTLAW Topic No. 371.
C.J.S. Taxation § 1102.

6–3.1–16–11   Adjusted basis reduction

Sec. 11. For purposes of IC 6–3, the adjusted basis of:

(1) the structure, if the historic property is a structure; or

(2) the entire property, if the historic property is not a structure;

shall be reduced by the amount of a credit granted under this chapter.

As added by P.L.77–1993, SEC.1.

Library References

Taxation ⚏996.1, 1047.
WESTLAW Topic No. 371.
C.J.S. Taxation §§ 1097 to 1098.

6–3.1–16–12   Recapture

Sec. 12. (a) A credit claimed under this chapter shall be recaptured from the taxpayer if:

(1) the property is transferred less than five (5) years after completion of the certified preservation or rehabilitation work; or

(2) less than five (5) years after completion of the certified preservation or rehabilitation, additional modifications to the property are undertaken that do not meet the standards of the division.

(b) If the recapture of a credit is required under this section, an amount equal to the credit recaptured shall be added to the tax liability of the taxpayer for the taxable year during which the credit is recaptured.

As added by P.L.77–1993, SEC.1.

Library References

Taxation ⚏1047.
WESTLAW Topic No. 371.
C.J.S. Taxation § 1098.

6–3.1–16–13   Carryover; carryback

Sec. 13. (a) If the credit provided by this chapter exceeds a taxpayer's state tax liability for the taxable year for which the credit is first claimed, the excess may be carried over to succeeding taxable years and used as a credit against

147

the tax otherwise due and payable by the taxpayer under IC 6–2.1 or IC 6–3 during those taxable years. Each time that the credit is carried over to a succeeding taxable year, the credit is to be reduced by the amount that was used as a credit during the immediately preceding taxable year. The credit provided by this chapter may be carried forward and applied to succeeding taxable years for fifteen (15) taxable years following the unused credit year.

(b) A credit earned by a taxpayer in a particular taxable year shall be applied against the taxpayer's tax liability for that taxable year before any credit carryover is applied against that liability under subsection (a).

(c) A taxpayer is not entitled to any carryback or refund of any unused credit. *As added by P.L.77–1993, SEC.1.*

Library References

Taxation ☞1047.
WESTLAW Topic No. 371.
C.J.S. Taxation § 1098.

6–3.1–16–14 Annual limit

Sec. 14. The amount of tax credits allowed under this chapter may not exceed:

(1) seven hundred fifty thousand dollars ($750,000) in the state fiscal year beginning July 1, 1997, and the state fiscal year beginning July 1, 1998; and

(2) four hundred fifty thousand dollars ($450,000) in a state fiscal year that begins July 1, 1999, or thereafter.

As added by P.L.77–1993, SEC.1. Amended by P.L.54–1997, SEC.5.

Historical and Statutory Notes

P.L.54–1997, Sec.5, amended the section by adding Subsec. (1); and designating Subsec. (2) and inserting "that begins July 1, 1999, or thereafter" therein.

Library References

Taxation ☞1047, 1073.
WESTLAW Topic No. 371.
C.J.S. Taxation §§ 1098, 1103.

6–3.1–16–15 Rules

Sec. 15. The following may adopt rules under IC 4–22–2 to carry out this chapter:

(1) The department of state revenue.

(2) The division.

As added by P.L.77–1993, SEC.1.

Chapter 17

Indiana Riverboat Building Credit

6–3.1–17–1   "Qualified investment" defined

Sec. 1.   As used in this chapter, "qualified investment" means costs incurred to build or refurbish a riverboat in Indiana that are approved by the department of commerce under section 7 of this chapter.

As added by P.L.19–1994, SEC.10.

Library References

Taxation ⚭1047.
WESTLAW Topic No. 371.
C.J.S. Taxation § 1098.

6–3.1–17–2   "Riverboat" defined

Sec. 2.   As used in this chapter, "riverboat" has the meaning set forth in IC 4–33–2–17.

As added by P.L.19–1994, SEC.10.

6–3.1–17–3   "State tax liability" defined

Sec. 3.   As used in this chapter, "state tax liability" means a taxpayer's total tax liability that is incurred under:

(1) IC 6–2.1 (the gross income tax);

(2) IC 6–3–1 through IC 6–3–7 (the adjusted gross income tax);

(3) IC 6–3–8 (the supplemental net income tax);

(4) IC 6–5–10 (the bank tax);

(5) IC 6–5–11 (the savings and loan association tax);

(6) IC 27–1–18–2 (the insurance premiums tax);

(7) IC 6–5.5 (the financial institutions tax); and

(8) IC 6–2.5 (state gross retail and use tax);

as computed after the application of the credits that under IC 6–3.1–1–2 are to be applied before the credit provided by this chapter.

As added by P.L.19–1994, SEC.10.

6–3.1–17–4 "Taxpayer" defined

Sec. 4.   As used in this chapter, "taxpayer" means an individual or entity that has any state tax liability.

As added by P.L.19–1994, SEC.10.

6–3.1–17–5 Entitlement to and amount of credit

Sec. 5.   (a) A taxpayer is entitled to a credit against the taxpayer's state tax liability for a taxable year if the taxpayer makes a qualified investment in that taxable year.

(b) The amount of the credit to which a taxpayer is entitled is equal to fifteen percent (15%) multiplied by the qualified investment made by the taxpayer during the taxable year.

As added by P.L.19–1994, SEC.10.

Library References

Taxation ⚲1047, 1073.
WESTLAW Topic No. 371.
C.J.S. Taxation §§ 1098, 1103.

6–3.1–17–6 Carryover of credit

Sec. 6.   (a) If the amount determined under section 5(b) of this chapter for a taxpayer in a taxable year exceeds the taxpayer's state tax liability for that taxable year, the taxpayer may carry the excess over to the following taxable years.   The amount of the credit carryover from a taxable year shall be reduced to the extent that the carryover is used by the taxpayer to obtain a credit under this chapter for any subsequent taxable year.

(b) A taxpayer is not entitled to a carryback or refund of any unused credit.

As added by P.L.19–1994, SEC.10.

Library References

Taxation ⚲1047.
WESTLAW Topic No. 371.
C.J.S. Taxation § 1098.

6–3.1–17–7 Determination of qualified investment

Sec. 7.   (a) To be entitled to a credit under this chapter, a taxpayer must request the department of commerce to determine whether costs incurred to build or refurbish a riverboat are qualified investments.

(b) The request under subsection (a) must be made before the costs are incurred.

(c) The department of commerce shall find that costs are a qualified investment to the extent that the costs result:

(1) from work performed in Indiana to build or refurbish a riverboat; and

(2) in taxable income to any other Indiana taxpayer;
as determined under the standards adopted by the department of commerce.
As added by P.L.19–1994, SEC.10.

6–3.1–17–8   Claim for credit

Sec. 8.   To receive the credit provided by this chapter, a taxpayer must claim the credit on the taxpayer's state tax return or returns in the manner prescribed by the department.   The taxpayer shall submit to the department the certification of credit by the department of commerce, proof of payment of the certified qualified investment, and all information that the department determines is necessary for the calculation of the credit provided by this chapter and for the determination of whether an investment cost is a qualified investment cost.
As added by P.L.19–1994, SEC.10.

6–3.1–17–9   Aggregate monetary limitation on credits

Sec. 9.   (a) The amount of tax credits allowed under this chapter may not exceed one million dollars ($1,000,000) in a state fiscal year.

(b) The department shall record the time of filing of each application for allowance of a credit under section 8 of this chapter and shall approve the applications, if they otherwise qualify for a tax credit under this chapter, in the chronological order in which the applications are filed in the state fiscal year.

(c) When the total credits approved under this section equal the maximum amount allowable in a state fiscal year, no application thereafter filed for that same fiscal year shall be approved.   However, if an applicant for whom a credit has been approved fails to file the statement of proof of payment required under section 8 of this chapter, an amount equal to the credit previously allowed or set aside for the applicant may be allowed to any subsequent applicant in the year.   In addition, the department may, if the applicant so requests, approve a credit application, in whole or in part, with respect to the next succeeding state fiscal year.
As added by P.L.19–1994, SEC.10.

Chapter 18

Individual Development Account Tax Credit

Cross References

Commerce department, individual development account fund, see IC 4–4–28–13.

6–3.1–18–1 "Community development corporation" defined

Sec. 1. As used in this chapter, "community development corporation" has the meaning set forth in IC 4–4–28–2.

As added by P.L.15–1997, SEC.2.

Historical and Statutory Notes

P.L.15–1997, Sec.2, eff. Jan. 1, 1998.

P.L.15–1997, Sec.6, eff. Jan. 1, 1998, provides:

"A tax credit provided under IC 6–3.1–18, as added by this act, may be claimed only for taxes owed in taxable years that begin after December 31, 1997."

6–3.1–18–2 "Fund" defined

Sec. 2. As used in this chapter, "fund" refers to an individual development account fund established by a community development corporation under IC 4–4–28–13.

As added by P.L.15–1997, SEC.2.

6–3.1–18–3 "Individual development account" defined

Sec. 3. As used in this chapter, "individual development account" has the meaning set forth in IC 4–4–28–5.

As added by P.L.15–1997, SEC.2.

6–3.1–18–4 "Pass through entity" defined

Sec. 4. As used in this chapter, "pass through entity" means:

(1) a corporation that is exempt from the adjusted gross income tax under IC 6–3–2–2.8(2);

(2) a partnership;

(3) a limited liability company; or

(4) a limited liability partnership.

As added by P.L.15–1997, SEC.2.

6–3.1–18–5 "State tax liability" defined

Sec. 5. As used in this chapter, "state tax liability" means a taxpayer's total tax liability incurred under:

(1) IC 6–2.1 (the gross income tax);

(2) IC 6–3–1 through IC 6–3–7 (the adjusted gross income tax);

(3) IC 6–3–8 (the supplemental corporate net income tax); and

(4) IC 6–5.5 (the financial institutions tax);

as computed after the application of all credits that under IC 6–3.1–1–2 are to be applied before the credit provided by this chapter.

As added by P.L.15–1997, SEC.2.

6–3.1–18–6 Income tax credit

Sec. 6. (a) Subject to the limitations provided in subsection (b) and sections 7, 8, 9, 10, and 11 of this chapter, the department shall grant a tax credit against any gross, adjusted gross, or supplemental net income tax due equal to fifty percent (50%) of the amount contributed by a person or an individual to a fund if the contribution is not less than one hundred dollars ($100) and not more than fifty thousand dollars ($50,000).

(b) The credit provided by this chapter shall only be applied against any income tax liability owed by the taxpayer after the application of any credits that under IC 6–3.1–1–2 must be applied before the credit provided by this chapter.

As added by P.L.15–1997, SEC.2. Amended by P.L.4–1999, SEC.4.

Historical and Statutory Notes

P.L.4–1999, Sec.4, emerg. eff. March 31, 1999, amended the section by substituting "one hundred dollars ($100)" for "one thousand dollars ($1,000)" in Subsec. (a).

Library References

Taxation ⚖1047, 1073.
WESTLAW Topic No. 371.
C.J.S. Taxation §§ 1098, 1103.

6–3.1–18–7 Application of tax credit to pass through entities; calculation

Sec. 7. If a pass through entity is entitled to a credit under section 6 of this chapter but does not have state tax liability against which the tax credit may be applied, a shareholder, partner, or member of the pass through entity is entitled to a tax credit equal to:

(1) the tax credit determined for the pass through entity for the taxable year; multiplied by

(2) the percentage of the pass through entity's distributive income to which the shareholder, partner, or member is entitled.

As added by P.L.15–1997, SEC.2.

Library References

Taxation ☜1047, 1073.
WESTLAW Topic No. 371.
C.J.S. Taxation §§ 1098, 1103.

6–3.1–18–8   Additional income tax credits

Sec. 8.   The credit provided under section 7 of this chapter is in addition to a tax credit to which a shareholder, partner, or member of a pass through entity is otherwise entitled under IC 6–2.1, IC 6–3, this article, or IC 6–5.5. However, a pass through entity and a shareholder, partner, or member of the pass through entity may not claim more than one (1) credit for the same qualified expenditure.

As added by P.L.15–1997, SEC.2.

Library References

Taxation ☜1047.
WESTLAW Topic No. 371.
C.J.S. Taxation § 1098.

6–3.1–18–9   Application for tax credit; proof of payment

Sec. 9.   (a) A person that or an individual who desires to claim a tax credit as provided in this chapter shall file with the department, in the form approved by the department, an application stating the amount of the contribution that the person or individual proposes to make that would qualify for a tax credit and the amount sought to be claimed as a credit.

(b) The department shall promptly notify an applicant whether, or the extent to which, the tax credit is allowable in the state fiscal year in which the application is filed, as provided in section 6 of this chapter. If the credit is allowable in that state fiscal year, the applicant shall within thirty (30) days after receipt of the notice file with the department a statement, in the form and accompanied by the proof of payment as the department may prescribe, setting forth that the amount to be claimed as a credit under this chapter has been paid to a fund as provided in section 6 of this chapter.

(c) The department may disallow any credit claimed under this chapter for which the statement or proof of payment is not filed within the thirty (30) day period.

As added by P.L.15–1997, SEC.2.

6–3.1–18–10　Amount of tax credits allowed

Sec. 10.　(a) The amount of tax credits allowed under this chapter may not exceed five hundred thousand dollars ($500,000) in any state fiscal year.

(b) The department shall:

(1) record the time of filing of each application for allowance of a credit required under section 9 of this chapter;　and

(2) approve the applications, if they otherwise qualify for a tax credit under this chapter, in the chronological order in which the applications are filed in the state fiscal year.

(c) When the total credits approved under this section equal the maximum amount allowable in any state fiscal year, an application filed after that time for the same fiscal year may not be approved.　However, if an applicant for whom a credit has been approved fails to file the statement of proof of payment required under section 9 of this chapter, an amount equal to the credit previously allowed or set aside for the applicant may be allowed to any subsequent applicant in the year.　In addition, the department may, if the applicant so requests, approve a credit application, in whole or in part, with respect to the next succeeding state fiscal year.

As added by P.L.15–1997, SEC.2.

Library References

Taxation ⚬1047, 1073.
WESTLAW Topic No. 371.
C.J.S. Taxation §§ 1098, 1103.

6–3.1–18–11　Tax credit available only in year paid

Sec. 11.　A tax credit shall be allowable under this chapter only for the taxable year of the taxpayer in which the contribution qualifying for the credit is paid.

As added by P.L.15–1997, SEC.2.

Library References

Taxation ⚬1047.
WESTLAW Topic No. 371.
C.J.S. Taxation § 1098.

Chapter 19

Community Revitalization Enhancement District Tax Credit

6–3.1–19–1   "State and local tax liability" defined

Sec. 1.   As used in this chapter, "state and local tax liability" means a taxpayer's total tax liability incurred under:

(1) IC 6–2.1 (the gross income tax);

(2) IC 6–3–1 through IC 6–3–7 (the adjusted gross income tax);

(3) IC 6–3–8 (the supplemental net income tax);

(4) IC 6–3.5–1.1 (county adjusted gross income tax);

(5) IC 6–3.5–6 (county option income tax);

(6) IC 6–3.5–7 (county economic development income tax);

(7) IC 6–5–10 (the bank tax);

(8) IC 6–5–11 (the savings and loan association tax);

(9) IC 6–5.5 (the financial institutions tax); and

(10) IC 27–1–18–2 (the insurance premiums tax);

as computed after the application of all credits that under IC 6–3.1–1–2 are to be applied before the credit provided by this chapter.
As added by P.L.125–1998, SEC.3.

Historical and Statutory Notes

P.L.125–1998, Sec.3, eff. Jan. 1, 1999.

P.L.125–1998, Sec.25, eff. Jan. 1, 1999, provides:

"IC 6–3.1–19, as added by this act, applies only to taxable years beginning after December 31, 1998."

6–3.1–19–2   "Qualified investment" defined

Sec. 2.   As used in this chapter, "qualified investment" means the amount of a taxpayer's expenditures that is:

(1) for redevelopment or rehabilitation of property located within a community revitalization enhancement district designated under IC 36–7–13;

(2) made under a plan adopted by an advisory commission on industrial development under IC 36–7–13; and

(3) approved by the department of commerce before the expenditure is made.
As added by P.L.125–1998, SEC.3.

Library References

Taxation ⚯1047.
WESTLAW Topic No. 371.
C.J.S. Taxation § 1098.

6–3.1–19–3 Entitlement to credit; amount; assignment

Sec. 3. (a) Subject to section 5 of this chapter, a taxpayer is entitled to a credit against the taxpayer's state and local tax liability for a taxable year if the taxpayer makes a qualified investment in that year.

(b) The amount of the credit to which a taxpayer is entitled is the qualified investment made by the taxpayer during the taxable year multiplied by twenty-five percent (25%).

(c) A taxpayer may assign any part of the credit to which the taxpayer is entitled under this chapter to a lessee of property redeveloped or rehabilitated under section 2 of this chapter. A credit that is assigned under this subsection remains subject to this chapter.

(d) An assignment under subsection (c) must be in writing and both the taxpayer and the lessee must report the assignment on their state tax return for the year in which the assignment is made, in the manner prescribed by the department. The taxpayer may not receive value in connection with the assignment under subsection (c) that exceeds the value of the part of the credit assigned.

As added by P.L.125–1998, SEC.3.

Library References

Taxation ⬤1047, 1073.
WESTLAW Topic No. 371.
C.J.S. Taxation §§ 1098, 1103.

6–3.1–19–4 Credit carryover; carryback or refund unavailable

Sec. 4. If the amount of the credit determined under section 3 of this chapter for a taxable year exceeds the taxpayer's state tax liability for that taxable year, the taxpayer may carry the excess over to the immediately following taxable years. The amount of the credit carryover from a taxable year shall be reduced to the extent that the carryover is used by the taxpayer to obtain a credit under this chapter for any subsequent taxable year. A taxpayer is not entitled to a carryback or refund of any unused credit.

As added by P.L.125–1998, SEC.3.

Library References

Taxation ⬤1047.
WESTLAW Topic No. 371.
C.J.S. Taxation § 1098.

6–3.1–19–5 Ineligibility for credit to extent of reduction or cessation of operations in Indiana

Sec. 5. (a) Except as provided in subsection (b), a taxpayer is not entitled to claim the credit provided by this chapter to the extent that the taxpayer substantially reduces or ceases its operations in Indiana in order to relocate them within the district.

(b) Notwithstanding subsection (a), a taxpayer's substantial reduction or cessation of operations in Indiana in order to relocate operations to a district does not make a taxpayer ineligible for a credit under this chapter if:

(1) the taxpayer had existing operations in the district; and

(2) the operations relocated to the district are an expansion of the taxpayer's operations in the district.

(c) A determination that a taxpayer is not entitled to the credit provided by this chapter as a result of a substantial reduction or cessation of operations applies to credits that would otherwise arise in the taxable year in which the substantial reduction or cessation occurs and in all subsequent years. Determinations under this section shall be made by the department of state revenue. *As added by P.L.125–1998, SEC.3.*

Library References

Taxation ⚷1047.
WESTLAW Topic No. 371.
C.J.S. Taxation § 1098.

6–3.1–19–6 Method of claiming credit; submission of information

Sec. 6. To receive the credit provided by this section, a taxpayer must claim the credit on the taxpayer's annual state tax return or returns in the manner prescribed by the department of state revenue. The taxpayer shall submit to the department of state revenue all information that the department determines is necessary for the calculation of the credit provided by this chapter and for the determination of whether an expenditure was for a qualified investment. *As added by P.L.125–1998, SEC.3.*

Library References

Taxation ⚷1047, 1079.1.
WESTLAW Topic No. 371.
C.J.S. Taxation §§ 1098, 1102.

Chapter 21 [1]

Earned Income Tax Credit

[1] IC 6–3.1 contains no chapter 20.

Section

6–3.1–21–1   **Creation of credit**

Sec. 1. This chapter creates the Indiana earned income tax credit.
As added by P.L.273–1999, SEC.227.

Historical and Statutory Notes

P.L.273–1999, Sec.227, emerg. eff. retroactive to Jan. 1, 1999.

P.L.273–1999, Sec.229, emerg. eff. retroactive to Jan. 1, 1999, provides:

"IC 6–3.1–21, as added by this act, applies to taxable years beginning after December 31, 1998."

Library References

Words and Phrases (Perm.Ed.)

6–3.1–21–2   **"Earned income" defined**

Sec. 2. As used in this chapter, "earned income" means the sum of the:

(1) wages, salaries, tips, and other employee compensation; and

(2) net earnings from self-employment (as computed under Section 32(c)(2) of the Internal Revenue Code [1]);

of an individual taxpayer, and the individual's spouse, if the individual files a joint adjusted gross income tax return.
As added by P.L.273–1999, SEC.227.

[1] 26 U.S.C.A. § 32(c)(2).

Library References

Words and Phrases (Perm.Ed.)

6–3.1–21–3   **"Indiana total income" defined**

Sec. 3. As used in this chapter, "Indiana total income" means gross income (as defined in Section 61 of the Internal Revenue Code [1]) for an individual, and if the individual files a joint return, the individual's spouse, for a year.
As added by P.L.273–1999, SEC.227.

[1] 26 U.S.C.A. § 61.

Library References

Words and Phrases (Perm.Ed.)

6–3.1–21–4   **"Qualifying child" defined**

Sec. 4. As used in this chapter, "qualifying child" has the meaning set forth in Section 32(c)(3) of the Internal Revenue Code.[1]
As added by P.L.273–1999, SEC.227.

[1] 26 U.S.C.A. § 32(c)(3).

Library References

Words and Phrases (Perm.Ed.)

6–3.1–21–5   Individuals entitled to credit

Sec. 5.   An individual who, in a year, has:

(1) at least one (1) qualifying child;

(2) Indiana total income from all sources of not more than twelve thousand dollars ($12,000); and

(3) Indiana total income from earned income that is at least eighty percent (80%) of the individual's Indiana total income;

is entitled to a credit against the taxpayer's adjusted gross income tax liability for the taxable year in the amount determined in section 6 of this chapter. *As added by P.L.273–1999, SEC.227.*

Library References

Taxation ☞1047.
WESTLAW Topic No. 371.
C.J.S. Taxation § 1098.

6–3.1–21–6   Amount of credit

Sec. 6.   The credit authorized under section 5 of this chapter is equal to three and four-tenths percent (3.4%) of:

(1) twelve thousand dollars ($12,000); minus

(2) the amount of the individual's Indiana total income.

If the credit amount exceeds the taxpayer's adjusted gross income tax liability for the taxable year, the excess shall be refunded to the taxpayer. *As added by P.L.273–1999, SEC.227.*

Library References

Taxation ☞1047, 1073.
WESTLAW Topic No. 371.
C.J.S. Taxation §§ 1098, 1103.

6–3.1–21–7   Joint credit application

Sec. 7.   (a) If a husband and wife file a joint Indiana income tax return for a year, a joint credit application must be used under this chapter for that year.

(b) If a husband and wife file separate Indiana income tax returns for a year, separate credit applications must be used under this chapter for that year. *As added by P.L.273–1999, SEC.227.*

Library References

Taxation ☞1079.1.
WESTLAW Topic No. 371.
C.J.S. Taxation § 1102.

6–3.1–21–8   Claim for credit on return;   submission of information

Sec. 8.   To obtain a credit under this chapter, a taxpayer must claim the credit on the taxpayer's annual state tax return or returns in the manner prescribed by the department of state revenue.   The taxpayer shall submit to the department of state revenue all information that the department of state revenue determines is necessary for the calculation of the credit provided by this chapter.

As added by P.L.273–1999, SEC.227.

Library References

Taxation ⊕1047, 1079.1.
WESTLAW Topic No. 371.
C.J.S. Taxation §§ 1098, 1102.

6–3.1–21–9   Application of credit to TANF

Sec. 9.   (a) The division of family and children shall apply the refundable portion of the credits provided under this chapter as expenditures toward Indiana's maintenance of effort under the federal Temporary Assistance to Needy Families (TANF) program (45 CFR 265).

(b) The department of state revenue shall collect and provide the data requested by the division of family and children that is necessary to comply with this section.

As added by P.L.273–1999, SEC.227.

6–3.1–21–10   Expiration of chapter

Sec. 10.   This chapter expires December 31, 2001.

As added by P.L.273–1999, SEC.227.

ARTICLE 3.5

LOCAL TAXATION

WESTLAW Computer Assisted Legal Research

WESTLAW supplements your legal research in many ways. WESTLAW allows you to
- update your research with the most current information
- expand your library with additional resources
- retrieve current, comprehensive history and citing references to a case with KeyCite

For more information on using WESTLAW to supplement your research, see the WESTLAW Electronic Research Guide, which follows the Preface.

Cross References

Motor vehicle license branch operation contracts, see IC 9–16–1–4.
Professional sports development area, covered taxes defined, see IC 36–7–31.3–4.

Chapter 1

County Adjusted Gross Income Tax Law

6–3.5–1–1 to 6–3.5–1–12 Repealed

(Repealed by P.L.73–1983, SEC.3.)

Historical and Statutory Notes

P.L. 73–1983 provided in Section 27, containing emergency clause, that the act takes effect March 15, 1983.

The repealed chapter related to the county adjusted gross income tax law.

For provisions relating to recodification and continuation of the subject matter of the repealed sections, see Historical Note under section 6–3.5–1.1–1.

COUNTY TAX

DISPOSITION TABLE

Showing where the subject matter of the repealed sections of Title 6 is now covered in new sections of Title 6, West's Annotated Indiana Code.

Chapter 1.1

County Adjusted Gross Income Tax

6–3.5–1.1–1   Definitions

Sec. 1. As used in this chapter:

"Adjusted gross income" has the same definition that the term is given in IC 6–3–1–3.5(a), except that in the case of a county taxpayer who is not a resident of a county that has imposed the county adjusted gross income tax, the term includes only adjusted gross income derived from his principal place of business or employment.

"Civil taxing unit" means any entity having the power to impose ad valorem property taxes except a school corporation. The term does not include a solid waste management district that is not entitled to a distribution under section 1.3 of this chapter. However, in the case of a consolidated city, the term "civil taxing unit" includes the consolidated city and all special taxing districts, all special service districts, and all entities whose budgets and property tax levies are subject to review under IC 36–3–6–9.

"County council" includes the city-county council of a consolidated city.

"County taxpayer" as it relates to a county for a year means any individual:

(1) who resides in that county on the date specified in section 16 of this chapter; or

(2) who maintains his principal place of business or employment in that county on the date specified in section 16 of this chapter and who does not on that same date reside in another county in which the county adjusted gross income tax, the county option income tax, or the county economic development income tax is in effect.

"Department" refers to the Indiana department of state revenue.

"Nonresident county taxpayer" as it relates to a county for a year means any county taxpayer for that county for that year who is not a resident county taxpayer of that county for that year.

"Resident county taxpayer" as it relates to a county for a year means any county taxpayer who resides in that county on the date specified in section 16 of this chapter.

"School corporation" means any public school corporation established under Indiana law.

As added by P.L.73–1983, SEC.2. Amended by P.L.44–1984, SEC.12; P.L.22–1988, SEC.3; P.L.96–1995, SEC.1.

Historical and Statutory Notes

P.L. 73–1983, Sec.2, emerg. eff. March 15, 1983, added this chapter.

Sections 25 and 26 of P.L.73–1983 provided:

"Section 25. (a) Sections 1 and 2 of this act comprise a codification and rearrangement of IC 6–3.5–1. Whenever this act repeals and re-enacts provisions of IC 6–3.5–1 in the same form or restated form, the substantive operation and effect of those provisions continue uninterrupted.

"(b) This act does not affect any:

"(1) rights or liabilities accrued;

"(2) penalties incurred;

"(3) crimes committed; or

"(4) proceedings begun;

"before the effective date of this act. Those rights, liabilities, penalties, crimes, and proceedings continue and shall be imposed and enforced under IC 6–3.5–1 as if this act had not been enacted."

"Section 26. The general assembly may, by concurrent resolution, preserve any of the background materials related to this act."

P.L.44–1984, Sec.12, emerg. eff. March 7, 1984, modified definition of "County taxpayer"

by deleting "who" from the end of the introductory paragraph, by inserting "who" at beginning of Subds. (1) and (2), and by inserting "or the county option income tax" in Subd. (2).

P.L. 22–1988, Sec.3, emerg. eff. retroactive to Jan. 1, 1988, and by section 10 applicable to "taxable years that begin after December 31, 1987", inserted in Cl. (2) of the definition of county taxpayer "or the county economic development income tax".

P.L. 22–1988, Sec.10, emerg. eff. March 3, 1988, provides:

"Sections 3, 4, and 6 of this act apply to taxable years that begin after December 31, 1987."

P.L.96–1995, Sec.1, emerg. eff. May 5, 1995, amended the section by inserting the second sentence in the paragraph defining a "civil taxing unit."

Formerly:

IC 6–3.5–1–1.
Acts 1973, P.L.50, SEC.7.
Acts 1977(ss), P.L.5, SEC.1.
Acts 1979, P.L.73, SEC.1.
Acts 1981, P.L.11, SEC.31.

Constitutional Provisions

Article 10, § 8, provides:

"The general assembly may levy and collect a tax upon income, from whatever source de-

rived, at such rates, in such manner, and with such exemptions as may be prescribed by law."

Cross References

Adjusted gross income tax act, see IC 6–3–1–1 et seq.
Administration, enforcement, and collection of tax, department of state revenue, see IC 6–8.1–1–1 et seq.
Community revitalization enhancement district tax credit, state and local tax liability, see IC 6–3.1–19–1.
Gross income tax law, see IC 6–2.1–1–1 et seq.
Industrial development fund, state and local income taxes, see IC 36–7–13–3.8.
Library property taxes, replacement credits, see IC 6–3.5–7–23.
Outstanding tax warrants, list, see IC 6–8–3–17.
Rural development fund, qualifications for grants, see IC 4–4–9–4.
Withholding instructions, adjusted gross income tax, see IC 6–3–4–8, 6–3–4–12, 6–3–4–13.

Library References

Counties ☞189 to 194.
WESTLAW Topic No. 104.
C.J.S. Counties §§ 227 to 234.

6–3.5–1.1–1.3　Districts not entitled to distribution

Sec. 1.3. (a) This section applies to a county solid waste management district (as defined in IC 13–11–2–47) or a joint solid waste management district (as defined in IC 13–11–2–113).

(b) A district may not receive a distribution under this chapter unless a majority of the members of each of the county fiscal bodies of the counties within the district passes a resolution approving the distribution.

As added by P.L.96–1995, SEC.2.   Amended by P.L.1–1996, SEC.47.

Historical and Statutory Notes

P.L.96–1995, Sec.2, emerg. eff. May 5, 1995.

P.L.1–1996, Sec.47, amended the section by substituting "IC 13–11–2–47" for "IC 13–9.5–1–

7" and "IC 13–11–2–113" for "IC 13–9.5–1–18" in Subsec. (a).

6–3.5–1.1–2   Authorization; rate of tax; form and adoption of ordinance

Sec. 2.   (a) The county council of any county in which the county option income tax will not be in effect on July 1 of a year under an ordinance adopted during a previous calendar year may impose the county adjusted gross income tax on the adjusted gross income of county taxpayers of its county effective July 1 of that year.

(b) Except as provided in section 2.5 or 3.5 of this chapter, the county adjusted gross income tax may be imposed at a rate of one-half of one percent (0.5%), three-fourths of one percent (0.75%), or one percent (1%) on the adjusted gross income of resident county taxpayers of the county. Any county imposing the county adjusted gross income tax must impose the tax on the nonresident county taxpayers at a rate of one-fourth of one percent (0.25%) on their adjusted gross income. If the county council elects to decrease the county adjusted gross income tax, the county council may decrease the county adjusted gross income tax rate in increments of one-tenth of one percent (0.1%).

(c) To impose the county adjusted gross income tax, the county council must, after January 1 but before April 1 of a year, adopt an ordinance. The ordinance must substantially state the following:

"The _____ County Council imposes the county adjusted gross income tax on the county taxpayers of _____ County. The county adjusted gross income tax is imposed at a rate of _____ percent (_____%) on the resident county taxpayers of the county and one-fourth of one percent (0.25%) on the nonresident county taxpayers of the county. This tax takes effect July 1 of this year.".

(d) Any ordinance adopted under this section takes effect July 1 of the year the ordinance is adopted.

(e) The auditor of a county shall record all votes taken on ordinances presented for a vote under the authority of this section and immediately send a certified copy of the results to the department by certified mail.

(f) If the county adjusted gross income tax had previously been adopted by a county under IC 6–3.5–1 (before its repeal on March 15, 1983) and that tax was in effect at the time of the enactment of this chapter, then the county adjusted gross income tax continues in that county at the rates in effect at the time of enactment until the rates are modified or the tax is rescinded in the manner prescribed by this chapter. If a county's adjusted gross income tax is continued under this subsection, then the tax shall be treated as if it had been imposed under this chapter and is subject to rescission or reduction as authorized in this chapter.

As added by P.L.73–1983, SEC.2. Amended by P.L.44–1984, SEC.13; P.L.3–1990, SEC.24; P.L.35–1990, SEC.12; P.L.42–1994, SEC.1; P.L.119–1998, SEC.6.

Historical and Statutory Notes

P.L.44–1984, Sec.13, emerg. eff. March 7, 1984, modified Subsec. (a) by inserting "in which the county option income tax will not be in effect on July 1 of a year under an ordinance adopted during a previous calendar year", and by adding "effective July 1 of that year".

P.L.3–1990, Sec.24, emerg. eff. March 13, 1990, in Subsec. (f), deleted "before its repeal on March 15, 1983" preceding "IC 6–3.5–1".

P.L.35–1990, Sec.12, emerg. eff. April 1, 1990, in Subsec. (e), substituted "send a certified copy of" for "certify", and inserted "by certified mail".

P.L.42–1994, Sec.1, emerg. eff. March 18, 1994, in Subsec. (b), inserted the second sentence relating to election to decrease county

adjusted gross income tax; and in Subsec. (f), in the second sentence, inserted "and is subject to rescission or reduction as authorized in this chapter".

P.L.119–1998, Sec.6, amended the section by inserting "Except as provided in section 2.5 or 3.5 of this chapter," in Subsec. (b).

Formerly:

IC 6–3.5–1–2.
IC 6–3.5–1–4.
Acts 1973, P.L.50, SEC.7.
Acts 1974, P.L.22, SEC.1.
Acts 1977, P.L.2, SEC.31.
Acts 1977, P.L.78, SEC.5.

Library References

Counties ⚮190(1).
WESTLAW Topic No. 104.
C.J.S. Counties §§ 227 to 232.

6–3.5–1.1–2.5 Additional tax for jail and juvenile detention center in county with population between 37,000 and 37,800.

Sec. 2.5. (a) This section applies only to a county having a population of more than thirty-seven thousand (37,000) but less than thirty-seven thousand eight hundred (37,800).

(b) The county council of a county described in subsection (a) may, by ordinance, determine that additional county adjusted gross income tax revenue is needed in the county to fund the operation and maintenance of a jail and juvenile detention center opened after July 1, 1998.

(c) Notwithstanding section 2 of this chapter, if the county council adopts an ordinance under subsection (b), the county council may impose the county adjusted gross income tax at a rate of one and one-tenth percent (1.1%) on adjusted gross income. However, a county may impose the county adjusted gross income tax at a rate of one and one-tenth percent (1.1%) for only four (4) years. After the county has imposed the county adjusted gross income tax at a rate of one and one-tenth percent (1.1%) for four (4) years, the rate is reduced to one percent (1%). If the county council imposes the county adjusted gross income tax at a rate of one and one-tenth percent (1.1%), the county council may decrease the rate or rescind the tax in the manner provided under this chapter.

(d) If a county imposes the county adjusted gross income tax at a rate of one and one-tenth percent (1.1%) under this section, the revenue derived from a tax rate of one-tenth percent (0.1%) on adjusted gross income:

    (1) shall be paid to the county treasurer;

    (2) may be used only to pay the costs of operating a jail and juvenile detention center opened after July 1, 1998; and

    (3) may not be considered by the state board of tax commissioners in determining the county's maximum permissible property tax levy limit under IC 6–1.1–18.5.

As added by P.L.119–1998, SEC.7.

6–3.5–1.1–3   Increase of tax rate; ordinance; requisites

Sec. 3. (a) The county council may increase the county adjusted gross income tax rate imposed upon the resident county taxpayers of the county. To increase the rate, the county council must, after January 1 but before April 1 of a year, adopt an ordinance. The ordinance must substantially state the following:

    "The _____ County Council increases the county adjusted gross income tax rate imposed upon the resident county taxpayers of the county from _____ percent (_____%) to _____ percent (_____%). This tax rate increase takes effect July 1 of this year.".

(b) Any ordinance adopted under this section takes effect July 1 of the year the ordinance is adopted.

(c) The auditor of a county shall record all votes taken on ordinances presented for a vote under the authority of this section and immediately send a certified copy of the results to the department by certified mail.

As added by P.L.73–1983, SEC.2. Amended by P.L.35–1990, SEC.13.

Historical and Statutory Notes

P.L.35–1990, Sec.13, emerg. eff. March 20, 1990.

P.L.35–1990, Sec.13, in Subsec. (c), substituted "send a certified copy of" for "certify", and inserted "by certified mail".

Formerly:

IC 6–3.5–1–4.

Acts 1973, P.L.50, SEC.7.

Acts 1974, P.L.22, SEC.1.

Library References

Counties ☞189 to 194.
WESTLAW Topic No. 104.
C.J.S. Counties §§ 227 to 234.

6–3.5–1.1–3.1   Decrease in county adjusted gross income tax rate; adoption of ordinance; procedures

Sec. 3.1. (a) The county council may decrease the county adjusted gross income tax rate imposed upon the resident county taxpayers of the county. To decrease the rate, the county council must, after January 1 but before April 1 of a year, adopt an ordinance. The ordinance must substantially state the following:

"The _____ County Council decreases the county adjusted gross income tax rate imposed upon the resident county taxpayers of the county from ____ percent (__) to ____ percent (__). This tax rate decrease takes effect July 1 of this year.".

(b) A county council may not decrease the county adjusted gross income tax rate if the county or any commission, board, department, or authority that is authorized by statute to pledge the county adjusted gross income tax has pledged the county adjusted gross income tax for any purpose permitted by IC 5–1–14 or any other statute.

(c) Any ordinance adopted under this section takes effect July 1 of the year the ordinance is adopted.

(d) The auditor of a county shall record all votes taken on ordinances presented for a vote under the authority of this section and immediately send a certified copy of the results to the department by certified mail.

(e) Notwithstanding IC 6–3.5–7, and except as provided in subsection (f), a county council that decreases the county adjusted gross income tax rate in a year may not in the same year adopt or increase the county economic development income tax under IC 6–3.5–7.

(f) This subsection applies only to a county having a population of more than one hundred seven thousand (107,000) but less than one hundred eight thousand (108,000). The county council may adopt or increase the county economic development income tax rate under IC 6–3.5–7 in the same year that the county council decreases the county adjusted gross income tax rate if the county economic development income tax rate plus the county adjusted gross income tax rate in effect after the county council decreases the county adjusted gross income tax rate is less than the county adjusted gross income tax rate in effect before the adoption of an ordinance under this section decreasing the rate of the county adjusted gross income tax.

As added by P.L.42–1994, SEC.2. Amended by P.L.10–1997, SEC.13.

Historical and Statutory Notes

P.L.42–1994, Sec.2, emerg. eff. March 18, 1994.

P.L.10–1997, Sec.13, emerg. eff. May 13, 1997, amended the section by inserting "and except as provided in subsection (f)," in Subsec. (e); and adding Subsec. (f).

P.L.10–1997, Sec.40, emerg. eff. May 13, 1997, provides:

"(a) This section applies only to a county having a population of more than one hundred seven thousand (107,000) but less than one hundred eight thousand (108,000).

"(b) The following are hereby legalized and validated:

"(1) Any action taken by a county council in adopting the county economic development income tax, if the action would have been valid under IC 6–3.5–1.1–3.1, as amended by this act.

"(2) Any action of a county in adopting a capital improvement plan under IC 6–3.5–7–15, following the adoption of the county economic development income tax as permitted by IC 6–3.5–1.1–3.1, as amended by this act.

"(c) Notwithstanding IC 6–3.5–7–5, a county council that reduced its county adjusted gross income tax rate in 1997 may adopt an ordinance to impose the county economic development income tax before May 31, 1997."

6–3.5–1.1–3.5 Additional tax for jail and justice center in county with population between 12,600 and 13,000

Sec. 3.5. (a) This section applies only to a county having a population of more than twelve thousand six hundred (12,600) but less than thirteen thousand (13,000).

(b) The county council of a county described in subsection (a) may, by ordinance, determine that additional county adjusted gross income tax revenue is needed in the county to fund the operation and maintenance of a jail and justice center.

(c) Notwithstanding section 2 of this chapter, if the county council adopts an ordinance under subsection (b), the county council may impose the county adjusted gross income tax at a rate of one and three-tenths percent (1.3%) on adjusted gross income. However, a county may impose the county adjusted gross income tax at a rate of one and three-tenths percent (1.3%) for only four (4) years. After the county has imposed the county adjusted gross income tax at a rate of one and three-tenths percent (1.3%) for four (4) years, the rate is reduced to one percent (1%). If the county council imposes the county adjusted gross income tax at a rate of one and three-tenths percent (1.3%), the county council may decrease the rate or rescind the tax in the manner provided under this chapter.

(d) If a county imposes the county adjusted gross income tax at a rate of one and three-tenths percent (1.3%) under this section, the revenue derived from a tax rate of three-tenths percent (0.3%) on adjusted gross income:

(1) shall be paid to the county treasurer;

(2) may be used only to pay the costs of operating and maintaining a jail and justice center; and

(3) may not be considered by the state board of tax commissioners under any provision of IC 6–1.1–18.5, including the determination of the county's maximum permissible property tax levy.

(e) Notwithstanding section 3 of this chapter, the county fiscal body may adopt an ordinance under this section before June 1.
As added by P.L.119–1998, SEC.8.

Historical and Statutory Notes

P.L.119–1998, Sec.9, emerg. eff. March 13, 1998.

6–3.5–1.1–4 Duration of tax; rescission of tax; ordinance

Sec. 4. (a) The county adjusted gross income tax imposed by a county council under this chapter remains in effect until rescinded.

(b) Except as provided in subsection (e), the county council may rescind the county adjusted gross income tax by adopting an ordinance to rescind the tax after January 1 but before June 1 of a year.

(c) Any ordinance adopted under this section takes effect July 1 of the year the ordinance is adopted.

(d) The auditor of a county shall record all votes taken on ordinances presented for a vote under the authority of this section and immediately send a certified copy of the results to the department by certified mail.

(e) A county council may not rescind the county adjusted gross income tax or take any action that would result in a civil taxing unit in the county having a smaller certified share than the certified share to which the civil taxing unit was entitled when the civil taxing unit pledged county adjusted gross income tax if the civil taxing unit or any commission, board, department, or authority that is authorized by statute to pledge county adjusted gross income tax has pledged county adjusted gross income tax for any purpose permitted by IC 5–1–14 or any other statute. The prohibition in this section does not apply if the civil taxing unit pledges legally available revenues to fully replace the civil taxing unit's certified share that has been pledged.

As added by P.L.73–1983, SEC.2. Amended by P.L.35–1990, SEC.14.

Historical and Statutory Notes

P.L.35–1990, Sec.14, emerg. eff. March 20, 1990.

P.L.35–1990, Sec.14, in Subsec. (b), inserted "Except as provided in subsection (e)"; in Subsec. (d), substituted "send a certified copy of" for "certify", and inserted "by certified mail"; and added Subsec. (e).

Formerly:

IC 6–3.5–1–6.
Acts 1973, P.L.50, SEC.7.
Acts 1977, P.L.81, SEC.2.

Library References

Counties ☜190(1).
WESTLAW Topic No. 104.
C.J.S. Counties §§ 227 to 232.

Notes of Decisions

Rescission of tax   1

_____

1. Rescission of tax

After April 21st, 1977, a county could rescind the county adjusted gross income tax authorized by prior law only by passing a rescission ordinance between January 1st and July 1st of the year in which the rescission was to take effect, and rescission of the tax would take effect on July 1st of such year. 1977 Op.Atty.Gen. No. 14.

6–3.5–1.1–5   Tax in effect part of year; computation

Sec. 5.   (a) Except as provided in subsections (b) through (c), if the county adjusted gross income tax is not in effect during a county taxpayer's entire taxable year, then the amount of county adjusted gross income tax that the county taxpayer owes for that taxable year equals the product of:

(1) the amount of county adjusted gross income tax the county taxpayer would owe if the tax had been imposed during the county taxpayer's entire taxable year; multiplied by

(2) a fraction:

(A) The numerator of the fraction equals the number of days during the county taxpayer's taxable year during which the county adjusted gross income tax was in effect.

(B) The denominator of the fraction equals the total number of days in the county taxpayer's taxable year.

(b) If a county taxpayer:

(1) is unemployed for a part of the taxpayer's taxable year;

(2) was not discharged for just cause (as defined in IC 22–4–15–1(e)); and

(3) has no earned income for the part of the taxpayer's taxable year that the tax was in effect;

the county taxpayer's adjusted gross income for the taxable year is reduced by the amount of the taxpayer's earned income for the taxable year.

(c) A taxpayer who qualifies under subsection (b) must file a claim for a refund for the difference between the county adjusted gross income tax owed, as determined under subsection (a), and the tax owed, as determined under subsection (b). A claim for a refund must be on a form approved by the department and include all supporting documentation reasonably required by the department.

As added by P.L.73–1983, SEC.2. Amended by P.L.96–1987, SEC.1.

Historical and Statutory Notes

P.L.96–1987, Sec.1, emerg. eff. retroactive to Jan. 1, 1986, designated Subsec. (a), added exception at the beginning thereof, and added Subsecs. (b) and (c).

Section 15(b) of P.L.96–1987 provides that Section 1 of this act applies to taxable years that begin after Dec. 31, 1985.

Formerly:

IC 6–3.5–1–5.

Acts 1973, P.L.50, SEC.7.

Library References

Counties ⚬193.
WESTLAW Topic No. 104.
C.J.S. Counties § 233.

6–3.5–1.1–6   Credit for taxes imposed by governmental entities outside of state

Sec. 6. (a) Except as provided in subsection (b), if for a particular taxable year a county taxpayer is liable for an income tax imposed by a county, city, town, or other local governmental entity located outside of Indiana, that county taxpayer is entitled to a credit against his county adjusted gross income tax liability for that same taxable year. The amount of the credit equals the amount of tax imposed by the other governmental entity on income derived from sources outside Indiana and subject to the county adjusted gross income tax. However, the credit provided by this section may not reduce a county taxpayer's county adjusted gross income tax liability to an amount less than would have been owed if the income subject to taxation by the other governmental entity had been ignored.

(b) The credit provided by this section does not apply to a county taxpayer to the extent that the other governmental entity provides for a credit to the taxpayer for the amount of county adjusted gross income taxes owed under this chapter.

(c) To claim the credit provided by this section, a county taxpayer must provide the department with satisfactory evidence that he is entitled to the credit.

As added by P.L.73–1983, SEC.2.

Historical and Statutory Notes

Formerly:
  IC 6–3.5–1–11.

Acts 1973, P.L.50, SEC.7.
Acts 1977 (ss), P.L.4, SEC.20.

6–3.5–1.1–7   Credit for the elderly; computation

Sec. 7.   (a) If for a particular taxable year a county taxpayer is, or a county taxpayer and his spouse who file a joint return are, allowed a credit for the elderly or the totally disabled under Section 22 of the Internal Revenue Code, the county taxpayer is, or the county taxpayer and his spouse are, entitled to a credit against his or their county adjusted gross income tax liability for that same taxable year.   The amount of the credit equals the lesser of:

(1) the product of:

(A) his or their credit for the elderly or the totally disabled for that same taxable year; multiplied by

(B) a fraction, the numerator of which is the county adjusted gross income tax rate imposed against the county taxpayer, or the county taxpayer and his spouse, and the denominator of which is fifteen hundredths (0.15); or

(2) the amount of county adjusted gross income tax imposed on the county taxpayer, or the county taxpayer and his spouse.

(b) If a county taxpayer and his spouse file a joint return and are subject to different county adjusted gross income tax rates for the same taxable year, they shall compute the credit under this section by using the formula provided by subsection (a), except that they shall use the average of the two (2) county adjusted gross income tax rates imposed against them as the numerator referred to in subsections (a)(1)(B).

As added by P.L.73–1983, SEC.2.   Amended by P.L.23–1986, SEC.5; P.L.63–1988, SEC.9.

Historical and Statutory Notes

P.L.23–1986, Sec.5, eff. Jan. 1, 1987, in Subsec. (a), inserted "or the totally disabled" twice, in the first sentence and Subd. (1)(A); and substituted subsection "(a)(1)(B)" for "(a)(1)" at the end of Subsec. (b).

Section 23(b) of P.L.23–1986 provides that Section 5 of this act applies to taxable years that begin after Dec. 31, 1986.

P.L. 63–1988, Sec.9, emerg. eff. retroactive to Jan. 1, 1988, substituted in the first sentence of subsec. (a) "Section 22 of the Internal Revenue Code" for "Section 37 of the Internal Revenue Code, as defined by IC 6–3–1–11".

Section 16 of P.L. 63–1988, provides that the amendment to this section "apply to taxable years that begin after December 31, 1987."

Formerly:
IC 6–3.5–1–2.
Acts 1973, P.L.50, SEC.7.
Acts 1977, P.L.2, SEC.31.
Acts 1977, P.L.78, SEC.5.

Library References

Counties ⊆193.
WESTLAW Topic No. 104.
C.J.S. Counties § 233.

6–3.5–1.1–8   Accounts in state general fund; deposits

Sec. 8.   (a) A special account within the state general fund shall be established for each county adopting the county adjusted gross income tax.   Any revenue derived from the imposition of the county adjusted gross income tax by a county shall be deposited in that county's account in the state general fund.

(b) Any income earned on money held in an account under subsection (a) becomes a part of that account.

(c) Any revenue remaining in an account established under subsection (a) at the end of a fiscal year does not revert to the state general fund.
As added by P.L.73–1983, SEC.2.

Historical and Statutory Notes

Formerly:
IC 6–3.5–1–7.
Acts 1973, P.L.50, SEC.7.

Acts 1974, P.L.22, SEC.2.
Acts 1977 (ss), P.L.5, SEC.3.
Acts 1979, P.L.73, SEC.3.

Cross References

Limitations on public school corporation tax levies, property tax law, see IC 6–1.1–19–1 et seq.

Library References

States ⊆122.
WESTLAW Topic No. 360.
C.J.S. States § 224.

6–3.5–1.1–9   Distribution of revenue; certification

Sec. 9.   (a) Revenue derived from the imposition of the county adjusted gross income tax shall, in the manner prescribed by this section, be distributed to the county that imposed it.   The amount to be distributed to a county during an ensuing calendar year equals the amount of county adjusted gross income tax revenue that the department, after reviewing the recommendation of the state budget agency, estimates will be received from that county during the twelve (12) month period beginning July 1 of the immediately preceding calendar year and ending June 30 of the ensuing calendar year.

(b) Before July 2 of each calendar year, the department, after reviewing the recommendation of the state budget agency, shall estimate and certify to the county auditor of each adopting county the amount of county adjusted gross income tax revenue that will be collected from that county during the twelve (12) month period beginning July 1 of that calendar year and ending June 30 of the immediately succeeding calendar year. The amount certified is the county's "certified distribution" for the immediately succeeding calendar year. The amount certified may be adjusted under subsection (c) or (d).

(c) The department may certify to an adopting county an amount that is greater than the estimated twelve (12) month revenue collection if the department, after reviewing the recommendation of the state budget agency, determines that there will be a greater amount of revenue available for distribution from the county's account established under section 8 of this chapter.

(d) The department may certify an amount less than the estimated twelve (12) month revenue collection if the department, after reviewing the recommendation of the state budget agency, determines that a part of those collections need to be distributed during the current calendar year so that the county will receive its full certified distribution for the current calendar year.

As added by P.L.73–1983, SEC.2. Amended by P.L.23–1986, SEC.6.

Historical and Statutory Notes

P.L.23–1986, Sec.6, eff. May 1, 1986, inserted "after reviewing the recommendation of the state budget agency," four times where appearing in Subsecs. (a) to (d).

Formerly:
IC 6–3.5–1–7.

Acts 1973, P.L.50, SEC.7.
Acts 1974, P.L.22, SEC.2.
Acts 1977 (ss), P.L.5, SEC.3.
Acts 1979, P.L.73, SEC.3.

Library References

States ⬡123.
WESTLAW Topic No. 360.
C.J.S. States § 226.

6–3.5–1.1–9.5 Reduction of balance of county's special account

Sec. 9.5. (a) The county council of a county may adopt an ordinance to reduce the required six (6) month balance of that county's special account to a three (3) month balance for that county.

(b) To reduce the balance, a county council must adopt an ordinance. The ordinance must substantially state the following:

"The _____ County council elects to reduce the required county income tax special account balance from a six (6) month balance to a three (3) month balance within ninety (90) days after the adoption of this ordinance.".

(c) Not more than thirty (30) days after adopting an ordinance under subsection (b), the county council shall deliver a copy of the ordinance to the budget agency.

(d) Not later than:

(1) sixty (60) days after a county council adopts an ordinance under subsection (b); and

(2) December 31 of each year;

the budget agency shall make the calculation described in subsection (e). Not later than ninety (90) days after the ordinance is adopted, the budget agency shall make an initial distribution to the county auditor of the amount determined under subsection (e) STEP FOUR. Subsequent distributions needed to distribute any amount in the county income tax special account that exceeds a three (3) month balance, as determined under STEP FOUR of subsection (e), shall be made in January of the ensuing calendar year after the calculation is made.

(e) The budget agency shall make the following calculation:

STEP ONE: Determine the cumulative balance in a county's account established under section 8 of this chapter.

STEP TWO: Divide the amount estimated under section 9(b) of this chapter before any adjustments are made under section 9(c) or 9(d) of this chapter by twelve (12).

STEP THREE: Multiply the STEP TWO amount by three (3).

STEP FOUR: Subtract the amount determined in STEP THREE from the amount determined in STEP ONE.

(f) For the purposes of this subsection and subsection (g), "civil taxing unit" includes a city or town that existed on January 1 of the year in which the distribution is made. The county auditor shall distribute an amount received under subsection (d) to the civil taxing units in the same manner as the certified distribution is distributed and not later than thirty (30) days after the county auditor receives the amount. However, the county auditor shall distribute an amount to a civil taxing unit that does not have a property tax levy in the year of the distribution based on an estimate certified by the state board of tax commissioners. The state board of tax commissioners shall compute and certify an amount for a civil taxing unit that does not have a property tax levy equal to the amount to be distributed multiplied by a fraction in which:

(1) the numerator of the fraction equals an estimate of the budget of that civil taxing unit for:

(A) that calendar year, if the civil taxing unit has adopted a resolution indicating that the civil taxing unit will not adopt a property tax in the ensuing calendar year; or

(B) the ensuing calendar year, if clause (A) does not apply; and

(2) the denominator of the fraction equals the aggregate attributed levies (as defined in IC 6–3.5–1.1–15) of all civil taxing units of that county for that calendar year plus the sum of the budgets estimated under subdivision (1) for each civil taxing unit that does not have a property tax levy in the year of the distribution.

176

(g) The civil taxing units may use the amounts received under subsection (f) for any item for which the particular civil taxing unit's certified shares may be used. The amount distributed shall not be included in the computation under IC 6–1.1–18.5–3.

As added by P.L.58–1996, SEC.1.

Historical and Statutory Notes

P.L.58–1996, Sec.1, emerg. eff. March 15, 1996.

6–3.5–1.1–10   Distribution of revenue; time; use

Sec. 10.   (a) One-half (½) of each adopting county's certified distribution for a calendar year shall be distributed from its account established under section 8 of this chapter to the appropriate county treasurer on May 1 and the other one-half (½) on November 1 of that calendar year.

(b) Except for revenue that must be used to pay the costs of operating a jail and juvenile detention center under section 2.5(d) of this chapter or revenue that must be used to pay the costs of operating and maintaining a jail and justice center under section 3.5(d) of this chapter, distributions made to a county treasurer under subsection (a) shall be treated as though they were property taxes that were due and payable during that same calendar year. The certified distribution shall be distributed and used by the taxing units and school corporations as provided in sections 11 through 15 of this chapter.

(c) All distributions from an account established under section 8 of this chapter shall be made by warrants issued by the auditor of the state to the treasurer of the state ordering the appropriate payments.

As added by P.L.73–1983, SEC.2.   Amended by P.L.119–1998, SEC.9.

Historical and Statutory Notes

P.L.119–1998, Sec.9, amended the section by inserting "Except for revenue that must be used to pay the costs of operating a jail and juvenile detention center under section 2.5(d) of this chapter or revenue that must be used to pay the costs of operating and maintaining a jail and justice center under section 3.5(d) of this chapter," in Subsec. (b).

Formerly:

IC 6–3.5–1–7.
Acts 1973, P.L.50, SEC.7.
Acts 1974, P.L.22, SEC.2.
Acts 1977 (ss), P.L.5, SEC.3.
Acts 1979, P.L.73, SEC.3.

Library References

States ☞123.
WESTLAW Topic No. 360.
C.J.S. States § 226.

6–3.5–1.1–11   Allocation of certified distribution

Sec. 11.   (a) Except for revenue that must be used to pay the costs of operating a jail and juvenile detention center under section 2.5(d) of this chapter or revenue that must be used to pay the costs of operating and maintaining a jail and justice center under section 3.5(d) of this chapter, the certified distribution received by a county treasurer shall, in the manner prescribed in this section, be allocated, distributed, and used by the civil taxing units and school corporations of the county as certified shares and property tax replacement credits.

(b) Before August 2 of each calendar year, each county auditor shall determine the part of the certified distribution for the next succeeding calendar year that will be allocated as property tax replacement credits and the part that will be allocated as certified shares. The percentage of a certified distribution that will be allocated as property tax replacement credits or as certified shares depends upon the county adjusted gross income tax rate for resident county taxpayers in effect on August 1 of the calendar year that precedes the year in which the certified distribution will be received. The percentages are set forth in the following table:

COUNTY ADJUSTED GROSS INCOME TAX RATE	PROPERTY TAX REPLACEMENT CREDITS	CERTIFIED SHARES
0.5%	50%	50%
0.75%	33 1/3%	66 2/3%
1%	25%	75%

(c) The part of a certified distribution that constitutes property tax replacement credits shall be distributed as provided under sections 12, 13, and 14 of this chapter.

(d) The part of a certified distribution that constitutes certified shares shall be distributed as provided by section 15 of this chapter.

As added by P.L.73–1983, SEC.2. Amended by P.L.119–1998, SEC.10.

Historical and Statutory Notes

P.L.119–1998, Sec.10, amended the section by inserting "Except for revenue that must be used to pay the costs of operating a jail and juvenile detention center under section 2.5(d) of this chapter or revenue that must be used to pay the costs of operating and maintaining a jail and justice center under section 3.5(d) of this chapter," in Subsec. (a).

Formerly:

IC 6–3.5–1–7.
Acts 1973, P.L.50, SEC.7.
Acts 1974, P.L.22, SEC.2.
Acts 1977 (ss), P.L.5, SEC.3.
Acts 1979, P.L.73, SEC.3.

Library References

States ☞123.
WESTLAW Topic No. 360.
C.J.S. States § 226.

6–3.5–1.1–12 Allocation of property tax replacement credits; amount; formula; certification

Sec. 12.   (a) The part of a county's certified distribution for a calendar year that is to be used as property tax replacement credits shall be allocated by the county auditor among the civil taxing units and school corporations of the county.

(b) Except as provided in section 13 of this chapter, the amount of property tax replacement credits that each civil taxing unit and school corporation in a county is entitled to receive during a calendar year equals the product of:

(1) that part of the county's certified distribution that is dedicated to providing property tax replacement credits for that same calendar year; multiplied by

(2) a fraction:

(A) The numerator of the fraction equals the sum of the total property taxes being collected by the civil taxing unit or school corporation during that calendar year, plus with respect to a civil taxing unit, the amount of federal revenue sharing funds and certified shares received by it during that calendar year to the extent that they are used to reduce its property tax levy below the limit imposed by IC 6–1.1–18.5 for that same calendar year.

(B) The denominator of the fraction equals the sum of the total property taxes being collected by all civil taxing units and school corporations, plus the amount of federal revenue sharing funds and certified shares received by all civil taxing units in the county to the extent that they are used to reduce the civil taxing units' property tax levies below the limits imposed by IC 6–1.1–18.5 for that same calendar year.

(c) The state board of tax commissioners shall provide each county auditor with the amount of property tax replacement credits that each civil taxing unit and school corporation in the auditor's county is entitled to receive. The county auditor shall then certify to each civil taxing unit and school corporation the amount of property tax replacement credits it is entitled to receive (after adjustment made under section 13 of this chapter) during that calendar year. The county auditor shall also certify these distributions to the county treasurer.
As added by P.L.73–1983, SEC.2.

Historical and Statutory Notes

Formerly:
IC 6–3.5–1–7.
Acts 1973, P.L.50, SEC.7.

Acts 1974, P.L.22, SEC.2.
Acts 1977 (ss), P.L.5, SEC.3.
Acts 1979, P.L.73, SEC.3.

Library References

States ⊷123.
WESTLAW Topic No. 360.
C.J.S. States § 226.

6–3.5–1.1–13 Allocation of replacement credits; tax levy not due in same year as credit distribution; amount; formula; adjustments

Sec. 13. (a) If a civil taxing unit or school corporation of an adopting county does not impose a property tax levy that is first due and payable in a calendar year in which property tax replacement credits are being distributed, that civil taxing unit or school corporation is entitled to receive a proportion of the property tax replacement credits to be distributed within the county. The amount such a civil taxing unit or school corporation is entitled to receive during that calendar year equals the product of:

(1) the part of the county's certified distribution that is to be used to provide property tax replacement credits during that calendar year; multiplied by

(2) a fraction:

(A) The numerator of the fraction equals the budget of that civil taxing unit or school corporation for that calendar year.

(B) The denominator of the fraction equals the aggregate budgets of all civil taxing units and school corporations of that county for that calendar year.

(b) If for a calendar year a civil taxing unit or school corporation is allocated a proportion of a county's property tax replacement credits by this section then the formula used in section 12 of this chapter to determine all other civil taxing units' and school corporations' property tax replacement credits shall be changed for that same year by reducing the amount dedicated to providing property tax replacement credits by the amount of property tax replacement credits allocated under this section for that same calendar year. The state board of tax commissioners shall make any adjustments required by this section and provide them to the appropriate county auditors.

As added by P.L.73–1983, SEC.2.

Historical and Statutory Notes

Formerly:
IC 6–3.5–1–7.
Acts 1973, P.L.50, SEC.7.

Acts 1974, P.L.22, SEC.2.
Acts 1977 (ss), P.L.5, SEC.3.
Acts 1979, P.L.73, SEC.3.

Library References

States ☞123.
WESTLAW Topic No. 360.
C.J.S. States § 226.

6–3.5–1.1–14 Replacement credits; determination limited; multiple county taxing units; effect upon budget, property tax rates, and school funds

Sec. 14. (a) In determining the amount of property tax replacement credits civil taxing units and school corporations of a county are entitled to receive during a calendar year, the state board of tax commissioners shall consider only property taxes imposed on tangible property that was assessed in that county.

(b) If a civil taxing unit or a school corporation is located in more than one (1) county and receives property tax replacement credits from one (1) or more of the counties, then the property tax replacement credits received from each county shall be used only to reduce the property tax rates that are imposed within the county that distributed the property tax replacement credits.

(c) A civil taxing unit shall treat any property tax replacement credits that it receives or is to receive during a particular calendar year as a part of its property tax levy for that same calendar year for purposes of fixing its budget and for purposes of the property tax levy limits imposed by IC 6–1.1–18.5.

(d) A school corporation shall treat any property tax replacement credits that the school corporation receives or is to receive during a particular calendar year as a part of its property tax levy for its general fund, debt service fund, capital projects fund, transportation fund, and special education preschool fund in proportion to the levy for each of these funds for that same calendar year for purposes of fixing its budget and for purposes of the property tax levy limits imposed by IC 6–1.1–19. A school corporation shall allocate the property tax replacement credits described in this subsection to all five (5) funds in proportion to the levy for each fund.

As added by P.L.73–1983, SEC.2. Amended by P.L.25–1995, SEC.56.

Historical and Statutory Notes

P.L.25–1995, Sec.56, amended the section by deleting "or school corporation" following "A civil taxing unit" in Subsec. (c), deleting "IC 6–1.1–19 or" prior to "IC 6–1.1–18.5" in Subsec. (c), and adding Subsec. (d).

Acts 1973, P.L.50, SEC.7.
Acts 1974, P.L.22, SEC.2.
Acts 1977 (ss), P.L.5, SEC.3.
Acts 1979, P.L.73, SEC.3.

Formerly:
IC 6–3.5–1–7.

Library References

States ⚷123.
WESTLAW Topic No. 360.
C.J.S. States § 226.

6–3.5–1.1–15   Attributed levy; allocation of certified shares

Sec. 15.   (a) As used in this section, "attributed levy" of a civil taxing unit means the sum of:

(1) the ad valorem property tax levy of the civil taxing unit that is currently being collected at the time the allocation is made; plus

(2) the current ad valorem property tax levy of any special taxing district, authority, board, or other entity formed to discharge governmental services or functions on behalf of or ordinarily attributable to the civil taxing unit; plus

(3) the amount of federal revenue sharing funds and certified shares that were used by the civil taxing unit (or any special taxing district, authority, board, or other entity formed to discharge governmental services or functions on behalf of or ordinarily attributable to the civil taxing unit) to

reduce its ad valorem property tax levies below the limits imposed by IC 6–1.1–18.5; plus

(4) in the case of a county, an amount equal to the property taxes imposed by the county in 1999 for the county's welfare fund and welfare administration fund.

(b) The part of a county's certified distribution that is to be used as certified shares shall be allocated only among the county's civil taxing units. Each civil taxing unit of a county is entitled to receive a percentage of the certified shares to be distributed in the county equal to the ratio of its attributed levy to the total attributed levies of all civil taxing units of the county.

(c) The local government tax control board established by IC 6–1.1–18.5–11 shall determine the attributed levies of civil taxing units that are entitled to receive certified shares during a calendar year. If the ad valorem property tax levy of any special taxing district, authority, board, or other entity is attributed to another civil taxing unit under subsection (b)(2), then the special taxing district, authority, board, or other entity shall not be treated as having an attributed levy of its own. The local government tax control board shall certify the attributed levy amounts to the appropriate county auditor. The county auditor shall then allocate the certified shares among the civil taxing units of his county.

(d) Certified shares received by a civil taxing unit shall be treated as additional revenue for the purpose of fixing its budget for the calendar year during which the certified shares will be received. The certified shares may be allocated to or appropriated for any purpose, including property tax relief or a transfer of funds to another civil taxing unit whose levy was attributed to the civil taxing unit in the determination of its attributed levy.

As added by P.L.73–1983, SEC.2. Amended by P.L.273–1999, SEC.69.

Historical and Statutory Notes

P.L.273–1999, Sec.69, eff. Jan. 1, 2000, added Subsec. (a)(4).

Formerly:
  IC 6–3.5–1–7.
  IC 6–3.5–1–8.

Acts 1973, P.L.50, SEC.7.
Acts 1974, P.L.22, SEC.2.
Acts 1977, P.L.81, SEC.3.
Acts 1977 (ss), P.L.5, SECS.3, 4.
Acts 1979, P.L.73, SEC.3.

Library References

Words and Phrases (Perm.Ed.)
States ☞123.

WESTLAW Topic No. 360.
C.J.S. States § 226.

6–3.5–1.1–16   County residency and place of business or employment; determination

Sec. 16. (a) For purposes of this chapter, an individual shall be treated as a resident of the county in which he:

(1) maintains a home if the individual maintains only one (1) in Indiana;

(2) if subdivision (1) does not apply, is registered to vote;

(3) if neither subdivision (1) or (2) applies, registers his personal automobile; or

(4) if neither subdivision (1), (2), or (3) applies, spends the majority of his time spent in Indiana during the taxable year in question.

(b) The residence or principal place of business or employment of an individual is to be determined on January 1 of the calendar year in which the individual's taxable year commences. If an individual changes the location of his residence or principal place of employment or business to another county in Indiana during a calendar year, his liability for county adjusted gross income tax is not affected.

(c) Notwithstanding subsection (b), if an individual becomes a county taxpayer for purposes of IC 36–7–27 during a calendar year because the individual:

(1) changes the location of the individual's residence to a county in which the individual begins employment or business at a qualified economic development tax project (as defined in IC 36–7–27–9); or

(2) changes the location of the individual's principal place of employment or business to a qualified economic development tax project and does not reside in another county in which the county adjusted gross income tax is in effect;

the individual's adjusted gross income attributable to employment or business at the qualified economic development tax project is taxable only by the county containing the qualified economic development tax project.

As added by P.L.73–1983, SEC.2. Amended by P.L.42–1994, SEC.3.

Historical and Statutory Notes

P.L.42–1994, Sec.3, added Subsec. (c) relating to individuals who become county taxpayers for purposes of IC 36–7–27.

Acts 1973, P.L.50, SEC.7.
Acts 1977 (ss), P.L.4, SEC.19.

Formerly:
    IC 6–3.5–1–9.

Library References

Counties ☜189 to 194.
WESTLAW Topic No. 104.
C.J.S. Counties §§ 227 to 232.

6–3.5–1.1–17   Reciprocity agreements between local governmental entities

Sec. 17. (a) The county council of any adopting county may adopt an ordinance to enter into reciprocity agreements with the taxing authority of any city, town, municipality, county, or other similar local government entity of any other state. Such a reciprocity agreement must provide that the income of resident county taxpayers is exempt from income taxation by the other local governmental entity to the extent that income of the residents of the other local governmental entity is exempt from the county adjusted gross income tax in the adopting county.

(b) A reciprocity agreement entered into under subsection (a) may not become effective until it is also made effective in the other local governmental entity that is a party to the agreement.

(c) The form and effective date of any reciprocity agreement described in this section must be approved by the department.

As added by P.L.73–1983, SEC.2.

Historical and Statutory Notes

Formerly:
IC 6–3.5–1–11.

Acts 1973, P.L.50, SEC.7.
Acts 1977 (ss), P.L.4, SEC.20.

Library References

Counties ☜190(1).
WESTLAW Topic No. 104.
C.J.S. Counties § 227 to 232.

6–3.5–1.1–18 Adjusted gross income tax provisions; applicability; employer's annual withholding report

Sec. 18. (a) Except as otherwise provided in this chapter, all provisions of the adjusted gross income tax law (IC 6–3) concerning:

(1) definitions;

(2) declarations of estimated tax;

(3) filing of returns;

(4) remittances;

(5) incorporation of the provisions of the Internal Revenue Code;

(6) penalties and interest;

(7) exclusion of military pay credits for withholding; and

(8) exemptions and deductions;

apply to the imposition, collection, and administration of the tax imposed by this chapter.

(b) The provisions of IC 6–3–1–3.5(a)(6), IC 6–3–3–3, IC 6–3–3–5, and IC 6–3–5–1 do not apply to the tax imposed by this chapter.

(c) Notwithstanding subsections (a) and (b), each employer shall report to the department the amount of withholdings attributable to each county. This report shall be submitted annually along with the employer's annual withholding report.

As added by P.L.73–1983, SEC.2. Amended by P.L.82–1983, SEC.9; P.L.23–1986, SEC.7; P.L.57–1997, SEC.4.

Historical and Statutory Notes

P.L. 82–1983, Sec.9, emerg. eff. March 15, 1983, in Subsec. (a)(8), substituted "exemptions and deductions" for "duties of the secretary of state and treasurer of state".

P.L. 23–1986, Sec.7, eff. Jan. 1, 1987, added Subsec. (c).

Section 23(b) of P.L.23–1986 provides that Section 7 of this act applies to taxable years that begin after Dec. 31, 1986.

P.L.57–1997, Sec.4, emerg. eff. retroactive to Jan. 1, 1997, amended the section by substitut-

ing "IC 6–3–1–3.5(a)(6)," for "IC 6–3–1–3.5(a)(5)," in Subsec. (b).

Formerly:
IC 6–3.5–1–10.
Acts 1973, P.L.50, SEC.7.
Acts 1979, P.L.69, SEC.2.
Acts 1980, P.L.54, SEC.8.

Library References

Counties ☞189 to 194.
WESTLAW Topic No. 104.
C.J.S. Counties §§ 227 to 232.

6–3.5–1.1–19   Citation to prior law; continued effect of rules

Sec. 19.   (a) If a provision of the prior county adjusted gross income tax law (IC 6–3.5–1) has been replaced in the same form or in a restated form, by a provision of this chapter, then a citation to the provision of the prior law shall be construed as a citation to the corresponding provision of this chapter.

(b) Any rule adopted under, and applicable to, the prior county adjusted gross income tax law (IC 6–3.5–1) continues in effect under this chapter if the provisions under which it was adopted and to which it was applicable were replaced, in the same or restated form, by corresponding provisions of this chapter.
As added by P.L.73–1983, SEC.2.

Library References

Counties ☞189 to 194.
WESTLAW Topic No. 104.
C.J.S. Counties §§ 227 to 232.

6–3.5–1.1–21 [1]   Annual report; county adjusted gross income tax accounts

Sec. 21.   Before February 1 of each year, the department shall submit a report to each county treasurer indicating the balance in the county's adjusted gross income tax account as of the end of the preceding year.
As added by P.L.23–1986, SEC.8.

[1] IC 6–3.5–1.1 contains no section 20.

Historical and Statutory Notes

P.L.23–1986, Sec.8, eff. May 1, 1986, added this section.

6–3.5–1.1–22   Obligations or leases entered into by civil taxing unit; public sale

Sec. 22.   Notwithstanding any other law, if a civil taxing unit desires to issue obligations or enter into leases payable wholly or in part by the county adjusted gross income tax, the obligations of the civil taxing unit or any lessor may be sold at public sale in accordance with IC 5–1–11 or at negotiated sale.
As added by P.L.35–1990, SEC.15.

Historical and Statutory Notes

P.L.35–1990, Sec.15, emerg. eff. March 20, 1990.

Chapter 2 .

Employment Tax

6–3.5–2–1   Definitions

Sec. 1. As used in this chapter:

(1) "Agency" means a board, commission, division, bureau, committee, authority, military body, college, university, or other instrumentality.

(2) "Compensation" means gross income from services rendered as that term is defined by section 61(a) of the Internal Revenue Code.[1]

(3) "Employee" means any individual permitted to work for remuneration by any employer, but excluding any individual performing:

(i) agricultural labor as that term is defined in IC 22–2–2–3(m);

(ii) domestic service solely on a daily basis in a private home;

(iii) newspaper carrier delivery or distribution service if the individual is under the age of eighteen (18) years; or

(iv) services in the employ of one's father, mother, son, daughter, or spouse.

(4) "Full time employee" means an employee who received compensation from employment of at least nine hundred dollars ($900) in any calendar quarter of a year from an employer who is subject to the tax imposed by this chapter; "full time employee" shall include a self-employed person who receives compensation from employment of at least nine hundred dollars ($900) in any calendar quarter of a year.

(5) "Employer" means any natural person, receiver, administrator, executor, trustee, trustee in bankruptcy, trust, estate, firm, partnership (general or

limited), joint venture, company, limited liability company, or any form of unincorporated business, corporation (foreign or domestic, for profit or not-for-profit) who or which is doing business within the county.

(6) "Doing business within the county" means employing individuals to work in whole or in part, within the county and one (1) of the following:

(i) maintaining a fixed place of business in the county;

(ii) owning or leasing property within the county;

(iii) maintaining a stock of tangible personal property within the county;

(iv) employing or loaning capital or property within the county; or

(v) employing persons as employees or independent contractors, to solicit business within the county.

(7) "Person" includes a sole proprietorship, partnership, association, corporation, limited liability company, fiduciary, or individual.

(8) "Principally employed in the county" means an employee who devotes more than fifty percent (50%) of the time which he works for his employer to services which he performs in the taxing county.

(9) "Political subdivision" means a county, township, town, city, separate municipal corporation, special taxing district, or public school corporation.

(10) "County council" includes a city-county council of a consolidated city.

As amended by Acts 1981, P.L.11, SEC.32; P.L.2–1987, SEC.22; P.L.8–1993, SEC.91.

[1] 26 U.S.C.A. § 61(a).

Historical and Statutory Notes

Acts 1981, P.L. 11, § 32, in Subd. (3)(i), deleted "1971" following "IC"; in Subd. (10), deleted "established under IC1971, 18–4" following "consolidated city"; and made other nonsubstantive grammatical changes.

Acts 1981, P.L. 11 was a part of a codification, revision and rearrangement of laws relating to local government.

P.L.2–1987, Sec.22, amended this section emergency effective retroactive to Jan. 1, 1987.

P.L.2–1987 provides in Section 54 that this act applies to taxable years beginning after Dec. 31, 1986.

P.L.8–1993, Sec.91, inserted "limited liability company" in the definitions of "employer" and "person".

Formerly:

Acts 1975, P.L.62, SEC.1.

6–3.5–2–2   Counties over 400,000 but less than 700,000; ordinance imposing tax; maximum rate

Sec. 2.   Before July 1 of any year, the county council of a county having a population of more than four hundred thousand (400,000) but less than seven hundred thousand (700,000) may adopt an ordinance to impose an employment tax on each employer and employee described in section 3 of this chapter.   The county council may impose the employment tax at a rate not to exceed fifty cents ($0.50) per employee per month.   Any tax so imposed shall be paid by the employer for each full-time employee and by each such employee at the same rate. A self-employed person shall be subject to tax only as an employee. No other county may adopt an ordinance to impose an employment tax under this chapter.

As amended by Acts 1979, P.L.74, SEC.1; P.L.12–1992, SEC.28.

Historical and Statutory Notes

Acts 1979, P.L. 74, § 1, emerg. eff. March 1, 1979, in the first sentence, inserted "with a population of not less than 500,000 and not more than 600,000 according to the last decennial census," and added the final sentence.

P.L.12–1992, Sec.28, emerg. eff. April 1, 1992, revised population descriptions to accommodate the 1990 federal census.

Formerly:

Acts 1975, P.L.62, SEC.1.

Library References

Taxation ⬯111.1.
WESTLAW Topic No. 371.
C.J.S. Social Security and Public Welfare §§ 165, 192, 194.

I.L.E. Taxation § 66.

6–3.5–2–3   Employers and employees subject to tax

Sec. 3. If the county council adopts an ordinance to impose the employment tax, employers and employees are subject to the tax if:

(1) in the case of an employer, he employs at least one (1) full time employee who is principally employed in the county during any portion of a month after the date such ordinance is adopted; and

(2) in the case of an employee, he is principally employed in the county by an employer described in clause (1) of this section during any portion of a month after the date the ordinance is adopted.

Historical and Statutory Notes

Formerly:
Acts 1975, P.L.62, SEC.1.

Library References

Taxation ⬯111.8.
WESTLAW Topic No. 371.
C.J.S. Social Security and Public Welfare § 175.

I.L.E. Taxation §§ 20, 21.

6–3.5–2–4   Persons exempt from tax

Sec. 4. The following persons are exempt from the employment tax:

(1) the United States;

(2) an agency of the United States;

(3) this state;

(4) an agency of this state;

(5) a political subdivision of this state; and

(6) a taxpayer described in IC 6–2.1–3–19, IC 6–2.1–3–20, IC 6–2.1–3–21, and IC 6–2.1–3–22.

However, employees of such persons are not exempt from the employment tax.

As amended by Acts 1981, P.L.77, SEC.16.

Historical and Statutory Notes

Acts 1981, P.L. 77, § 16, emerg. eff. April 29, 1981, rewrote Cl. (6) which prior thereto read:

"(6) a person described in IC1971, 6–2–1–7(i)."

Acts 1981, P.L. 77 was a part of a codification of the laws relating to gross income tax.

Formerly:
Acts 1975, P.L.62, SEC.1.

Cross References

Fraternal or social organizations, business leagues, gross income tax exemptions, see IC 6–2.1–3–21.
Fraternities, sororities or student cooperative housing associations, gross income tax exemptions, see IC 6–2.1–3–19.
Hospitals, labor unions, religious institutions, schools, pension trusts, gross income tax exemptions, see IC 6–2.1–3–22.
Religious, charitable, scientific, literary, educational or civic organizations, gross income tax exemptions, see IC 6–2.1–3–20.

Library References

Taxation ⚮111.21.
WESTLAW Topic No. 371.
C.J.S. Social Security and Public Welfare § 191.

I.L.E. Taxation §§ 37, 38.

6–3.5–2–5   Rescission of tax

Sec. 5.   Before July 1 of any year, the county council may adopt an ordinance to rescind the employment tax. If the county council adopts such an ordinance, the tax does not apply after December 31 of the year the ordinance is adopted.

However, if the adoption of the employment tax is conditioned upon any other county adopting the tax, the county council may rescind the tax before it becomes effective if the other county does not adopt the tax.

Historical and Statutory Notes

Formerly:
Acts 1975, P.L.62, SEC.1.

6–3.5–2–6   Increasing or decreasing tax

Sec. 6.   Before July 1 of any year, the county council may adopt an ordinance to increase or decrease the employment tax rate. The new tax rate shall become effective on January 1 of the year immediately following the year in which the ordinance is adopted.

Historical and Statutory Notes

Formerly:
  Acts 1975, P.L.62, SEC.1.

6–3.5–2–7 Copies of ordinances

Sec. 7. If a county council adopts an ordinance to impose, rescind, or change the rate of the employment tax, the county council shall send a copy of the ordinance to the county auditor and to the county treasurer.

Historical and Statutory Notes

Formerly:
  Acts 1975, P.L.62, SEC.1.

6–3.5–2–8 Quarterly payments

Sec. 8. An employer described in section 3 of this chapter shall pay employment tax for each calendar quarter equal to the sum of the following:

(1) for each month during which the employer employed at least one (1) full time employee who was principally employed in the county during that month, the tax for such month equals the total number of full time employees principally employed within the county during that month multiplied by the current tax rate; and

(2) for each employee described in clause (1) of this section the employer is required to withhold the tax imposed on the employee for that month under this chapter. The employer shall withhold the tax from the employee, as an agent for the county. Notwithstanding the amount of employment tax collected from its employees, each employer is liable to the county for the tax imposed on its employees under this chapter. Every employer and every officer, employee or member of the employer who is responsible for withholding the taxes from employees is personally liable for the taxes. The taxes to be withheld by the employer constitute a trust fund in the hands of the employer and are owned by the county.

Historical and Statutory Notes

Formerly:
  Acts 1975, P.L.62, SEC.1.

Library References

Taxation ⏀515.
WESTLAW Topic No. 371.
C.J.S. Social Security and Public Welfare §§ 203, 207, 208.

C.J.S. Taxation §§ 607, 618, 630, 1082.
I.L.E. Taxation §§ 106, 108.

6–3.5–2–9 Filing returns; recordkeeping requirement

Sec. 9. Each employer described in section 3 of this chapter shall pay the total employment tax due for each calendar quarter to the county treasurer within thirty (30) days after the end of the quarter. Concurrently with the payment of the tax, the employer shall file an employment tax return with the county treasurer on a form prescribed by the state board of accounts. Each employer within the county shall maintain for a period of five (5) years adequate records to determine its tax liability for a calendar quarter. Upon request of the county treasurer, the Indiana department of revenue shall conduct an audit of an employer's employment tax records.

Historical and Statutory Notes

Formerly:
  Acts 1975, P.L.62, SEC.1.

6–3.5–2–10   County mass transportation fund; deposit of revenue

Sec. 10. The county treasurer shall deposit all employment tax revenues in a fund to be known as the "_____ county mass transportation fund". Money which is credited to a county's mass transportation fund may be used only to purchase, establish, operate, repair, or maintain a public mass transportation system. The county council may, in the manner provided by law, appropriate money from the fund to a public corporation which is authorized to purchase, establish, operate, repair, or maintain such a system if the system is located, either entirely or partially, within the county.

Historical and Statutory Notes

Formerly:
  Acts 1975, P.L.62, SEC.1.

Library References

Counties ☜155.
WESTLAW Topic No. 104.
C.J.S. Counties § 197.

6–3.5–2–11   Tokens for public passenger transportation

Sec. 11. The county council may establish a method of[1] provide to each taxpayer at the time the employment tax is paid, tokens, coupons or indicia, equal to the tax paid, which are acceptable for passenger transportation on any transportation facility operated by or under contract with the county or public transportation authority.

[1.] So in enrolled Indiana Code. Probably should read "to."

Historical and Statutory Notes

Formerly:
  Acts 1975, P.L.62, SEC.1.

6–3.5–2–12   Estimated tax revenues

Sec. 12. On or before August 1st of each year, the auditor of a county which has adopted the employment tax shall provide the county council with an estimate of the employment tax revenues to be credited to the county mass transportation fund during the next calendar year. The county shall show the estimated employment tax revenues in its budget estimate for that calendar year.

Historical and Statutory Notes

Formerly:
  Acts 1975, P.L.62, SEC.1.

6–3.5–2–13   Interest penalties

  Sec. 13.   If an employer fails to pay all or any part of the employment tax due for a calendar quarter within the time prescribed by section 9 of this chapter, he shall pay interest on the unpaid amount at the rate of twelve percent (12%) per year.

Historical and Statutory Notes

Formerly:
  Acts 1975, P.L.62, SEC.1.

Library References

Taxation ☞901.
WESTLAW Topic No. 371.

C.J.S. Taxation § 1207.
I.L.E. Taxation § 126.

Chapter 3

Occupation Income Tax

6–3.5–3–1 to 6–3.5–3–14   Repealed

(Repealed by P.L.28–1997, SEC.31.)

Historical and Statutory Notes

  Former IC 6–3.5–3–1 to 6–3.5–3–14 related to occupation income tax.

Formerly:
  Acts 1975, P.L.63, SEC.1.

Acts 1976, P.L.17, SECS.1, 2.
Acts 1977, P.L. 82, SECS.1, 2.
P.L.73–1983, SEC.13.
P.L.8–1989, SECS.27 to 30.

Chapter 4

County Motor Vehicle Excise Surtax

6–3.5–4–1   Definitions

Sec. 1.   As used in this chapter:

"Branch office" means a branch office of the bureau of motor vehicles.

"County council" includes the city-county council of a county that contains a consolidated city of the first class.

"Motor vehicle" means a vehicle which is subject to the annual license excise tax imposed under IC 6–6–5.

"Net annual license excise tax" means the tax due under IC 6–6–5 after the application of the adjustments and credits provided by that chapter.

"Surtax" means the annual license excise surtax imposed by a county council under this chapter.

As added by Acts 1980, P.L.10, SEC.4.

Historical and Statutory Notes

Acts 1980, P.L. 10, § 4, emerg. eff. March 3,
1980, added this chapter.

Cross References

Amount of service charge on each surtax collection, see IC 9–29–3–1.
Motor vehicle excise tax, see IC 6–6–5–1 et seq.

6–3.5–4–2   Imposition and rate of surtax; application of tax; wheel tax; duration

Sec. 2.   (a) The county council of any county may, subject to the limitation imposed by subsection (c), adopt an ordinance to impose an annual license excise surtax at the same rate or amount on each motor vehicle listed in subsection (b) that is registered in the county.   The county council may impose the surtax either:

(1) at a rate of not less than two percent (2%) nor more than ten percent (10%); or

(2) at a specific amount of at least seven dollars and fifty cents ($7.50) and not more than twenty-five dollars ($25).

However, the surtax on a vehicle may not be less than seven dollars and fifty cents ($7.50). The county council shall state the surtax rate or amount in the ordinance which imposes the tax.

(b) The license excise surtax applies to the following vehicles:

(1) Passenger vehicles.

(2) Motorcycles.

(3) Trucks with a declared gross weight that does not exceed eleven thousand (11,000) pounds.

(c) The county council may not adopt an ordinance to impose the surtax unless it concurrently adopts an ordinance under IC 6–3.5–5 to impose the wheel tax.

(d) Notwithstanding any other provision of this chapter or IC 6–3.5–5, ordinances adopted by a county council before June 1, 1983, to impose or change the annual license excise surtax and the annual wheel tax in the county remain in effect until the ordinances are amended or repealed under this chapter or IC 6–3.5–5.

As added by Acts 1980, P.L.10, SEC.4.   Amended by P.L.85–1983, SEC.1;   P.L. 255–1996, SEC.1.

Historical and Statutory Notes

P.L. 85–1983, Sec.1, eff. June 1, 1983, rewrote the section, which had read:

"(a) After January 1 but before July 1 of any year, the county council of any county may, subject to the limitation imposed by subsection (b), adopt an ordinance to impose an annual license excise surtax on each motor vehicle registered in the county. The county council may impose the surtax at a rate of not less than two percent (2%) nor more than ten percent (10%). The county council shall state the initial surtax rate in the ordinance which imposes the tax.

"(b) The county council may not adopt an ordinance to impose the surtax unless it concur-

rently adopts an ordinance under IC 6–3.5–5 to impose the wheel tax."

P.L.255–1996, Sec.1, emerg. eff. retroactive to July 1, 1996, amended the section by inserting "or amount" and "either" in Subsec. (a); designating Subsec. (a)91); adding Subsec. (a)(2); inserting "or amount" in the final sentence in Subsec. (a); and making other nonsubstantive changes.

Governor's veto of P.L.255–1996 of the 1996 Regular Session was overridden by the General Assembly on Jan. 30, 1997.

Cross References

Distressed road loans, availability, see IC 8–14–8–4.

Library References

Automobiles ⇌25, 46.
WESTLAW Topic No. 48A.

C.J.S. Motor Vehicles §§ 60, 61, 137.
I.L.E. Taxation §§ 183 to 185, 191 to 200.

6–3.5–4–3   Motor vehicles subject to tax

Sec. 3.   If a county council adopts an ordinance imposing the surtax after December 31 but before July 1 of the following year, a motor vehicle is subject to the tax if it is registered in the county after December 31 of the year in which the ordinance is adopted. If a county council adopts an ordinance imposing the surtax after June 30 but before the following January 1, a motor vehicle is subject to the tax if it is registered in the county after December 31 of the year following the year in which the ordinance is adopted. However, in the first year the surtax is effective, the surtax does not apply to the registration of a motor vehicle for the registration year that commenced in the calendar year preceding the year the surtax is first effective.

As added by Acts 1980, P.L.10, SEC.4. Amended by P.L.85–1983, SEC.2; P.L.43–1994, SEC.1.

Historical and Statutory Notes

P.L. 85–1983, Sec.2, eff. June 1, 1983, inserted "after December 31 but before July 1 of the following year" in the first sentence; and added the second sentence.

P.L.43–1994, Sec.1, emerg. eff. retroactive to Jan. 1, 1994, added the third sentence.

Library References

Automobiles ☞45.
WESTLAW Topic No. 48A.

C.J.S. Motor Vehicles § 136.
I.L.E. Taxation §§ 183 to 185, 191 to 200.

6–3.5–4–4   Rescission of surtax and wheel tax

Sec. 4. (a) After January 1 but before July 1 of any year, the county council may, subject to the limitations imposed by subsection (b), adopt an ordinance to rescind the surtax. If the county council adopts such an ordinance, the surtax does not apply to a motor vehicle registered after December 31 of the year the ordinance is adopted.

(b) The county council may not adopt an ordinance to rescind the surtax unless it concurrently adopts an ordinance under IC 6–3.5–5 to rescind the wheel tax. In addition, the county council may not adopt an ordinance to rescind the surtax if any portion of a loan obtained by the county under IC 8–14–8 is unpaid, or if any bonds issued by the county under IC 8–14–9 are outstanding.

As added by Acts 1980, P.L.10, SEC.4. Amended by Acts 1981, P.L.88, SEC.1.

Historical and Statutory Notes

Acts 1981, P.L. 88, § 1, emerg. eff. May 5, 1981, in the first sentence of Subsec. (a), substituted "limitations" for "limitation", and added the second sentence in Subsec. (b).

Cross References

Distressed roads, financial assistance to counties, see IC 8–14–8–1 et seq.
Local county road and bridge board, see IC 8–14–9–2 et seq.

Library References

Taxation ☞1205.
WESTLAW Topic No. 371.

C.J.S. Taxation § 1231.
I.L.E. Taxation §§ 183 to 185, 191 to 200.

6–3.5–4–5   Increase or decrease of surtax; rate

Sec. 5.   (a) The county council may, subject to the limitations imposed by subsection (b), adopt an ordinance to increase or decrease the surtax rate or amount.   The new surtax rate or amount must be within the range of rates or amounts prescribed by section 2 of this chapter.   A new rate or amount that is established by an ordinance that is adopted after December 31 but before July 1 of the following year applies to motor vehicles registered after December 31 of the year in which the ordinance to change the rate or amount is adopted.   A new rate or amount that is established by an ordinance that is adopted after June 30 but before January 1 of the following year applies to motor vehicles registered after December 31 of the year following the year in which the ordinance is adopted.

(b) The county council may not adopt an ordinance to decrease the surtax rate or amount under this section if any portion of a loan obtained by the county under IC 8–14–8 is unpaid, or if any bonds issued by the county under IC 8–14–9 are outstanding.

As added by Acts 1980, P.L.10, SEC.4.   Amended by Acts 1981, P.L.88, SEC.2; P.L.85–1983, SEC.3; P.L.255–1996, SEC.2.

Historical and Statutory Notes

Acts 1981, P.L. 88, § 2, emerg. eff. May 5, 1981, designated Subsec. (a); in the first sentence in Subsec. (a), inserted "subject to the limitations imposed by subsection (b);" and added Subsec. (b).

P.L. 85–1983, Sec.3, eff. June 1, 1983, rewrote Subsec. (a), which had read:

"(a) After January 1 but before July 1 of any year, the county council may, subject to the limitations imposed by subsection (b), adopt an ordinance to increase or decrease the surtax

rate.   The new surtax rate must be within the range of rates prescribed by section 2 of this chapter, and it applies to motor vehicles registered after December 31 of the year in which the ordinance to change the rate is adopted."

P.L.255–1996, Sec.2, emerg. eff. retroactive to July 1, 1996, amended the section by inserting "or amount" and "or amounts" throughout.

Governor's veto of P.L.255–1996 of the 1996 Regular Session was overridden by the General Assembly on Jan. 30, 1997.

Cross References

Distressed roads, financial assistance to counties, see IC 8–14–8–1 et seq.
Local county road and bridge board, see IC 8–14–9–2 et seq.

Library References

Automobiles ⊜25, 46.
WESTLAW Topic No. 48A.

C.J.S. Motor Vehicles §§ 60, 61, 137.
I.L.E. Taxation §§ 183 to 185, 191 to 200.

6–3.5–4–6   Adopted ordinance; transmittal of copy to commissioner of bureau of motor vehicles

Sec. 6.   If a county council adopts an ordinance to impose, rescind, or change the rate or amount of the surtax, the county council shall send a copy of the ordinance to the commissioner of the bureau of motor vehicles.

As added by Acts 1980, P.L.10, SEC.4.   Amended by P.L.255–1996, SEC.3.

Historical and Statutory Notes

P.L.255–1996, Sec.3, emerg. eff. retroactive to July 1, 1996, amended the section by inserting "or amount".

Governor's veto of P.L.255–1996 of the 1996 Regular Session was overridden by the General Assembly on Jan. 30, 1997.

6–3.5–4–7   Registration of motor vehicle; surtax; amount; collection

Sec. 7. A person may not register a motor vehicle in a county that has adopted the surtax unless the person pays the surtax due, if any, to the bureau of motor vehicles. The amount of the surtax due equals the greater of seven dollars and fifty cents ($7.50), the amount established under section 2 of this chapter, or the product of:

   (1) the amount determined under section 7.3 of this chapter for the vehicle, as adjusted under section 7.4 of this chapter; multiplied by

   (2) the surtax rate in effect at the time of registration.

The bureau of motor vehicles shall collect the surtax due, if any, at the time a motor vehicle is registered. However, the bureau may utilize its branch offices to collect the surtax.

As added by Acts 1980, P.L.10, SEC.4. Amended by P.L.85–1983, SEC.4; P.L.33–1990, SEC.11; P.L.255–1996, SEC.4; P.L.11–1999, SEC.1.

Historical and Statutory Notes

P.L. 85–1983, Sec.4, eff. June 1, 1983, inserted "greater of seven dollars and fifty cents ($7.50) or the" in the second sentence.

P.L.33–1990, Sec.11, eff. Jan. 1, 1991, substituted "(1) the amount determined under section 7.3 of this chapter for the vehicle" for "(i) the net annual license excise tax imposed with respect to the registration of that vehicle"; redesignated Subsec. (ii) as Subsec. (2); and made a gender related change.

P.L.255–1996, Sec.4, emerg. eff. retroactive to July 1, 1996, amended the section by inserting "the amount established under section 2 of this chapter,".

Governor's veto of P.L.255–1996 of the 1996 Regular Session was overridden by the General Assembly on Jan. 30, 1997.

P.L.11–1999, Sec.1, eff. Jan. 1, 2000, amended the section by inserting "as adjusted under section 7.4 of this chapter;" after "vehicle" in Subsec. (1).

Cross References

Registration of motor vehicles, see IC 9–18–2–29 et seq.

Library References

Automobiles ⬤45, 46, 48.
WESTLAW Topic No. 48A.
C.J.S. Motor Vehicles §§ 136, 137, 142, 145.

I.L.E. Taxation §§ 117, 183 to 185, 191 to 200.

6–3.5–4–7.3   Surtax; amount; schedule

Sec. 7.3. (a) The amount of surtax imposed by rate under this chapter shall be based upon the classification and age of a vehicle as determined by the bureau of motor vehicles under IC 6–6–5, in accordance with the schedule set out in subsection (b).

(b) The schedule to be used in determining the amount to be used in section 7 of this chapter is as follows:

Year of Manufacture	I	II	III	IV	V
1st	$ 12	$ 36	$ 60	$ 96	$132
2nd	12	30	51	84	114
3rd	12	27	42	72	96
4th	12	24	33	60	78
5th	12	18	24	48	66
6th	12	12	18	36	54
7th	12	12	12	24	42
8th	12	12	12	18	24
9th	12	12	12	12	12
10th and thereafter	12	12	12	12	12

Year of Manufacture	VI	VII	VIII	IX	X
1st	$168	$ 206	$246	$300	$344
2nd	147	184	220	268	298
3rd	126	154	186	230	260
4th	104	127	156	196	224
5th	82	101	128	164	191
6th	63	74	98	130	157
7th	49	60	75	104	129
8th	30	40	54	80	106
9th	18	21	34	40	50
10th and thereafter	12	12	12	12	12

Year of Manufacture	XI	XII	XIII	XIV	XV
1st	$413	$ 500	$600	$700	$812
2nd	358	434	520	607	705
3rd	312	378	450	529	614
4th	269	326	367	456	513
5th	229	278	300	389	420
6th	188	228	242	319	338
7th	155	188	192	263	268
8th	127	129	129	181	181
9th	62	62	62	87	87
10th and thereafter	21	26	30	36	42

Year of Manufacture	XVI	XVII
1st	$938	$1,063
2nd	814	922
3rd	709	795
4th	611	693
5th	521	591
6th	428	483
7th	353	383
8th	258	258
9th	125	125
10th and thereafter	49	55

As added by P.L.33–1990, SEC.12. Amended by P.L.255–1996, SEC.5.

Historical and Statutory Notes

P.L.33–1990, Sec.12, eff. Jan. 1, 1991.

P.L.255–1996, Sec.5, emerg. eff. retroactive to July 1, 1996, amended the section by inserting "rate under" in Subsec. (a).

Governor's veto of P.L.255–1996 of the 1996 Regular Session was overridden by the General Assembly on Jan. 30, 1997.

6–3.5–4–7.4 Surtax adjustment

Sec. 7.4. (a) If a vehicle has been acquired or brought into Indiana, or for any other reason becomes subject to registration after the regular annual registration date in the year on or before which the owner of the vehicle is required under the motor vehicle registration laws of Indiana to register vehicles, the amount of surtax computed under section 7.3 of this chapter shall be reduced in the same manner as the excise tax is reduced under IC 6–6–5–7.

(b) The owner of a vehicle who sells the vehicle in a year in which the owner has paid the surtax imposed by this chapter is entitled to receive a credit that is calculated in the same manner and subject to the same requirements as the credit for the excise tax under IC 6–6–5–7.

(c) If the name of the owner of a vehicle is legally changed and the change has caused a change in the owner's annual registration date, the surtax liability of the owner shall be adjusted in the same manner as excise taxes are adjusted under IC 6–6–5–7.

As added by P.L.11–1999, SEC.2.

Historical and Statutory Notes

P.L.11–1999, Sec.2, eff. Jan. 1, 2000.

6–3.5–4–8 Collections by branch office; disposition

Sec. 8. The surtax collected by a branch office shall be deposited daily by the branch manager in a separate account in a depository designated by the state board of finance.

As added by Acts 1980, P.L.10, SEC.4.

Library References

Automobiles ⊙48.
WESTLAW Topic No. 48A.
C.J.S. Motor Vehicles §§ 142, 145.

6–3.5–4–9 Collections by branch office; remittance to county treasurer; report

Sec. 9. On or before the tenth day of the month following the month in which surtax is collected at a branch office, the branch office manager shall remit the surtax to the county treasurer of the county that imposed the surtax. Concurrently with the remittance, the branch office manager shall file a surtax collections report with the county treasurer and the county auditor. The branch manager shall prepare the report on forms prescribed by the state board of accounts.

As added by Acts 1980, P.L.10, SEC.4.

Library References

Automobiles ⚖48.
WESTLAW Topic No. 48A.
C.J.S. Automobiles §§ 142, 145.

6–3.5–4–10 Collections by branch office; report to bureau of motor vehicles

Sec. 10. Each branch office manager shall report surtax collections, if any, to the bureau of motor vehicles at the same time that registration fees are reported.

As added by Acts 1980, P.L.10, SEC.4.

Library References

Automobiles ⚖48.
WESTLAW Topic No. 48A.
C.J.S. Motor Vehicles §§ 142, 145.

6–3.5–4–11 Collections by bureau of motor vehicles; remittance to county treasurer; report to county auditor

Sec. 11. If surtax is collected directly by the bureau of motor vehicles, instead of at a branch office, the commissioner of the bureau shall:

(1) remit the surtax to, and file a surtax collections report with, the appropriate county treasurer; and

(2) file a surtax collections report with the county auditor;

in the same manner and at the same time that a branch office manager is required to remit and report under section 9 of this chapter.

As added by Acts 1980, P.L.10, SEC.4.

Library References

Automobiles ⚖48, 49.   I.L.E. Taxation §§ 118, 183 to 185, 191 to
WESTLAW Topic No. 48A.   200.
C.J.S. Motor Vehicles §§ 142, 143, 145.

6–3.5–4–12 Appropriation of money derived from surtax

Sec. 12. In the case of a county that contains a consolidated city, the city-county council may appropriate money derived from the surtax to the department of transportation established by IC 36–3–5–4 for use by the department under law. The city-county council may not appropriate money derived from the surtax for any other purpose.

As added by Acts 1980, P.L.10, SEC.4. Amended by Acts 1982, P.L.33, SEC.7.

Historical and Statutory Notes

Acts 1982, P.L.33, Sec.7, emerg. eff. Feb. 24, 1982, in the first sentence deleted "of the first class" following "consolidated city," and substi-tuted "city-county" for "county," "IC 36–3–5–4" for "IC 18–4–10" and "law" for "that chapter"; and in the second sentence, substituted "city-county" for "county."

The 1982 act was a part of a codification, revision and rearrangement of laws relating to local government.

Library References

Automobiles ⊕49.
WESTLAW Topic No. 48A.

C.J.S. Motor Vehicles § 143.
I.L.E. Taxation §§ 183 to 185, 191 to 200.

6–3.5–4–13   Surtax fund; allocation; distribution; use

Sec. 13.   (a) In the case of a county that does not contain a consolidated city of the first class, the county treasurer shall deposit the surtax revenues in a fund to be known as the "_____ County Surtax Fund".

(b) Before the twentieth day of each month, the county auditor shall allocate the money deposited in the county surtax fund during that month among the county and the cities and the towns in the county.   The county auditor shall allocate the money to counties, cities, and towns under IC 8–14–2–4(c)(1) through IC 8–14–2–4(c)(3).

(c) Before the twenty-fifth day of each month, the county treasurer shall distribute to the county and the cities and towns in the county the money deposited in the county surtax fund during that month.   The county treasurer shall base the distribution on allocations made by the county auditor for that month under subsection (b).

(d) A county, city, or town may only use the surtax revenues it receives under this section to construct, reconstruct, repair, or maintain streets and roads under its jurisdiction.

As added by Acts 1980, P.L.10, SEC.4.   Amended by P.L.85–1983, SEC.5.

Historical and Statutory Notes

P.L. 85–1983, Sec.5, eff. June 1, 1983, re-wrote Subsec. (b), which had read:

"(b) Before the twentieth day of each month, the county auditor shall allocate the money deposited in the county surtax fund during that month among the county and the cities and the towns in the county.   The county auditor shall allocate to each city and town an amount equal to the product of the amount of money deposit-ed in the fund during that month, multiplied by a fraction.   The numerator of the fraction is the number of miles of roads and streets under the jurisdiction of the city or town, and the denomi-nator of the fraction is the total miles of roads and streets under the jurisdiction of the county and the cities and towns in the county.   The county auditor shall allocate the remainder of the money deposited in the fund during that month to the county."

Library References

Automobiles ⊕48.
WESTLAW Topic No. 48A.

C.J.S. Motor Vehicles §§ 142, 145.
I.L.E. Taxation §§ 183 to 185, 191 to 200.

6–3.5–4–14   Estimate of revenues; distribution

Sec. 14.   (a) On or before August 1 of each year, the auditor of a county that contains a consolidated city of the first class and that has adopted the surtax shall provide the county council with an estimate of the surtax revenues to be received by the county during the next calendar year.   The county shall show the estimated surtax revenues in its budget estimate for the calendar year.

(b) On or before August 1 of each year, the auditor of a county that does not contain a consolidated city of the first class and that has adopted the surtax shall provide the county and each city and town in the county with an estimate of the surtax revenues to be distributed to that unit during the next calendar year. The county, city, or town shall show the estimated surtax revenues in its budget estimate for the calendar year.

As added by Acts 1980, P.L.10, SEC.4.

Library References

Automobiles ⬅49.
WESTLAW Topic No. 48A.

C.J.S. Motor Vehicles § 143.
I.L.E. Taxation §§ 183 to 185, 191 to 200.

6–3.5–4–15   Service charge for surtax

Sec. 15. Each license branch shall collect the service charge prescribed under IC 9–29 for the surtax collected with respect to each vehicle registered by that branch.

As added by Acts 1980, P.L.10, SEC.4. Amended by P.L.42–1986, SEC.3; P.L.2–1991, SEC.37.

Historical and Statutory Notes

P.L. 42–1986, Sec.3, eff. July 1, 1988, rewrote the section, which had read:

"As compensation for collecting the surtax imposed under this chapter, each branch office manager is entitled to retain fifteen cents ($.15) of the surtax collected with respect to each

vehicle registered by his branch office. The branch office manager shall withhold this compensation from the surtax collections that he deposits and remits under sections 8 and 9 of this chapter."

P.L.2–1991, Sec.37, substituted "IC 9–29" for "IC 9–1.5".

Library References

Automobiles ⬅48.
WESTLAW Topic No. 48A.

C.J.S. Motor Vehicles §§ 142, 145.
I.L.E. Taxation § 118.

6–3.5–4–16   Violations; offense

Sec. 16. (a) The owner of a motor vehicle who knowingly registers the vehicle without paying surtax imposed under this chapter with respect to that registration commits a Class B misdemeanor.

(b) An employee of the bureau of motor vehicles, an employee of a branch office, or the manager of a branch office who recklessly issues a registration on any motor vehicle without collecting surtax imposed under this chapter with respect to that registration commits a Class B misdemeanor.

As added by Acts 1980, P.L.10, SEC.4.

Cross References

Penalty for class B misdemeanor, see IC 35–50–3–3.

Chapter 5

County Wheel Tax

6–3.5–5–1   Definitions

Sec. 1. As used in this chapter:

"Branch office" means a branch office of the bureau of motor vehicles.

"Bus" has the meaning set forth in IC 9–13–2–17(a).

"County council" includes the city-county council of a county that contains a consolidated city of the first class.

"Political subdivision" has the meaning set forth in IC 34–6–2–110.

"Recreational vehicle" has the meaning set forth in IC 9–13–2–150.

"Semitrailer" has the meaning set forth in IC 9–13–2–164(a).

"State agency" has the meaning set forth in IC 34–4–16.5–2.

"Tractor" has the meaning set forth in IC 9–13–2–180.

"Trailer" has the meaning set forth in IC 9–13–2–184(a).

"Truck" has the meaning set forth in IC 9–13–2–188(a).

"Wheel tax" means the tax imposed under this chapter.

As added by Acts 1980, P.L.10, SEC.5. Amended by P.L.3–1989, SEC.40; P.L.2–1991, SEC.38; P.L.1–1998, SEC.79.

Historical and Statutory Notes

Acts 1980, P.L. 10, § 5 emerg. eff. March 3, 1980, added this chapter.

P.L.3–1989, Sec.40, emerg. eff. May 5, 1989, made corrective changes.

P.L.2–1991, Sec.38, made Title 9 citation changes throughout the section.

P.L.1–1998, Sec.79, amended the section by substituting "IC 34–6–2–110" for "IC 34–4–

16.5–2" in the definition o f"Political subdivision".

Cross References

Amount of service charge on each wheel tax collection, see IC 9–29–3–2.
Bureau of motor vehicles, definitions, see IC 9–13–2–1.

Library References

Words and Phrases (Perm.Ed.)

6–3.5–5–2 Imposition of tax; annual license excise tax; rate

Sec. 2. (a) The county council of any county may, subject to the limitation imposed by subsection (b), adopt an ordinance to impose an annual wheel tax on each vehicle which:

(1) is included in one (1) of the classes of vehicles listed in section 3 of this chapter;

(2) is not exempt from the wheel tax under section 4 of this chapter; and

(3) is registered in the county.

(b) The county council of a county may not adopt an ordinance to impose the wheel tax unless it concurrently adopts an ordinance under IC 6–3.5–4 to impose the annual license excise surtax.

(c) The county council may impose the wheel tax at a different rate for each of the classes of vehicles listed in section 3 of this chapter. In addition, the county council may establish different rates within the classes of buses, semitrailers, trailers, tractors, and trucks based on weight classifications of those vehicles that are established by the bureau of motor vehicles for use throughout Indiana. However, the wheel tax rate for a particular class or weight classification of vehicles may not be less than five dollars ($5) and may not exceed forty dollars ($40). The county council shall state the initial wheel tax rates in the ordinance that imposes the tax.

As added by Acts 1980, P.L.10, SEC.5. Amended by P.L.85–1983, SEC.6.

Historical and Statutory Notes

P.L. 85–1983, Sec.6, eff. June 1, 1983, in Subsec. (a), deleted "After January 1 but before July 1 of any year" from the beginning of the first sentence; and, in Subsec. (c), inserted the second sentence, and in the third sentence, inserted "or weight classification."

Library References

Automobiles ⚖21.
WESTLAW Topic No. 48A.

C.J.S. Motor Vehicles § 59.
I.L.E. Taxation § 60.

6–3.5–5–3 Vehicles subject to tax

Sec. 3. The wheel tax applies to the following classes of vehicles:
(1) buses;

(2) recreational vehicles;

(3) semitrailers;

(4) tractors;

(5) trailers; and

(6) trucks.

As added by Acts 1980, P.L.10, SEC.5.

Library References

Automobiles ☜45.   C.J.S. Motor Vehicles § 136.
WESTLAW Topic No. 48A.   I.L.E. Taxation §§ 25, 26.

6–3.5–5–4   Exempt vehicles

Sec. 4.   A vehicle is exempt from the wheel tax imposed under this chapter if the vehicle is:

(1) owned by this state;

(2) owned by a state agency of this state;

(3) owned by a political subdivision of this state;

(4) subject to the annual license excise surtax imposed under IC 6–3.5–4; or

(5) a bus owned and operated by a religious or nonprofit youth organization and used to haul persons to religious services or for the benefit of their members.

As added by Acts 1980, P.L.10, SEC.5.

Library References

Automobiles ☜45.   C.J.S. Motor Vehicles § 136.
WESTLAW Topic No. 48A.   I.L.E. Taxation § 51.

6–3.5–5–5   Registration of vehicles

Sec. 5.   If a county council adopts an ordinance imposing the wheel tax after December 31 but before July 1 of the following year, a vehicle described in section 2(a) of this chapter is subject to the tax if it is registered in the county after December 31 of the year in which the ordinance is adopted.   If a county council adopts an ordinance imposing the wheel tax after June 30 but before the following January 1, a vehicle described in section 2(a) of this chapter is subject to the tax if it is registered in the county after December 31 of the year following the year in which the ordinance is adopted.   However, in the first year the tax is effective, the tax does not apply to the registration of a motor vehicle for the registration year that commenced in the calendar year preceding the year the tax is first effective.

As added by Acts 1980, P.L.10, SEC.5.   Amended by P.L.85–1983, SEC.7; P.L.43–1994, SEC.2.

Historical and Statutory Notes

P.L. 85–1983, Sec.7, eff. June 1, 1983, insert-   P.L.43–1994, Sec.2, emerg. eff. retroactive to
ed "after December 31 but before July 1 of the   Jan. 1, 1994, added the third sentence.
following year" in the first sentence; and added
the second sentence.

Library References

Automobiles ☞45.   C.J.S. Motor Vehicles § 136.
WESTLAW Topic No. 48A.   I.L.E. Taxation §§ 25, 26.

6–3.5–5–6   Rescission of wheel tax and annual license excise surtax

Sec. 6.   (a) After January 1 but before July 1 of any year, the county council may, subject to the limitations imposed by subsection (b), adopt an ordinance to rescind the wheel tax.   If the county council adopts such an ordinance, the wheel tax does not apply to a vehicle registered after December 31 of the year the ordinance is adopted.

(b) The county council may not adopt an ordinance to rescind the wheel tax unless it concurrently adopts an ordinance under IC 6–3.5–4 to rescind the annual license excise surtax.   In addition, the county council may not adopt an ordinance to rescind the wheel tax if any portion of a loan obtained by the county under IC 8–14–8 is unpaid, or if any bonds issued by the county under IC 8–14–9 are outstanding.

As added by Acts 1980, P.L.10, SEC.5.   Amended by Acts 1981, P.L.88, SEC.3.

Historical and Statutory Notes

Acts 1981, P.L. 88, § 3, emerg. eff. May 5,   for "limitation" in the first sentence; and added
1981, in Subsec. (a), substituted "limitations"   the second sentence in Subsec. (b).

Cross References

Distressed roads, financial assistance to counties, see IC 8–14–8–1 et seq.
Local county road and bridge board, see IC 8–14–9–2 et seq.

6–3.5–5–7   Increase or decrease of tax; rates

Sec. 7.   (a) The county council may, subject to the limitations imposed by subsection (b), adopt an ordinance to increase or decrease the wheel tax rates. The new wheel tax rates must be within the range of rates prescribed by section 2 of this chapter.   New rates that are established by an ordinance that is adopted after December 31 but before July 1 of the following year apply to vehicles registered after December 31 of the year in which the ordinance to change the rates is adopted.   New rates that are established by an ordinance that is adopted after June 30 but before July 1 of the following year apply to motor vehicles registered after December 31 of the year following the year in which the ordinance is adopted.

(b) The county council may not adopt an ordinance to decrease the wheel tax rate under this section if any portion of a loan obtained by the county under IC

8–14–8 is unpaid, or if any bonds issued by the county under IC 8–14–9 are outstanding.

As added by Acts 1980, P.L.10, SEC.5. Amended by Acts 1981, P.L.88, SEC.4; P.L.85–1983, SEC.8.

Historical and Statutory Notes

Acts 1981, P.L. 88, § 5, emerg. eff. May 5, 1981, designated Subsec. (a); in the first sentence of Subsec. (a), inserted "subject to the limitations imposed by subsection (b);" and added Subsec. (b).

P.L. 85–1983, Sec.8, eff. June 1, 1983, rewrote Subsec. (a), which had read:

"(a) After January 1 but before July 1 of any year, the county council may, subject to the limitations imposed by subsection (b), adopt an ordinance to increase or decrease the wheel tax rates. The new wheel tax rates must be within the range of rates prescribed by section 2 of this chapter, and they apply to vehicles registered after December 31 of the year in which the ordinance to change the rates is adopted."

Cross References

Distressed roads, financial assistance to counties, see IC 8–14–8–1 et seq.
Local county road and bridge board, see IC 8–14–9–2 et seq.

6–3.5–5–8 Adopted ordinance; transmittal of copy to commissioner of bureau of motor vehicles

Sec. 8. If a county council adopts an ordinance to impose, rescind, or change the rates of the wheel tax, the county council shall send a copy of the ordinance to the commissioner of the bureau of motor vehicles.

As added by Acts 1980, P.L.10, SEC.5.

6–3.5–5–8.5 Credit upon sale of vehicle

Sec. 8.5. (a) Every owner of a vehicle for which the wheel tax has been paid for the owner's registration year is entitled to a credit if during that registration year the owner sells the vehicle. The amount of the credit equals the wheel tax paid by the owner for the vehicle that was sold. The credit may only be applied by the owner against the wheel tax owed for a vehicle that is purchased during the same registration year.

(b) An owner of a vehicle is not entitled to a refund of any part of a credit that is not used under this section.

As added by P.L.86–1983, SEC.1.

Historical and Statutory Notes

P.L. 86–1983, Sec.1, emerg. eff. Jan. 1, 1983, added this section.

Library References

Automobiles ⬥50.
WESTLAW Topic No. 48A.
C.J.S. Motor Vehicles § 142.

6–3.5–5–9   Registration of motor vehicle; wheel tax; amount; collection

Sec. 9. A person may not register a vehicle in a county which has adopted the wheel tax unless he pays the wheel tax due, if any, to the bureau of motor vehicles. The amount of the wheel tax due is based on the wheel tax rate, for that class of vehicle, in effect at the time of registration. The bureau of motor vehicles shall collect the wheel tax due, if any, at the time a motor vehicle is registered. However, the bureau may utilize its branch offices to collect the wheel tax.

As added by Acts 1980, P.L.10, SEC.5.

Cross References

Registration of motor vehicles, see IC 9–18–2–29 et seq.

Library References

Automobiles ☞46.
WESTLAW Topic No. 48A.

C.J.S. Motor Vehicles § 137.
I.L.E. Taxation §§ 25, 26.

6–3.5–5–10   Collections by branch office; disposition

Sec. 10. The wheel tax collected by a branch office shall be deposited daily by the branch manager in a separate account in a depository designated by the state board of finance.

As added by Acts 1980, P.L.10, SEC.5.

Library References

Automobiles ☞48.
WESTLAW Topic No. 48A.
C.J.S. Motor Vehicles §§ 142, 145.

6–3.5–5–11   Collections by branch office; remittance to county treasurer; report

Sec. 11. On or before the tenth day of the month following the month in which wheel tax is collected at a branch office, the branch office manager shall remit the wheel tax to the county treasurer of the county that imposed the wheel tax. Concurrently with the remittance, the branch office manager shall file a wheel tax collections report with the county treasurer and the county auditor. The branch manager shall prepare the report on forms prescribed by the state board of accounts.

As added by Acts 1980, P.L.10, SEC.5.

Library References

Automobiles ☞48.
WESTLAW Topic No. 48A.

C.J.S. Motor Vehicles §§ 142, 145.
I.L.E. Taxation § 120.

6–3.5–5–12   Collections by branch office; report to bureau of motor vehicles

Sec. 12.   Each branch office manager shall report wheel tax collections, if any, to the bureau of motor vehicles at the same time that registration fees are reported.
As added by Acts 1980, P.L.10, SEC.5.

Library References

Automobiles ☞48.   C.J.S. Motor Vehicles §§ 142, 145.
WESTLAW Topic No. 48A.   I.L.E. Taxation § 120.

6–3.5–5–13   Collections by bureau of motor vehicles; remittance to county treasurer; report to county auditor

Sec. 13.   If the wheel tax is collected directly by the bureau of motor vehicles, instead of at a branch office, the commissioner of the bureau shall:

(1) remit the wheel tax to, and file a wheel tax collections report with, the appropriate county treasurer; and

(2) file a wheel tax collections report with the county auditor;

in the same manner and at the same time that a branch office manager is required to remit and report under section 11 of this chapter.
As added by Acts 1980, P.L.10, SEC.5.

Library References

Automobiles ☞48.   C.J.S. Motor Vehicles §§ 142, 145.
WESTLAW Topic No. 48A.   I.L.E. Taxation § 120.

6–3.5–5–14   Appropriation of money derived from wheel tax

Sec. 14.   (a) In the case of a county that contains a consolidated city, the city-county council may appropriate money derived from the wheel tax to:

(1) the department of transportation established by IC 36–3–5–4 for use by the department under law; or

(2) an authority established under IC 36–7–23.

(b) The city-county council may not appropriate money derived from the wheel tax for any other purpose.
As added by Acts 1980, P.L.10, SEC.5.   Amended by Acts 1982, P.L.33, SEC.8; P.L.346–1989(ss), SEC.1.

Historical and Statutory Notes

Acts 1982, P.L.33, Sec.8, emerg. eff. Feb. 24, 1982, in the first sentence, deleted "of the first class" following "consolidated city," and substituted "city-county" for "county," "IC 36–3–5–4" for "IC 18–4–10" and "law" for "that chap-ter"; and in the second sentence, substituted "city-county" for "county."

The 1982 act was a part of a codification, revision and rearrangement of laws relating to local government.

P.L.346–1989(ss), Sec.1, inserted internal des- | authorities established under chapter 36–7–23
ignations and added Subsec. (a)(2), relating to | (Multiple County Infrastructure Authorities).

Library References

Automobiles ☞49.
WESTLAW Topic No. 48A.
C.J.S. Motor Vehicles § 143.

6–3.5–5–15   Wheel tax fund; allocation; distribution; use

Sec. 15.   (a) In the case of a county that does not contain a consolidated city, the county treasurer shall deposit the wheel tax revenues in a fund to be known as the "County Wheel Tax Fund".

(b) Before the twentieth day of each month, the county auditor shall allocate the money deposited in the county wheel tax fund during that month among the county and the cities and the towns in the county.   The county auditor shall allocate the money to counties, cities, and towns under IC 8–14–2–4(c)(1) through IC 8–14–2–4(c)(3).

(c) Before the twenty-fifth day of each month, the county treasurer shall distribute to the county and the cities and towns in the county the money deposited in the county wheel tax fund during that month.   The county treasurer shall base the distribution on allocations made by the county auditor for that month under subsection (b).

(d) A county, city, or town may only use the wheel tax revenues it receives under this section:

(1) to construct, reconstruct, repair, or maintain streets and roads under its jurisdiction; or

(2) as a contribution to an authority established under IC 36–7–23.

As added by Acts 1980, P.L.10, SEC.5.   Amended by P.L.85–1983, SEC.9; P.L. 346–1989(ss), SEC.2.

Historical and Statutory Notes

P.L.85–1983, Sec.9, eff. June 1, 1983, rewrote the second sentence of Subsec. (b), which prior thereto read:

"The county auditor shall allocate to each city and town an amount equal to the product of the amount of money deposited in the fund during that month, multiplied by a fraction."

P.L.346–1989(ss), Sec.2, deleted "of the first class," following "a consolidated city," in Subsec. (a); and, in Subsec. (d), designated (d)(1), inserted "or " thereafter, and added (d)(2).

Library References

Automobiles ☞49.
WESTLAW Topic No. 48A.
C.J.S. Motor Vehicles § 143.

6–3.5–5–16   Estimate of revenues; distribution

Sec. 16.   (a) On or before August 1 of each year, the auditor of a county that contains a consolidated city of the first class and that has adopted the wheel tax shall provide the county council with an estimate of the wheel tax revenues to be received by the county during the next calendar year. The county shall show the estimated wheel tax revenues in its budget estimate for the calendar year.

(b) On or before August 1 of each year, the auditor of a county that does not contain a consolidated city of the first class and that has adopted the wheel tax shall provide the county and each city and town in the county with an estimate of the wheel tax revenues to be distributed to that unit during the next calendar year. The county, city, or town shall show the estimated wheel tax revenues in its budget estimate for the calendar year.

As added by Acts 1980, P.L.10, SEC.5.

Library References

Automobiles ⟋49.
WESTLAW Topic No. 48A.
C.J.S. Motor Vehicles § 143.

6–3.5–5–17 Service charge

Sec. 17. Each license branch shall collect the service charge prescribed under IC 9–29 for the wheel tax collected with respect to each vehicle registered by that branch.

As added by Acts 1980, P.L.10, SEC.5. Amended by P.L.42–1986, SEC.4; P.L.2–1991, SEC.39.

Historical and Statutory Notes

P.L. 42–1986, Sec.4, eff. July 1, 1988, rewrote the section, which had read:

"As compensation for collecting the wheel tax imposed under this chapter, each branch office manager is entitled to retain fifteen cents ($.15) of the wheel tax collected with respect to each

vehicle registered by his branch office. The branch office manager shall withhold this compensation from the wheel tax collections that he deposits and remits under sections 10 and 11 of this chapter."

P.L.2–1991, Sec.39, substituted "IC 9–29" for "IC 9–1.5".

Library References

Counties ⟋190.
WESTLAW Topic No. 104.

C.J.S. Counties §§ 227, 230 to 232.
I.L.E. Taxation § 118.

6–3.5–5–18 Violations; offense

Sec. 18. (a) The owner of a vehicle who knowingly registers the vehicle without paying wheel tax imposed under this chapter with respect to that registration commits a Class B misdemeanor.

(b) An employee of the bureau of motor vehicles, an employee of a branch office, or the manager of a branch office who recklessly issues a registration on any vehicle without collecting wheel tax imposed under this chapter with respect to that registration commits a Class B misdemeanor.

As added by Acts 1980, P.L.10, SEC.5.

Cross References

Penalty for class B misdemeanors, see IC 35–50–3–3.

Chapter 6

County Option Income Tax

212

Cross References

Professional sports development area, covered taxes defined, see IC 36–7–31–6.

6–3.5–6–1   Definitions

Sec. 1. As used in this chapter:

"Adjusted gross income" has the same definition that the term is given in IC 6–3–1–3.5. However, in the case of a county taxpayer who is not treated as a resident county taxpayer of a county, the term includes only adjusted gross income derived from his principal place of business or employment.

"Civil taxing unit" means any entity, except a school corporation, that has the power to impose ad valorem property taxes. The term does not include a solid waste management district that is not entitled to a distribution under section 1.3 of this chapter. However, in the case of a county in which a consolidated city is located, the consolidated city, the county, all special taxing districts, special service districts, included towns (as defined in IC 36–3–1–7), and all other political subdivisions except townships, excluded cities (as defined in IC 36–3–1–7), and school corporations shall be deemed to comprise one (1) civil taxing unit whose fiscal body is the fiscal body of the consolidated city.

"County income tax council" means a council established by section 2 of this chapter.

"County taxpayer", as it relates to a particular county, means any individual:

(1) who resides in that county on the date specified in section 20 of this chapter; or

(2) who maintains his principal place of business or employment in that county on the date specified in section 20 of this chapter and who does not reside on that same date in another county in which the county option income tax, the county adjusted income tax, or the county economic development income tax is in effect.

"Department" refers to the Indiana department of state revenue.

"Fiscal body" has the same definition that the term is given in IC 36–1–2–6.

"Resident county taxpayer", as it relates to a particular county, means any county taxpayer who resides in that county on the date specified in section 20 of this chapter.

"School corporation" has the same definition that the term is given in IC 6–1.1–1–16.

As added by P.L.44–1984, SEC.14. Amended by P.L.23–1986, SEC.9; P.L.22–1988, SEC.4; P.L.96–1995, SEC.3.

Historical and Statutory Notes

P.L.44–1984, Sec.14, emerg. eff. March 7, 1984, added this chapter.

P.L.23–1986, Sec.9, eff. Jan. 1, 1987, deleted "within that county" following employment at the end of the definition of "Adjusted gross income".

Section 23(b) of P.L.23–1986 provides that Section 9 of this act applies to taxable years that begin after Dec. 31, 1986.

P.L.22–1988, Sec.4, emerg. eff. retroactive to Jan. 1, 1988, and by section 10 applicable to "taxable years that begin after December 31, 1987" inserted in Cl. (2) of the definition of county taxpayer "or the county economic development income tax".

P.L.22–1988, Sec.10, emerg. eff. March 3, 1988, provides:

"Sections 3, 4, and 6 of this act apply to taxable years that begin after December 31, 1987."

P.L.96–1995, Sec.3, emerg. eff. May 5, 1995, amended the section by inserting the second sentence in the paragraph defining a "civil taxing unit."

P.L.98–1995, Sec.2, eff. Jan. 1, 1996, provides:

"This section applies to county option income tax distributions made under IC 6–3.5–6 after December 31, 1995."

P.L.2–1996, Sec.296, emerg. eff. March 10, 1996, amended P.L.98–1995, Sec.2, to provide:

"I.C. 6–3.5–6–18.5, as amended by P.L.98–1995, applies to county option income tax distributions made under I.C. 6–3.5–6 after December 31, 1995."

Cross References

Community revitalization enhancement district tax credit, state and local tax liability, see IC 6–3.1–19–1.
Funding of military base reuse area, pledge of, or covenant to increase, revenues, see IC 36–7–30–21.
Industrial development fund, state and local income taxes, see IC 36–7–13–3.8.
Redevelopment districts, pledge of distributive share of county option income tax, see IC 36–7–15.1–48.
Rural development fund, qualifications for grants, see IC 4–4–9–4.

6–3.5–6–1.3   Districts not entitled to distribution

Sec. 1.3. (a) This section applies to a county solid waste management district (as defined in IC 13–11–2–47) or a joint solid waste management district (as defined in IC 13–11–2–113).

(b) A district may not receive a distribution under this chapter unless a majority of the members of each of the county fiscal bodies of the counties within the district passes a resolution approving the distribution.
As added by P.L.96–1995, SEC.4. Amended by P.L.1–1996, SEC.48.

Historical and Statutory Notes

P.L.96–1995, Sec.4, emerg. eff. May 5, 1995.

P.L.1–1996, Sec.48, amended the section by substituting "IC 13–11–2–47" for "IC 13–9.5–1–7" and "IC 13–11–2–113" for "IC 13–9.5–1–18" in Subsec. (a).

6–3.5–6–2   County income tax council; establishment; membership; ordinances

Sec. 2. (a) A county income tax council is established for each county in Indiana. The membership of each county's county income tax council consists of the fiscal body of the county and the fiscal body of each city or town that lies either partially or entirely within that county.

(b) Using procedures described in this chapter, a county income tax council may adopt ordinances to:

   (1) impose the county option income tax in its county;

(2) subject to section 12 of this chapter, rescind the county option income tax in its county;

(3) increase the county option income tax rate for the county;

(4) freeze the county option income tax rate for its county;

(5) increase the homestead credit in its county;

(6) subject to section 12.5 of this chapter, decrease the county option income tax rate for the county; or

(7) subject to section 17.5 of this chapter, elect to reduce the required balance in the county special account.

(c) An ordinance adopted in a particular year under this chapter to impose or rescind the county option income tax or to increase its tax rate is effective July 1 of that year.

As added by P.L.44–1984, SEC.14. Amended by P.L.2–1989, SEC.14; P.L.42–1994, SEC.4.

Historical and Statutory Notes

P.L.2–1989, Sec.14, emerg. eff. May 5, 1989.

P.L.2–1989, Sec.14, in Subsec. (b)(2), inserted "subject to section 12 of this chapter".

P.L.42–1994, Sec.4, emerg. eff. March 18, 1994, inserted Subsec. (b)(6) relating to decrees

in county option income tax rates; and inserted Subsec. (b)(7) relating to reduction of required balance in county special account.

6–3.5–6–3 County income tax council; allocation of votes

Sec. 3. (a) In the case of a city or town that lies within more than one (1) county, the county auditor of each county shall base the allocations required by subsection (b) on the population of that part of the city or town that lies within the county for which the allocations are being made.

(b) Every county income tax council has a total of one hundred (100) votes. Every member of the county income tax council is allocated a percentage of the total one hundred (100) votes that may be cast. The percentage that a city or town is allocated for a year equals the same percentage that the population of the city or town bears to the population of the county. The percentage that the county is allocated for a year equals the same percentage that the population of all areas in the county not located in a city or town bears to the population of the county. On or before January 1 of each year, the county auditor shall certify to each member of the county income tax council the number of votes, rounded to the nearest one hundredth (0.01), it has for that year.

As added by P.L.44–1984, SEC.14.

6–3.5–6–4 Resolutions; transmittal to county auditor

Sec. 4. (a) A member of the county income tax council may exercise its votes by passing a resolution and transmitting the resolution to the auditor of the county. However, in the case of an ordinance to impose, rescind, increase, decrease, or freeze the county rate of the county option income tax, the member must transmit the resolution to the county auditor by the appropriate time described in section 8, 9, 10, or 11 of this chapter. The form of a resolution is as follows:

"The _____ (name of civil taxing unit's fiscal body) casts its ___ votes ___ (for or against) the proposed ordinance of the _____ County Income Tax Council, which reads as follows:".

(b) A resolution passed by a member of the county income tax council exercises all votes of the member on the proposed ordinance, and those votes may not be changed during the year.

As added by P.L.44–1984, SEC.14. Amended by P.L.42–1994, SEC.5.

Historical and Statutory Notes

P.L.42–1994, Sec.5, emerg. eff. March 18, 1994, in the second sentence, inserted "decrease".

6–3.5–6–5   Ordinances; procedure for proposal; voting

Sec. 5.   Any member of a county income tax council may present an ordinance for passage. To do so, the member must pass a resolution to propose the ordinance to the county income tax council and distribute a copy of the proposed ordinance to the auditor of the county. The auditor of the county shall treat any proposed ordinance presented to the auditor under this section as a casting of all that member's votes in favor of that proposed ordinance. Subject to the limitations of section 6 of this chapter, the auditor of the county shall deliver copies of a proposed ordinance the auditor receives to all members of the county income tax council within ten (10) days after receipt. Once a member receives a proposed ordinance from the auditor of the county, the member shall vote on it within thirty (30) days after receipt.

As added by P.L.44–1984, SEC.14. Amended by P.L.28–1997, SEC.17.

Historical and Statutory Notes

P.L.28–1997, Sec.17, eff. Jan. 1, 1998, amended the section by deleting "If a member does not vote within thirty (30) days, the county auditor shall treat the member as having voted no on the proposed ordinance." from the end of the section; and making changes to reflect gender neutral language.

6–3.5–6–6   Ordinances; limitation of number; effect of passage on proposed ordinances; proposed ordinances with same effect

Sec. 6.   (a) A county income tax council may pass only one (1) ordinance described in section 2(b)(1), 2(b)(2), 2(b)(3), 2(b)(4), or 2(b)(6) of this chapter in one (1) year. Once an ordinance described in section 2(b)(1), 2(b)(2), 2(b)(3), 2(b)(4), or 2(b)(6) of this chapter has been passed, the auditor of the county shall:

(1) cease distributing proposed ordinances of those types for the rest of the year; and

(2) withdraw from the membership any other of those types of proposed ordinances.

Any votes subsequently received by the auditor of the county on proposed ordinances of those types during that same year are void.

(b) The county income tax council may not vote on, nor may the auditor of the county distribute to the members of the county income tax council, any proposed ordinance during a year, if previously during that same year the auditor of the county received and distributed to the members of the county income tax council a proposed ordinance whose passage would have substantially the same effect.

As added by P.L.44–1984, SEC.14. Amended by P.L.42–1994, SEC.6.

Historical and Statutory Notes

P.L.42–1994, Sec.6, emerg. eff. March 18, 1994, in Subsec. (a), in the first and second sentences, inserted a reference to section 2(b)(6); and made nonsubstantive changes.

6–3.5–6–7 Ordinances; hearing; notice

Sec. 7. (a) Before a member of the county income tax council may propose an ordinance or vote on a proposed ordinance, the member must hold a public hearing on the proposed ordinance and provide the public with notice of the time and place where the public hearing will be held.

(b) The notice required by subsection (a) must be given in accordance with IC 5–3–1.

(c) The form of the notice required by this section must be in substantially the following form:

"NOTICE OF COUNTY OPTION INCOME TAX ORDINANCE VOTE.

The fiscal body of the _____ (insert name of civil taxing unit) hereby declares that on _____ (insert date) at _____ (insert the time of day) a public hearing will be held at _____ (insert location) concerning the following resolution to propose an ordinance (or proposed ordinance) that is before the members of the county income tax council. Members of the public are cordially invited to attend the hearing for the purpose of expressing their views.

(Insert a copy of the proposed ordinance or resolution to propose an ordinance.)".

As added by P.L.44–1984, SEC.14.

6–3.5–6–8 Imposition of tax; time; rate of tax; necessity and form of ordinance; recording of votes

Sec. 8. (a) The county income tax council of any county in which the county adjusted gross income tax will not be in effect on July 1 of a year under an ordinance adopted during a previous calendar year may impose the county option income tax on the adjusted gross income of county taxpayers of its county effective July 1 of that same year.

(b) The county option income tax may initially be imposed at a rate of two-tenths of one percent (0.2%) on the resident county taxpayers of the county and at a rate of five hundredths of one percent (0.05%) for all other county taxpayers.

(c) To impose the county option income tax, a county income tax council must, after January 1 but before April 1 of the year, pass an ordinance. The ordinance must substantially state the following:

"The _____ County Income Tax Council imposes the county option income tax on the county taxpayers of _____ County. The county option income tax is imposed at a rate of two-tenths of one percent (0.2%) on the resident county taxpayers of the county and at a rate of five hundredths of one percent (0.05%) on all other county taxpayers. This tax takes effect July 1 of this year.".

(d) If the county option income tax is imposed on the county taxpayers of a county, then the county option income tax rate that is in effect for resident county taxpayers of that county increases by one-tenth of one percent (0.1%) on each succeeding July 1 until the rate equals six-tenths of one percent (0.6%).

(e) The county option income tax rate in effect for the county taxpayers of a county who are not resident county taxpayers of that county is at all times one-fourth (¼) of the tax rate imposed upon resident county taxpayers.

(f) The auditor of a county shall record all votes taken on ordinances presented for a vote under this section and immediately send a certified copy of the results to the department by certified mail.

As added by P.L.44–1984, SEC.14. Amended by P.L.35–1990, SEC.16.

Historical and Statutory Notes

P.L.35–1990, Sec.16, emerg. eff. March 20, 1990 added Subsec. (f).

6–3.5–6–9 Increase of tax rate

Sec. 9. (a) If on January 1 of a calendar year the county option income tax rate in effect for resident county taxpayers equals six tenths of one percent (0.6%), then the county income tax council of that county may after January 1 and before April 1 of that year pass an ordinance to increase its tax rate for resident county taxpayers. If a county income tax council passes an ordinance under this section, its county option income tax rate for resident county taxpayers increases by one tenth of one percent (0.1%) each succeeding July 1 until its rate reaches a maximum of one percent (1%).

(b) The auditor of the county shall record any vote taken on an ordinance proposed under the authority of this section and immediately send a certified copy of the results to the department by certified mail.

As added by P.L.44–1984, SEC.14. Amended by P.L.35–1990, SEC.17.

Historical and Statutory Notes

P.L.35–1990, Sec.17, emerg. eff. March 20, 1990, in Subsec. (b), substituted "send a certi- fied copy of" for "certify", and inserted "by certified mail".

6–3.5–6–9.5   Repealed

(Repealed by P.L.2–1989, SEC.56.)

Historical and Statutory Notes

P.L.2–1989, Sec.56, emerg. eff. May 5, 1989.

Former IC 6–3.5–6–9.5 related to increase of tax rate and use of revenues.

Formerly:

P.L.84–1987, SEC.2.
P.L.22–1988, SEC.5.

6–3.5–6–10   Effect of adoption of county option income tax and county adjusted gross income tax in same county

Sec. 10. If during a particular calendar year the county council of a county adopts an ordinance to impose the county adjusted gross income tax in its county on July 1 of that year and the county option income tax council of the county adopts an ordinance to impose the county option income tax in the county on July 1 of that year, the county option income tax takes effect in that county and the county adjusted gross income tax shall not take effect in that county.

As added by P.L.44–1984, SEC.14.

6–3.5–6–11   Freeze of tax rate; adoption, duration, rescission of ordinance

Sec. 11. (a) The county income tax council of any county may adopt an ordinance to permanently freeze the county option income tax rates at the rate in effect for its county on January 1 of a year.

(b) To freeze the county option income tax rates a county income tax council must, after January 1 but before April 1 of a year, adopt an ordinance. The ordinance must substantially state the following:

"The _____ County Income Tax Council permanently freezes the county option income tax rates at the rate in effect on January 1 of the current year.".

(c) An ordinance adopted under the authority of this section remains in effect until rescinded. The county income tax council may rescind such an ordinance after January 1 but before April 1 of any calendar year. Such an ordinance shall take effect July 1 of that same calendar year.

(d) If a county income tax council rescinds an ordinance as adopted under this section the county option income tax rate shall automatically increase by one-tenth of one percent (0.01%) until:

(1) the tax rate is again frozen under another ordinance adopted under this section; or

(2) the tax rate equals six tenths of one percent (0.6%) (if the frozen tax rate equaled an amount less than six tenths of one percent (0.6%)) or one

percent (1%) (if the frozen tax rate equaled an amount in excess of six tenths of one percent (0.6%)).

(e) The county auditor shall record any vote taken on an ordinance proposed under the authority of this section and immediately send a certified copy of the results to the department by certified mail.

As added by P.L.44–1984, SEC.14. Amended by P.L.35–1990, SEC.18.

Historical and Statutory Notes

P.L.35–1990, Sec.18, emerg. eff. March 20, 1990.

P.L.35–1990, Sec.18, in Subsec. (e), substituted "send a certified copy of" for "certify", and inserted "by certified mail".

6–3.5–6–12   Duration of tax; rescission of tax; record of votes

Sec. 12. (a) The county option income tax imposed by a county income tax council under this chapter remains in effect until rescinded.

(b) Subject to subsection (c), the county income tax council of a county may rescind the county option income tax by passing an ordinance to rescind the tax after January 1 but before April 1 of a year.

(c) A county income tax council may not rescind the county option income tax or take any action that would result in a civil taxing unit in the county having a smaller distributive share than the distributive share to which it was entitled when it pledged county option income tax, if the civil taxing unit or any commission, board, department, or authority that is authorized by statute to pledge county option income tax, has pledged county option income tax for any purpose permitted by IC 5–1–14 or any other statute.

(d) The auditor of a county shall record all votes taken on a proposed ordinance presented for a vote under the authority of this section and immediately send a certified copy of the results to the department by certified mail.
As added by P.L.44–1984, SEC.14. Amended by P.L.2–1989, SEC.15; P.L.35–1990, SEC.19; P.L.28–1997, SEC.18.

Historical and Statutory Notes

P.L.2–1989, Sec.15, emerg. eff. May 5, 1989.

P.L.2–1989, Sec.15, in Subsec. (b), inserted "Subject to subsection (c),"; redesignated Subsec. (c) as (d); and inserted new Subsec. (c).

P.L.35–1990, Sec.19, emerg. eff. March 20, 1990.

P.L.35–1990, Sec.19, in Subsec. (d) substituted "send a certified copy of" for "certify", and inserted "by certified mail".

P.L.28–1997, Sec.18, eff. Jan. 1, 1998, amended the section by substituting "April" for "June" in Subsec. (b).

6–3.5–6–12.5   Decrease in county option income tax rate; adoption of ordinance; procedures

Sec. 12.5. (a) The county income tax council may adopt an ordinance to decrease the county option income tax rate in effect.

(b) To decrease the county option income tax rate, the county income tax council must adopt an ordinance after January 1 but before April 1 of a year. The ordinance must substantially state the following:

"The _____ County Income Tax Council decreases the county option income tax rate from __ percent (__%) to __ percent (__%). This ordinance takes effect July 1 of this year.".

(c) A county income tax council may not decrease the county option income tax if the county or any commission, board, department, or authority that is authorized by statute to pledge the county option income tax has pledged the county option income tax for any purpose permitted by IC 5–1–14 or any other statute.

(d) An ordinance adopted under this subsection takes effect July 1 of the year in which the ordinance is adopted.

(e) The county auditor shall record the votes taken on an ordinance under this subsection and shall send a certified copy of the ordinance to the department by certified mail not more than thirty (30) days after the ordinance is adopted.

(f) Notwithstanding IC 6–3.5–7, a county income tax council that decreases the county option income tax in a year may not in the same year adopt or increase the county economic development income tax under IC 6–3.5–7. *As added by P.L.42–1994, SEC.7.*

Historical and Statutory Notes

P.L.42–1994, Sec.7, emerg. eff. March 18, 1994.

6–3.5–6–13 Increase of homestead credit percentage

Sec. 13.   (a) A county income tax council of a county in which the county option income tax is in effect may adopt an ordinance to increase the percentage credit allowed for homesteads in its county under IC 6–1.1–20.9–2.

(b) A county income tax council may not increase the percentage credit allowed for homesteads by an amount that exceeds eight percent (8%).

(c) The increase of the homestead credit percentage must be uniform for all homesteads in a county.

(d) In the ordinance that increases the homestead credit percentage, a county income tax council may provide for a series of increases or decreases to take place for each of a group of succeeding calendar years.

(e) An ordinance may be adopted under this section after January 1 but before June 1 of a calendar year.

(f) An ordinance adopted under this section takes effect on January 1 of the next succeeding calendar year.

(g) Any ordinance adopted under this section for a county is repealed for a year if on January 1 of that year the county option income tax is not in effect. *As added by P.L.44–1984, SEC.14. Amended by P.L.3–1989, SEC.41.*

221

Historical and Statutory Notes

P.L.3–1989, Sec.41, emerg. eff. May 5, 1989,
made corrective changes.

6–3.5–6–14 Taxpayer subject to different tax rates; rate of tax

Sec. 14. If for any taxable year a county taxpayer is subject to different tax rates for the county option income tax imposed by a particular county, the taxpayer's county option income tax rate for that county and that taxable year is the rate determined in the last STEP of the following STEPS:

STEP ONE: Multiply the number of months in the taxpayer's taxable year that precede July 1 by the rate in effect before the rate change.

STEP TWO: Multiply the number of months in the taxpayer's taxable year that follow June 30 by the rate in effect after the rate change.

STEP THREE: Divide the sum of the amounts determined under STEPS ONE and TWO by twelve (12).

As added by P.L.44–1984, SEC.14.

6–3.5–6–15 Tax not in effect entire taxable year

Sec. 15. If the county option income tax is not in effect during a county taxpayer's entire taxable year, the amount of county option income tax that the county taxpayer owes for that taxable year equals the product of:

(1) the amount of county option income tax the county taxpayer would owe if the tax had been imposed during the county taxpayer's entire taxable year; multiplied by

(2) a fraction. The numerator of the fraction equals the number of days in the county taxpayer's taxable year during which the county option income tax was in effect. The denominator of the fraction equals the total number of days in the county taxpayer's taxable year.

However, if the taxpayer files state income tax returns on a calendar year basis, the fraction to be applied under this section is one-half (½).

As added by P.L.44–1984, SEC.14.

6–3.5–6–16 Deposit of revenue in special account

Sec. 16. (a) A special account within the state general fund shall be established for each county that adopts the county option income tax. Any revenue derived from the imposition of the county option income tax by a county shall be deposited in that county's account in the state general fund.

(b) Any income earned on money held in an account under subsection (a) becomes a part of that account.

(c) Any revenue remaining in an account established under subsection (a) at the end of a fiscal year does not revert to the state general fund.

As added by P.L.44–1984, SEC.14.

6–3.5–6–17   Distribution of revenue to counties

Sec. 17. (a) Revenue derived from the imposition of the county option income tax shall, in the manner prescribed by this section, be distributed to the county that imposed it. The amount that is to be distributed to a county during an ensuing calendar year equals the amount of county option income tax revenue that the department, after reviewing the recommendation of the state budget agency, estimates will be received from that county during the twelve (12) month period beginning July 1 of the immediately preceding calendar year and ending June 30 of the ensuing calendar year.

(b) Before June 16 of each calendar year, the department, after reviewing the recommendation of the state budget agency, shall estimate and certify to the county auditor of each adopting county the amount of county option income tax revenue that will be collected from that county during the twelve (12) month period beginning July 1 of that calendar year and ending June 30 of the immediately succeeding calendar year. The amount certified is the county's "certified distribution" for the immediately succeeding calendar year. The amount certified may be adjusted under subsection (c) or (d).

(c) The department may certify to an adopting county an amount that is greater than the estimated twelve (12) month revenue collection if the department, after reviewing the recommendation of the state budget agency, determines that there will be a greater amount of revenue available for distribution from the county's account established under section 16 of this chapter.

(d) The department may certify an amount less than the estimated twelve (12) month revenue collection if the department, after reviewing the recommendation of the state budget agency, determines that a part of those collections needs to be distributed during the current calendar year so that the county will receive its full certified distribution for the current calendar year.

(e) One-twelfth ($\frac{1}{12}$) of each adopting county's certified distribution for a calendar year shall be distributed from its account established under section 16 of this chapter to the appropriate county treasurer on the first day of each month of that calendar year.

(f) Upon receipt, each monthly payment of a county's certified distribution shall be allocated among, distributed to, and used by the civil taxing units of the county as provided in sections 18 and 19 of this chapter.

(g) All distributions from an account established under section 16 of this chapter shall be made by warrants issued by the auditor of state to the treasurer of the state ordering the appropriate payments.

As added by P.L.44–1984, SEC.14. Amended by P.L.23–1986, SEC.10.

Historical and Statutory Notes

P.L.23–1986, Sec.10, eff. May 1, 1986, inserted ", after reviewing the recommendation of the state budget agency," four times where appear-ing in Subsecs. (a) to (d); and made a nonsubstantive change in Subsec. (g).

6–3.5–6–17.4 **Counties with population between 36,700 and 37,000; ordinance to reduce county's special account balance; calculation and distribution of amount**

Sec. 17.4. (a) This section applies only to a county having a population of more than thirty-six thousand seven hundred (36,700) but less than thirty-seven thousand (37,000).

(b) The county income tax council of a county may adopt an ordinance to reduce the required six (6) month balance of that county's special account to a three (3) month balance for that county.

(c) To reduce the balance a county income tax council must adopt an ordinance. The ordinance must substantially state the following:

"The _____ County Income Tax Council elects to reduce the required county income tax special account balance from a six (6) month balance to a three (3) month balance within ninety (90) days after the adoption of this ordinance.".

(d) Not more than thirty (30) days after adopting an ordinance under subsection (c), the county income tax council shall deliver a copy of the ordinance to the budget agency.

(e) Not later than:

(1) sixty (60) days after a county income tax council adopts an ordinance under subsection (c); and

(2) December 31 of each year;

the budget agency shall make the calculation described in subsection (f). Not later than ninety (90) days after the ordinance is adopted, the budget agency shall make an initial distribution to the county auditor of the amount determined under subsection (f) STEP FOUR. Subsequent distributions needed to distribute any amount in the county income tax special account that exceeds a three (3) month balance, as determined under subsection (f) STEP FOUR, shall be made in January of the ensuing calendar year after the calculation is made.

(f) The budget agency shall make the following calculation:

STEP ONE: Determine the cumulative balance in a county's account established under section 16 of this chapter.

STEP TWO: Divide the amount estimated under section 17(b) of this chapter before any adjustments are made under section 17(c) or 17(d) of this chapter by twelve (12).

STEP THREE: Multiply the STEP TWO amount by three (3).

STEP FOUR: Subtract the amount determined in STEP THREE from the amount determined in STEP ONE.

(g) The county auditor shall distribute an amount received under subsection (e) to the civil taxing units in the same manner as the certified distribution is distributed and not later than thirty (30) days after the county auditor receives the amount.

(h) The civil taxing units may use the amounts received under subsection (g) for any item for which the particular civil taxing unit's certified distribution may be used.

As added by P.L.97–1995, SEC.1.

Historical and Statutory Notes

P.L.97–1995, Sec.1, emerg. eff. March 28, 1995.

6–3.5–6–17.5 Reduction of county's special account balance; adoption of ordinance; procedures; distribution; use of funds

Sec. 17.5. (a) This section does not apply to a county containing a consolidated city.

(b) The county income tax council of any county may adopt an ordinance to reduce the required six (6) month balance of that county's special account to a three (3) month balance for that county on January 1 of a year.

(c) To reduce the balance a county income tax council must, after January 1 but before April 1 of a year, adopt an ordinance. The ordinance must substantially state the following:

"The _____ County Income Tax Council elects to reduce the required county income tax special account balance from a six (6) month balance to a three (3) month balance.".

(d) On or before December 31 of each year, the budget agency shall make the following calculation:

STEP ONE: Determine the cumulative balance in a county's account established under section 16 of this chapter.

STEP TWO: Divide the amount estimated under section 17(b) of this chapter before any adjustments are made under section 17(c) or 17(d) of this chapter by twelve (12).

STEP THREE: Multiply the STEP TWO amount by three (3).

STEP FOUR: Subtract the amount determined in STEP THREE from the amount determined in STEP ONE.

(e) The amount determined in STEP FOUR of subsection (d) shall be distributed to the county auditor in January of the ensuing calendar year.

(f) The county auditor shall distribute the amount received under subsection (e) to the civil taxing units in the same manner as the certified distribution is distributed and not later than thirty (30) days after the county auditor receives the amount.

(g) The civil taxing units may use the amounts received under subsection (f) as follows:

(1) For the later of 1995 or the first calendar year in which the county adopts an ordinance under subsection (c) and:

(A) for each civil taxing unit that is a county, city, or town, for the purposes authorized under IC 36–9–14.5–2 or IC 36–9–15.5–2 (whichever applies and regardless of whether the civil taxing unit has established a cumulative capital development fund under IC 36–9–14.5 or IC 36–9–15.5); and

(B) for each civil taxing unit that is a township or a special taxing district, for any item for which the civil taxing unit may issue a general obligation bond.

(2) For each year after the year to which subdivision (1) applies and for all civil taxing units, for any item for which the particular civil taxing unit's certified distribution may be used.

As added by P.L.42–1994, SEC.8.

Historical and Statutory Notes

P.L.42–1994, Sec.8, emerg. eff. March 18, 1994.

6–3.5–6–17.6   Counties containing a consolidated city; budget agency calculations; payment of outstanding obligations for qualified economic development tax project; distributions

Sec. 17.6. (a) This section applies to a county containing a consolidated city.

(b) On or before July 15 of each year, the budget agency shall make the following calculation:

STEP ONE: Determine the cumulative balance in a county's account established under section 16 of this chapter as of the end of the current calendar year.

STEP TWO: Divide the amount estimated under section 17(b) of this chapter before any adjustments are made under section 17(c) or 17(d) of this chapter by twelve (12).

STEP THREE: Multiply the STEP TWO amount by three (3).

STEP FOUR: Subtract the amount determined in STEP THREE from the amount determined in STEP ONE.

(c) For 1995, the budget agency shall certify the STEP FOUR amount to the county auditor on or before July 15, 1994. Not later than January 31, 1995, the auditor of state shall distribute the STEP FOUR amount to the county auditor to be used to retire outstanding obligations for a qualified economic development tax project (as defined in IC 36–7–27–9).

(d) After 1995, the STEP FOUR amount shall be distributed to the county auditor in January of the ensuing calendar year. The STEP FOUR amount shall be distributed by the county auditor to the civil taxing units within thirty

(30) days after the county auditor receives the distribution. Each civil taxing unit's share equals the STEP FOUR amount multiplied by the quotient of:

    (1) the maximum permissible property tax levy under IC 6–1.1–18.5 for the civil taxing unit, plus, for a county, an amount equal to the property taxes imposed by the county in 1999 for the county's welfare administration fund; divided by

    (2) the sum of the maximum permissible property tax levies under IC 6–1.1–18.5 for all civil taxing units of the county, plus an amount equal to the property taxes imposed by the county in 1999 for the county's welfare administration fund.

As added by P.L.42–1994, SEC.9. Amended by P.L.273–1999, SEC.70.

Historical and Statutory Notes

P.L.42–1994, Sec.9, emerg. eff. March 18, 1994.

P.L.273–1999, Sec.70, eff. Jan. 1, 2000, inserted "plus, for a county, an amount equal to the property taxes imposed by the county in 1999 for the county's welfare administration fund;" in Subsec. (d)(1) and "plus an amount equal to the property taxes imposed by the county in 1999 for the county's welfare administration fund" in Subsec. (d)(2).

6–3.5–6–18 Use of revenue by county auditors; distribution of revenue to civil taxing units and school corporations; qualified economic development tax projects

Sec. 18. (a) The revenue a county auditor receives under this chapter shall be used to:

    (1) replace the amount, if any, of property tax revenue lost due to the allowance of an increased homestead credit within the county;

    (2) fund the operation of a public communications system and computer facilities district as provided in an election, if any, made by the county fiscal body under IC 36–8–15–19(b);

    (3) fund the operation of a public transportation corporation as provided in an election, if any, made by the county fiscal body under IC 36–9–4–42;

    (4) make payments permitted under IC 36–7–15.1–17.5;

    (5) make payments permitted under subsection (I [1]); and

    (6) make distributions of distributive shares to the civil taxing units of a county.

(b) The county auditor shall retain from the payments of the county's certified distribution, an amount equal to the revenue lost, if any, due to the increase of the homestead credit within the county. This money shall be distributed to the civil taxing units and school corporations of the county as though they were property tax collections and in such a manner that no civil taxing unit or school corporation shall suffer a net revenue loss due to the allowance of an increased homestead credit.

(c) The county auditor shall retain the amount, if any, specified by the county fiscal body for a particular calendar year under subsection[1] (I), IC 36–7–15.1–

17.5, IC 36–8–15–19(b), and IC 36–9–4–42 from the county's certified distribution for that same calendar year. The county auditor shall distribute amounts retained under this subsection to the county.

(d) All certified distribution revenues that are not retained and distributed under subsections (b) and (c) shall be distributed to the civil taxing units of the county as distributive shares.

(e) The amount of distributive shares that each civil taxing unit in a county is entitled to receive during a month equals the product of the following:

(1) The amount of revenue that is to be distributed as distributive shares during that month; multiplied by

(2) A fraction. The numerator of the fraction equals the total property taxes that are first due and payable to the civil taxing unit during the calendar year in which the month falls, plus, for a county, an amount equal to the property taxes imposed by the county in 1999 for the county's welfare fund and welfare administration fund. The denominator of the fraction equals the sum of the total property taxes that are first due and payable to all civil taxing units of the county during the calendar year in which the month falls, plus an amount equal to the property taxes imposed by the county in 1999 for the county's welfare fund and welfare administration fund.

(f) The state board of tax commissioners shall provide each county auditor with the fractional amount of distributive shares that each civil taxing unit in the auditor's county is entitled to receive monthly under this section.

(g) Notwithstanding subsection (e), if a civil taxing unit of an adopting county does not impose a property tax levy that is first due and payable in a calendar year in which distributive shares are being distributed under this section, that civil taxing unit is entitled to receive a part of the revenue to be distributed as distributive shares under this section within the county. The fractional amount such a civil taxing unit is entitled to receive each month during that calendar year equals the product of the following:

(1) The amount to be distributed as distributive shares during that month; multiplied by

(2) A fraction. The numerator of the fraction equals the budget of that civil taxing unit for that calendar year. The denominator of the fraction equals the aggregate budgets of all civil taxing units of that county for that calendar year.

(h) If for a calendar year a civil taxing unit is allocated a part of a county's distributive shares by subsection (g), then the formula used in subsection (e) to determine all other civil taxing units' distributive shares shall be changed each month for that same year by reducing the amount to be distributed as distributive shares under subsection (e) by the amount of distributive shares allocated under subsection (g) for that same month. The state board of tax commissioners shall make any adjustments required by this subsection and provide them to the appropriate county auditors.

(I [1]) Notwithstanding any other law, a county fiscal body may pledge revenues received under this chapter to the payment of bonds or lease rentals to finance a qualified economic development tax project under IC 36–7–27 in that county or in any other county if the county fiscal body determines that the project will promote significant opportunities for the gainful employment or retention of employment of the county's residents.

As added by P.L.44–1984, SEC.14. Amended by P.L.225–1986, SEC.10; P.L.32–1986, SEC.2; P.L.84–1987, SEC.3; P.L.2–1989, SEC.16; P.L.28–1993, SEC.7; P.L.273–1999, SEC.71.

[1] So in enrolled act; probably should read "i".

Historical and Statutory Notes

P.L.225–1986, Sec.10, eff. March 6, 1986, in Subsec. (a), deleted "and" following "counties;" at the end of Subd. (1), inserted Subd. (2), and redesignated former Subd. (2) as Subd. (3) [now subd. (5)]; in Subsec. (b), substituted "the" for "a" preceding "county's certified distribution"; inserted Subsec. (c); redesignated former Subsecs. (c) through (g) as (d) through (h); and, in Subsec. (d), substituted "subsections (b) and (c)" for "subsection (b)"; in Subsec. (g), substituted "subsection (e)" for "subsection (d)"; and, in Subsec. (h), substituted references to Subsecs. (g), and (e), respectively, for references to Subsecs. (f) and (d).

P.L. 32–1986, SEC.2, emerg. eff. March 12, 1986, substituted "IC 36–8–15–19(b)" for "IC 36–8–15–19(a)" in Subsecs. (a)(2) and (c).

P.L. 84–1987, Sec.3, emerg. eff. May 6, 1987, added Subsecs. (a)(3), (4) and renumbered former (a)(3) as (a)(5); and added citations in Subsec. (c).

P.L.2–1989, Sec.16, emerg. eff. May 5, 1989, in Subsec. (a)(4), deleted "fund any economic development projects under IC 36–7–15.2–5 or" preceding "make payments" and deleted "related to those projects;" preceding "and".

P.L.28–1993, Sec.7, emerg. eff. Feb. 12, 1993, inserted subsec. (a)(5) and redesignated former subsec. (a)(5) as subsec. (a)(6), in subsec. (c) inserted "subsection (i),", and added subsec. (i).

P.L.273–1999, Sec.71, eff. Jan. 1, 2000, rewrote Subsec. (e)(2) and made other nonsubstantive changes. Prior to amendment, Subsec. (e)(2) read:

"(2) a fraction. The numerator of the fraction equals the total property taxes that are first due and payable to the civil taxing unit during the calendar year in which the month falls. The denominator of the fraction equals the total property taxes that are first due and payable to all civil taxing units of the county during the calendar year in which the month falls."

6–3.5–6–18.5 Distributive shares to civil taxing units in counties containing a consolidated city

Sec. 18.5. (a) This section applies to a county containing a consolidated city.

(b) Notwithstanding section 18(e) of this chapter, the distributive shares that each civil taxing unit in a county containing a consolidated city is entitled to receive during a month equals the following:

(1) For the calendar year beginning January 1, 1995, calculate the total amount of revenues that are to be distributed as distributive shares during that month multiplied by the following factor:

Center Township	.0251
Decatur Township	.00217
Franklin Township	.0023
Lawrence Township	.01177
Perry Township	.01130
Pike Township	.01865

Warren Township	.01359
Washington Township	.01346
Wayne Township	.01307
Lawrence–City	.00858
Beech Grove	.00845
Southport	.00025
Speedway	.00722
Indianapolis/Marion County	.86409

(2) Notwithstanding subdivision (1), for the calendar year beginning January 1, 1995, the distributive shares for each civil taxing unit in a county containing a consolidated city shall be not less than the following:

Center Township	$1,898,145
Decatur Township	$164,103
Franklin Township	$173,934
Lawrence Township	$890,086
Perry Township	$854,544
Pike Township	$1,410,375
Warren Township	$1,027,721
Washington Township	$1,017,890
Wayne Township	$988,397
Lawrence–City	$648,848
Beech Grove	$639,017
Southport	$18,906
Speedway	$546,000

(3) For each year after 1995, calculate the total amount of revenues that are to be distributed as distributive shares during that month as follows:

STEP ONE: Determine the total amount of revenues that were distributed as distributive shares during that month in calendar year 1995.

STEP TWO: Determine the total amount of revenue that the department has certified as distributive shares for that month under section 17 of this chapter for the calendar year.

STEP THREE: Subtract the STEP ONE result from the STEP TWO result.

STEP FOUR: If the STEP THREE result is less than or equal to zero (0), multiply the STEP TWO result by the ratio established under subdivision (1).

STEP FIVE: Determine the ratio of:

(A) the maximum permissible property tax levy under IC 6–1.1–18.5 and IC 6–1.1–18.6 for each civil taxing unit for the calendar year in which the month falls, plus, for a county, an amount equal to the property taxes imposed by the county in 1999 for the county's welfare fund and welfare administration fund; divided by

(B) the sum of the maximum permissible property tax levies under IC 6–1.1–18.5 and IC 6–1.1–18.6 for all civil taxing units of the county during the calendar year in which the month falls, and an

230

amount equal to the property taxes imposed by the county in 1999 for the county's welfare fund and welfare administration fund.

STEP SIX: If the STEP THREE result is greater than zero (0), the STEP ONE amount shall be distributed by multiplying the STEP ONE amount by the ratio established under subdivision (1).

STEP SEVEN: For each taxing unit determine the STEP FIVE ratio multiplied by the STEP TWO amount.

STEP EIGHT: For each civil taxing unit determine the difference between the STEP SEVEN amount minus the product of the STEP ONE amount multiplied by the ratio established under subdivision (1). The STEP THREE excess shall be distributed as provided in STEP NINE only to the civil taxing units that have a STEP EIGHT difference greater than or equal to zero (0).

STEP NINE: For the civil taxing units qualifying for a distribution under STEP EIGHT, each civil taxing unit's share equals the STEP THREE excess multiplied by the ratio of:

(A) the maximum permissible property tax levy under IC 6–1.1–18.5 and IC 6–1.1–18.6 for the qualifying civil taxing unit during the calendar year in which the month falls, plus, for a county, an amount equal to the property taxes imposed by the county in 1999 for the county's welfare fund and welfare administration fund; divided by

(B) the sum of the maximum permissible property tax levies under IC 6–1.1–18.5 and IC 6–1.1–18.6 for all qualifying civil taxing units of the county during the calendar year in which the month falls, and an amount equal to the property taxes imposed by the county in 1999 for the county's welfare fund and welfare administration fund.

As added by P.L.42–1994, SEC.10.   Amended by P.L.98–1995, SEC.1; P.L.273–1999, SEC.72.

Historical and Statutory Notes

P.L.98–1995, Sec.1, eff. Jan. 1, 1996, amended the section by substituting "section 17 of this chapter" for "IC 6–3.5–6–17" in STEP TWO of Subsec. (b)(3); inserting "and IC 6–1.1–18.6" throughout STEP FIVE of Subsec. (b)(3); deleting "The STEP THREE excess shall be distributed as provided in STEP SEVEN only to the civil taxing units that have a ratio under STEP FIVE that is greater than the ratio for that civil taxing unit under subdivision (1)" from the end of STEP SIX of Subsec. (b)(3); deleting former STEP SEVEN of Subsec. (b)(3); and by adding STEP SEVEN through STEP NINE of Subsec. (b)(3).   Prior to amendment, STEP SEVEN of Subsec. (b)(3) read:

"STEP SEVEN: For the civil taxing units qualifying for a distribution under STEP SIX, each civil taxing unit's share equals the STEP THREE excess multiplied by the ratio of:

"(A) the maximum permissible property tax levy under IC 6–1.1–18.5 for the qualifying civil taxing unit during the calendar year in which the month falls; divided by

"(B) the sum of the maximum permissible property tax levies under IC 6–1.1–18.5 for all qualifying civil taxing units of the county during the calendar year in which the month falls."

For related provisions of P.L.2–1996, Sec.296, see Historical and Statutory Note under IC 6–3.5–6–1.

P.L.273–1999, Sec.72, eff. Jan. 1, 2000, inserted "plus, for a county, an amount equal to the property taxes imposed by the county in 1999 for the county's welfare fund and welfare administration fund;" and "an amount equal to the property taxes imposed by the county in 1999 for the county's welfare fund and welfare administration fund" in "STEP FIVE" AND "STEP NINE" in Subsec. (b)(3).

6–3.5–6–19   Distributive shares of civil taxing units; determination; budget

Sec. 19.   (a) Except as provided in sections 17.6(d), 18(e), and 18.5(b)(3) of this chapter, in determining the fractional share of distributive shares the civil taxing units of a county are entitled to receive under section 18 of this chapter during a calendar year, the state board of tax commissioners shall consider only property taxes imposed on tangible property subject to assessment in that county.

(b) In determining the amount of distributive shares a civil taxing unit is entitled to receive under section 18(g) of this chapter, the state board of tax commissioners shall consider only the percentage of the civil taxing unit's budget that equals the ratio that the total assessed valuation that lies within the civil taxing unit and the county that has adopted the county option tax bears to the total assessed valuation that lies within the civil taxing unit.

(c) The distributive shares to be allocated and distributed under this chapter shall be treated by each civil taxing unit as additional revenue for the purpose of fixing its budget for the budget year during which the distributive shares is to be distributed to the civil taxing unit.

(d) In the case of a civil taxing unit that includes a consolidated city its fiscal body may distribute any revenue it receives under this chapter to any governmental entity located in its county except an excluded city, a township, or a school corporation.

As added by P.L.44–1984, SEC.14.   Amended by P.L.225–1986, SEC.11; P.L.273–1999, SEC.73.

Historical and Statutory Notes

P.L.225–1986, Sec.11, emerg. eff. March 6, 1986, in Subsec. (b), substituted "section 18(g)" for "section 18(f)".

P.L.273–1999, Sec.73, eff. Jan. 1, 2000, inserted "Except as provided in sections 17.6(d), 18(e), and 18.5(b)(3) of this chapter," at the beginning of Subsec. (a).

6–3.5–6–20   County residents; determination

Sec. 20.   (a) For purposes of this chapter, an individual shall be treated as a resident of the county in which he:

(1) maintains a home, if the individual maintains only one (1) in Indiana;

(2) if subdivision (1) does not apply, is registered to vote;

(3) if subdivision (1) or (2) does not apply, registers his personal automobile; or

(4) if subdivision (1), (2), or (3) does not apply, spends the majority of his time spent in Indiana during the taxable year in question.

(b) The residence or principal place of business or employment of an individual is to be determined on January 1 of the calendar year in which the individual's taxable year commences. If an individual changes the location of his residence or principal place of employment or business to another county in Indiana during a calendar year, his liability for county option income tax is not affected.

(c) Notwithstanding subsection (b), if an individual becomes a county taxpayer for purposes of IC 36–7–27 during a calendar year because the individual:

(1) changes the location of the individual's residence to a county in which the individual begins employment or business at a qualified economic development tax project (as defined in IC 36–7–27–9); or

(2) changes the location of the individual's principal place of employment or business to a qualified economic development tax project and does not reside in another county in which the county option income tax is in effect;

the individual's adjusted gross income attributable to employment or business at the qualified economic development tax project is taxable only by the county containing the qualified economic development tax project.

As added by P.L.44–1984, SEC.14. Amended by P.L.42–1994, SEC.11.

Historical and Statutory Notes

P.L.42–1994, Sec.11, added Subsec. (c) relating to individuals who become county taxpayers for purpose of IC 36–7–27.

6–3.5–6–21 Reciprocity agreements

Sec. 21. (a) Using procedures provided under this chapter, the county income tax council of any adopting county may pass an ordinance to enter into reciprocity agreements with the taxing authority of any city, town, municipality, county, or other similar local governmental entity of any other state. The reciprocity agreements must provide that the income of resident county taxpayers is exempt from income taxation by the other local governmental entity to the extent income of the residents of the other local governmental entity is exempt from the county option income tax in the adopting county.

(b) A reciprocity agreement adopted under this section may not become effective until it is also made effective in the other local governmental entity that is a party to the agreement.

(c) The form and effective date of any reciprocity agreement described in this section must be approved by the department.

As added by P.L.44–1984, SEC.14.

6–3.5–6–22 Adjusted gross income tax provisions; applicability; employer's annual withholding report

Sec. 22. (a) Except as otherwise provided in subsection (b) and the other provisions of this chapter, all provisions of the adjusted gross income tax law (IC 6–3) concerning:

(1) definitions;

(2) declarations of estimated tax;

(3) filing of returns;

(4) deductions or exemptions from adjusted gross income;

(5) remittances;

(6) incorporation of the provisions of the Internal Revenue Code;

(7) penalties and interest; and

(8) exclusion of military pay credits for withholding;

apply to the imposition, collection, and administration of the tax imposed by this chapter.

(b) The provisions of IC 6-3-1-3.5(a)(6), IC 6-3-3-3, IC 6-3-3-5, and IC 6-3-5-1 do not apply to the tax imposed by this chapter.

(c) Notwithstanding subsections (a) and (b), each employer shall report to the department the amount of withholdings attributable to each county. This report shall be submitted along with the employer's other withholding report. *As added by P.L.44-1984, SEC.14. Amended by P.L.23-1986, SEC.11; P.L.57-1997, SEC.5.*

Historical and Statutory Notes

P.L.23-1986, Sec.11, eff. Jan. 1, 1987, added Subsec. (c).

Section 23(b) of P.L.23-1986 provides that Section 11 of this act applies to taxable years that begin after Dec. 31, 1986.

P.L.57-1997, Sec.5, emerg. eff. retroactive to Jan. 1, 1997, amended the section by substituting "IC 6-3-1-3.5(a)(6)," for "IC 6-3-1-3.5(a)(5)," in Subsec. (b).

6-3.5-6-23 Credit for income tax imposed by local governmental entity outside Indiana

Sec. 23. (a) Except as provided in subsection (b), if for a particular taxable year a county taxpayer is liable for an income tax imposed by a county, city, town, or other local governmental entity located outside of Indiana, that county taxpayer is entitled to a credit against the county option income tax liability for that same taxable year. The amount of the credit equals the amount of tax imposed by the other governmental entity on income derived from sources outside Indiana and subject to the county option income tax. However, the credit provided by this section may not reduce a county taxpayer's county option income tax liability to an amount less than would have been owed if the income subject to taxation by the other governmental entity had been ignored.

(b) The credit provided by this section does not apply to a county taxpayer to the extent that the other governmental entity provides for a credit to the taxpayer for the amount of county option income taxes owed under this chapter.

(c) To claim the credit provided by this section, a county taxpayer must provide the department with satisfactory evidence that the taxpayer is entitled to the credit. *As added by P.L.23-1986, SEC.12.*

Historical and Statutory Notes

P.L.23–1986, Sec.12, eff. Jan. 1, 1987, added this section.

Section 23(b) of P.L.23–1986 provides that Section 12 of this act applies to taxable years that begin after Dec. 31, 1986.

6–3.5–6–24 Credit for elderly or totally disabled persons

Sec. 24. (a) If for a particular taxable year a county taxpayer is, or a county taxpayer and the taxpayer's spouse who file a joint return are, allowed a credit for the elderly or the totally disabled under Section 22 of the Internal Revenue Code, the county taxpayer is, or the county taxpayer and the taxpayer's spouse are, entitled to a credit against the county option income tax liability for that same taxable year. The amount of the credit equals the lesser of:

(1) the product of:

(A) the credit for the elderly or the totally disabled for that same taxable year; multiplied by

(B) a fraction, the numerator of which is the county option income tax rate imposed against the county taxpayer, or the county taxpayer and the taxpayer's spouse, and the denominator of which is fifteen-hundredths (0.15); or

(2) the amount of county option income tax imposed on the county taxpayer, or the county taxpayer and the taxpayer's spouse.

(b) If a county taxpayer and the taxpayer's spouse file a joint return and are subject to different county option income tax rates for the same taxable year, they shall compute the credit under this section by using the formula provided by subsection (a), except that they shall use the average of the two (2) county option income tax rates imposed against them as the numerator referred to in subsection (a)(1)(B).

As added by P.L.23–1986, SEC.13. Amended by P.L.63–1988, SEC.10.

Historical and Statutory Notes

P.L.23–1986, Sec.13, eff. Jan. 1, 1987, added this section.

Section 23(b) of P.L.23–1986 provides that Section 13 of this act applies to taxable years that begin after Dec. 31, 1986.

P.L. 63–1988, Sec.10, emerg. eff. retroactive to Jan. 1, 1988, substituted in the first sentence

of Subsec. (a) "Section 22 of the Internal Revenue Code" for "Section 37 of the Internal Revenue Code, as defined by IC 6–3–1–11".

Section 16 of P.L. 63–1988, provides that the amendment to this section "apply to taxable years that begin after December 31, 1987."

6–3.5–6–25 Public sale of obligations

Sec. 25. Notwithstanding any other law, if a civil taxing unit desires to issue obligations, or enter into leases, payable wholly or in part by the county option income tax, the obligations of the civil taxing unit or any lessor may be sold at public sale in accordance with IC 5–1–11 or at negotiated sale.

As added by P.L.2–1989, SEC.17.

Historical and Statutory Notes

P.L.2–1989, Sec.17, emerg. eff. May 5, 1989.

Chapter 7

County Economic Development Income Tax

Library References

Counties ☞190(1).
Taxation ☞979.
WESTLAW Topic Nos. 104, 371.

C.J.S. Counties § 227, 230 to 232.
C.J.S. Taxation § 1096.

6–3.5–7–1   "Adjusted gross income" defined

Sec. 1. (a) Except as otherwise provided in this section, as used in this chapter, "adjusted gross income" has the meaning set forth in IC 6–3–1–3.5(a).

(b) In the case of a county taxpayer who is not a resident of a county that has imposed the county economic development income tax, the term "adjusted gross income" includes only adjusted gross income derived from the taxpayer's principal place of business or employment.

(c) In the case of a county taxpayer who is a resident of a county having a population of more than nineteen thousand (19,000) but less than nineteen thousand three hundred (19,300), the term "adjusted gross income" does not include adjusted gross income that is:

    (1) earned in a county that is:

        (A) located in another state; and

        (B) adjacent to the county in which the taxpayer resides; and

    (2) subject to an income tax imposed by a county, city, town, or other local governmental entity in the other state.

As added by P.L.380–1987(ss), SEC.6. Amended by P.L.66–1991, SEC.1; P.L.12–1992, SEC.29.

Historical and Statutory Notes

P.L. 380–1987(ss), Sec.6, added this chapter emergency effective upon passage May 7, 1987.

Section 22 of P.L. 380–1987(ss) provides:

"The provisions of this act are severable in the manner provided by IC 1–1–1–8(b)."

P.L.66–1991, Sec.1, emerg. eff. retroactive to Jan. 1, 1991.

P.L.66–1991, Sec.1, divided this section into Subsecs. (a) and (b); in Subsec. (a), added "Except as otherwise provided in this section," at the beginning, and deleted "However," at the

end; in Subsec. (b), inserted " 'adjusted gross income' "; and added Subsec. (c).

P.L.66–1991, Sec.2 provides:

"This act applies to taxable years that begin after December 31, 1990."

P.L.12–1992, Sec.29, emerg. eff. April 1, 1992, revised population descriptions to accommodate the 1990 federal census.

For related provisions of P.L.124–1999, Sec.4, see Historical and Statutory Notes under IC 6–3.5–7–23.

Cross References

Community revitalization enhancement district tax credit, state and local tax liability, see IC 6–3.1–19–1.

Funding of military base reuse area, pledge of, or covenant to increase, revenues, see IC 36–7–30–21.

Industrial development fund, state and local income taxes, see IC 36–7–13–3.8.

Rural development fund, qualifications for grants, see IC 4–4–9–4.

6–3.5–7–1.5 "Capital project" defined

Sec. 1.5. As used in this chapter, "capital project" includes substance removal or remedial action in a designated unit.

As added by P.L.44–1994, SEC.1.

Historical and Statutory Notes

P.L.44–1994, Sec.1, emerg. eff. March 17, 1994.

6–3.5–7–2   "County council" defined

Sec. 2.   As used in this chapter, "county council" includes the city-county council of a consolidated city.

As added by P.L.380–1987(ss), SEC.6.

6–3.5–7–3   "County taxpayer" defined

Sec. 3.   As used in this chapter, "county taxpayer" as it relates to a county for a year means any individual who:

(1) resides in that county on the date specified in section 17 of this chapter; or

(2) maintains a principal place of business or employment in that county on the date specified in section 17 of this chapter and who does not on that same date reside in another county in which the county adjusted gross income tax, the county option income tax, or the county economic development income tax is in effect.

As added by P.L.380–1987(ss), SEC.6.   Amended by P.L.22–1988, SEC.6.

Historical and Statutory Notes

P.L. 22–1988, Sec.6, emerg. eff. retroactive to Jan. 1, 1988, and by section 10 applicable to "taxable years that begin after December 31, 1987" inserted in Cl. (2) "or the county economic development income tax".

P.L. 22–1988, Sec.10, emerg. eff. March 3, 1988, provides:

"Sections 3, 4, and 6 of this act apply to taxable years that begin after December 31, 1987."

6–3.5–7–4   "Department" defined

Sec. 4.   As used in the chapter, "department" refers to the department of state revenue.

As added by P.L.380–1987(ss), SEC.6.

6–3.5–7–4.3   "Designated unit" defined

Sec. 4.3.   As used in this chapter, "designated unit" refers to a county having a population of more than one hundred twenty-nine thousand (129,000) but less than one hundred thirty thousand six hundred (130,600).

As added by P.L.44–1994, SEC.2.

Historical and Statutory Notes

P.L.44–1994, Sec.2, emerg. eff. March 17, 1994.

6–3.5–7–4.6   "Remedial action" defined

Sec. 4.6.   As used in this chapter, "remedial action" has the meaning set forth in IC 13–11–2–185.

As added by P.L.44–1994, SEC.3.   Amended by P.L.1–1996, SEC.49.

Historical and Statutory Notes

P.L.44–1994, Sec.3, emerg. eff. March 17, 1994.

P.L.1–1996, Sec.49, amended the section by substituting "IC 13–11–2–185" for "IC 13–7–8.7–1".

6–3.5–7–4.7   "Removal" defined

Sec. 4.7. As used in this chapter, "removal" has the meaning set forth in IC 13–11–2–187.

As added by P.L.44–1994, SEC.4. Amended by P.L.1–1996, SEC.50.

Historical and Statutory Notes

P.L.44–1994, Sec.4, emerg. eff. March 17, 1994.

P.L.1–1996, Sec.50, amended the section by substituting "IC 13–11–2–187" for "IC 13–7–8.7–1".

6–3.5–7–4.8   "Substance" defined

Sec. 4.8. As used in this chapter, "substance" has the meaning set forth in IC 13–11–2–98 for "hazardous substance".

As added by P.L.44–1994, SEC.5. Amended by P.L.1–1996, SEC.51.

Historical and Statutory Notes

P.L.44–1994, Sec.5, emerg. eff. March 17, 1994.

P.L.1–1996, Sec.51, amended the section by substituting "IC 13–11–2–98" for "IC 13–7–8.7–1".

6–3.5–7–5   Imposition of tax; procedures; rate of tax; ordinance; effective date; vote

Sec. 5. (a) Except as provided in subsection (c), the county economic development income tax may be imposed on the adjusted gross income of county taxpayers. The entity that may impose the tax is:

(1) the county income tax council (as defined in IC 6–3.5–6–1) if the county option income tax is in effect on January 1 of the year the county economic development income tax is imposed;

(2) the county council if the county adjusted gross income tax is in effect on January 1 of the year the county economic development tax is imposed; or

(3) the county income tax council or the county council, whichever acts first, for a county not covered by subdivision (1) or (2).

To impose the county economic development income tax, a county income tax council shall use the procedures set forth in IC 6–3.5–6 concerning the imposition of the county option income tax.

(b) Except as provided in subsections (c) and (g), the county economic development income tax may be imposed at a rate of:

(1) one-tenth percent (0.1%);

(2) two-tenths percent (0.2%);

(3) twenty-five hundredths percent (0.25%);

(4) three-tenths percent (0.3%);

(5) thirty-five hundredths percent (0.35%);

(6) four-tenths percent (0.4%);

(7) forty-five hundredths percent (0.45%); or

(8) five-tenths percent (0.5%);

on the adjusted gross income of county taxpayers.

(c) Except as provided in subsection (h) or (i), the county economic development income tax rate plus the county adjusted gross income tax rate, if any, that are in effect on January 1 of a year may not exceed one and twenty-five hundredths percent (1.25%). Except as provided in subsection (g), the county economic development tax rate plus the county option income tax rate, if any, that are in effect on January 1 of a year may not exceed one percent (1%).

(d) To impose the county economic development income tax, the appropriate body must, after January 1 but before April 1 of a year, adopt an ordinance. The ordinance must substantially state the following:

"The _____ County _____ imposes the county economic development income tax on the county taxpayers of _____ County. The county economic development income tax is imposed at a rate of _____ percent (___%) on the county taxpayers of the county. This tax takes effect July 1 of this year.".

(e) Any ordinance adopted under this section takes effect July 1 of the year the ordinance is adopted.

(f) The auditor of a county shall record all votes taken on ordinances presented for a vote under the authority of this section and immediately send a certified copy of the results to the department by certified mail.

(g) This subsection applies to a county having a population of more than one hundred twenty-nine thousand (129,000) but less than one hundred thirty thousand six hundred (130,600). In addition to the rates permitted by subsection (b), the:

(1) county economic development income tax may be imposed at a rate of:

(A) fifteen-hundredths percent (0.15%);

(B) two-tenths percent (0.2%); or

(C) twenty-five hundredths percent (0.25%); and

(2) county economic development income tax rate plus the county option income tax rate that are in effect on January 1 of a year may equal up to one and twenty-five hundredths percent (1.25%);

if the county income tax council makes a determination to impose rates under this subsection and section 22 of this chapter.

(h) For a county having a population of more than thirty-seven thousand (37,000) but less than thirty-seven thousand eight hundred (37,800), the county economic development income tax rate plus the county adjusted gross income tax rate that are in effect on January 1 of a year may not exceed one and thirty-five hundredths percent (1.35%) if the county has imposed the county adjusted gross income tax at a rate of one and one-tenth percent (1.1%) under IC 6–3.5–1.1–2.5.

(i) For a county having a population of more than twelve thousand six hundred (12,600) but less than thirteen thousand (13,000), the county economic development income tax rate plus the county adjusted gross income tax rate that are in effect on January 1 of a year may not exceed one and fifty-five hundredths percent (1.55%).

As added by P.L.380–1987(ss), SEC.6. Amended by P.L.35–1990, SEC.20; P.L.28–1993, SEC.8; P.L.44–1994, SEC.6; P.L.99–1995, SEC.1; P.L.119–1998, SEC.11.

Historical and Statutory Notes

P.L.35–1990, Sec.20, emerg. eff. March 20, 1990.

P.L.35–1990, Sec.20, in Subsec. (f), substituted "send a certified copy of" for "certify", and inserted "by certified mail".

P.L.28–1993, Sec.8, emerg. eff. Feb. 12, 1993, added subsec. (g).

P.L.28–1993, Sec.16, provides:

"The following are hereby legalized and validated:

"(1) Any action taken by a county income tax council in adopting the county economic development income tax, if the action would have been valid under IC 6–3.5–7–5, as amended by this act.

"(2) Any action of a county in adopting a capital improvement plan under IC 6–3.5–7–15, if the action would have been valid under IC 6–3.5–7, as amended by this act.

"(3) Any action taken by a county fiscal body in determining that an excise tax should be continued, if the action would have been valid under IC 6–9–20–3, as amended by this act.

"(4) Any action of a county, a county building authority, an eligible entity (as defined in IC 36–9–13), the executive of an eligible entity, or the state board of tax commissioners, if the action would have been valid under IC 36–9–13.1, as added by this act."

P.L.44–1994, Sec.6, emerg. eff. March 17, 1994, in Subsec. (b), inserted a reference to Subsec. (h) in the introduction; in Subsec. (c), inserted the exception as provided in Subsecs. (g) and (h) at the beginning of the second sentence; and added Subsec. (h).

P.L.99–1995, Sec.1, emerg. eff. April 29, 1995, amended the section by deleting former Subsec. (g); redesignating former Subsec. (h) as Subsec. (g); and changing references to Subsec.

(h) to references to Subsec. (g). Prior to amendment, former Subsec. (g) read:

"(g) This subsection applies only to a county having a population of more than one hundred sixty thousand (160,000) but less than two hundred thousand (200,000). Notwithstanding subsection (c), the county economic development income tax rate plus the county option income tax rate that are in effect on January 1 of a year may equal up to one and twenty five hundredths percent (1.25%) if the county income tax council determines that the combined rate in excess of one percent (1%) is necessary for financing a government building to be subleased to the federal government or an agency or department of the federal government under IC 36–9–13.1. An action to contest the validity of the determination under this subsection must be instituted not more than ten (10) days after the determination."

P.L.99–1995, Sec.15, emerg. eff. April 29, 1995, provides:

"(a) This section applies to a county having a population of more than one hundred sixty thousand (160,000) but less than two hundred thousand (200,000).

"(b) An ordinance adopted by a county income tax council after July 1, 1992, but before July 1, 1993, to impose a county option income tax or county economic development income tax (as authorized under IC 6–3.5–7–5(g), before its amendment by this act) to finance a government building to be subleased to the federal government or an agency or a department of the federal government under IC 36–9–13.1 (before its repeal by this act) is invalid."

P.L.10–1997, Sec.40, emerg. eff. May 13, 1997, provides:

"(a) This section applies only to a county having a population of more than one hundred seven thousand (107,000) but less than one hundred eight thousand (108,000).

"(b) The following are hereby legalized and validated:

"(1) Any action taken by a county council in adopting the county economic development income tax, if the action would have been valid under IC 6–3.5–1.1–3.1, as amended by this act.

"(2) Any action of a county in adopting a capital improvement plan under IC 6–3.5–7–15, following the adoption of the county economic development income tax as permitted by IC 6–3.5–1.1–3.1, as amended by this act.

"(c) Notwithstanding IC 6–3.5–7–5, a county council that reduced its county adjusted gross income tax rate in 1997 may adopt an ordinance to impose the county economic development income tax before May 31, 1997."

P.L.119–1998, Sec.11, amended the section by inserting "Except as provided in subsection (h) or (i)," in Subsec. (c); and adding Subsecs. (h) and (i).

For related provisions of P.L.124–1999, Sec.4, see Historical and Statutory Notes under IC 6–3.5–7–23.

Cross References

Grants to municipalities, establishment of revolving fund, see IC 5–1–14–14.

Library References

Counties ⊜190(1).
WESTLAW Topic No. 104.
C.J.S. Counties § 279.

6–3.5–7–6   Rate decrease or increase; limitations; ordinance; effective date; vote

Sec. 6. (a) The body imposing the tax may decrease or increase the county economic development income tax rate imposed upon the county taxpayers as long as the resulting rate does not exceed the rates specified in section 5(b) and 5(c) or 5(g) of this chapter. The rate imposed under this section must be adopted at one (1) of the rates specified in section 5(b) of this chapter. To decrease or increase the rate, the appropriate body must, after January 1 but before April 1 of a year, adopt an ordinance. The ordinance must substantially state the following:

"The _____ County _____ increases (decreases) the county economic development income tax rate imposed upon the county taxpayers of the county from _____ percent (__%) to _____ percent (__%). This tax rate increase (decrease) takes effect July 1 of this year.".

(b) Any ordinance adopted under this section takes effect July 1 of the year the ordinance is adopted.

(c) The auditor of a county shall record all votes taken on ordinances presented for a vote under the authority of this section and immediately send a certified copy of the results to the department by certified mail.

As added by P.L.380–1987(ss), SEC.6. Amended by P.L.35–1990, SEC.21; P.L.44–1994, SEC.7; P.L.99–1995, SEC.2; P.L.119–1998, SEC.12.

Historical and Statutory Notes

P.L.35–1990, Sec.21, emerg. eff. March 20, 1990.

P.L.35–1990, Sec.21, in Subsec. (c), substituted "send a certified copy of" for "certify", and inserted "by certified mail".

P.L.44–1994, Sec.7, emerg. eff. March 17, 1994, in Subsec. (a), inserted a reference to section 5(h) of this chapter in the first sentence.

P.L.99–1995, Sec.2, emerg. eff. April 29, 1995, amended the section by substituting "5(g)" for "5(h)" in Subsec. (a).

P.L.119–1998, Sec.12, emerg. eff. retroactive to Jan. 1, 1998, amended the section by inserting the second sentence in Subsec. (a).

Library References

Counties ☞190(2).
WESTLAW Topic No. 104.
C.J.S. Counties § 279.

Notes of Decisions

Validity   1

_____

1. Validity

Economic development income tax statute that effectively permitted only one county to take advantage of increased tax rate set forth in statute, by making special rate available only to counties with population of more than 129,000 but less than 130,600, was "local or special statute," for purposes of constitutional provision prohibiting certain local and special laws. (Per Justice Dickson with one Justice concurring, two Justices concurring in result, and one Justice concurring in part.) State v. Hoovler, 1996, 668 N.E.2d 1229, rehearing denied, motion granted 673 N.E.2d 767.

Economic development income tax statute, which authorized increased tax rate to be available to only one county, but which did not authorize any new property valuations or changes in system of tax gathering, was not constitutionally prohibited local or special law providing for "assessment and collection of tax-

es" for county purposes. (Per Justice Dickson with one Justice concurring, two Justices concurring in result, and one Justice concurring in part.) State v. Hoovler, 1996, 668 N.E.2d 1229, rehearing denied, motion granted 673 N.E.2d 767.

While economic development income tax statute used narrow population range to effectively authorize only one county to impose increased tax rates, legislature's apparent intent to benefit that county, which was only one in state facing environmental cleanup liability, was not matter necessarily subject to general law uniformly applicable in all counties, as would make statute unconstitutional local or special law, even though special legislative classification created by population restriction failed to bear rational relationship to subject matter in question and reason for classification did not inhere in statute. (Per Justice Dickson with one Justice concurring, two Justices concurring in result, and one Justice concurring in part.) State v. Hoovler, 1996, 668 N.E.2d 1229, rehearing denied, motion granted 673 N.E.2d 767.

6–3.5–7–7   Tax effective until rescission; rescinding ordinance; effective date; vote

Sec. 7.   (a) The county economic development income tax imposed under this chapter remains in effect until rescinded.

(b) Subject to section 14 of this chapter, the body imposing the county economic development income tax may rescind the tax by adopting an ordinance to rescind the tax after January 1 but before April 1 of a year.

(c) Any ordinance adopted under this section takes effect July 1 of the year the ordinance is adopted.

(d) The auditor of a county shall record all votes taken on ordinances presented for a vote under the authority of this section and immediately send a certified copy of the results to the department by certified mail.

As added by P.L.380–1987(ss), SEC.6. Amended by P.L.35–1990, SEC.22; P.L.28–1997, SEC.19.

Historical and Statutory Notes

P.L.35–1990, Sec.22, emerg. eff. March 20, 1990, in Subsec. (d), substituted "send a certified copy of" for "certify", and inserted "by certified mail".

P.L.28–1997, Sec.19, eff. Jan. 1, 1998, amended the section by substituting "April" for "June" in Subsec. (b).

6–3.5–7–8   Tax effective for less than taxable year; calculation

Sec. 8. If the county economic development income tax is not in effect during a county taxpayer's entire taxable year, then the amount of county economic development income tax that the county taxpayer owes for that taxable year equals the product of:

(1) the amount of county economic development income tax the county taxpayer would owe if the tax had been imposed during the county taxpayer's entire taxable year; multiplied by

(2) a fraction. The numerator of the fraction equals the number of days during the county taxpayer's taxable year during which the county economic development income tax was in effect. The denominator of the fraction equals three hundred sixty-five (365).

As added by P.L.380–1987(ss), SEC.6.

6–3.5–7–9   Credits for elderly or totally disabled; calculation

Sec. 9. (a) If for a taxable year a county taxpayer is (or a county taxpayer and a county taxpayer's spouse who file a joint return are) allowed a credit for the elderly or the totally disabled under Section 22 of the Internal Revenue Code,[1] the county taxpayer is (or the county taxpayer and the county taxpayer's spouse are) entitled to a credit against the county taxpayer's (or the county taxpayer's and the county taxpayer's spouse's) county economic development income tax liability for that same taxable year. The amount of the credit equals the lesser of:

(1) the product of:

(A) the county taxpayer's (or the county taxpayer's and the county taxpayer's spouse's) credit for the elderly or the totally disabled for that same taxable year; multipled by

(B) a fraction. The numerator of the fraction is the county economic development income tax rate imposed against the county taxpayer (or against the county taxpayer and the county taxpayer's spouse). The denominator of the fraction is fifteen-hundredths (0.15); or

(2) the amount of county economic development income tax imposed on the county taxpayer (or the county taxpayer and the county taxpayer's spouse).

(b) If a county taxpayer and the county taxpayer's spouse file a joint return and are subject to different county economic development income tax rates for the same taxable year, they shall compute the credit under this section by using the formula provided by subsection (a), except that they shall use the average of the two (2) county economic development income tax rates imposed against them as the numerator referred to in subsection (a)(1)(B).

As added by P.L.380–1987(ss), SEC.6. Amended by P.L.63–1988, SEC.11.

1. 26 U.S.C.A. § 22.

Historical and Statutory Notes

P.L. 63–1988, Sec.11, emerg. eff. retroactive to Jan. 1, 1988, substituted "22" for "37" in the reference to the Internal Revenue Code in the first sentence of Subsec. (a).

Section 16 of P.L. 63–1988, provides that the amendment to this section "apply to taxable years that begin after December 31, 1987."

6–3.5–7–10   County economic development income tax special account

Sec. 10. (a) A special account within the state general fund shall be established for each county adopting the county economic development income tax. Any revenue derived from the imposition of the county economic development income tax by a county shall be credited to that county's account in the state general fund.

(b) Any income earned on money credited to an account under subsection (a) becomes a part of that account.

(c) Any revenue credited to an account established under subsection (a) at the end of a fiscal year may not be credited to any other account in the state general fund.

As added by P.L.380–1987(ss), SEC.6.

6–3.5–7–11   Distribution of tax revenue; procedure

Sec. 11. (a) Revenue derived from the imposition of the county economic development income tax shall, in the manner prescribed by this section, be distributed to the county that imposed it.

(b) Before July 2 of each calendar year, the department, after reviewing the recommendation of the budget agency, shall estimate and certify to the county auditor of each adopting county the amount of county economic development income tax revenue that will be collected from that county during the twelve (12) month period beginning July 1 of that calendar year and ending June 30 of the following calendar year. The amount certified is the county's certified distribution, which shall be distributed on the dates specified in section 16 of this chapter for the following calendar year. The amount certified may be adjusted under subsection (c) or (d).

(c) The department may certify to an adopting county an amount that is greater than the estimated twelve (12) month revenue collection if the department, after reviewing the recommendation of the budget agency, determines that there will be a greater amount of revenue available for distribution from the county's account established under section 10 of this chapter.

(d) The department may certify an amount less than the estimated twelve (12) month revenue collection if the department, after reviewing the recommendation of the budget agency, determines that a part of those collections need to

be distributed during the current calendar year so that the county will receive its full certified distribution for the current calendar year.
As added by P.L.380–1987(ss), SEC.6.

6–3.5–7–12 Certified distribution; amount; adoption of ordinance; exception; fractional amounts (first version)

Note: This version of section amended by P.L.124–1999, SEC.1. See also following version of this section, amended by P.L.273–1999, SEC.74.

Sec. 12. (a) Except as provided in section 23 of this chapter, the county auditor shall distribute in the manner specified in this section the certified distribution to the county.

(b) Except as provided in subsections (c) and (h) and section 15 of this chapter, the amount of the certified distribution that the county and each city or town in a county is entitled to receive during May and November of each year equals the product of:

(1) The amount of the certified distribution for that month; multiplied by

(2) A fraction. The numerator of the fraction equals the total property taxes that are first due and payable to the county, city, or town during the calendar year in which the month falls. The denominator of the fraction equals the total property taxes that are first due and payable to the county and all cities and towns of the county during the calendar year in which the month falls.

(c) This subsection applies to a county council or county income tax council that imposes a tax under this chapter after June 1, 1992. The body imposing the tax may adopt an ordinance before July 1 of a year to provide for the distribution of certified distributions under this subsection instead of a distribution under subsection (b). The following apply if an ordinance is adopted under this subsection:

(1) The ordinance is effective January 1 of the following year.

(2) The amount of the certified distribution that the county and each city and town in the county is entitled to receive during May and November of each year equals the product of:

(A) the amount of the certified distribution for the month; multiplied by

(B) a fraction. For a city or town, the numerator of the fraction equals the population of the city or the town. For a county, the numerator of the fraction equals the population of the part of the county that is not located in a city or town. The denominator of the fraction equals the sum of the population of all cities and towns located in the county and the population of the part of the county that is not located in a city or town.

(3) The ordinance may be made irrevocable for the duration of specified lease rental or debt service payments.

(d) The body imposing the tax may not adopt an ordinance under subsection (c) if, before the adoption of the proposed ordinance, any of the following have pledged the county economic development income tax for any purpose permitted by IC 5–1–14 or any other statute:

    (1) The county.

    (2) A city or town in the county.

    (3) A commission, a board, a department, or an authority that is authorized by statute to pledge the county economic development income tax.

(e) The state board of tax commissioners shall provide each county auditor with the fractional amount of the certified distribution that the county and each city or town in the county is entitled to receive under this section.

(f) Money received by a county, city, or town under this section shall be deposited in the unit's economic development income tax fund.

(g) In determining the fractional amount of the certified distribution the county and its cities and towns are entitled to receive under subsection (b) during a calendar year, the state board of tax commissioners shall consider only property taxes imposed on tangible property subject to assessment in that county.

(h) In a county having a consolidated city, only the consolidated city is entitled to the certified distribution, subject to the requirements of section 15 of this chapter.

As added by P.L.380–1987(ss), SEC.6. Amended by P.L.47–1992, SEC.1; P.L.28–1993, SEC.9; P.L.99–1995, SEC.3; P.L.124–1999, SEC.1.

> *Note: See also following version of this section, amended by P.L.273–1999, SEC.74.*

6–3.5–7–12   **Certified distribution; amount; adoption of ordinance; exception; fractional amounts (second version)**

> *Note: This version of section amended by P.L.273–1999, SEC.74. See also preceding version of this section, amended by P.L.124–1999, SEC.1.*

Sec. 12. (a) The county auditor shall distribute in the manner specified in this section the certified distribution to the county.

(b) Except as provided in subsections (c) and (h) and section 15 of this chapter, the amount of the certified distribution that the county and each city or town in a county is entitled to receive during May and November of each year equals the product of the following:

    (1) The amount of the certified distribution for that month; multiplied by

    (2) A fraction. The numerator of the fraction equals the sum of the following:

        (A) Total property taxes that are first due and payable to the county, city, or town during the calendar year in which the month falls; plus

(B) For a county, an amount equal to the property taxes imposed by the county in 1999 for the county's welfare fund and welfare administration fund.

The denominator of the fraction equals the sum of the total property taxes that are first due and payable to the county and all cities and towns of the county during the calendar year in which the month falls, plus an amount equal to the property taxes imposed by the county in 1999 for the county's welfare fund and welfare administration fund.

(c) This subsection applies to a county council or county income tax council that imposes a tax under this chapter after June 1, 1992. The body imposing the tax may adopt an ordinance before July 1 of a year to provide for the distribution of certified distributions under this subsection instead of a distribution under subsection (b). The following apply if an ordinance is adopted under this subsection:

(1) The ordinance is effective January 1 of the following year.

(2) The amount of the certified distribution that the county and each city and town in the county is entitled to receive during May and November of each year equals the product of:

(A) the amount of the certified distribution for the month; multiplied by

(B) a fraction. For a city or town, the numerator of the fraction equals the population of the city or the town. For a county, the numerator of the fraction equals the population of the part of the county that is not located in a city or town. The denominator of the fraction equals the sum of the population of all cities and towns located in the county and the population of the part of the county that is not located in a city or town.

(3) The ordinance may be made irrevocable for the duration of specified lease rental or debt service payments.

(d) The body imposing the tax may not adopt an ordinance under subsection (c) if, before the adoption of the proposed ordinance, any of the following have pledged the county economic development income tax for any purpose permitted by IC 5–1–14 or any other statute:

(1) The county.

(2) A city or town in the county.

(3) A commission, a board, a department, or an authority that is authorized by statute to pledge the county economic development income tax.

(e) The state board of tax commissioners shall provide each county auditor with the fractional amount of the certified distribution that the county and each city or town in the county is entitled to receive under this section.

(f) Money received by a county, city, or town under this section shall be deposited in the unit's economic development income tax fund.

(g) Except as provided in subsection (b)(2)(B), in determining the fractional amount of the certified distribution the county and its cities and towns are entitled to receive under subsection (b) during a calendar year, the state board of tax commissioners shall consider only property taxes imposed on tangible property subject to assessment in that county.

(h) In a county having a consolidated city, only the consolidated city is entitled to the certified distribution, subject to the requirements of section 15 of this chapter.

As added by P.L.380–1987(ss), SEC.6. Amended by P.L.47–1992, SEC.1; P.L.28– 1993, SEC.9; P.L.99–1995, SEC.3; P.L.273–1999, SEC.74.

Note: See also preceding version of this section, amended by P.L.124– 1999, SEC.1.

Historical and Statutory Notes

P.L.47–1992, Sec.1, eff. June 1, 1992, modified internal references; inserted Subsecs. (c) and (d); and redesignated former Subsecs. (c) to (f) as (e) to (h).

P.L.28–1993, Sec.9, emerg. eff. Feb. 12, 1993, added subsec. (i).

P.L.99–1995, Sec.3, emerg. eff. April 29, 1995, amended the section by deleting former Subsec. (i), which read:

"(i) This subsection applies only to a county having a population of more than one hundred sixty thousand (160,000) but less than two hundred thousand (200,000). Notwithstanding sections 11 and 16 of this chapter, a certified distribution may not be made to the county until the department receives a certification from the county auditor that the federal government has granted a defense project for the county. If a rescission of the income tax occurs before a distribution, a county taxpayer that has paid the income tax is entitled to a refund of the income taxes paid under this chapter. The refund may be claimed by a county taxpayer at the time the county taxpayer files an annual income tax return. Notwithstanding IC 6–3, the refund amount is equal to the entire income tax paid under this chapter regardless of the taxable year in which the tax is paid, plus interest for the taxable years preceding the most recent taxable year. The interest rate to be paid on that portion of the refund is the interest rate earned on the balance credited to the county's account. If a certified distribution is made, then notwith-

standing subsections (b) through (h) and section 13.1(a) of this chapter, the entire certified distribution shall be distributed to the county and shall be deposited in the defense project fund established under IC 36–9–13.1, which shall be considered the county's economic development fund for the purposes of this chapter."

P.L.124–1999, Sec.1, emerg. eff. May 3, 1999, inserted "Except as provided in section 23 of this chapter," in Subsec. (a).

P.L.273–1999, Sec.74, eff. Jan. 1, 2000, rewrote Subsec. (b) and inserted "Except as provided in subsection (b)(2)(B)," at the beginning of Subsec. (g). Prior to amendment, Subsec. (b) read:

"(b) Except as provided in subsections (c) and (h) and section 15 of this chapter, the amount of the certified distribution that the county and each city or town in a county is entitled to receive during May and November of each year equals the product of:

"(1) the amount of the certified distribution for that month; multiplied by

"(2) a fraction. The numerator of the fraction equals the total property taxes that are first due and payable to the county, city, or town during the calendar year in which the month falls. The denominator of the fraction equals the total property taxes that are first due and payable to the county and all cities and towns of the county during the calendar year in which the month falls."

6–3.5–7–13   Repealed

(Repealed by P.L.1–1990, SEC.80.)

Historical and Statutory Notes

P.L.1–1990, Sec.80, emerg. eff. March 20,
1990.

See, now, IC 6–3.5–7–13.1.

The repealed section related to the economic
development income tax fund.

6–3.5–7–13.1   Economic development income tax funds; deposits; uses

Sec. 13.1. (a) The fiscal officer of each county, city, or town for a county in which the county economic development tax is imposed shall establish an economic development income tax fund. Except as provided in section 23 of this chapter, the revenue received by a county, city, or town under this chapter shall be deposited in the unit's economic development income tax fund.

(b) Except as provided in sections 15 and 23 of this chapter, revenues from the county economic development income tax may be used as follows:

(1) By a county, city, or town for economic development projects, for paying, notwithstanding any other law, under a written agreement all or a part of the interest owed by a private developer or user on a loan extended by a financial institution or other lender to the developer or user if the proceeds of the loan are or are to be used to finance an economic development project, for the retirement of bonds under section 14 of this chapter for economic development projects, for leases under section 21 of this chapter, or for leases or bonds entered into or issued prior to the date the economic development income tax was imposed if the purpose of the lease or bonds would have qualified as a purpose under this chapter at the time the lease was entered into or the bonds were issued.

(2) By a county, city, or town for:

(A) the construction or acquisition of, or remedial action with respect to, a capital project for which the unit is empowered to issue general obligation bonds or establish a fund under any statute listed in IC 6–1.1–18.5–9.8;

(B) the retirement of bonds issued under any provision of Indiana law for a capital project;

(C) the payment of lease rentals under any statute for a capital project;

(D) contract payments to a nonprofit corporation whose primary corporate purpose is to assist government in planning and implementing economic development projects;

(E) operating expenses of a governmental entity that plans or implements economic development projects;

(F) to the extent not otherwise allowed under this chapter, funding substance removal or remedial action in a designated unit; or

(G) funding of a revolving fund established under IC 5–1–14–14.

(c) As used in this section, an economic development project is any project that:

(1) the county, city, or town determines will:

    (A) promote significant opportunities for the gainful employment of its citizens;

    (B) attract a major new business enterprise to the unit; or

    (C) retain or expand a significant business enterprise within the unit; and

  (2) involves an expenditure for:

    (A) the acquisition of land;

    (B) interests in land;

    (C) site improvements;

    (D) infrastructure improvements;

    (E) buildings;

    (F) structures;

    (G) rehabilitation, renovation, and enlargement of buildings and structures;

    (H) machinery;

    (I) equipment;

    (J) furnishings;

    (K) facilities;

    (L) administrative expenses associated with such a project, including contract payments authorized under subsection (b)(2)(D);

    (M) operating expenses authorized under subsection (b)(2)(E); or

    (N) to the extent not otherwise allowed under this chapter, substance removal or remedial action in a designated unit;

or any combination of these.

As added by P.L.1–1990, SEC.81. Amended by P.L.17–1991, SEC.9; P.L.44–1994, SEC.8; P.L.27–1995, SEC.6; P.L.124–1999, SEC.2.

Historical and Statutory Notes

P.L.1–1990, Sec.81, emerg. eff. upon passage March 20, 1990.

P.L.17–1991, Sec.9, in Subsec. (b)(1), inserted: "for paying, notwithstanding any other law, under a written agreement all or a part of the interest owed by a private developer or user on a loan extended by a financial institution or other lender to the developer or user if the proceeds of the loan are or are to be used to finance an economic development project".

P.L.44–1994, Sec.8, emerg. eff. March 17, 1994, in Subsec. (b)(2), inserted references to acquisition of, and remedial actions with respect to, the specified capital projects in Clause (A), and added Clause (F); and in Subsec. (c)(2), added Clause (N).

P.L.27–1995, Sec.6, amended the section by adding Subsec. (b)(2)(G); and making other nonsubstantive changes.

P.L.124–1999, Sec.2, emerg. eff. May 3, 1999, inserted "Except as provided in section 23 of this chapter," in Subsec. (a); and substituted "sections 15 and 23" for "section 15" in the introductory clause in Subsec. (b).

Formerly:

IC 6–3.5–7–13.
P.L.380–1987(ss).
P.L.22–1988, SEC.7.
P.L.2–1989, SEC.18.
P.L.346–1989(ss), SEC.3.

6–3.5–7–14   Bonds; debt service requirements; sale; covenant protecting bondholders

Sec. 14. (a) The fiscal body of a county, city, or town may issue bonds payable from the county economic development income tax. The bonds must be for economic development projects (as defined in section 13.1 of this chapter).

(b) The fiscal body of a county, city, or town may issue bonds payable from the county economic development income tax for any capital project for which the fiscal body is authorized to issue general obligation bonds. The bonds issued under this section may be payable from the county economic development income tax if the county option income tax or the county adjusted gross income tax is also in effect in the county at the time the bonds are issued.

(c) If there are bonds outstanding that have been issued under this section, or leases in effect under section 21 of this chapter, the body that imposed the county economic development income tax may not reduce the county economic development income tax rate below a rate that would produce one and twenty-five hundredths (1.25) times the total of the highest annual debt service on the bonds to their final maturity, plus the highest annual lease payments, unless:

  (1) the body that imposed the economic development income tax; or

  (2) any city, town, or county;

pledges all or a portion of its distributive share for the life of the bonds or the term of the lease, in an amount that is sufficient, when combined with the amount pledged by the city, town, or county that issued the bonds, to produce one and twenty-five hundredths (1.25) times the total of the highest annual debt service plus the highest annual lease payments.

(d) For purposes of subsection (c), the determination of a tax rate sufficient to produce one and twenty-five hundredths (1.25) times the total of the highest annual debt service plus the highest annual lease payments shall be based on an average of the immediately preceding three (3) years tax collections, if the tax has been imposed for the last preceding three (3) years. If the tax has not been imposed for the last preceding three (3) years, the body that imposed the tax may not reduce the rate below a rate that would produce one and twenty-five hundredths (1.25) times the total of the highest annual debt service, plus the highest annual lease payments, based upon a study by a qualified public accountant or financial advisor.

(e) IC 6–1.1–20 does not apply to the issuance of bonds under this section.

(f) Bonds issued under this section may be sold at a public sale in accordance with IC 5–1–11 or may be sold at a negotiated sale.

(g) After a sale of bonds under this section, the county auditor shall prepare a debt service schedule for the bonds.

(h) The general assembly covenants that it will not repeal or amend this chapter in a manner that would adversely affect owners of outstanding bonds issued, or payment of any lease rentals due, under this section.

As added by P.L.380–1987(ss), SEC.6.   Amended by P.L.2–1989, SEC.19; P.L.1–1990, SEC.82; P.L.19–1994, SEC.11.

Historical and Statutory Notes

P.L.2–1989, Sec.19, emerg. eff. May 5, 1989.

P.L.2–1989, Sec.19, rewrote Subsec. (d) which prior thereto read:

"(d) IC 6–1.1–20, except for:

"(1) IC 6–1.1–20–3; and

"(2) IC 6–1.1–20–4;

"applies to the issuance of bonds under this section."

The 1989 amendment also in Subsec. (g), inserted "or payment of any lease rentals due,".

P.L.1–1990, Sec.82, emerg. eff. March 20, 1990, made corrective changes.

P.L.19–1994, Sec.11, emerg. eff. March 18, 1994, inserted the first occurrence of "payable from the county economic development income tax" in Subsec. (b), rewrote Subsec. (c), designated and rewrote Subsec. (d), and redesignated former Subsecs. (d) through (g) as Subsecs. (e) through (h), respectively.

6–3.5–7–15   Capital improvement plan; retention of certified distribution pending adoption of plan; components of plan

Sec. 15.   (a) The executive of a county, city, or town may:

(1) adopt a capital improvement plan specifying the uses of the revenues to be received under this chapter; or

(2) designate the county or a city or town in the county as the recipient of all or a part of its share of the distribution.

(b) If a designation is made under subsection (a)(2), the county treasurer shall transfer the share or part of the share to the designated unit unless that unit does not have a capital improvement plan.

(c) A county, city, or town that fails to adopt a capital improvement plan may not receive:

(1) its fractional amount of the certified distribution; or

(2) any amount designated under subsection (c)(2);

for the year or years in which the unit does not have a plan.   The county treasurer shall retain the certified distribution and any designated distribution for such a unit in a separate account until the unit adopts a plan.   Interest on the separate account becomes part of the account.   If a unit fails to adopt a plan for a period of three (3) years, then the balance in the separate account shall be distributed to the other units in the county based on property taxes first due and payable to the units during the calendar year in which the three (3) year period expires.

(d) A capital improvement plan must include the following components:

(1) Identification and general description of each project that would be funded by the county economic development income tax.

(2) The estimated total cost of the project.

(3) Identification of all sources of funds expected to be used for each project.

(4) The planning, development, and construction schedule of each project.

(e) A capital improvement plan:

(1) must encompass a period of no less than two (2) years; and

(2) must incorporate projects the cost of which is at least seventy-five percent (75%) of the fractional amount certified distribution expected to be received by the county, city, or town in that period of time.

(f) In making a designation under subsection (a)(2), the executive must specify the purpose and duration of the designation. If the designation is made to provide for the payment of lease rentals or bond payments, the executive may specify that the designation and its duration are irrevocable.

As added by P.L.380–1987(ss), SEC.6. Amended by P.L.22–1988, SEC.8; P.L.17–1991, SEC.10.

Historical and Statutory Notes

P.L. 22–1988, Sec.8, emerg. eff. March 3, 1988, substituted "or" for "and" at the end of Subsec. (a)(1), added Subsec. (c)(2) as an alternative to Subsec. (c)(1), and substituted in the second sentence of Subsec. (c) "certified distribution and any designated distribution" for "distribution", and added Subsec. (f).

P.L.17–1991, Sec.10, in Subsec. (a)(2), inserted "all or a part of".

For provision of P.L.28-1993, Sec.16, validating actions under this section, see Historical and Statutory Notes under §6–3.5–7–5.

For related provisions of P.L.10–1997, see Historical and Statutory Note under IC 6–3.5–7–5.

6–3.5–7–16   Certified distribution dates; distribution by warrant

Sec. 16. (a) On May 1 of each year, one-half (½) of each county's certified distribution for a calendar year shall be distributed from its account established under section 10 of this chapter to the county treasurer. The other one-half (½) shall be distributed on November 1 of that calendar year.

(b) All distributions from an account established under section 10 of this chapter shall be made by warrants issued by the auditor of state to the treasurer of state ordering the appropriate payments.

As added by P.L.380–1987(ss), SEC.6.

6–3.5–7–17   Residence or principal place of business; determination

Sec. 17. (a) For purposes of this chapter, an individual shall be treated as a resident of the county in which the individual:

(1) maintains a home if the individual maintains only one (1) home in Indiana;

(2) if subdivision (1) does not apply, is registered to vote;

(3) if subdivision (1) or (2) does not apply, registers the individual's personal automobile; or

(4) if subdivision (1), (2), or (3) does not apply, spends the majority of the individual's time in Indiana during the taxable year in question.

(b) The residence or principal place of business or employment of an individual is to be determined on January 1 of the calendar year in which the individual's taxable year commences. If an individual changes location of residence or principal place of employment or business to another county in Indiana during a calendar year, the individual's liability for county economic development income tax is not affected.

(c) Notwithstanding subsection (b), if an individual becomes a county taxpayer for purposes of IC 36–7–27 during a calendar year because the individual:

(1) changes the location of the individual's residence to a county in which the individual begins employment or business at a qualified economic development tax project (as defined in IC 36–7–27–9); or

(2) changes the location of the individual's principal place of employment or business to a qualified economic development tax project and does not reside in another county in which the county economic development income tax is in effect;

the individual's adjusted gross income attributable to employment or business at the qualified economic development tax project is taxable only by the county containing the qualified economic development tax project.

As added by P.L.380–1987(ss), SEC.6.   Amended by P.L.44–1994, SEC.9.

Historical and Statutory Notes

P.L.44–1994, Sec.9, in Subsec. (a), made a nonsubstantive language change in Subd. (1); and added Subsec. (c).

6–3.5–7–18   Application of adjusted gross income tax law and other statutory provisions; withholdings report

Sec. 18. (a) Except as otherwise provided in this chapter, all provisions of the adjusted gross income tax law (IC 6–3) concerning:

(1) definitions;

(2) declarations of estimated tax;

(3) filing of returns;

(4) remittances;

(5) incorporation of the provisions of the Internal Revenue Code;

(6) penalties and interest;

(7) exclusion of military pay credits for withholding; and

(8) exemptions and deductions;

apply to the imposition, collection, and administration of the tax imposed by this chapter.

(b) The provisions of IC IC 6–3–1–3.5(a)(6), IC 6–3–3–3, IC 6–3–3–5, and IC 6–3–5–1 do not apply to the tax imposed by this chapter.

(c) Notwithstanding subsections (a) and (b), each employer shall report to the department the amount of withholdings attributable to each county. This report shall be submitted annually along with the employer's annual withholding report.

As added by P.L.380–1987(ss), SEC.6.   Amended by P.L.57–1997, SEC.6.

Historical and Statutory Notes

P.L.57–1997, Sec.6, emerg. eff. retroactive to Jan. 1, 1997, amended the section by substituting "IC 6–3–1–3.5(a)(6)," for "IC 6–3–1–3.5(a)(5)," in Subsec. (b).

6–3.5–7–19 Annual report of economic development income tax account year-end balance

Sec. 19. Before February 1 of each year, the department shall submit a report to each county treasurer indicating the amount credited to the county's economic development income tax account as of the end of the preceding year.

As added by P.L.380–1987(ss), SEC.6.

6–3.5–7–20 "Listed tax" and "income tax" status for tax administration purposes

Sec. 20. The economic development income tax is a listed tax and an income tax for the purposes of IC 6–8.1.

As added by P.L.380–1987(ss), SEC.6.

6–3.5–7–21 Leases; terms; public hearing; approval; execution; notice; action contesting validity; purchase of leased facility

Sec. 21. (a) A unit may enter into a lease with a leasing body (as defined in IC 5–1–1–1) of any property that could be financed with the proceeds of bonds issued under this chapter with a lessor for a term not to exceed fifty (50) years, and the lease may provide for payments from revenues under this chapter, any other revenue available to the unit, or any combination of these sources.

(b) A lease may provide that payments by the unit to the lessor are required only to the extent and only for the period that the lessor is able to provide the leased facilities in accordance with the lease. The terms of each lease must be based upon the value of the facilities leased and may not create a debt of the unit for purposes of the Constitution of the State of Indiana.

(c) A lease may be entered into by the executive of the unit only after a public hearing at which all interested parties are provided the opportunity to be heard. After the public hearing, the executive may approve the execution of the lease on behalf of the unit if the executive finds that the service to be provided throughout the term of the lease will serve the public purpose of the unit and is in the best interests of its residents. Any lease approved by the executive must also be approved by an ordinance of the fiscal body of the unit.

(d) Upon execution of a lease providing for payments by the unit in whole or in part from taxes under this chapter and upon approval of the lease by the unit's fiscal body, the executive of the unit shall publish notice of the execution of the lease and its approval in accordance with IC 5–3–1.

(e) Except as provided in this section, no approvals of any governmental body or agency are required before the unit enters into a lease under this section.

(f) An action to contest the validity of the lease or to enjoin the performance of any of its terms and conditions must be brought within thirty (30) days after the publication of the notice of the execution and approval of the lease.

(g) If a unit exercises an option to buy a leased facility from a lessor, the unit may subsequently sell the leased facility, without regard to any other statute, to the lessor at the end of the lease term at a price set forth in the lease or at fair market value established at the time of the sale by the executive of the unit through auction, appraisal, or arms length negotiation. If the facility is sold at auction, after appraisal, or through negotiation, the unit shall conduct a hearing after public notice in accordance with IC 5–3–1 before the sale. Any action to contest the sale must be brought within fifteen (15) days of the hearing.

As added by P.L.380–1987(ss), SEC.6. Amended by P.L.28–1993, SEC.10; P.L.99–1995, SEC.4.

Historical and Statutory Notes

P.L.28–1993, Sec.10, emerg. eff. Feb. 12, 1993, added Subsec. (h) and redesignated former Subsec. (h) as Subsec. (g).

P.L.99–1995, Sec.4, emerg. eff. April 29, 1995, amended the section by deleting former Subsec. (h), which read:

"(h) This section does not apply to the use of the economic development income tax for lease payments by a county having a population of more than one hundred sixty thousand (160,-000) but less than two hundred thousand (200,-000)."

6–3.5–7–22 Substance removal and remedial action funds

Sec. 22. (a) This section only applies to a designated unit.

(b) The county income tax council may, by ordinance, determine that economic development income tax money is needed in the county to fund substance removal and remedial action, including the repayment of bonds or other debt incurred for substance removal or remedial action, and the actions taken to fund substance removal and remedial action serve a public purpose by promoting public health, welfare, and safety.

(c) If the county income tax council makes a determination under subsection (b), the county income tax council may adopt a tax rate under section 5(g) of this chapter. The tax rate may not be imposed at a rate or for a time greater than is necessary to fund substance removal and remedial action in the county, including the repayment of bonds or other debt incurred for substance removal or remedial action.

(d) The county treasurer shall establish a substance removal and remedial action fund to be used only for the purposes described in this section. County economic development income tax revenues derived from the tax rate imposed under section 5(g) of this chapter shall be deposited in the substance removal and remedial action fund before making a certified distribution under section 12 of this chapter.

(e) The county income tax council may, by ordinance, appropriate or pledge any part of the substance removal and remediation action fund to a political subdivision or to an entity formed by an interlocal cooperation agreement under IC 36–1–7 for the purposes set forth in this chapter in the county.

(f) The county auditor shall distribute the amount specified in the ordinance to the designated political subdivision or to an entity formed by an interlocal cooperation agreement under IC 36–1–7 from the substance removal and remedial action fund.

(g) Bonds issued by a political subdivision or an entity formed by an interlocal cooperation agreement under IC 36–1–7 payable from the substance removal and remedial action fund do not constitute debt of a designated unit or a city or town in the designated unit, and the bonds shall contain a statement on their face to that effect and to the effect that the bonds are payable solely from money in the substance removal and remedial action fund, and other available funds, and are not supported by the full faith and credit of the county, city, or town.

As added by P.L.44–1994, SEC.10. Amended by P.L.99–1995, SEC.5.

Historical and Statutory Notes

P.L.44–1994, Sec.10, emerg. eff. March 17, 1994.

P.L.99–1995, Sec.5, emerg. eff. April 29, 1995, amended the section by changing refer-ences to section 5(h) to references to section 5(g).

6–3.5–7–23   Library property taxes; replacement credits

Sec. 23. (a) This section applies only to a county having a population of at least forty-five thousand (45,000) but not more than forty-seven thousand (47,000).

(b) The county council may by ordinance determine that, in order to promote the development of libraries in the county and thereby encourage economic development, it is necessary to use economic development income tax revenue to replace library property taxes in the county. However, a county council may adopt an ordinance under this subsection only if all territory in the county is included in a library district.

(c) If the county council makes a determination under subsection (b), the county council may designate the county economic development income tax revenue generated by the tax rate adopted under section 5 of this chapter, or revenue generated by a portion of the tax rate, as revenue that will be used to replace public library property taxes imposed by public libraries in the county. The county council may not designate for library property tax replacement purposes any county economic development income tax revenue that is generated by a tax rate of more than fifteen-hundredths percent (0.15%).

(d) The county treasurer shall establish a library property tax replacement fund to be used only for the purposes described in this section. County economic development income tax revenues derived from the portion of the tax rate designated for property tax replacement credits under subsection (c) shall be deposited in the library property tax replacement fund before certified distributions are made under section 12 of this chapter.

(e) The amount of county economic development income tax revenue dedicated to providing library property tax replacement credits shall, in the manner prescribed in this section, be allocated to public libraries operating in the county and shall be used by those public libraries as property tax replacement credits. The amount of property tax replacement credits that each public library in the county is entitled to receive during a calendar year under this section equals the lesser of:

(1) the product of:

(A) the amount of revenue deposited by the county auditor in the library property tax replacement fund; multiplied by

(B) a fraction described as follows:

(i) The numerator of the fraction equals the sum of the total property taxes that would have been collected by the public library during the previous calendar year from taxpayers located within the library district if the property tax replacement under this section had not been in effect.

(ii) The denominator of the fraction equals the sum of the total property taxes that would have been collected during the previous year from taxpayers located within the county by all public libraries that are eligible to receive property tax replacement credits under this section if the property tax replacement under this section had not been in effect; or

(2) the total property taxes that would otherwise be collected by the public library for the calendar year if the property tax replacement credit under this section were not in effect.

The state board of tax commissioners shall make any adjustments necessary to account for the expansion of a library district. However, a public library is eligible to receive property tax replacement credits under this section only if it has entered into reciprocal borrowing agreements with all other public libraries in the county. If the total amount of county economic development income tax revenue deposited by the county auditor in the library property tax replacement fund for a calendar year exceeds the total property tax liability that would otherwise be imposed for public libraries in the county for the year, the excess shall remain in the library property tax replacement fund and shall be used for library property tax replacement purposes in the following calendar year.

(f) Notwithstanding subsection (e), if a public library did not impose a property tax levy during the previous calendar year, that public library is entitled to receive a part of the property tax replacement credits to be distributed for the calendar year. The amount of property tax replacement credits the public library is entitled to receive during the calendar year equals the product of:

(1) the amount of revenue deposited in the library property tax replacement fund; multiplied by

(2) a fraction. The numerator of the fraction equals the budget of the public library for that calendar year. The denominator of the fraction equals the aggregate budgets of public libraries in the county for that calendar year.

If for a calendar year a public library is allocated a part of the property tax replacement credits under this subsection, then the amount of property tax credits distributed to other public libraries in the county for the calendar year shall be reduced by the amount to be distributed as property tax replacement credits under this subsection. The state board of tax commissioners shall make any adjustments required by this subsection and provide the adjustments to the county auditor.

(g) The state board of tax commissioners shall inform the county auditor of the amount of property tax replacement credits that each public library in the county is entitled to receive under this section. The county auditor shall certify to each public library the amount of property tax replacement credits that the public library is entitled to receive during that calendar year. The county auditor shall also certify these amounts to the county treasurer.

(h) A public library receiving property tax replacement credits under this section shall allocate the credits among each fund for which a distinct property tax levy is imposed. The amount that must be allocated to each fund equals:

(1) the amount of property tax replacement credits provided to the public library under this section; multiplied by

(2) the amount determined in **STEP THREE** of the following formula:

STEP ONE: Determine the property taxes that would have been collected for each fund by the public library during the previous calendar year if the property tax replacement under this section had not been in effect.

STEP TWO: Determine the sum of the total property taxes that would have been collected for all funds by the public library during the previous calendar year if the property tax replacement under this section had not been in effect.

STEP THREE: Divide the STEP ONE amount by the STEP TWO amount.

However, if a public library did not impose a property tax levy during the previous calendar year or did not impose a property tax levy for a particular fund during the previous calendar year, but the public library is imposing a property tax levy in the current calendar year or is imposing a property tax levy for the particular fund in the current calendar year, the state board of tax commissioners shall adjust the amount of property tax replacement credits allocated among the various funds of the public library and shall provide the adjustment to the county auditor. If a public library receiving property tax replacement credits under this section does not impose a property tax levy for a particular fund that is first due and payable in a calendar year in which the property tax replacement credits are being distributed, the public library is not required to allocate to that fund a part of the property tax replacement credits to be distributed to the public library.

(i) For each public library that receives property tax credits under this section, the state board of tax commissioners shall certify to the county auditor the property tax rate applicable to each fund after the property tax replacement credits are allocated.

(j) A public library shall treat property tax replacement credits received during a particular calendar year under this section as a part of the public library's property tax levy for each fund for that same calendar year for purposes of fixing the public library's budget and for purposes of the property tax levy limits imposed by IC 6–1.1–18.5.

(k) The property tax replacement credits that are received under this section do not reduce the total county tax levy that is used to compute the state property tax replacement credit under IC 6–1.1–21. For the purpose of computing and distributing certified distributions under IC 6–3.5–1.1 and tax revenue under IC 6–5–10, IC 6–5–11, IC 6–5–12, IC 6–5.5, or IC 6–6–5, the property tax replacement credits that are received under this section shall be treated as though they were property taxes that were due and payable during that same calendar year.

As added by P.L.124–1999, SEC.3.

Historical and Statutory Notes

P.L.124–1999, Sec.4, emerg. eff. May 3, 1999, provides:

"(a) Notwithstanding IC 6–3.5–7–5, the county council of a county described in IC 6–3.5–7–23, as added by this act, may after January 1 but before June 15 of a year adopt an ordinance to impose the county economic development income tax under IC 6–3.5–7.

"(b) This section expires January 1, 2000."

Chapter 8.5

City Option Hospital Income Tax

6–3.5–8.5–1 to 6–3.5–8.5–15   Repealed

(Repealed by P.L.156–1995, SEC.9.)

Historical and Statutory Notes

P.L.156–1995, Sec.9, emerg. eff. retroactive to January 1, 1995.

The repealed sections related to city option hospital income tax.

Formerly:

P.L.27–1992, SEC.2.
P.L.2–1993, SEC.58.
P.L.227–1993(ss), SECS.63 to 67.

ARTICLE 4

INHERITANCE AND ESTATE TAX

Historical and Statutory Notes

P.L.1–1993, Sec.41, which was part of a correction bill, emerg. eff. upon passage May 4, 1993, repealed Article 6–4, which had been previously repealed in 1976.

Chapter 1

Inheritance and Estate Tax

6–4–1–1 to 6–4–1–40   Repealed

(Repealed by Acts 1976, P.L.18, SEC.2; P.L.1–1993, SEC.41.)

Historical and Statutory Notes

Acts 1976, P.L. 18, provided in § 7, containing emergency clause, that the act takes effect Feb. 18, 1976.

The former chapter related to inheritance and estate taxes.

DISPOSITION TABLE

Showing where the subject matter of the repealed sections of Title 6 of the Indiana Code was covered in new sections of Title 6, West's Annotated Indiana Code.

Repealed Sections	New Sections	Repealed Sections	New Sections
6–4–1–1	6–4.1–2–1 to 6–4.1–2–7, 6–4.1–3–6, 6–4.1–3–7	6–4–1–7	6–4.1–4–1 to 6–4.1–4–6, 6–4.1–4–9, 6–4.1–5–2, 6–4.1–5–5, 6–4.1–5 –7, 6–4.1–5–8, 6–4.1–5–10, 6–4.1–5–12, 6–4.1–9–6, 6–4.1–12–2
6–4–1–2	6–4.1–1–3, 6–4.1–5–1		
6–4–1–3	6–4.1–3–1, 6–4.1–3–2 to 6–4.1–3–4, 6–4.1–3–8 to 6–4.1–3–12		
		6–4–1–8	6–4.1–5–2, 6–4.1–5–5, 6–4.1–5–10, 6–4.1–7–1, 6–4.1–7–2, 6–4.1–12–2 to 6–4.1–12–4
6–4–1–4	6–4.1–3–13 to 6–4.1–3–15		
6–4–1–5	6–4.1–6–1 to 6–4.1–6–4, 6–4.1–6–6		
		6–4–1–9	6–4.1–5–3, 6–4.1–5–4,
6–4–1–6	6–4.1–12–1		

263

Formerly:

IC 6–4–1–26.
IC 6–4–1–35.5.
IC 6–4–1–35.6.
IC 6–4–1–40.
Acts 1931, c. 75, ss. 27, 41.
Acts 1971, P.L.66, SECS.1, 2.

Chapter 2

Exemption: Gifts Or Bequests Of Annuities To Educational Institutions

6–4–2–1 Repealed

(Repealed by Acts 1976, P.L.18, SEC.2; P.L.1–1993, SEC.41.)

Historical and Statutory Notes

Acts 1976, P.L. 18, provided in § 7, containing emergency clause, that the act takes effect Feb. 18, 1976.

The former chapter related to exemptions from inheritance and estate taxes for gifts to educational institutions.

Formerly:

Acts 1921, c. 260, s. 2.

ARTICLE 4.1

DEATH TAXES

WESTLAW Computer Assisted Legal Research

WESTLAW supplements your legal research in many ways. WESTLAW allows you to

- update your research with the most current information

- expand your library with additional resources

- retrieve current, comprehensive history and citing references to a case with KeyCite

For more information on using WESTLAW to supplement your research, see the WESTLAW Electronic Research Guide, which follows the Preface.

Cross References

Airport authorities, bonds and interest exempt from taxation, see IC 8–22–3–17, 8–22–3–18.1.
Airport development authority, property exempt from taxation, see IC 8–22–3.7–21.
Airport facilities, exemptions from taxation, see IC 8–21–9–31.
Building and loan associations, disposition of unpledged stock of decedent, waiver required, see IC 28–1–21–38.
Civic center building authority, property exempt from taxation, see IC 36–10–10–24.
County hospital building authorities, tax exemptions, see IC 16–22–6–34.
Financing of housing, tax exemption for bonds, see IC 5–20–2–14.
Hospital bonding authorities, tax exemption, see IC 5–1–4–26.
Indiana bond bank, exemption from taxation, see IC 5–1.5–9–9.
Indiana development finance authority, property exempt from taxation, see IC 4–4–11–36.1.
Indiana educational facilities authority, tax exemptions, see IC 20–12–63–27.
Indiana political subdivision risk management commission, bond proceeds and interest exempt from taxation, see IC 27–1–29–17.
Indiana port commission, property exempt from taxation, see IC 8–10–1–27.
Industrial loan and investment companies, payment after death of certificate holder, waiver required, see IC 28–5–2–2.
Intelenet commission, property exempt from taxation, see IC 5–21–2–15.

Little Calumet River basin development commission, exemption from taxes or assessments, see IC 14–13–2–28.
Local public improvement bond banks, exemption from taxation, see IC 5–1.4–9–9.
Marion County convention and recreational facilities authority, property exempt from taxation, see IC 36–10–9.1–22.
Marion County redevelopment authority, property exempt from taxation, see IC 36–9–25–27.
Multiple county infrastructure authority, property exempt from taxation, see IC 36–7–23–48.
Municipal bonds, proceeds and interest exempt from taxation, see IC 6–8–5–1.
Probate law, claims defined, see IC 29–1–1–3.
Recreational development commission, property exempt from taxation or assessment, see IC 14–14–1–46.
Redevelopment authorities, property exempt from taxation, see IC 36–7–14.5–23.
Regional transportation authorities, bonds and interest exempt from taxation, see IC 36–9–3–31.
Reopened estates, inheritance tax, see IC 29–1–17–14.
Sewage works, construction bonds and interest exempt from taxation, see IC 36–9–25–27.
State office building commission, exemption of property from taxes, see IC 4–13.5–4–6.
Transportation system lease financing, exemption from taxation, see IC 8–14.5–6–12.
Underground petroleum storage tank excess liability fund, tax exemption for bonds and other property of authority, see IC 4–4–11.2–29.
White River state park development commission, exemption from taxes or assessments, see IC 14–13–1–38.

Chapter 1

Definitions and Rules of Construction

Library References

Taxation ⊸860.
WESTLAW Topic No. 371.

C.J.S. Taxation § 1135.
I.L.E. Taxation § 232.

6–4.1–1–1   Application to article

Sec. 1. The definitions and rules of construction contained in this chapter apply throughout this article unless the context clearly requires otherwise.
As added by Acts 1976, P.L.18, SEC.1.

Historical and Statutory Notes

Acts 1976, P.L. 18, § 1, emerg. eff. Feb. 18, 1976, added this article.

The 1976 act reenacted the provisions of this article as part of a codification, revision and rearrangement of laws relating to death taxes.

Acts 1976, P.L. 18, provided in §§ 3, 4 and 6:

"Section 3. (a) This act is intended to be a codification and restatement of applicable or corresponding provisions of laws repealed by this act. The substantive operation and effect of any law repealed by this act shall continue without interruption if that law is reenacted, in the same or restated form, by this act.

"(b) A rule or regulation promulgated under a law repealed by this act and in effect before the effective date of this act shall remain in full force and effect until it is amended, repealed, or rescinded.

"(c) This act does not effect any:

"(1) rights or liabilities accrued;

"(2) penalties incurred; or

"(3) proceedings begun;

"before the effective date of this act. These rights, liabilities, and proceedings are continued; and punishments, penalties, or forfeitures shall be imposed and enforced under the repealed laws as if this act had not been enacted.

"(d) All crimes committed, before the effective date of this act, under laws repealed by this act shall be prosecuted and remain punishable under the repealed laws as if this act had not been enacted.

"Section 4. A citation to a law repealed by this act shall be construed as a citation to the appropriate provision of this act if the repealed law is reenacted, in the same or restated form, by this act."

"Section 6. If a provision of this act or its application to a person or circumstance is held invalid, the invalidity does not affect other provisions or applications of the act which can be given effect without the invalid provision or application, and to this end the provisions of this act are severable."

Administrative Code References

Definitions, see 45 IAC 4.1–1–1 et seq.

Law Review and Journal Commentaries

Amendments of 1977 to Indiana Inheritance Tax Law. William L. Tracy, 21 Res Gestae 488 (1977).

Death taxes. Thomas B. Allington, 10 Ind. L.Rev. 340 (1976).

Death taxes: Survey of recent law. John W. Boyd, 11 Ind.L.Rev. 292 (1978); 12 Ind.L.Rev. 320, 326 (1979).

Inheritance taxation. 21 Ind.L.J. 119 (1946).

Jurisdiction of the states to tax, recent developments. 5 Ind.L.J. 507 (1930).

Reasonable cause for late filing of estate tax returns. 11 Ind.L.Rev. 621 (1978).

Taxable gifts: a tax-saving strategy. Nicolas H. Schmelzer, 41 Res Gestae 16 (April 1998).

Taxation; department of revenue: Survey of recent law. Marc S. Weinstein, 13 Ind.L.Rev. 1 (1980).

United States Code Annotated

Federal estate tax, see 26 U.S.C.A. § 2001 et seq.

6–4.1–1–2 "Appropriate probate court" defined

Sec. 2. "Appropriate probate court" means the probate court which has jurisdiction over the determination of the inheritance tax imposed as a result of a resident decedent's death.

As added by Acts 1976, P.L.18, SEC.1.

Library References

Words and Phrases (Perm. Ed.)

6–4.1–1–3 Classes of transferees defined; adopted child as natural child

Sec. 3. (a) "Class A transferee" means a transferee who is a lineal ancestor or lineal descendant of the transferor.

(b) "Class B transferee" means a transferee who is a:

(1) brother or sister of the transferor;

(2) descendant of a brother or sister of the transferor; or

(3) spouse, widow, or widower of a child of the transferor.

(c) "Class C transferee" means a transferee, except a surviving spouse, who is neither a Class A nor a Class B transferee.

(d) For purposes of this section, a legally adopted child is to be treated as if he were the natural child of his adopting parent. For purposes of this section, if a relationship of loco parentis has existed for at least ten (10) years and if the relationship began before the child's fifteenth birthday, the child is to be considered the natural child of the loco parentis parent.

As added by Acts 1976, P.L.18, SEC.1. Amended by Acts 1979, P.L.75, SEC.1.

Historical and Statutory Notes

Acts 1979, P.L. 75, § 1, eff. July 1, 1979, deleted "surviving spouse," in Subsec. (a) before "lineal ancestor"; and inserted "except a surviving spouse" in Subsec. (c).

Acts 1979, P.L. 75, provided in § 16(b):

"(b) The remainder of this act takes effect July 1, 1979, and applies to inheritance and estate taxes imposed as a result of the deaths of decedents who die after June 30, 1979."

Formerly:
IC 6–4–1–2.
Acts 1931, c. 75, s. 2.
Acts 1965, c. 302, s. 1.
Acts 1975, P.L.64, SEC.1.

Notes of Decisions

Brother or sister 1
Loco parentis relationship 3
Spouse, widow or widower of child 2

___

1. Brother or sister

Brothers and sisters of half blood and their descendants are in the same class as those of whole blood as concerns rate of inheritance tax and amount of exemption. 1936 Op.Atty.Gen. p. 306.

2. Spouse, widow or widower of child

Though testatrix' deceased son's wife, who was sole surviving beneficiary under the will, had remarried prior to testatrix' death, wife was a "widow" within meaning of this section providing that, for inheritance tax purposes, a "class B transferee" was a widow of a child of the transferor. Matter of Souder's Estate, App. 3 Dist.1981, 421 N.E.2d 12.

3. Loco parentis relationship

Child's claim of Class A transferee status for inheritance tax purposes when her natural mother died did not estop child from subsequently claiming Class A transferee status when she was named as residuary legatee in will of her stepmother, with whom she stood in loco parentis. State, Dept. of State Revenue v. National Bank of Logansport, App. 2 Dist.1980, 402 N.E.2d 1008.

6–4.1–1–4 "Federal death tax credit" defined

Sec. 4. "Federal death tax credit" means the maximum federal estate tax credit provided, with respect to estate, inheritance, legacy, or succession taxes, under Section 2011 or Section 2102 of the Internal Revenue Code.[1]

As added by Acts 1976, P.L.18, SEC.1. Amended by Acts 1977(ss), P.L.6, SEC.1; P.L.87–1983, SEC.1; P.L.2–1987, SEC.23.

[1] 26 U.S.C.A. §§ 2011 or 2102.

Historical and Statutory Notes

Acts 1977 (ss), P.L. 6, § 1, emerg. eff. retroactively to Jan. 1, 1977, inserted "maximum" before "federal estate tax"; and substituted "1977" for "1976" following "January 1".

P.L. 87–1983, Sec.1, emerg. eff. Jan. 1, 1983, substituted "January 1, 1983" for "January 1, 1977."

Section 7 of P.L. 87–1983 provides that this act applies to the estates of decedents who die after Dec. 31, 1982.

P.L. 2–1987, Sec.23, emergency effective retroactive to Jan. 1, 1987, deleted "of 1954, as amended and in effect on January 1, 1983" following "Code".

P.L. 2–1987 provides in Section 54 that this act applies to taxable years beginning after Dec. 31, 1986.

Law Review and Journal Commentaries

Amendments of 1977 to Indiana Inheritance Tax Law. William L. Tracy, 21 Res Gestae 488 (1977).

Death taxes. Thomas B. Allington, 10 Ind. L.Rev. 340 (1976).

6–4.1–1–5 "Intangible personal property" defined

Sec. 5. "Intangible personal property" means incorporeal property, such as money, deposits, credits, shares of stock, bonds, notes, other evidences of indebtedness, and other evidences of property interests.

As added by Acts 1976, P.L.18, SEC.1.

Historical and Statutory Notes

Formerly:

IC 6–4–1–32.
Acts 1931, c. 75, s. 33.

Library References

Inheritance tax considerations in connection with transfers of securities owned by a deceased person, see Galanti, 18 Indiana Practice § 15.7.

Notes of Decisions

In general   1
Property interest   2

_____

1. In general

Interest incorporeal in nature is interest in intangible personal property. Indiana Dept. of State Revenue, Inheritance Tax Div. v. Estate of Puschel, 1991, 582 N.E.2d 923.

2. Property interest

Transfer of beneficial interests in charitable remainder unitrust, including as asset a beneficial interest in land trust holding Indiana real property, was not subject to inheritance tax; interest transferred was incorporeal in nature and transfer was therefore of intangible personal property. Blood v. Poindexter, 1989, 534 N.E.2d 768.

6–4.1–1–6 "Intestate succession" defined

Sec. 6. "Intestate succession" means a property interest transfer which is effected by the statute of descent and distribution or by operation of law, as the result of the death of an individual who fails to make a complete disposition of the property under a valid will.

As added by Acts 1976, P.L.18, SEC.1.

Historical and Statutory Notes

Formerly:
  IC 6–4–1–32.
  Acts 1931, c. 75, s. 33.

6–4.1–1–7 "Non-resident decedent" defined

Sec. 7. "Non-resident decedent" means an individual who was not domiciled in Indiana at the time of his death.

As added by Acts 1976, P.L.18, SEC.1.

6–4.1–1–8 "Person" defined

Sec. 8. "Person" includes a sole proprietorship, partnership, association, corporation, limited liability company, fiduciary, individual, and the department of state revenue.

As added by Acts 1976, P.L.18, SEC.1. Amended by P.L.8–1993, SEC.92.

Historical and Statutory Notes

  P.L.8–1993, Sec.92, inserted "limited liability company".

6–4.1–1–9 "Personal representative" defined

Sec. 9. "Personal representative" means a person who is appointed to administer a decedent's estate by a court which has jurisdiction over the estate.

As added by Acts 1976, P.L.18, SEC.1.

6–4.1–1–10 "Probate court" defined

Sec. 10. "Probate court" means a court of this state which has jurisdiction over probate matters.

As added by Acts 1976, P.L.18, SEC.1.

6–4.1–1–11 "Resident decedent" defined

Sec. 11. "Resident decedent" means an individual who was domiciled in Indiana at the time of his death.

As added by Acts 1976, P.L.18, SEC.1.

6–4.1–1–12 Repealed

(Repealed by P.L.58–1990, SEC.6.)

Historical and Statutory Notes

Former IC 6–4.1–1–12 related to the definition of state death tax.

Formerly:
Acts 1976, P.L.18, SEC.1.

6–4.1–1–13   "Tangible personal property" defined

Sec. 13. "Tangible personal property" means corporeal personal property,
such as goods, wares, and merchandise.

As added by Acts 1976, P.L.18, SEC.1.

Historical and Statutory Notes

Formerly:
   IC 6–4–1–32.
   Acts 1931, c. 75, s. 33.

6–4.1–1–14   "Taxable transfer" defined

Sec. 14. "Taxable transfer" means a property interest transfer which is
described in clauses (1) and (2) of IC 6–4.1–2–1 and which is not exempt from
the inheritance tax under sections 1 through 7 of IC 6–4.1–3.

As added by Acts 1976, P.L.18, SEC.1.

6–4.1–1–15   Gender; singular as plural

Sec. 15. (a) Whenever a masculine gender pronoun is used in this article, it
refers to the masculine, feminine, or neuter, whichever is appropriate.

(b) The singular form of any noun as used in this article includes the plural,
and the plural includes the singular, where appropriate.

As added by Acts 1976, P.L.18, SEC.1.

Cross References

Construction of statutes, see IC 1–1–4–1.

Chapter 2

Imposition of the Inheritance Tax

6–4.1–2–1   Time of imposition; transfers subject to tax

Sec. 1. (a) An inheritance tax is imposed at the time of a decedent's death on certain property interest transfers made by him. The transfer of a property interest is subject to the tax if:

(1) the property transferred is described in:

(i) section 2 of this chapter if the property is transferred by a resident decedent; or

(ii) section 3 of this chapter if the property is transferred by a non-resident decedent;

(2) the transfer is described in section 4 of this chapter; and

(3) neither the transfer nor the property is exempt from the inheritance tax under IC 6–4.1–3.

(b) For purposes of this article, a transfer described in section 4 of this chapter is considered a transfer made by the deceased transferor regardless of when the transferee acquires the property interest.

As added by Acts 1976, P.L.18, SEC.1.

Historical and Statutory Notes

Acts 1976, P.L. 18, § 1, emerg. eff. Feb. 18, 1976, added this article.

The 1976 act added and reenacted the provisions of this chapter as part of a codification, revision and rearrangement of laws relating to death taxes.

Formerly:

IC 6–4–1–1.

Acts 1931, c. 75, s. 1.

Cross References

Indiana family college savings programs, individual account not asset, see IC 21–9–7–3.

Administrative Code References

Time of imposition, see 45 IAC 4.1–2–1.

Transfers subject to tax, see 45 IAC 4.1–2–5 et seq.

Law Review and Journal Commentaries

Conflict between domicile and situs as basis of tax jurisdiction. 12 Ind.L.J. 87 (1936).

Death taxes: Survey of recent law. John W. Boyd, 11 Ind.L.Rev. 292 (1978).

Determination of domicile of taxpayer subject to state inheritance tax. 14 Ind.L.J. 464 (1939).

Determination of items taxable as income in respect of a decedent. 28 Ind.L.J. 46 (1952).

Inheritance tax and retirement plan death benefits. Robert T. Wildman, 20 Res Gestae 162 (1976).

Stock redemptions from a closely held corporation in order to pay estate tax. 23 Ind.L.J. 89 (1948).

Surviving spouses' rights. John S. Grimes, 10 Ind.L.Rev. 675 (1977).

Taxability of non-residents on stock of domestic corporations. 7 Ind.L.J. 495 (1932).

Taxation. 9 Ind.L.Rev. 336 (1975).

Validity of estate tax levied on gross estate of decedent domiciled within New York. 13 Ind. L.J. 414 (1938).

Library References

Taxation ☞877.
WESTLAW Topic No. 371.

C.J.S. Taxation § 1142.
I.L.E. Taxation §§ 233 to 235.

United States Code Annotated

Federal estate tax, liability for payment, see 26 U.S.C.A. § 2002.
Imposition and rate of federal estate tax, see 26 U.S.C.A. § 2001.

Notes of Decisions

Renunciation of interest   2
Taxable transfers   3
Time of imposition   1

1. Time of imposition

If beneficiary receives less than fee interest in property transferred by reason of owner's death, inheritance tax is calculated pursuant to actuarial tables as of date of death. Estate of Hibbs v. Indiana Dept. of State Revenue, Inheritance Tax Div., 1994, 636 N.E.2d 204.

If life estate with remainder is created upon death of property owner, both life tenant and remainderman will pay inheritance tax on their proportionate interests, based on interests' values at date of owner's death. Estate of Hibbs v. Indiana Dept. of State Revenue, Inheritance Tax Div., 1994, 636 N.E.2d 204.

Inheritance tax may be imposed on certain inter vivos transfers, but its collection is postponed until death of transferor. In re Grotrian's Estate, App. 3 Dist.1980, 405 N.E.2d 69.

For purposes of former statute making inheritance tax due and payable at time of transfer, transfer occurred at time of death of deceased, and therefore estate was liable for interest from date of death, even though will was not discovered and estate was consequently not opened until several years thereafter. 1937 Op.Atty. Gen. p. 134.

2. Renunciation of interest

Will beneficiary's renunciation of interest in decedent's estate related back to time of decedent's death; there was no transfer of portion of decedent's estate which she renounced and there was thus no basis for assessment of inheritance tax to her. Matter of Wisely's Estate, App. 2 Dist.1980, 402 N.E.2d 14.

3. Taxable transfers

See, generally, Notes of Decisions under § 6–4.1–2–4.

State inheritance tax is imposed, not on the property itself, but rather on the transfer of ownership of the property. Department of State Revenue, Inheritance Tax Div. v. Estate of Hardy, 1998, 703 N.E.2d 705.

Inheritance tax is not a tax on the property of a decedent's estate but a tax on the privilege of succeeding to the property rights of the decedent. Estate of McNicholas v. State, App. 4 Dist.1991, 580 N.E.2d 978, transfer denied.

If will is admitted to probate and never set aside, property is transferred under the will and must be taxed as such. Estate of McNicholas v. State, App. 4 Dist.1991, 580 N.E.2d 978, transfer denied.

Where will was admitted to probate and court was without authority to invalidate or set aside the will, and court could only approve family settlement agreement between the beneficiaries, inheritance tax was to be based on distribution under the will rather than the distribution effected by the settlement agreement. Estate of McNicholas v. State, App. 4 Dist.1991, 580 N.E.2d 978, transfer denied.

6–4.1–2–2   Property transfers of resident decedent

Sec. 2.   (a) The inheritance tax applies to a property interest transfer made by a resident decedent if the interest transferred is in:

(1) real property located in this state;

(2) tangible personal property which does not have an actual situs outside this state; or

(3) intangible personal property regardless of where it is located.

(b) The inheritance tax does not apply to a property interest transfer made by a resident decedent if the interest transferred is in:

(1) real property located outside this state, regardless of whether the property is held in a trust or whether the trustee is required to distribute the property in-kind; or

(2) real property located in this state, if:

(A) the real property was transferred to an irrevocable trust during the decedent's lifetime;

(B) the transfer to the trust was not made in contemplation of the transferor's death, as determined under IC 6–4.1–2–4; and

(C) the decedent does not have a retained interest in the trust.

As added by Acts 1976, P.L.18, SEC.1. As amended by P.L.78–1993, SEC.1.

Historical and Statutory Notes

P.L.78–1993, Sec.1, designated Subsec. (a) and added Subsec. (b).

Section 4 of P.L. 78–1993, provides:

"This act does not apply to individuals who die before July 1, 1993."

Formerly:

IC 6–4–1–1.

Acts 1931, c. 75, s. 1.

Library References

Taxation ☞864.
WESTLAW Topic No. 371.
C.J.S. Taxation §§ 1115, 1138, 1140.

I.L.E. Taxation §§ 233 to 235.
Galanti, 18 Indiana Practice § 15.7.

Notes of Decisions

Real property in trust   1

—————

1. Real property in trust

Interest of beneficiaries in real property held in trust was interest in intangible personal property, and therefore subject to inheritance tax, where trust agreement was silent as to whether distribution of property had to be in kind or in cash, trust gave trustee broad discretionary powers to deal with and administer trust corpus, including explicit power to make distributions whether in cash or in kind, and trustee's discretion to distribute property in cash or in kind was unrestricted by beneficiaries' wishes. Indiana Dept. of State Revenue, Inheritance Tax Div. v. Estate of Nichols, 1995, 659 N.E.2d 694.

If character of beneficial interest in trust on date of decedent's death was real property, it was not subject to inheritance tax, since trust property was located outside Indiana, but if character of that interest was intangible property, it was taxable. Indiana Dept. of State Revenue, Inheritance Tax Div. v. Estate of Puschel, 1991, 582 N.E.2d 923.

Property interest transferred from trust upon death of resident grantor, who was also the lifetime beneficiary, constituted incorporeal interest in intangible personal property subject to inheritance tax, even though out-of-state real property was transferred, where transfer of value rather than transfer of real property itself was grantor's intent. Indiana Dept. of State Revenue, Inheritance Tax Div. v. Estate of Puschel, 1991, 582 N.E.2d 923.

6–4.1–2–3   Property transfers of non-resident decedent

Sec. 3. The inheritance tax applies to a property interest transfer made by a nonresident decedent if the interest transferred is in:

(1) real property located in this state, regardless of whether the property is held in a trust or whether the trustee is required to distribute the property in-kind, unless:

(A) the real property was transferred to an irrevocable trust during the decedent's lifetime;

(B) the transfer to the trust was not made in contemplation of the transferor's death, as determined under IC 6–4.1–2–4; and

(C) the decedent does not have a retained interest in the trust; or

(2) tangible personal property which has an actual situs in this state.

As added by Acts 1976, P.L.18, SEC.1.   Amended by Acts 1979, P.L.75, SEC.2; P.L.78–1993, SEC.2.

Historical and Statutory Notes

Acts 1979, P.L. 75, § 2, eff. July 1, 1979, deleted Cls. (3) through (6) which read:

"(3) shares of stock or evidences of indebtedness issued by a national bank which is located in this state;

"(4) shares of stock or evidences of indebtedness issued by an Indiana corporation;

"(5) evidences of indebtedness issued by Indiana residents; or

"(6) any other intangible personal property which is physically located in this state."

P.L.78–1993, Sec.2, inserted provisions of Cl. (1) following "real property located in this state."

For applicability of P.L.78–1993, see the Historical and Statutory Notes under § 6–4.1–2–2.

Formerly:

IC 6–4–1–1.

IC 6–4–1–32.

Acts 1931, c. 75, ss. 1, 33.

Cross References

Determination of tax due from non-resident decedents, see IC 6–4.1–5–14.

Law Review and Journal Commentaries

Multiple inheritance taxation of intangible property in different states.   15 Ind.L.J. 156 (1939).

Practical aspects of multiple state taxation of nonresidents' intangibles.   24 Notre Dame Law. 41 (1948).

Library References

Taxation ⟲867(1).

WESTLAW Topic No. 371.

C.J.S. Taxation §§ 1116, 1141.

I.L.E. Taxation §§ 233 to 235.

United States Code Annotated

Federal estate tax, nonresidents not citizens of United States, see 26 U.S.C.A. § 2101 et seq.

Notes of Decisions

Real property interest   1

_____

1.   Real property interest

Transfer of beneficial interests in charitable remainder unitrust, including as asset a benefi-cial interest in land trust holding Indiana real property, was not subject to inheritance tax; interest transferred was incorporeal in nature and transfer was therefore of intangible personal property.   Blood v. Poindexter, 1989, 534 N.E.2d 768.

6–4.1–2–4   Transfers of interests in property; transfers in contemplation of death; transfers for consideration

Sec. 4. (a) The inheritance tax applies to transfers of property interests described in subsection (d) and to the following types of property interest transfers:

(1) transfers which are made under a deceased transferor's will or under the laws of intestate succession, as a result of the transferor's death;

(2) transfers which are made in contemplation of the transferor's death;

(3) transfers which are made in such a manner that they are intended to take effect in possession or enjoyment at or after the transferor's death;

(4) transfers which are made in payment of a claim against the transferor's estate if:

(A) the claim results from a contract or antenuptial agreement made by the transferor; and

(B) payment of the amount claimed is due at or after the transferor's death under the terms of the transferor's will or the contract;

(5) those jointly held property transfers described in section 5 of this chapter;

(6) those transfers which are made by a trust deed in the manner described in section 6 of this chapter; and

(7) those transfers which are made to an executor or trustee in the manner described in section 7 of this chapter.

(b) A transfer is presumed to have been made in contemplation of the transferor's death if it is made within one (1) year before the transferor's date of death. However, the presumption is rebuttable.

(c) If a transfer described in subsection (a)(1), (a)(2), (a)(3), or (a)(4) is made for valuable consideration, the value of the property so transferred equals the remainder of:

(1) the total value of the property transferred; minus

(2) the equivalent in money value of the consideration received by the transferor.

For purposes of this subsection, the term "consideration" does not include love or affection.

(d) If at the time of death a surviving spouse has been entitled to income from a property interest that was the subject of a previous transfer exempt from inheritance tax under IC 6–4.1–3–7(b) or IC 6–4.1–3–7 (c), then the value of the property interest at the time of death of the surviving spouse is subject to the inheritance tax as if it were a transfer of property owned by the surviving spouse. The value of a property interest subject to inheritance tax under this section includes the value of each gift of any part of the property interest made by the surviving spouse in contemplation of death.

As added by Acts 1976, P.L.18, SEC.1.   Amended by Acts 1982, P.L.55, SEC.1; P.L.58–1990, SEC.1.

Historical and Statutory Notes

Acts 1982, P.L.55, Sec.1, emerg. eff. Jan. 1, 1982, in Subsec. (a), in the introduction, inserted "transfers of property interests described in subsection (d) and to"; and added Subsec. (d).

Section 3 of Acts 1982, P.L.55, provided:

"Because an emergency exists this act takes effect on January 1, 1982, and applies to the estates of decedents who die after December 31, 1981."

P.L.58–1990, Sec.1, eff. Jan. 1, 1991, in Subsec. (b), substituted "one (1) year" for "two (2) years"; and made other nonsubstantive changes throughout the section.

P.L.58–1990, Sec.5, eff. Jan. 1, 1991, provides:

"Section 1 of this act does not apply to decedents who die before January 1, 1991."

Formerly:

IC 6–4–1–1.
Acts 1931, c. 75, s. 1.

Administrative Code References

Inheritance tax, jointly owned property, transfers prior to payment of tax, see 45 IAC 4.1–8–3.
Transfer in contemplation of death, see 45 IAC 4.1–2–6.
Transfers in general, see 45 IAC 4.1–2–5 et seq.

Law Review and Journal Commentaries

Death taxes: Survey of recent law. John W. Boyd, 12 Ind.L.Rev. 320, 326 (1979).

Inheritance tax: Survey of recent law. Debra A. Falender, 17 Ind.L.Rev. 392 (1984).

Validity of statute creating conclusive presumption with respect to transfers made in contemplation of death. 8 Ind.L.J. 143 (1932).

Library References

Taxation ☞878(1), 879(1).
WESTLAW Topic No. 371.
C.J.S. Taxation §§ 1117, 1142, 1147.
I.L.E. Taxation §§ 233 to 235.

Co-ownership of property, tenancy by the entirety, see Smithburn, 14 Indiana Practice § 3.32.

WESTLAW Electronic Research

See WESTLAW Electronic Research Guide following the Preface.

United States Code Annotated

Federal estate tax, gross estate,
    Joint interests, see 26 U.S.C.A. § 2040.
    Powers of appointment, see 26 U.S.C.A. § 2041.
    Transfers for insufficient consideration, see 26 U.S.C.A. § 2043.
    Transfers taking effect at death, see 26 U.S.C.A. § 2037.
    Transfers with retained life estate, see 26 U.S.C.A. § 2036.
    Transfers within 3 years of decedent's death, see 26 U.S.C.A. § 2035.

Notes of Decisions

1. In general

When farm lessees exercised their option to purchase farm following death of testatrix/owner, paid purchase price and received deed, farm ceased to be part of probate estate, with price paid instead becoming part of estate, and, thus, farm was not therefore liable for use to satisfy debts, expenses of administration and taxes pursuant to provision of will that such claims be paid out of "probate estate"; substantial difference between option price and valuation placed on farm for inheritance tax purposes did not warrant attachment of portion of inheritance taxes to farm on ground that it was probate asset for short time, particularly as doing so would impose burden on lessees, which would have been contrary to intention expressed by testatrix. Matter of Estate of Saylors, App. 1996, 671 N.E.2d 905.

Inheritance is tax on right of heirs to succeed to property, and not tax on property itself. Matter of Estate of Saylors, App.1996, 671 N.E.2d 905.

Inheritance tax is generally not paid from residue of estate unless will so directs. Matter of Estate of Saylors, App.1996, 671 N.E.2d 905.

Inheritance tax is imposed on transfer of ownership of either legal or beneficial interest in property, but is not imposed on property itself. Estate of Hibbs v. Indiana Dept. of State Revenue, Inheritance Tax Div., 1994, 636 N.E.2d 204.

Prerequisites to establishing liability for inheritance tax under ownership theory are a transfer from decedent of an interest in property which decedent owned at death. State, Dept. of Revenue, Inheritance Tax Division v. Monroe County State Bank, App. 1 Dist.1979, 390 N.E.2d 1104, 181 Ind.App. 176.

2. Transfers in contemplation of death

Expectation of death, when determining whether transfers of property are subject to state inheritance tax, need not be imminent, but it is not general expectation of death which all human beings entertain. Indiana Dept. of State Revenue, Inheritance Tax Div. v. Estate of Baldwin, 1995, 652 N.E.2d 124.

To determine whether transfer of property was prompted by expectation of death, subjecting property to state inheritance tax, courts must determine transferor's state of mind toward death; objective facts may be overcome by evidence of subjective motives. Indiana Dept. of State Revenue, Inheritance Tax Div. v. Estate of Baldwin, 1995, 652 N.E.2d 124.

Presumption that property transferred to daughter and son-in-law within one year of elderly person's death, was made in contemplation of death and subject to state inheritance tax, was rebutted by showing that transfer was made to qualify for Medicaid during anticipated nursing home stay; transferor's motive was life-related, rather than in expectation of death. Indiana Dept. of State Revenue, Inheritance Tax Div. v. Estate of Baldwin, 1995, 652 N.E.2d 124.

Where money was given within two years of decedent's death when decedent was 90 years old and notes received in return were interest free and unsecured, and no valuable consideration was offered by "borrower" who eventually inherited approximately three quarters of decedent's estate, transfers represented "taxable gifts" made in contemplation of death. Indiana Dept. of State Revenue, Inheritance Tax Div. v. Cohen's Estate, App. 1 Dist.1982, 436 N.E.2d 832.

Conclusion that transfers of real estate within two years of decedent's death were not made in contemplation of death and, hence, were not taxable was supported by substantial evidence indicating that decedent did not have an expectation of death in the narrow or general sense of the word but, rather, living motives for the transfer, namely his good physical and mental health, the absence of recent or prolonged illness, the absence of depression or strong emotional response to his wife's death, the continued life of his two sisters, his desire to be relieved of business and management worries, his desire to discharge moral obligations and reward the efforts of his children, and his desire to reduce his income taxes and provide for his future financial security. Indiana Dept. of Revenue, Inheritance Tax Division v. Flanders' Estate, App. 2 Dist.1980, 408 N.E.2d 172.

In making the "in contemplation of death" determination with respect to taxable inter vivos transfers, courts consider objective facts from which state of mind may be inferred and subjective motives for transfer, namely, testamentary motives (distribution in anticipation of death and/or for purpose of avoiding death taxes) or living motives (distribution for purposes associated with life). Indiana Dept. of Revenue, Inheritance Tax Division v. Flanders' Estate, App. 2 Dist.1980, 408 N.E.2d 172.

Although gifts of $30,000 to nieces in each of years 1973 and 1974 were made within two years of transferor's death, the fact that transfers were property received upon death of transferor's sister and that transferor thought that such property should have gone to her nieces and nephews rather than to her could be considered by probate court in determining whether transfers were made in contemplation of death. State v. Bower, App. 3 Dist.1978, 372 N.E.2d 1227, 175 Ind.App. 540.

Under inheritance tax act [repealed; see, now, § 6–4.1–1–1 et seq.], which provided that any transfer of property made by person within two years prior to death was to be deemed to have been made "in contemplation of death", quoted words meant that thought of death was impelling cause of transfer. 1943 Op.Atty.Gen. p. 380.

3. Life estates

Net effect of qualified terminable interest property (QTIP) election in connection with transfer of life estate in property to surviving spouse is to defer payment of inheritance tax until death of surviving spouse. Department of State Revenue, Inheritance Tax Div. v. Phelps, 1998, 697 N.E.2d 506.

Effect of qualified terminable interest property (QTIP) election in connection with transfer by decedent of life estate in property to surviving spouse is that when surviving spouse dies, surviving spouse's qualifying income interest for life is treated as fee interest for purposes of determining the inheritance tax due upon its transfer to remaindermen; thus, remaindermen will pay inheritance tax on value of entire property at date of death of surviving spouse. Department of State Revenue, Inheritance Tax Div. v. Phelps, 1998, 697 N.E.2d 506.

Under qualified terminable interest property (QTIP) election, income interest in property passes to surviving spouse for life and inheritance tax is deferred until death of surviving spouse. Estate of Hibbs v. Indiana Dept. of State Revenue, Inheritance Tax Div., 1994, 636 N.E.2d 204.

Personal representative of estate must elect qualified terminable interest property (QTIP) treatment for income interest in property to pass to surviving spouse for life and inheritance tax to be deferred until death of surviving spouse. Estate of Hibbs v. Indiana Dept. of State Revenue, Inheritance Tax Div., 1994, 636 N.E.2d 204.

Testator's will, revocable trust instruments, and original and amended estate tax return were sufficient "writings attached to the return" to qualify for qualified terminable interest property (QTIP) election and to defer inheritance tax until surviving spouse's death. Estate of Hibbs

v. Indiana Dept. of State Revenue, Inheritance Tax Div., 1994, 636 N.E.2d 204.

Language by which testator "directed" personal representative to qualify property as qualified terminable interest property (QTIP) was sufficient straightforward command and thus indicated affirmative unequivocal intent to elect QTIP treatment and to defer inheritance tax until surviving spouse's death. Estate of Hibbs v. Indiana Dept. of State Revenue, Inheritance Tax Div., 1994, 636 N.E.2d 204.

Real property held originally by decedent and her husband as tenants by the entireties and then transferred by them to their children, subject to joint and successive life estates in grantors, became wholly subject to inheritance tax at time of death of decedent, the last grantor, since transferees took possession of entire property at that time. Indiana Dept. of State Revenue, Inheritance Tax Div. v. Smith, 1985, 473 N.E.2d 611.

Conveyance of property subject to life estate in an individual grantor was a transfer "intended to take effect in possession or enjoyment at or after the death of the transferor" within meaning of IC1971, 6–4–1–1 [repealed; see, now, § 6–4.1–1–1 et seq.]. State, Dept. of State Revenue, Inheritance Tax Division v. Union Bank & Trust Co., App. 1 Dist.1978, 380 N.E.2d 1279, 177 Ind.App. 632.

Whenever real estate which is held by entireties is transferred, subject to joint and successive life estates in grantors, without valuable and sufficient consideration in money or money's worth, such transfer should be taxed in estate of last grantor to die. State, Dept. of State Revenue, Inheritance Tax Division v. Union Bank & Trust Co., App. 1 Dist.1978, 380 N.E.2d 1279, 177 Ind.App. 632.

4. Power of appointment

No transfer of property from decedent had occurred, and thus, decedent's interest in marital trust set up by his predeceased wife was not a "taxable asset" under inheritance tax, where, although decedent had unlimited power to invade the corpus and had general testamentary power of appointment, decedent did not exercise his power of appointment in favor of himself, his estate, or someone else. Indiana Dept. of State Revenue, Inheritance Tax Div. v. Estate of Morris, App. 4 Dist.1985, 486 N.E.2d 1100, rehearing denied, transfer denied.

Exercise of power of appointment is no longer a taxable event for inheritance tax purposes. Indiana Dept. of State Revenue, Inheritance Tax Div. v. Hungate's Estate, 1982, 439 N.E.2d 1148.

Where, under her husband's will, decedent had complete and unconditional power of appointment with respect to corpus of trust, exercisable by her alone and at her sole discretion during her lifetime and also at her death, in favor of herself, her estate, or any other person, decedent possessed an equitable ownership interest in the corpus of the trust, subject to inheritance tax at her death. Indiana Dept. of State Revenue, Inheritance Tax Div. v. Hungate's Estate, 1982, 439 N.E.2d 1148.

Exercise of power of appointment is a "transfer" within inheritance tax statutes, which require both that there be a transfer from decedent and an interest in property which decedent owned at death. Indiana Dept. of State Revenue, Inheritance Tax Div. v. Hungate's Estate, 1982, 439 N.E.2d 1148.

Wife's partial exercise of power of appointment over trust created by husband's will by appointing property to her own estate did not constitute taxable transfer since those who received the property or benefit by the appointment took from the donor husband and not donee wife. Matter of Martindale's Estate, App. 2 Dist.1981, 423 N.E.2d 662.

Wife did not at her death have a property interest in trust corpus set up by husband's will which would impose liability on her estate for inheritance tax on the trust corpus where wife's power to invade and exhaust the corpus was only an inter vivos general power of appointment. Matter of Martindale's Estate, App. 2 Dist.1981, 423 N.E.2d 662.

Exercise of a general power to appoint beneficiary of a remainder, said power effective at appointer's death, coupled with a life estate in corpus is not a sufficient property interest as to indicate ownership for inheritance tax purposes inasmuch as appointer has no property right in corpus which he can enjoy during his lifetime. State, Dept. of Revenue, Inheritance Tax Division v. Monroe County State Bank, App. 1 Dist. 1979, 390 N.E.2d 1104, 181 Ind.App. 176.

5. Death benefits payable to survivor

Inheritance tax statute [repealed; see, now, § 6–4.1–2–5] pertaining to joint tenancies was to be read in conjunction with provision [repealed; see, now, this section] concerning transfers which would be taxable and excluding those for which good and valuable consider-

ation had been given. State v. George, 1980, 401 N.E.2d 680, 273 Ind. 26.

Even if arrangement between employer and employee for payment of annuity to widow after death of employee involved deferred compensation, there was no sufficient property interest in employee to meet "ownership" test for taxability under inheritance tax statute [now, § 6–4.1–1–1 et seq.]. Matter of Bannon's Estate, App. 1 Dist.1976, 358 N.E.2d 215, 171 Ind.App. 610.

Where deceased employee had no interest in annuity which was payable to his widow under terms of employment agreement, there was no transfer from decedent and annuity was not subject to inheritance tax. Matter of Bannon's Estate, App. 1 Dist.1976, 358 N.E.2d 215, 171 Ind.App. 610.

Death of husband before payment of entire purchase prices on contracts under which he and wife had conditionally sold real estate they had held by entireties did not result in a "transfer," and the interest in the remaining unpaid portion of the prices thus was not subject to inheritance tax. State v. Weinstein's Estate, App.1967, 228 N.E.2d 23, 141 Ind.App. 395, rehearing denied 229 N.E.2d 741, 141 Ind.App. 399.

The death benefits, payable as provided by various retirement fund statutes were taxable under Acts 1931, c. 75, s. 1 [repealed; see, now, this section] and the value of the survivorship annuity benefits, (except the portion not attributable to the employee's contributions plus interest thereon payable upon election by the surviving spouse as noted above) payable under the particular funds and statutes, was also taxable for inheritance tax purposes. 1963 Op.Atty. Gen. No. 27.

Neither the lump-sum benefits payable under 45 U.S.C.A. § 228e of the railroad retirement act (now, omitted), nor those payable under 42 U.S.C.A. § 402 of the social security act, when payable directly to eligible beneficiaries, constituted transfers which were subject to the tax imposed by the Indiana inheritance tax law, Acts 1931, c. 75 [repealed; see, now, 6–4.1–1–1 et seq.] from which follows the ultimate conclusion that such lump-sum benefits were not taxable under that act. 1961 Op.Atty.Gen. No. 60.

6–4.1–2–5   **Joint ownership with rights of survivorship**

Sec. 5. If property is held by two (2) or more individuals jointly with rights of survivorship, the exercise of the rights of the surviving joint owner or owners to the immediate ownership or possession and enjoyment of the property upon the death of one (1) of the joint owners is a transfer to which the inheritance tax applies. The value of the property so transferred equals the remainder of (1) the total value of the jointly held property, minus (2) the value of that portion of the jointly held property which the surviving joint owner or owners prove belonged to him or them.

As added by Acts 1976, P.L.18, SEC.1. Amended by Acts 1982, P.L.56, SEC.1.

Historical and Statutory Notes

Acts 1982, P.L.56, Sec.1, eff. June 1, 1982, deleted "and never belonged to the deceased joint owner" at the end of the second sentence.

Formerly:
IC 6–4–1–1.
Acts 1931, c. 75, s. 1.

Administrative Code References

Inheritance tax, jointly owned property, transfers prior to payment of tax, see 45 IAC 4.1–2–9.

Library References

Taxation ☞878(1).
WESTLAW Topic No. 371.

C.J.S. Taxation §§ 1117, 1142.
I.L.E. Taxation §§ 233 to 235.

United States Code Annotated

Federal estate tax, gross estate, joint interests, see 26 U.S.C.A. § 2040.

Notes of Decisions

In general **1**
Contributions by parties **4**
Successive life estates **3**
Tenancy by entirety **2**

1. In general

Inheritance tax statute [repealed; see, now, this section] discussing joint tenancies was to be read in conjunction with paragraph [repealed; see, now, § 6–4.1–2–4] stating those transfers which would be taxable and excluding those for which good and valuable consideration had been given. State v. George, 1980, 401 N.E.2d 680, 273 Ind. 26.

Even if property did belong to brother in and prior to 1960, sister was entitled to exclusion from inheritance tax where facts showed that she gave good and valuable consideration for her one-half interest in property held in joint tenancy at time of his death; and she was not required to show that such property belonged to her and never belonged to brother. State v. George, 1980, 401 N.E.2d 680, 273 Ind. 26.

2. Tenancy by entirety

Death of husband before payment of entire purchase prices on contracts under which he and wife had conditionally sold real estate they had held by entireties did not result in a "transfer", and the interest in the remaining unpaid portion of the prices thus was not subject to inheritance tax. State v. Weinstein's Estate, App.1967, 228 N.E.2d 23, 141 Ind.App. 395,

rehearing denied 229 N.E.2d 741, 141 Ind.App. 399.

3. Successive life estates

Real property held originally by decedent and her husband as tenants by the entireties and then transferred by them to their children, subject to joint and successive life estates in grantors, became wholly subject to inheritance tax at time of death of decedent, the last grantor, since transferees took possession of entire property at that time. Indiana Dept. of State Revenue, Inheritance Tax Div. v. Smith, 1985, 473 N.E.2d 611.

Whenever real estate which is held by entireties is transferred, subject to joint and successive life estates in grantors, without valuable and sufficient consideration in money or money's worth, such transfer should be taxed in estate of last grantor to die. State, Dept. of State Revenue, Inheritance Tax Division v. Union Bank & Trust Co., App. 1 Dist.1978, 380 N.E.2d 1279, 177 Ind.App. 632.

4. Contributions by parties

Surviving joint tenant's exercise of his right of survivorship to real property incurred no state inheritance tax, where surviving joint tenant had contributed 100% of purchase price of the subject property, and there was no evidence that decedent had contributed anything for her joint interest in the property. Department of State Revenue, Inheritance Tax Div. v. Estate of Hardy, 1998, 703 N.E.2d 705.

For purposes of state inheritance tax, the taxability of the exercise of survivorship rights to all property is to be measured by the contribution of the survivor to the property. Department of State Revenue, Inheritance Tax Div. v. Estate of Hardy, 1998, 703 N.E.2d 705.

6–4.1–2–6   Transfers by deed of trust with powers reserved in transferor

Sec. 6. If a transferor transfers property by a deed of trust in such a manner that he reserves to:

   (1) himself any interest; or

   (2) himself and others powers of revocation, alteration, or amendment which if exercised would cause the property to revert to the transferor;

then the inheritance tax imposed as a result of the transferor's death applies to the transfer. The value of the property so transferred equals the value of the property subject to the powers, and in respect to which the powers remain unexercised, at the time of the transferor's death.

As added by Acts 1976, P.L.18, SEC.1.

Historical and Statutory Notes

Formerly:
  IC 6–4–1–1.
  Acts 1931, c. 75, s. 1.

Law Review and Journal Commentaries

Revocable living trust—traps and pratfalls. Donald E. Esmont, 36 Res Gestae 458 (1993).

Inheritance tax: Survey of recent law. Debra A. Falender, 17 Ind.L.Rev. 392 (1984).

Library References

Taxation ☞878(1), 883.
WESTLAW Topic No. 371.
C.J.S. Taxation §§ 1117, 1142, 1151.

Notes of Decisions

Possibility of reverter   1

———

1. Possibility of reverter

Possibility of reverter, though remote, was subject to inheritance taxation in estate of trustor, and under IC 1971, 6–4–1–1 [repealed; see, now, this section] providing that transfer of property by deed of trust wherein trustor reserves to himself any income or interest shall on death of trustor be taxable to extent of value of property "subject to" such power and in respect to which such powers remain unexercised, entire trust was subject to inheritance taxation in trustor's estate. State, Indiana Dept. of State Revenue Inheritance Tax Division v. Daley, App. 4 Dist.1982, 434 N.E.2d 149.

6–4.1–2–7   Transfers to executor as trustee in lieu of fee

Sec. 7. If an individual transfers property to an executor or trustee in lieu of his fee, the inheritance tax applies to the transfer if the value of the property transferred exceeds the fee that would have been due if the transfer had not been made. The value of the property so transferred equals the amount of the excess.

As added by Acts 1976, P.L.18, SEC.1.

Historical and Statutory Notes

Formerly:
IC 6–4–1–1.
Acts 1931, c. 75, s. 1.

Library References

Taxation ☞890.
WESTLAW Topic No. 371.

C.J.S. Taxation § 1169.
I.L.E. Taxation §§ 233 to 235.

Chapter 3

Inheritance Tax Exemptions and Deductions

6–4.1–3–1   Exempt transfers

Sec. 1.   Each transfer described in section 2055(a) of the Internal Revenue Code [1] is exempt from the inheritance tax.

As added by Acts 1976, P.L.18, SEC.1.   Amended by Acts 1976, P.L.19, SEC.1.

[1]   26 U.S.C.A. § 2055(a).

Historical and Statutory Notes

Acts 1976, P.L. 18, § 1, emerg. eff. Feb. 18, 1976, added this article.

Acts 1976, P.L. 18 added the provisions of this chapter as part of a codification and restatement of the laws relating to death taxes.

See, also, Historical Note under § 6-4.1-1-1 for effect of recodification and severability provisions of Acts 1976, P.L. 18.

Acts 1976, P.L. 19, § 1, emerg. eff. July 1, 1976, rewrote the section which prior thereto read:

"Subject to the limitations contained in sections 2, 3, and 4 of this chapter, the following transfers are exempt from the inheritance tax:

"(1) a transfer to or for the use of a municipal corporation of this state;

"(2) a transfer to a public institution to be used exclusively for a public purpose;

"(3) a transfer to a trust for the sole benefit of a charitable, educational, or religious organization; and

"(4) a transfer to a transferee which is organized for charitable, educational or religious purposes."

Acts 1976, P.L. 19, provided in § 4(a):

"Because an emergency exists, Sections 1 and 3 of this act take effect July 1, 1976, and apply to transfers made by individuals who die after June 30, 1976."

Formerly:

IC 6-4-1-3.
Acts 1931, c. 75, s. 3.
Acts 1947, c. 311, s. 1.
Acts 1963, c. 265, s. 1.
Acts 1975, P.L.64, SEC.2.

Law Review and Journal Commentaries

Death taxes: Survey of recent tax law. Thomas B. Allington, 10 Ind.L.Rev. 340 (1976).

Library References

Taxation ⬤872.
WESTLAW Topic No. 371.

C.J.S. Taxation §§ 1157 to 1159.
I.L.E. Taxation § 236.

United States Code Annotated

Federal gross estate, valuation, see 26 U.S.C.A. § 2031 et seq.

Notes of Decisions

In general   1
Charitable purposes   2

1. In general

Section 6-4.1-3-1 et seq. governing property exempt from inheritance tax, as amended by Acts 1976, P.L. 19, § 1, which incorporated by reference standards of Internal Revenue Code [26 U.S.C.A. § 2055(a)] governing transfers for public, charitable, and religious uses for purposes of estate tax, did not refer to any specific date on which such federal statute was in effect, and thus better interpretation of Indiana statute was that it incorporated federal statute as it read on date amendment was adopted February 25, 1976, so that subsequent amendments to section by Congress did not affect Indiana statute. Indiana Dept. of State Revenue, Inheritance Tax Division v. Wallace's Estate, App. 1 Dist.1980, 408 N.E.2d 150.

Adoption of § 6-4.1-3-1.5 governing inheritance tax exemption for transfer of property to cemetery association came too late to apply to bequest for use of cemetery, which did not qualify for exemption under this section governing property exempt from inheritance tax, and there was no reason to believe that General Assembly was merely clarifying meaning of latter section when it enacted former section and thus former section provided no basis for relief to executor. Indiana Dept. of State Revenue, Inheritance Tax Division v. Wallace's Estate, App. 1 Dist.1980, 408 N.E.2d 150.

2. Charitable purposes

Funds spent by foundations for education and research, which went to subsidize seminars and research projects aimed at advancing goals of foundations, as well as for gifts and contributions, were within exemption under section 6-4-1-3 [repealed (see, now, section 6-4.1-3-1)] from inheritance taxes for transfers to any corporation, institution, society, association, or trust formed for charitable, educational, or religious purposes. Matter of Goodrich's Estate, App. 4 Dist.1982, 439 N.E.2d 1155.

Fact that an organization's benefits are limited to particular group or limited number of people does not mean that organization cannot be regarded as exclusively charitable, educational or religious. In re Albersmeier's Estate, App. 3 Dist.1981, 425 N.E.2d 245.

Bequest of entire residuary estate of decedent to bank and trust company in trust for Masonic lodge for holding of property interest and accumulation of income until lodge had sufficient funds together with trust property to provide for purchase of site for, and construction of, temple for the lodge was exempt from state inheritance tax. In re Albersmeier's Estate, App. 3 Dist. 1981, 425 N.E.2d 245.

Where part of income from testamentary trust fund was to be used to purchase wreath for each pair of graves on certain lots annually at Christmas time and bouquet for each grave in those lots on Decoration Day each year, bequest to trust fund was not intended to be used by trustee exclusively for any of purposes permissible under Internal Revenue Code section [26 U.S.C.A. § 2055(a)], which governs transfers for public, charitable, and religious uses for purposes of estate tax, and standards of which were incorporated by reference into this section governing property exempt from inheritance tax. Indiana Dept. of State Revenue, Inheritance Tax Division v. Wallace's Estate, App. 1 Dist.1980, 408 N.E.2d 150.

6–4.1–3–1.5   Transfer to cemetery association

Sec. 1.5.   (a) As used in this section, "cemetery" and "cemetery purposes" have the same meaning as the definitions of those terms contained in IC 23–14–33.

(b) The transfer of property to a cemetery association is exempt from the inheritance tax if the property is used for cemetery purposes.

As added by Acts 1980, P.L.57, SEC.1.   Amended by P.L.52–1997, SEC.2.

Historical and Statutory Notes

Acts 1980, P.L. 57, § 1, eff. July 1, 1980, added this section.

P.L.52–1997, Sec.2, amended the section by substituting "IC 23–14–33" for "IC 23–14–1–1" in Subsec. (a).

Cross References

Cemeteries, deposits or bequests for care, see IC 23–14–53–2.

Administrative Code References

Cemeteries, bequests to or for the use of cemeteries, see 45 IAC 4.1–3–2.

6–4.1–3–2 to 6–4.1–3–4   Repealed

(Repealed by Acts 1976, P.L.19, SEC.3.)

Historical and Statutory Notes

Acts 1976, P.L. 19, provided in § 4(a), containing emergency clause, that § 3 takes effect July 1, 1976.

The former sections related to limits on exemptions from the tax.

Formerly:

Acts 1976, P.L.18, SEC.1.

6–4.1–3–5   Repealed

(Repealed by Acts 1980, P.L.57, SEC.29.)

Historical and Statutory Notes

Acts 1980, P.L. 57, provided in § 30(b), containing emergency clause, that § 29 takes effect retroactively to July 1, 1979.

The former section related to tax exemptions for transfers of personal property.

Formerly:

Acts 1976, P.L.18, SEC.1.

6–4.1–3–6   Life insurance proceeds

Sec. 6. The proceeds from life insurance on the life of a decedent are exempt from the inheritance tax imposed as a result of his death unless the proceeds become subject to distribution as part of his estate and subject to claims against his estate.

As added by Acts 1976, P.L.18, SEC.1.

Historical and Statutory Notes

Formerly:
  IC 6–4–1–1.
  Acts 1931, c. 75, s. 1.

Library References

Taxation ⊂872.
WESTLAW Topic No. 371.

C.J.S. Taxation §§ 1157 to 1159.
I.L.E. Taxation § 236.

WESTLAW Electronic Research

See WESTLAW Electronic Research Guide following the Preface.

United States Code Annotated

Federal estate tax, inclusion of life insurance proceeds, see 26 U.S.C.A. § 2042.

Notes of Decisions

Liberal construction   1
Proceeds   2
Trusts   3

1. Liberal construction

IC 1971, 6–4–1–1 [repealed; see, now, this section] exempting from inheritance tax all proceeds of life insurance payable other than to decedent's estate should be liberally construed in favor of taxpayer. In re Cassner's Estate, App. 2 Dist.1975, 325 N.E.2d 487, 163 Ind.App. 588.

2. Proceeds

Where pension plan required that "initial life insurance protection" equal to 100 times the monthly retirement stipends be bought, there was a risk element sufficient to warrant conclusion that money paid under such insurance policies, on employee's death before actual retirement, constituted "life insurance proceeds" rather than death benefits from pension plan for purposes of determining whether such money was subject to state inheritance tax, though executrix of employee's estate exempted such money from federal taxation as an annuity. State Dept. of Revenue, Inheritance Tax Division v. Estate of Powell, App. 1 Dist.1975, 333 N.E.2d 92, 165 Ind.App. 482.

Court in determining whether term "proceeds" in IC1971, 6–4–1–3 [repealed; see, now, this section] exempting from inheritance tax all proceeds of life insurance payable other than to decedent's estate included termination, accumulated and postmortem dividends payable other than to decedent's estate would not ignore presumption that legislature in enacting statute was aware of other tax statutes, including federal tax statutes that treat "proceeds" as including all termination, post mortem and accumulated dividends. In re Cassner's Estate, App. 2 Dist. 1975, 325 N.E.2d 487, 163 Ind.App. 588.

3. Trusts

Life insurance, if there exists the essential elements of risk shifting, in simple or mixed form is not subject to inheritance tax even though trust into which insurance proceeds are paid is established and maintained by third-party employer. State Dept. of Revenue, Inheritance Tax Division v. Estate of Powell, App. 1 Dist.1975, 333 N.E.2d 92, 165 Ind.App. 482.

Life insurance proceeds paid to cotrustees of an inter vivos trust established by decedent were not includable in decedent's estate for inheritance tax purposes, notwithstanding that provisions of trust indenture vested trustees with discretionary power to pay specified claims against decedent's estate, where, by designating cotrustees as beneficiaries of life policies and by transferring ownership of policies to trustees, decedent effectively precluded proceeds from being subject to distribution as a part of his estate. In re Osland's Estate, App. 1 Dist.1975, 328 N.E.2d 448, 164 Ind.App. 282.

6–4.1–3–6.5 Annuity payments

Sec. 6.5. An annuity, or other payment, described in Section 2039(a) of the Internal Revenue Code[1] is exempt from the inheritance tax imposed as a result of a decedent's death to the same extent that the annuity or other payment is excluded from the decedent's federal gross estate under Section 2039 of the Internal Revenue Code.[2]

As added by Acts 1977(ss), P.L.6, SEC.2. Amended by Acts 1980, P.L.57, SEC.2; P.L.87–1983, SEC.2; P.L.2–1987, SEC.24.

[1] 26 U.S.C.A. § 2039(a).
[2] 26 U.S.C.A. § 2039.

Historical and Statutory Notes

Acts 1977 (ss), P.L. 6, § 2, emerg. eff. July 1, 1977, added this section.

Acts 1977 (ss), P.L. 6, provided in § 12(b):

"Because an emergency exists, Sections 2 through 11 of this act take effect July 1, 1977, and Sections 2, 3, and 7 of this act apply to transfers made by individuals who die after June 30, 1977."

Acts 1980, P.L. 57, § 2, emerg. eff. retroactively to Jan. 1, 1979, substituted "1979" for "1977" following "January 1".

Acts 1980, P.L. 57, provided in § 30(a):

"Because an emergency exists, Sections 2 and 30 of this act take effect retroactively to January 1, 1979, and Section 2 applies to inheritance taxes imposed with respect to decedents who die after December 31, 1978."

P.L. 87–1983, Sec.2, emerg. eff. Jan. 1, 1983, substituted "January 1, 1983" for "January 1, 1979."

Section 7 of P.L. 87–1983 provided that this act applies to the estates of decedents who die after Dec. 31, 1982.

P.L. 2–1987, Sec.24, emergency effective retroactive to Jan. 1, 1987, deleted "of 1954, as amended and in effect on January 1, 1983" following "Code".

P.L. 2–1987 provides in Section 54 that this act applies to taxable years beginning after Dec. 31, 1986.

Law Review and Journal Commentaries

Amendments of 1977 to Indiana Inheritance Tax Law. William L. Tracy, 21 Res Gestae 488 (1977).

Library References

Taxation ⊕872.
WESTLAW Topic No. 371.

C.J.S. Taxation §§ 1157 to 1159.
I.L.E. Taxation § 236.

Notes of Decisions

Life insurance proceeds 1

___

1. Life insurance proceeds

Where pension plan required that "initial life insurance protection" equal to 100 times the monthly retirement stipends be bought, there was a risk element sufficient to warrant conclusion that money paid under such insurance policies, on employee's death before actual retirement, constituted "life insurance proceeds" rather than death benefits from pension plan for purposes of determining whether such money was subject to state inheritance tax, though executrix of employee's estate exempted such money from federal taxation as an annuity. State Dept. of Revenue, Inheritance Tax Division v. Estate of Powell, App. 1 Dist.1975, 333 N.E.2d 92, 165 Ind.App. 482.

6–4.1–3–7 Transfers of property by decedent to surviving spouse; qualifying income interest for life; election

Sec. 7. (a) Each property interest which a decedent transfers to his surviving spouse is exempt from the inheritance tax imposed as a result of his death.

(b) For the purpose of subsection (a), "property interest which a decedent transfers to his surviving spouse" includes a property interest from which the surviving spouse is entitled for life to income or payments and which otherwise qualifies for deduction from the gross estate of the decedent under Section 2056(b)(5) or 2056(b)(6) of the Internal Revenue Code.[1]

(c) The personal representative of the decedent's estate or the trustee or transferee of property transferred by the decedent may, for the purpose of the exemption established by subsection (a), elect to treat property passing from the decedent in which the surviving spouse has a qualifying income interest for life as a property interest which a decedent transfers to his surviving spouse. For purposes of this section, "qualifying income interest for life" means a qualifying income interest for life (as defined in Section 2056(b)(7) of the Internal Revenue Code).[2]

(d) The election referred to in subsection (c) shall be made in writing and shall be attached to the inheritance tax return, if one is required to be filed. The election, once made, is irrevocable.

As added by Acts 1976, P.L.18, SEC.1. Amended by Acts 1979, P.L.75, SEC.3; Acts 1982, P.L.55, SEC.2; P.L.2–1987, SEC.25.

[1] 26 U.S.C.A. § 2056(b)(5) or (6).
[2] 26 U.S.C.A. § 2056(b)(7).

Historical and Statutory Notes

Acts 1979, P.L. 75, § 3, eff. July 1, 1979, rewrote the section which prior thereto read:

"Real property which is held jointly by a decedent and his spouse as tenants by the entirety is exempt from the inheritance tax imposed as a result of his death."

See, also, Historical Note under § 6–4.1–1–3 for decedents' estates affected by Acts 1979, P.L. 75.

Acts 1982, P.L. 55, Sec.2, emerg. eff. Jan. 1, 1982, added Subsecs. (b) to (d).

Section 3 of Acts 1982, P.L. 55, provided:

"Because an emergency exists this act takes effect on January 1, 1982, and applies to the estates of decedents who die after December 31, 1981."

P.L. 2–1987, Sec.25, emergency effective retroactive to Jan. 1, 1987, deleted "of 1954" following "Code" in Subsec. (b), and "as amended and in effect on January 1, 1982" at the end of Subsecs. (b) and (c).

P.L. 2–1987 provides in Section 54 that this act applies to taxable years beginning after Dec. 31, 1986.

Formerly:
IC 6–4–1–1.
Acts 1931, c. 75, s. 1.

Cross References

Transfers exempt from inheritance tax under section 6–4.1–3–7(b) or (c), taxability at time of death of surviving spouse, see IC 6–4.1–2–4.

Administrative Code References

Inheritance tax, jointly held property,
    Terminable interest property, see 45 IAC 4.1–2–8.
    Transfers to surviving spouse, see 45 IAC 4.1–3–5.

Law Review and Journal Commentaries

Surviving spouses' rights. John S. Grimes, 10 Ind.L.Rev. 675 (1977).

Library References

Taxation ⊱875(1).
WESTLAW Topic No. 371.
C.J.S. Taxation § 1163.

United States Code Annotated

Joint interests, federal estate tax, see 26 U.S.C.A. § 2040.

Notes of Decisions

In general   1
QTIP election   2

―――――

1. In general

When decedent spouse transfers life estate in property to surviving spouse, no inheritance tax is due on that transfer. Department of State Revenue, Inheritance Tax Div. v. Phelps, 1998, 697 N.E.2d 506.

2. QTIP election

While no inheritance tax is due when decedent spouse transfers life estate in property to surviving spouse, transfer of remainder interest is ordinarily subject to inheritance tax; this tax may be avoided, or, more accurately, postponed, by making qualified terminable interest property (QTIP) election. Department of State Revenue, Inheritance Tax Div. v. Phelps, 1998, 697 N.E.2d 506.

Qualified terminable interest property (QTIP) election allows decedent to transfer qualifying income interest for life to surviving spouse, while exempting transfer of remainder to other beneficiaries from inheritance tax. Department of State Revenue, Inheritance Tax Div. v. Phelps, 1998, 697 N.E.2d 506.

Surviving spouse has qualifying income interest for life in property transferred by decedent, so that qualified terminable interest property (QTIP) election is permissible, if surviving spouse is entitled to all of the income for life, and if, during his or her lifetime, no one has power to appoint any part of property to any person other than him or her. Department of State Revenue, Inheritance Tax Div. v. Phelps, 1998, 697 N.E.2d 506.

Net effect of qualified terminable interest property (QTIP) election in connection with transfer of life estate in property to surviving spouse is to defer payment of inheritance tax until death of surviving spouse. Department of State Revenue, Inheritance Tax Div. v. Phelps, 1998, 697 N.E.2d 506.

Effect of qualified terminable interest property (QTIP) election in connection with transfer by decedent of life estate in property to surviving spouse is that when surviving spouse dies, surviving spouse's qualifying income interest for life is treated as fee interest for purposes of determining the inheritance tax due upon its transfer to remaindermen; thus, remaindermen will pay inheritance tax on value of entire property at date of death of surviving spouse. Department of State Revenue, Inheritance Tax Div. v. Phelps, 1998, 697 N.E.2d 506.

To obtain qualified terminable interest property (QTIP) treatment in connection with transfer of life estate to surviving spouse as result of decedent's death, person filing inheritance tax return must elect QTIP treatment; election must be in writing, and must manifest an affirmative, unequivocal intent to elect QTIP treatment. Department of State Revenue, Inheritance Tax Div. v. Phelps, 1998, 697 N.E.2d 506.

Under qualified terminable interest property (QTIP) election, income interest in property passes to surviving spouse for life and inheritance tax is deferred until death of surviving spouse. Estate of Hibbs v. Indiana Dept. of State Revenue, Inheritance Tax Div., 1994, 636 N.E.2d 204.

Testator's will, revocable trust instruments, and original and amended estate tax return were sufficient "writings attached to the return" to qualify for qualified terminable interest property (QTIP) election and to defer inheritance tax until surviving spouse's death. Estate of Hibbs v. Indiana Dept. of State Revenue, Inheritance Tax Div., 1994, 636 N.E.2d 204.

Regulation setting forth means to elect qualified terminable interest property (QTIP) treatment of property and to defer inheritance tax until surviving spouse's death could not be applied retroactively and, thus, testator's will and trust documents attached to inheritance tax return were sufficient to elect QTIP treatment. Estate of Hibbs v. Indiana Dept. of State Revenue, Inheritance Tax Div., 1994, 636 N.E.2d 204.

6–4.1–3–8   Repealed

(Repealed by Acts 1979, P.L.75, SEC.15.)

Historical and Statutory Notes

Acts 1979, P.L. 75, provided in § 16(b) that § 15 takes effect July 1, 1979.

The former section related to the tax exemption for transfers to a surviving spouse.

Formerly:

Acts 1976, P.L.18, SEC.1.
Acts 1977 (ss), P.L.6, SEC.3.

6–4.1–3–8.5   Repealed

(Repealed by Acts 1982, P.L.56, SEC.6.)

Historical and Statutory Notes

Acts 1982, P.L. 56, provided in Section 8(e) that Section 6 takes effect June 1, 1982.

The former section related to the tax exemption for a child of the transferor.

Formerly:

Acts 1979, P.L.75, SEC.4.

6–4.1–3–9   Repealed

(Repealed by Acts 1982, P.L.56, SEC.7.)

Historical and Statutory Notes

Acts 1982, P.L. 56, provided in Section 8(a), containing emergency clause, that Section 7 takes effect retroactively on Feb. 18, 1976.

The repealed section exempted from the inheritance tax a portion of property interests transferred to children less than 21 years of age.

See, now, IC 6–4.1–3–9.1.

The subject matter of the repealed section could also have been found in section 6–4.1–3–9.2 which was also repealed in 1982.

6–4.1–3–9.1   Repealed

(Repealed by P.L.254–1997(ss), SEC.37.)

Historical and Statutory Notes

Former IC 6–4.1–3–9.1 related to portion of property interests transferred to children under taxable transfer.

Formerly:

IC 6–4–1–3.
IC 6–4.1–3–9.
Acts 1931, c. 75, s. 3.

Acts 1947, c. 311, s. 1.
Acts 1963, c. 265, s. 1.
Acts 1975, P.L.64, SEC.2.
Acts 1976, P.L.18, SEC.1.
Acts 1979, P.L.75, SEC.5.
Acts 1980, P.L.57, SEC.3.
Acts 1981, P.L.89, SEC.1.
Acts 1982, P.L.56, SEC.2.

6–4.1–3–9.2 Repealed

(Repealed by Acts 1982, P.L.56, SEC.6.)

Historical and Statutory Notes

Acts 1982, P.L. 56, provided in Section 8(e) that Section 6 takes effect June 1, 1982.

Formerly:
IC 6–4–1–3.
IC 6–4.1–3–9.
Acts 1931, c. 75, s. 3.
Acts 1947, c. 311, s. 1.

Acts 1963, c. 265, s. 1.
Acts 1975, P.L.64, SEC.2.
Acts 1976, P.L.18, SEC.1.
Acts 1979, P.L.75, SEC.5.
Acts 1980, P.L.57, SEC.3.
Acts 1981, P.L.89, SEC.1.
Acts 1982, P.L.56, SEC.3.

6–4.1–3–9.5, 6–4.1–3–9.7 Repealed

(Repealed by P.L.254–1997(ss), SEC.37.)

Historical and Statutory Notes

Former IC 6–4.1–3–9.5 related to portion of property interests transferred to children 21 years of age or older under taxable transfer.

Former IC 6–4.1–3–9.7 related to portion of property interests transferred to parents.

Formerly:

Acts 1980, P.L.57, SEC.4.
Acts 1981, P.L.90, SEC.1.
Acts 1982, P.L.56, SECS.4, 5.

6–4.1–3–10 Portion of property interests transferred to Class A transferee under taxable transfer

Sec. 10.   The first one hundred thousand dollars ($100,000) of property interests transferred to a Class A transferee under a taxable transfer or transfers is exempt from the inheritance tax.

As added by Acts 1976, P.L.18, SEC.1.   Amended by Acts 1979, P.L.75, SEC.6; Acts 1980, P.L.57, SEC.5; Acts 1981, P.L.90, SEC.2; P.L.87–1983, SEC.3; P.L. 254–1997(ss), SEC.9.

Historical and Statutory Notes

Acts 1979, P.L. 75, Sec.6, eff. July 1, 1979, substituted "section 8.5 or 9" for "section 8 or section 9".

Acts 1980, P.L. 57, Sec.5, eff. July 1, 1980, substituted "9 or 9.5" for "or 9" following "8.5".

Acts 1981, P.L. 90, Sec.2, eff. July 1, 1981, inserted "or 9.7" and deleted "or" following "8.5, 9".

P.L. 87–1983, Sec.3, emerg. eff. Jan. 1, 1983, substituted "9.1" for "8.5, 9".

Section 7 of P.L. 87–1983 provided that this act applies to the estates of decedents who die after Dec. 31, 1982.

P.L.254–1997(ss), Sec.9, amended the section by substituting "one hundred thousand dollars ($100,000)" for "two thousand dollars ($2,000)"; and deleting "except a transferee entitled to an exemption under section 9.1, 9.5, or 9.7 of this chapter," after "Class A transferee".

Formerly:
IC 6–4–1–3.
Acts 1931, c. 75, s. 3.
Acts 1947, c. 311, s. 1.
Acts 1963, c. 265, s. 1.
Acts 1975, P.L.64, SEC.2.

Cross References

Classes of transferees defined, see IC 6–4.1–1–3.

6–4.1–3–11 Portion of property interest transferred to class B transferee under taxable transfer

Sec. 11. The first five hundred dollars ($500) of property interests transferred to a Class B transferee under a taxable transfer or transfers is exempt from the inheritance tax.
As added by Acts 1976, P.L.18, SEC.1.

Historical and Statutory Notes

Formerly:
IC 6–4–1–3.
Acts 1931, c. 75, s. 3.

Acts 1947, c. 311, s. 1.
Acts 1963, c. 265, s. 1.
Acts 1975, P.L.64, SEC.2.

Cross References

Classes of transferees defined, see IC 6–4.1–1–3.

6–4.1–3–12 Portion of property interest transferred to class C transferee under taxable transfer

Sec. 12. The first one hundred dollars ($100) of property interests transferred to a Class C transferee under a taxable transfer or transfers is exempt from the inheritance tax.
As added by Acts 1976, P.L.18, SEC.1.

Historical and Statutory Notes

Formerly:
IC 6–4–1–3.
Acts 1931, c. 75, s. 3.

Acts 1947, c. 311, s. 1.
Acts 1963, c. 265, s. 1.
Acts 1975, P.L.64, SEC.2.

Cross References

Classes of transferees defined, see IC 6–4.1–1–3.

6–4.1–3–12.5 Affidavit stating exemptions from tax

Sec. 12.5. The department of state revenue shall prescribe the form of an affidavit that may be used to state that no inheritance tax is due after applying the exemptions under this article.
As added by P.L.254–1997(ss), SEC.10.

6–4.1–3–13 Items deductible from value of property interests transferred by resident decedent by will, intestate succession, or under trust

Sec. 13. (a) For purposes of this section, the term "property subject to the inheritance tax" means property transferred by a decedent under a taxable transfer.

(b) The following items, and no others, may be deducted from the value of property interests transferred by a resident decedent under his will, under the laws of intestate succession, or under a trust:

(1) the decedent's debts which are lawful claims against his resident estate;

(2) taxes on the decedent's real property which is located in this state and subject to the inheritance tax, if the real property taxes were a lien at the time of the decedent's death;

(3) taxes on decedent's personal property which is located in this state and subject to the inheritance tax, if the personal property taxes are a personal obligation of the decedent or a lien against the property and if the taxes were unpaid at the time of the decedent's death;

(4) taxes imposed on the decedent's income to date of death, if the taxes were unpaid at the time of his death;

(5) inheritance, estate, or transfer taxes, other than federal estate taxes, imposed by other jurisdictions with respect to intangible personal property which is subject to the inheritance tax;

(6) mortgages or special assessments which, at the time of decedent's death, were a lien on any of decedent's real property which is located in this state and subject to the inheritance tax;

(7) decedent's funeral expenses;

(8) amounts, not to exceed one thousand dollars ($1,000), paid for a memorial for the decedent;

(9) expenses incurred in administering property subject to the inheritance tax, including but not limited to reasonable attorney fees, personal representative fees, and trustee fees;

(10) the amount of any allowance provided to the resident decedent's children by IC 29–1–4–1; and

(11) The value of any property actually received by a resident decedent's surviving spouse in satisfaction of the allowance provided by IC 29–1–4–1, regardless of whether or not a claim for that allowance has been filed under IC 29–1–14.

(c) The amounts which are deductible under subsection (b)(6) of this section are deductible only from the value of the real property encumbered by the mortgage or special assessment.

As added by Acts 1976, P.L.18, SEC.1. Amended by Acts 1976, P.L.20, SEC.1; Acts 1979, P.L.75, SEC.7; Acts 1980, P.L.57, SEC.6; Acts 1981, P.L.89, SEC.2.

Historical and Statutory Notes

Acts 1976, P.L. 20, § 1, emerg. eff. retroactive to March 1, 1976, added Cl. (10) in Subsec. (b).

Acts 1976, P.L. 20, provided in § 3:

"Because an emergency exists, this act takes effect retroactively to March 1, 1976 and applies to inheritance taxes imposed on transfers made by decedents who die after February 29, 1976."

Acts 1979, P.L. 75, § 7, emerg. eff. retroactive to March 1, 1976, except amendments to Subsec. (b)(8) and (10) which took effect July 1, 1979, inserted "or under a trust" in the introductory clause of Subsec. (b); in Subsec. (b)(8), substituted "one thousand dollars ($1,000)" for "five hundred dollars ($500)"; and in Subsec. (b)(10) deleted "dependent" before "children".

Acts 1979, P.L. 75, provided in § 16:

"(a) Because an emergency exists, Section 7 of this act, except the amendments to IC 6–4.1–3–13(b)(8) and (10), and Sections 8 and 16 of this act take effect retroactively to March 1, 1976.

"(b) The remainder of this act takes effect July 1, 1979, and applies to inheritance and estate taxes imposed as a result of the deaths of decedents who die after June 30, 1979."

Acts 1980, P.L. 57, § 6, emerg. eff. retroactive to July 1, 1979, deleted "surviving spouse or" before "children" in Subsec. (b)(10).

Acts 1980, P.L. 57, provided in § 30(b):

"Because an emergency exists, Sections 6, 7, and 29 of this act take effect retroactively to July 1, 1979, and apply to inheritance taxes imposed with respect to decedents who die after June 30, 1979."

Acts 1981, P.L. 89, § 2, emerg. eff. retroactive to July 1, 1979, added Cl. (11) to Subsec. (b).

Acts 1981, P.L. 89, provided in § 3(b):

"Because an emergency exists, Sections 2 and 3 of this act take effect retroactively to July 1, 1979, and Section 2 of this act applies to inheritance taxes imposed with respect to decedents who have died, or who die, after June 30, 1979."

Formerly:

IC 6–4–1–4.
Acts 1931, c. 75, s. 4.
Acts 1947, c. 182, s. 1.
Acts 1965, c. 302, s. 2.

Administrative Code References

Inheritance tax, deductions, see 45 IAC 4.1–3–7 et seq.

Law Review and Journal Commentaries

Death taxes: Survey of recent tax law. Thomas B. Allington, 10 Ind.L.Rev. 340 (1976).

Deductibility of statutory survivors allowance. Norbert Engler, 20 Res Gestae 370 (1976).

Library References

Taxation ⟐895(6).
WESTLAW Topic No. 371.

C.J.S. Taxation § 1183 et seq.
I.L.E. Taxation §§ 233 to 235, 240.

WESTLAW Electronic Research

See WESTLAW Electronic Research Guide following the Preface.

United States Code Annotated

Federal estate tax, deductions, see 26 U.S.C.A. § 2051 et seq.

Notes of Decisions

Administrative expenses 8
Allocation of deductions 7
Co-ownership 3
Debts 1
Federal tax 2
Funeral expenses 4
Survivor or family allowance 5

Will contest judgment 6

_____

1. Debts

Inheritance tax order which was entered after personal representative allowed and paid, with written consent of those affected by decedent's will, his own claim for personal services was to be reversed due to his failure to follow procedures under § 29–1–14–17 to establish his claim as a "lawful claim." In re Feusner's Estate, App. 3 Dist.1980, 411 N.E.2d 166.

2. Federal tax

Where claim has been made for a reduction of federal taxes paid upon property outside of state of Indiana, the federal estate tax must be considered as a debt of the estate being administered. 1917–1920 Op.Atty.Gen. p. 514.

3. Co-ownership

For purposes of inheritance tax computation, estate executor should not have been permitted to list as a deduction a mortgage lien on certain real property owned by decedent and his surviving spouse by tenancy by entirety. Indiana Dept. of Revenue, Inheritance Tax Division v. Security Bank & Trust Co., App. 1 Dist.1979, 393 N.E.2d 197, 181 Ind.App. 543.

Under Inheritance Tax Act of 1931, § 4, tenant in common, upon inheriting interest of cotenant, could not deduct taxes, which were lien on entire property, in arriving at value, for inheritance tax purposes, of interest inherited, but was entitled to deduct for such purposes only one-half thereof. 1937 Op.Atty.Gen. p. 545.

4. Funeral expenses

Although the former Inheritance Tax Act fixed no limit on amount of funeral expenses, the law would not permit the deduction of an unreasonable sum. 1936 Op.Atty.Gen. p. 58.

The erection of a mausoleum at cost of $10,000 could not be allowed as tax exempt funeral expense, and its cost over $500 allowed by former statute for a memorial was properly taxable. 1936 Op.Atty.Gen. p. 58.

5. Survivor or family allowance

Under Subsec. (b)(10) of this section (as it read prior to amendment in 1980), an absolute

deduction for the survivor's allowance was created regardless of whether the allowance was actually never paid or was paid from an estate already vested in survivor. 1977 Op.Atty.Gen. No. 27.

6. Will contest judgment

Where judgment was rendered in will contest requiring payment by administrator of a specified sum to contestors, thereby indicating on its face that amount payable was to be received by contestors in compromise settlement of their contest, such a sum was not an allowable deduction in administrator's computation of transfer tax. Indiana Dept. of State Revenue, Inheritance Tax Division v. Kitchin, App.1949, 86 N.E.2d 96, 119 Ind.App. 422.

7. Allocation of deductions

While subsec. (b) of this section does not prohibit pro rating of deductions, it certainly does not mandate such a procedure. Matter of Estate of Pfeiffer, App. 1 Dist.1983, 452 N.E.2d 448.

With respect to the inheritance tax, logic dictates that an inheritance tax deduction must be attributed only to the party which expends the resources which constitute the deduction. Matter of Estate of Pfeiffer, App. 1 Dist.1983, 452 N.E.2d 448.

8. Administrative expenses

Generally, expenses of administering decedent's estate and payment of other debts and expenses are chargeable to decedent's real and personal property. Matter of Estate of Saylors, App.1996, 671 N.E.2d 905.

Sole heir executor could deduct expenses of selling estate real estate prior to distribution as administrative expenses from the gross estate for inheritance tax purposes even where sale of real estate was for executor's own benefit. Matter of Estate of Cook, App. 1 Dist.1988, 529 N.E.2d 853.

6–4.1–3–14 Items deductible from value of property interests transferred by resident decedent other than by will, intestate succession, or under trust

Sec. 14. (a) Except as provided in subsection (b), the following items, and no others, may be deducted from the value of property interests which are transferred by a resident decedent but which are not transferred by the decedent's will, under the laws of intestate succession, or under a trust:

(1) Those taxes described in section 13(b)(5) of this chapter.

(2) Liens against the property interests that are transferred.

(3) The decedent's debts, funeral expenses, and estate administration expenses, including reasonable attorney's fees incurred in filing the inheritance tax return.

(b) In addition, any portion of the deduction provided by section 13(b)(10) of this chapter which is not needed to reduce to zero (0) the value of the property referred to in section 13 of this chapter may be deducted from the value of any other propety[1] transferred by the resident decedent to the decedent's children who are entitled to the allowance provided by IC 29–1–4–1. If more than one (1) of the decedent's children are entitled to the allowance, the deduction provided by this subsection shall be divided equally among all the decedent's children who are entitled to the allowance.

As added by Acts 1976, P.L.18, SEC.1. Amended by Acts 1976, P.L.20, SEC.2; Acts 1979, P.L.75, SEC.8; Acts 1980, P.L.57, SEC.7; P.L.94–1989, SEC.1.

[1] So in enrolled 1989 Act. Probably should read "property".

Historical and Statutory Notes

Acts 1976, P.L. 20, § 2, emerg. eff. retroactive to March 1, 1976, added the last paragraph.

See, also, Historical Note under § 6–4.1–3–13 for decedents' estates affected by Acts 1976, P.L. 20.

Acts 1979, P.L. 75, § 8, emerg. eff. retroactive to March 1, 1976, inserted "or under a trust" in the introductory clause of first paragraph; and in the last paragraph inserted "of this chapter" following "section 13(b)(10)", substituted "property referred to in section 13(b) of this chapter" for "probate property transferred by the resident decedent", and substituted "other" for "non-probate" before "property transferred."

Acts 1980, P.L. 57, § 7, emerg. eff. retroactive to July 1, 1979, in the first sentence of the last paragraph substituted "the resident decedent to his children who are" for "him to the individual or individuals;" and in the second sentence of the last paragraph substituted "one (1) of the decedent's children are" for "one (1) individual is" and substituted "his children who are" for "the individuals".

See, also, Historical Note under § 6–4.1–3–13 for decedents' estates affected by Acts 1980, P.L. 57.

P.L.94–1989, Sec.1, in Subsec. (a), inserted "Except as provided in subsection (b)"; substituted "the decedent's" for "his"; in Subsec. (a)(2), substituted "against" for "subject to which"; inserted Subsec. (a)(3); deleted the last sentence of Subsec. (a) which read:

"However, the amount of the decedent's debts or funeral expenses paid by a surviving joint owner of property held jointly with the decedent may be deducted from the value of the jointly held property if the assets of decedent's estate are insufficient to pay the debts or funeral expenses."

In addition, P.L.94–1989, Sec.1, in Subsec. (b), substituted "the decedent's" for "his" in the first and second sentences; substituted "subsection" for "paragraph" in the second sentence; and made nonsubstantive changes throughout the section.

Formerly:

IC 6–4–1–4.

Acts 1931, c. 75, s. 4.

Acts 1947, c. 182, s. 1.

Acts 1965, c. 302, s. 2.

Administrative Code References

Inheritance tax, deductions, see 45 IAC 4.1–3–7 et seq.

Law Review and Journal Commentaries

Death taxes: Survey of recent tax law. Thomas B. Allington, 10 Ind.L.Rev. 340 (1976).

Deductibility of statutory survivors allowance. Norbert Engler, 20 Res Gestae 370 (1976).

Library References

Taxation ☜895(6).
WESTLAW Topic No. 371.

C.J.S. Taxation § 1183.
I.L.E Taxation §§ 362, 367.

Notes of Decisions

Debts and funeral expenses 2
Liens 1

_____

1. Liens

For purposes of inheritance tax computation, estate executor should not have been permitted to list as a deduction a mortgage lien on certain real property owned by decedent and his surviving spouse by tenancy by entirety. Indiana Dept. of Revenue, Inheritance Tax Division v. Security Bank & Trust Co., App. 1 Dist.1979, 393 N.E.2d 197, 181 Ind.App. 543.

2. Debts and funeral expenses

Under this section providing that amount of decedent's debts and funeral expenses could be deducted from value of jointly held property "if the assets of decedent's estate are insufficient to pay the debts or funeral expenses," fact that assets of estate were not liquid and would have to be sold to obtain funds to pay such expenses was of no moment, and thus, where decedent's total assets, including real estate, exceeded covered debts and expenses, surviving joint tenant in bank account who paid funeral expenses and other costs was not entitled to claim such sums as deductions from joint bank account for inheritance tax purposes. Indiana Dept. of State Revenue, Inheritance Tax Div. v. Estate of Smith, App. 1 Dist.1984, 460 N.E.2d 1263.

6–4.1–3–15   Items deductible from value of property interests transferred by non-resident decedent

Sec. 15. The following items, and no others, may be deducted from the value of property interests transferred by a non-resident decedent:

(1) taxes, other than federal estate taxes;

(2) those administration expenses described in section 13(b)(9) of this chapter;

(3) liens against the property so transferred; and

(4) claims against the decedent's domiciliary estate which are allowed by the court having jurisdiction over that estate and which will not be paid from that estate because it is exhausted.

As added by Acts 1976, P.L.18, SEC.1.

Historical and Statutory Notes

Formerly:
IC 6–4–1–4.
Acts 1931, c. 75, s. 4.

Acts 1947, c. 182, s. 1.
Acts 1965, c. 302, s. 2.

Administrative Code References

Inheritance tax, deductions, see 45 IAC 4.1–3–13.

Library References

Taxation ⟨key⟩895(8).
WESTLAW Topic No. 371.

C.J.S. Taxation § 1186.
I.L.E. Taxation §§ 233 to 235, 240.

Chapter 4

Filing Requirements

6–4.1–4–0.5   Inheritance tax return; fair market value of property interests transferred in excess of exemptions

Sec. 0.5.   No inheritance tax return is required under this chapter unless the total fair market value of the property interests transferred by the decedent to a transferee under a taxable transfer or transfers exceeds the exemption provided to the transferee under sections 9.1 through 12 of IC 6–4.1–3. For purposes of this section, the fair market value of a property interest is its fair market value as of the appraisal date prescribed by IC 6–4.1–5–1.5.

As added by Acts 1977(ss), P.L.6, SEC.4. Amended by Acts 1979, P.L.75, SEC.9; Acts 1980, P.L.57, SEC.8; P.L.87–1983, SEC.4.

Historical and Statutory Notes

Acts 1977 (ss), P.L. 6, § 4, emerg. eff. July 1, 1977, added this section.

Acts 1979, P.L. 75, § 9, eff. July 1, 1979, substituted "8.5" for "8" following "under sections" in the first sentence.

Acts 1980, P.L. 57, § 8, eff. July 1, 1980, deleted "or statement" following "tax return" in the first sentence; and substituted "as of the appraisal date prescribed by IC 6–4.1–5–1.5" for "at the time of the decedent's death" in the second sentence.

P.L. 87–1983, Sec.4, emerg. eff. Jan. 1, 1983, substituted "9.1" for "8.5" in the first sentence.

Section 7 of P.L. 87–1983 provided that this act applies to the estates of decedents who die after Dec. 31, 1982.

Law Review and Journal Commentaries

Amendments of 1977 to Indiana Inheritance Tax Law. William L. Tracy, 21 Res Gestae 488 (1977).

Library References

Taxation ⊂⊃893.
WESTLAW Topic No. 371.

C.J.S. Taxation § 1190.
I.L.E. Taxation §§ 233 to 236.

6–4.1–4–1   Inheritance tax return; filing time; contents

Sec. 1.   (a) Except as otherwise provided in section 0.5 of this chapter or in IC 6–4.1–5–8, the personal representative of a resident decedent's estate or the trustee or transferee of property transferred by the decedent shall file an inheritance tax return with the appropriate probate court within twelve (12) months after the date of the decedent's death. The person filing the return shall file it under oath on the forms prescribed by the department of state revenue. The return shall:

(1) contain a statement of all property interests transferred by the decedent under taxable transfers;

(2) indicate the fair market value, as of the appraisal date prescribed by IC 6–4.1–5–1.5, of each property interest included in the statement;

(3) contain an itemized list of all inheritance tax deductions claimed with respect to property interests included in the statement;

(4) contain a list which indicates the name and address of each transferee of the property interests included in the statement and which indicates the total value of the property interests transferred to each transferee; and

(5) contain the name and address of the attorney for the personal representative or for the person filing the return.

(b) If the decedent died testate, the person filing the return shall attach a copy of the decedent's will to the return.

As added by Acts 1976, P.L.18, SEC.1. Amended by Acts 1977(ss), P.L.6, SEC.5; Acts 1980, P.L.57, SEC.9; P.L.67–1988, SEC.1.

Historical and Statutory Notes

Acts 1976, P.L. 18, § 1, emerg. eff. Feb. 18, 1976, added this article.

The 1976 act added the provisions of this chapter as part of a codification and restatement of laws relating to death taxes.

As enacted by Acts 1976, P.L. 18, this section read:

"The personal representative of a resident decedent's estate or the trustee or transferee of property transferred by the decedent shall file an inheritance tax return with the appropriate probate court within twelve (12) months after the date of the decedent's death. The person filing the return shall file it under oath on the forms prescribed by the department of state revenue. The return shall:

"(1) contain a statement of all property interest transferred by the decedent under taxable transfers;

"(2) indicate the fair market value, at the time of the decedent's death, of the property included in the statement;

"(3) indicate the assessed value, at the time of decedent's death, of any real property interest included in the statement;

"(4) contain an itemized list of all inheritance tax deductions claimed with respect to property interest included in the statement; and

"(5) contain a list which indicates the name and address of each transferee of the property interests included in the statement and which indicates the total value of the property interests transferred to each transferee.

"If the decedent died testate, the person filing the return shall attach a copy of the decedent's will to the return."

Acts 1977 (ss), P.L. 6, § 5, emerg. eff. July 1, 1977, in provisions now constituting subsec. (a), at the beginning of the first sentence, inserted "Except as otherwise provided in section 0.5 of this chapter or in IC 6–4.1–5–8"; substituted "interests" for "interest" in Cls. (1) and (4); and inserted "interest" following "property" in Cl. (2).

Acts 1980, P.L. 57, § 9, eff. July 1, 1980, in provisions now constituting Subsec. A, substituted "as of the appraisal date prescribed by IC 6–4.1–5–1.5" for "at the time of the decedent's death", "each" for "the" preceding "property" and "interest" for "interests" following "property" in Cl. (2); deleted former Cl. (3) of the section as added in 1976; and renumbered former Cls. (4) and (5) as "(3)" and "(4)", respectively.

P.L. 67–1988, § 1, designated Subsecs. (a) and (b); and added Subsec. (a)(5) relating to the name and address of the attorney.

Formerly:

IC 6–4–1–7.
Acts 1931, c. 75, s. 7.
Acts 1933, c. 229, s. 1.
Acts 1937, c. 285, s. 1.
Acts 1957, c. 318, s. 1.

Cross References

Personal property tax returns, filing by fiduciaries, see IC 6–1.1–36–6.

Administrative Code References

Inheritance tax returns, filing requirements, see 45 IAC 4.1–4–1 et seq.

Law Review and Journal Commentaries

Death taxes: Survey of recent law. John W. Boyd, 12 Ind.L.Rev. 320, 326 (1979).

Reasonable cause for late filing of estate tax returns. 11 Ind.L.Rev. 621 (1978).

Library References

Taxation ☞893.
WESTLAW Topic No. 371.

C.J.S. Taxation § 1190.
I.L.E. Taxation § 239.

Notes of Decisions

Fair market value   1

1. Fair market value

"Fair market value" of an item is that which a willing buyer, under no compulsion to buy, would pay a willing seller, under no compulsion to sell, for the item. Second Nat. Bank of Richmond v. State Dept. of State Revenue, Inheritance Tax Division, App. 1 Dist.1977, 366 N.E.2d 694, 174 Ind.App. 168.

For state estate tax purposes, the fair market value of United States treasury bonds, which were not scheduled to mature for more than 20 years, was the price of such bonds on the open market rather than their face value at which United States treasury was required to redeem them in payment of federal estate taxes. Second Nat. Bank of Richmond v. State Dept. of State Revenue, Inheritance Tax Division, App. 1 Dist.1977, 366 N.E.2d 694, 174 Ind.App. 168.

6–4.1–4–2   Extension of filing time; subsequent extensions

Sec. 2.   If the appropriate probate court finds that because of an unavoidable delay an inheritance tax return cannot be filed within twelve (12) months after the date of decedent's death, the court may extend the period for filing the return. After the expiration of the first extension period, the court may grant a subsequent extension if the person seeking the extension files a written motion which states the reason for the delay in filing the return. For purposes of sections 3 and 6 of this chapter, an inheritance tax return is not due until the last day of any extension period or periods granted by the court under this section.

As added by Acts 1976, P.L.18, SEC.1.

Historical and Statutory Notes

Formerly:
IC 6–4–1–7.
Acts 1931, c. 75, s. 7.

Acts 1933, c. 229, s. 1.
Acts 1937, c. 285, s. 1.
Acts 1957, c. 318, s. 1.

Law Review and Journal Commentaries
Reasonable cause for late filing of estate tax
returns. 11 Ind.L.Rev. 621 (1978).

6–4.1–4–3 Failure to file; court ordered appearance upon request of interested parties

Sec. 3. The appropriate probate court shall order a person who fails to file an inheritance tax return on or before the date the return is due to appear before the court to state why the return has not been filed if an interested party files a motion asking the court to take that action. In addition, the court may on its own motion order the person to enter such an appearance.

As added by Acts 1976, P.L.18, SEC.1.

Historical and Statutory Notes

Formerly:
IC 6–4–1–7.
Acts 1931, c. 75, s. 7.

Acts 1933, c. 229, s. 1.
Acts 1937, c. 285, s. 1.
Acts 1957, c. 318, s. 1.

Library References

Taxation ☞893.
WESTLAW Topic No. 371.
C.J.S. Taxation § 1190.

6–4.1–4–4 Court order; appearance upon request of interested parties

Sec. 4. The appropriate probate court may order a personal representative of a resident decedent's estate to file an inheritance tax return on or before a date fixed by the court if the personal representative appears before the court in response to an order issued by the court under section 3 of this chapter.

As added by Acts 1976, P.L.18, SEC.1.

Historical and Statutory Notes

Formerly:
IC 6–4–1–7.
Acts 1931, c. 75, s. 7.

Acts 1933, c. 229, s. 1.
Acts 1937, c. 285, s. 1.
Acts 1957, c. 318, s. 1.

6–4.1–4–5 Removal of personal representative; grounds

Sec. 5. The appropriate probate court may order the removal of the personal representative of a resident decedent's estate and appoint a successor to take the removed personal representative's place if:

(1) the personal representative fails to appear before the court in response to an order issued by it under section 3 of this chapter; or

(2) the personal representative fails to file an inheritance tax return on or before the date fixed by the court under section 4 of this chapter.

As added by Acts 1976, P.L.18, SEC.1.

Historical and Statutory Notes

Formerly: Acts 1933, c. 229, s. 1.
  IC 6–4–1–7.   Acts 1937, c. 285, s. 1.
  Acts 1931, c. 75, s. 7.   Acts 1957, c. 318, s. 1.

Cross References

Removal of personal representative, see IC 29–1–10–6.

Library References

Executors and Administrators ⊙35(1).   C.J.S. Executors and Administrators § 90.
WESTLAW Topic No. 162.   I.L.E. Taxation § 232.

6–4.1–4–6   Penalties for failure to file return; waiver

Sec. 6. (a) Except as provided in subsection (b) of this section, the appropriate probate court shall charge a person who fails to file an inheritance tax return on or before the due date a penalty in an amount which equals:

(1) fifty cents ($0.50) per day for each day that the return is delinquent; or

(2) fifty dollars ($50);

whichever is less. The court shall include the penalty in the inheritance tax decree which it issues with respect to the decedent's estate. The person to whom the penalty is charged shall pay it to the treasurer of the county in which the resident decedent was domiciled at the time of the resident decedent's death.

(b) The appropriate probate court may waive the penalty otherwise required under subsection (a) of this section if the court finds that the person had a justifiable excuse for not filing the return on or before the due date.

As added by Acts 1976, P.L.18, SEC.1. Amended by P.L.86–1995, SEC.6.

Historical and Statutory Notes

P.L.86–1995, Sec.6, emerg. eff. retroactive to Jan. 1, 1994, amended the section by substituting "resident decedent was domiciled at the time of the resident decedent's death" for "court is sitting" in Subsec. (a)(2).

Acts 1931, c. 75, s. 7.
Acts 1933, c. 229, s. 1.
Acts 1937, c. 285, s. 1.
Acts 1957, c. 318, s. 1.

Formerly:
  IC 6–4–1–7.

Law Review and Journal Commentaries

Reasonable cause for late filing of estate tax returns. 11 Ind.L.Rev. 621 (1978).

Library References

Taxation ⊙906.   C.J.S. Taxation § 1207.
WESTLAW Topic No. 371.   I.L.E. Taxation § 239.

Notes of Decisions

Justifiable excuse   1

_____

1. Justifiable excuse

Where the inexperienced taxpayer, wholly unaware of the time requirements for filing a federal estate tax return, and where those time requirements were different from Indiana filing dates, selected a competent tax expert, supplied him with all necessary and relevant informa-tion, requested him to prepare all necessary documents including tax returns, relied upon his doing so, and maintained contact with him from time to time during the estate administra-tion, but where the expert neglected to timely file the estate tax return, "reasonable cause" existed for the taxpayer's failure to timely file, and the taxpayer was thus not subject to imposi-tion of a penalty. Rohrabaugh v. U. S., C.A.7 (Ind.)1979, 611 F.2d 211.

6–4.1–4–7 Non-resident decedent; inheritance tax return

Sec. 7.   (a) Except as otherwise provided in section 0.5 of this chapter, the personal representative of a nonresident decedent's estate or the trustee or transferee of property transferred by the decedent shall file an inheritance tax return with the department of state revenue within twelve (12) months after the date of the decedent's death. The person filing the return shall file it under oath on the forms prescribed by the department of state revenue. The return shall:

(1) contain a statement of all property interests transferred by the decedent under taxable transfers;

(2) indicate the fair market value, as of the appraisal date prescribed by IC 6–4.1–5–1.5, of each property interest included in the statement;

(3) contain an itemized list of all inheritance tax deductions claimed with respect to property interests included in the statement;

(4) contain a list which indicates the name and address of each transferee of the property interests included in the statement and which indicates the total value of the property interests transferred to each transferee; and

(5) contain the name and address of the attorney for the personal represen-tative or for the person filing the return.

(b) If the decedent died testate, the person filing the return shall attach a copy of the decedent's will to the return.

As added by Acts 1976, P.L.18, SEC.1.   Amended by Acts 1977(ss), P.L.6, SEC.6; Acts 1980, P.L.57, SEC.10; P.L.67–1988, SEC.2.

Historical and Statutory Notes

Acts 1977 (ss), P.L. 6, § 6, emerg. eff. July 1, 1977, in provisions now constituting Subsec. (a), at the beginning of the first sentence insert-ed "Except as otherwise provided in section 0.5 of this chapter;" and substituted "statement" for "schedule" in the second sentence.

Acts 1980, P.L.57, § 10, eff. July 1, 1980, rewrote the section, which had read:

"Except as otherwise provided in section 0.5 of this chapter, each person who has possession of or control over a nonresident decedent's property described in IC 6–4.1–2–3 shall file an itemized statement of that property with the department of state revenue. The person shall file the statement within six (6) months after the date of the nonresident decedent's death on forms prescribed by the department of state revenue."

P.L. 67–1988, Sec.2, designated Subsecs. (a) and (b); and added Subsec. (a)(5), relating to the name and address of the attorney.

DETERMINATION OF TAX

Formerly:
IC 6–4–1–20.
Acts 1931, c. 75, s. 20.

Administrative Code References

Inheritance tax returns, nonresident decedents property, filing requirements, see 45 IAC 4.1–4–1,
45 IAC 4.1–4–2.

6–4.1–4–8   Federal estate tax return; filing with state

Sec. 8.   If a federal estate tax return is filed for a decedent's estate and if a
tax is imposed under this article as a result of the decedent's death, the
personal representative of the decedent's estate or the trustee or transferee of
property transferred by the decedent shall:

(1) concurrently with the filing of the federal estate tax return file a signed
copy of that return with the department of state revenue; and

(2) file a copy of the final determination of federal estate tax, whether
issued by the internal revenue service or a federal court, with the department of state revenue within thirty (30) days after it is received.

As added by Acts 1976, P.L.18, SEC.1.

Historical and Statutory Notes

Formerly:
IC 6–4–1–38.
Acts 1931, c. 75, s. 39.

Acts 1965, c. 276, s. 2.
Acts 1974, P.L.24, SEC.2.

Library References

Taxation ☞893.
WESTLAW Topic No. 371.

C.J.S. Taxation § 1190.
I.L.E. Taxation § 239.

6–4.1–4–9   Filing fee prohibited

Sec. 9.   A person may not be required to pay a fee to file an inheritance tax
return.

As added by Acts 1976, P.L.18, SEC.1.   Amended by Acts 1980, P.L.57, SEC.11.

Historical and Statutory Notes

Acts 1980, P.L. 57, § 11, eff. July 1, 1980,
deleted "or statement" following "tax return."

Formerly:
IC 6–4–1–7.

Acts 1931, c. 75, s. 7.
Acts 1933, c. 229, s. 1.
Acts 1937, c. 285, s. 1.
Acts 1957, c. 318, s. 1.

Chapter 5

Determination of Inheritance Tax

Section

6–4.1–5–1   Tax rates; transfers to Classes A, B and C transferees

Sec. 1.   (a) For purposes of this section, the net taxable value of property interests transferred by a decedent to a particular transferee equals the remainder of:

(1) the total fair market value of the property interests transferred by the decedent to the transferee under a taxable transfer or transfers; minus

(2) the total amount of exemptions and deductions provided under sections 9.1 through 15 of IC 6–4.1–3 with respect to the property interests so transferred.

(b) The inheritance tax imposed on a decedent's transfer of property interests to a particular Class A transferee is prescribed in the following table:

NET TAXABLE VALUE OF PROPERTY INTERESTS TRANSFERRED	INHERITANCE TAX
$25,000 or less	1% of net taxable value
over $25,000 but not over $50,000	$250, plus 2% of net taxable value over $25,000
over $50,000 but not over $200,000	$750, plus 3% of net taxable value over $50,000
over $200,000 but not over $300,000	$5,250, plus 4% of net taxable value over $200,000
over $300,000 but not over $500,000	$9,250, plus 5% of net taxable value over $300,000
over $500,000 but not over $700,000	$19,250, plus 6% of net taxable value over $500,000

NET TAXABLE VALUE
OF PROPERTY
INTERESTS
TRANSFERRED   INHERITANCE TAX

over $700,000 but not
   over $1,000,000 . . . . $31,250, plus 7% of net taxable value
                     over $700,000

over $1,000,000 but not
   over $1,500,000 . . . . $52,250, plus 8% of net taxable value
                     over $1,000,000

over $1,500,000 . . . . $92,250, plus 10% of net taxable value
                     over $1,500,000

(c) The inheritance tax imposed on a decedent's transfer of property interests to a particular Class B transferee is prescribed in the following table:

NET TAXABLE VALUE
OF PROPERTY
INTERESTS
TRANSFERRED   INHERITANCE TAX

$100,000 or less . . . . 7% of net taxable value

over $100,000 but not
   over $500,000 . . . . $7,000, plus 10% of net taxable value
                     over $100,000

over $500,000 but not
   over $1,000,000 . . . . $47,000, plus 12% of net taxable value
                     over $500,000

over $1,000,000 . . . . $107,000, plus 15% of net taxable val-
                     ue over $1,000,000

(d) The inheritance tax imposed on a decedent's transfer of property interests to a particular Class C transferee is prescribed in the following table:

NET TAXABLE VALUE
OF PROPERTY
INTERESTS
TRANSFERRED   INHERITANCE TAX

$100,000 or less . . . . 10% of net taxable value

over $100,000 but not
   over $1,000,000 . . . . $10,000, plus 15% of net taxable value
                     over $100,000

over $1,000,000 . . . . $145,000, plus 20% of net taxable val-
                     ue over $1,000,000

As added by Acts 1976, P.L.18, SEC.1. Amended by Acts 1977(ss), P.L.6, SEC.7; Acts 1979, P.L.75, SEC.10; Acts 1980, P.L.57, SEC.12; P.L.87–1983, SEC.5.

Historical and Statutory Notes

Acts 1976, P.L. 18, § 1, emerg. eff. Feb. 18, 1976, added this article.

The 1976 act added the provisions of this chapter as part of a codification, and restatement of laws relating to death taxes.

Acts 1977 (ss), P.L. 6, § 7, emerg. eff. July 1, 1977, in Subsec. (a) substituted "by" for "from" before "the decedent".

Acts 1979, P.L. 75, § 10, eff. July 1, 1979, substituted "8.5" for "8" in Subsec. (a) following "sections".

Acts 1980, P.L. 57, § 12, eff. July 1, 1980, in Subsec. (a) deleted "on the date of the decedent's death" following "fair market value".

P.L. 87–1983, Sec.5, emerg. eff. Jan. 1, 1983, substituted "9.1" for "8.5" in Cl. (2) of Subsec. (a).

Section 7 of P.L. 87–1983 provided that this act applies to the estates of decedents who die after Dec. 31, 1982.

Formerly:

IC 6–4–1–2.

Acts 1931, c. 75, s. 2.

Acts 1965, c. 302, s. 1.

Acts 1975, P.L.64, SEC.1.

Cross References

Classes of transferees, defined, see IC 6–4.1–1–3.

Law Review and Journal Commentaries

Amendments of 1977 to Indiana Inheritance Tax Law. William L. Tracy, 21 Res Gestae 488 (1977).

Library References

Taxation ⟜886½.
WESTLAW Topic No. 371.

C.J.S. Taxation § 1181.
I.L.E. Taxation § 241.

United States Code Annotated

Deductions in computing federal taxable estate, see 26 U.S.C.A. § 2051 et seq.
Valuation, federal estate tax, see 26 U.S.C.A. § 2032, 2032A.

Notes of Decisions

Classes of transferees 1
Rate of taxation 2

----

1. Classes of transferees

Though testatrix' deceased son's wife, who was sole surviving beneficiary under the will, had remarried prior to testatrix' death, wife was a "widow" within meaning of § 6–4.1–1–3 providing that, for inheritance tax purposes, a "class B transferee" was a widow of a child of the transferor. Matter of Souder's Estate, App. 3 Dist.1981, 421 N.E.2d 12.

Where first brother died intestate in 1941 survived by father, mother and second brother, father and mother, by intestate succession took undivided one-half interest as joint tenants while other one-half interest passed to second brother, second brother, by 1942 deed, conveyed his interest to father and mother as tenants by entirety, father and mother, later in 1942, conveyed by deed fee simple remainder interest in property to second brother reserving to themselves a life estate for and during their natural lives, second brother died intestate in 1950 and his remainder interest passed to his

spouse, father died in 1955, and mother died in 1977, the 1942 transfer by which father and mother conveyed fee simple remainder interest to second brother was subject to inheritance tax as transfer by decedent to Class A transferee and not to Class B transferee. In re Grotrian's Estate, App. 3 Dist.1980, 405 N.E.2d 69.

Inheritance tax is to be measured by relationship of transferor to transferee under deed. In re Grotrian's Estate, App. 3 Dist.1980, 405 N.E.2d 69.

2. Rate of taxation

Where a man died and left widow property valued at $95,000, inheritance for tax purposes should have been considered to be $80,000 and of this $10,000 was taxable at 1%, $25,000 at 2%, and the balance at 3%. Indiana Dept. of State Revenue, Inheritance Tax Division v. Short, App.1956, 131 N.E.2d 154, 126 Ind.App. 242.

Under former inheritance tax act providing for increased rate when market value of property or interest to which any person became beneficially entitled exceeded $25,000, where value of property was in excess of $25,000, higher rate of tax was properly assessed on all property which passed to heirs or legatees. 1913–1914 Op.Atty.Gen. p. 85.

6–4.1–5–1.5 Fair market value; appraisal date

Sec. 1.5. (a) For purposes of determining the fair market value of each property interest transferred by a decedent, the appraisal date for the property interest is the date used to value the property interest for federal estate tax purposes. However, if no federal estate tax return is filed for the decedent's estate, the appraisal date for each property interest transferred by the decedent is the date of the decedent's death.

(b) The finally determined federal estate tax value of a property interest is presumed to be the fair market value of the property interest for Indiana inheritance tax purposes, unless the federal estate tax value is determined under Section 2032A of the Internal Revenue Code.[1] However, the presumption is rebuttable. A property interest that is valued for federal estate tax purposes under Section 2032A of the Internal Revenue Code shall be valued for Indiana inheritance tax purposes at its fair market value on the appraisal date prescribed by subsection (a).

As added by Acts 1980, P.L.57, SEC.13.

[1] 26 U.S.C.A. § 2032A.

Historical and Statutory Notes

Acts 1980, P.L. 57, § 13, eff. July 1, 1980, added this section.

Administrative Code References

Inheritance tax, stocks and bonds, appraisal of fair market value, methods of determining, see 45 IAC 4.1–5–3.

Law Review and Journal Commentaries

Protecting client assets—How to acquire cost effective appraisals of coin, stamp and paper money collections and accumulations. Donn H. Wray and James M. Hackett, 34 Res Gestae 110 (1990).

Library References

Taxation ☞895(1).
WESTLAW Topic No. 371.

C.J.S. Taxation § 1171.
I.L.E. Taxation § 239.

Notes of Decisions

Fair market value   1
Future interests   3
Securities and stocks   2

————

1. Fair market value

Inheritance tax on property transfer made by decedent is based on fair market value of property interest on date of decedent's death, or on date used for valuation of property interest for federal estate tax purposes. Department of State Revenue, Inheritance Tax Div. v. Phelps, 1998, 697 N.E.2d 506.

Date of decedent's death is appraisal date for determining fair market value of property interest transferred by a decedent if no federal estate tax return is filed. Sibbitt v. Indiana Dept. of

Revenue, App. 1 Dist.1990, 563 N.E.2d 146, rehearing denied, transfer denied.

"Fair market value" is what a willing buyer, under no compulsion to buy, would pay a willing seller, under no compulsion to sell, for the item. Second Nat. Bank of Richmond v. State Dept. of State Revenue, Inheritance Tax Division, App. 1 Dist.1977, 366 N.E.2d 694, 174 Ind.App. 168.

2. Securities and stocks

United States Treasury bonds, commonly known as "Flower Bonds," are to be valued at price determined in the open market and not at par for purposes of the Indiana inheritance and estate tax, despite provisions in bonds which allow them to be redeemed at their par or face value in payment of federal estate taxes. State v. Bower, App. 3 Dist.1978, 372 N.E.2d 1227, 175 Ind.App. 540.

For state estate tax purposes, the fair market value of United States Treasury bonds, which were not scheduled to mature for more than 20 years, was the price of such bonds on the open market rather than their face value at which United States Treasury was required to redeem them in payment of federal estate taxes. Second Nat. Bank of Richmond v. State Dept. of State Revenue, Inheritance Tax Division, App. 1 Dist.1977, 366 N.E.2d 694, 174 Ind.App. 168.

3. Future interests

Language in will that testator's heir "shall have a life estate in [two parcels of testator's real property], at the then fair market value as appraised," was clearly intended to specify value of heir's interest in parcels for tax purposes, and did not indicate intent by testator that heir was merely granted option to purchase parcels. In re Estate of Grimm, App.1999, 705 N.E.2d 483, rehearing denied, transfer denied.

If beneficiary receives less than fee interest in property transferred by reason of owner's death, inheritance tax is calculated pursuant to actuarial tables as of date of death. Estate of Hibbs v. Indiana Dept. of State Revenue, Inheritance Tax Div., 1994, 636 N.E.2d 204.

If life estate with remainder is created upon death of property owner, both life tenant and remainderman will pay inheritance tax on their proportionate interests, based on interests' values at date of owner's death. Estate of Hibbs v. Indiana Dept. of State Revenue, Inheritance Tax Div., 1994, 636 N.E.2d 204.

Ordinarily, where testator has devised future estates, the present value of the future estate, life estates, and remainders, are determined at his death according to appropriate statutory methods, tables, and actuarial formulae; then the tax is assessed and paid during administration by the personal representative. Indiana Dept. of State Revenue, Inheritance Tax Division v. Puett's Estate, App. 1 Dist.1982, 435 N.E.2d 298.

6–4.1–5–2 Referral of return to tax appraiser; duties

Sec. 2. Within ten (10) days after an inheritance tax return for a resident decedent is filed with the probate court, the court shall refer the return to the county inheritance tax appraiser. The county inheritance tax appraiser shall:

(1) investigate the facts concerning taxable transfers made by the decedent before his death;

(2) review the return for mistakes and omissions; and

(3) appraise each property interest, transferred by the decedent under a taxable transfer, at its fair market value as of the appraisal date prescribed by IC 6–4.1–5–1.5.

As added by Acts 1976, P.L.18, SEC.1. Amended by Acts 1980, P.L.57, SEC.14.

Historical and Statutory Notes

Acts 1980, P.L. 57, § 14, eff. July 1, 1980, in Cl. (3) substituted "appraisal date prescribed by IC 6–4.1–5–1.5" for "date of the decedent's death."

Formerly:
IC 6–4–1–7.

IC 6–4–1–8.
Acts 1931, c. 75, ss. 7, 8.
Acts 1933, c. 229, s. 1.
Acts 1937, c. 285, s. 1.
Acts 1957, c. 318, ss. 1, 2.
Acts 1965, c. 324, s. 1.

Notes of Decisions

Appraisal   1
Cash assets   2
Fees and expenses   3

1. Appraisal

An "appraisal" is a valuation or estimation of value placed upon an item of property or interest therein for inheritance tax purposes. Matter of Waltz' Estate, App. 3 Dist.1980, 408 N.E.2d 558.

2. Cash assets

A decedent's estate, consisting entirely of money, need not be appraised for the computation of inheritance tax. 1915–1916 Op.Atty. Gen. p. 101.

3. Fees and expenses

Fees and expenses in appraising an estate for inheritance taxes were to be drawn from the inheritance tax fund in the hands of the treasurer. State v. Smith, 1920, 127 N.E. 545, 190 Ind. 690.

6–4.1–5–3   Notice of appraisal

Sec. 3.   Before he makes the appraisal required under section 2(3) of this chapter, the county inheritance tax appraiser shall give notice of the time and place of the appraisal, by mail, to:

(1) each person known to have an interest in the property interests to be appraised, including the department of state revenue; and

(2) any person designated by the probate court.

The county inheritance tax appraiser shall appraise the property interests at the time and place stated in the notice.

As added by Acts 1976, P.L.18, SEC.1.

6–4.1–5–4   Subpoena; witness fees

Sec. 4.   In order to make the appraisal required under section 2(3) of this chapter, the county inheritance tax appraiser may:

(1) issue subpoenas;

(2) compel the appearance of witnesses before him; and

(3) examine witnesses under oath.

Each witness examined with respect to the appraisal is entitled to receive a fee in the same amount paid to a witness subpoenaed to appear before a court of record. The county treasurer shall, from county funds not otherwise appropriated, pay the witness fee which is provided for under this section and which is allowed by the probate court under section 10 of this chapter.

As added by Acts 1976, P.L.18, SEC.1.

Historical and Statutory Notes

Formerly:
  IC 6–4–1–9.

Acts 1931, c. 75, s. 9.
Acts 1957, c. 318, s. 3.

Cross References

Witness fees, see IC 33–19–1–5 et seq.

Library References

Taxation ☞895(3).
Witnesses ☞7 to 15, 25, 27.
WESTLAW Topic Nos. 371, 410.

C.J.S. Taxation § 1171.
C.J.S. Witnesses §§ 13, 19 to 26, 37, 41.
I.L.E. Taxation § 242.

6–4.1–5–5   Refiling return following appraisal; appraiser's review

Sec. 5. After an inheritance tax return filed for a resident decedent is examined by the county inheritance tax appraiser and the probate court, the court shall order the person responsible for filing the return to complete the return and refile it if the court finds that the return is incomplete. When the return is refiled, the court shall refer the refiled return to the county inheritance tax appraiser for review by him.

As added by Acts 1976, P.L.18, SEC.1.

Historical and Statutory Notes

Formerly:
  IC 6–4–1–7.
  IC 6–4–1–8.

Acts 1931, c. 75, ss. 7, 8.
Acts 1957, c. 318, ss. 1, 2.
Acts 1965, c. 324, s. 1.

Library References

Taxation ☞893.
WESTLAW Topic No. 371.

C.J.S. Taxation § 1190.
I.L.E. Taxation § 242.

6–4.1–5–6   Appraisal report; preparation; filing

Sec. 6. After completing the duties assigned to him under section 2 of this chapter, the county inheritance tax appraiser shall prepare an appraisal report. The appraisal report shall:

    (1) contain a list of the property interests described in section 2(3) of this chapter; and

    (2) indicate the fair market value of the property interests.

The county inheritance tax appraiser shall file one (1) copy of the report with the probate court, and he shall file another copy of the report with the department of state revenue. The appraiser shall attach the depositions of any witnesses examined with respect to the appraisal and any other information which the court may require to the appraisal report which he files with the court.

As added by Acts 1976, P.L.18, SEC.1. Amended by Acts 1980, P.L.57, SEC.15.

Historical and Statutory Notes

Acts 1980, P.L. 57, § 15, eff. July 1, 1980, substituted "2" for "1" in the first sentence; and in Cl. (2) deleted "as of the date of the decedent's death" following "property interests".

IC 6–4–1–10.
Acts 1931, c. 75, ss. 9, 10.
Acts 1957, c. 318, s. 3.
Acts 1973, P.L.48, SEC.2.

Formerly:
IC 6–4–1–9.

Library References

Taxation ☞895(1).
WESTLAW Topic No. 371.

C.J.S. Taxation § 1171.
I.L.E. Taxation § 242.

6–4.1–5–7 Petition for order of no inheritance tax due

Sec. 7. If the personal representative of a resident decedent's estate or the trustee or transferee of property transferred by the decedent believes that no inheritance tax is imposed under this article as a result of the decedent's death, he may file a verified petition with the appropriate probate court requesting that the court enter an order stating that no inheritance tax is due. The petitioner must include in the petition a statement of the value of the property interests transferred by the decedent.

As added by Acts 1976, P.L.18, SEC.1.

Historical and Statutory Notes

Formerly:
IC 6–4–1–7.
Acts 1931, c. 75, s. 7.

Acts 1933, c. 229, s. 1.
Acts 1937, c. 285, s. 1.
Acts 1957, c. 318, s. 1.

6–4.1–5–8 Hearing upon petition for order of no inheritance tax due; rehearing

Sec. 8. If a petition is filed under section 7 of this chapter, the probate court may hold a hearing on the petition. If the court elects to hold a hearing, it shall give notice of the hearing in the same manner prescribed for giving the notice required under section 9 of this chapter. After the probate court completes its examination of the petition, the court may enter an order stating that no inheritance tax is due as a result of the decedent's death. If the court enters such an order, the petitioner is not required to file an inheritance tax return. However, a person may petition the appropriate probate court under IC 6–4.1–7 for a rehearing on the court's order or for a reappraisal of the property interests transferred by the decedent.

As added by Acts 1976, P.L.18, SEC.1.

Historical and Statutory Notes

Formerly:
  IC 6–4–1–7.
  Acts 1931, c. 75, s. 7.

Acts 1933, c. 229, s. 1.
Acts 1937, c. 285, s. 1.
Acts 1957, c. 318, s. 1.

Notes of Decisions

Prior law   1

1. Prior law

Under Tax Act of 1919, § 160, if court, upon application of auditor of state or county treasurer or other interested party, or on its own motion, determined that an estate was not subject to tax, no notice was required inasmuch as

no hearing to determine tax was held. 1917–1920 Op.Atty.Gen. p. 510.

Under Acts 1931, c. 75, §§ 7, 8 all inheritance tax schedules in counties of less than 400,000 population were to be transmitted to the county assessor for appraisement of the property, and a court could not enter a decree finding no inheritance tax payable after examining the schedule without appraisement. 1931–1932 Op.Atty. Gen. p. 743.

6–4.1–5–9   Hearing on tax appraiser's report; notice

Sec. 9. (a) When the county inheritance tax appraiser files an appraisal report with the probate court, the court shall give twenty (20) days notice of the time and place of a hearing on the report. The court shall give the notice by mail to all persons known to be interested in the resident decedent's estate, including the department of state revenue.

(b) If the address of a person interested in a resident decedent's estate is unknown, the probate court shall give notice of the time and place of the appraisal report hearing by publication. The court shall publish the notice not less than three (3) successive weeks before the hearing in a newspaper published in the county.

As added by Acts 1976, P.L.18, SEC.1.

Historical and Statutory Notes

Formerly:
  IC 6–4–1–10.

Acts 1931, c. 75, s. 10.
Acts 1973, P.L.48, SEC.2.

6–4.1–5–10   Orders of inheritance tax and witness fees due; form

Sec. 10. (a) After the hearing required by section 9 of this chapter, the probate court shall determine the fair market value of the property interests transferred by the resident decedent and the amount of inheritance tax due as a result of his death. The court shall then enter an order stating the amount of inheritance tax due and the fees due witnesses under section 4 of this chapter. If the court finds that no inheritance tax is due, the court shall include a statement to that effect in the order.

(b) The court shall prepare the order required by this section on the form prescribed by the department of state revenue. The court shall include in the order a description of all Indiana real property owned by the resident decedent at the time of his death. The probate court shall spread the order of record in the office of the clerk of the circuit court. The clerk shall maintain the orders in a looseleaf ledger.

As added by Acts 1976, P.L.18, SEC.1. Amended by Acts 1980, P.L.57, SEC.16.

Historical and Statutory Notes

Acts 1980, P.L. 57, § 16, eff. July 1, 1980, in Subsec. (a) in the first sentence deleted "on the date of the resident decedent's death" following "market value", and substituted "the resident decedent" for "him".

Formerly:
IC 6–4–1–7.
IC 6–4–1–8.

IC 6–4–1–9.
IC 6–4–1–10.
Acts 1931, c. 75, ss. 7 to 10.
Acts 1933, c. 229, s. 1.
Acts 1937, c. 285, s. 1.
Acts 1957, c. 318, ss. 1 to 3.
Acts 1965, c. 324, s. 1.
Acts 1973, P.L.48, SEC.2.

Administrative Code References

Inheritance tax, value of estate and payment, see 45 IAC 4.1–9–4, 45 IAC 4.1–5–11, 45 IAC 4.1–5–12.

Library References

Taxation ⚯900(2).
WESTLAW Topic No. 371.

C.J.S. Taxation § 1202.
I.L.E. Taxation § 242.

6–4.1–5–11   Court determination of inheritance tax due; copies to interested persons

Sec. 11.   The court shall immediately mail a copy of its determination of the fair market value of the property interests transferred by a resident decedent and the inheritance tax due as a result of the decedent's death to all persons interested in the decedent's estate, including the department of state revenue and the county treasurer.

As added by Acts 1976, P.L.18, SEC.1.

Historical and Statutory Notes

Formerly:
IC 6–4–1–10.

Acts 1931, c. 75, s. 10.
Acts 1973, P.L.48, SEC.2.

Cross References

Enforcement of payment of tax, statute of limitations, need to comply with this section, see IC 6–4.1–9–11.

Library References

Taxation ⚯900(5).
WESTLAW Topic No. 371.

C.J.S. Taxation § 1205.
I.L.E. Taxation § 242.

Notes of Decisions

Review   1

___

1. Review

Under former inheritance tax statutes, the judicial determination of the value of the estate of the decedent, and of the inheritance tax thereon, was a judgment, which was subject to review under former statute [see, now, § 6–4.1–7–1] providing for rehearing and to appeal under former statute providing for appeal. Indiana Dept. of Revenue Inheritance Tax Division v. Callaway's Estate, 1953, 110 N.E.2d 903, 232 Ind. 1.

6–4.1–5–12   Repealed

(Repealed by P.L.305–1987, SEC.38.)

Historical and Statutory Notes

P.L. 305–1987 provided in Section 43 that the act takes effect July 1, 1987.

The repealed section established appraisal charges when no inheritance tax was due.

Formerly:

IC 6–4–1–7.

Acts 1931, c. 75, s. 7.
Acts 1933, c. 229, s. 1.
Acts 1937, c. 285, s. 1.
Acts 1957, c. 318, s. 1.
Acts 1976, P.L.18, SEC.1.
P.L. 171–1984, SEC.4.
P.L. 192–1986, SEC.4.

6–4.1–5–13   Appointment of temporary guardian

Sec. 13.   A probate court shall appoint a temporary guardian to represent an individual if, at any time during the proceedings to determine the inheritance tax imposed as a result of a resident decedent's death, the court finds that the individual:

(1) is under eighteen (18) years of age or incapacitated (as defined in IC 29–3–1–7.5); and

(2) has an interest in the resident decedent's estate which is adverse to an interest which another person has in the estate.

As added by Acts 1976, P.L.18, SEC.1.   Amended by P.L.33–1989, SEC.5.

Historical and Statutory Notes

P.L.33–1989, Sec.5, substituted "temporary" for "special"; and, in Subd. (1), substituted "incapacitated (as defined in IC 29–3–1–7.5)".

Formerly:

IC 6–4–1–10.

Acts 1931, c. 75, s. 10.
Acts 1973, P.L.48, SEC.2.

6–4.1–5–14   Appraisal and determination of tax due on nonresident decedent's estate; determination without court intervention

Sec. 14.   The department of state revenue shall determine the inheritance tax imposed as a result of a non-resident decedent's death. The department may appraise the property transferred by the decedent and determine the inheritance tax due without the intervention of a court.

As added by Acts 1976, P.L.18, SEC.1.

Historical and Statutory Notes

Formerly:

IC 6–4–1–20.
Acts 1931, c. 75, s. 20.

Cross References

Property transfers of nonresident decedents, imposition of inheritance tax, see IC 6–4.1–2–3.

6–4.1–5–15   Orders with respect to nonresident decedent's estate; filing fees

Sec. 15.   (a) The department of state revenue shall, with respect to a nonresident decedent's estate, enter an order which:

(1) states the fair market value of all property interests transferred by the decedent under taxable transfers;

(2) describes all Indiana real property so transferred by the decedent; and

(3) states the inheritance tax imposed as a result of the decedent's death.

(b) The clerk of the circuit court of each county in which real property described in the order is located shall spread a copy of the order of record.
As added by Acts 1976, P.L.18, SEC.1. Amended by Acts 1980, P.L.57, SEC.17; P.L.171–1984, SEC.5; P.L.192–1986, SEC.5; P.L.305–1987, SEC.8.

Historical and Statutory Notes

Acts 1980, P.L. 57, Sec.17, eff. July 1, 1980, in Cl. (1), deleted "on the date of the decedent's death" following "market value".

P.L.171–1984, Sec.5, emerg. eff. March 1, 1984, substituted "charge the fee provided in IC 33–17–6–4" for "not charge a fee which exceeds three dollars ($3.00)".

P.L.192–1986, SEC.5, eff. July 1, 1987, made a statutory translation and other nonsubstantive changes.

P.L.305–1987, SEC.8, eff. July 1, 1987, designated Subsections, and deleted "upon payment of the fee provided in IC 33–18–33–15".

Formerly:

IC 6–4–1–23.

Acts 1931, c. 75, s. 23.

6–4.1–5–16   Notice of taxes due upon nonresident decedent's estate

Sec. 16.   The department of state revenue shall, by mail, give notice of the inheritance tax due as a result of a nonresident decedent's death to the personal representative of the decedent's estate or the trustee of property transferred by the decedent.   However, if there is no personal representative or trustee, the department shall give the notice to each person liable for payment of the tax. Unless an appeal is initiated under IC 6–4.1–7–5 within ninety (90) days after the notice is given, the inheritance tax stated by the department in the notice is final.
As added by Acts 1976, P.L.18, SEC.1.

Historical and Statutory Notes

Formerly:

IC 6–4–1–20.
Acts 1931, c. 75, s. 20.

6–4.1–5–17   Transfers by will; property not specifically bequeathed or devised

Sec. 17.   When property is transferred by will and is not specifically bequeathed or devised, the property is, for purposes of this article, to be treated as if it were transferred proportionately to and divided pro rata among all the general legatees and devisees named in the transferor's will, including all transfers under a residuary clause of the will.
As added by Acts 1976, P.L.18, SEC.1.

Historical and Statutory Notes

Formerly:
  IC 6–4–1–33.
  Acts 1931, c. 75, s. 34.

Library References

Taxation ⊕878(1).
WESTLAW Topic No. 371.

C.J.S. Taxation §§ 1117, 1142.
I.L.E. Taxation §§ 233 to 235.

Chapter 6

Special Procedures for Appraising and Taxing Certain Property Interests

6–4.1–6–1 Mortality standards and actuarial tables; valuation of future interests

Sec. 1. (a) For purposes of this article, county inheritance tax appraisers and the department of state revenue shall, if possible, appraise each future, contingent, defeasible, or life interest in property and each annuity by using the rules, methods, standards of mortality, and actuarial tables used by the Internal Revenue Service on October 1, 1988, for federal estate tax purposes.

(b) Except as otherwise provided in this chapter, the value of a future interest in specific property equals the remainder of:

(1) the total value of the property; minus

(2) the value of all other interests in the property.

(c) Unless otherwise provided by the transferor, the inheritance tax imposed on the transfer of each of the interests is payable from the property in which the interests exist.

As added by Acts 1976, P.L.18, SEC.1. Amended by P.L.95–1989, SEC.1.

Historical and Statutory Notes

Acts 1976, P.L. 18, § 1, emerg. eff. Feb. 18, 1976, added this article.

The 1976 act added the provisions of this chapter as part of a codification and restatement of laws relating to death taxes.

P.L.95–1989, Sec.1, emerg. eff. April 26, 1989, in Subsec. (a), deleted "currently" follow-

ing "actuarial tables" and inserted "on October 1, 1988".

Formerly:

  IC 6–4–1–5.
  Acts 1931, c. 75, s. 5.
  Acts 1965, c. 302, s. 3.

MORTALITY AND LIFE TABLES

For Mortality Tables from the Life Insurance Fact Book 1990 and Life Tables from the National Center for Health Statistics, see tables following Article 18 of Title 34, Civil Procedure.

FEDERAL ESTATE TAX PRESENT WORTH TABLES

For the updated tables and regulations concerning valuation of annuities, life estates, terms for years, remainders, and reversions for estates of decedents, see tables in 26 CFR § 20.2031–7.

Library References

Taxation ☞895(1).
WESTLAW Topic No. 371.

C.J.S. Taxation § 1171.
I.L.E. Taxation § 239.

Notes of Decisions

Life estates   1
Renunciation of interest   2

1. Life estates

If beneficiary receives less than fee interest in property transferred by reason of a decedent's death, such as a life estate or a future interest, fair market value of that interest is calculated by using actuarial tables. Department of State Revenue, Inheritance Tax Div. v. Phelps, 1998, 697 N.E.2d 506.

If beneficiary receives less than fee interest in property transferred by reason of owner's death, inheritance tax is calculated pursuant to actuarial tables as of date of death. Estate of Hibbs v. Indiana Dept. of State Revenue, Inheritance Tax Div., 1994, 636 N.E.2d 204.

If life estate with remainder is created upon death of property owner, both life tenant and remainderman will pay inheritance tax on their proportionate interests, based on interests' values at date of owner's death. Estate of Hibbs v. Indiana Dept. of State Revenue, Inheritance Tax Div., 1994, 636 N.E.2d 204.

Under circumstances in which beneficiary receiving a life estate from testator dies shortly after testator, the internal revenue service permits valuation of beneficiary's life estate upon known facts rather than standard mortality tables for inheritance tax purposes. Matter of Waltz' Estate, App. 3 Dist.1980, 408 N.E.2d 558.

2. Renunciation of interest

Regardless of whether disclaimer of beneficiary of testamentary trust was timely submitted under either probate renunciation statute [IC1971, 29–1–6–4 (repealed; see, now, §§ 32–3–2–2 to 32–3–2–4, 32–3–2–10 and 32–3–2–13)] or trust renunciation statute [IC1971, 30–4–2–3 (repealed; see, now, § 32–3–2–6)], renunciation could have had no effect on valuation of her interest for inheritance tax purposes where probate renunciation statute provided that "succession so renounced shall be subject to the same Indiana inheritance tax that would have been assessed if there [had been] no renunciation." Matter of Newell's Estate, App. 4 Dist.1980, 408 N.E.2d 552.

6–4.1–6–2   Property interests which may be divested

Sec. 2. County inheritance tax appraisers and the department of state revenue shall appraise a property interest which may be divested because of an act or omission of the transferee as if there were no possibility of divestment.

As added by Acts 1976, P.L.18, SEC.1.

Historical and Statutory Notes

Formerly:
   IC 6–4–1–5.

Acts 1931, c. 75, s. 5.
Acts 1965, c. 302, s. 3.

Cross References

Future estates, life estates, remainders, creation, see IC 32–1–2–34.

6–4.1–6–3   Agreements with department for computing taxes

Sec. 3.   (a) The department of state revenue and a taxpayer may enter into an agreement under which the department will compute the inheritance tax due with respect to a taxable transfer if:

(1) it is impossible to compute the present value of the property interest transferred; or

(2) the tax imposed on the transfer cannot be computed because a contingency makes it impossible to determine who will take the property.

The personal representative of an estate or the trustee of a trust may, without court authorization, enter into such an agreement with the department on behalf of the estate or trust.

(b) When the department of state revenue enters into an agreement with a taxpayer under this section, the tax computed by the department is payable from the property interest transferred.

As added by Acts 1976, P.L.18, SEC.1.

Historical and Statutory Notes

Formerly: Acts 1931, c. 75, s. 5.
  IC 6–4–1–5.   Acts 1965, c. 302, s. 3.

6–4.1–6–4   Manner of property distribution;   circumstances where court determination required;   finality

Sec. 4.   For purposes of determining the inheritance tax imposed on a decedent's transfer of specific property, the appropriate probate court shall, so far as possible, determine the manner in which the property will probably be distributed if:

(1) a contingency makes it impossible to determine each transferee's exact interest in the property; and

(2) the department of state revenue and the taxpayer fail, within a reasonable time, to enter into an agreement under section 3 of this chapter.

Unless the court's determination is appealed, it is final and binding on all parties.

As added by Acts 1976, P.L.18, SEC.1.

Historical and Statutory Notes

Formerly: Acts 1931, c. 75, s. 5.
  IC 6–4–1–5.   Acts 1965, c. 302, s. 3.

Library References

Taxation ☞900(1).   C.J.S. Taxation § 1201.
WESTLAW Topic No. 371.   I.L.E. Taxation § 242.

United States Code Annotated

Transfers taking effect at death, federal estate taxes, see 26 U.S.C.A. § 2037.

6–4.1–6–5 Appraisal of limited, contingent, dependent, or determinable interests

Sec. 5. If a probate court files an application with the department of state revenue asking the department to appraise a property interest which is limited, contingent, dependent, or determinable upon a life in being, including but not limited to a life or remainder interest, the department shall, if possible, appraise the property interest. The department shall base its appraisal on the facts stated by the court in the application, and the department shall certify its appraisal in duplicate to the court. The department's certification is competent evidence that the appraisal is correct.

As added by Acts 1976, P.L.18, SEC.1.

Historical and Statutory Notes

Formerly:
  IC 6–4–1–28.
  Acts 1931, c. 75, s. 29.

6–4.1–6–6 Contingent or defeasible future interests; appraisal

Sec. 6. (a) If proceedings have not been instituted under this chapter to determine the inheritance tax imposed on the decedent's transfer of a contingent or defeasible future interest in property or if the tax imposed on such a transfer is postponed under subsection (b) of this section, the county inheritance tax appraiser or the department of state revenue shall, notwithstanding the provisions of IC 6–4.1–5, appraise the property interest at its fair market value when the transferee of the interest obtains the beneficial enjoyment or possession of the property.

(b) The inheritance tax imposed on the decedent's transfer of a contingent or defeasible interest in property accrues and is due when the transferee of the interest obtains the beneficial enjoyment or possession of the property if the fair market value of the property interest as of the appraisal date prescribed by IC 6–4.1–5–1.5 cannot otherwise be ascertained under this chapter.

As added by Acts 1976, P.L.18, SEC.1. Amended by Acts 1980, P.L.57, SEC.18.

Historical and Statutory Notes

Acts 1980, P.L. 57, § 18, eff. July 1, 1980, in subsec. (b) substituted "as of the appraisal date prescribed by IC 6–4.1–5–1.5" for "at the time of the decedent's death."

Formerly:
  IC 6–4–1–5.
  Acts 1931, c. 75, s. 5.
  Acts 1965, c. 302, s. 3.

United States Code Annotated

Interest of decedent in property, federal estate tax, see 26 U.S.C.A. § 2033.

Notes of Decisions

Accrual of interest   1

---

1. Accrual of interest

Inheritance tax accrues and becomes a lien on decedent's property at the time of decedent's death, except that the tax imposed on the transfer of a contingent or defeasible interest accrues and is due on when the transferee of the interest obtains the beneficial enjoyment or possession of the property. Estate of McNicholas v. State, App. 4 Dist.1991, 580 N.E.2d 978, transfer denied.

Chapter 7

Review of Inheritance Tax Appraisals and Tax Determinations

Section

6–4.1–7–1   Rehearing

Sec. 1. A person who is dissatisfied with an inheritance tax determination made by a probate court with respect to a resident decedent's estate may obtain a rehearing on the determination. To obtain the rehearing, the person must file a petition for rehearing with the probate court within one hundred twenty (120) days after the determination is made. In the petition, the person must state the grounds for the rehearing. The probate court shall base the rehearing on evidence presented at the original hearing plus any additional evidence which the court elects to hear.

As added by Acts 1976, P.L.18, SEC.1. Amended by P.L.48–1992, SEC.1.

Historical and Statutory Notes

Acts 1976, P.L. 18, § 1, emerg. eff. Feb. 18, 1976, added this article.

The 1976 act added the provisions of this chapter as part of a codification, and restatement of laws relating to death taxes.

P.L.48–1992, Sec.1, substituted "one hundred twenty (120)" for "ninety (90)" following "within" in the second sentence.

P.L.48–1992, Sec.3, provides:

"This act does not apply to a petition for rehearing or redetermination that is based on a determination or final determination made before July 1, 1992."

Formerly:

IC 6–4–1–8.
IC 6–4–1–11.
Acts 1931, c. 75, ss. 8, 11.
Acts 1957, c. 318, s. 2.
Acts 1965, c. 324, s. 1.

Library References

Taxation ⊕900(1).
WESTLAW Topic No. 371.

C.J.S. Taxation § 1201.
I.L.E. Taxation §§ 243 to 246.

WESTLAW Electronic Research

See WESTLAW Electronic Research Guide following the Preface.

Notes of Decisions

1. In general

Language of IC1971, 6–4–1–11 [repealed; see, now this section] allowing determination made by probate court with respect to resident decedent's estate to obtain hearing on determination if petition is filed within 90 days after determination is made was all inclusive and applied to any basis for seeking a redetermination of the tax. Matter of Waltz' Estate, App. 3 Dist.1980, 408 N.E.2d 558.

Where there is a procedure set forth, as in statute dealing with rehearing and redetermination of inheritance taxes, such procedure is controlling. Indiana Dept. of State Revenue, Inheritance Tax Division v. Bandelier, App.1952, 104 N.E.2d 133, 122 Ind.App. 200.

Proceedings for rehearing and redetermination of inheritance taxes are in the nature of special proceedings. Indiana Dept. of State Revenue, Inheritance Tax Division v. Bandelier, App.1952, 104 N.E.2d 133, 122 Ind.App. 200.

2. Purpose

When IC1971, 6–4–1–11 [repealed; see, now, this section] allowing person dissatisfied with inheritance tax determination made by probate court with respect to resident decedent's estate to obtain hearing on determination if petition was filed within 90 days after determination was made is construed in pari materia with IC1971, 6–4–1–12 [repealed; see, now, § 6–4.1–7–2] allowing person dissatisfied with an appraisal approved by probate court with respect to resident decedent's estate to obtain reappraisal of property interest involved if petition was filed for reappraisal within one year after court entered order determining inheritance tax due, it was legislative purpose that despite broad language of statute allowing hearing on determination, petitions to challenge an appraisal of property interest could be brought within one year of determination. Matter of Waltz' Estate, App. 3 Dist.1980, 408 N.E.2d 558.

3. Burden of proof

Plaintiffs maintaining action for redetermination of value of estate and amount of inheritance tax due, on basis of claimed exemption, had burden of proving such exemption. Indiana Dept. of State Revenue, Inheritance Tax Division v. Griffith's Estate, App.1959, 156 N.E.2d 395, 129 Ind.App. 278.

4. Petition—In general

The object of a petition for a rehearing and redetermination of inheritance and transfer taxes is to point out mistakes of law or of fact, or both, which it is claimed court made in reaching its conclusion. Indiana Dept. of State Revenue, Inheritance Tax Division v. Bandelier, App. 1952, 104 N.E.2d 133, 122 Ind.App. 200.

5. —— Timeliness of petition

Court lacked jurisdiction to enter second order determining new amount of inheritance tax when executor of estate attempted to file new affidavit for inheritance tax appraisement after sale of second farm at less than appraised value six years after first inheritance tax order was issued without following appropriate procedures or observing statutory time limitations. Sibbitt v. Indiana Dept. of Revenue, App. 1 Dist.1990, 563 N.E.2d 146, rehearing denied, transfer denied.

Where estate did not file its petition for reduction of penalty interest within 90 days of amended order determining inheritance tax due, trial court, pursuant to this section, did not have jurisdiction of the cause. Indiana Dept. of State Revenue, Inheritance Tax Div. v. Estate of Broyles, App. 1 Dist.1983, 457 N.E.2d 250.

Failure to comply with statutory time limits for seeking rehearing on inheritance tax determination deprives court of jurisdiction of subject matter at issue, but this section providing for such rehearing by probate court is not exclusive remedy, and taxpayer may file claim for refund, in which event court does not lack jurisdiction to determine appeal from denial of claim for refund. Indiana Dept. of Revenue, Inheritance Tax Division v. Binhack's Estate, App. 1 Dist.1981, 426 N.E.2d 714.

The filing of a petition for a redetermination of the inheritance and transfer tax due, or the filing of a petition for refund and appealing the same to the court within the time fixed by §§ 6–4.1–10–1, 6–4.1–10–4 and this section is jurisdictional, a precondition to or the essence of the right itself, and after the passage of the time allotted by statute the right itself is lost, the court does not have jurisdiction to hear it, and jurisdiction cannot be conferred, even by agreement. Matter of Compton's Estate, App. 1 Dist. 1980, 406 N.E.2d 365.

Where administratrix listed and valued savings bonds in joint tenancy schedule with the note that the entire consideration was furnished by the surviving joint tenant and that, therefore, the funds were not to be considered part of the property taxable, IC1971, 6–4–1–11 [repealed; see, now, this section] providing for application for rehearing within 90 days after judgment determining tax was applicable to the state's claim that the bonds had been improperly omitted from the property taxable; IC1971, 6–4–1–12 [repealed; see, now, § 6–4.1–7–2] providing for petition for reappraisal within one or two years after judgment is limited to issue of valuation of the property of the estate. In re Hogg's Estate, App.1971, 276 N.E.2d 898, 150 Ind.App. 650.

6. Grounds for rehearing

A petition for reduction of interest on inheritance tax due is within ambit of this section providing that a person who is dissatisfied with an inheritance tax determination may obtain a rehearing on the determination, since penalty interest relates to ultimate computation of the amount of inheritance tax due. Indiana Dept.

of State Revenue, Inheritance Tax Div. v. Estate of Broyles, App. 1 Dist.1983, 457 N.E.2d 250.

A further hearing was required to redetermine inheritance tax due to failure of personal representative to follow procedures under § 29–1–14–17 in allowing his own claim to be paid from the estate even though, in its petition to redetermine inheritance tax, state had opportunity to establish that the claim was result of fraud, collusion, or was contrary to law since the state only elected to attack manner in which the claim was allowed. In re Feusner's Estate, App. 3 Dist.1980, 411 N.E.2d 166.

7. Scope of review

This section which provides that a person dissatisfied with an inheritance tax determination may obtain a rehearing on the determination gives a court free rein to review any factor which makes up the final determination of the inheritance tax due. Indiana Dept. of State Revenue, Inheritance Tax Div. v. Estate of Broyles, App. 1 Dist.1983, 457 N.E.2d 250.

This section provides no limitation either on reasons for request for redetermination of tax or on factors which court might consider relating to manner in which tax is calculated. Indiana Dept. of Revenue, Inheritance Tax Division v. Binhack's Estate, App. 1 Dist.1981, 426 N.E.2d 714.

6–4.1–7–2   Reappraisal; petition; time of filing

Sec. 2. A person who is dissatisfied with an appraisal approved by a probate court with respect to a resident decedent's estate may obtain a reappraisal of the property interest involved. To obtain the reappraisal, the person must file a petition for reappraisal with the probate court within one (1) year after the court enters an order determining the inheritance tax due as a result of the decedent's death. However, if the original appraisal is fraudulently or erroneously made, the person may file the reappraisal petition within two (2) years after the court enters the order.

As added by Acts 1976, P.L.18, SEC.1.

Historical and Statutory Notes

Formerly:
IC 6–4–1–8.
IC 6–4–1–12.

Acts 1931, c. 75, ss. 8, 12a.
Acts 1957, c. 318, s. 5.

Library References

Taxation ☞900(4).
WESTLAW Topic No. 371.

C.J.S. Taxation § 1198.
I.L.E. Taxation §§ 243 to 246.

Notes of Decisions

Discretion in making reappraisal 3

Timeliness of filing 2

Validity of prior law   1

---

1. Validity of prior law

Presumption of validity of former statute providing tax commissioners with a means of obtaining reappraisal of the property and assets of a decedent's estate, was fortified by acquiescence, through approximately twenty years, during which neither the people, the courts, nor the legislature changed such statute. Indiana Dept. of Revenue Inheritance Tax Division v. Callaway's Estate, 1953, 110 N.E.2d 903, 232 Ind. 1.

The prior inheritance tax statute which provided tax commissioners with means of obtaining reappraisal of the value of the property and assets of a decedent's estate and which attempted to permit the mandatory setting aside of the probate court judgment determining amount of inheritance tax, constituted unconstitutional infringement by legislature upon judicial department of government. Indiana Dept. of Revenue Inheritance Tax Division v. Callaway's Estate, 1953, 110 N.E.2d 903, 232 Ind. 1.

2. Timeliness of filing

Court lacked jurisdiction to enter second order determining new amount of inheritance tax when executor of estate attempted to file new affidavit for inheritance tax appraisement after sale of second farm at less than appraised value six years after first inheritance tax order was issued without following appropriate procedures or observing statutory time limitations. Sibbitt v. Indiana Dept. of Revenue, App. 1 Dist.1990, 563 N.E.2d 146, rehearing denied, transfer denied.

When IC1971, 6–4–1–11 [repealed; see, now, § 6–4.1–7–1] allowing person dissatisfied with inheritance tax determination made by probate court with respect to resident decedent's estate to obtain hearing on determination if petition is filed within 90 days after determination is made was construed in pari materia with IC1971, 6–4–1–12 [repealed; see, now, this section] allowing person dissatisfied with an appraisal approved by probate court with respect to resident decedent's estate to obtain reappraisal of property interest involved if petition is filed for reappraisal within one year after court enters order determining inheritance tax due, it was legislative purpose that despite broad language of statute allowing hearing on determination, petitions to challenge an appraisal of property interest could be brought within one year of determination. Matter of Waltz' Estate, App. 3 Dist.1980, 408 N.E.2d 558.

Petition for reappraisal, for inheritance tax purposes, of beneficiary's life interest in charitable remainder trust which was filed by administrator of testator's estate on basis that beneficiary had died within a few days after testator's death and that life estate should thus be valued upon beneficiary's actual life expectancy rather than standard mortality tables, was not barred because it was not filed within 90 days after original determination of inheritance tax. Matter of Waltz' Estate, App. 3 Dist.1980, 408 N.E.2d 558.

Where administratrix listed and valued savings bonds in joint tenancy schedule with the note that the entire consideration was furnished by the surviving joint tenant and that, therefore, the funds were not to be considered part of the property taxable, IC1971, 6–4–1–11 [repealed; see, now, § 6–4.1–7–1] providing for application for rehearing within 90 days after judgment determining tax was applicable to the state's claim that the bonds had been improperly omitted from the property taxable; IC1971, 6–4–1–12 [repealed; now this section] providing for petition for reappraisal within one or two years after judgment is limited to issue of valuation of the property of the estate. In re Hogg's Estate, App.1971, 276 N.E.2d 898, 150 Ind.App. 650.

3. Discretion in making reappraisal

The language in this section and §§ 6–4.1–7–3 and 6–4.1–7–4 governing reappraisal of inheritance taxes assessed is discretionary. Matter of Waltz' Estate, App. 3 Dist.1980, 408 N.E.2d 558.

It is within discretion of trial court to grant or deny a reappraisal of inheritance taxes due and, hence, an abuse of that discretion is standard of review on appeal. Indiana Dept. of Revenue, Inheritance Tax Division v. Flanders' Estate, App. 2 Dist.1980, 408 N.E.2d 172.

Denial of petition filed by the inheritance tax division of the department of revenue for reappraisal of decedent's four-tenths undivided interest in real estate encumbered by a ten-year lease with no right of partition based on a $1,000 per acre valuation was not erroneous nor contrary to logic. Indiana Dept. of Revenue, Inheritance Tax Division v. Flanders' Estate, App. 2 Dist.1980, 408 N.E.2d 172.

6–4.1–7–3   Appointment of reappraiser; powers; compensation

Sec. 3. When a reappraisal petition is filed under section 2 of this chapter, the probate court may appoint a competent person to reappraise the property interests transferred by the resident decedent under taxable transfers. An appraiser appointed by the court under this section has the same powers and duties, including the duty to give notice of the appraisal and the duty to make an appraisal report to the court, as the county inheritance tax appraiser. The appointed appraiser is entitled to receive an amount fixed by the court and approved by the department of revenue as compensation for his services. After the probate court certifies to the county treasurer the amount of compensation due the appointed appraiser, the county treasurer shall pay the appraiser from county funds not otherwise appropriated.

As added by Acts 1976, P.L.18, SEC.1.

Historical and Statutory Notes

Formerly:
  IC 6–4–1–12.

Acts 1931, c. 75, s. 12a.
Acts 1957, c. 318, s. 5.

Library References

Taxation ⚖900(4).
WESTLAW Topic No. 371.

C.J.S. Taxation § 1198.
I.L.E. Taxation §§ 243 to 246.

Notes of Decisions

Discretion in making reappraisal 1

——————

1. Discretion in making reappraisal
  The language in this section and §§ 6–4.1–7–2 and 6–4.1–7–4 governing reappraisal of inheri-

tance taxes assessed is discretionary. Indiana Dept. of Revenue, Inheritance Tax Division v. Flanders' Estate, App. 2 Dist.1980, 408 N.E.2d 172.

6–4.1–7–4   Report or reappraisal; redetermination of taxes; filing of redetermination

Sec. 4. (a) After the appraiser, if any, appointed under section 3 of this chapter files his appraisal report, the probate court shall redetermine the inheritance tax due with respect to the property interests transferred by the resident decedent. In making the redetermination, the court shall follow the same procedures it is required to follow under IC 6–4.1–5–9, IC 6–4.1–5–10, and IC 6–4.1–5–11 when making an original inheritance tax determination.

(b) The probate court's redetermination of the inheritance tax due supersedes the court's original determination. The court shall file a copy of the redetermination with the clerk of the court.

As added by Acts 1976, P.L.18, SEC.1. Amended by P.L.1–1991, SEC.54.

Historical and Statutory Notes

P.L.1–1991, Sec.54, emerg. eff. April 23, 1991, substituted "IC 6–4.1–5–9, IC 6–4.1–5–10, and IC 6–4.1–5–11" for "sections 9, 10, and 11 of IC 6–4.1–5" in Subsec. (a).

Formerly:
  IC 6–4–1–12.
  Acts 1931, c. 75, s. 12a.
  Acts 1957, c. 318, s. 5.

Notes of Decisions

Discretion in making reappraisal 1

___

1. **Discretion in making reappraisal**
The language in this section and §§ 6–4.1–7–2 and 6–4.1–7–3 governing reappraisal of inheri-

tance taxes assessed is discretionary. Indiana Dept. of Revenue, Inheritance Tax Division v. Flanders' Estate, App. 2 Dist.1980, 408 N.E.2d 172.

6–4.1–7–5 Non-resident decedent's property; appeal of department determination; procedures

Sec. 5. (a) A person who is dissatisfied with an inheritance tax determination or an appraisal made by the department of state revenue with respect to property interests transferred by a non-resident decedent may appeal the department's decision to:

(1) the probate court of the county, if any, in which administration of the decedent's estate is pending; or

(2) the probate court of any county in which any of the decedent's property was located at the time of his death, if no administration of the decedent's estate is pending in Indiana.

(b) To initiate the appeal, the person must:

(1) file a complaint within ninety (90) days after the date that the department mails the notice required by IC 6–4.1–5–16; and

(2) pay, or give security to pay, the court cost resulting from the appeal and the inheritance tax to be fixed by the court.

(c) When an appeal is initiated under this section, the court may decide all questions concerning the fair market value of property interests transferred by the decedent or concerning the inheritance tax due as a result of the decedent's death.

As added by Acts 1976, P.L.18, SEC.1. Amended by Acts 1980, P.L.57, SEC.19.

Historical and Statutory Notes

Acts 1980, P.L. 57, § 19, eff. July 1, 1980, designated Subsecs. (a) and (b); added Cls. (1) and (2) in Subsec. (a); and deleted "the probate court of Marion County" following "decision to" in the introductory clause of Subsec. (a).

Formerly:

IC 6–4–1–21.

Acts 1931, c. 75, s. 21.

Library References

Taxation ⬥900.
WESTLAW Topic No. 371.

C.J.S. Taxation § 1201.
I.L.E. Taxation §§ 243 to 246.

Notes of Decisions

Construction with other statutes 1

___

1. **Construction with other statutes**
Rehearing statute [IC1971, 6–4–1–21 (repealed; see, now, this section)], which afforded

taxpayer method of contesting tax determination at appraisal and assessment stage, and refund statute [IC1971, 6–4–1–17 (repealed; see, now, § 6–4.1–10–1 et seq.)] which enabled taxpayer to pay tax as assessed and subsequently seek refund if tax was "erroneously, wrongfully or illegally imposed * * * or in any manner wrongfully collected," provided alternative methods by which a taxpayer could obtain relief, and thus executors' failure to protest estate tax assessment did not preclude relief under the refund statute, but on the contrary, refund statute provided a separate vehicle by which executors could proceed in probate court. State v. Davies, App. 2 Dist.1978, 379 N.E.2d 501, 177 Ind.App. 288.

6–4.1–7–6   Probate court determination of tax due as provisional estimate; redetermination resulting from federal estate tax valuation

Sec. 6.   (a) The department of state revenue may accept a probate court's determination of the inheritance tax due as a result of a decedent's death as a provisional estimate of the inheritance tax imposed.

(b) If the final determination of federal estate tax shows a change in the fair market value of the assets of a decedent's estate or a change in deductions, the department of state revenue may petition or cause other persons to petition the probate court which has jurisdiction for a redetermination of the inheritance tax imposed as a result of the decedent's death. The petition must be filed within sixty (60) days after a copy of the final determination of federal estate tax is filed with the department as required by IC 6–4.1–4–8. An inheritance tax redetermination which is made under this section is limited to modifications based on either a change in the fair market value of the assets of the decedent's estate or a change in deductions.

As added by Acts 1976, P.L.18, SEC.1.   Amended by Acts 1979, P.L.75, SEC.11; P.L.48–1992, SEC.2.

Historical and Statutory Notes

Acts 1979, P.L. 75, § 11, eff. July 1, 1979, inserted "or a change in deductions" in the first sentence of Subsec. (b); and in the third sentence of Subsec. (b), substituted "either a" for "the" and added "or a change in deductions."

P.L.48–1992, Sec.2, in Subsec. (b), substituted "sixty (60)" for "thirty (30)" following "within" in the second sentence.

For related provisions of P.L.48–1992, see Historical and Statutory Note under section 6–4.1–7–1.

Formerly:
IC 6–4–1–38.
Acts 1931, c. 75, s. 39.
Acts 1965, c. 276, s. 2.
Acts 1974, P.L.24, SEC.2.

Notes of Decisions

Exemptions not previously claimed   4
Jurisdiction   2
Receipt of taxes   3
Timeliness of filing   1

---

1.   Timeliness of filing

Court lacked jurisdiction to enter second order determining new amount of inheritance tax when executor of estate attempted to file new affidavit for inheritance tax appraisement after sale of second farm at less than appraised value six years after first inheritance tax order was issued without following appropriate procedures or observing statutory time limitations. Sibbitt v. Indiana Dept. of Revenue, App. 1 Dist.1990, 563 N.E.2d 146, rehearing denied, transfer denied.

Failure to comply with statutory time limits for seeking rehearing on inheritance tax determination deprives court of jurisdiction of subject matter at issue, but section 6–4.1–7–1 providing for such rehearing by probate court is not exclusive remedy, and taxpayer may file claim for refund, in which event court does not lack jurisdiction to determine appeal from denial of claim for refund. Indiana Dept. of Revenue, Inheritance Tax Division v. Binhack's Estate, App. 1 Dist.1981, 426 N.E.2d 714.

State was not required to file its petition within 30 days of date on which state gained knowledge of federal line adjustments indicating that additional assets should have been included in schedule of all property filed for decedent's estate, and thus petition filed within 30 days after copy of final determination of federal estate tax was filed with department of state revenue was. timely. Matter of Adamson's Estate, App. 1 Dist.1980, 403 N.E.2d 355.

State was not required to file its petition for redetermination of inheritance tax, based upon omitted assets, within 90 days of probate court's order determining amount of inheritance tax due, but rather was required to file its petition within 30 days after copy of final determination of federal estate tax was filed with department of state revenue. Matter of Adamson's Estate, App. 1 Dist.1980, 403 N.E.2d 355.

2. Jurisdiction

Department of state revenue, which countersigned a receipt given by county treasurer evidencing receipt of inheritance taxes, was not required to treat circuit court's determination of inheritance tax due as a provisional estimate in order to preserve its right to seek a redetermination of inheritance tax; thus, circuit court had subject matter jurisdiction to entertain de-

partment's petition for redetermination, which was filed within 30 days of department's receipt of copy of final determination of federal estate tax. In re Coffman's Estate, App. 1 Dist.1979, 391 N.E.2d 861, 181 Ind.App. 348.

3. Receipt of taxes

Execution of countersigned receipt by inheritance tax division did not prevent the state from subsequently seeking a redetermination of inheritance tax. Matter of Adamson's Estate, App. 1 Dist.1980, 403 N.E.2d 355.

4. Exemptions not previously claimed

Once the department of state revenue filed its petition for reevaluation of estate assets to conform to federal estate tax evaluations, an equal right was not conferred upon the estate to relitigate the exemption not theretofore taken or claimed by the estate, and counterclaim wherein estate sought to obtain tax benefits afforded charitable remainder trusts after trust had been modified to bring it into compliance with federal standards should not have been allowed. Matter of Compton's Estate, App. 1 Dist.1980, 406 N.E.2d 365.

6–4.1–7–7 Redetermination of inheritance tax; appeal

Sec. 7. A probate court's redetermination of inheritance tax under this chapter may be appealed to the tax court in accordance with the rules of appellate procedure.

As added by P.L.59–1990, SEC.1.

Notes of Decisions

1. In general

Tax Court has jurisdiction to review appeals from final determination of probate court concerning amount of inheritance tax due. Department of State Revenue, Inheritance Tax Div. v. Phelps, 1998, 697 N.E.2d 506.

Tax Court acts as true appellate tribunal in reviewing final determinations by probate court of inheritance tax due. Estate of Hibbs v. Indiana Dept. of State Revenue, Inheritance Tax Div., 1994, 636 N.E.2d 204.

2. Standard of review

In reviewing final determination of probate court concerning amount of state inheritance tax due, Tax Court acts as a true appellate tribunal; accordingly, the Court affords probate court's factual findings a great deal of deference, but the Court reviews the legal conclu-

sions of probate court de novo. Department of State Revenue, Inheritance Tax Div. v. Estate of Hardy, 1998, 703 N.E.2d 705.

In reviewing of final determination of probate court concerning amount of inheritance tax due, Tax Court acts as true appellate tribunal, and accordingly, affords probate court a great deal of deference in its role as finder of fact, but reviews legal conclusions of probate court de novo. Department of State Revenue, Inheritance Tax Div. v. Phelps, 1998, 697 N.E.2d 506.

On appeal from probate court's final determination concerning amount of state inheritance tax due, Tax Court acts as true appellate tribunal, and will not reweigh evidence nor judge credibility of witnesses, but will affirm probate court's judgment upon any legal theory supported by evidence introduced at trial; more specifically, Tax Court will reverse probate court's judgment only if there is no substantial evidence of probative value to support judgment. Indiana Dept. of State Revenue, Inheritance Tax Div. v. Estate of Nichols, 1995, 659 N.E.2d 694.

State tax court acts as true appellate tribunal when reviewing probate court's final determination concerning amount of state inheritance tax

due; court will not reweigh evidence or judge credibility of witnesses, but will affirm probate court's judgment upon any legal theory supported by evidence introduced at trial. Indiana Dept. of State Revenue, Inheritance Tax Div. v. Estate of Baldwin, 1995, 652 N.E.2d 124.

Chapter 8

Inheritance Tax Lien and Limitations on the Transfer of Decedent's Property

Library References

Taxation ☞902.
WESTLAW Topic No. 371.
C.J.S. Taxation §§ 1214 to 1219.

6–4.1–8–1   Attachment and termination of lien; persons liable for inheritance tax

Sec. 1.   The inheritance tax imposed as a result of a decedent's death is a lien on the property transferred by him.   Except as otherwise provided in IC 6–4.1–6–6(b), the inheritance tax accrues and the lien attaches at the time of the decedent's death.   The lien terminates when the inheritance tax is paid or five (5) years after the date of the decedent's death, whichever occurs first.   In addition to the lien, the transferee of the property and any personal representative or trustee who has possession of or control over the property are personally liable for the inheritance tax.

As added by Acts 1976, P.L.18, SEC.1.

Historical and Statutory Notes

Acts 1976, P.L. 18, § 1, emerg. eff. Feb. 18, 1976, added this article.

The 1976 act added the provisions of this chapter as part of a codification, revision and restatement of laws relating to death taxes.

Formerly:
    IC 6–4–1–16.

IC 6–4–1–29.
Acts 1931, c. 75, ss. 16, 30.
Acts 1937, c. 159, s. 1.
Acts 1951, c. 75, s. 1.
Acts 1957, c. 204, s. 1.

Administrative Code References

Inheritance tax, liability for tax and liens, see 45 IAC 4.1–7–1 et seq.

Law Review and Journal Commentaries

Inheritance tax: Survey of recent law. Debra
A. Falender, 17 Ind.L.Rev. 392 (1984).

Library References

Taxation ⬭902.
WESTLAW Topic No. 371.
C.J.S. Taxation §§ 1214 to 1219.
I.L.E. Taxation §§ 1232.

Inheritance tax considerations in connection with transfers of securities owned by a deceased person, see Galanti, 18 Indiana Practice § 15.7.

Notes of Decisions

In general   1
Realty encumbered   2
Termination of lien   3
Transferees liability   4

1. In general

Where will was admitted to probate and court was without authority to invalidate or set aside the will, and court could only approve family settlement agreement between the beneficiaries, inheritance tax was to be based on distribution under the will rather than the distribution effected by the settlement agreement. Estate of McNicholas v. State, App. 4 Dist.1991, 580 N.E.2d 978, transfer denied.

Indiana inheritance tax or Indiana death tax statute is not tax on property, but tax on rights of heirs to succeed to that property; inheritance tax is levied upon distributee's share, not upon decedent's estate as with federal estate tax. Indiana Dept. of State Revenue, Inheritance Tax Div. v. Cohen's Estate, App. 1 Dist.1982, 436 N.E.2d 832.

2. Realty encumbered

Will provision disposing of balance of estate after payment of all expenses, taxes, fees, costs and bequests plainly directed that all taxes, including state inheritance tax normally levied on distributee's share, be paid before residue was determined and divided. Matter of Estate of Kirby, App. 1 Dist.1986, 498 N.E.2d 64, rehearing denied, transfer denied.

Where conveyance of realty by decedent to his sons was subject to inheritance tax as a gift or grant intended to take effect in possession or enjoyment at or after the death of the decedent, any inheritance or transfer taxes due by the grantees were a lien on the realty transferred and the trial court should have determined the tax and established it as a lien on the property. Indiana Dept. of State Revenue, Inheritance Tax

Division v. Mertz, App.1949, 88 N.E.2d 917, 119 Ind.App. 601.

3. Termination of lien

If no proceeding was taken to determine inheritance tax within five years of decedent's death, no inheritance tax was due and all property of decedent was free and clear of lien. State, Indiana Dept. of State Revenue, Inheritance Tax Division v. Lees, App. 2 Dist.1980, 418 N.E.2d 226.

Former statutory provision [Acts 1937, c. 159, § 1] that if no proceeding were taken to determine the inheritance tax on property of any deceased person within ten years after his death, it shall be conclusively presumed that no tax is due, operated not only to remove the lien of the tax but also to make presumption of payment conclusive so that there was no tax due. In re Batt's Estate, 1942, 41 N.E.2d 365, 220 Ind. 193.

4. Transferees liability

Generally, inheritance tax is levied upon distributee's share and, unlike federal estate taxes which are debt of estate, imposes personal liability upon transferee for payment of tax. Matter of Estate of Saylors, App.1996, 671 N.E.2d 905.

When there is an effective disclaimer of an interest in a decedent's estate, disclaimed property passes as if the disclaimant had predeceased the person creating the interest and there is no inheritance tax to the disclaimant. Estate of McNicholas v. State, App. 4 Dist.1991, 580 N.E.2d 978, transfer denied.

Inheritance tax accrues and becomes a lien on decedent's property at the time of decedent's death, except that the tax imposed on the transfer of a contingent or defeasible interest accrues and is due on when the transferee of the interest obtains the beneficial enjoyment or possession of the property. Estate of McNicholas v. State,

App. 4 Dist.1991, 580 N.E.2d 978, transfer denied.

Will provision disposing of residue of estate after payment of all expenses, taxes, fees, costs and bequests, clearly and unambiguously provided that residuary legatees receive their bequests subject to payment of all taxes, including federal estate taxes. Matter of Estate of Kirby, App. 1 Dist.1986, 498 N.E.2d 64, rehearing denied, transfer denied.

Federal estate taxes are debts of estate whereas Indiana inheritance taxes impose personal liability upon transferee for payment of tax. Indiana Dept. of State Revenue, Inheritance Tax Div. v. Cohen's Estate, App. 1 Dist.1982, 436 N.E.2d 832.

In view of former statute, making inheritance taxes a lien on property taken by transferees and providing for collections from transferees by administrator, executor, or trustee, the residuary estate was not chargeable generally with the inheritance tax upon other transfers unless expressly so charged by the will. Nation v. Green, 1919, 123 N.E. 163, 188 Ind. 697.

Where an Indiana resident, who died intestate, gave various sums of money to several persons before his death, the administrator was not bound to account for the tax accruing from the gifts. Furthermore, the tax lien followed only the gifts, and the donees were solely responsible for payment in this situation. 1943 Op.Atty.Gen. p. 156.

6–4.1–8–2   Transfers prohibited until tax paid; limited transfers

Sec. 2.   (a) The personal representative of a decedent's estate or the trustee of property transferred by the decedent may not transfer or deliver property to a transferee unless the inheritance tax imposed with respect to the transfer has been paid.

(b) If money is transferred by the decedent to a transferee for a limited period of time, the personal representative or trustee shall retain the total inheritance tax imposed on all the interests in the money.

(c) If property other than money is transferred by the decedent to a transferee for a limited period of time, the transferees of the interests in the property shall pay to the personal representative or trustee the inheritance tax imposed on the interests.   The personal representative or trustee shall apply to the appropriate probate court for a determination of the amount which each transferee is required to pay under this subsection.

As added by Acts 1976, P.L.18, SEC.1.

Historical and Statutory Notes

Formerly:
  IC 6–4–1–16.
  Acts 1931, c. 75, s. 16.

Library References

Inheritance tax considerations in connection with transfers of securities owned by a deceased person, see Galanti, 18 Indiana Practice § 15.7.

Notes of Decisions

Tax on distributive shares   1

———

1.   Tax on distributive shares
  While personal representative must pay inheritance taxes before he may be discharged, he must, in absence of agreement or direction in will, deduct tax payable by each beneficiary from his distributive share, or, where tangible property is received, collect tax from beneficiary.   Indiana Dept. of State Revenue, Inheri-

tance Tax Div. v. Cohen's Estate, App. 1 Dist.
1982, 436 N.E.2d 832.

6–4.1–8–3   Sale of property to pay decedent's debts

Sec. 3.   In order to pay the inheritance tax imposed as a result of a decedent's death, the personal representative of the decedent's estate or the trustee of property transferred by the decedent may sell property transferred by the decedent.   The personal representative or trustee may sell the property in the same manner that he is authorized to sell property to pay the decedent's debts.

As added by Acts 1976, P.L.18, SEC.1.

Historical and Statutory Notes

Formerly:
  IC 6–4–1–16.
  Acts 1931, c. 75, s. 16.

Cross References

Sale, mortgage, lease or exchange of real or personal property belonging to estate, payment of claims and taxes, see IC 29–1–15–3.

6–4.1–8–4   Personal property; consent to transfer

Sec. 4.   (a) A person who has possession of or control over personal property held jointly by a resident decedent and another person may not transfer the property to the surviving joint tenant, unless:

    (1) the surviving joint tenant is the decedent's surviving spouse; or

    (2) the property is money held in a joint checking account;

without the written consent of the department of state revenue or the county assessor of the county in which the resident decedent was domiciled at the time of the decedent's death.

(b) Except as provided in subsection (c), a person who has possession of or control over personal property held in a trust that is subject to the Indiana inheritance or estate tax at the time of a resident decedent's death may not transfer the property to a beneficiary or any other person, unless the beneficiary or other person is the decedent's surviving spouse, without the written consent of the department of state revenue or the county assessor of the county in which the resident decedent was domiciled at the time of the decedent's death.

(c) A person who has possession of or control over personal property held in trust may transfer the property without the written consent of the department of state revenue or the county assessor of the county in which the resident decedent was domiciled at the time of the decedent's death under the following conditions:

    (1) The transferee is domiciled in Indiana.

(2) The transferee completes a sworn affidavit on a form prescribed by the department of state revenue that states:

(A) the transfer of the personal property is not subject to Indiana inheritance or estate tax; and

(B) the reasons the transfer is not subject to tax.

(3) A copy of the affidavit required under subdivision (2) is immediately filed with the department of state revenue.

(d) A person who has possession of or control over a resident decedent's personal property (except proceeds payable under a life insurance policy) may not transfer the property to any other person, unless:

(1) the other person is the decedent's surviving spouse; or

(2) the property is money held in a checking account;

without the written consent of the department of state revenue or the county assessor of the county in which the resident decedent was domiciled at the time of the decedent's death.

(e) The department of state revenue or the appropriate county assessor may consent to a transfer if the department or the county assessor believes that the transfer will not jeopardize the collection of inheritance tax.

(f) The department of state revenue shall send a copy of any consent to transfer that it issues under this section to the county assessor of the county in which the resident decedent was domiciled at the time of the decedent's death.

As added by Acts 1976, P.L.18, SEC.1. Amended by Acts 1977(ss), P.L.6, SEC.8; Acts 1980, P.L.57, SEC.20; Acts 1981, P.L.91, SEC.1; P.L.59–1996, SEC.1.

Historical and Statutory Notes

Acts 1977 (ss), P.L. 6, § 8, emerg. eff. July 1, 1977, designated the paragraph formerly constituting the entire section as Subsec. (a); added Subsecs. (b), (c) and (d); added "or the county assessor of the county in which the resident decedent was domiciled at the time of his death" at the end of Subsec. (a); and deleted a former last sentence of Subsec. (a) which read, "The department may consent to the transfer if it believes that the transfer will not jeopardize the collection of inheritance tax."

Acts 1980, P.L. 57, § 20, eff. July 1, 1980, in Subsec. (a), inserted "unless the surviving joint tenant is the decedent's surviving spouse" following "to the surviving joint tenant"; and, in Subsec. (b), inserted "unless the other person is the decedent's surviving spouse" following

"may not transfer the property to any other person."

Acts 1981, P.L. 91, § 1, in Subsec. (a), substituted Cls. (1) and (2) for "the surviving joint tenant is the decedent's surviving spouse"; and in Subsec. (b), substituted Cls. (1) and (2) for "the other person is the decedent's surviving spouse."

P.L.59–1996, Sec.1, amended the section by substituting "the decedent's" for "his" in Subsecs. (a)(2), (d)(2), and (f); adding new Subsecs. (b) and (c); and redesignating former Subsecs. (b) through (d) as (d) through (f).

Formerly:

IC 6–4–1–18.

Acts 1931, c. 75, s. 18.

Administrative Code References

Inheritance tax, transfer of jointly owned property,
    Transfers of jointly held property, consent required, see 45 IAC 4.1–8–1 et seq.

Law Review and Journal Commentaries

Amendments of 1977 to Indiana Inheritance Tax Law. William L. Tracy, 21 Res Gestae 488 (1977).

Library References

Executors and Administrators ⊕158.
Taxation ⊕878(1).
WESTLAW Topic Nos. 162, 371.
C.J.S. Executors and Administrators § 305.
C.J.S. Taxation §§ 1117, 1142.

I.L.E. Taxation §§ 233 to 235, 252 to 256.
Inheritance tax considerations in connection with transfers of securities owned by a deceased person, see Galanti, 18 Indiana Practice § 15.7.

Notes of Decisions

Purpose of law 1
Right to disclaim 2

_____

1. Purpose of law

Purpose of inheritance tax statute [IC 6–4.1–8–4(a)(1982 Ed.)] governing personal property held jointly by decedent and others is to provide assurance that inheritance taxes will be paid. Indiana Dept. of State Revenue, Inheritance Tax Div. v. Estate of Parker, App. 3 Dist.1985, 485 N.E.2d 1387.

2. Right to disclaim

Execution by decedent's daughter of application for consent to transfer her interest in certif-

icates of deposit in names of decedent, his wife, and daughter, as joint tenants with right of survivorship, did not forfeit daughter's right to disclaim, for inheritance tax purposes, even though bank could have transferred or reissued certificates thereafter, absent evidence or contention that daughter demanded or received any principal or interest on certificates in question, or that she made any effort to assign, convey, or encumber certificates or her interest therein. Indiana Dept. of State Revenue, Inheritance Tax Div. v. Estate of Parker, App. 3 Dist.1985, 485 N.E.2d 1387.

6–4.1–8–4.5   Repealed

(Repealed by Acts 1982, P.L.57, SEC.1.)

Historical and Statutory Notes

Acts 1982, P.L. 57, provided in Section 2 that the act takes effect June 1, 1982, and applies to property that is transferred by decedents who die after May 31, 1982.

The repealed section pertained to transfers to surviving spouses and required notice to the

department of state revenue or the county assessor when such transfers were made.

Formerly:

Acts 1980, P.L.57, SEC.21.
Acts 1981, P.L.91, SEC.2.

6–4.1–8–4.6   Checking account; notice of transfer of funds to person other than surviving spouse

Sec. 4.6.   A person who has possession of or control over money held in a checking account in which a resident decedent had a legal interest shall notify the department or the county assessor of the county in which the resident decedent was domiciled at the time of death, when money is transferred from the account to a person, other than the resident decedent's surviving spouse.

As added by P.L.26–1985, SEC.11.

Historical and Statutory Notes

P.L.26–1985, Sec.11, eff. July 1, 1986, added this section.

Subsection (c) of section 22 of P.L.26–1985 provided:

"(c) Section 11 applies to property belonging to decedents who die after June 30, 1986."

6–4.1–8–5   Life insurance proceeds

Sec. 5. (a) Within ten (10) days after life insurance proceeds are paid to a resident decedent's estate, the life insurance company shall give notice of the payment to the department of state revenue.

(b) The department of state revenue shall send a copy of any notice which it receives under subsection (a) to the county assessor of the county in which the resident decedent was domiciled at the time of his death.

As added by Acts 1976, P.L.18, SEC.1. Amended by Acts 1977(ss), P.L.6, SEC.9; P.L.157–1992, SEC.1; P.L.6–1999, SEC.1.

Historical and Statutory Notes

Acts 1977 (ss), P.L. 6, § 9, emerg. eff. July 1, 1977, added Subsec. (c); and rewrote Subsecs. (a) and (b) which prior thereto read:

"(a) Except as provided in subsection (b) of this section, a person who has possession of or control over a resident decedent's personal property or safe deposit box may not transfer the property to the personal representative of the decedent's estate or the trustee or transferee of property transferred by the decedent nor open the box unless reasonable notice of the time and nature of the transfer or the time of the box opening is given to the department of state revenue or the county assessor. In addition, the person shall permit the department or the county assessor to examine and list the property to be transferred or the contents of the safe deposit box.

"(b) A person may transfer a resident decedent's bank or savings account to the personal representative of the decedent's estate if, at the time the transfer is made, the person making the transfer notifies the department of state revenue or the county assessor of the transfer."

P.L.157–1992, Sec.1, in Subsec.(a), inserted "Except as provided in subsection (d),"; and inserted Subsec.(d) relating to joint tenants.

Governor's veto of S.E.A.116 (P.L.157–1992), passed by the 107th General Assembly, was overridden by the 108th General Assembly on April 29, 1993. The effective date of P.L.157–1992 is July 1, 1993.

P.L.6–1999, Sec.1, rewrote the section. Prior to amendment, the section read:

"Sec. 5. (a) Except as provided in subsection (d), a person who has possession of or control over a resident decedent's safe deposit box may not open the box unless reasonable notice of the time and place of the box opening is given to the department of state revenue or the county assessor of the county in which the resident decedent was domiciled at the time of his death. In addition, the person shall permit the department or the county assessor to examine and list the contents of the safe deposit box.

"(b) Within ten (10) days after life insurance proceeds are paid to a resident decedent's estate, the life insurance company shall give notice of the payment to the department of state revenue.

"(c) The department of state revenue shall send a copy of any safe deposit box inventory which it prepares under subsection (a), and a copy of any notice which it receives under subsection (b), to the county assessor of the county in which the resident decedent was domiciled at the time of his death.

"(d) A person who has possession of or control over a safe deposit box held by two (2) individuals as joint tenants is not required, on the death of one (1) of the joint tenants, to:

"(1) notify the department of state revenue or the county assessor before opening the safe deposit box; or

"(2) permit the department or the county assessor to examine and list the contents of the safe deposit box;

"if, at the time of the joint tenant's death, the joint tenants were married to each other."

336

P.L.6–1999, Sec. 3, provides:

"IC 6–4.1–8–5, as amended by this act, applies to the estate of an individual who dies after June 30, 1999."

Formerly:
IC 6–4–1–19.
Acts 1931, c. 75, s. 19.
Acts 1965, c. 302, s. 4.
Acts 1974, P.L.24, SEC.1.

Library References

Taxation ⚯865.
WESTLAW Topic No. 371.

C.J.S. Taxation §§ 1115, 1118, 1140, 1150.
I.L.E. Taxation §§ 250, 251.

Notes of Decisions

Sealing of safe deposit boxes   1

---

1. Sealing of safe deposit boxes

Taxing officials have no authority to demand that all safe deposit boxes be sealed and the contents checked by taxing authorities in the absence of facts showing the presence of property belonging to the decedent in the box. 1938 Op.Atty.Gen. p. 151.

6–4.1–8–6   Repealed

(Repealed by P.L.6–1999, SEC.2.)

Historical and Statutory Notes

Former IC 6–4.1–8–6 related to safe deposit box examination and confidentiality of information.

Formerly:
IC 6–4–1–19.

Acts 1931, c. 75, s. 19.
Acts 1965, c. 302, s. 4.
Acts 1974, P.L.24, SEC.1.
Acts 1976, P.L.18, SEC.1.

6–4.1–8–7   Violations of IC 6–4.1–8–4 or IC 6–4.1–8–5; penalties

Sec. 7.   If a person violates a provision of section 4 or 5 of this chapter, he is liable for the taxes imposed under this article as a result of the resident decedent's death and is subject to an additional penalty not to exceed one thousand dollars ($1,000).   The department of state revenue shall initiate an action in the name of this state to collect the taxes and the penalty which the person is liable for under this section.

As added by Acts 1976, P.L.18, SEC.1.   Amended by Acts 1980, P.L.57, SEC.22; P.L.87–1983, SEC.6.

Historical and Statutory Notes

Acts 1980, P.L. 57, § 22, eff. July 1, 1980, substituted "section 4, 4.5, or 5" for "section 4, or section 5" in the first sentence.

P.L. 87–1983, Sec.6, emerg. eff. Jan. 1, 1983, deleted "4.5" following "section 4" in the first sentence.

Section 7 of P.L. 87–1983 provided that this act applies to the estates of decedents who die after Dec. 31, 1982.

Formerly:
IC 6–4–1–18.
IC 6–4–1–19.
Acts 1931, c. 75, ss. 18, 19.
Acts 1965, c. 302, s. 4.
Acts 1974, P.L.24, SEC.1.

6–4.1–8–8   Repealed

(Repealed by P.L.6–1999, SEC.2.)

Historical and Statutory Notes

Former IC 6–4.1–8–8 related to violation of
IC 6–4.1–8–6.

Formerly:

IC 6–4–1–19.

Acts 1931, c. 75, s. 19.
Acts 1965, c. 302, s. 4.
Acts 1974, P.L.24, SEC.1.
Acts 1976, P.L.18, SEC.1.
Acts 1978, P.L.2, SEC.624.

Chapter 9

General Inheritance Tax Collection Provisions

6–4.1–9–1   Due date for taxes; interest on delinquent portion; unavoidable delays

Sec. 1. (a) Except as otherwise provided in IC 6–4.1–6–6 (b), the inheritance tax imposed as a result of a decedent's death is due eighteen (18) months
after his date of death. If a person liable for payment of inheritance tax does

not pay the tax on or before the due date, he shall, except as provided in subsection (b) of this section, pay interest on the delinquent portion of the tax at the rate of ten percent (10%) per year from the date of the decedent's death to the date payment is made.

(b) If an unavoidable delay, such as necessary litigation, prevents a determination of the amount of inheritance tax due, the appropriate probate court, in the case of a resident decedent, or the department of state revenue, in the case of a non-resident decedent, may reduce the rate of interest imposed under this section, for the time period beginning on the date of the decedent's death and ending when the cause of delay is removed, to six percent (6%) per year. *As added by Acts 1976, P.L.18, SEC.1.*

Historical and Statutory Notes

Acts 1976, P.L. 18, § 1, emerg. eff. Feb. 18, 1976, added this article.

The 1976 act added the provisions of this chapter as part of a codification, reenactment, revision and rearrangement of laws relating to death taxes.

Formerly:

IC 6–4–1–13.
IC 6–4–1–30.
Acts 1931, c. 75, ss. 13, 31.

Cross References

Contingent or defeasible future interests, inheritance tax due date, see IC 6–4.1–6–6.

Administrative Code References

Inheritance tax payment, due date and interest, see 45 IAC 4.1–9–1, 45 IAC 4.1–9–3.

Library References

Taxation ⏝901, 905(1).
WESTLAW Topic No. 371.

C.J.S. Taxation §§ 1207, 1223.
I.L.E. Taxation §§ 250, 251.

WESTLAW Electronic Research

See WESTLAW Electronic Research Guide following the Preface.

United States Code Annotated

Time for filing federal estate tax return, see 26 U.S.C.A. § 6075.

Notes of Decisions

Discharge of taxes due 4
Inter vivos transfers 6
Interest on unpaid taxes 5
Liability for tax 2
Purpose 1
Time of payment 3

1. Purpose

The purpose of penalty and interest provisions for late payment of taxes is to insure compliance with the tax laws, prompt payment of taxes, and to penalize noncompliance, not to generate additional revenue for the state. Nell v. Tracy, App. 1 Dist.1984, 459 N.E.2d 432.

2. Liability for tax

In the collection of the inheritance tax under former statute, the executor, administrator, or trustee did not necessarily act in his capacity as such, but as an agent named by the state to act for the state in making such collection, and was made personally responsible therefor. Nation v. Green, 1919, 123 N.E. 163, 188 Ind. 697.

3. Time of payment

Taxpayer's mailing of tax payment by United States certified mail, return receipt requested, on April 28, 1981, was a timely payment of inheritance tax due on April 30, 1981, despite fact that the payment was not received by department of revenue until May 4, 1981. Nell v. Tracy, App. 1 Dist.1984, 459 N.E.2d 432.

Inheritance tax accrues at death of testator or intestate and it is duty of administrator or executor to see that same is paid within time prescribed by statute or suffer penalty. 1917–1920 Op.Atty.Gen. p. 170.

4. Discharge of taxes due

Nothing but payment will discharge taxes due from a decedent's estate. Cullop v. City of Vincennes, App.1904, 72 N.E. 166, 34 Ind.App. 667.

5. Interest on unpaid taxes

Court order which required estate to pay an additional $2,120.74 plus interest at 10% was proper, inasmuch as estate's first payment on inheritance tax deficiency prior to the order was applied first to interest then due, leaving a balance of principal and interest in the amount of the court's order. Indiana Dept. of State Revenue, Inheritance Tax Div. v. Estate of Rogers, App. 1 Dist.1984, 459 N.E.2d 69.

Trial judge has absolute discretion to reduce penalty interest rate from ten percent to six percent if an unavoidable delay prevents a determination of inheritance tax due; however, once a determination of the inheritance tax due is made, then the interest rate to be charged on the delinquent tax amount is ten percent. Indiana Dept. of State Revenue, Inheritance Tax Div. v. Estate of Broyles, App. 1 Dist.1983, 457 N.E.2d 250.

After the order determining value of estate and amount of tax has been entered, interest should be charged on any unpaid inheritance tax at the rate of 10 per cent per annum, provided eighteen months have elapsed from date of decedent's death; and, when both inheritance tax and interest thereon are due, any partial payment made must be applied first to the satisfaction of interest before any part of such payment is applied to principal. 1962 Op.Atty.Gen. No. 17.

The county treasurer was required to accept the payment of inheritance tax without interest after the expiration of 18 months from the date of accrual when proper proof was submitted that tender of payment had been made within 18 months of the date of death, even though no court order had been previously entered. 1955 Op.Atty.Gen. No. 24.

For purposes of former statute making inheritance tax due and payable at time of transfer, transfer occurred at time of death of deceased, and therefore estate would be liable for interest from date of death, even though will was not discovered and estate was consequently not opened until several years thereafter. 1937 Op. Atty.Gen. p. 134.

Where inheritance tax is not paid within 18 months after decedent's death, interest shall be charged and collected at rate of 10 percent from time of decedent's death unless there was unavoidable cause for delay, in which case interest shall be at rate of 6% per annum until cause of delay is removed, after which 10 percent shall be charged. 1917–1920 Op.Atty.Gen. p. 170.

6. Inter vivos transfers

Inheritance tax may be imposed on certain inter vivos transfers, but its collection is postponed until death of transferor. In re Grotrian's Estate, App. 3 Dist.1980, 405 N.E.2d 69.

6–4.1–9–1.5 Due date for taxes where petition for redetermination of inheritance taxes

Sec. 1.5. If inheritance tax is imposed because a petition is filed under IC 6–4.1–7–6, the inheritance tax so imposed is, notwithstanding section 1 of this chapter, not due until thirty (30) days after notice of the final determination of federal estate tax is received by a person liable for paying the inheritance tax. If any inheritance tax so imposed is not paid on or before the due date, the person liable for paying the tax shall pay interest on the delinquent tax at the rate of six percent (6%) per year from the due date until the tax is paid.

As added by Acts 1976, P.L.19, SEC.2.

Historical and Statutory Notes

Acts 1976, P.L. 19, § 2, emerg. eff. Feb. 25, 1976, added this section.

Cross References

Redetermination of inheritance tax resulting from federal estate tax valuation, see IC 6–4.1–7–6.

Law Review and Journal Commentaries

Death taxes: Survey of recent tax law. Thomas B. Allington, 10 Ind.L.Rev. 340 (1976).

6–4.1–9–2 Reduction of taxes for payment within one year of death

Sec. 2. If the inheritance tax imposed as a result of a decedent's death is paid within one (1) year after his date of death, the person making the payment is entitled to a five percent (5%) reduction in the inheritance tax due. When payment is so made, the person collecting the tax shall grant the five percent (5%) reduction to the payor.

As added by Acts 1976, P.L.18, SEC.1.

Historical and Statutory Notes

Formerly:
IC 6–4–1–13.
Acts 1931, c. 75, s. 13.

Administrative Code References

Inheritance tax, payment, discount on tax, time limitation, see 45 IAC 4.1–9–2.

Library References

Taxation ☞903.
WESTLAW Topic No. 371.

C.J.S. Taxation § 1220.
I.L.E. Taxation §§ 250, 251.

Notes of Decisions

Strict compliance 1
Tender of taxes due 2

___

1. Strict compliance

A five per cent discount was allowed on inheritance tax only if the tax was paid within one year of decedent's death and no discount could be allowed in cases where tax was paid more than a year after decedent's death, irrespective of the reasons occasioning a delay in payments. 1915–1916 Op.Atty.Gen. p. 553.

2. Tender of taxes due

The county treasurer was required to accept payment of inheritance taxes tendered within one year from the date of accrual (the date of death of decedent), and was required to allow the 5% discount when such tender was made within one year after accrual even though no court order had been entered prior to such tender. 1955 Op.Atty.Gen. No. 24.

6–4.1–9–3 Inheritance tax due as result of non-resident decedent's death; book showing tax due

Sec. 3. The department of state revenue shall maintain a book which indicates the amount of inheritance tax due as a result of a non-resident decedent's death. When the department gives an inheritance tax notice required by IC 6–4.1–5–16, the department shall concurrently enter in the book the amount of inheritance tax stated in the notice. The book required by this section is a public record.

As added by Acts 1976, P.L.18, SEC.1.

Historical and Statutory Notes

Formerly:
 IC 6–4–1–22.
 Acts 1931, c. 75, s. 22.

6–4.1–9–4 Tax payments resulting from non-resident decedent's death; monthly reports

Sec. 4. A person who is liable for inheritance tax imposed as a result of a non-resident decedent's death shall pay the tax to the department of state revenue. The department shall collect the tax and shall issue a receipt to the person who pays it. On the first Monday of each month, the department shall report and remit to the state treasurer the inheritance tax collected by it during the preceding month under this section. The report must indicate the estates for which the inheritance taxes were paid.

As added by Acts 1976, P.L.18, SEC.1.

Historical and Statutory Notes

Formerly:
 IC 6–4–1–22.
 Acts 1931, c. 75, s. 22.

Administrative Code References

Inheritance tax, payments for non-resident decedents, see 45 IAC 4.1–9–4, 45 IAC 4.1–9–5.

6–4.1–9–5 Collection and payment of taxes; receipts

Sec. 5. (a) A person who is liable for inheritance tax imposed as a result of a resident decedent's death shall pay the tax to the treasurer of the county in which the resident decedent was domiciled at the time of the resident decedent's death. If such a person believes that more inheritance tax is due as a result of the resident decedent's death than the amount of tax determined by the court under IC 6–4.1–5–10, the person may, without obtaining another court determination, pay the additional tax and any interest due on the additional tax to the county treasurer.

(b) The county treasurer shall collect the tax, shall issue a receipt for the tax payment in duplicate, and shall send one (1) copy of the receipt to the department of state revenue. The department shall countersign the receipt, shall affix its seal to the receipt, and shall return the signed and sealed receipt to the payor. The department shall also charge the county treasurer with the amount of inheritance tax collected by him.

As added by Acts 1976, P.L.18, SEC.1. Amended by Acts 1979, P.L.75, SEC.12; Acts 1980, P.L.57, SEC.23; P.L.86–1995, SEC.7.

Historical and Statutory Notes

Acts 1979, P.L. 75, § 12, eff. July 1, 1979, designated Subsecs. (a) and (b); and added the second sentence in Subsec. (a).

Acts 1980, P.L. 57, § 23, emerg. eff. March 3, 1980, substituted "IC 6–4.1–5–10" for "IC 6–4.1–5–11" in the second sentence of Subsec. (a).

P.L.86–1995, Sec.7, emerg. eff. retroactive to Jan. 1, 1994, amended the section by substitut-ing "resident decedent was domiciled at the time of the resident decedent's death" for "inheritance tax due is determined" in Subsec. (a).

Formerly:

IC 6–4–1–13.

Acts 1931, c. 75, s. 13.

Administrative Code References

Inheritance tax payments,
    Compromise on tax due, see 45 IAC 4.1–9–6.
    Payment and collection of taxes, see 45 IAC 4.1–9–4, 45 IAC 4.1–9–5.

Library References

Taxation ☞905(1).
WESTLAW Topic No. 371.

C.J.S. Taxation § 1223.
I.L.E. Taxation §§ 250, 251.

Notes of Decisions

Receipt, effect   1

_____

1. Receipt, effect
    Execution of countersigned receipt by inheritance tax division did not prevent the state from subsequently seeking a redetermination of inheritance tax. Matter of Adamson's Estate, App. 1 Dist.1980, 403 N.E.2d 355.

6–4.1–9–6 Apportionment of receipts between county and state; transfer to county and state

Sec. 6. (a) With respect to the inheritance tax imposed as a result of a resident decedent's death, the county in which the tax is collected shall receive eight percent (8%) of the inheritance tax paid as a result of the decedent's death. On the first day of January, April, July, and October of each year, the county treasurer shall, except as provided in subsection (b), transfer to the county general fund the amount due the county under this section. This state shall receive the remaining ninety-two percent (92%) of the inheritance taxes, all the interest charges collected by the county treasurer under section 1 or 1.5 of this chapter, and all the penalties collected by the county treasurer under IC 6–4.1–4–6.

(b) In a county having a consolidated city, the amount due the county under this section shall be transferred to the general fund of the consolidated city.

As added by Acts 1976, P.L.18, SEC.1. Amended by Acts 1980, P.L.57, SEC.24; Acts 1981, P.L.11, SEC.33; P.L.86–1995, SEC.8.

Historical and Statutory Notes

Acts 1980, P.L. 57, § 24, emerg. eff. March 3, 1980, substituted "section 1 or 1.5 of this chapter" for "IC 6–4.1–9–1" in the third sentence of present Subsec. (a).

Acts 1981, P.L. 11, § 33, designated Subsec. (a) and added Subsec. (b); and substituted "subsection (b)" for "IC 19–5–3–18(a)(9)" in the second sentence of present Subsec. (a).

Acts 1981, P.L. 11, was a part of a codification, revision and rearrangement of laws relating to local government.

P.L.86–1995, Sec.8, emerg. eff. retroactive to Jan. 1, 1994, amended the section by substituting "collected" for "determined" and "the decedent's" for "his" in Subsec. (a).

Formerly:
IC 6–4–1–7.

IC 6–4–1–14.
IC 6–4–1–35.
IC 19–5–3–18.
Acts 1931, c. 75, ss. 7, 14, 36.
Acts 1933, c. 229, s. 1.
Acts 1937, c. 285, s. 1.
Acts 1947, c. 13, s. 1.
Acts 1957, c. 318, ss. 1, 6.
Acts 1967, c. 311, s. 19.
Acts 1969, c. 235, s. 10.

Cross References

Penalties for failure to file return, see IC 6–4.1–4–6.

Notes of Decisions

Mandate 1

_____

1. Mandate

Although action to compel Indiana revenue board to pay counties the amounts due under former statute [see, now, this section] providing for sharing of inheritance taxes between the state and counties in which such taxes were collected was required to be brought in nature of an action for mandate, such did not preclude award of interest on amount which board was mandated to pay the counties. Indiana Revenue Bd. v. State ex rel. Bd. of Com'rs of Hendricks County, 1979, 385 N.E.2d 1131, 270 Ind. 365.

6–4.1–9–7   County treasurer's quarterly report of collections; warrants

Sec. 7.   (a) On the first day of January, April, July, and October of each year, each county treasurer shall, under oath, send a written inheritance tax report to the department of state revenue.   Each report shall state the amount of inheritance taxes collected by the county treasurer during the preceding three (3) months and shall indicate the estates for which the taxes were paid, who paid the taxes, and when the taxes were paid.   The county treasurer shall prepare each report on the form prescribed by the state board of accounts.

(b) On the first day of January, April, July, and October of each year, each county auditor shall issue a warrant to the state treasurer for the amount of inheritance taxes, interest charges, and penalties which the state is to receive under section 6 of this chapter.   The county treasurer shall stamp and countersign the warrant.   The county treasurer shall send the warrant to the department of state revenue not more than thirty (30) days after the county treasurer is required to send the related inheritance tax report for the preceding three (3) months under subsection (a).

As added by Acts 1976, P.L.18, SEC.1.   Amended by P.L.30–1994, SEC.7.

Historical and Statutory Notes

P.L.30–1994, Sec.7, substituted "not more than thirty (30) days after the county treasurer is required to send the related " for "with his" in Subsec. (b), and added "under subsection (a) at the end of Subsec. (b).

Formerly:
IC 6–4–1–14.
Acts 1931, c. 75, s. 14.
Acts 1947, c. 13, s. 1.
Acts 1957, c. 318, s. 6.

6–4.1–9–8   Disposition of warrant from county; quietus

Sec. 8.   (a) The department of state revenue shall receipt and account for each warrant which it receives under section 7(b) of this chapter.   The department shall then forward the warrant to the state treasurer.   The state treasurer shall deposit the warrants in a special account within the state general fund to be known as the Inheritance Tax Account.

(b) At the end of each month, the state auditor shall issue a quietus to the department of state revenue for the money collected by the department under section 7(b) of this chapter.   The state auditor shall issue the quietus under the same terms and conditions established for issuing a quietus to similar state agencies.

As added by Acts 1976, P.L.18, SEC.1.

Historical and Statutory Notes

Formerly:
IC 6–4–1–14.
IC 6–4–1–35.

Acts 1931, c. 75, ss. 14, 36.
Acts 1947, c. 13, s. 1.
Acts 1957, c. 318, s. 6.

6–4.1–9–9   Audit of quarterly reports; report and disposition of shortages and excessive payments

Sec. 9.   The department of state revenue shall audit the quarterly inheritance tax reports required by section 7 of this chapter.   The department shall report any shortage which it discovers to the appropriate county treasurer and county auditor.   If the department notifies them of a shortage, the county treasurer and county auditor shall promptly issue a warrant to the state treasurer for the balance due the state.   If the department, through its audit, discovers that an excessive payment has been made, the amount of the excess shall be refunded in the same manner that refunds are made under IC 6–4.1–10.

As added by Acts 1976, P.L.18, SEC.1.

Historical and Statutory Notes

Formerly:
IC 6–4–1–14.
Acts 1931, c. 75, s. 14.

Acts 1947, c. 13, s. 1.
Acts 1957, c. 318, s. 6.

Cross References

Refund of inheritance tax erroneously or illegally collected, see IC 6–4.1–10–1 et seq.

6–4.1–9–10   Repealed

(Repealed by P.L.30–1994, SEC.8.)

Historical and Statutory Notes

Former IC 6–4.1–9–10 related to nonpayment by county to department of state revenue.

Formerly:
IC 6–4–1–14.

Acts 1931, c. 75, s. 14.
Acts 1947, c. 13, s. 1.
Acts 1957, c. 318, s. 6.
Acts 1976, P.L.18, SEC.1.

6–4.1–9–11 Action for failure to pay inheritance tax; payment of tax after prosecution

Sec. 11. (a) If the department of state revenue believes that a person has failed to pay inheritance tax for which the person is liable under a court order, the department may file in the appropriate probate court an action in the name of the state to enforce payment of the tax. This action must be commenced within ten (10) years after the date of the order imposing the tax unless the court has not complied with IC 6–4.1–5–11. Every person who is liable for the inheritance tax is liable to the department of state revenue for payment of the tax. The amounts collected under this section shall be distributed under section 6 of this chapter.

(b) When an action has been successfully prosecuted under this section, the person who is liable for the inheritance tax due from any property which is subject to the inheritance tax shall then pay the amount due from the person to the department of state revenue.

As added by Acts 1976, P.L.18, SEC.1. Amended by P.L.26–1985, SEC.12; P.L.60–1996, SEC.1.

Historical and Statutory Notes

P.L.26–1985, Sec.12, eff. July 1, 1986, in Subsec. (a), inserted the fourth sentence.

P.L.60–1996, Sec.1, rewrote the section, which previously read:

"(a) If a county treasurer believes that a person has failed to pay inheritance tax for which he is liable, the county treasurer shall give the county prosecuting attorney written notice of the person's failure to pay. When the prosecuting attorney receives such a notice, he shall ask the appropriate probate court to order the person to appear before the court to show why the tax has not been paid. If the court believes that inheritance tax is due and that payment of the tax cannot be enforced under the other provisions of this article, the court shall direct the prosecuting attorney to initiate an action in the name of the county to enforce payment of the tax. This action must be commenced within ten (10) years after the date of the order imposing

the tax unless the court has not complied with IC 6–4.1–5–11. Every person who is liable for the inheritance tax is liable to the county in whose name the action is initiated.

"(b) When an action is initiated under this section, the personal representative of the decedent's estate or the trustee of property transferred by the decedent shall deduct the inheritance tax due from any property which the personal representative or trustee has possession of or control over and which is subject to the lien established for that inheritance tax under IC 6–4.1–8–1. The personal representative or trustee shall then pay the amount so deducted to the county treasurer."

Formerly:

IC 6–4–1–15.
Acts 1931, c. 75, s. 15.

Cross References

County prosecuting attorneys, actions to collect unpaid taxes, see IC 6–8.1–3–13.

Court ordered sale, mortgage, lease or exchange of personal or real property, payment of inheritance tax, see IC 29–1–15–3.

United States Code Annotated

Federal estate tax, authority to bring civil action for collection of tax, see 26 U.S.C.A. § 7404.

Notes of Decisions

Limitation of actions 2
Parties 1

___

1. Parties

Action to enforce payment of inheritance taxes was ineffective where Attorney General rather than county prosecuting attorney initiated proceeding, and Attorney General's office failed to order administrator to appear and show cause why tax had not been paid. In re Estate of Dukes, App. 4 Dist.1983, 453 N.E.2d 1179.

2. Limitation of actions

Action to enforce payment of inheritance taxes is subject to residual statute of limitations [section 34–1–2–3] providing, inter alia, that all actions not limited by any other statute shall be brought within ten years unless cause of action arose before September 1, 1982, in which case action must be brought within 15 years. In re Estate of Dukes, App. 4 Dist.1983, 453 N.E.2d 1179.

Obligation to pay inheritance tax, and thus cause of action to enforce payment thereof, accrued at time decedent died; therefore, under applicable 15-year statute of limitations [section 34–1–2–3], action initiated more than 15 years after date of decedent's death was untimely. In re Estate of Dukes, App. 4 Dist.1983, 453 N.E.2d 1179.

6–4.1–9–12 Appointment of resident or special administrator for non-resident decedent's estate

Sec. 12. The Probate Court of Marion County may appoint a resident or special administrator for a non-resident decedent's estate if the department of state revenue shows:

(1) that the department has reason to believe that a property interest transferred by the decedent under a taxable transfer has not been appraised for inheritance tax purposes in the manner required by this article and that the property involved is located in this state; or

(2) that the inheritance tax imposed as a result of the decedent's death, as determined by the department, has not been paid and it has been at least two (2) years since the decedent died.

A resident or special administrator appointed by the court under this section has the same powers and duties as a general administrator.

As added by Acts 1976, P.L.18, SEC.1.

Historical and Statutory Notes

Formerly:
    IC 6–4–1–25.
    Acts 1931, c. 75, s. 26.

6–4.1–9–13 Repealed

(Repealed by Acts 1979, P.L.75, SEC.15.)

Historical and Statutory Notes

Acts 1979, P.L. 75, provided in § 16(b) that § 15 takes effect July 1, 1979.

The former section related to tax receipts in personal representatives' reports.

Formerly:

Acts 1976, P.L.18, SEC.1.

Chapter 10

Refund of Inheritance Tax Erroneously or Illegally Collected

Library References

Taxation ☜904.
C.J.S. Taxation § 1222.

WESTLAW Topic No. 371.
I.L.E. Taxation § 371.

6–4.1–10–1 Refund for illegally or erroneously collected tax; time for filing

Sec. 1. (a) A person may file with the department of state revenue a claim for the refund of inheritance or Indiana estate tax which has been erroneously or illegally collected. Except as provided in section 2 of this chapter, the person must file the claim within three (3) years after the tax is paid or within one (1) year after the tax is finally determined, whichever is later.

(b) The amount of the refund that a person is entitled to receive under this chapter equals the amount of the erroneously or illegally collected tax, plus interest at the rate of six percent (6%) per annum computed from the date the tax was paid to the date it is refunded.

As added by Acts 1976, P.L.18, SEC.1. Amended by Acts 1980, P.L.57, SEC.25.

Historical and Statutory Notes

Acts 1976, P.L. 18, § 1, emerg. eff. Feb. 18, 1976, added this article.

The 1976 act added the provisions of this chapter as part of a codification, reenactment, revision and rearrangement of laws relating to death taxes.

Acts 1980, P.L. 57, § 25, eff. July 1, 1980, designated Subsec. (a); added Subsec. (b); and in Subsec. (a) in the first sentence, inserted "or

Indiana estate", and substituted "has been" for "is" and, in the second sentence, deleted "by the highest court hearing the matter" following "finally determined".

Formerly:

IC 6–4–1–17.
IC 6–4–1–24.
Acts 1931, c. 75, ss. 17, 24.
Acts 1937, c. 159, ss. 2, 3.

WESTLAW Electronic Research

See WESTLAW Electronic Research Guide following the Preface.

Notes of Decisions

1. Validity of prior law

Acts 1937, c. 159, s. 2 [repealed; see, now, this chapter] providing that state board of tax commissioners was authorized and empowered to order refund and repayment, without interest, of all taxes erroneously, wrongfully, or illegally imposed on estates, inheritances, bequests, legacies, devises, successions, gifts, or other similar transfers of property and of all such taxes that were excessive in amount or in any manner wrongfully collected by the state, was not unconstitutional because of the power given the board. 1939 Op.Atty.Gen. p. 88.

2. In general

Rehearing statute [repealed; see, now, § 6–4.1–7–5], which afforded taxpayer method of contesting tax determination at appraisal and assessment stage, and refund statute [repealed; see, now, this chapter] which enabled taxpayer to pay tax as assessed and subsequently seek refund if tax was "erroneously, wrongfully or illegally imposed * * * or in any manner wrongfully collected," provided alternative methods by which a taxpayer could obtain relief, and thus executors' failure to protest estate tax assessment did not preclude relief under the refund statute but on the contrary, refund statute provided a separate vehicle by which executors could proceed in probate court. State v. Davies, App. 2 Dist.1978, 379 N.E.2d 501, 177 Ind.App. 288.

Executors' claim for refund of estate tax on intangible personal property of nonresident decedent located in Indiana fell within scope of IC1971, 6–4–1–17 [repealed; see, now, this chapter] which allowed refund for tax erroneously, wrongfully or illegally imposed, not just when tax was "erroneously paid." State v. Davies, App. 2 Dist.1978, 379 N.E.2d 501, 177 Ind.App. 288.

3. Rules and regulations

Under inheritance tax act of 1931, s. 38, the state board of tax commissioners had power to make such regulations as were necessary to accomplish the purpose of the act, and they could make provision for refunding to individual heir of amount advanced upon his own account for payment of additional estate tax im-

posed, if claim of heir with internal revenue department of federal government for refund had been rejected. 1934 Op.Atty.Gen. p. 118.

4. Time for filing

Court lacked jurisdiction to enter second order determining new amount of inheritance tax when executor of estate attempted to file new affidavit for inheritance tax appraisement after sale of second farm at less than appraised value six years after first inheritance tax order was issued without following appropriate procedures or observing statutory time limitations. Sibbitt v. Indiana Dept. of Revenue, App. 1 Dist.1990, 563 N.E.2d 146, rehearing denied, transfer denied.

Failure to comply with statutory time limits for seeking rehearing on inheritance tax determination deprives court of jurisdiction of subject matter at issue, but section 6–4.1–7–1 providing for such rehearing by probate court is not exclusive remedy, and taxpayer may file claim for refund, in which event court does not lack jurisdiction to determine appeal from denial of claim for refund. Indiana Dept. of Revenue, Inheritance Tax Division v. Binhack's Estate, App. 1 Dist.1981, 426 N.E.2d 714.

The filing of a petition for a redetermination of the inheritance and transfer tax due, or the filing of a petition for refund and appealing the same to the court within the time fixed by §§ 6–4.1–7–1, 6–4.1–10–4 and this section is jurisdictional, a precondition to or the essence of the right itself, and after the passage of the time allotted by these sections the right itself is lost, the court does not have jurisdiction to hear it, and jurisdiction cannot be conferred, even by agreement. Matter of Compton's Estate, App. 1 Dist.1980, 406 N.E.2d 365.

Where administratrix erroneously paid inheritance tax through no fault of state officials in 1929 and refund was requested in 1934, provision of Acts 1931, c. 75, s. 24 [repealed; see, now, this section], which contained requirement that application for refunds by non-residents be made within year from date of payment barred application for return or refund on any part of the inheritance tax paid by administratrix. 1935 Op.Atty.Gen. p. 329.

Even if inheritance tax was erroneously paid, where application for refund thereof was not filed for more than three years after payment of such tax, state auditor was without authority to authorize the refund in absence of judgment of a court. 1923–1924 Op.Atty.Gen. p. 22.

6–4.1–10–2   Time limits for filing for property interests under IC 6–4.1–6

Sec. 2.   The time limits prescribed in section 1 of this chapter for filing a refund claim do not apply if the claim is for the refund of inheritance tax which has been determined in the manner provided in IC 6–4.1–6.
As added by Acts 1976, P.L.18, SEC.1.

Historical and Statutory Notes

Formerly:
IC 6–4–1–17.

Acts 1931, c. 75, s. 17.
Acts 1937, c. 159, s. 2.

Cross References

Special procedures for appraising and taxing certain property interests, see IC 6–4.1–6–1 et seq.

6–4.1–10–3   Orders for refund; funds from which payable; credit

Sec. 3.   (a) The department of state revenue shall review each claim for refund and shall enter an order either approving, partially approving, or disapproving the refund.   If the department either approves or partially approves a claim for refund, the department shall send a copy of the order to:

(1) the treasurer of the county that collected the tax, if the refund applies to inheritance tax collected as a result of a resident decedent's death; or

(2) the treasurer of state, if the refund applies to tax collected by the department.

The county or state treasurer, as the case may be, shall pay the refund from money which is under his control and which has not otherwise been appropriated.   The county or state treasurer shall receive a credit for the amount so refunded.   The county treasurer shall claim the credit on his inheritance tax report for the quarter in which the refund is paid.

(b) Within five (5) days after entering an order with respect to a claim for refund filed under section 1 of this chapter, the department shall send a copy of the order to the person who filed the claim.
As added by Acts 1976, P.L.18, SEC.1.   Amended by Acts 1980, P.L.57, SEC.26.

Historical and Statutory Notes

Acts 1980, P.L. 57, § 26, eff. July 1, 1980, rewrote the section which prior thereto read:

"The department of state revenue may order any county treasurer or the state treasurer to refund, without interest, inheritance tax which has been erroneously or illegally collected to the person who appears to be entitled to the refund. The county or state treasurer shall refund the tax from money which is under his control and which has not otherwise been appropriated.

The county or state treasurer shall receive a credit for the amount of tax so refunded. The county treasurer shall claim the credit on his inheritance tax report for the quarter in which the refund is paid."

Formerly:

IC 6–4–1–17.
Acts 1931, c. 75, s. 17.
Acts 1937, c. 159, s. 2.

Library References

Taxation ☞904.   C.J.S. Taxation § 1222.
WESTLAW Topic No. 371.   I.L.E. Taxation §§ 247 to 249.

6–4.1–10–4   Appeal of refund order; complaint; jurisdiction

Sec. 4.   (a) A person who files a claim for the refund of inheritance or Indiana estate tax may appeal any refund order which the department of state revenue enters with respect to his claim.   To initiate the appeal, the person must, within ninety (90) days after the department enters the order, file a complaint in which the department is named as the defendant.

(b) The court which has jurisdiction over an appeal initiated under this section is:

(1) the probate court of the county in which administration of the estate is pending, if the appeal involves either a resident or a nonresident decedent's estate and administration of the estate is pending;

(2) the probate court of the county in which the decedent was domiciled at the time of his death, if the appeal involves a resident decedent's estate and no administration of the estate is pending in Indiana; or

(3) the probate court of any county in which any of the decedent's property was located at the time of his death, if the appeal involves a nonresident decedent's estate and no administration of the estate is pending in Indiana.

As added by Acts 1976, P.L.18, SEC.1.   Amended by Acts 1980, P.L.57, SEC.27.

Historical and Statutory Notes

Acts 1980, P.L. 57, § 27, eff. July 1, 1980, rewrote the section which prior thereto read:

"A person who files a claim for the refund of inheritance tax may appeal any refund order which the department of state revenue enters with respect to his claim. To initiate the appeal, the person must, within ninety (90) days after the department enters the order, file a complaint in which the department is named as the defendant. If the inheritance tax is imposed as the result of a resident decedent's death, the person must file the complaint in the probate court which originally determined the amount of tax due. If the inheritance tax is imposed as a result of a non-resident decedent's death, person must file the complaint in the Probate Court of Marion County."

Formerly:

IC 6–4–1–17.
Acts 1931, c. 75, s. 17.
Acts 1937, c. 159, s. 2.

Notes of Decisions

Jurisdiction   1

—————

1. Jurisdiction

The filing of a petition for a redetermination of the inheritance and transfer tax due, or the filing of a petition for refund and appealing the same to the court within the time fixed by §§ 6– 4.1–7–1, 6–4.1–10–1 and this section is jurisdictional, a precondition to or the essence of the right itself, and after the passage of the time allotted by these sections the right itself is lost, the court does not have jurisdiction to hear it, and jurisdiction cannot be conferred, even by agreement. Matter of Compton's Estate, App. 1 Dist.1980, 406 N.E.2d 365.

6–4.1–10–5   Probate court determination; appeal

Sec. 5.   When an appeal is initiated under section 4 of this chapter, the probate court shall determine the amount of any tax refund due.   Either party may appeal the probate court's decision to the tax court in accordance with the rules of appellate procedure.

As added by Acts 1976, P.L.18, SEC.1. Amended by Acts 1980, P.L.57, SEC.28; P.L.59–1990, SEC.2.

Historical and Statutory Notes

Acts 1980, P.L. 57, § 28, eff. July 1, 1980, deleted "inheritance" before "tax refund" in the first sentence.

P.L.59–1990, Sec.2, in the first sentence, substituted "shall" for "may", and in the second sentence inserted "to the tax court in accordance with the rules of appellate procedure".

Formerly:

IC 6–4–1–17.

Acts 1931, c. 75, s. 17.
Acts 1937, c. 159, s. 2.

6–4.1–10–6   Annual appropriation to pay refund

Sec. 6. Amounts sufficient to pay the refunds provided for under this chapter are annually appropriated.

As added by Acts 1976, P.L.18, SEC.1.

Historical and Statutory Notes

Formerly:
  IC 6–4–1–17.

Acts 1931, c. 75, s. 17.
Acts 1937, c. 159, s. 2.

Chapter 11

Indiana Estate Tax

Library References

Taxation ☞856.
WESTLAW Topic No. 371.
C.J.S. Taxation §§ 1111 to 1120, 1131.

6–4.1–11–1   Imposition of estate tax

Sec. 1. A tax to be known as the "Indiana estate tax" is imposed upon a resident or nonresident decedent's estate.

As added by Acts 1976, P.L.18, SEC.1. Amended by P.L.58–1990, SEC.2.

Historical and Statutory Notes

Acts 1976, P.L. 18, § 1, emerg. eff. Feb. 18, 1976, added this article.

The 1976 act added and reenacted the provisions of this chapter as part of a codification, revision and rearrangement of laws relating to death taxes.

P.L.58–1990, Sec.2, inserted "resident or nonresident"; and deleted "if the federal death tax credit allowed against the federal estate tax imposed as a result of his death exceeds the total state death taxes actually paid as a result of his death" following "decedent's estate".

Formerly:
IC 6–4–1–37.
Acts 1931, c. 75, s. 38.
Acts 1965, c. 276, s. 1.

Cross References

"Federal death tax credit" defined, see IC 6–4.1–1–4.
Imposition of inheritance tax, see IC 6–4.1–2–1 et seq.

Law Review and Journal Commentaries

Death taxes: Survey of recent law. John W. Boyd, 11 Ind.L.Rev. 292 (1978).

Malpractice claims in estate planning. Richard B. Urda, Jr., 41 Res Gestae 12 (March 1998).

Surviving spouses' rights. John S. Grimes, 10 Ind.L.Rev. 675 (1977).

Library References

Taxation ⊜856.
WESTLAW Topic No. 371.

C.J.S. Taxation §§ 1111 to 1120, 1131.
I.L.E. Taxation § 232.

Notes of Decisions

Taxes paid foreign states   1

_____

1. Taxes paid foreign states

Florida estate tax paid by estate of Indiana resident was similar in purpose and character to Indiana estate tax and thus could not be subtracted from estate's federal death tax credit in arriving at Indiana estate tax owed. Indiana Dept. of State Revenue, Inheritance Tax Div. v. Estate of Pearson, App. 2 Dist.1986, 498 N.E.2d 990, rehearing denied, affirmed 521 N.E.2d 350.

IC1971, 6–4–1–37 [repealed; see, now, this section] permitting a deduction from estate tax for "death taxes" paid other states had to be construed as excluding "pickup taxes" paid other states from allowable deduction even though such construction resulted in imposition of state taxes which, in total, exceeded credit allowed by federal law for such taxes whenever a resident decedent died possessed of property in another state that levied pickup taxes similar to those levied in state. State v. Purdue Nat. Bank of Lafayette, App. 2 Dist.1976, 355 N.E.2d 414, 171 Ind.App. 76.

6–4.1–11–2   Computation for residents and non-residents; determination of value of Indiana gross estate

Sec. 2.   (a) The Indiana estate tax is the amount determined in STEP FOUR of the following formula:

STEP ONE: Divide:

(A) the value of the decedent's Indiana gross estate; by

(B) the value of the decedent's total gross estate for federal estate tax purposes.

STEP TWO: Multiply:

(A) the quotient determined under STEP ONE; by

(B) the federal state death tax credit allowable against the decedent's federal estate tax.

The product is the Indiana portion of the federal state death tax credit.

STEP THREE: Subtract:

(A) the amount of all Indiana inheritance taxes actually paid as a result of the decedent's death; from

(B) the product determined under **STEP TWO**.

STEP FOUR: Determine the greater of the following:

(A) The remainder determined under **STEP THREE**.

(B) Zero (0).

(b) For purposes of this section, the value of a nonresident decedent's Indiana gross estate equals the total fair market value on the appraisal date of tangible personal property and real estate which had an actual situs in Indiana at the time of the decedent's death and which is included in the decedent's gross estate for federal estate tax purposes under Sections 2031 through 2044 of the Internal Revenue Code.

(c) For purposes of this section, the value of a resident decedent's Indiana gross estate equals the total fair market value on the appraisal date of personal property and real estate that had an actual situs in Indiana at the time of the decedent's death and all intangible personal property wherever located that is included in the decedent's gross estate for federal estate tax purposes.

(d) For purposes of this section, the value of a resident or nonresident decedent's total gross estate for federal estate tax purposes equals the total fair market value on the appraisal date of the property included in the decedent's gross estate for federal estate tax purposes under Sections 2031 through 2044 of the Internal Revenue Code.

(e) For purposes of determining the value of a decedent's Indiana gross estate and the decedent's total gross estate, the appraisal date for each property interest is the date on which the property interest is valued for federal estate tax purposes.

(f) The estate tax does not apply to a property interest transfer made by a resident decedent if the interest transferred is in:

(1) real property located outside Indiana, regardless of whether the property is held in a trust or whether the trustee is required to distribute the property in-kind; or

(2) real property located in Indiana, if:

(A) the real property was transferred to an irrevocable trust during the decedent's lifetime;

(B) the transfer to the trust was not made in contemplation of the transferor's death, as determined under IC 6–4.1–2–4; and

(C) the decedent does not have a retained interest in the trust.

As added by Acts 1976, P.L.18, SEC.1. Amended by Acts 1979, P.L.75, SEC.13; P.L.58–1990, SEC.3; P.L.78–1993, SEC.3.

Historical and Statutory Notes

Acts 1979, P.L. 75, § 13, eff. July 1, 1979, added Subsecs. (c), (d) and (e).

P.L.58–1990, Sec.3, rewrote Subsec. (a); deleted former Subsec. (b); redesignated former Subsec. (c) as Subsec. (b) and in that subsection, substituted "personal property and real estate" for "property"; inserted Subsec. (c); in Subsec. (d), inserted "resident or" and "for

federal estate tax purposes"; and in Subsec. (e), substituted "the decedent's" for "his".

P.L.78–1993, Sec.3, added Subsec. (f).

Formerly:

IC 6–4–1–37.
Acts 1931, c. 75, s. 38.
Acts 1965, c. 276, s. 1.

Law Review and Journal Commentaries

Malpractice claims in estate planning. Richard B. Urda, Jr., 41 Res Gestae 12 (March 1998).

Library References

Taxation ☞886½.
WESTLAW Topic No. 371.

C.J.S. Taxation § 1181.
I.L.E. Taxation § 239.

Notes of Decisions

Federal tax credit construed 1

---

1. Federal tax credit construed

The phrase "federal tax credit allowed" in this section governing proper calculation of Indiana estate tax meant actual federal estate tax paid, rather than maximum federal estate tax credit available, and thus, Department of Revenue was not entitled to tax estate based on difference between maximum allowable federal estate tax and state inheritance tax paid. State, Dept. of Revenue v. Estate of Eberbach, 1989, 535 N.E.2d 1194.

6–4.1–11–3 Accrual of tax; time for payment

Sec. 3. (a) The Indiana estate tax accrues at the time of the decedent's death. Except as provided in subsection (b) of this section, the Indiana estate tax is due eighteen (18) months after the date of the decedent's death.

(b) Any Indiana estate tax, which results from a final change in the amount of federal estate tax, is due:

(1) eighteen (18) months after the date of the decedent's death; or

(2) one (1) month after final notice of the federal estate tax due is given to the person liable for the tax;

whichever is later.

As added by Acts 1976, P.L.18, SEC.1.

Historical and Statutory Notes

Formerly:
IC 6–4–1–30.
IC 6–4–1–39.

Acts 1931, c. 75, ss. 31, 40.
Acts 1965, c. 276, s. 3.

6–4.1–11–4   Late payments; interest

Sec. 4.   If Indiana estate tax is not paid on or before the due date, the person liable for the tax shall pay interest on the delinquent portion of the tax from the due date until it is paid at the rate of six percent (6%) per year. *As added by Acts 1976, P.L.18, SEC.1.*

Historical and Statutory Notes

Formerly: Acts 1931, c. 75, s. 40.
  IC 6–4–1–39.   Acts 1965, c. 276, s. 3.

6–4.1–11–5   Indiana estate tax as credit against inheritance tax

Sec. 5.   A person is entitled to claim the amount of Indiana estate tax paid under this chapter as a credit against inheritance tax imposed under this article if:

(1) the inheritance tax is imposed after the Indiana estate tax is paid; and

(2) both taxes are imposed as a result of the same decedent's death.

As added by Acts 1976, P.L.18, SEC.1.

Historical and Statutory Notes

Formerly: Acts 1931, c. 75, s. 38.
  IC 6–4–1–37.   Acts 1965, c. 276, s. 1.

6–4.1–11–6   Collection of tax; remittance; deposit, distribution to counties

Sec. 6.   (a) The department of state revenue shall collect the Indiana estate tax and the interest charges imposed under this chapter. The department shall remit the money which it collects under this chapter to the state treasurer, and the state treasurer shall deposit the money in the state general fund.

(b) Before August 15 of each year, the treasurer of state shall distribute to each county the amount determined under subsection (c) for the county. There is appropriated from the state general fund the amount necessary to make the distributions under this section.

(c) The department of state revenue shall determine the inheritance tax replacement amount for each county, using the following formula:

STEP ONE: Determine the amount of inheritance tax revenue retained by each county in each state fiscal year beginning with the state fiscal year that began July 1, 1990, and ending with the state fiscal year that ends June 30, 1997.

STEP TWO: Determine the average annual amount of inheritance tax revenue retained by each county using five (5) of the seven (7) state fiscal years described in STEP ONE after excluding the two (2) years in which each county retained its highest and lowest totals of inheritance tax revenue.

STEP THREE: Determine the remainder of the STEP TWO amount minus the amount of inheritance taxes retained by the county during the immediately preceding state fiscal year.

As added by Acts 1976, P.L.18, SEC.1. Amended by P.L.254–1997(ss), SEC.11.

Historical and Statutory Notes

P.L.254–1997(ss), Sec.11, amended the section by designating Subsec. (a); and adding Subsecs. (b) and (c).

Formerly:
  IC 6–4–1–31.

IC 6–4–1–35.
Acts 1931, c. 75, ss. 32, 36.
Acts 1937, c. 159, s. 5.

Library References

Taxation ⚖️905(1).
WESTLAW Topic No. 371.

C.J.S. Taxation § 1223.
I.L.E. Taxation §§ 250, 251.

6–4.1–11–7   Estate tax owing; final determination; appeal

Sec. 7. A probate court's final determination concerning the amount of Indiana estate tax owing under this chapter may be appealed to the tax court in accordance with the rules of appellate procedure.

As added by P.L.59–1990, SEC.3.

Library References

Interlocutory appeals, appeals from the Indiana tax court, see Stroud, 4A Indiana Practice § 15.25 (2d ed.).

Chapter 11.5

Indiana Generation–Skipping Transfer Tax

6–4.1–11.5–1   "Federal generation-skipping transfer tax"

Sec. 1. As used in this chapter, "federal generation-skipping transfer tax" means the tax imposed by Chapter 13 of Subtitle B of the Internal Revenue Code.

As added by P.L.67–1991, SEC.1.

6–4.1–11.5–2   "Federal generation-skipping transfer tax credit"

Sec. 2. As used in this chapter, "federal generation-skipping transfer tax credit" means the maximum allowable federal generation-skipping transfer tax credit under Section 2604 of the Internal Revenue Code [1] for state generation-skipping transfer taxes.

As added by P.L.67–1991, SEC.1.

[1] 26 U.S.C.A. § 2604.

6–4.1–11.5–3   "Generation-skipping transfer"

Sec. 3. As used in this chapter, "generation-skipping transfer" includes every transfer subject to the tax imposed under Chapter 13 of Subtitle B of the Internal Revenue Code [1] if:

(1) the original transferor is a resident of Indiana on the date of the original transfer; or

(2) the transferor is not a resident of Indiana and the transferred property is:

(A) real property located in Indiana; or

(B) tangible personal property that is legally located in Indiana.

As added by P.L.67–1991, SEC.1.

[1] 26 U.S.C.A. § 2601 et seq.

6–4.1–11.5–4   "Original transferor"

Sec. 4. As used in this chapter, "original transferor" means a donor, grantor, testator, or trustor who by gift, grant, will, or trust makes a transfer of real or personal property that results in the imposition of the federal generation-skipping transfer tax under the Internal Revenue Code.

As added by P.L.67–1991, SEC.1.

6–4.1–11.5–5   "Transfer tax"

Sec. 5. As used in this chapter, "transfer tax" means the Indiana generation-skipping transfer tax imposed under section 7 of this chapter.

As added by P.L.67–1991, SEC.1.

6–4.1–11.5–6 "Transferred property"

Sec. 6. As used in this chapter, "transferred property" means real or personal property, whether located in Indiana or in another jurisdiction, the transfer of which gives rise to federal generation-skipping transfer tax.
As added by P.L.67–1991, SEC.1.

Library References

Taxation ☞877.
WESTLAW Topic No. 371.
C.J.S. Taxation § 1142.

6–4.1–11.5–7 Generation-skipping transfer tax

Sec. 7. The Indiana generation-skipping transfer tax is imposed upon every generation-skipping transfer.
As added by P.L.67–1991, SEC.1.

Library References

Taxation ☞877.
WESTLAW Topic No. 371.
C.J.S. Taxation § 1142.

6–4.1–11.5–8 Amount of transfer tax

Sec. 8. (a) The transfer tax is the amount determined in the following formula:

STEP ONE: Divide:

(A) the value of the transferred property that is legally located in Indiana; by

(B) the total value of the transferred property.

STEP TWO: Multiply:

(A) the quotient determined under STEP ONE; by

(B) the federal generation-skipping transfer tax credit.

STEP THREE: Determine the remainder of:

(A) the federal generation-skipping transfer tax credit; minus

(B) the generation-skipping transfer taxes paid to states other than Indiana.

STEP FOUR: Determine the greater of:

(A) the STEP TWO amount; or

(B) the STEP THREE amount.

(b) For purposes of this section, the value of the transferred property equals the final value of the property determined for federal generation-skipping transfer tax purposes.
As added by P.L.67–1991, SEC.1.

Library References

Taxation ☞886.5.
WESTLAW Topic No. 371.
C.J.S. Taxation § 1181.

6–4.1–11.5–9   Due date of transfer tax

Sec. 9.   The transfer tax is due eighteen (18) months after the date of death of the person whose death resulted in the generation-skipping transfer.
As added by P.L.67–1991, SEC.1.

Library References

Taxation ☞887.
WESTLAW Topic No. 371.
C.J.S. Taxation § 1166.

6–4.1–11.5–10   Payment of transfer tax

Sec. 10.   The transfer tax shall be paid to the department of state revenue.
As added by P.L.67–1991, SEC.1.

Library References

Taxation ☞903.
WESTLAW Topic No. 371.
C.J.S. Taxation § 1220.

6–4.1–11.5–11   Federal generation-skipping transfer tax credit; contents of filing

Sec. 11.   A person who is required to file a return reporting a generation-skipping transfer that reflects a federal generation-skipping transfer tax credit under federal statutes and regulations shall, on or before the date specified in section 9 of this chapter, file the following with the department of state revenue:

(1) A copy of the federal return.

(2) A schedule indicating:

(A) the value of the transferred property legally located in Indiana; and

(B) the results of the formula set forth in section 8 of this chapter.

As added by P.L.67–1991, SEC.1.

6–4.1–11.5–12   Delinquent tax payment; interest

Sec. 12.   If the transfer tax is not paid on or before the due date set under section 9 of this chapter, the person who is required to pay the tax shall pay, in addition to the tax, interest on the delinquent portion of the tax at the rate of six percent (6%) per year. Interest under this section shall be charged from the due date of the tax until the date the tax is paid.

As added by P.L.67–1991, SEC.1.

Library References

Taxation ☞901.
WESTLAW Topic No. 371.
C.J.S. Taxation § 1207.

Chapter 12

General Administrative Provisions

6–4.1–12–1   Jurisdiction of probate court to determine inheritance tax

Sec. 1.   The probate court of the county:

(1) in which a resident decedent was domiciled at the time of the decedent's death; or

(2) in which the resident decedent's estate is being administered, if different from the county described in subdivision (1);

has jurisdiction to determine the inheritance tax imposed as a result of the resident decedent's death and to hear all matters related to the tax determination. However, if two (2) or more courts in a county have probate jurisdiction, the first court acquiring jurisdiction under this article acquires exclusive jurisdiction over the inheritance tax determination.

As added by Acts 1976, P.L.18, SEC.1. Amended by Acts 1977(ss), P.L.6, SEC.11; P.L.86–1995, SEC.9.

Historical and Statutory Notes

Acts 1976, P.L. 18, § 1, emerg. eff. Feb. 18, 1976, added this article.

The 1976 act added the provisions of this chapter as part of a codification, reenactment, revision and rearrangement of laws relating to death taxes.

361

Acts 1977(ss), P.L. 6, § 11, emerg. eff. July 1, 1977, at the beginning of the first sentence substituted "The" for "Each", "the county in which a resident decedent was domiciled at the time of his death" for "this state" and "the" for "a" following "as a result of."

P.L.86–1995, Sec.9, emerg. eff. retroactive to January 1, 1994, amended the section by designating Subsec. (1) and adding Subsec. (2).

P.L.86–1995, Sec.11, emerg. eff. retroactive to January 1, 1994, provides:

"(a) IC 6–4.1–12–1, as amended by this act, does not apply to the determination of inheritance tax for an estate of a resident decedent if the estate was opened before January 1, 1994.

"(b) This section expires January 1, 1999."

Formerly:

IC 6–4–1–6.

Acts 1931, c. 75, s. 6.

Cross References

Nonresident decedents, determination of inheritance tax due, see IC 6–4.1–5–14.

Library References

Courts ☜198.
Taxation ☜900(5).
WESTLAW Topic Nos. 106, 371.

C.J.S. Taxation § 1205.
I.L.E. Taxation § 232.

6–4.1–12–2 County assessor as inheritance tax appraiser; appointment of other; fees

Sec. 2. Each county assessor shall serve as the county inheritance tax appraiser for the county he serves. However, the appropriate probate court shall appoint a competent and qualified resident of the county to appraise property transferred by a resident decedent if the county assessor is:

(1) beneficially interested as an heir of the decedent's estate;

(2) the personal representative of the decedent's estate; or

(3) related to the decedent or a beneficiary of the decedent's estate within the third degree of consanguinity or affinity.

A person who is appointed to act as the county inheritance tax appraiser under this section shall receive a fee for his services. The court, subject to the approval of the department of state revenue, shall set the fee.

As added by Acts 1976, P.L.18, SEC.1.

Historical and Statutory Notes

Formerly:

IC 6–4–1–7.
IC 6–4–1–8.
Acts 1931, c. 75, ss. 7, 8.

Acts 1933, c. 229, s. 1.
Acts 1937, c. 285, s. 1.
Acts 1957, c. 318, ss. 1, 2.
Acts 1965, c. 324, s. 1.

Cross References

Review and appraisal of inheritance tax return, see IC 6–4.1–5–2.

Library References

Taxation ☜895(2).
WESTLAW Topic No. 371.

C.J.S. Taxation § 1195.
I.L.E. Taxation §§ 232, 239.

6–4.1–12–3   Repealed

(Repealed by Acts 1982, P.L.1, SEC.71.)

Historical and Statutory Notes

Acts 1982, P.L. 1, provided in Section 72, containing emergency clause, that the act takes effect April 1, 1982.

The repealed section provided for stenographic assistants and inheritance tax deputies in counties of 150,000 or more population.

Formerly:
IC 6–4–1–8.
Acts 1931, c. 75, s. 8.
Acts 1957, c. 318, s. 2.
Acts 1965, c. 324, s. 1.
Acts 1976, P.L.18, SEC.1.

6–4.1–12–4   Equipment costs

Sec. 4.   The county assessor shall receive funds from the county to pay the actual cost of equipment which he needs to perform the duties assigned to him under this article.

As added by Acts 1976, P.L.18, SEC.1.

Historical and Statutory Notes

Formerly:
IC 6–4–1–8.
Acts 1931, c. 75, s. 8.

Acts 1957, c. 318, s. 2.
Acts 1965, c. 324, s. 1.

6–4.1–12–5   Compromise agreements concerning tax or interest on delinquency

Sec. 5.   (a) If one (1) of the conditions listed in subsection (b) of this section exists, the department of state revenue may, with the advice and approval of the attorney general, enter into a compromise agreement concerning the amount of any inheritance tax, or interest charges on delinquent inheritance tax, to be collected under this article.   The department may enter into such an agreement with the personal representative of a decedent's estate or with the transferee of property transferred by the decedent.

(b) The department may enter into a compromise agreement under this section only if the department and the attorney general believe that a substantial doubt exists as to:

(1) the right to impose the tax under applicable Indiana law;

(2) the constitutionality, under either the Indiana or United States Constitutions, of the imposition of the tax;

(3) the correct value of property transferred under a taxable transfer;

(4) the correct amount of tax due;

(5) the collectability of the tax; or

(6) whether the decedent was a resident or a non-resident of this state.

(c) After payment of the inheritance tax agreed to by the parties to a compromise agreement entered into under this section, the issue of the amount of tax to be collected may be reopened only if the agreement was entered into fraudulently.

As added by Acts 1976, P.L.18, SEC.1.

Historical and Statutory Notes

Formerly:
IC 6–4–1–27.
IC 6–4–1–36.

Acts 1931, c. 75, ss. 28, 37.
Acts 1937, c. 159, s. 4.

Cross References

Future, contingent, defeasible or life interests in property, appraisal, see IC 6–4.1–6–1 et seq.

Library References

Taxation ☞901.
WESTLAW Topic No. 371.

C.J.S. Taxation § 1207.
I.L.E. Taxation §§ 247 to 249.

6–4.1–12–6 Powers and duties of department of state revenue

Sec. 6. The department of state revenue:

(1) shall supervise the enforcement of this article;

(2) shall supervise the collection of taxes imposed under this article;

(3) shall investigate the manner in which this article is administered and enforced in the various counties of this state;

(4) shall provide the forms and books required to implement this article;

(5) shall promulgate any rules or regulations which are necessary for the interpretation or the enforcement of this article;

(6) may investigate any facts or circumstances which are relevant to the taxes imposed under this article;

(7) shall provide the inheritance tax administrator with a secretary; and

(8) may provide the inheritance tax administrator with assistants, clerks, or stenographers.

As added by Acts 1976, P.L.18, SEC.1.

Historical and Statutory Notes

Formerly:
IC 6–4–1–31.
IC 6–4–1–34.

Acts 1931, c. 75, ss. 32, 35.
Acts 1937, c. 159, s. 5.

Cross References

Department of state revenue, see IC 6–8.1–2–1 et seq.

Notes of Decisions

Compliance with requirements   1
Regulations   2

1. Compliance with requirements

Inheritance tax return to which decedent's estate had attached only a copy of will and revocable trust agreement, and had not attached written form complying with requirements established by Department of Revenue for qualified terminable interest property (QTIP) elections, was insufficient to make proper QTIP election. Department of State Revenue, Inheritance Tax Div. v. Phelps, 1998, 697 N.E.2d 506.

Failure of decedent's estate to attach valid form making qualified terminable interest property (QTIP) election to initial inheritance tax return prevented transfer to decedent's surviving spouse from being treated as QTIP transfer, even though estate contended filed later return to which valid QTIP election form had been attached; later return, whether viewed as supplemental or amended return, could not cure initial failure to make valid election. Department of State Revenue, Inheritance Tax Div. v. Phelps, 1998, 697 N.E.2d 506.

Decedent's estate cannot cure failure to attach qualified terminable interest property (QTIP) election to initial inheritance tax return it files by filing subsequent inheritance tax returns containing QTIP election. Department of State Revenue, Inheritance Tax Div. v. Phelps, 1998, 697 N.E.2d 506.

2. Regulations

Regulation adopted by Department of Revenue regarding permissible form for qualified terminable interest property (QTIP) election was issued pursuant to Department's statutory authority, and has force of law. Department of State Revenue, Inheritance Tax Div. v. Phelps, 1998, 697 N.E.2d 506.

Regulations promulgated by Department of State Revenue under its statutory authority to issue regulations interpreting state's inheritance tax laws have the force of law; however, the Department has no authority to issue regulations that add to the law as enacted or extend its powers. Department of State Revenue, Inheritance Tax Div. v. Estate of Hardy, 1998, 703 N.E.2d 705.

6–4.1–12–6.5   Determination of department of state revenue resulting in tax increase; statement in rules

Sec. 6.5.   All changes in the department of state revenue's interpretations of IC 6–4.1 that could increase a person's tax liability must be stated in rules promulgated under IC 4–22–2.   In no event may a change in a departmental interpretation of IC 6–4.1 that could increase a person's tax liability take effect before the date on which it is promulgated in a rule.

As added by Acts 1979, P.L.75, SEC.14.

Historical and Statutory Notes

Acts 1979, P.L. 75, § 14, eff. July 1, 1979, added this section.

Library References

Taxation ☞446½.
WESTLAW Topic No. 371.

C.J.S. Taxation §§ 499, 501.
I.L.E. Taxation §§ 232, 241.

6–4.1–12–7   Investigative powers of department of state revenue; witness fees

Sec. 7.   For the purpose of conducting an investigation described under clause (3) or clause (6) of section 6 of this chapter, the department of state revenue may:

(1) subpoena evidence;

(2) subpoena witnesses;

(3) administer oaths; or

(4) take testimony concerning any matter.

Each witness examined by the department is entitled to receive a fee equal to the same fee paid witnesses subpoenaed to appear before a court of record. The witness fee shall be paid in the same manner that erroneous tax payments are refunded under IC 6–4.1–10.

As added by Acts 1976, P.L.18, SEC.1.

Historical and Statutory Notes

Formerly:
  IC 6–4–1–31.

Acts 1931, c. 75, s. 32.
Acts 1937, c. 159, s. 5.

Cross References

Witness fees, see IC 33–19–1–5 et seq.

6–4.1–12–8 Inheritance tax administrator; appointment; salary

Sec. 8. The governor shall, with the advice of the department of state revenue, appoint a state inheritance tax administrator. The inheritance tax administrator shall receive a salary to be fixed in the manner prescribed in IC 4–12–1–13. In addition, he shall receive the same mileage and travel allowances which other state employees receive.

As added by Acts 1976, P.L.18, SEC.1.

Historical and Statutory Notes

Formerly:
  IC 6–4–1–31.

Acts 1931, c. 75, s. 32.
Acts 1937, c. 159, s. 5.

Library References

Taxation ⟠895(2).
WESTLAW Topic No. 371.

C.J.S. Taxation § 1195.
I.L.E. Taxation § 232.

6–4.1–12–9 Powers and duties of inheritance tax administrator

Sec. 9. The inheritance tax administrator:

(1) shall supervise the administration of this article;

(2) shall, on behalf of the department of state revenue, perform the administrative duties assigned to the department under this article;

(3) shall file reports with the department of state revenue on the first day of January, April, July, and October of each year;

(4) may, with the approval of the governor, employ special auditors or appraisers to appraise any property interest which is transferred by a decedent under a taxable transfer; and

(5) may, with the approval of the governor, employ special counsel to advise the administrator or to represent the administrator or the department of state revenue in any proceeding initiated by or against the administrator or the department.

As added by Acts 1976, P.L.18, SEC.1.

Historical and Statutory Notes

Formerly:
IC 6–4–1–31.

Acts 1931, c. 75, s. 32.
Acts 1937, c. 159, s. 5.

Library References

Taxation ☞895(3).
WESTLAW Topic No. 371.

C.J.S. Taxation § 1196.
I.L.E. Taxation §§ 232, 250, 251.

6–4.1–12–10   Special auditor, appraiser or counsel; compensation

Sec. 10.   A special auditor, appraiser, or counsel appointed by the inheritance tax administrator under section 9 of this chapter shall receive compensation for his services in an amount fixed by the administrator and the governor. When a claim for the compensation is approved by the administrator and the governor, the state auditor shall issue a warrant to the claimant in the amount so approved.   The state auditor shall draw the warrant on taxes collected under this article.   The state treasurer shall pay the warrant.

As added by Acts 1976, P.L.18, SEC.1.

Historical and Statutory Notes

Formerly:
IC 6–4–1–31.

Acts 1931, c. 75, s. 32.
Acts 1937, c. 159, s. 5.

6–4.1–12–11   Information and investigations concerning non-resident's estates

Sec. 11.   The department of state revenue and the inheritance tax administrator shall gather information and make investigations concerning the estates of non-residents whose deaths result in the imposition of a tax under this article.

As added by Acts 1976, P.L.18, SEC.1.

Historical and Statutory Notes

Formerly:
IC 6–4–1–31.

Acts 1931, c. 75, s. 32.
Acts 1937, c. 159, s. 5.

6–4.1–12–12   Disclosure of inheritance tax information; offense

Sec. 12.   (a) The department, the department's counsel, agents, clerks, stenographers, other employees, or former employees, or any other person who gains access to the inheritance tax files shall not divulge any information disclosed by the documents required to be filed under this article.   However, disclosure may be made in the following cases:

(1) To comply with an order of a court.

(2) To the members and employees of the department.

(3) To the members and employees of county offices and courts to the extent they need the information for inheritance tax purposes. IC 5–14–3–6.5 does not apply to this subdivision.

(4) To the governor.

(5) To the attorney general.

(6) To any other legal representative of the state in any action pertaining to the tax due under this article.

(7) To any authorized officer of the United States, when the recipient agrees that the information is confidential and will be used solely for official purposes.

(8) Upon the receipt of a certified request, to any designated officer of a tax department of any other state, district, territory, or possession of the United States, when the state, district, territory, or possession permits the exchange of like information with the taxing officials of Indiana and when the recipient agrees that the information is confidential and will be used solely for tax collection purposes.

(9) Upon receipt of a written request, to the director of the division of family and children and to any county director of family and children, when the recipient agrees that the information is confidential and will be used only in connection with their official duties.

(10) To the attorney listed on the inheritance tax return under IC 6–4.1–4–1 or IC 6–4.1–4–7.

(11) To a devisee, an heir, a successor in interest, or a surviving joint tenant of the decedent for whom an inheritance tax return was filed or, upon the receipt of a written request, to an agent or attorney of a devisee, an heir, a successor in interest, or a surviving joint tenant of the decedent.

(b) Any person who knowingly violates this section:

(1) commits a Class C misdemeanor; and

(2) shall be immediately dismissed from the person's office or employment, if the person is an officer or employee of the state.

As added by P.L.26–1985, SEC.13. Amended by P.L.67–1988, SEC.3; P.L.58–1990, SEC.4; P.L.2–1992, SEC.70; P.L.4–1993, SEC.10; P.L.5–1993, SEC.22.

Historical and Statutory Notes

P.L.26–1985, Sec.13, eff. July 1, 1986, added this section.

P.L. 67–1988, Sec.3, added Subsec. (a)(10), permitting disclosures to the attorney listed on the inheritance tax return.

P.L.58–1990, Sec.4, inserted Subsec. (a)(11), permitting disclosures to devisees, heirs, successors in interest, or surviving joint tenants.

P.L.2–1992, Sec.70, emerg. eff. Feb. 14, 1992, substituted "director" for "administrator" and "division of family and children" for "department of public welfare" in Subsec. (a)(9).

P.L.4–1993, Sec.10, and P.L.5–1993, Sec.22, by identical language, in Subsec. (a)(9), substituted a reference to county directors of family and children for a reference to county welfare directors.

Library References

Taxation ⚖️905(1).
WESTLAW Topic No. 371.
C.J.S. Taxation § 1223.

ARTICLE 5

FINANCIAL INSTITUTION TAXES

WESTLAW Computer Assisted Legal Research

WESTLAW supplements your legal research in many ways. WESTLAW allows you to

- update your research with the most current information
- expand your library with additional resources
- retrieve current, comprehensive history and citing references to a case with KeyCite

For more information on using WESTLAW to supplement your research, see the WESTLAW Electronic Research Guide, which follows the Preface.

Chapter 1

Intangibles Tax

6–5–1–1 to 6–5–1–34   Repealed

(Repealed by Acts 1977, P.L.84, SEC.2.)

Historical and Statutory Notes

Acts 1977, P.L. 84, provided in § 7, containing emergency clause, that the act takes effect April 12, 1977.

The former chapter related to the intangibles tax.

Formerly:
IC 6–5–1–9.
IC 6–5–1–12 to 6–5–1–16.
IC 6–5–1–18.
IC 6–5–1–20 to 6–5–1–22.
IC 6–5–1–25 to 6–5–1–29.
IC 6–5–1–32.

Acts 1933, c. 81, ss. 10, 15, 16, 17, 20, 21, 26, 32, 33, 35 to 40.
Acts 1935, c. 294, s. 4.
Acts 1945, c. 51, s. 2.
Acts 1947, c. 198, s. 1.

Acts 1951, c. 278, s. 3.
Acts 1955, c. 287, s. 4.
Acts 1957, c. 348, s. 2.
Acts 1959, c. 317, s. 3.
Acts 1965, c. 226, ss. 4, 12, 13.
Acts 1971, P.L.67, SECS.4, 8.

DISPOSITION TABLE

Showing where the subject matter of the repealed sections of Title 6 of the Indiana Code is now covered in new sections of Title 6, West's Annotated Indiana Code.

Repealed Sections	New Sections
6–5–1–1(a)	6–5.1–1–1, 6–5.1–5–7 (13 to 17)
6–5–1–1(b)	6–5.1–5–6, 6–5.1–5–7 (1 to 12, 15 to 17, and 20)
6–5–1–1(c)	6–5.1–3–1
6–5–1–1(c)(1)	6–5.1–1–2
6–5–1–1(c)(2)	6–5.1–1–3
6–5–1–1(d)	6–5.1–1–4
6–5–1–1(e)	—
6–5–1–1(f)	6–5.1–1–5
6–5–1–1(g)	—
6–5–1–1(h)	—
6–5–1–1(i)	6–5.1–1–6
6–5–1–1(j)	—
6–5–1–1(k)	6–5.1–1–7, 6–5.1–2–1(c), 6–5.1–5–7(17)
6–5–1–2	6–5.1–2–1(a), (b), 6–5.1–5–7(17)
6–5–1–3	6–5.1–2–2
6–5–1–4	6–5.1–3–2, 6–5.1–3–3
6–5–1–5	6–5.1–3–2(d), 6–5.1–3–4, 6–5.1–3–5, 6–5.1–8–2(b), (c) [Repealed]
6–5–1–6	6–5.1–3–5, 6–5.1–3–6
6–5–1–7	6–5.1–3–7, 6–5.1–7–1 [Repealed]
6–5–1–8	6–5.1–1–2
6–5–1–9	—
6–5–1–10	6–5.1–6–1, 6–5.1–6–2, 6–5.1–8–3 [Repealed], 6–5.1–8–5(a) [Repealed], 6–5.1–9–3
6–5–1–11	6–5.1–6–1(a), 6–5.1–8–3 [Repealed], 6–5.1–8–4(b) [Repealed]
6–5–1–12	6–5.1–9–5(e) [Repealed]
6–5–1–13	6–5.1–9–5(a), (b) [Repealed]
6–5–1–14	—
6–5–1–15	6–5.1–6–4 [Repealed], 6–5.1–8–1 [Repealed], 6–5.1–8–2(b), (d) [Repealed], 6–5.1–8–3 [Repealed], 6–5.1–8–5(a)(3) [Repealed]
6–5–1–16	6–5.1–9–5(c), (d) [Repealed], 6–5.1–9–6(b) [Repealed]
6–5–1–17	6–5.1–8–10
6–5–1–18	6–5.1–8–4(a), (b) [Repealed]
6–5–1–19	6–5.1–5–4
6–5–1–20	—
6–5–1–21	6–5.1–8–6 [Repealed]
6–5–1–22	6–5.1–8–1 [Repealed]
6–5–1–23	6–5.1–6–3, 6–5.1–8–1 [Repealed], 6–5.1–8–2(a) to (c) [Repealed], 6–5.1–8–7 [Repealed], 6–5.1–8–8 [Repealed]
6–5–1–24(a)	6–5.1–9–2 to 6–5.1–9–4
6–5–1–24(b)	6–5.1–9–6(a) [Repealed]
6–5–1–25	6–5.1–8–9 [Repealed]
6–5–1–26	—
6–5–1–27	6–5.1–9–1 [Repealed]
6–5–1–28	—
6–5–1–29	—
6–5–1–30	6–5.1–7–2
6–5–1–31(a)	6–5.1–4–1, 6–5.1–6–1(a)
6–5–1–31(b)	6–5.1–4–2
6–5–1–31(c)	6–5.1–4–3
6–5–1–31(d)	6–5.1–4–4, 6–5.1–4–5
6–5–1–31(e)	6–5.1–4–4, 6–5.1–8–3 [Repealed]
6–5–1–31(f)	6–5.1–4–4, 6–5.1–8–4(b) [Repealed]
6–5–1–31(g)	6–5.1–4–3
6–5–1–32	6–5.1–8–11 [Repealed]
6–5–1–33	6–5.1–5–2
6–5–1–34	6–5.1–5–7(19)

Chapter 2

Exemption—Intangibles Held By Nonprofit Organizations

6–5–2–1, 6–5–2–2 Repealed

(Repealed by Acts 1977, P.L.84, SEC.2.)

Historical and Statutory Notes

Acts 1977, P.L. 84, provided in § 7, containing emergency clause, that the act takes effect April 12, 1977.

The former chapter related to intangibles tax exemptions for intangibles held by nonprofit organizations.

For subject matter of former § 6–5–2–1, see now, § 6–5.1–5–1.

Formerly:

IC 6–5–2–2.
Acts 1945, c. 170, s. 3.

Chapter 3

Exemption—Certain Pension Profit Sharing And Stock Bonus Trusts

6–5–3–1 Repealed

(Repealed by Acts 1977, P.L.84, SEC.2.)

Historical and Statutory Notes

Acts 1977, P.L. 84, provided in § 7, containing emergency clause, that the act takes effect April 12, 1977.

The former chapter related to intangibles tax exemptions for certain pensions, profit sharing plans and stock bonus trusts.

See, now, IC 6–5.1–5–5.

Chapter 3.5

Exemption For Certain Individuals

6–5–3.5–1, 6–5–3.5–2 Repealed

(Repealed by Acts 1977, P.L.84, SEC.2.)

Historical and Statutory Notes

Acts 1977, P.L. 84, provided in § 7, containing emergency clause, that the act takes effect April 12, 1977.

The former chapter related to intangibles tax exemptions for individuals whose annual household income did not exceed $10,000.

See, now, IC 6–5.1–5–3.

Chapter 4

Penalties For Nonpayment Of Intangibles Tax

6-5-4-1　Repealed

(Repealed by Acts 1977, P.L.84, SEC.2.)

Historical and Statutory Notes

Acts 1977, P.L. 84, provided in § 7, containing emergency clause, that the act takes effect April 12, 1977.

The former chapter related to penalties for nonpayment of intangibles tax.

Formerly:

Acts 1965, c. 226, s. 14.

Chapter 5

Deputy Assessor For Intangibles

6-5-5-1　Repealed

(Repealed by Acts 1977, P.L.84, SEC.2.)

Historical and Statutory Notes

Acts 1977, P.L. 84, provided in § 7, containing emergency clause, that the act takes effect April 12, 1977.

The former chapter related to the deputy assessor for intangibles.

Formerly:

Acts 1935, c. 201, s. 1.
Acts 1949, c. 244, s. 1.
Acts 1955, c. 116, s. 1.

Chapter 6

Bank Tax

6-5-6-1 to 6-5-6-16　Repealed

(Repealed by P.L.88–1983, SEC.14.)

Historical and Statutory Notes

P.L. 88–1983 provided in Section 17 that the act takes effect June 1, 1983.

The repealed sections, dealing generally with financial institution taxes, defined terms, set out the types of property assessed, and set out tax payment procedures.

Formerly:

IC 6-5-6-3.
Acts 1933, c. 83, s. 3.
Acts 1973, P.L.52, SEC.1.

DISPOSITION TABLE

Showing where the subject matter of the repealed sections of Title 6 is now covered in new sections of Title 6, West's Annotated Indiana Code.

Repealed Sections	New Sections	Repealed Sections	New Sections
6–5–6–1	6–5–10–1	6–5–6–9	6–5–10–9
6–5–6–2	6–5–10–3	6–5–6–10	6–5–10–10
6–5–6–3	None	6–5–6–11	6–5–10–5
6–5–6–4	6–5–10–3		6–5–10–7
6–5–6–5	6–5–10–3	6–5–6–12	6–5–10–6
6–5–6–6	6–5–10–2	6–5–6–13	6–5–10–3
6–5–6–7	6–5–10–8	6–5–6–14	6–5–10–14
6–5–6–8	6–5–10–4	6–5–6–15	6–5–10–12
		6–5–6–16	6–5–10–17

6–5–6–17 Repealed

(Repealed by Acts 1980, P.L.61, SEC.15; P.L.88–1983, SEC.14.)

Historical and Statutory Notes

Acts 1980, P.L. 61, provided in § 16 that the act takes effect Jan. 1, 1981.

The former section related to the failure to file a return and penalties therefor.

Provisions pertaining to filing of tax forms and penalties imposed by the department of state revenue are now contained in §§ 6–8.1–6–1 et seq. and 6–8.1–10–1 et seq.

Formerly:
Acts 1933, c. 83, s. 17.
Acts 1935, c. 298, s. 5.
Acts 1975, P.L.65, SEC.8.

6–5–6–18 to 6–5–6–20 Repealed

(Repealed by P.L.88–1983, SEC.14.)

Historical and Statutory Notes

P.L.88–1983 provided in Section 17 that the act takes effect June 1, 1983.

For subject matter of former section 6–5–6–18, see sections 6–5–10–15, 6–5–10–16.

Formerly:
IC 6–5–6–19.

IC 6–5–6–20.
Acts 1933, c. 83, ss. 19, 20.
Acts 1937, c. 235, s. 1.

6–5–6–21 to 6–5–6–24 Repealed

(Repealed by Acts 1980, P.L.61, SEC.15; P.L.88–1983, SEC.14.)

Historical and Statutory Notes

Acts 1980, P.L. 61, provided in § 16 that the act takes effect Jan. 1, 1981.

Former §§ 6–5–6–21 and 6–5–6–22 related to the administration of the chapter.

Former § 6–5–6–23 related to investigatory powers.

Former § 6–5–6–24 related to penalties for unpaid tax.

Provisions pertaining to penalties by and the powers and duties of the department of state revenue are now contained in §§ 6–8.1–10–1 et seq. and 6–8.1–3–1 et seq.

Formerly:
Acts 1975, P.L.65, SECS.10 to 13.
Acts 1977, P.L.2, SEC.32.
Acts 1978, P.L.2, SEC.626.

6–5–6–25 Repealed

(Repealed by P.L.88–1983, SEC.14.)

Historical and Statutory Notes

P.L.88–1983 provided in Section 17 that the act takes effect June 1, 1983.

The repealed section related to refunding of excess payments, received by local units of government, to the state treasurer.

See, now, IC 6–5–10–13.

For construction and savings provisions relating to the repealed section, see the note under section 6–5–10–1.

Formerly:

Acts 1975, P.L.65, SEC.14.

6–5–6–26 to 6–5–6–28 Repealed

(Repealed by Acts 1980, P.L.61, SEC.15; P.L.88–1983, SEC.14.)

Historical and Statutory Notes

Acts 1980, P.L. 61, provided in § 16 that the act takes effect Jan. 1, 1981.

Former § 6–5–6–26 related to incorrect returns.

Former § 6–5–6–27 related to refunds for overpayment.

Former § 6–5–6–28 related to confidential information.

Provisions pertaining to filing, refunds and confidential information are now contained in §§ 6–8.1–6–1 et seq., 6–8.1–7–1 et seq. and 6–8.1–9–1 et seq.

Formerly:

Acts 1975, P.L.65, SECS.15 to 17.
Acts 1978, P.L.2, SEC.627.

6–5–6–29 Repealed

(Repealed by P.L.88–1983, SEC.14.)

Historical and Statutory Notes

P.L.88–1983 provided in Section 17 that the act takes effect June 1, 1983.

The repealed section set out the procedure for payments under protest.

See, now, IC 6–5–10–11.

Formerly:
Acts 1975, P.L.65, SEC.18.

6–5–6–30 Repealed

(Repealed by Acts 1980, P.L.61, SEC.15; P.L.88–1983, SEC.14.)

Historical and Statutory Notes

Acts 1980, P.L. 61, provided in § 16 that the act takes effect Jan. 1, 1981.

The former section related to department records.

Provisions pertaining to records of the department of state revenue are now contained in § 6–8.1–3–6.

Formerly:

Acts 1975, P.L.65, SEC.19.

6–5–6–31 Repealed

(Repealed by P.L.88–1983, SEC.14.)

Historical and Statutory Notes

P.L.88–1983 provided in Sections 17 that the act takes effect June 1, 1983.

The repealed section provided for severability.

Formerly:

Acts 1975, P.L.65, SEC.20.

Chapter 7

Construction Of Bank Tax

6–5–7–1   Repealed

(Repealed by P.L.88–1983, SEC.14.)

Historical and Statutory Notes

P.L.88–1983 provided in Section 17 that this act takes effect June 1, 1983.

The repealed section related to the construction of certain financial institutions tax statutes

in the event of judicially-determined partial invalidity.

Formerly:

Acts 1939, c. 158, s. 2.

Chapter 8

Savings And Loan Association Tax

6–5–8–1 to 6–5–8–9   Repealed

(Repealed by P.L.88–1983, SEC.14.)

Historical and Statutory Notes

P.L. 88–1983 provided in Section 17 that the act takes effect June 1, 1983.

The repealed sections, relating generally to taxation of savings and loan associations, defined terms and provided for the assessment, imposition, rate, computation, payment and allocation of tax.

Formerly:

IC 6–5–8–2.
IC 6–5–8–3.
Acts 1933, c. 82, ss. 2, 3.
Acts 1933, c. 82, s. 3.

DISPOSITION TABLE

Showing where the subject matter of the repealed sections of Title 6 is now covered in new sections of Title 6, West's Annotated Indiana Code.

Repealed Sections	New Sections	Repealed Sections	New Sections
6–5–8–1	6–5–11–1	6–5–8–6	6–5–11–3
6–5–8–2	None	6–5–8–6.5	6–5–11–4
6–5–8–3	None		6–5–11–5
6–5–8–4	6–5–11–2	6–5–8–7	6–5–11–6
		6–5–8–7.1	6–5–11–7
6–5–8–5	6–5–11–2	6–5–8–8	6–5–11–4
6–5–8–5.1	6–5–11–2	6–5–8–9	6–5–11–11

6–5–8–10   Repealed

(Repealed by Acts 1980, P.L.61, SEC.15; P.L.88–1983, SEC.14.)

Historical and Statutory Notes

Acts 1980, P.L. 61, provided in § 16 that the act takes effect Jan. 1, 1981.

The former section related to penalties for failure to pay taxes or to report when due.

Provisions pertaining to penalties are now contained in §§ 6–8.1–10–1 et seq.

Formerly:
Acts 1933, c. 82, s. 10.

6–5–8–11 to 6–5–8–14   Repealed

(Repealed by P.L.88–1983, SEC.14.)

Historical and Statutory Notes

P.L.88–1983 provided in Section 17 that the act takes effect June 1, 1983.

The repealed sections, dealing generally with the savings and loan association tax, provided for liens in the event of unpaid tax, offenses for failure to file and fraudulent statements, and procedures in the event of liquidation.

The subject matter of the repealed sections is now covered in new sections of Title 6 as follows:

Repealed Sections	New Sections
6–5–8–11	6–5–11–8
6–5–8–12	6–5–11–10
6–5–8–13	None
6–5–8–14	6–5–11–9

Formerly:
IC 6–5–8–13.
Acts 1933, c. 82, s. 13.

Chapter 9

Production Credit Association Tax

6–5–9–1 to 6–5–9–12   Repealed

(Repealed by P.L.88–1983, SEC.14.)

Historical and Statutory Notes

P.L.88–1983 provided in Section 17 that the act takes effect June 1, 1983.

The repealed chapter assessed a tax against production credit associations and their property.

Formerly:
IC 6–5–9–2.
IC 6–5–9–3.
Acts 1949, c. 29, ss. 2, 3.

DISPOSITION TABLE

Showing where the subject matter of the repealed sections of Title 6 is now covered in new sections of Title 6, West's Annotated Indiana Code.

Repealed Sections	New Sections	Repealed Sections	New Sections
6–5–9–1	6–5–12–1	6–5–9–4	6–5–12–2
6–5–9–2	None	6–5–9–5	6–5–12–2
6–5–9–3	None		

Chapter 10

Bank Tax

Library References

Taxation ⊂⇒125 to 131.
WESTLAW Topic No. 371.
C.J.S. Taxation §§ 143 to 149.

6–5–10–1 Definitions

Sec. 1. As used in this chapter:

"Assessed value" means assessed value as defined in IC 6–1.1–1–3.

"Bank" means a:

(1) bank, trust company, savings bank, bank of discount and deposit, or loan and trust and safe deposit company organized under the law of this state; or

(2) national banking association organized under the law of the United States and engaged in business in this state.

378

The term "bank" does not include an international banking facility.

"Department" means the department of state revenue.

"Deposit" means money that is deposited in a bank, that is evidenced by any means, and that may be withdrawn, on demand or otherwise, by:

(1) the owner of the money;

(2) the trustee of the money; or

(3) a person who has a beneficial interest in the money.

"Deposits of another financial institution" means deposits that are owned by and may be withdrawn by another bank, a savings association, or an international banking facility located in Indiana.

"International banking facility" means an international banking facility as defined in Regulation D of the Board of Governors of the Federal Reserve System (12 CFR 204).

"Liquidating agent" means a person, an official, or a department that is in charge of the assets of a bank that has ceased business.

"Nonresident deposit" means a deposit that:

(1) is owned by a person, firm, limited liability company, or corporation that resides or is domiciled outside Indiana; and

(2) does not have a business situs in Indiana.

"Public deposit" means a deposit that is owned by and may be withdrawn by:

(1) this state;

(2) a political subdivision of this state;

(3) an agency of this state;

(4) the United States; or

(5) a department, an agency, or an instrumentality of the United States.

"Taxable deposits" means taxable deposits as defined in section 2 of this chapter.

"Taxable shares" means the capital, surplus, and undivided profits of a bank minus the assessed value of all real estate that is owned by the bank or leased by the bank and used for banking purposes.

"Taxable surplus and profits" means the total surplus and undivided profits of a savings bank minus the assessed value of all real estate owned by the savings bank or leased by the savings bank and used for banking purposes.

"Taxpayer" means an entity that is liable for the tax imposed under this chapter.

As added by P.L.88–1983, SEC.1. Amended by P.L.79–1983, SEC.3; P.L.42–1993, SEC.5; P.L.79–1998, SEC.12.

Historical and Statutory Notes

P.L.88–1983, Sec.1, eff. June 1, 1983, added this chapter.

Sections 15 and 16 of P.L.88–1983 provided:

"Section 15. (a) This act is intended to be a codification and restatement of applicable or corresponding provisions of IC 6–5–6, IC 6–5–7, IC 6–5–8, and IC 6–5–9. If this act repeals and replaces a provision in the same form or in a restated form, the substantive operation and effect of that provision continues uninterrupted.

"(b) This act does not affect any:

"(1) rights or liabilities accrued;

"(2) penalties incurred;

"(3) offenses committed; or

"(4) proceedings begun;

"before the effective date of this act. Those rights, liabilities, penalties, offenses, and proceedings continue and shall be imposed and enforced under IC 6–5–6, IC 6–5–7, IC 6–5–8, or IC 6–5–9 as if this act had not been enacted.

"Section 16. The general assembly may, by concurrent resolution, preserve any of the background materials related to this act."

P.L.79–1983, Sec.3, eff. July 1, 1983, added the second sentence in the definition of "Bank"; and, in the definition of "Deposits of another financial institution", inserted "or an international banking facility"; and inserted the definition of "International banking facility".

Section 5(c) of P.L.79–1983 provided that Section 3 of this act first applies to taxes that accrue and are computed under IC 6–5–6 for months and years that begin after June 30, 1983.

P.L.42–1993, Sec.5, emerg. eff. May 13, 1993, deleted a reference to private banks in the definition of "Bank"; inserted a reference to a limited liability company in the definition of "Nonresident deposit"; and made nonsubstantive language changes throughout.

P.L.79–1998, Sec.12, amended the section by substituting "savings" for "building and loan" under the definition of "Deposits of another financial institution".

Formerly:

IC 6–5–6–1.
Acts 1933, c. 83, s. 1.
Acts 1935, c. 298, s. 1.
Acts 1975, P.L.65, SEC.1.

Cross References

Administration, enforcement, and collection of tax, department of state revenue, see IC 6–8.1–1–1 et seq.
Community revitalization enhancement district tax credit, state and local tax liability, see IC 6–3.1–19–1.
County supplemental school distribution fund, deposits and distributions, see 21–2–12–6.1.
Industrial loan and investment companies, intangible taxation in manner of banks and trust companies, see IC 28–5–1–23.
Institutions subject to bank tax, personal property not subject to property tax assessment and taxation, see IC 6–1.1–2–6.
Military base recovery tax credit,
  Against other taxes owed, priority of application, see IC 6–3.1–11.5–24.
  State tax liability, see IC 6–3.1–11.5–14.
Library property taxes, replacement credits, see IC 6–3.5–7–23.
National banking and savings and loan association credit, see IC 6–2.1–4.5–1 et seq.

Library References

Notes of Decisions

Banks 1
Taxable shares 2
Taxable surplus 3

---

1. Banks

Organization which, through its agencies, made loans, but indulged in no other elements

of banking, were not banks within purview of chapter 83 of Acts of 1933 [now this chapter] imposing an intangible tax. 1934 Op.Atty.Gen. p. 57.

2. Taxable shares

While board of review had to exercise discretion in fixing value of capital stock of a bank, deduction of the assessed value of realty in which surplus was invested from valuation of the stock was an administrative matter, commanded by statute to be made from statement which should have been furnished by the bank. Smith v. Stephens, 1910, 91 N.E. 167, 173 Ind. 564.

Prior statute providing that, where the capital stock of a domestic corporation is invested in tangible property returned for taxation, the stock shall not be assessed to the extent that it is so invested, contemplated the ascertainment of the cash value of the stock; and, if its value exceeded that of the tangible property in which it was invested, it was taxable on the excess, but if the tangible property exceeded the capital stock in value, the stock was not taxable. Smith v. Stephens, 1910, 91 N.E. 167, 173 Ind. 564.

Real estate taken by a bank in payment of a debt, and that owned by it and necessary for its immediate accommodation, is a part of its capital stock, and therefore not subject to taxation as real estate, where the taxation of the capital stock is otherwise provided for. State Bank v. Brackenridge, 1845, 7 Blackf. 395.

3. Taxable surplus

Proper basis for assessment of surplus of bank invested in realty was value of capital, surplus,

and undivided profits, not including any amount represented in the real estate, but where value of real estate was not included by bank in making its returns, bank was not entitled to further deduction of assessed value of the real estate. Smith v. Stephens, 1910, 91 N.E. 167, 173 Ind. 564.

In absence of a contrary showing, land in which the surplus of a bank is invested would be presumed equal in value to the amount invested therein for the purposes of taxation. Smith v. Stephens, 1910, 91 N.E. 167, 173 Ind. 564.

Under prior statute, providing that the assessed valuation of realty owned by a bank shall be deducted from the valuation of the capital or capital stock of the bank, while the board of review must exercise discretion in fixing the value of the stock, the deduction of the assessed value of realty in which the surplus is invested from the valuation of the stock is an administrative matter, commanded by the statute to be made from the statement which should be furnished by the bank. Smith v. Stephens, 1910, 91 N.E. 167, 173 Ind. 564.

6–5–10–2 "Taxable deposits" defined

Sec. 2. (a) Subject to the limitations established in subsections (b) and (c), "taxable deposits" is the remainder of the total deposits in the bank minus:

(1) public deposits, nonresident deposits, and deposits of another financial institution in the bank; and

(2) obligations of the United States, an instrumentality of the United States, this state, or an agency or political subdivision of this state, that are owned by the bank.

(b) The amount subtracted under subsection (a)(2) may not exceed one-half (½) of the remainder of the total deposits in the bank minus public deposits, nonresident deposits, and deposits of another financial institution in the bank.

(c) The amount of the obligations of the United States or an instrumentality of the United States that is used under subsection (a)(2) is the average of the amount of those obligations owned by the bank at the end of each business day during the calendar month in which the value of the taxable deposits is determined.

As added by P.L.88–1983, SEC.1.

Historical and Statutory Notes

Formerly:

IC 6–5–6–6.
Acts 1933, c. 83, s. 6.

Acts 1935, c. 298, s. 2.
Acts 1943, c. 32, s. 1.
Acts 1975, P.L.65, SEC.2.

Library References

Taxation ⟨⟩126.
WESTLAW Topic No. 371.

C.J.S. Taxation §§ 143, 144.
I.L.E. Taxation §§ 32, 33.

Notes of Decisions

Deposits   2
Exempt investments of capital stock   3
Validity of prior laws   1

ers, was not invalid as denying the equal protection of the laws, for the classification was reasonable. Board of Com'rs of Johnson County v. Johnson, 1909, 89 N.E. 590, 173 Ind. 76.

1. Validity of prior laws

Acts 1903, p. 64, c. 29, § 27 [repealed], authorizing unincorporated banks to deduct for purposes of taxation amount of their deposits from moneys, credits, and other assets other than real estate was not invalid. Board of Com'rs of Johnson County v. Johnson, 1909, 89 N.E. 590, 173 Ind. 76.

Acts 1903, p. 64, c. 29, § 27, authorizing unincorporated banks to deduct for purposes of taxation the amount of their deposits from moneys, credits, and other assets other than real estate, while individuals could only deduct their indebtedness from credits proper, and while unincorporated banks could deduct the assessed value of their real estate and tangible property and indebtedness in fixing the value of the shares which were taxed to the individual own-

2. Deposits

Money on deposit in a savings bank is regarded for taxation as the chattel of the depositor, and not as a credit due him, and hence is taxable to the depositor. Beard v. People's Sav. Bank, App.1913, 101 N.E. 325, 53 Ind.App. 185.

3. Exempt investments of capital stock

Capital stock of national bank invested in government bonds was not taxable by state as against bank. Beard v. People's Sav. Bank, App.1913, 101 N.E. 325, 53 Ind.App. 185.

That the capital of the bank was invested in United States bonds did not affect the right of the state to tax the shares under the act of Congress. A tax upon the shares of a bank was not a tax upon the property or capital of the bank. Wright v. Stilz, 1866, 27 Ind. 338.

6–5–10–3   Imposition of tax; rate; payment; lien

Sec. 3.   (a) A tax is imposed at the rate of one-fourth of one percent (0.25%) per year on the value of all taxable deposits, taxable shares, and taxable surplus and profits.

(b) Taxable deposits, taxable shares, and taxable surplus and profits shall be assessed to their respective owners.

(c) Except as provided in section 14 of this chapter, each bank shall, on the last day of each month, determine the tax on taxable deposits in the bank, taxable shares of the bank, and taxable surplus and profits of the bank. Except as provided in sections 11 and 14 of this chapter, the entity liable for the tax shall pay the tax to the treasurer of the county in which the bank is located before the twenty-first day of the following month.

(d) Except as provided in section 14 of this chapter, the tax imposed by this chapter on taxable deposits and taxable shares becomes a lien on those taxable deposits and taxable shares, and the tax imposed by this chapter on taxable surplus and profits becomes a lien on the assets and property of the bank, at the time that the bank is required to determine the tax under subsection (c).

As added by P.L.88–1983, SEC.1.

Historical and Statutory Notes

Formerly:

IC 6–5–6–2.
IC 6–5–6–4.
IC 6–5–6–5.
IC 6–5–6–13.

Acts 1933, c. 83, s. 2.
Acts 1933, c. 83, s. 4.
Acts 1933, c. 83, s. 5.
Acts 1933, c. 83, s. 13.
Acts 1975, P.L.65, SEC.6.

Cross References

Industrial loan and investment companies, applicability of bank tax, see IC 28–5–1–23.
Investment credits against bank tax, see IC 6–3.1–5–1 et seq.
Purchases qualifying for investment credit, exemption from bank tax, see IC 6–3.1–5–11.

Law Review and Journal Commentaries

Taxation of state bank shares owned by Delaware corporation in Minnesota. 13 Ind.L.J. 79 (1937).

Library References

Taxation ⊕125 to 131.
WESTLAW Topic No. 371.

C.J.S. Taxation §§ 143 to 149.
I.L.E. Taxation §§ 32, 33.

WESTLAW Electronic Research

See WESTLAW Electronic Research Guide following the Preface.

United States Code Annotated

State taxation of national banks, see 12 U.S.C.A. § 548.

United States Supreme Court

Tax on net earnings of banks, interest received on obligations of the United States and other states, see Memphis Bank & Trust Co. v. Garner, 1983, 103 S.Ct. 692, 459 U.S. 392, 74 L.Ed.2d 562.

Notes of Decisions

Construction with federal statute 2
National banks 3
Validity of prior laws 1

----

1. Validity of prior laws

Acts 1933, cc. 81 to 83 [§ 6–5–1–1 et seq. (repealed; see, now, § 6–5.1–1–1 et seq.); § 6–5–6–1 et seq. (repealed; see, now, § 6–5–10–1 et seq.); and § 6–5–8–1 et seq. (repealed; see, now, § 6–5–11–1 et seq.)] providing for the taxation of intangibles, building and loan associations, and banks and trust companies were not unconstitutional as granting special privileges or immunities to certain classes, or as abridging the privileges or immunities of citizens of the United States, or denying any person equal protection of the law. Lutz v. Arnold, 1935, 193 N.E. 840, 208 Ind. 480, rehearing overruled 196 N.E. 702, 208 Ind. 480.

Acts 1933, cc. 81 to 83 [§ 6–5–1–1 et seq. (repealed; see, now, § 6–5.1–1–1 et seq.); § 6–5–6–1 et seq. (repealed; see, now, § 6–5–11–1 et seq.)], providing for taxation of intangibles, building and loan associations, and banks and trust companies were not unconstitutional because of the exemption of certain intangibles from personal property taxes nor unconstitutional as "local" or "special" laws under Const. Art. 4, § 22. Lutz v. Arnold, 1935, 193 N.E. 840, 208 Ind. 480, rehearing overruled 196 N.E. 702, 208 Ind. 480.

Acts 1903, p. 64, c. 29, § 27, providing for the taxation of unincorporated banks, was not invalid as a local or special act, for it provided for a reasonable classification, and was of uniform operation throughout the state, and operated alike on all coming within the classification. Board of Com'rs of Johnson County v. Johnson, 1909, 89 N.E. 590, 173 Ind. 76.

Where the tax law of a state allows taxpayers to deduct their debts from the assessed value of a class of credits which constitute a material portion of the moneyed capital of the state in the hands of its citizens, but denies to the owners of national bank stock the right to deduct their debts from the assessed value of such stock, it is such a discrimination, in view of the provisions of federal law, relating to national banks, as renders the state law to that extent inoperative. Wasson v. First Nat. Bank, 1886, 8 N.E. 97, 107 Ind. 206.

A tax laid by a state on banks, "on a valuation equal to the amount of their capital stock paid in, or secured to be paid in," is a tax on the property of the institution; and, when that property consists of stocks of the federal government, the law laying the tax is void. Whitney v. City of Madison, 1864, 23 Ind. 331.

2. Construction with federal statute

Act Cong. June 30, 1864 (13 Stat. 218), declaring that all bonds, treasury notes, and other obligations of the United States shall be exempt from state taxation, and that the words "obligation or other security of the United States" meant all bonds, national currency, United States notes, and other representations of value

which could have been or could be issued under any act of congress, did not exempt the notes of national banks from state taxation. Board of Com'rs of Montgomery County v. Elston, 1869, 32 Ind. 27, 2 Am.Rep. 327.

3. National banks

National banks are agents and instrumentalities of federal government, and cannot be taxed by states without consent of Congress. Davis v. Sexton, 1936, 200 N.E. 233, 210 Ind. 138.

Tax on cash value of national bank shares was not illegal on ground that competing moneyed capital in substantial amount in hands of individual citizens was allowed debt deduction while right was denied to capital invested in bank shares, where bona fide indebtedness was deducted in arriving at value of bank shares. Davis v. Sexton, 1936, 200 N.E. 233, 210 Ind. 138.

The shares of national banks are by the act of Congress authorizing such associations placed within the reach of the taxing power of the states, subject to certain conditions, which were intended to prevent any discrimination against such shares. Wright v. Stilz, 1866, 27 Ind. 338.

6–5–10–4   Election to pay taxes; notice; effectiveness

Sec. 4.   On the last day of each month, each bank shall elect whether it will pay the taxes imposed by this chapter on its taxable shares, taxable deposits, or both.   Each bank shall file a written notice of the election with the auditor of the county in which it is located before the sixteenth day of the succeeding month.   The election remains in effect unless it is revoked in writing by the bank.

As added by P.L.88–1983, SEC.1.

Historical and Statutory Notes

Formerly:
  IC 6–5–6–8.
  Acts 1933, c. 83, s. 8.

Library References

Taxation ⚯128, 130.
WESTLAW Topic No. 371.
C.J.S. Taxation §§ 146, 148.

6–5–10–5   Banks electing to pay taxes; deductions from and charges to shareholders and depositors prohibited

Sec. 5.   A bank that pays the tax imposed by this chapter may not:

  (1) deduct the amount of the tax from the dividends of its shareholders or from any deposits; or

(2) charge the tax to any of its shareholders or depositors, or collect the tax from them.

As added by P.L.88–1983, SEC.1.

Historical and Statutory Notes

Formerly:

IC 6–5–6–11.
Acts 1933, c. 83, s. 11.

Acts 1939, c. 158, s. 1.
Acts 1971, P.L.68, SEC.1.
Acts 1975, P.L.65, SEC.5.
Acts 1981, P.L.77, SEC.17.

Library References

Taxation ⚭125 to 131.
WESTLAW Topic No. 371.

C.J.S. Taxation §§ 143 to 149.
I.L.E. Taxation §§ 32, 33, 104, 105.

6–5–10–6   Banks electing not to pay taxes; discharge of liens by deductions from dividends, deposits and interest

Sec. 6.   (a) A bank that has elected to not pay the tax imposed by this chapter on its taxable shares or taxable deposits shall discharge each lien created under section 3(d) of this chapter on those taxable shares or taxable deposits by deducting amounts under subsection (b) and paying those amounts to the treasurer of the county in which the bank is located.

(b) Except as provided in subsection (d), a bank that is required to discharge a lien under subsection (a) shall deduct the amount of tax owed on a taxable:

(1) share from any dividend on that share; and

(2) deposit from that deposit or from any interest on that deposit.

(c) If there is a lien on a taxable deposit or a taxable share as provided in section 3(d) of this chapter, and if a bank pays the taxable deposit to the depositor or pays the dividends on the taxable share to the shareholder, then the bank is liable for the tax on the deposit or taxable share.

(d) A bank may not deduct the amount of tax under subsection (b), or collect the amount from or charge the amount to the depositor or shareholder, if it does not deduct the amount under subsection (b) within twenty (20) days of the date that:

(1) a lien on the taxable deposit is created under section 3(d) of this chapter; or

(2) a dividend on the taxable share is payable.

As added by P.L.88–1983, SEC.1.

Historical and Statutory Notes

Formerly:

IC 6–5–6–12.
Acts 1933, c. 83, s. 12.

6–5–10–7　Banks electing to pay taxes; credit against taxes paid

Sec. 7.　(a) For purposes of this section, "taxable year" has the same meaning as the definition of taxable year contained in IC 6–2.1–1–15.

(b) A bank that elects to pay the tax imposed by this chapter and that is not a national banking association is entitled to a credit against the tax in the amount of the tax paid by the bank under IC 6–2.1. If the credit for a taxable year exceeds the amount of tax for which the bank is liable under this chapter for that taxable year, the bank may claim the excess:

(1) first, against the tax that it paid under this chapter in any one (1) or more of the thirty-six (36) months that immediately precede the taxable year; and

(2) second, if additional excess credit remains, against the tax for which it is liable under this chapter in any one (1) or more of the thirty-six (36) months that immediately succeed the taxable year.

(c) Notwithstanding anything in this chapter or IC 6–2.1 to the contrary, the department shall pay to a taxpayer any refund to which the taxpayer is entitled that is attributable to a credit claimed under subsection (a).
As added by P.L.88–1983, SEC.1.

Historical and Statutory Notes

Formerly:

IC 6–5–6–11.
Acts 1933, c. 83, s. 11.

Acts 1939, c. 158, s. 1.
Acts 1971, P.L.68, SEC.1.
Acts 1975, P.L.65, SEC.5.
Acts 1981, P.L.77, SEC.17.

Cross References

Financial institutions tax fund, distributions to counties, see IC 6–5.5–8–2.

Notes of Decisions

Credit against taxes paid　1

—————

1.　Credit against taxes paid

State gross retail tax was not an allowable credit which could be taken by banks and trust companies when reporting and remitting to county treasurers the tax assessed under Acts 1933, c. 83 [now this chapter]. 1966 Op.Atty. Gen. No. 47.

6–5–10–8　Monthly statements to county auditor

Sec. 8.　(a) Before the twenty-first day of each month, an officer of each bank that is not under the supervision of a liquidating agent shall deliver a statement in duplicate to the auditor of the county in which the bank is located. The officer shall deliver the statement on forms prescribed and furnished by the department, shall sign the statement under penalty of perjury, and shall include the following information, current as of the fifth day of the month in which the statement is to be delivered:

(1) The number of shares of the bank.

(2) The amount of capital stock, surplus, and undivided profits of the bank.

(3) The assessed value of all real estate that is owned by the bank or leased by the bank and used for banking purposes.

(4) The amount of all deposits, public deposits, nonresident deposits, and deposits of another financial institution in the bank.

(5) The amount of obligations of the United States, an instrumentality of the United States, this state, or an instrumentality or political subdivision of this state that are owned by the bank.

(6) The amount of all taxable deposits in the bank, taxable shares of the bank, and taxable surplus and profits of the bank.

(7) Subject to subsection (b), the amount of taxable deposits in the principal office and in each branch office of the bank.

(8) The amount of tax that is due in that month under this chapter.

(9) If the bank is not a national banking association, the amount of credit that the bank claims for taxes paid under IC 6–2.1 against the tax for which it is liable in that month under this chapter.

(b) For purposes of subsection (a)(7), a bank that does not maintain a system of separate accounts for its branches shall:

(1) determine the proportion of taxable deposits in its principal and branch offices on January 5 of each year by taking an actual tally of its taxable deposits in those offices on that date; and

(2) allocate the value of taxable deposits among its principal and branch offices in each subsequent month of that calendar year in the proportion determined under subsection (b)(1).

As added by P.L.88–1983, SEC.1.

Historical and Statutory Notes

Formerly:

IC 6–5–6–7.

Acts 1933, c. 83, s. 7.

Acts 1935, c. 298, s. 3.
Acts 1943, c. 32, s. 2.
Acts 1957, c. 77, s. 1.
Acts 1975, P.L.65, SEC.3.

Library References

Taxation ☞126.
WESTLAW Topic No. 371.

C.J.S. Taxation §§ 143, 144.
I.L.E. Taxation §§ 32, 33.

Notes of Decisions

Value of shares   1

_____

1. Value of shares
Gross assessment of shares of stock of a bank at 75 percent of aggregate capital stock was not subject to objection that it did not specify value of each share where such valuation was ascertainable by simple computation by auditor. Citizens' Nat. Bank v. Klauss, App.1911, 93 N.E. 681, 47 Ind.App. 50.

6–5–10–9   Banks electing not to pay taxes; submission of lists of shareholders and depositors to county auditor

Sec. 9.   (a) A bank that elects to not pay the tax on its taxable shares shall prepare a list each month of the names and addresses of its shareholders and the number of shares of stock owned by each of them on the last day of the preceding month.

(b) A bank that elects to not pay the tax on its taxable deposits shall prepare a list each month of the names and addresses of its depositors and the amount of deposits owned by each of them on the last day of the preceding month.

(c) A bank shall verify each list prepared under subsection (a) or (b) under oath and submit it before the sixteenth day of the month in which it is prepared to the auditor of the county in which the bank is located.

As added by P.L.88–1983, SEC.1.

Historical and Statutory Notes

Formerly:
IC 6–5–6–9.
Acts 1933, c. 83, s. 9.

Library References

Taxation ☞126.
WESTLAW Topic No. 371.
C.J.S. Taxation §§ 143, 144.

6–5–10–10   Distribution of statements received by county auditor; filing of certificate with county treasurer

Sec. 10.   Upon receipt of each statement delivered under section 8 of this chapter, the county auditor shall:

(1) file one (1) copy in his office;

(2) send one (1) copy to the department; and

(3) file a certificate before the twenty-first day of the month with the county treasurer that:

(A) shows the tax liability of the bank as indicated on the statement; and

(B) allocates the tax liability on taxable shares and taxable deposits among the principal and branch offices of the bank in the proportion that taxable deposits are allocated under section 8(b) of this chapter.

As added by P.L.88–1983, SEC.1.

Historical and Statutory Notes

Formerly: Acts 1957, c. 77, s. 2.
  IC 6–5–6–10.   Acts 1975, P.L.65, SEC.4.
  Acts 1933, c. 83, s. 10.

Library References

Taxation ☞126.
WESTLAW Topic No. 371.
C.J.S. Taxation §§ 143, 144.

6–5–10–11   Taxpayers intending to claim refunds; payments to be held in escrow; disposition

Sec. 11.   (a) A taxpayer that intends to claim a refund under IC 6–8.1–9 of any tax imposed under this chapter may pay the tax and any interest or penalty to the department.   The department shall deliver all amounts paid to it to the treasurer of state, who shall hold the money in escrow.

(b) If a taxpayer:

(1) is found liable by the department for the tax or any part of the tax, and does not appeal to a court within the period prescribed in IC 6–8.1–9–1; or

(2) is found liable by a court for the tax or any part of the tax, and has exhausted all judicial appeals;

then the treasurer of state shall pay the amount of the tax for which the taxpayer is found liable to the treasurer of the county in which the principal office of the taxpayer is located.

(c) If:

(1) the department determines that the taxpayer is not liable for the tax or any part of the tax; or

(2) a court determines that the taxpayer is not liable for the tax or any part of the tax and the department has exhausted all judicial appeals;

then the treasurer of state shall pay to the taxpayer the amount of the tax for which the taxpayer is not found liable and any interest or penalties paid by the taxpayer on that amount.

(d) If the taxpayer does not claim a refund within the period prescribed in IC 6–8.1–9–1, the treasurer of state shall pay the amount of the tax paid by the taxpayer under subsection (a) to the treasurer of the county in which the principal office of the taxpayer is located.

(e) The treasurer of each county shall allocate the amounts that he receives under subsections (b) and (d) in the manner shown on the certificate filed by the auditor of that county under section 10 of this chapter.

As added by P.L.88–1983, SEC.1.

Historical and Statutory Notes

Formerly:
  IC 6–5–6–29.
  Acts 1975, P.L.65, SEC.18.

6–5–10–12 County treasurers; accounting and allocation of taxes paid; distribution of allocated amounts to local units of government

Sec. 12. The treasurer of each county shall:

(1) keep an account of all taxes paid to him under this chapter;

(2) allocate those taxes among the principal and branch offices of each bank in the same proportion that tax liability is allocated on the certificate of the county auditor filed under section 10 of this chapter; and

(3) pay the amount allocated to each principal and branch office to local units of government in the same proportion that those local units receive property taxes on the real property of the principal or branch office.

As added by P.L.88–1983, SEC.1.

Historical and Statutory Notes

Formerly: Acts 1933, c. 83, s. 15.
IC 6–5–6–15.   Acts 1957, c. 77, s. 3.

6–5–10–13 Local units of government; payments to state treasurer

Sec. 13. A local unit of government shall pay to the treasurer of state:

(1) the amount of any payment received by the local unit that is refunded to the taxpayer under IC 6–8.1–9–1; and

(2) any interest on that amount that is paid to the taxpayer under IC 6–8.1–9–2(c).

As added by P.L.88–1983, SEC.1.

Historical and Statutory Notes

Formerly: Acts 1975, P.L.65, SEC.14.
IC 6–5–6–25.   Acts 1980, P.L.61, SEC.7.

Cross References

Financial institutions tax fund, distributions to counties, see IC 6–5.5–8–2.

6–5–10–14 Banks under supervision of liquidating agents

Sec. 14. (a) A bank that is under the supervision of a liquidating agent shall determine the tax imposed by this chapter on taxable deposits and taxable shares as of the date that deposits are distributed to depositors and the date that liquidating dividends are distributed to shareholders, and the entity liable for the tax shall pay the tax on or before those dates.

(b) The tax on those taxable deposits and taxable shares becomes a lien on the deposits or shares at the time that the liquidating agent is appointed.

(c) The tax rate established in section 3 of this chapter is applied to the taxable deposits and taxable shares for the period from the date of the lien to the date of distribution of the deposits or liquidating dividends.

(d) The liquidating agent of a bank shall deliver a statement to the auditor of the county in which the bank is located, on forms provided by the department, showing the amount of:

(1) taxable deposits that the bank will distribute to depositors; and

(2) liquidating dividends that the bank will distribute to shareholders.

(e) The tax imposed by this chapter on the taxable deposits in a bank in liquidation, and on its taxable shares, is an expense of liquidation of the bank.
As added by P.L.88–1983, SEC.1.

Historical and Statutory Notes

Formerly:
IC 6–5–6–14.
Acts 1933, c. 83, s. 14.

Acts 1935, c. 298, s. 4.
Acts 1975, P.L.65, SEC.7.

Library References

Taxation ☞126.
WESTLAW Topic No. 371.

C.J.S. Taxation §§ 143, 144.
I.L.E. Taxation §§ 32, 33.

6–5–10–15 Offenses pertaining to required statements and to books of bank

Sec. 15. A person who:

(1) fails to deliver a statement under section 8 or 14 of this chapter;

(2) makes a false statement of any information required on a statement delivered under section 8 or 14 of this chapter with intent to defraud this state or to evade the payment of tax under this chapter; or

(3) makes a false entry in the books of a bank, or keeps more than one (1) set of books for the bank, with intent to defraud this state or to evade the payment of tax under this chapter;

commits a Class B misdemeanor.
As added by P.L. 88–1983, SEC.1.

Historical and Statutory Notes

Formerly:
IC 6–5–6–18.
Acts 1933, c. 83, s. 18.

Acts 1975, P.L.65, SEC.9.
Acts 1978, P.L.2, SEC.625.
P.L.16–1983, SEC.3.

6–5–10–16 Taxpayers; offenses

Sec. 16. A taxpayer that:

(1) recklessly fails to permit the department to examine any books, records, or returns under IC 6–8.1;

(2) recklessly fails to permit the department to inspect or appraise any property under IC 6–8.1;

(3) knowingly fails to offer testimony or produce any record under IC 6–8.1; or

(4) recklessly fails to keep for three (3) years after the tax is due the documents necessary to determine the amount of tax for which it is liable under this chapter;

commits a Class B misdemeanor.
As added by P.L. 88–1983, SEC.1.

Historical and Statutory Notes

Formerly:
IC 6–5–6–18.
Acts 1933, c. 83, s. 18.

Acts 1975, P.L.65, SEC.9.
Acts 1978, P.L.2, SEC.625.
P.L.16–1983, SEC.3.

6–5–10–17 Bank tax in lieu of other taxes

Sec. 17. The tax imposed by this chapter is in lieu of any other tax, except the tax imposed under IC 6–2.1 and IC 6–4.1, on the:

(1) shares of stock, surplus, undivided profits, reserves, and deposits of a bank; and

(2) owners of the items listed in subsection (1).
As added by P.L.88–1983, SEC.1.

Historical and Statutory Notes

Formerly:
IC 6–5–6–16.
Acts 1933, c. 83, s. 16.

Cross References

Institutions subject to bank tax, certain property not subject to property tax assessment and taxation, see IC 6–1.1–2–6.

Library References

Taxation ⊕125 to 131.
WESTLAW Topic No. 371.
C.J.S. Taxation §§ 143 to 149.

Notes of Decisions

Personal property tax   1

_____

1. Personal property tax

A bank is not relieved under Acts 1933, c. 83, s. 16 [now this section] of the payment of the property tax on personal property that had accrued at the time of the foreclosure proceedings. The tax was a lien against the property at that time and there is no reason why the bank should be relieved of the payment of the tax. 1940 Op.Atty.Gen. p. 59.

Chapter 11

Savings and Loan Association Tax

Library References

Taxation ⊕132 to 135.
WESTLAW Topic No. 371.
C.J.S. Taxation §§ 157, 158.

6–5–11–1   Definitions

Sec. 1. As used in this chapter:

"Association" means an entity organized under IC 28–4 (before its repeal) that was engaged in business in this state on June 30, 1997, as a:

(1) building and loan association;

(2) rural loan and savings association; or

(3) guaranty loan and savings association.

"Nonresident shareholder" means an individual, firm, limited liability company, or corporation that resides or is domiciled outside Indiana and that owns investment shares that do not have a business situs in Indiana.

"Surplus" means a sinking fund established to provide against contingent losses, undivided profits, or any surplus fund, regardless of name.

"Taxing district" means a geographical area within which property is taxed by the same taxing units at the same total rate.

"Taxing unit" means an entity that has the power to impose ad valorem property taxes.

As added by P.L.88–1983, SEC.2. Amended by P.L.8–1993, SEC.93; P.L.79–1998, SEC.13.

Historical and Statutory Notes

P.L.88–1983, Sec.2, eff. June 1, 1983, added this chapter.

Sections 15 and 16 of P.L. 88–1983 provided:

"Section 15. (a) This act is intended to be a codification and restatement of applicable or corresponding provisions of IC 6–5–6, IC 6–5–7, IC 6–5–8, and IC 6–5–9. If this act repeals and replaces a provision in the same form or in a restated form, the substantive operation and effect of that provision continues uninterrupted.

"(b) This act does not affect any:

"(1) rights or liabilities accrued;

"(2) penalties incurred;

"(3) offenses committed; or

"(4) proceedings begun;

"before the effective date of this act. Those rights, liabilities, penalties, offenses, and proceedings continue and shall be imposed and enforced under IC 6–5–6, IC 6–5–7, IC 6–5–8, or IC 6–5–9 as if this act had not been enacted.

"Section 16. The general assembly may, by concurrent resolution, preserve any of the background materials related to this act."

P.L.8–1993, Sec.93, inserted "limited liability company" in the definition of "nonresident shareholder".

P.L.79–1998, Sec.13, amended the section by inserting "organized under IC 28–4 (before its repeal) that was"; inserting "on June 30, 1997"; and substituting "as" for "that is" in the definition of "association".

Formerly:

IC 6–5–8–1.

Acts 1933, c. 82, s. 1.

Acts 1935, c. 263, s. 1.

Cross References

Administration, enforcement, and collection of tax, department of state revenue, see IC 6–8.1–1–1 et seq.

Community revitalization enhancement district tax credit, state and local tax liability, see IC 6–3.1–19–1.

Industrial loan and investment companies, intangible tax law applicable, see IC 28–5–1–23.

Military base recovery tax credit,

  Against other taxes owed, priority of application, see IC 6–3.1–11.5–24.

  State tax liability, see IC 6–3.1–11.5–14.

Library property taxes, replacement credits, see IC 6–3.5–7–23.

National banking and savings and loan association credit, see IC 6–2.1–4.5–1.

Library References

Taxation ⬤132 to 135.
WESTLAW Topic No. 371.

C.J.S. Taxation §§ 157, 158.
Words and Phrases (Perm.Ed.)

6–5–11–2 Imposition of tax; rate

Sec. 2. (a) An excise tax is imposed on each association at the rate of fourteen hundredths of one percent (0.14%) per year on the remainder of the paid-in value of its issued and outstanding capital stock and the value of its surplus minus the following:

(1) Subject to subsection (b), the assessed value of all real property owned by the association and subject to taxation.

(2) The value of investment shares of the association that are owned by credit unions and nonresident shareholders.

(3) The value of shares of the association that are owned by or held for the use and benefit of any corporation, institution, foundation, trust, or association that operates exclusively for religious, charitable, educational, hospital, scientific, fraternal, civic, or cemetery purposes and not for private profit.

(4) The amount of any mortgage loan on which foreclosure proceedings have been filed.

(5) The amount of any loan secured by a pledge of investment stock of the association.

(6) The amount invested by the association in shares of stock of any federal home loan bank.

(7) The amount of deposits of the association in any federal home loan bank.

(8) Subject to subsection (c), the amount of obligations of the United States government, an instrumentality of the United States government, this state, or an instrumentality or political subdivision of this state that are owned by the association.

(b) The assessed value used in subsection (a)(1) of real estate of the association that has been sold under contract may not exceed the lesser of the:

(1) balance due on the contract; or

(2) amount invested in the real estate by the association.

(c) The amount used in subsection (a)(8) may not exceed one-half ($\frac{1}{2}$) of the remainder of the surplus and the issued and outstanding capital stock of the association minus the values and amounts determined under subsections (a)(1) through (a)(7) and subsection (b).

As added by P.L.88–1983, SEC.2.

Historical and Statutory Notes

Formerly:

IC 6–5–8–4.
IC 6–5–8–5.
IC 6–5–8–5.1.
Acts 1933, c. 82, ss. 4, 5.

Acts 1935, c. 263, s. 2.
Acts 1945, c. 91, s. 1.
Acts 1965, c. 21, s. 1.
Acts 1967, c. 59, s. 1.
Acts 1978, P.L.46, SECS.1, 2.

Cross References

Investment credits against the savings and loan association tax, see IC 6–3.1–5–1 et seq.
Purchasers qualifying for investment credit, exemption from the savings and loan association tax, see IC 6–3.1–5–11.

Notes of Decisions

In general   2
Deductions   4
Liability for tax   3
Nonresident shareholders   6
Validity of prior law   1
Value of stock   5

---

1. Validity of prior law

Statutes providing for the taxation of intangibles [repealed; see, now, § 6–5.1–1–1 et seq.], building and loan associations [now this chapter], and banks and trust companies [now § 6–5–10–1 et seq.] were not unconstitutional as granting special privileges or immunities to certain classes, or as abridging the privileges or immunities of citizens of the United States, or denying any person equal protection of the law. Lutz v. Arnold, 1935, 193 N.E. 840, 208 Ind. 480, rehearing overruled 196 N.E. 702, 208 Ind. 480.

Acts 1933, cc. 81 to 83, providing for the taxation of intangibles, building and loan associations, and banks and trust companies were not unconstitutional under Const. Art. 4, § 22 as "local" or "special" laws, nor because of the exemption of certain intangibles from personal property taxes. Lutz v. Arnold, 1935, 193 N.E. 840, 208 Ind. 480, rehearing overruled 196 N.E. 702, 208 Ind. 480.

Acts 1933, c. 82 [now, this chapter] providing for taxation of intangibles was not arbitrary and unreasonable because applicable to persons only and not to banks, trust companies, and building and loan associations, in view of other statutes providing for the taxation of such companies. Lutz v. Arnold, 1935, 193 N.E. 840, 208 Ind. 480, rehearing overruled 196 N.E. 702, 208 Ind. 480.

Taxation of building association on money loaned by it out of its earnings from interest and premiums on its loans to stockholders on their shares of stock as collateral, is not objectionable as double taxation on ground that same property had been assessed to shareholders. International Bldg. & Loan Ass'n v. Board of Com'rs of Marion County, App.1902, 65 N.E. 297, 30 Ind. App. 12.

Any law either directly or indirectly exempting stock in building and loan associations from taxation is unconstitutional. State ex rel. State ex rel. Morgan v. Workingmen's Bldg. & Loan Fund & Sav. Ass'n, 1899, 53 N.E. 168, 152 Ind. 278.

2. In general

Declaration in a statute providing for the taxation of intangibles, that tax thereby imposed is an excise tax, must be accepted unless the declaration is incompatible with the effect of the statute. Lutz v. Arnold, 1935, 193 N.E. 840, 208 Ind. 480, rehearing overruled 196 N.E. 702, 208 Ind. 480.

An "excise tax" is a tax imposed on performance of an act, engaging in an occupation or enjoyment of a privilege, and every form of tax not imposed directly on property must constitute an "excise" if it is a valid tax of any description. Lutz v. Arnold, 1935, 193 N.E. 840, 208 Ind. 480, rehearing overruled 196 N.E. 702, 208 Ind. 480.

3. Liability for tax

Fact that savings and loan association owns capital stock of a federal loan association does not relieve it from excise tax imposed by Acts 1933, c. 82, upon the capital stock and surplus as taxed by s. 5 [now this section]. 1934 Op. Atty.Gen. p. 305.

4. Deductions

Investment in realty purchased by building and loan association for resale to stockholders, association having no lien or interest to protect by purchase, and realty being resold on contracts for substantially exact cost pursuant to prior statute, and value of such investment being carried in contingent and reserve funds was deductible therefrom for tax purposes, notwithstanding stockholders under contracts assumed taxes on realty. Showalter v. Fletcher Ave. Sav. & Loan Ass'n, App.1934, 190 N.E. 127, 100 Ind.App. 378.

The tax imposed by Acts 1933, c. 82, § 5 [now this section] was not upon securities in which building and loan association might have some of its funds invested but was an excise tax upon association for privilege of exercising its franchise and transacting its business, and therefore such association could not, for purposes of computing its tax liability, deduct amount of funds invested by it in bonds issued by Home Owners' Loan Corporation. 1937 Op.Atty.Gen. p. 72.

Under tax law of 1919, building and loan associations which carried non-taxable securities as part of their contingent and reserve funds were entitled to a deduction of such non-taxables in the valuation of such contingent and reserve funds. 1927–1928 Op.Atty.Gen. p. 309.

5. Value of stock

Stock in building association, whether paid up, prepaid, running, or otherwise, is taxable at its true cash value. State v. Real Estate Bldg. & Loan Fund Ass'n, 1898, 51 N.E. 1061, 151 Ind. 502.

Liberty bonds, under tax law of 1919, owned by building and loan association were not taxable as property but could be considered in fixing value of stock of an association held by an individual. 1917–1920 Op.Atty.Gen. p. 209.

6. Nonresident shareholders

If shares of stock in a building and loan association were outside the state of Indiana but some of its shares were held by residents within the state, the shares would have been taxable to the holder under the General Intangibles Tax Act [repealed; see, now, § 6–5.1–1–1 et seq.]. 1942 Op.Atty.Gen. p. 223.

6–5–11–3   Credits against tax

Sec. 3.   (a) An association is entitled to a credit against the tax imposed under this chapter in the amount of taxes paid:

(1) on gross income under IC 6–2.1; and

(2) on personal property under IC 6–1.1.

(b) An association may claim the credit on any return or returns that it files after it pays the tax for which the credit is allowed.

As added by P.L.88–1983, SEC.2.

Historical and Statutory Notes

Formerly:
IC 6–5–8–6.
Acts 1933, c. 82, s. 6.

Acts 1943, c. 68, s. 1.
Acts 1965, c. 21, s. 2.
Acts 1977, P.L.83, SEC.2.

Library References

Taxation ☞133.
WESTLAW Topic No. 371.

C.J.S. Taxation §§ 157, 158.
I.L.E. Taxation §§ 32, 33, 36.

6–5–11–4   Computation and payment of tax; reports to county auditor

Sec. 4.   Each association shall compute the tax imposed by this chapter as of the last day of each calendar month, and shall pay the tax on or before the twenty-first day of the following month. At the time that an association pays the tax, it shall file a report in duplicate with the auditor of each county in which it has an office. The report shall be verified by the secretary of the association, and shall show the computation of the amount of tax due from the association under this chapter.

As added by P.L.88–1983, SEC.2.

Historical and Statutory Notes

Formerly:
IC 6–5–8–6.5.

IC 6–5–8–8.
Acts 1933, c. 82, s. 8.

Acts 1935, c. 263, s. 3.
Acts 1967, c. 59, s. 2.
Acts 1977, P.L.83, SECS. 3, 5.

Library References

Taxation ⟊133.
WESTLAW Topic No. 371.
C.J.S. Taxation §§ 157, 158.

Notes of Decisions

Sufficiency of reports 1

---

1. Sufficiency of reports

Return of building association that all its funds were loaned out to members on mortgag-es which had been duly assessed for taxation, is insufficient where it is not alleged that all of the members are borrowers. Co-operative Bldg. & Loan Ass'n v. State ex rel. Daniels, 1901, 60 N.E. 146, 156 Ind. 463.

6–5–11–5   Payments to county treasurer

Sec. 5.   Each association shall pay to the treasurer of each county in which it has an office the product of the tax determined under section 2 of this chapter multiplied by a fraction:

(1) The numerator of the fraction is the total deposits in the offices of the association in the county.

(2) The denominator of the fraction is the total deposits in the association.
As added by P.L.88–1983, SEC.2.

Historical and Statutory Notes

Formerly:
IC 6–5–8–6.5.
Acts 1977, P.L.83, SEC.3.

6–5–11–6   County treasurer; apportionment of taxes collected; distribution to taxing units

Sec. 6.   (a) The county treasurer shall apportion to each of the county's taxing districts in which an association has an office an amount equal to the product of the excise tax collected by the treasurer from that association under this chapter multiplied by a fraction:

(1) The numerator of the fraction is the total deposits in the association's offices in that taxing district.

(2) The denominator of the fraction is the total deposits in the association's offices in the county.

(b) The county treasurer shall distribute the excise taxes apportioned to each taxing district among the taxing units in that district in the proportion and manner that real property taxes are distributed.
As added by P.L.88–1983, SEC.2.

Historical and Statutory Notes

Formerly:
  IC 6–5–8–7.

Acts 1933, c. 82, s. 7.
Acts 1977, P.L.83, SEC.4.

Cross References

County supplemental school distribution fund, see IC 21–2–12–6.1.

Library References

Taxation ⚚133, 909.
WESTLAW Topic No. 371.
C.J.S. Taxation §§ 157, 158, 1059, 1086.

I.L.E. Taxation §§ 32, 33, 183 to 185, 191 to 200.

6–5–11–7   Annual determination of amounts taxing units are entitled to receive; distributions from general fund

Sec. 7. (a) After January 1 but before March 1 of each year, each county auditor shall determine for each taxing unit of the county the lesser of:

(1) twice the amount received by the taxing unit from taxes collected under IC 6–5–8 (repealed June 1, 1983) for the period from July 1, 1977, through December 31, 1977; and

(2) the amount the taxing unit would have received from taxes collected under IC 6–5–8 (repealed June 1, 1983) or this chapter for the immediately preceding calendar year if the tax rate had been one-fourth of one percent (0.25%).

(b) If the amount determined under subsection (a) for a particular taxing unit and a particular calendar year is greater than the amount the taxing unit actually received from taxes collected under IC 6–5–8 (repealed June 1, 1983) or this chapter for the immediately preceding calendar year, the taxing unit is entitled to receive the amount of the difference from the state general fund.

(c) After January 1 but before March 10 of each calendar year, each county auditor shall certify to the auditor of state the amount to be distributed to each taxing unit of the county under this section during that calendar year. Before April 1 of the calendar year in which the certification is made, the auditor of state shall issue a warrant drawn on the state general fund to the county treasurer. The auditor of state shall issue the warrant in an amount equal to the total of the amounts certified by the county auditor.

(d) Each county treasurer shall distribute the money that he receives during a particular calendar year under subsection (c) among the taxing units of the county at the same time that he makes the first distribution of property taxes to those taxing units. The county treasurer shall base the distributions on the amount certified for each taxing unit by the county auditor under subsection (c).

As added by P.L.88–1983, SEC.2. Amended by P.L.3–1990, SEC.25.

Historical and Statutory Notes

P.L.3–1990, Sec.25, emerg. eff. March 13, 1990.

Acts 1978, P.L.46, SEC.3.
Acts 1979, P.L.76, SEC.1.

Formerly:
 IC 6–5–8–7.1.

Library References

Taxation ☞909.
WESTLAW Topic No. 371.
C.J.S. Taxation §§ 1059, 1086.

I.L.E. Taxation §§ 32, 33, 183 to 185, 191 to 200.

Notes of Decisions

Review 1

_____

1. Review

Tax Court has jurisdiction to review appeals from final determinations of probate court concerning amount of estate tax due. West's A.I.C. 6–4.1–11–7. Indiana Dept. of State Revenue,

Inheritance Tax Div. v. Estate of Puschel, 1991, 582 N.E.2d 923.

On appeal from probate court's determination of inheritance tax due, Tax Court's task is to determine whether probate court correctly applied law to undisputed facts. Indiana Dept. of State Revenue, Inheritance Tax Div. v. Estate of Puschel, 1991, 582 N.E.2d 923.

6–5–11–8 Delinquent taxes and penalties; assessment; lien; collection and distribution

Sec. 8. (a) The county treasurer shall enter on the tax duplicates of the county the amount of any tax imposed under this chapter that is delinquent, and the amount of any penalty on that tax, and shall assess and charge those amounts as omitted tax against the association liable for the tax. At the time of the entry, those amounts become a lien against all property of the association that owes the tax.

(b) The county treasurer shall collect delinquent taxes and penalties in the manner that he collects other delinquent taxes, and he shall distribute penalties on delinquent taxes in the manner that he distributes tax collections under this chapter.

As added by P.L.88–1983, SEC.2.

Historical and Statutory Notes

Formerly:
 IC 6–5–8–11.

Acts 1933, c. 82, s. 11.
Acts 1935, c. 263, s. 4.

Library References

Taxation ☞133, 544.
WESTLAW Topic No. 371.
C.J.S. Social Security and Public Welfare §§ 204, 205.

C.J.S. Taxation §§ 157, 158, 241, 640, 641, 1088.
I.L.E. Taxation §§ 32, 33, 98.

6–5–11–9 Associations in liquidation

Sec. 9. The entity or individual in charge of an association in liquidation may pay the tax imposed by this chapter and file reports:

(1) as required in section 4 of this chapter; or

(2) with the written consent of the department of state revenue, at the time and in the manner that liquidating agents of banks pay tax and file reports under IC 6–5–10.

As added by P.L.88–1983, SEC.2.

Historical and Statutory Notes

Formerly:
IC 6–5–8–14.

Acts 1933, c. 82, s. 15.
Acts 1935, c. 263, s. 5.

Library References

WESTLAW Topic No. 371.
C.J.S. Social Security and Public Welfare §§ 203, 207, 208.

Taxation ☞133, 517.
C.J.S. Taxation §§ 157, 158, 609, 614, 1082.

6–5–11–10 Offenses pertaining to reports

Sec. 10. A secretary of an association who fails to file any report required by this chapter or who makes a false or fraudulent statement of any of the facts required in any report required by this chapter commits a Class C infraction.

As added by P.L.88–1983, SEC.2.

Historical and Statutory Notes

Formerly:
IC 6–5–8–12.

Acts 1933, c. 82, s. 12.
Acts 1978, P.L.2, SEC.628.

Cross References

Penalty for infractions, see IC 34–28–5–4.

Library References

Taxation ☞126, 325.
WESTLAW Topic No. 371.

C.J.S. Taxation §§ 143, 144, 388.
I.L.E. Taxation §§ 32, 33.

6–5–11–11 Liability for other taxes

Sec. 11. (a) The tax imposed by this chapter is in lieu of any other tax on the mortgages, notes, and contracts for sale of real property of the association.

(b) Neither the association nor an owner of its shares of capital stock is liable for any other tax, except the tax imposed by IC 6–2.1 and IC 6–4.1, on the shares of capital stock and surplus of the association.

As added by P.L.88–1983, SEC.2.

Historical and Statutory Notes

Formerly:
IC 6–5–8–9.

Acts 1933, c. 82, s. 9.
Acts 1935, c. 200, s. 1.

Library References

Taxation ⊕135.
WESTLAW Topic No. 371.
C.J.S. Taxation § 157.

Notes of Decisions

Validity of prior law   1

———

1. Validity of prior law

Statutes providing for taxation of intangibles [repealed; see, now, § 6–5.1–1–1 et seq.] build-ing and loan associations [now this chapter], and banks and trust companies [now § 6–5–10–1 et seq.] were not unconstitutional because of the exemption of certain intangibles from personal property taxes. Lutz v. Arnold, 1935, 193 N.E. 840, 208 Ind. 480, rehearing overruled 196 N.E. 702, 208 Ind. 480.

Chapter 12

Production Credit Association Tax

Library References

Taxation ⊕114.
WESTLAW Topic No. 371.
C.J.S. Taxation §§ 127, 156, 261.

6–5–12–1   "Association" defined

Sec. 1. As used in this chapter, "association" means a production credit association engaged in business in Indiana that is organized and chartered under 12 U.S.C. 2091 and that is not exempt from state taxation under the laws of the United States.

As added by P.L.88–1983, SEC.3.

Historical and Statutory Notes

P.L.88–1983, Sec.3, eff. June 1, 1983, added this chapter.

Sections 15 and 16 of P.L.88–1983 provided:

"Section 15.   (a) This act is intended to be a codification and restatement of applicable or corresponding provisions of IC 6–5–6, IC 6–5–7, IC 6–5–8, and IC 6–5–9. If this act repeals and replaces a provision in the same form or in a restated form, the substantive operation and effect of that provision continues uninterrupted.

"(b) This act does not affect any:

"(1) rights or liabilities accrued;

"(2) penalties incurred;

"(3) offenses committed; or

"(4) proceedings begun;

"before the effective date of this act. Those rights, liabilities, penalties, offenses, and proceedings continue and shall be imposed and enforced under IC 6–5–6, IC 6–5–7, IC 6–5–8, or IC 6–5–9 as if this act had not been enacted.

"Section 16. The general assembly may, by concurrent resolution, preserve any of the background materials related to this act."

Formerly:

IC 6–5–9–1.

Acts 1949, c. 29, s. 1.

Cross References

Defrauding a financial institution, see IC 35–43–5–8.
Library property taxes, replacement credits, see IC 6–3.5–7–23.
National banking and savings and loan association credit, see IC 6–2.1–4.5–1.

Library References

Words and Phrases (Perm.Ed.)

6–5–12–2   Imposition of tax; rate

Sec. 2. An excise tax is imposed on each association at the rate of one-fourth of one percent (0.25%) per year on the sum of the following:

(1) Paid-in value of its issued and outstanding capital stock.

(2) Amount of its reserve account for bad and doubtful debts.

(3) Amount of its guaranty fund.

(4) Amount of its undistributed earnings.

(5) Amount of its unpaid balance of outstanding loans less:

(A) the assessed value of all its real estate and tangible personal property;

(B) the unpaid balance of loans that it has sold or discounted and that are held by others; and

(C) cash it has on hand and in banks.

As added by P.L.88–1983, SEC.3.

Historical and Statutory Notes

Formerly:
IC 6–5–9–4.

IC 6–5–9–5.
Acts 1949, c. 29, ss. 4, 5.

Library References

Taxation ⟜114.
WESTLAW Topic No. 371.

C.J.S. Taxation §§ 127, 156, 261.
I.L.E. Taxation §§ 22, 24, 61, 64.

6–5–12–3   Credits against tax

Sec. 3. An association is entitled to a credit against the tax imposed under this chapter in the amount of the gross income tax paid under IC 6–2.1–1. The association may claim the credit on any return or returns filed after the gross income tax has been paid.

As added by P.L.88–1983, SEC.3.

Historical and Statutory Notes

Formerly:
  IC 6–5–9–6.
  Acts 1949, c. 29, s. 6.

6–5–12–4   Computation and payment of tax; reports to county auditor

Sec. 4.   (a) Each association shall compute the tax imposed under this chapter as of the last day of each calendar month.   Before the twenty-first day of the next succeeding month, the association shall pay the tax and file a report, in duplicate, verified by the secretary-treasurer of the association.   In the report, the association shall enter each of the values and amounts specified in section 2 of this chapter and the amount of the tax due under this chapter.

(b) The association shall pay the tax to the treasurer of the county where it has its principal place of business and shall file the report with the auditor of that county.

As added by P.L.88–1983, SEC.3.

Historical and Statutory Notes

Formerly: IC 6–5–9–8.
  IC 6–5–9–6.   Acts 1949, c. 29, ss. 6, 8.

6–5–12–5   County treasurer; distribution of taxes paid

Sec. 5.   The county treasurer shall distribute the tax paid under this chapter in the proportion and manner he distributes real estate taxes.

As added by P.L.88–1983, SEC.3.

Historical and Statutory Notes

Formerly:
  IC 6–5–9–7.
  Acts 1949, c. 29, s. 7.

Library References

Taxation ⚬114, 909.
WESTLAW Topic No. 371.
C.J.S. Taxation §§ 127, 156, 261, 1059, 1086.

6–5–12–6   Delinquent or unreported taxes; penalty

Sec. 6.   An association failing to pay or report any tax due under this chapter shall pay a penalty in the amount of one percent (1%) per month of the tax that is delinquent or unreported.

As added by P.L.88–1983, SEC.3.

Historical and Statutory Notes

Formerly:
  IC 6–5–9–10.
  Acts 1949, c. 29, s. 10.

6–5–12–7 Delinquent taxes and penalties; assessment; lien; collection and distribution

Sec. 7. (a) The county treasurer shall enter, on the tax duplicates of the county, the amount of the tax imposed under this chapter that is delinquent and the amount of any penalty on that tax and shall assess and charge those amounts as omitted tax against the association liable for the tax. At the time of the entry, those amounts become a lien against all property of the association that owes the tax.

(b) The county treasurer shall collect delinquent taxes and penalties in the manner he collects other delinquent taxes and penalties, and he shall distribute them in the manner that taxes collected under this chapter are distributed.
As added by P.L.88–1983, SEC.3.

Historical and Statutory Notes

Formerly:
 IC 6–5–9–11.
 Acts 1949, c. 29, s. 11.

6–5–12–8 Offenses pertaining to reports

Sec. 8. A secretary-treasurer of an association who:

(1) fails to file any report required by this chapter; or

(2) makes a false or fraudulent statement of any of the facts required in any report required by this chapter;

commits a Class C infraction.
As added by P.L.88–1983, SEC.3.

Historical and Statutory Notes

Formerly: Acts 1949, c. 29, s. 12.
 IC 6–5–9–12.   Acts 1978, P.L.2, SEC.629.

Cross References

Penalty for infractions, see IC 34–28–5–4.

Library References

Taxation ⏀325.   C.J.S. Taxation § 388.
WESTLAW Topic No. 371.   I.L.E. Taxation § 117.

6–5–12–9 Liability for other taxes

Sec. 9. (a) The tax imposed under this chapter is in lieu of any other tax on an association's shares of capital stock and intangible property.

(b) Neither the association nor an owner of its shares of capital stock is liable for any other tax, except the taxes imposed by IC 6–2.1 and IC 6–4.1, on the shares of capital stock and surplus of the association.
As added by P.L.88–1983, SEC.3.

Historical and Statutory Notes

Formerly:

IC 6–5–9–9.

Acts 1949, c. 29, s. 9.

Library References

Taxation ⚖114.

WESTLAW Topic No. 371.

C.J.S. Taxation §§ 127, 156, 261.

ARTICLE 5.1

INTANGIBLES TAX

Chapter 1

Definitions

6–5.1–1–1 to 6–5.1–1–7   Repealed

(Repealed by P.L.80–1989, SEC.18.)

Historical and Statutory Notes

P.L.80–1989 provided in Section 19, containing emergency clause, that the act takes effect retroactive to Nov. 10, 1988.

Former IC 6–5.1–1–1 to 6–5.1–1–7 related to definitions.

Formerly:
 IC 6–5–1–1.
 IC 6–5–1–8.

Acts 1933, c. 81, ss. 1, 9.
Acts 1935, c. 294, s. 1.
Acts 1943, c. 134, s. 1.
Acts 1955, c. 287, s. 3.
Acts 1959, c. 317, s. 2.
Acts 1965, c. 226, ss. 1, 3.
Acts 1967, c. 308, s. 1.
Acts 1971, P.L.67, SECS.1, 3.
Acts 1977, P.L.84, SEC.1.

Chapter 2

Imposition

6–5.1–2–1, 6–5.1–2–2   Repealed

(Repealed by P.L.80–1989, SEC.18.)

Historical and Statutory Notes

P.L.80–1989 provided in Section 19, containing emergency clause, that the act takes effect retroactive to Nov. 10, 1988.

Former IC 6–5.1–2–1 related to privileges taxed.

Former IC 6–5.1–2–2 related to tax rate.

Formerly:
 IC 6–5–1–1 to 6–5–1–3.

Acts 1933, c. 81, ss. 1 to 3.
Acts 1935, c. 294, s. 1.
Acts 1943, c. 134, s. 1.
Acts 1965, c. 226, s. 1.
Acts 1967, c. 308, s. 1.
Acts 1971, P.L.67, SEC.1.
Acts 1977, P.L.84, SEC.1.
Acts 1979, P.L.77, SEC.1.
Acts 1980, P.L.39, SEC.10.

Chapter 3

Valuation

6–5.1–3–1 to 6–5.1–3–7   Repealed

(Repealed by P.L.80–1989, SEC.18.)

Historical and Statutory Notes

P.L.80–1989 provided in Section 19, containing emergency clause, that the act takes effect retroactive to Nov. 10, 1988.

Former IC 6–5.1–3–1 to 6–5.1–3–7 related to valuation.

Formerly:
IC 6–5–1–1.
IC 6–5–1–4 to 6–5–1–7.
Acts 1933, c. 81, s. 1, 4 to 7.
Acts 1935, c. 294, ss. 1 to 3.

Acts 1943, c. 134, s. 1.
Acts 1945, c. 51, s. 1.
Acts 1955, c. 18, s. 1.
Acts 1955, c. 287, s. 1.
Acts 1957, c. 348, s. 1.
Acts 1959, c. 317, s.1.
Acts 1965, c. 226, ss. 1, 2.
Acts 1967, c. 308, ss. 1, 2.
Acts 1971, P.L.67, SECS.1, 2.
Acts 1977, P.L.84, SEC.1.

Chapter 4

Qualified Credit Company Election

6–5.1–4–1 to 6–5.1–4–5.1   Repealed

(Repealed by P.L.80–1989, SEC.18.)

Historical and Statutory Notes

P.L.80–1989 provided in Section 19, containing emergency clause, that the act takes effect retroactive to Nov. 10, 1988.

Former IC 6–5.1–4–1 to 6–5.1–4–5.1 related to qualified credit company election.

Formerly:
IC 6–5–1–31.

Acts 1933, c. 81, s. 41b.
Acts 1957, c. 153, s. 1.
Acts 1971, P.L.67, SEC.7.
Acts 1977, P.L.84, SEC.1.
Acts 1979, P.L.77, SEC.2.
Acts 1979, P.L.78, SEC.1.

Chapter 5

Exemptions

6–5.1–5–1 to 6–5.1–5–9   Repealed

(Repealed by P.L.80–1989, SEC.18.)

Historical and Statutory Notes

P.L.80–1989 provided in Section 19, containing emergency clause, that the act takes effect retroactive to Nov. 10, 1988.

Former IC 6–5.1–5–1 to 6–5.1–5–9 related to exemptions.

Formerly:
IC 6–5–1–1.
IC 6–5–1–2.
IC 6–5–1–19.
IC 6–5–1–33.
IC 6–5–1–34.
IC 6–5–2–1.

IC 6–5–3–1.
IC 6–5–3.5–1.
IC 6–5–3.5–2.
IC 6–8–5–1.
Acts 1933, c. 81, ss. 1, 2, 31.
Acts 1935, c. 294, s.1.
Acts 1943, c. 134, s. 1.
Acts 1945, c. 170, s. 1.
Acts 1947, c. 346, s. 1.
Acts 1953, c. 255, s. 1.
Acts 1959, c. 154, s. 1.
Acts 1965, c. 226, ss. 1, 11.
Acts 1967, c. 308, s. 1.

Acts 1971, P.L.67, SECS.1, 9.
Acts 1975, P.L.47, SEC.2.
Acts 1975, P.L.353, SEC.1.
Acts 1977, P.L.84, SEC.1.

Acts 1980, P.L.8, SEC.58.
Acts 1980, P.L.61, SEC.8.
Acts 1981, P.L.92, SEC.1.
P.L.79–1983, SEC.4.
P.L.17–1985, SEC.4.

Chapter 6

Reporting

6–5.1–6–1 to 6–5.1–6–3   Repealed

(Repealed by P.L.80–1989, SEC.18.)

Historical and Statutory Notes

P.L.80–1989 provided in Section 19, containing emergency clause, that the act takes effect retroactive to Nov. 10, 1988.

Former IC 6–5.1–6–1 to 6–5.1–6–3 related to reporting.

Formerly:

IC 6–5–1–10.
IC 6–5–1–11.
IC 6–5–1–23.
IC 6–5–1–31.

Acts 1933, c. 81, ss. 13, 13b, 35½, 41b.
Acts 1945, c. 51, s. 4.
Acts 1951, c. 278, s. 1.
Acts 1953, c. 49, s. 1.
Acts 1955, c. 287, s. 7.
Acts 1957, c. 348, s. 3.
Acts 1957, c. 153, s. 1.
Acts 1959, c. 317, s. 5.
Acts 1965, c. 226, ss. 5, 6.
Acts 1967, c. 308, ss. 3, 4.
Acts 1971, P.L.67, SECS.5 to 7.

6–5.1–6–4   Repealed

(Repealed by Acts 1980, P.L.61, SEC.15; P.L.80–1989, SEC.18.)

Historical and Statutory Notes

Acts 1980, P.L. 61, provided in § 16 that the act takes effect Jan. 1, 1981.

The former section related to informational reports.

Formerly:

Acts 1977, P.L.84, SEC.1.

Chapter 7

Refunds

6–5.1–7–1   Repealed

(Repealed by Acts 1980, P.L.61, SEC.15; P.L.80–1989, SEC.18.)

Historical and Statutory Notes

Acts 1980, P.L. 61, provided in § 16 that the act takes effect Jan. 1, 1981.

The former section related to claims for refunds for taxes wrongfully paid.

Provisions pertaining to refunds by the department of state revenue are now contained in § 6–8.1–9–1 et seq.

Formerly:
Acts 1977, P.L.84, SEC.1.

6–5.1–7–2   Repealed

(Repealed by P.L.80–1989, SEC.18.)

Historical and Statutory Notes

P.L.80–1989 provided in Section 19, containing emergency clause, that the act takes effect retroactive to Nov. 10, 1988.

Former IC 6–5.1–7–2 related to void promissory notes secured by mortgages.

Formerly:
IC 6–5–1–30.
Acts 1933, c. 81, s. 40a.
Acts 1951, c. 82, s. 1.
Acts 1977, P.L.84, SEC.1.

Chapter 8

Administration

6–5.1–8–1 to 6–5.1–8–9   Repealed

(Repealed by Acts 1980, P.L.61, SEC.15; P.L.80–1989, SEC.18.)

Historical and Statutory Notes

Acts 1980, P.L. 61, provided in § 16 that the act takes effect Jan. 1, 1981.

The former sections related to the administration of the intangibles tax law.

Provisions pertaining to the powers and duties of the department of state revenue are now contained in § 6–8.1–3–1 et seq.

Formerly:
Acts 1977, P.L.84, SEC.1.

6–5.1–8–10   Repealed

(Repealed by P.L.80–1989, SEC.18.)

Historical and Statutory Notes

P.L.80–1989 provided in Section 19, containing emergency clause, that the act takes effect retroactive to Nov. 10, 1988.

Former IC 6–5.1–8–10 related to proceeds of tax to state general fund.

Formerly:
IC 6–5–1–17.

Acts 1933, c. 81, s. 22.
Acts 1965, c. 226, s. 8.
Acts 1969, c. 426, s. 1.
Acts 1973, P.L.51, SEC.1.
Acts 1977, P.L.84, SEC.1.

6–5.1–8–11   Repealed

(Repealed by Acts 1980, P.L.61, SEC.15; P.L.80–1989, SEC.18.)

Historical and Statutory Notes

Acts 1980, P.L. 61, provided in § 16 that the act takes effect Jan. 1, 1981.

The former section related to assessment notices upon failure to pay the tax or upon improper reporting of tax.

Provisions pertaining to assessments and notices from the department of state revenue are now contained in § 6–8.1–5–1.

Formerly:

Acts 1977, P.L.84, SEC.1.

Chapter 9

Penalties and Sanctions

6–5.1–9–1   Repealed

(Repealed by Acts 1980, P.L.61, SEC.15; P.L.80–1989, SEC.18.)

Historical and Statutory Notes

Acts 1980, P.L. 61, provided in § 16 that the act takes effect Jan. 1, 1981.

The former section related to disclosure of information by members or agents of the department.

Provisions pertaining to confidentiality by the department of state revenue are now contained in § 6–8.1–7–1 et seq.

Formerly:

Acts 1977, P.L.84, SEC.1.
Acts 1978, P.L.2, SEC.630.

6–5.1–9–2 to 6–5.1–9–4   Repealed

(Repealed by P.L.80–1989, SEC.18.)

Historical and Statutory Notes

P.L.80–1989 provided in Section 19, containing emergency clause, that the act takes effect retroactive to Nov. 10, 1988.

Former IC 6–5.1–9–2 related to unlawful acts.

Former IC 6–5.1–9–3 related to swearing to or verifying false returns.

Former IC 6–5.1–9–4 related to business associations and false returns.

Formerly:

IC 6–5–1–10.
IC 6–5–1–24.

IC 35–1–90–1.
Acts 1905, c. 169, s. 474.
Acts 1927, c. 203, s. 7.
Acts 1933, c. 81, ss. 13, 36.
Acts 1955, c. 287, s. 7.
Acts 1957, c. 348, s. 3.
Acts 1959, c. 317, s. 5.
Acts 1965, c. 226, s. 5.
Acts 1967, c. 308, ss. 3, 9.
Acts 1971, P.L.67, SEC.5.
Acts 1977, P.L.84, SEC.1.
Acts 1978, P.L.2, SECS.631 to 633.

6–5.1–9–5 to 6–5.1–9–6   Repealed

(Repealed by Acts 1980, P.L.61, SEC.15; P.L.80–1989, SEC.18.)

Historical and Statutory Notes

Acts 1980, P.L. 61, provided in § 16 that the act takes effect Jan. 1, 1981.

Former §§ 6–5.1–9–5 and 6–5.1–9–5.5 related to delinquent taxes.

Former § 6–5.1–9–6 related to jurisdiction for criminal prosecutions and civil actions.

Provisions pertaining to collections, penalties, powers and duties of the department of state revenue are now contained in §§ 6–8.1–3–13, 6–8.1–8–1 et seq. and 6–8.1–10–1 et seq.

Formerly:

Acts 1977, P.L.84, SECS.1, 2.
Acts 1977, P.L.86, SEC.1.

ARTICLE 5.5

TAXATION OF FINANCIAL INSTITUTIONS

WESTLAW Computer Assisted Legal Research

WESTLAW supplements your legal research in many ways. WESTLAW allows you to

- update your research with the most current information
- expand your library with additional resources
- retrieve current, comprehensive history and citing references to a case with KeyCite

For more information on using WESTLAW to supplement your research, see the WESTLAW Electronic Research Guide, which follows the Preface.

Cross References

Airport authorities, bonds and interest exempt from taxation, see IC 8–22–3–17, 8–22–3–18.1.
Airport development authority, property exempt from taxation, see IC 8–22–3.7–21.
Airport facilities, exemptions from taxation, see IC 8–21–9–31.
Civic center building authority, property exempt from taxation, see IC 36–10–10–24.
Commerce department, interest rates for individual development accounts, see IC 4–4–28–14.
County hospital building authorities, tax exemptions, see IC 16–22–6–34.
Financing of housing, tax exemption for bonds, see IC 5–20–2–14.
Hospital bonding authorities, tax exemption, see IC 5–1–4–26.
Indiana bond bank, exemption from taxation, see IC 5–1.5–9–9.
Indiana development finance authority, property exempt from taxation, see IC 4–4–11–36.1.
Indiana educational facilities authority, tax exemptions, see IC 20–12–63–27.
Indiana political subdivision risk management commission, bonds proceeds and interest exempt from taxation, see IC 27–1–29–17.
Indiana port commission, property exempt from taxation, see IC 8–10–1–27.
Intelenet commission, property exempt from taxation, see IC 5–21–2–15.
Little Calumet River basin development commission, exemption from taxes or assessments, see IC 14–13–2–28.
Local public improvement bond banks, exemption from taxation, see IC 5–1.4–9–9.
Marion County convention and recreational facilities authority, property exempt from taxation, see IC 36–10–9.1–22.
Marion County redevelopment authority, property exempt from taxation, see IC 36–9–25–27.
Multiple county infrastructure authority, property exempt from taxation, see IC 36–7–23–48.

Chapter 1

Definitions

6–5.5–1–1　Application of definitions

Sec. 1.　The definitions in this chapter apply throughout this article.

As added by P.L.347–1989(ss), SEC.1.

Historical and Statutory Notes

P.L.347–1989(ss), Sec.1, eff. Jan. 1, 1990, added this article.

P.L.347–1989(ss), Sec.30, as amended by P.L. 21–1990, Sec.60, emerg. eff. Jan. 1, 1990, provides:

"(a) Except as provided in subsection (b), this act applies for IC 6–2.1, IC 6–3, IC 6–5, and IC 6–5.5 to taxable years that begin after December 31, 1989.

"(b) Any holding company or regulated financial corporation with a fiscal year beginning before and ending on or after January 1, 1990, may:

"(1) change the company's or corporation's fiscal year to a calendar year beginning January 1, 1990, and file a final short year return for the tax under IC 6–2.1, IC 6–3, and IC 6–5; or

"(2) file the final short year return designated in subdivision (1) without changing the company's or corporation's fiscal year and file a short year return under IC 6–5.5 for the period from January 1, 1990, to the end of the corporation's fiscal year.

"(c) Any taxes imposed under IC 6–5–10 and IC 6–5–11 for taxable years that begin before January 1, 1990, and end in 1990, shall be administered, determined, collected, refunded, and distributed under those chapters, unless the regulated financial institution is governed by subsection (a).

"(d) This applies to property taxes first due and payable after December 31, 1989."

Cross References

Library property taxes, replacement credits, see IC 6–3.5–7–23.

Administrative Code References

Intercompany transactions, see 45 IAC 1.1–4–5.

6–5.5–1–2   "Adjusted gross income" defined

Sec. 2.   (a) Except as provided in subsections (b) through (d), "adjusted gross income" means taxable income as defined in Section 63 of the Internal Revenue Code, [1] adjusted as follows:

(1) Add the following amounts:

(A) An amount equal to a deduction allowed or allowable under Section 166, Section 585, or Section 593 of the Internal Revenue Code.[2]

(B) An amount equal to a deduction allowed or allowable under Section 170 of the Internal Revenue Code.[3]

(C) An amount equal to a deduction or deductions allowed or allowable under Section 63 of the Internal Revenue Code [1] for taxes based on or measured by income and levied at the state level by a state of the United States or levied at the local level by any subdivision of a state of the United States.

(D) The amount of interest excluded under Section 103 of the Internal Revenue Code [4] or under any other federal law, minus the associated expenses disallowed in the computation of taxable income under Section 265 of the Internal Revenue Code.[5]

(E) An amount equal to the deduction allowed under Section 172 or 1212 of the Internal Revenue Code [6] for net operating losses or net capital losses.

(F) For a taxpayer that is not a large bank (as defined in Section 585(c)(2) of the Internal Revenue Code [7]), an amount equal to the recovery of a debt, or part of a debt, that becomes worthless to the extent a deduction was allowed from gross income in a prior taxable year under Section 166(a) of the Internal Revenue Code.[8]

(2) Subtract the following amounts:

(A) Income that the United States Constitution or any statute of the United States prohibits from being used to measure the tax imposed by this chapter.

(B) Income that is derived from sources outside the United States, as defined by the Internal Revenue Code.

(C) An amount equal to a debt or part of a debt that becomes worthless, as permitted under Section 166(a) of the Internal Revenue Code.[8]

(D) An amount equal to any bad debt reserves that are included in federal income because of accounting method changes required by Section 585(c)(3)(A) or Section 593 of the Internal Revenue Code.[9]

(b) In the case of a credit union, "adjusted gross income" for a taxable year means the total transfers to undivided earnings minus dividends for that taxable year after statutory reserves are set aside under IC 28–7–1–24.

(c) In the case of an investment company, "adjusted gross income" means the company's federal taxable income multiplied by the quotient of:

(1) the aggregate of the gross payments collected by the company during the taxable year from old and new business upon investment contracts issued by the company and held by residents of Indiana; divided by

(2) the total amount of gross payments collected during the taxable year by the company from the business upon investment contracts issued by the company and held by persons residing within Indiana and elsewhere.

(d) As used in subsection (c), "investment company" means a person, copartnership, association, limited liability company, or corporation, whether domestic or foreign, that:

(1) is registered under the Investment Company Act of 1940 (15 U.S.C. 80a–1 et seq.); and

(2) solicits or receives a payment to be made to itself and issues in exchange for the payment:

(A) a so-called bond;

(B) a share;

(C) a coupon;

(D) a certificate of membership;

(E) an agreement;

(F) a pretended agreement; or

(G) other evidences of obligation;

entitling the holder to anything of value at some future date, if the gross payments received by the company during the taxable year on outstanding investment contracts, plus interest and dividends earned on those contracts (by prorating the interest and dividends earned on investment contracts by the same proportion that certificate reserves (as defined by the Investment Company Act of 1940) is to the company's total assets) is at least fifty percent (50%) of the company's gross payments upon investment contracts plus gross income from all other sources except dividends from subsidiaries for the taxable year. The term "investment contract" means an instrument listed in clauses (A) through (G).

As added by P.L.347–1989(ss), SEC.1. Amended by P.L.21–1990, SEC.15; P.L.68–1991, SEC.1; P.L.8–1993, SEC.94; P.L.28–1997, SEC.20; P.L.119–1998, SEC.13; P.L.273–1999, SEC.52.

[1] 26 U.S.C.A. § 63.
[2] 26 U.S.C.A. § 166, 585, or 593.
[3] 26 U.S.C.A. § 170.
[4] 26 U.S.C.A. § 103.
[5] 26 U.S.C.A. § 265.
[6] 26 U.S.C.A. § 172 or 1212.
[7] 26 U.S.C.A. § 585(c)(2).
[8] 26 U.S.C.A. § 166(a).
[9] 26 U.S.C.A. § 585(c)(3)(A) OR 593.

Historical and Statutory Notes

P.L.21–1990, Sec.15, emerg. eff. retroactive to Jan. 1, 1990, inserted "state or a" in Subsec. (a)(7).

P.L.68–1991, Sec.1, emerg. eff. retroactive to Jan. 1, 1990.

P.L.68–1991, Sec.1, substituted "Section 585(c)(3)(A)" for "Section 585(c)(1)(A)" in Subsec. (a)(4); inserted "or levied at the local level by any subdivision of a state of the United States," preceding "or for taxes on property" in Subsec. (a)(7); and rewrote Subsec. (d)(2), which had read:

"(2) solicits or receives a payment to be made to itself and issues in exchange for the payment:

"(A) a so-called bond;

"(B) a share;

"(C) a coupon;

"(D) a certificate of membership;

"(E) an agreement;

"(F) a pretended agreement; or

"(G) another evidence of obligation;

"entitling the holder to anything of value at some future date, if the gross payments to the holder equal at least fifty percent (50%) of the sum of the company's gross payments on all investment contracts plus the company's gross income from all other sources, except dividends from subsidiaries, for the taxable year. The term 'gross payments' means the amount received during the taxable year on outstanding investment contracts, plus interest and dividends earned on those contracts. The interest and dividends earned on investment contracts are determined by dividing certificate reserves (as defined by the Investment Company Act of

1940) by the company's total assets. The term 'investment contract' means an instrument listed in clauses (A) through (G)."

P.L.8–1993, Sec.94, inserted "limited liability company" in Subsec.(d).

P.L.28–1997, Sec.20, eff. Jan. 1, 1998, amended the section by deleting former Subsecs. (a)(1) through (a)(4); redesignating former Subsec. (a)(5) through (a)(9) as Subsecs. (a)(1) and (a)(1)(A) through (a)(1)(E); and adding Subsecs. (a)(1)(F) and (a)(2). Prior to deletion, former Subsecs. (a)(1) through (a)(4) read:

"(1) Subtract income that the United States Constitution or any statute of the United States prohibits from being used to measure the tax imposed by this chapter.

"(2) Subtract income that is derived from sources outside the United States, as defined by the Internal Revenue Code.

"(3) Subtract an amount equal to a debt or portion of a debt that becomes worthless, as permitted under Section 166(a) of the Internal Revenue Code.

"(4) Subtract an amount equal to any bad debt reserves that are included in federal income because of accounting method changes required by Section 585(c)(3)(A) of the Internal Revenue Code."

P.L.119–1998, Sec.13, emerg. eff. retroactive to Jan. 1, 1998, amended the section by inserting "or Section 593" in Subsec. (a)(2)(D).

P.L.273–1999, Sec.52, emerg. eff. retroactive to Jan. 1, 1999, deleted "or for taxes on property levied by any subdivision of any state of the United States" from the end of Subsec. (a)(1)(C).

Library References

Words and Phrases (Perm.Ed.)

Notes of Decisions

Procedural issues   1
Value-added tax   2

———

1. Procedural issues

Concession by Department of State Revenue during proceeding relating to prior tax year that, if agricultural credit association was determined to be a federal instrumentality, it was immune from state taxation, did not operate under doctrine of res judicata to bar Department from relitigating issue of whether status as federal instrumentality made association immune from state taxation in proceeding relating to subsequent tax year. Farm Credit Services

of Mid-America v. Department of State Revenue, 1999, 705 N.E.2d 1089.

2. Value-added tax

Michigan Single Business Tax (MSBT) paid by financial institution which did business in Indiana was not tax based on or measured by income, and thus was not required to be added back to institution's federal taxable income to calculate its Indiana adjusted gross income, for purposes of determining its Financial Institution Tax (FIT) liability; while taxable income was one portion of MSBT base formula, adjustments radically altered income element, and MSBT was in actuality a tax based on value added. First Chicago NBD Corp. v. Department of State Revenue, 1999, 708 N.E.2d 631.

6–5.5–1–3   "Business of a financial institution" defined

Sec. 3. "Business of a financial institution" has the meaning set forth in section 17(d) of this chapter.

As added by P.L.347–1989(ss), SEC.1.

6–5.5–1–4   "Commercial domicile" defined

Sec. 4. "Commercial domicile" means:

  (1) for a regulated financial corporation:

    (A) the taxing jurisdiction under the laws of which it is organized; or

    (B) if it is organized under the laws of the United States, the place designated as its principal office with the regulatory authority;

  (2) if it is a foreign bank, the state where it has established a federal agency or federal branch under Section 4 of the International Banking Act of 1978 (12 U.S.C. 3102) or if it transacts business in more than one (1) state, its home state as provided in Section 5(c) of the International Banking Act of 1978 (12 U.S.C. 3103(c)); or

  (3) for all other entities, the principal place from which the trade or business of the entity is directed or managed.

As added by P.L.347–1989(ss), SEC.1.

6–5.5–1–5   "Compensation" defined

Sec. 5. "Compensation" means wages, salaries, commissions, and any other form of remuneration paid to employees for personal services.

As added by P.L.347–1989(ss), SEC.1.

6–5.5–1–6   "Corporation" defined

Sec. 6.   "Corporation" means an entity that is:

(1) a corporation (as defined in Internal Revenue Code Section 7701(a)(3)) for federal income tax purposes, including an entity taxed as a corporation under the Internal Revenue Code; and

(2) organized under the laws of the United States, this state, any other taxing jurisdiction, or a foreign government.

As added by P.L.347–1989(ss), SEC.1.   Amended by P.L.21–1990, SEC.16.

Historical and Statutory Notes

P.L.21–1990, Sec.16, emerg. eff. retroactive to Jan. 1, 1990.

P.L.21–1990, Sec.16, in the introductory sentence, inserted "an entity that is"; and in Sub-sec. (1), inserted "including an entity taxed as a corporation under the Internal Revenue Code", and deleted "that is" following "and".

6–5.5–1–7   "Department" defined

Sec. 7.   "Department" refers to the department of state revenue.
As added by P.L.347–1989(ss), SEC.1.

6–5.5–1–8   "Employee" defined

Sec. 8.   "Employee" has the same meaning as it has for purposes of federal income tax withholding under Sections 3401 through 3404 of the Internal Revenue Code.
As added by P.L.347–1989(ss), SEC.1.

6–5.5–1–9   "Foreign bank" defined

Sec. 9.   "Foreign bank" means an entity organized under the laws of a foreign country, a territory of the United States, Puerto Rico, Guam, American Samoa, or the Virgin Islands that engages in the business of a financial institution or a subsidiary or affiliate organized under those laws of such an entity.   The term includes foreign commercial banks, foreign merchant banks, and other foreign institutions that engage in banking activities that are usually in connection with the business of a financial institution in the countries where the foreign institutions are organized or operating.
As added by P.L.347–1989(ss), SEC.1.

6–5.5–1–10   "Gross income" defined

Sec. 10.   "Gross income" means gross income (as defined in Section 61 of the Internal Revenue Code) for federal income tax purposes.
As added by P.L.347–1989(ss), SEC.1.

6–5.5–1–11   "Internal Revenue Code" defined

Sec. 11.   "Internal Revenue Code" has the meaning set forth in IC 6–3–1–11.
As added by P.L.347–1989(ss), SEC.1.

6–5.5–1–12 "Nonresident taxpayer" defined

Sec. 12. "Nonresident taxpayer" means a taxpayer that:

(1) is transacting business within Indiana, as provided in IC 6–5.5–3; and

(2) has its commercial domicile outside Indiana.

As added by P.L.347–1989(ss), SEC.1. Amended by P.L.68–1991, SEC.2.

Historical and Statutory Notes

P.L.68–1991, Sec.2, emerg. eff. retroactive to Jan. 1, 1990.

P.L.68–1991, Sec.2, deleted "in a taxing jurisdiction" preceding "outside Indiana" in Subsec. (2).

6–5.5–1–13 "Resident taxpayer" defined

Sec. 13. "Resident taxpayer" means a taxpayer that:

(1) is transacting business within Indiana, as provided in IC 6–5.5–3; and

(2) has its commercial domicile in Indiana.

As added by P.L.347–1989(ss), SEC.1.

6–5.5–1–14 "Subsidiary" defined

Sec. 14. "Subsidiary" means:

(1) a corporation fifty percent (50%) or more of whose voting stock; or

(2) an entity other than a corporation that is taxed as a corporation under the Internal Revenue Code and fifty percent (50%) of whose net worth;

is owned by another legal entity.

As added by P.L.347–1989(ss), SEC.1. Amended by P.L.21–1990, SEC.17.

Historical and Statutory Notes

P.L.21–1990, Sec.17, emerg. eff. retroactive to Jan. 1, 1990.

P.L.21–1990, Sec.17, in Subsec. (2), substituted "is taxed as a corporation under the Internal

Revenue Code and" for "has at least"; and made nonsubstantive changes throughout.

6–5.5–1–15 "Taxable year" defined

Sec. 15. "Taxable year", with respect to a taxpayer, means the taxable year of the taxpayer as shown on the taxpayer's return required to be filed under the Internal Revenue Code. If a taxpayer does not file a return under the Internal Revenue Code, the taxpayer's taxable year is the calendar year.

As added by P.L.347–1989(ss), SEC.1.

6–5.5–1–16 "Taxing jurisdiction" defined

Sec. 16. "Taxing jurisdiction" means a state of the United States, the District of Columbia, the Commonwealth of Puerto Rico, or a territory or possession of the United States.

As added by P.L.347–1989(ss), SEC.1.

6–5.5–1–17 "Taxpayer" defined

Sec. 17. (a) "Taxpayer" means a corporation that is transacting the business of a financial institution in Indiana, including any of the following:

(1) A holding company.

(2) A regulated financial corporation.

(3) A subsidiary of a holding company or regulated financial corporation.

(4) Any other corporation organized under the laws of the United States, this state, another taxing jurisdiction, or a foreign government that is carrying on the business of a financial institution.

(b) As used in this section, "holding company" means a corporation registered under the Bank Holding Company Act of 1956 (12 U.S.C. 1841 through 1849), as in effect on December 31, 1990, or registered as a savings and loan holding company other than a diversified savings and loan holding company (as defined in Section 10(a)(F) of the Home Owners' Loan Act of 1933 (12 U.S.C. 1467a(1)(F)), as in effect on December 31, 1990).

(c) As used in this section, "regulated financial corporation" means:

(1) an institution, the deposits, shares, or accounts of which are insured under the Federal Deposit Insurance Act (12 U.S.C. 1811 through 1833e), as in effect on December 31, 1990;

(2) an institution that is a member of a Federal Home Loan Bank;

(3) any other bank or thrift institution incorporated or organized under the laws of a state that is engaged in the business of receiving deposits;

(4) a credit union incorporated and organized under the laws of this state;

(5) a production credit association organized under 12 U.S.C. 2071, as in effect on December 31, 1990;

(6) a corporation organized under 12 U.S.C. 611 through 631 (an Edge Act corporation), as in effect on December 31, 1990;

(7) a federal or state agency or branch of a foreign bank (as defined in 12 U.S.C. 3101, as in effect on December 31, 1990); or

(8) a trust company formed under IC 28–12.

(d) For purposes of this section and when used in this article, "business of a financial institution" means the following:

(1) For a holding company, a regulated financial corporation, or a subsidiary of either, the activities that each is authorized to perform under federal or state law, including the activities authorized by regulation or order of the Federal Reserve Board for such a subsidiary under Section 4(c)(8) of the Bank Holding Company Act of 1956 (12 U.S.C. 1843(c)(8)), as in effect on December 31, 1990.

(2) For any other corporation described in subsection (a)(4), all of the corporation's business activities if eighty percent (80%) or more of the

corporation's gross income, excluding extraordinary income, is derived from one (1) or more of the following activities:

(A) Making, acquiring, selling, or servicing loans or extensions of credit. For the purpose of this subdivision, loans and extensions of credit include:

(i) secured or unsecured consumer loans;

(ii) installment obligations;

(iii) mortgage or other secured loans on real estate or tangible personal property;

(iv) credit card loans;

(v) secured and unsecured commercial loans of any type;

(vi) letters of credit and acceptance of drafts;

(vii) loans arising in factoring; and

(viii) any other transactions with a comparable economic effect.

(B) Leasing or acting as an agent, broker, or advisor in connection with leasing real and personal property that is the economic equivalent of the extension of credit if the transaction is not treated as a lease for federal income tax purposes.

(C) Operating a credit card, debit card, charge card, or similar business.

As used in this subdivision, "gross income" includes income from interest, fees, penalties, a market discount or other type of discount, rental income, the gain on a sale of intangible or other property evidencing a loan or extension of credit, and dividends or other income received as a means of furthering the activities set out in this subdivision.

As added by P.L.347–1989(ss), SEC.1. Amended by P.L.21–1990, SEC.18; P.L.8–1991, SEC.4; P.L.68–1991, SEC.3; P.L.1–1992, SEC.18; P.L.119–1998, SEC.14.

Historical and Statutory Notes

P.L.21–1990, Sec.18, emerg. eff. retroactive to Jan. 1, 1990.

P.L.21–1990, Sec.18, in Subsec. (c)(1), deleted "or by the National Credit Union Administration" following "Corporation"; in Subsec. (c)(5), substituted "2071" for "2041"; in Subsec. (c)(7), substituted "of federal or state" for "an", deleted "or subsidiary" following "branch", and inserted "(as defined in 12 U.S.C. 3101)"; in Subsec. (d)(1), substituted "For" for 'The business activities that", deleted "foreign bank" following "corporation", substituted "either, the activities that each" for "such an entity", and deleted "when carried out by the entity or subsidiary" following "perform"; in Subsec. (d)(2), in the introductory sentence, substituted "For" for 'The business activities

of", and inserted "described in subsection (a)(4), all of the corporation's business activities"; in Subsec. (d)(2)(B), substituted "if the transaction is not treated as a lease for federal income tax purposes" for "(as defined by the Federal Reserve Board in 12 C.F.R. 225.25(b)(5))"; in Subsec. (d)(2)(C), inserted "debit card, charge card, or similar"; and made nonsubstantive changes throughout.

P.L.8–1991, Sec.4, emerg. eff. upon passage May 5, 1991.

P.L.8–1991, Sec.4, in Subsec. (b), deleted "Federal" preceding "Bank Holding", inserted "(12 U.S.C. 1841 through 1849), as in effect on December 31, 1990,", and substituted "10(a)(F) of the Home Owners' Loan Act of 1933 (12 U.S.C. 1467a(1)(F), as in effect on December 31,

1990'' for "408(a)(1)(F) of the Federal National Housing Act (12 U.S.C. 1730(a)(1)(F)"; in Subsec. (c)(1), inserted "(12 U.S.C. 1811 through 1833e), as in effect on December 31, 1990;" and deleted "by the Federal Savings and Loan Insurance Corporation" following "or"; and, in Subsecs. (c)(5), (6), and (7), inserted "as in effect on December 31, 1990".

P.L.68–1991, Sec.3, eff. Jan. 1, 1992.

P.L.68–1991, Sec.3, inserted Subsec. (c)(8).

P.L.1–1992, Sec.18, emerg. eff. Feb. 21, 1992, corrected the conflicting versions of this section as amended by P.L.8–1991, Sec.4, and as amended by P.L.68–1991, Sec.3.

P.L.119–1998, Sec.14, emerg. eff. retroactive to Jan. 1, 1998, amended the section by substituting "IC 28–12" for "IC 28–1–4" in Subsec. (c)(8).

6–5.5–1–18   "Unitary business" defined

Sec. 18.   (a) "Unitary business" means business activities or operations that are of mutual benefit, dependent upon, or contributory to one another, individually or as a group, in transacting the business of a financial institution.   The term may be applied within a single legal entity or between multiple entities and without regard to whether each entity is a corporation, a partnership, a limited liability company, or a trust, provided that each member is either a holding company, a regulated financial corporation, a subsidiary of either, a corporation that conducts the business of a financial institution under IC 6–5.5–1–17(d)(2), or any other entity, regardless of its form, that conducts activities that would constitute the business of a financial institution under IC 6–5.5–1–17(d)(2) if the activities were conducted by a corporation.   The term "unitary group" includes those entities that are engaged in a unitary business transacted wholly or partially within Indiana.

(b) Unity is presumed whenever there is unity of ownership, operation, and use evidenced by centralized management or executive force, centralized purchasing, advertising, accounting, or other controlled interaction among entities that are members of the unitary group, as described in subsection (a).   However, the absence of these centralized activities does not necessarily evidence a nonunitary business.

(c) Unity of ownership, when a corporation is involved, does not exist unless that corporation is a member of a group of two (2) or more business entities and more than fifty percent (50%) of the voting stock of each member of the group is directly or indirectly owned by:

(1) a common owner or common owners, either corporate or noncorporate; or

(2) one (1) or more of the member corporations of the group.

As added by P.L.347–1989(ss), SEC.1.   Amended by P.L.21–1990, SEC.19; P.L.8–1993, SEC.95.

Historical and Statutory Notes

P.L.21–1990, Sec.19, emerg. eff. retroactive to Jan. 1, 1990.

P.L.21–1990, Sec.19, in the second sentence, inserted "provided that each member is either a holding company, a regulated financial corporation, a subsidiary of either, a corporation that conducts the business of a financial institution under IC 6–5.5–1–17(d)(2), or any other entity, regardless of its form, that conducts activities that would constitute the business of a financial institution under IC 6–5.5–1–17(d)(2) if the activities were conducted by a corporation", and in the third sentence inserted "transacted", deleted "within" following "wholly", inserted "partially" and deleted "and without" preceding "Indiana"; in Subsec. (b), in the first sentence, substituted "members of the unitary group, as described in subsection (a)" for "holding companies, regulated financial institutions, or engaged in the business of a financial institution".

P.L.8–1993, Sec.95, inserted "a limited liability company" in the second sentence of Subsec.(a).

6–5.5–1–19   "Partnership" defined

Sec. 19.   "Partnership" means an association of two (2) or more entities formed to conduct a business, including but not limited to;

(1) a limited partnership, a syndicate, a group, a pool, a joint venture, or an incorporated association; or

(2) a similar entity if the income for federal income tax purposes is taxed to the equity participants in that business, however characterized.

As added by P.L.21–1990, SEC.20.

Historical and Statutory Notes

P.L.21–1990, Sec.20, emerg. eff. retroactive to Jan. 1, 1990.

Chapter 2

Imposition of Tax

6–5.5–2–1   Computation of franchise tax

Sec. 1.   (a) There is imposed on each taxpayer a franchise tax measured by the taxpayer's adjusted gross income or apportioned income for the privilege of exercising its franchise or the corporate privilege of transacting the business of a financial institution in Indiana.   The amount of the tax for a taxable year shall be determined by multiplying eight and one-half percent (8.5%) times the remainder of:

(1) the taxpayer's adjusted gross income or apportioned income; minus

(2) the taxpayer's deductible Indiana net operating losses as determined under this section; minus

(3) the taxpayer's net capital losses minus the taxpayer's net capital gains computed under the Internal Revenue Code for each taxable year or part of

a taxable year beginning after December 31, 1989, multiplied by the apportionment percentage applicable to the taxpayer under IC 6–5.5–2 for the taxable year of the loss.

A net capital loss for a taxable year is a net capital loss carryover to each of the five (5) taxable years that follow the taxable year in which the loss occurred.

(b) The amount of net operating losses deductible under subsection (a) is an amount equal to the net operating losses computed under the Internal Revenue Code, adjusted for the items set forth in IC 6–5.5–1–2, that are:

(1) incurred in each taxable year, or part of a year, beginning after December 31, 1989; and

(2) attributable to Indiana.

(c) The following apply to determining the amount of net operating losses that may be deducted under subsection (a):

(1) The amount of net operating losses that is attributable to Indiana is the taxpayer's total net operating losses under the Internal Revenue Code for the taxable year of the loss, adjusted for the items set forth in IC 6–5.5–1–2, multiplied by the apportionment percentage applicable to the taxpayer under IC 6–5.5–2 for the taxable year of the loss.

(2) A net operating loss for any taxable year is a net operating loss carryover to each of the fifteen (15) taxable years that follow the taxable year in which the loss occurred.

(d) The following provisions apply to a combined return computing the tax on the basis of the income of the unitary group when the return is filed for more than one (1) taxpayer member of the unitary group for any taxable year:

(1) Any net capital loss or net operating loss attributable to Indiana in the combined return shall be prorated between each taxpayer member of the unitary group by the quotient of:

(A) the receipts of that taxpayer member attributable to Indiana under section 4 of this chapter; divided by

(B) the receipts of all taxpayer members of the unitary group attributable to Indiana.

(2) The net capital loss or net operating loss for that year, if any, to be carried forward to any subsequent year shall be limited to the capital gains or apportioned income for the subsequent year of that taxpayer, determined by the same receipts formula set out in subdivision (1).

As added by P.L.347–1989(ss), SEC.1. Amended by P.L.21–1990, SEC.21; P.L.68–1991, SEC.4; P.L.1–1992, SEC.19.

Historical and Statutory Notes

P.L.347–1989(ss), Sec.1, eff. Jan. 1, 1990, added this article.

P.L.21–1990, Sec.21, emerg. eff. retroactive to Jan. 1, 1990.

P.L.21–1990, Sec.21, in Subsec. (a)(3), deleted "apportioned" following "taxpayer's" substituted "minus the taxpayer's" for "in an amount not to exceed the apportioned", inserted "computed under the Internal Revenue Code, substituted "each" for "the", and inserted "or part of a taxable year beginning after December 31, 1989, multiplied by the apportionment percentage applicable to the taxpayer under IC 6–5.5–2 for the taxable year of the loss", and inserted the last sentence; in Subsec. (b), in the introductory sentence, deleted "for net operating losses" preceding "adjusted"; in Subsec. (b)(1), inserted "each", and substituted "year, or part of a year, beginning" for "years ending"; in Subsec. (c)(2), substituted "A" for "The amount of", substituted "loss for any taxable year is a net operating loss carryover to each of" for "losses determined under subdivision (1) may be deducted under subsection (a) during", and deleted "not to exceed the amount of the loss" following "loss occurred".

P.L.68–1991, Sec.4, emerg. eff. retroactive to Jan. 1, 1990.

P.L.68–1991, Sec.4, rewrote the introductory paragraph of Subsec. (a); and added Subsec. (d). The introductory paragraph of Subsec. (a) had read:

"(a) There is imposed on each taxpayer a franchise tax measured by net income for the privilege of exercising its franchise or transacting business within Indiana. The amount of the tax for a taxable year shall be determined by multiplying eight and one half percent (8.5%) times the remainder of:"

P.L.1–1992, Sec.19, emerg. eff. Feb. 21, 1992, made corrective changes.

Library References

Taxation ⚮125, 165, 386, 397.
WESTLAW Topic No. 371.
C.J.S. Taxation §§ 143, 190, 424, 428.

Notes of Decisions

1. Validity

Intangibles tax did not violate commerce clause of the United States Constitution pursuant to *Darnell* opinion; *Darnell* opinion was dispositive of commerce clause issue, where *Darnell* had not been implicitly overruled by subsequent Supreme Court decisions and present intangible tax statute was substantially like tax statute at issue in *Darnell*. Indiana Dept. of State Revenue v. Felix, 1991, 571 N.E.2d 287, certiorari dismissed 112 S.Ct. 1073, 502 U.S. 1084, 117 L.Ed.2d 278.

Legislature was not required to exempt all intangibles from tax to meet uniformity requirements of State Constitution; legislature could discriminate within intangible personal property class consistently with uniformity requirement of constitution. Indiana Dept. of State Revenue v. Felix, 1991, 571 N.E.2d 287, certiorari dismissed 112 S.Ct. 1073, 502 U.S. 1084, 117 L.Ed.2d 278.

2. Validity of prior law

Taxing shares of foreign corporations owned by citizens under former statute [see, now, § 6–5.1–1–1 et seq.] did not deny equal protection of laws because with domestic corporations the property, and not the shares, was taxed. Darnell v. State of Indiana, U.S.Ind.1912, 33 S.Ct. 120, 226 U.S. 390, 57 L.Ed. 267.

Statute providing for the taxation of intangibles [repealed; see, now, § 6–5.1–1–1 et seq.] was applicable to postal savings certificates and was not unconstitutional as contrary to U.S.C.A.Const. Art. 1, § 8 and Art. 6 vesting in Congress power to borrow money on credit of the United States and providing that Constitution and laws made in pursuance thereof shall be the supreme law of the land. Lutz v. Arnold, 1935, 193 N.E. 840, 208 Ind. 480, rehearing overruled 196 N.E. 702, 208 Ind. 480.

Statutes providing for the taxation of intangibles [Acts 1933, c. 81, (repealed; see, now, § 6–5.1–1–1 et seq.)], building and loan associations [Acts 1933, c. 82; now, § 6–5–11–1 et seq.], and banks and trust companies [Acts 1933, c. 83; now, § 6–5–10–1 et seq.] were not unconstitutional as 10 "local" or "special" laws. Lutz v. Arnold, 1935, 193 N.E. 840, 208 Ind. 480, rehearing overruled 196 N.E. 702, 208 Ind. 480.

Statutes providing for the taxation of intangibles [repealed; see, now, § 6–5.1–1–1 et seq.], building and loan associations [now § 6–5–11–1 et seq.], and banks and trust companies [now, § 6–5–10–1 et seq.] were not unconstitutional as granting special privileges or immunities to certain classes, or as abridging the privileges or immunities of citizens of the United States, or denying any person equal protection of the law. Lutz v. Arnold, 1935, 193 N.E. 840, 208 Ind. 480, rehearing overruled 196 N.E. 702, 208 Ind. 480.

Statute providing for taxation of intangibles [repealed; see, now, § 6–5.1–1–1 et seq.] was an excise tax and, as such, not subject to Const. Art. 10, § 1 stating that general assembly shall provide by law for a uniform and equal rate of assessment and taxation on all property not specially exempted by law. Lutz v. Arnold, 1935, 193 N.E. 840, 208 Ind. 480, rehearing overruled 196 N.E. 702, 208 Ind. 480.

3. Purpose

Legislature, by enacting Intangible Tax Act [repealed; see, now, § 6–5.1–1–1 et seq.] did not intend to impair validity of existing obligations, such as notes, but only intended to suspend effectiveness and force of such obligations for all purposes until requirements of Act were satisfied by payment of tax in one of modes provided therein. Gradeless v. Gradeless, App.1943, 49 N.E.2d 398, 114 Ind.App. 10.

Intangible Tax Act [repealed; see, now, § 6–5.1–1–1 et seq.] was purely a "revenue measure", intended to expedite and enforce payment of moneys due state under provisions of the Act, by suspending effect for all purposes of all intangibles within purview of Act, such as notes, until such moneys were paid in full. Gradeless v. Gradeless, App.1943, 49 N.E.2d 398, 114 Ind.App. 10.

General purpose of General Intangibles Tax Act [repealed; see, now, § 6–5.1–1–1 et seq.] was to find more effective method of reaching intangibles for purpose of taxation, because property tax law had become ineffective in reaching such class of property. Zoercher v. Indiana Associated Telephone Corp., 1937, 7 N.E.2d 282, 211 Ind. 447.

4. Construction

Provision of General Intangibles Tax Act [repealed; see, now this section] relating to signing, executing, and issuing intangibles had to be construed with all other provisions of act, and whole act had to be construed together in order to determine meaning of act and intent of legislature. Zoercher v. Indiana Associated Telephone Corp., 1937, 7 N.E.2d 282, 211 Ind. 447.

Practical construction of General Intangibles Tax Act [repealed; see, now, § 6–5.1–1–1 et seq.] as shown by opinions of state board of tax commissioners and attorney general was influential, as respects interpretation by court, though not controlling. Zoercher v. Indiana Associated Telephone Corp., 1937, 7 N.E.2d 282, 211 Ind. 447.

5. Nature of tax

Financial institutions tax, described as franchise tax measured by taxpayer's adjusted gross income or apportioned income for privilege of exercising its franchise or corporate privilege of transacting business of financial institution in state, was not direct tax on federal and municipal bonds, but rather was excise tax on exercise of corporate privilege of operating as financial institution in state. Indiana Dept. of State Revenue v. Fort Wayne Nat. Corp., 1995, 649 N.E.2d 109, certiorari denied 116 S.Ct. 298, 516 U.S. 913, 133 L.Ed.2d 204.

An "excise tax" is a tax imposed on performance of an act, engaging in an occupation or enjoyment of a privilege, and every form of tax not imposed directly on property must constitute an "excise" if it is a valid tax of any description. Lutz v. Arnold, 1935, 193 N.E. 840, 208 Ind. 480, rehearing overruled 196 N.E. 702, 208 Ind. 480.

The intangibles tax is an excise tax as distinguished from a property tax. 1936 Op.Atty. Gen. p. 251.

The intangibles tax is imposed for right to exercise certain privileges inherent in intangibles. 1936 Op.Atty.Gen. p. 251.

6. Exemptions

Excise or franchise tax may be measured by taxpayer's income without being construed as income tax. Indiana Dept. of State Revenue v. Fort Wayne Nat. Corp., 1995, 649 N.E.2d 109, certiorari denied 116 S.Ct. 298, 516 U.S. 913, 133 L.Ed.2d 204.

State general exemption statute, exempting municipal bonds from taxation, did not preclude using tax exempt bond income in calculating financial institutions tax; only reasonable harmonization of general exemption statute and financial institutions tax statute was that bonds were exempt only from direct taxation. Indiana Dept. of State Revenue v. Fort Wayne Nat. Corp., 1995, 649 N.E.2d 109, certiorari denied 116 S.Ct. 298, 516 U.S. 913, 133 L.Ed.2d 204.

Tax exemption statutes must be construed strictly against one claiming exemption. Indiana Dept. of State Revenue v. Fort Wayne Nat. Corp., 1995, 649 N.E.2d 109, certiorari denied 116 S.Ct. 298, 516 U.S. 913, 133 L.Ed.2d 204.

7. Ownership and control of intangibles

To be taxed under the intangible tax statute [IC1971, 6–5–1–2 (repealed; see, now, this section)] taxpayer must either own or control intangible. Meridian Mortg. Co., Inc. v. State, App. 2 Dist.1979, 395 N.E.2d 433, 182 Ind.App. 328.

Corporation's trading in intangibles did not make it liable for intangible tax. Meridian Mortg. Co., Inc. v. State, App. 2 Dist.1979, 395 N.E.2d 433, 182 Ind.App. 328.

Although title to mortgages was in corporation's name and agreement between lending bank, title companies and corporation treated corporation as borrower, corporation was broker, it did not own or control mortgages and it was not subject to intangible taxes based on them, where arrangement was mechanism by bank to secure corporation's credit in support of mortgagors, corporation never had possession of mortgages, corporation had no discretion as to how mortgages would be handled, and mortgages were unconditionally assigned to bank which had right to monthly income payments and ultimately right to approve of and receive proceeds from sale of mortgages. Meridian Mortg. Co., Inc. v. State, App. 2 Dist.1979, 395 N.E.2d 433, 182 Ind.App. 328.

Under the General Intangibles Tax Act of 1933 [repealed; see, now, § 6–5.1–1–1 et seq.] it was the owner of the intangible who was liable for the tax, and ownership by some person liable for the tax was requisite to taxability, and consequently note and chattel mortgage made payable to citizen or corporation outside state could not be subjected to initial tax before delivery. 1934 Op.Atty.Gen. p. 421.

8. Receipt of income from intangibles

Taxpayer, by entering into a participation agreement with bank, was actually purchasing an interest in loan between bank and customer and, hence, was exercising a "taxable privilege" because it was receiving income from interest it had purchased. Indiana State Dept. of Revenue, Income Tax Division v. Valley Financial Services, Inc., App. 3 Dist.1982, 435 N.E.2d 68.

9. Issuance of intangibles

General Intangibles Tax Act [repealed; see, now, § 6–5.1–1–1 et seq.] did not impose tax upon issuer of intangibles, notwithstanding provision thereof that person should be taxed for privilege of, among other things, "signing, executing and issuing intangibles" and provision fixing penalty for violation of act by one signing or issuing intangibles, in view of definition of "intangibles" as evidence of indebtedness "issued," and many other provisions showing intention to tax owner of intangibles. Zoercher v. Indiana Associated Telephone Corp., 1937, 7 N.E.2d 282, 211 Ind. 447.

Domestic corporation, which issued bonds secured by indenture supplemental to prior indenture which contemplated later issue, and sold bonds without state to nonresidents, was not liable to taxation under General Intangibles Tax Act [repealed; see, now, § 6–5.1–1–1 et seq.] on account of signing, executing, and issuing bonds, sale and transfer thereof, or execution of supplemental indenture. Zoercher v. Indiana Associated Telephone Corp., 1937, 7 N.E.2d 282, 211 Ind. 447.

Former statute [see, now, this section] was not intended to impose tax upon issuers of intangibles, and therefore debtor who executed his note and mortgage to small loan company could not legally be charged with intangible tax required under law to be collected on such intangibles. 1937 Op.Atty.Gen. p. 162.

10. Corporations

Legislature may tax corporations based on amount of capital stock. State v. Siosi Oil Corp., 1936, 199 N.E. 232, 209 Ind. 394.

11. Trusts

The purpose of settlor in creating trust to avoid taxes would not render her liable for tax on stock of which she parted with title and control. Johnston v. State, 1937, 8 N.E.2d 590, 212 Ind. 375, rehearing denied 10 N.E.2d 40, 212 Ind. 375.

12. Tax stamps

Under agreement by which corporate stock was assigned to defendant with dividends payable to his sister until her death after payment of current obligations, fact that no intangible tax stamps were attached to the notes representing current obligations at the time they were paid did not preclude payment of the notes before declaration of dividends, since due to such failure, payment of the notes was merely abated until stamps in proper amount were attached thereto. Krull v. Pierce, App.1947, 71 N.E.2d 617, 117 Ind.App. 638.

Presence on, or absence from an intangible, such as a note, of tax stamps did not of itself determine whether tax on the intangible had been paid, nor constitute sole evidence of compliance or noncompliance with Intangible Tax Act [repealed; see, now, § 6–5.1–1–1 et seq.]. Gradeless v. Gradeless, App.1943, 49 N.E.2d 398, 114 Ind.App. 10.

6–5.5–2–2   Adjusted gross income of resident taxpayer not filing combined return

Sec. 2.   For a resident taxpayer that is not filing a combined return, the taxpayer's adjusted gross income equals all of the taxpayer's adjusted gross income from whatever source derived.

As added by P.L.347–1989(ss), SEC.1.   Amended by P.L.21–1990, SEC.22.

Historical and Statutory Notes

P.L.21–1990, Sec.22, emerg. eff. retroactive to Jan. 1, 1990.

P.L.21–1990, Sec.22, substituted "from whatever" for "regardless of the", and substituted "derived" for "of the income".

6–5.5–2–3   Apportioned income of nonresident taxpayer not filing combined return

Sec. 3.   For a nonresident taxpayer that is not filing a combined return, the taxpayer's apportioned income consists of the taxpayer's adjusted gross income for that year multiplied by the quotient of:

(1) the taxpayer's total receipts attributable to transacting business in Indiana, as determined under IC 6–5.5–4; divided by

(2) the taxpayer's total receipts from transacting business in all taxing jurisdictions, as determined under IC 6–5.5–4.

As added by P.L.347–1989(ss), SEC.1.

Library References

Taxation ☞397.
WESTLAW Topic No. 371.
C.J.S. Taxation § 428.

6–5.5–2–4   Apportioned income of taxpayer filing combined return for unitary group

Sec. 4.   For a taxpayer filing a combined return for its unitary group, the group's apportioned income for a taxable year consists of:

(1) the aggregate adjusted gross income, from whatever source derived, of the resident taxpayer members of the unitary group and the nonresident members of the unitary group; multiplied by

(2) the quotient of:

(A) all the receipts of the resident taxpayer members of the unitary group from whatever source derived plus the receipts of the nonresident taxpayer members of the unitary group that are attributable to transacting business in Indiana; divided by

(B) the receipts of all the members of the unitary group from transacting business in all taxing jurisdictions.

As added by P.L.347–1989(ss), SEC.1. Amended by P.L.68–1991, SEC.5.

Historical and Statutory Notes

P.L.68–1991, Sec.5, eff. Jan. 1, 1992.

P.L.68–1991, Sec.5, rewrote the section, which had read:

"For a taxpayer filing a combined return for its unitary group, the group's apportioned income consists of:

"(1) all of the adjusted gross income of the resident taxpayer members of the unitary group; plus

"(2) the adjusted gross income of all nonresident taxpayer members of the unitary group for the taxable year multiplied by the quotient of:

"(A) the receipts of the nonresident taxpayer members of the unitary group attributable to transacting business in Indiana, as determined under IC 6–5.5–4; divided by

"(B) the receipts of the nonresident taxpayer members of the unitary group from transacting business in all taxing jurisdictions, as determined under IC 6–5.5–4."

Library References

Taxation ⚖397.
WESTLAW Topic No. 371.
C.J.S. Taxation § 428.

6–5.5–2–5   Credit for resident taxpayer or resident member of unitary group

Sec. 5.   (a) A resident taxpayer or a resident member of a unitary group is entitled to a credit against the tax due under this article.

(b) The amount of the credit equals the lesser of:

(1) the amount of creditable tax actually paid by the resident taxpayer or member to any other taxing jurisdiction; or

(2) an amount equal to the amount of creditable tax that would be due at the tax rate set forth under this article on:

(A) the taxpayer's adjusted gross income or apportioned income that is subject to taxation by the other taxing jurisdiction; or

(B) the taxpayer's adjusted gross income or apportioned income that is attributable to the other taxing jurisdiction using the rules for attributing gross receipts under IC 6–5.5–4.

(c) As used in this section, "creditable tax" means in the case of a taxing jurisdiction that:

(1) measures its tax using net income:

(A) a direct net income tax; or

(B) a franchise or other tax measured by net income; or

(2) is not covered by subdivision (1):

(A) a tax based on deposits, investment capital or shares, net worth or capital, or a combination of these tax bases; or

(B) any other tax that is imposed instead of an income tax.

As added by P.L.347–1989(ss), SEC.1. Amended by P.L.68–1991, SEC.6.

Historical and Statutory Notes

P.L.68–1991, Sec.6, emerg. eff. retroactive to Jan. 1, 1990.

P.L.68–1991, Sec.6, rewrote Subsec. (b), which had read:

"(b) The amount of the credit equals the lesser of:

"(1) the amount of creditable tax actually paid by the resident taxpayer or member to

any other taxing jurisdiction on the resident taxpayer's or member's adjusted gross income; or

"(2) an amount equal to the amount of creditable tax that would be due at the tax rate set forth under this article on the lesser of:

"(A) the taxpayer's adjusted gross income that is subject to taxation by the other taxing jurisdiction; or

"(B) the taxpayer's adjusted gross income that is attributable to the other taxing juris- diction under the rules for attributing gross receipts under this article."

Library References

Taxation ⚖️386.
WESTLAW Topic No. 371.
C.J.S. Taxation § 424.

6–5.5–2–5.3   Credits; satisfactory evidence of payment

Sec. 5.3.   A credit provided in section 5 of this chapter may be allowed only after the taxpayer provides to the department satisfactory evidence of the payment of taxes to the other taxing jurisdiction.
As added by P.L.21–1990, SEC.23.

Historical and Statutory Notes

P.L.21–1990, Sec.23, emerg. eff. retroactive to Jan. 1, 1990.

6–5.5–2–6   Credit for nonresident taxpayer

Sec. 6.   (a) A nonresident taxpayer is entitled to a credit against the tax due under this article for the amount of net income tax, franchise tax, or other tax measured by net income that is due to the nonresident taxpayer's domiciliary state for a taxable year if:

(1) the receipt of interest or other income from a loan or loan transaction is attributed both to the taxpayer's domiciliary state under that state's laws and also to Indiana under IC 6–5.5–4; and

(2) the principal amount of the loan is at least two million dollars ($2,000,-000).

(b) The amount of the credit for each taxable year is the lesser of:

(1) the portion of the net income tax, franchise tax, or other tax measured by net income actually paid by the nonresident taxpayer to its domiciliary state that is attributable to the loan or loan transaction; or

(2) the portion of the franchise tax due to Indiana under this article that is attributable to the loan or loan transaction.

The amount determined under subdivisions (1) and (2) shall be reduced by the amount of any credit for the tax due from the nonresident taxpayer under this article (calculated without the allowance for the credit provided under this section) and that may be used by the nonresident taxpayer in calculating the income tax due under the laws of the nonresident taxpayer's domiciliary state.

(c) As used in this section:

(1) "loan" or "loan transaction" refers to an obligation created in a single transaction to pay or repay a sum of money attributed as provided in subsection (a)(1);

431

(2) the "principal amount" of a loan is limited to the principal amount specified in the loan documents at the time of making the loan and reasonably expected to be advanced during the term of the loan, even though there is more than one (1) advancement. If the loan is a participation loan (as defined in IC 6–5.5–4–13), the principal amount must be calculated separately for each participant and is equal to that portion of the loan committed by each participant; and

(3) a "taxpayer's domiciliary state" is the taxing jurisdiction in which its commercial domicile is located.

(d) The amount of tax attributable to a loan or loan transaction, under the laws of the taxpayer's domiciliary state or under this article, is the portion of the total tax due to each state in an amount equal to the same proportion as the receipts from the loan or loan transaction bear to the total of the taxpayer's receipts.

As added by P.L.347–1989(ss), SEC.1. Amended by P.L.21–1990, SEC.24; P.L.68–1991, SEC.7.

Historical and Statutory Notes

P.L.21–1990, Sec.24, emerg. eff. retroactive to Jan. 1, 1990.

P.L.21–1990, Sec.24, in Subsec. (a), inserted the last paragraph.

P.L.68–1991, Sec.7, emerg. eff. retroactive to Jan. 1, 1990.

P.L.68–1991, Sec.7, inserted ", franchise tax, or other tax measured by net income that is" in Subsec. (a); inserted ", franchise tax, or other tax measured by net income" in Subsec. (b)(1); substituted "franchise tax" for "net income tax" in Subsec. (b)(2); deleted Subsec. (c)(1); redesignated Subsecs. (c)(2) through (c)(4) as Subsecs. (c)(1) through (c)(3); and deleted Subsec. (e). Subsections (c)(1) and (e) had provided:

"(1) 'net income tax' means:

"(A) a direct net income tax; or

"(B) a franchise or other tax measured by net income;"

"(e) If the amount of tax for any taxable year to be paid for any loans or loan transactions by a nonresident taxpayer to its domiciliary state as provided in subsection (b)(1) is equal to or greater than the amount of tax due to Indiana under this article as provided in subsection (b)(2), computed by comparing the rate and base of the tax imposed by each state, the nonresident taxpayer may, in filing a tax return in Indiana:

"(1) exclude the receipt of interest or other income from those loans or loan transactions in calculating the tax due to Indiana in lieu of calculating the credit provided under this section; and

"(2) include in the return an estimate of the total of those receipts."

Library References

Taxation ⊗397.
WESTLAW Topic No. 371.
C.J.S. Taxation § 428.

6–5.5–2–7   Exempt organizations

Sec. 7. Notwithstanding any other provision of this article, there is no tax imposed on the adjusted gross income or apportioned income of the following:

(1) Insurance companies subject to the tax under IC 27–1–18–2 or IC 6–2.1.

(2) International banking facilities (as defined in Regulation D of the Board of Governors of the Federal Reserve System).

(3) Any corporation that is exempt from income tax under Section 1363 of the Internal Revenue Code.

(4) Any corporation exempt from federal income taxation under the Internal Revenue Code, except for the corporation's unrelated business income. However, this exemption does not apply to a corporation exempt from federal income taxation under Section 501(c)(14) of the Internal Revenue Code.

As added by P.L.347–1989(ss), SEC.1. Amended by P.L.21–1990, SEC.25; P.L.68–1991, SEC.8.

Historical and Statutory Notes

P.L.21–1990, Sec.25, emerg. eff. retroactive to Jan. 1, 1990.

P.L.21–1990, Sec.25, added Subsec. (4).

P.L.68–1991, Sec.8, emerg. eff. retroactive to Jan. 1, 1991.

P.L.68–1991, Sec.8, inserted the second sentence of Subsec. (4).

Library References

Taxation ⮑230.
WESTLAW Topic No. 371.
C.J.S. Taxation § 272.

Notes of Decisions

Annuities 3
Bank loans 6
Bonds 16
Certificates of deposit 15
Charitable deposits 10
Federal property, in general 7
Industrial loan and investment companies 1
Insurance policies 2
Judgments 4
Leases with option to purchase 13
Liens 5
National bank stock 8
Partnership interest 17
Personal service contracts 14
Postal savings deposits and certificates 11
Real estate sales contracts 12
Treasury notes 9

1. Industrial loan and investment companies

Under Acts 1935, c. 181, s. 21a [now, § 28–5–1–23] constituting the Loan and Investment Act, an undustrial loan and investment company is not liable for the payment of intangible tax upon loans made by it. 1944 Op.Atty.Gen. No. 88.

2. Insurance policies

Since Const. Art. 10, § 1, requires the general assembly to provide by law for uniform taxation, and prescribe such regulations as shall secure a just valuation for taxation of all property, except such as may be exempted by law,

where former statutes provided that all property not expressly exempted should be subject to taxation, and that "All other goods, chattels and personal property, and heretofore specifically mentioned, and their value," except exempt property should be taxable, even if life insurance policies were personal property within the tax law, they were not subject to taxation, where there was no statute providing any regulations for, or manner of, assessing or valuing such policies for taxation. State Bd. of Tax Com'rs v. Holliday, 1898, 49 N.E. 14, 150 Ind. 216.

Ordinarily life insurance policy is not taxable, but money due on life insurance policies which have matured and which have become a debt but which by contract independent of policies are loaned to insurance company, are taxable as a credit. 1925–1926 Op.Atty.Gen. p. 542.

3. Annuities

An annuity contract with a life insurance company, for which payment was made in single payment, was not subject to taxation under Indiana taxing laws. 1917–1920 Op.Atty.Gen. p. 516.

4. Judgments

A recovery on a claim which was filed and allowed as an open account representing the balance due on the purchase price of claimant's interest in a partnership which he had sold to decedent was not barred because no intangible tax had been paid, notwithstanding account was of a considerable amount, since the size did not change its character as an open account or tend to bring it within the terms of the intangible tax law. Newell v. Newell, 1938, 12 N.E.2d 344, 213 Ind. 261.

A judgment rendered in condemnation proceedings was not such a judgment as was subject to taxation under the Indiana Intangibles Tax Act [repealed; see, now, § 6–5.1–1–1 et seq.]. 1941 Op.Atty.Gen. p. 323.

Judgments on tax exempt securities were not "obligations" of governmental unit exempted from general intangible tax by Acts 1933, c. 81, s. 1 [repealed; see, now, this section]. 1940 Op.Atty.Gen. p. 151.

Judgments procured in the enforcement of Barrett Law bonds are subject to the intangible tax. 1940 Op.Atty.Gen. p. 151.

A judgment obtained on a poor relief claim was not a taxable intangible under Acts 1933, c. 81 [repealed; see, now, § 6–5.1–1–1 et seq.] 1934 Op.Atty.Gen. p. 70.

5. Liens

A mechanics lien for material is not taxable as an intangible. 1940 Op.Atty.Gen. p. 110.

6. Bank loans

Participation agreements by which taxpayer purchased an undivided interest in a loan which was previously made by bank to one of its customers were not entitled to the "parent-subsidiary exemption" from the tax on intangibles, since they were based, not on a written debt instrument from bank, but rather, on taxpayer's ownership of an undivided interest in original loan from bank to its customer. Indiana State Dept. of Revenue, Income Tax Division v. Valley Financial Services, Inc., App. 3 Dist.1982, 435 N.E.2d 68.

Money deposited by a subsidiary, The Commonwealth Loan Company of Indiana, in Chicago and New York banks for the sole purpose of maintaining lines of credit for the parent organization, Beneficial Loan Corporation of New Jersey, was exempt from intangible tax. 1954 Op.Atty.Gen. No. 1.

Under Acts 1933, c. 81, [repealed; see, now, § 6–5.1–1–1 et seq.] compensating balances retained in connection with loans made by bank were taxable as intangibles to Indiana owners of such balances unless such intangible had an actual business situs outside the state. 1942 Op.Atty.Gen. p. 154.

7. Federal property, in general

Act Cong. June 30, 1864 (13 Stat. 218), declaring that all bonds, treasury notes, and other obligations of the United States shall be exempt from state taxation, and that the words "obligation or other security of the United States" mean all bonds, national currency, United States notes, and other representations of value which may have been or may be issued under any act of congress, does not exempt the notes of national banks from state taxation. Board of Com'rs of Montgomery County v. Elston, 1869, 32 Ind. 27, 2 Am.Rep. 327.

A tax laid by a state on banks, "on a valuation equal to the amount of their capital stock paid in, or secured to be paid in," is a tax on the property of the institution; and, when that property consists of stocks of the federal government, the law laying the tax is void. Whitney v. City of Madison, 1864, 23 Ind. 331.

Where the federal government made a loan to a railroad, and sole beneficial interest in pledged securities made in connection with the loan was in the federal government, such securities were not taxable under the General Intangibles Tax Act [repealed; see, now, § 6–5.1–1–1 et seq.] until by sale or otherwise they should come into possession of an owner subject to the tax. 1936 Op.Atty.Gen. p. 123.

8. National bank stock

Capital stock of national bank invested in government bonds is not taxable by state as against bank. Beard v. People's Sav. Bank, App.1913, 101 N.E. 325, 53 Ind.App. 185.

The shares of national banks are, by the act of Congress authorizing such associations, placed within the reach of the taxing power of the states, subject to certain conditions, which were intended to prevent any discrimination against such shares. Wright v. Stilz, 1866, 27 Ind. 338.

9. Treasury notes

Where defendant on March 31st converted a general deposit of money into treasury notes, not taxable, and deposited the same in the bank for safe-keeping only, until April 11th, and then returned the notes to the general deposit, he was liable for a penalty. Durham v. State, App.1892, 32 N.E. 104, 6 Ind.App. 23.

United States treasury notes, commonly called greenbacks, are not subject to taxation. Ogden v. Walker, 1877, 59 Ind. 460.

United States treasury notes, popularly known as "greenbacks," are not liable to state taxation. Board of Com'rs of Montgomery County v. Elston, 1869, 32 Ind. 27, 2 Am.Rep. 327.

10. Charitable deposits

Acts of 1945, c. 170, [repealed; see, now, this section] restored the exemption granted charitable institutions under former laws and extended to charitable institutions full exemption from tax liability on intangibles; therefore, charitable deposits in banks and trust companies are non-taxable. 1955 Op.Atty.Gen. No. 44.

11. Postal savings deposits and certificates

Statute [repealed; see, now § 6–5.1–1–1 et seq.] providing for the taxation of intangibles was applicable to postal savings certificates. Lutz v. Arnold, 1935, 193 N.E. 840, 208 Ind. 480, rehearing overruled 196 N.E. 702, 208 Ind. 480.

The taxation of postal savings deposits under the General Intangibles Tax Act of 1933 [repealed; see, now, this article] was not a tax upon a United States agency, but it was a tax against the owner of the deposit, and was consequently not unconstitutional. 1934 Op.Atty. Gen. p. 151.

Postal savings deposits were taxable under the General Intangibles Tax Act of 1933 [repealed; see, now, § 6–5.1–1–1 et seq.] 1934 Op.Atty.Gen. p. 151.

12. Real estate sales contracts

So-called leases, under which lessees were to pay taxes and assessments, interest on principal, and keep the property insured for the benefit of the parties thereto, as their interest might appear, and requiring the grantor to deed the property to the grantee upon payment of the stipulated sums on or before maturity, were sale contracts, and were assessable to vendor for taxation. In re Spurgeon, App.1920, 126 N.E. 238, 72 Ind.App. 580.

The amount owing to a gas company under a contract conveying the equitable title to its plant with an agreement to convey legal title on completion of the payments was assessable for taxation. In re Assessment of Aurora Gaslight, Coke & Coal Co., App.1916, 113 N.E. 1012, 64 Ind.App. 690.

Under former statute which provided that agreements in the form of land contracts, options to purchase real estate and leases with option to purchase real estate which did not by their terms constitute enforcible promises to buy and to pay purchase price, should not have been subject to taxation, law governing assessments of contracts for taxation was not changed and statute only applied to contracts in which true intent was, not to effect a sale, but merely to create option to purchase. 1925–1926 Op. Atty.Gen. p. 538.

A real estate contract incorporating a title bond was evidence of an indebtedness owing by vendee to vendor, and had to be subjected to taxation under former statute which provided for assessment and taxation of evidences of indebtedness. 1915–1916 Op.Atty.Gen. p. 626.

13. Leases with option to purchase

Contracts in form of lease with option to purchase, are not taxable in hands of owners of real estate, unless they contain an enforcible provision for payment of all rent which may become due, which, in such event, may be said to represent purchase price. 1929–1930 Op. Atty.Gen. p. 549.

14. Personal service contracts

Where contract between electric company and customer provided that company agreed to erect and maintain electric signs which remained property of company, and customer agreed to keep sign for certain period and to pay specified monthly sum, contract was for personal services and excepted from provisions of Intangibles Tax Act [repealed; see, now, § 6–5.1–1–1 et seq.] 1943 Op.Atty.Gen. p. 422.

15. Certificates of deposit

A certificate of deposit issued by Indiana private bank was not subject to tax as an "intangible", defined by statute [repealed; see, now, this section] as not including certificates issued by banks. Erwin v. Erwin, App.1942, 41 N.E.2d 644, 111 Ind.App. 448.

16. Bonds

Bonds of municipality issued for payment of extensions to water plant system did not constitute indebtedness of municipal corporation in its governmental capacity, but bonds constituted charges only against special redemption fund created out of revenues of water plant system utility, and such bonds were not exempt from taxation. 1927–1928 Op.Atty.Gen. p. 262.

Former statute which authorized refunding of certain bonds by trustees was constitutional and valid and bonds issued under authority of the act were exempt from state and county taxes. 1923–1924 Op.Atty.Gen. p. 306.

Bonds issued by Indiana board of agriculture, pursuant to authority vested in it by former statute were exempt from taxation. 1923–1924 Op.Atty.Gen. p. 85.

17. Partnership interest

Since personal property, for the purposes of taxation, cannot be aggregated, but must be itemized, the good will of a newspaper conducted by a copartnership, being an incident of the business as a going concern, cannot be assessed as a tax on the property as a unit. Hart v. Smith, 1902, 64 N.E. 661, 159 Ind. 182, 95 Am.St.Rep. 280.

6–5.5–2–8   Partnerships; grantor or beneficiary of a trust; information return; withholding

Sec. 8.   (a) If a corporation is:

(1) transacting the business of a financial institution (as defined in IC 6–5.5–1–17(d)); and

(2) is a partner in a partnership or the grantor and beneficiary of a trust transacting business in Indiana and the partnership or trust is conducting in Indiana an activity or activities that would constitute the business of a financial institution if transacted by a corporation;

the corporation is a taxpayer under this article and shall, in calculating the corporation's tax liability under this article, include in the corporation's adjusted or apportioned income the corporation's percentage of the partnership or trust adjusted gross income or apportioned income.

(b) A partnership or trust covered by subsection (a):

(1) shall file an information return on an appropriate schedule, with capital and operating losses, modifications, and credits required by this article and any other items specified in the return form by the department. If the taxpayer is a nonresident, or is a member of a unitary group with nonresident members filing a combined return, the return must show the apportionment percentage and supporting amounts necessary to compute the tax under IC 6–5.5–4.   A partner's percentage share of the receipts of a taxpayer, for the purpose of apportionment, shall be calculated by using the partner's share of the partnership adjusted gross income;

(2) is subject to the provisions of IC 6–5.5–7–3 relating to taxpayers and IC 6–5.5–7–4 relating to persons when filing the information return;   and

(3) shall withhold from all nonresident corporate partners or beneficiaries an amount prescribed in withholding instructions issued by the department.   The amount required to be withheld shall be based upon the rate of tax prescribed in IC 6–5.5–2, unless the partner or beneficiary provides the partnership or trust with a written declaration that the partner or beneficiary is not subject to the tax.   In such a case the amount withheld shall be the amount prescribed in the withholding instructions issued by the department based upon the Indiana adjusted gross income tax rates.   The department shall issue procedures and directions for the withholding required by this subsection that are similar to those contained in IC 6–3–4 concerning the withholding of taxes.

As added by P.L.21–1990, SEC.26. Amended by P.L.68–1991, SEC.9.

Historical and Statutory Notes

P.L.21–1990, Sec.26, emerg. eff. retroactive to Jan. 1, 1990.

P.L.68–1991, Sec.9, emerg. eff. retroactive to Jan. 1, 1990.

P.L.68–1991, Sec.9, rewrote the section, which had provided:

"(a) If a corporation is a partner in a partnership or the grantor and beneficiary of a trust transacting business in Indiana, which would be the business of a financial institution if transacted by a corporation, the corporation is a taxpayer and shall pay the tax imposed by this article on the corporation's percentage of the partnership or trust adjusted gross income or apportioned income.

"(b) A partnership or trust shall file an information return on an appropriate schedule, with capital and operating losses, modifications, and credits required by this article and any other items specified in the return form by the department. If the taxpayer is a nonresident, or is a member of a unitary group with nonresident members filing a combined return, the return must show the apportionment percentage and supporting amounts necessary to compute the tax under IC 6–5.5–4. A partner's percentage share of the receipts of a taxpayer, for the purpose of apportionment, shall be calculated by using the partner's share of the partnership adjusted gross income.

"(c) A partnership or trust filing an information return under this section is subject to the provisions of IC 6–5.5–7–3 relating to taxpayers and IC 6–5.5–7–4 relating to persons.

"(d) A partnership or trust transacting business in Indiana, which if transacted by a corporation would constitute the business of a financial institution, shall withhold from all nonresident corporate partners or beneficiaries an amount prescribed in withholding instructions issued by the department. The amount required to be withheld shall be based upon the rate of tax prescribed in IC 6–5.5–2, unless the partner or beneficiary provides the partnership or trust with a written declaration that the partner or beneficiary is not subject to the tax. In such a case the amount withheld shall be the amount prescribed in the withholding instructions issued by the department based upon the Indiana adjusted gross income tax rates. The department shall issue procedures and directions for the withholding required by this subsection that are similar to those contained in IC 6–3–4 concerning the withholding of taxes."

Chapter 3

Business Transaction Rules

Section

6–5.5–3–1 Transacting business within state

Sec. 1. For the purposes of this article, a taxpayer is transacting business within Indiana in a taxable year only if the taxpayer:

(1) maintains an office in Indiana;

(2) has an employee, representative, or independent contractor conducting business in Indiana;

(3) regularly sells products or services of any kind or nature to customers in Indiana that receive the product or service in Indiana;

(4) regularly solicits business from potential customers in Indiana;

(5) regularly performs services outside Indiana that are consumed within Indiana;

(6) regularly engages in transactions with customers in Indiana that involve intangible property, including loans, but not property described in

437

section 8(5) of this chapter, and result in receipts flowing to the taxpayer from within Indiana;

(7) owns or leases tangible personal or real property located in Indiana; or

(8) regularly solicits and receives deposits from customers in Indiana.
As added by P.L.347–1989(ss), SEC.1.

Historical and Statutory Notes

P.L.347–1989(ss), Sec.1, eff. Jan. 1, 1990, added this article.

Library References

Taxation ☞125, 165.
WESTLAW Topic No. 371.
C.J.S. Taxation §§ 143, 190.

Notes of Decisions

Corporate stock, tax situs   4
Domicile of owner, tax situs   1
Multiple taxation, tax situs   2
Nonresidents, tax situs   5
Residence of corporation, tax situs   3

---

1.   Domicile of owner, tax situs

Under former statute which provided that "all property within the jurisdiction of this state, not expressly exempted, shall be subject to taxation," and under which credits were classed as personal property, if a bond, note, or other evidence of amount due the creditor was itself within the jurisdiction of the state, it was taxable, without regard to where the debtor lived, or where the debt was contracted. Buck v. Miller, 1896, 45 N.E. 647, 147 Ind. 586, 62 Am.St.Rep. 436, rehearing denied 47 N.E. 8, 147 Ind. 586, 62 Am.St.Rep. 436.

All debts, of every kind and nature, due to persons having a domicile in this state, are taxable to the creditor where he has his domicile. Foresman v. Byrns, 1879, 68 Ind. 247.

Personal property of an intangible character, which exists in rights of action, such as debts, bank stocks, etc., has no situs, other than the domicile of the owner, and is therefore only taxable at the place of his residence. Powell v. City of Madison, 1863, 21 Ind. 335.

2.   Multiple taxation, tax situs

Under former statute [see, now, § 6–5.1–1–1 et seq.], which provided for tax on intangibles of every person, including corporations, residing in or domiciled in state, without regard to where the tangibles were located, mere fact that the intangibles might also be physically located at the domicile of the owner in another state

where they might again be taxed, was no bar to imposition of tax, since there was no prohibition against multiple taxation of intangibles. 1944 Op.Atty.Gen. No. 105.

3.   Residence of corporation, tax situs

For purposes of IC1971, 6–5–1–2 [repealed; see, now, this section] imposing intangibles tax upon Indiana residents, corporation was resident of Missouri, its state of incorporation. Indiana Dept. of State Revenue v. Mercantile Mortg. Co., App. 2 Dist.1980, 412 N.E.2d 1252.

4.   Corporate stock, tax situs

Corporate stock is assessable only at owner's domicile. Croop v. Walton, 1927, 157 N.E. 275, 199 Ind. 262.

An owner of shares of stock in a foreign corporation was liable to taxation therefor where he resided, though a tax had been paid in the state where the corporation was located. Seward v. City of Rising Sun, 1881, 79 Ind. 351.

Shares of an insurance company are taxable where the owner is domiciled. City of Evansville v. Hall, 1859, 14 Ind. 27.

5.   Nonresidents, tax situs

Where an Indiana railroad corporation operated lines of road belonging to an Illinois railroad corporation under a contract to pay a specified per cent of the gross earnings as rentals, the funds set apart for and belonging to the Illinois corporation, being physically in Indiana in the possession of the receiver of the Indiana corporation, were subject to taxation for state and county purposes under former statute which provided that the personal property of nonresidents in the possession of any person or corporation as receiver should be assessed for state and county purposes, but only on an assessment against the Illinois corporation, or the receiver as trustee thereof. Clark v. Vandalia R. Co., 1909, 86 N.E. 851, 172 Ind. 409.

Where the receiver of an insolvent mutual benefit and assessment society had on deposit in a bank in Indiana a sum of money, a large portion of which had been turned over to him by receivers of other states, and which was to be paid to thousands of claimants, scattered over the country, all the money was subject to taxation by the county where it was deposited. Schmidt v. Failey, 1897, 47 N.E. 326, 148 Ind. 150.

Under former statute which provided that "personal property of non-residents of the state shall be assessed to the owner or to the person having the control thereof in the township, town or city where the same may be," etc., where a business was done in buying and selling property and making loans and investments, and the money, notes, and mortgages so used were retained in the state by the owner or his agent, they were subject to taxation, as well as any other kind of personal property. Buck v. Miller, 1896, 45 N.E. 647, 147 Ind. 586, 62 Am.St. Rep. 436, rehearing denied 47 N.E. 8, 147 Ind. 586, 62 Am.St.Rep. 436.

All debts, of every kind and nature, due from persons having a domicile in this state, to persons not having a domicile therein on the day named in the statute, unless in the hands of an agent doing business in this state, from which such debts have sprung, have no situs in this state, but have a situs where the creditor has his domicile, and are not taxable in Indiana. Foresman v. Byrns, 1879, 68 Ind. 247.

A nonresident firm which sold certain articles of machinery in the state on conditional sales contracts, which contracts were then shipped to office of nonresident's firm and payments thereon were made direct to such office, was not required to place intangibles tax stamps on such contracts on its anniversary date. 1941 Op. Atty.Gen. p. 301.

Under former statute [see, now, § 6–5.1–1–1 et seq.], where Indiana branch of foreign corporation received intangibles on assignment from outside the state, the intangibles tax applied and the tax stamp required should have been attached within ten days from the time the intangibles were assigned to the Indiana branch. 1941 Op.Atty.Gen. p. 241.

Under 1933 General Intangibles Tax Act [repealed; see, now, § 6–5.1–1–1 et seq.] foreign corporation financing automobiles in state would be required to pay tax on finance contract controlled by Indiana branch, even though contract were to finance non-resident's purchase of automobile from non-resident dealer. 1940 Op.Atty.Gen. p. 203.

6–5.5–3–2   Maintains office

Sec. 2.   For purposes of this chapter, a taxpayer is considered to maintain an office wherever the taxpayer has established a regular, continuous, and fixed place of business.

As added by P.L.347–1989(ss), SEC.1.

Library References

Taxation ☞125, 165.
WESTLAW Topic No. 371.
C.J.S. Taxation §§ 143, 190.

6–5.5–3–3   Conducting business

Sec. 3.   An employee, representative, or independent contractor is considered to be conducting business in Indiana if:

(1) the employee, representative, or independent contractor is regularly engaged in the business of the taxpayer in Indiana;

(2) the office from which the employee's, representative's, or independent contractor's activities are directed or controlled is located in Indiana and a majority of the employee's, representative's, or independent contractor's service is not performed in any other taxing jurisdiction; or

(3) a contribution to the Indiana employment security fund is required under IC 22–4–2 with respect to compensation paid to the employee.
As added by P.L.347–1989(ss), SEC.1. Amended by P.L.21–1990, SEC.27.

Historical and Statutory Notes

P.L.21–1990, Sec.27, emerg. eff. retroactive to Jan. 1, 1990.

P.L.21–1990, Sec.27, in the introductory sentence and in Subsec. (1), inserted "representa-

tive, or independent contractor"; in Subsec. (2), inserted "representative's or independent contractor's" in two places.

Library References

Taxation ⟋125, 165.
WESTLAW Topic No. 371.
C.J.S. Taxation §§ 143, 190.

6–5.5–3–4   Regularly solicit business; presumption

Sec. 4.   A person is presumed, subject to rebuttal, to regularly solicit business within Indiana if:

(1) the person conducts activities described in section 1(3), 1(5), and 1(6) of this chapter with twenty (20) or more customers within Indiana during the taxable year; or

(2) the sum of the person's assets, including the assets arising from loan transactions, and the absolute value of the person's deposits attributable to Indiana equal at least five million dollars ($5,000,000).

As added by P.L.347–1989(ss), SEC.1. Amended by P.L.21–1990, SEC.28; P.L.68–1991, SEC.10.

Historical and Statutory Notes

P.L.21–1990, Sec.28, emerg. eff. retroactive to Jan. 1, 1990.

P.L.21–1990, Sec.28, in Subsec. (1), substituted "customers" for "persons"; and in Subsec. (2), inserted "including the assets arising from loan transactions".

P.L.68–1991, Sec.10, emerg. eff. retroactive to Jan. 1, 1990.

P.L.68–1991, Sec.10, substituted "1(5), and 1(6)" for "through 1(6)" in Subsec. (1).

Library References

Taxation ⟋485(1).
WESTLAW Topic No. 371.
C.J.S. Social Security and Public Welfare §§ 199 to 201.

C.J.S. Taxation § 537.

6–5.5–3–5   Tangible assets, intangible assets and deposits attributable to state

Sec. 5.   For purposes of this chapter, tangible assets are attributable to this state if they are located in Indiana.   Intangible assets are attributable to this state if the income earned on those assets is attributable to this state under this article.   Deposits are attributed to this state if they are deposits made by this state or residents, political subdivisions, or agencies and instrumentalities of this state regardless of whether the deposits are accepted or maintained by the taxpayer at locations within Indiana.

As added by P.L.347–1989(ss), SEC.1.

Library References

Taxation ☞125, 165.
WESTLAW Topic No. 371.
C.J.S. Taxation §§ 143, 190.

Notes of Decisions

Intangibles held in foreign states by nonresidents, tax situs   3
Intangibles held in foreign states by state residents, tax situs   4
Property temporarily located in state, tax situs   2
Removal of intangibles from state, tax situs   1

---

1. Removal of intangibles from state, tax situs

Where proper situs of notes for purpose of taxation is in state, their liability to taxation cannot be avoided by temporarily removing them from state each year prior to assessment day. Buck v. Beach, 1904, 71 N.E. 963, 164 Ind. 37, 108 Am.St.Rep. 272, reversed 27 S.Ct. 712, 206 U.S. 392, 51 L.Ed. 1106, 11 Am.Ann. Cas. 732.

2. Property temporarily located in state, tax situs

Where notes or other choses in action are in the state temporarily, or in the hands of an attorney for collection, and the credits thereof are owned and held in another state by a nonresident of this state, the notes or bonds so owned and held cannot be taxed here, although secured by lien on property in this state. Buck v. Miller, 1896, 45 N.E. 647, 147 Ind. 586, 62 Am.St.Rep. 436, rehearing denied 47 N.E. 8, 147 Ind. 586, 62 Am.St.Rep. 436.

Notes and bonds belonging to and in the possession of a resident of another state, traveling through and temporarily residing in Indiana, are not liable to taxation. Herron v. Keeran, 1877, 59 Ind. 472, 26 Am.Rep. 87.

Bonds and notes of a nonresident, left in a bank for safe-keeping, or in an attorney's hands for collection, are not here taxable. Herron v. Keeran, 1877, 59 Ind. 472, 26 Am.Rep. 87.

3. Intangibles held in foreign states by nonresidents, tax situs

An assignment of stock to trustee domiciled in another state, pursuant to trust agreement providing for payment of income to settlor and her husband and for payment of principal to settlor's daughters on settlor's and husband's deaths, and authorizing revocation of trust by settlor with consent of husband, daughters, and sons-in-law, vested legal title in stock in trustee and right in husband and daughters to receive income and trust property, and hence stock was not taxable to settlor in state of her domicile. Johnston v. State, 1937, 8 N.E.2d 590, 212 Ind. 375, rehearing denied 10 N.E.2d 40, 212 Ind. 375.

Note or bond owned and held in another state by nonresident cannot be taxed in Indiana, though secured by lien on local property. Buck v. Miller, 1896, 45 N.E. 647, 147 Ind. 586, 62 Am.St.Rep. 436, rehearing denied 47 N.E. 8, 147 Ind. 586, 62 Am.St.Rep. 436.

Credits in favor of a nonresident, which were debits against citizens of this state, such credits resulting from loans evidenced by promissory notes held by such nonresident in another state, and secured by mortgages on real estate in this state, were not within the jurisdiction of this state, nor subject to taxation here. Senour v. Ruth, 1895, 39 N.E. 946, 140 Ind. 318.

4. Intangibles held in foreign states by state residents, tax situs

Domestic corporation's bills and accounts receivable having business situs in Illinois were not subject to taxation in Indiana. Miami Coal Co. v. Fox, 1931, 176 N.E. 11, 203 Ind. 99.

Shares of national bank stock located outside the state were not taxable to the owner thereof located within the state under the General Intangibles Tax Act [repealed; see, now, § 6–5.1–1–1 et seq.]. 1942 Op.Atty.Gen. p. 223.

Shares of state banks located outside the state but which were held by Indiana residents were taxable as intangibles under the General Intangibles Tax Act [repealed; see, now, § 6–5.1–1–1 et seq.]. 1942 Op.Atty.Gen. p. 223.

Mere establishing of deposits in out-of-state bank upon which checks could be drawn by home office of Indiana corporation to pay salesmen or to pay for material which was bought near or in out-of-state community would not be sufficient to localize possession and control of deposits in such community to acquire out-of-state business situs, and therefore such deposits would be subject to intangibles tax. 1941 Op. Atty.Gen. p. 395.

Under former statute which, provided for taxation of shares in foreign corporations, except national banks' shares owned by state inhabitants, national bank shares of an institution located in another state, owned by individuals or corporations of Indiana, could not be taxed in Indiana, but shares were required to be taxed in town or city where bank was located. 1891–1892 Op.Atty.Gen. p. 65.

6–5.5–3–6 Tangible property; located in state

Sec. 6. Except as otherwise provided in section 7 of this chapter, tangible property, including leased property, is considered to be located in Indiana if the property is physically situated in Indiana.
As added by P.L.347–1989(ss), SEC.1.

Library References

Taxation ☞125, 165.
WESTLAW Topic No. 371.
C.J.S. Taxation §§ 143, 190.

6–5.5–3–7 Moving property; located in state

Sec. 7. For purposes of this article, tangible personal property that is characteristically moving property, such as motor vehicles, rolling stock, aircraft, vessels, and mobile equipment, is considered to be located in Indiana if:

(1) the operation of the property is entirely in Indiana; or

(2) the operation of the property is not entirely in Indiana and:

(A) the operation outside Indiana is occasional and incidental to the operation in Indiana;

(B) the principal base of operations from which the property is sent out is in Indiana; or

(C) Indiana is the commercial domicile of the lessee or other user of the property and there is no principal base of operations.
As added by P.L.347–1989(ss), SEC.1.

Library References

Taxation ☞125, 165.
WESTLAW Topic No. 371.
C.J.S. Taxation §§ 143, 190.

6–5.5–3–8 Events not considered transacting business in state

Sec. 8. Notwithstanding any other provision of this chapter, a taxpayer, except for a trust company formed under IC 28–1–4, is not considered to be transacting business in Indiana if the only activities of the taxpayer in Indiana are or are in connection with any of the following:

(1) Maintaining or defending an action or suit.

(2) Filing, modifying, renewing, extending, or transferring a mortgage, deed of trust, or security interest.

(3) Acquiring, foreclosing, or otherwise conveying property in Indiana as a result of a default under the terms of a mortgage, deed of trust, or other security instrument relating to the property.

(4) Selling tangible personal property, if taxation under this article is precluded by 15 U.S.C. 381 through 384.

(5) Owning an interest in the following types of property, including those activities within Indiana that are reasonably required to evaluate and complete the acquisition or disposition of the property, the servicing of the property or the income from the property, the collection of income from the property, or the acquisition or liquidation of collateral relating to the property:

(A) An interest in a real estate mortgage investment conduit, a real estate investment trust, or a regulated investment company (as those terms are defined in the Internal Revenue Code).

(B) An interest in a loan backed security representing ownership or participation in a pool of promissory notes or certificates of interest that provide for payments in relation to payments or reasonable projections of payments on the notes or certificates.

(C) An interest in a loan or other asset from which the interest is attributed in IC 6–5.5–4–4, IC 6–5.5–4–5, and IC 6–5.5–4–6 and in which the payment obligations were solicited and entered into by a person that is independent and not acting on behalf of the owner.

(D) An interest in the right to service or collect income from a loan or other asset from which interest on the loan or other asset is attributed in IC 6–5.5–4–4, IC 6–5.5–4–5, and IC 6–5.5–4–6 and in which the payment obligations were solicited and entered into by a person that is independent and not acting on behalf of the owner.

(E) An amount held in an escrow or a trust account with respect to property described in this subdivision.

(6) Acting:

(A) as an executor of an estate;

(B) as a trustee of a benefit plan;

(C) as a trustee of an employees' pension, profit sharing, or other retirement plan;

(D) as a trustee of a testamentary or inter vivos trust or corporate indenture; or

(E) in any other fiduciary capacity, including holding title to real property in Indiana.

As added by P.L.347–1989(ss), SEC.1. Amended by P.L.68–1991, SEC.11.

Historical and Statutory Notes

P.L.68–1991, Sec.11, eff. Jan. 1, 1992.

P.L.68–1991, Sec.11, inserted ", except for a trust company formed under IC 28–1–4," in the introductory paragraph.

Library References

Taxation ⚷125, 165.
WESTLAW Topic No. 371.
C.J.S. Taxation §§ 143, 190.

Chapter 4

Rules for Attributing Receipts

6–5.5–4–1   Application of chapter

Sec. 1.   This chapter applies to the following:

(1) Nonresident taxpayers.

(2) Nonresident members of a unitary group that file a combined return.

As added by P.L.347–1989(ss), SEC.1.

Historical and Statutory Notes

P.L.347–1989(ss), Sec.1, eff. Jan. 1, 1990, added this article.

6–5.5–4–2   Definitions

Sec. 2.   For purposes of computing receipts or the receipts factor under this article the following apply:

(1) "Receipts" means gross income (as defined in IC 6–5.5–1–10), plus the gross income excluded under Section 103 of the Internal Revenue Code, less gross income derived from sources outside the United States. Howev-

444

er, upon the disposition of assets such as securities and money market transactions, when derived from transactions and activities in the regular course of the taxpayer's trade or business, receipts are limited to the gain (as defined in Section 1001 of the Internal Revenue Code) that is recognized upon the disposition.

(2) "Money market instruments" means federal funds sold and securities purchased under agreements to resell, commercial paper, banker's acceptances, and purchased certificates of deposit and similar instruments.

(3) "Securities" means United States Treasury securities, obligations of United States government agencies and corporations, obligations of state and political subdivisions, corporate stock and other securities, participations in securities backed by mortgages held by United States or state government agencies, loan backed securities and similar investments.

As added by P.L.347–1989(ss), SEC.1. Amended by P.L.21–1990, SEC.29; P.L.68– 1991, SEC.12.

Historical and Statutory Notes

P.L.21–1990, Sec.29, emerg. eff. retroactive to Jan. 1, 1990.

P.L.21–1990, Sec.29, in the introductory sentence, inserted "the following apply"; in Subsec. (1), in the first sentence, substituted "(as defined in IC 6–5.5–1–10)" for "including net taxable gain on", in the second sentence inserted "However, upon the" and inserted "receipts are limited to the gain (as defined in Section

1001 of the Internal Revenue Code) that is recognized upon the disposition".

P.L.68–1991, Sec.12, emerg. eff. retroactive to Jan. 1, 1990.

P.L.68–1991, Sec.12, in SubSec.1, rewrote the first sentence, which had read: " 'Receipts' includes all gross income (as defined in IC 6–5.5–1–10)".

6–5.5–4–3   Lease or rental of real or tangible personal property

Sec. 3. Receipts from the lease or rental of real or tangible personal property must be attributed to Indiana if the property is located in Indiana.

As added by P.L.347–1989(ss), SEC.1.

Library References

Taxation ☞397.
WESTLAW Topic No. 371.
C.J.S. Taxation § 428.

6–5.5–4–4   Secured loans or installment sales contracts; interest income and other receipts

Sec. 4.   Interest income and other receipts from assets in the nature of loans or installment sales contracts that are primarily secured by or deal with real or tangible personal property must be attributed to Indiana if the security or sale property is located in Indiana.

As added by P.L.347–1989(ss), SEC.1.

6–5.5–4–5   Unsecured consumer loans; interest income and other receipts

Sec. 5.   Interest income and other receipts from consumer loans not secured by real or tangible personal property must be attributed to Indiana if the loan is made to a resident of Indiana, whether at a place of business, by a traveling loan officer, by mail, by telephone, or by other electronic means.
As added by P.L.347–1989(ss), SEC.1.

6–5.5–4–6   Unsecured commercial loans or installment obligations; interest income and other receipts to be applied in state

Sec. 6.   Interest income and other receipts from commercial loans and installment obligations not secured by real or tangible personal property must be attributed to Indiana if the proceeds of the loan are to be applied in Indiana. If it cannot be determined where the funds are to be applied, the income and receipts are attributed to the state in which the business applied for the loan. As used in this section, "applied for" means initial inquiry (including customer assistance in preparing the loan application) or submission of a completed loan application, whichever occurs first.
As added by P.L.347–1989(ss), SEC.1.

6–5.5–4–7   Fee income and other receipts from letters of credit, acceptance of drafts and other guarantees of credit; apportionment

Sec. 7.   Fee income and other receipts from letters of credit, acceptance of drafts, and other devices for assuring or guaranteeing loans or credit must be apportioned in the same manner as interest income and other receipts from commercial loans are apportioned.
As added by P.L.347–1989(ss), SEC.1.

6–5.5–4–8 Credit cards; apportionment of service charges, interest income and fees

Sec. 8. Interest income, merchant discount, and other receipts including service charges from financial institution credit card and travel and entertainment credit card receivables and credit card holders' fees must be attributed to the state to which the card charges and fees are regularly billed.

As added by P.L.347–1989(ss), SEC.1.

Library References

Taxation ☞397.
WESTLAW Topic No. 371.
C.J.S. Taxation § 428.

United States Supreme Court

Credit card late payment fees, interest under National Bank Act, preemption of state law, see Smiley v. Citibank (South Dakota), N.A., 1996, 116 S.Ct. 1730.

6–5.5–4–9 Receipts from sale of assets; apportionment

Sec. 9. Receipts from the sale of an asset, tangible or intangible, must be apportioned in the manner that the income from the asset would be apportioned under this chapter.

As added by P.L.347–1989(ss), SEC.1.

Library References

Taxation ☞397.
WESTLAW Topic No. 371.
C.J.S. Taxation § 428.

6–5.5–4–10 Receipts from performance of fiduciary and other services; apportionment

Sec. 10. Receipts from the performance of fiduciary and other services must be attributed to the state in which the benefits of the services are consumed. If the benefits are consumed in more than one (1) state, the receipts from those benefits must be apportioned to Indiana on a pro rata basis according to the portion of the benefits consumed in Indiana.

As added by P.L.347–1989(ss), SEC.1.

Library References

Taxation ☞397.
WESTLAW Topic No. 371.
C.J.S. Taxation § 428.

6–5.5–4–11 Receipts from traveler's checks, money orders or savings bonds

Sec. 11. Receipts from the issuance of traveler's checks, money orders, or United States savings bonds must be attributed to the state in which the traveler's checks, money orders, or bonds are purchased.

As added by P.L.347–1989(ss), SEC.1.

Library References

Taxation ⟷397.
WESTLAW Topic No. 371.
C.J.S. Taxation § 428.

6–5.5–4–12 Receipts from investments of financial institution in state securities

Sec. 12. Receipts from investments of a financial institution in securities of this state and its political subdivisions, agencies, and instrumentalities must be attributed to Indiana.

As added by P.L.347–1989(ss), SEC.1.

Library References

Taxation ⟷397.
WESTLAW Topic No. 371.
C.J.S. Taxation § 428.

6–5.5–4–13 Participation loans; apportionment of interest income and other receipts

Sec. 13. Interest income and other receipts from a participating financial institution's portion of participation loans must be attributed under this chapter. A participation loan is a loan in which more than one (1) lender is a creditor to a common borrower.

As added by P.L.347–1989(ss), SEC.1.

Library References

Taxation ⟷397.
WESTLAW Topic No. 371.
C.J.S. Taxation § 428.

6–5.5–4–14, 6–5.5–4–15 Repealed

(Repealed by P.L.68–1991, SEC.18.)

Historical and Statutory Notes

P.L.68–1991 provided in Section 21, containing emergency clause, that Section 18 of the act takes effect retroactively to January 1, 1990.

Former IC 6–5.5–4–14 related to income connected and income unconnected with trade or business.

Former IC 6–5.5–4–15 related to apportionment of gross income receipts.

Formerly:
  P.L.347–1989(ss), SEC.1.

Chapter 5

Alternative Calculations; Combined Returns

Section
6–5.5–5–1   Members of unitary business; combined returns; fair representation of
                    taxpayer income within state; reapportionment
6–5.5–5–2   Members of unitary group; combined returns
6–5.5–5–3   Information or records required

6–5.5–5–1   Members of unitary business; combined returns; fair representation of taxpayer income within state; reapportionment

Sec. 1.   (a) Except as provided in this section, a unitary group consisting of at least two (2) taxpayers shall file a combined return covering all the operations of the unitary business and including all of the members of the unitary business.   However, only one (1) combined return needs to be filed, as provided in IC 6–5.5–6–1.

(b) If the department or taxpayer determines that the result of applying this section or article do not fairly represent the taxpayer's income within Indiana or the taxpayer's income within Indiana may be more fairly represented by a separate return, the taxpayer may petition for and the department may allow, or the department may require, in respect to all or a part of the taxpayer's business activity any of the following:

(1) Separate accounting.

(2) The filing of a separate return for the taxpayer.

(3) A reallocation of tax items between a taxpayer and a member of the taxpayer's unitary group.

(c) Income apportioned under this article must reflect a change in adjusted gross income that is required to comply with a department order under this section.

As added by P.L.347–1989(ss), SEC.1.   Amended by P.L.21–1990, SEC.30; P.L.68–1991, SEC.13.

Historical and Statutory Notes

P.L.347–1989(ss), Sec.1, eff. Jan. 1, 1990, added this article.

P.L.21–1990, Sec.30, emerg. eff. retroactive to Jan. 1, 1990.

P.L.21–1990, Sec.30, added Subsec. (a); re-designated Subsec. (a) as Subsec. (b); in Subsec. (b), in the introductory sentence, deleted "the other provisions of" following "applying", inserted "section or", substituted "do" for "does", and inserted "or the taxpayer's income within Indiana may be more fairly represented by a separate return"; inserted Subsec. (b)(2); redesignated Subsec. (b)(2) as Subsec. (b)(3); deleted Subsec. (b)(3), which read, "The filing of a combined return by each taxpayer transacting business in Indiana that is a member of a unitary group."; redesignated Subsec. (b) as Subsec. (c); and in Subsec. (c), substituted "this section" for "subsection (a)".

P.L.68–1991, Sec.13, emerg. eff. retroactive to Jan. 1, 1990.

P.L.68–1991, Sec.13, rewrote Subsec. (a), which had read:

"Except as provided in this section, each taxpayer who is a member of a unitary group shall file a combined return covering all the operations of the unitary business and including all of the members of the unitary business."

Library References

Taxation ☞366.1.
WESTLAW Topic No. 371.
C.J.S. Taxation §§ 431 to 432, 437, 439.

6–5.5–5–2   Members of unitary group; combined returns

Sec. 2.   A combined return must include the adjusted gross income of all members of the unitary group, even if some of the members would not otherwise be subject to taxation under this article.   The department may require a member of a unitary group to provide any information that is needed by the department to determine the unitary group's apportioned income under this article.   However, income of corporations or other entities organized in foreign countries, except a foreign bank (or its subsidiary) that transacts business in the United States, shall not be included in the combined return.   In addition, the taxpayer shall eliminate, in calculating adjusted gross income, all income and deductions from transactions between entities that are included in the unitary group.

As added by P.L.347–1989(ss), SEC.1.   Amended by P.L.21–1990, SEC.31.

Historical and Statutory Notes

P.L.21–1990, Sec.31, emerg. eff. retroactive to Jan. 1, 1990.

P.L.21–1990, Sec.31, deleted the first sentence, which read, "If it is required or permitted, under this article, each taxpayer that is a member of a unitary group shall file a combined

return covering all operations of the unitary business."; in the second sentence, substituted "A" for "The"; in the fourth sentence, substituted "the United States" for "Indiana", inserted "in calculating adjusted gross income", and substituted "income and deductions" for "dividends and receipts".

Library References

Taxation ☞366.1.
WESTLAW Topic No. 371.
C.J.S. Taxation §§ 431 to 432, 437, 439.

6–5.5–5–3   Information or records required

Sec. 3.   The department may require and the taxpayer shall furnish information or records that the department determines to be necessary for it to make the determination required under this article.   The department may require this information to be included in the taxpayer's return.

As added by P.L.347–1989(ss), SEC.1.

Library References

Taxation ☞366.1.
WESTLAW Topic No. 371.
C.J.S. Taxation §§ 431 to 432, 437, 439.

Chapter 6

Returns

6–5.5–6–1   Annual returns required

Sec. 1.   Annual returns with respect to the tax imposed by this article shall be made by every taxpayer:

(1) having for the taxable year adjusted gross income or apportioned income subject to taxation under this article; or

(2) that would have had adjusted gross income or apportioned income subject to taxation under this article, but had a loss for that taxable year.

However, taxpayer members of a unitary group are required to file only one (1) return covering all members of the unitary group. The taxpayer member that files the return may be designated by the members of the unitary group pursuant to consents executed by each member. Each taxpayer member of a unitary group is jointly and severally liable for the tax liability of all members of the unitary group.

As added by P.L.347–1989(ss), SEC.1.   Amended by P.L.68–1991, SEC.14.

Historical and Statutory Notes

P.L.347–1989(ss), Sec.1, eff. Jan. 1, 1990, added this article.

P.L.68–1991, Sec.14, emerg. eff. retroactive to Jan. 1, 1990.

P.L.68–1991, Sec.14, substituted "taxpayer members of a unitary group are" for "a unitary group is" following "However," in the second sentence; and inserted "taxpayer" preceding "member" in each of the third and fourth sentences.

Cross References

Unitary groups, combined returns filed by members, see IC 6–5.5–5–1.

Library References

Taxation ⚭366.1.
WESTLAW Topic No. 371.
C.J.S. Taxation §§ 431 to 432, 437, 439.

Notes of Decisions

Deductions 1
Receivers 2

Indianapolis v. Vajen, 1887, 12 N.E. 311, 111
Ind. 240.

2. Receivers

1. Deductions

Where a taxpayer, upon making out his assessment list for city taxes, gave the assessor notice of his indebtedness, and demanded the right to deduct it from his national bank stock, and, at the time he payed his tax, also demanded of the treasurer that such deduction be made, and the same was refused by both officers on the ground that it was not authorized by law, he was entitled, under former statute to recover the tax thus "erroneously assessed and collected," notwithstanding he did not make any statement of such stock or indebtedness upon his assessment list, and although he did not seek to have the erroneous assessment corrected by the board of equalization. City of

Where circuit court clerk who during his term received from judgment debtors and others funds to be applied to payment of judgments, interests in estates, etc., and trust funds so held were converted to clerk's own use, and official bond of clerk was insufficient to cover amount, and receiver was appointed to collect trust funds and to hold them subject to rights, interests, and trusts with which funds were charged in hands of clerk, and receiver recovered certain of funds but less than amount converted and amount of clerk's bonds, funds were taxable to persons for whose benefit defaulting clerk received them, and receiver was not required to make returns for taxation purposes on such funds. 1925–1926 Op.Atty.Gen. p. 546.

6–5.5–6–2 Time for filing returns; extensions

Sec. 2. Annual returns required by this chapter shall be filed with the department on or before the fifteenth day of the fourth month following the close of the taxpayer's taxable year. However, if a taxpayer receives an extension of time from the United States Internal Revenue Service for the filing of its federal income tax return for a taxable year, the department shall grant a similar extension of time to the taxpayer for the filing of a return required by this chapter for that taxable year. In addition, the department may grant an additional reasonable extension of time for filing a return required by this chapter.

As added by P.L.347–1989(ss), SEC.1.

Library References

Taxation ⊕366.1.
WESTLAW Topic No. 371.
C.J.S. Taxation §§ 431 to 432, 437, 439.

6–5.5–6–3 Quarterly estimated tax; annual tax liability exceeding one thousand dollars; quarterly payments by taxpayers whose quarterly payments exceed twenty thousand dollars

Sec. 3. (a) Each taxpayer subject to taxation under this article shall report and pay quarterly an estimated tax equal to twenty-five percent (25%) of the taxpayer's total estimated tax liability imposed by this article for the taxable year. The quarterly estimated payments shall be made on or before the last day of the month for the quarter ending on the last day of the preceding month, without assessment or notice and demand from the department. The department shall prescribe the manner and furnish the forms for reporting and payment.

(b) Subsection (a) is applicable only to taxpayers having a tax liability imposed under this article that exceeds one thousand dollars ($1,000) for the taxable year.

(c) If the department determines that a taxpayer's:

(1) estimated quarterly financial institutions tax liability for the current year; or

(2) average quarterly financial institutions tax payment for the preceding year;

exceeds ten thousand dollars ($10,000), the taxpayer shall pay the quarterly financial institutions taxes due by electronic fund transfer (as defined in IC 4–8.1–2–7) or by delivering in person or by overnight courier a payment by cashier's check, certified check, or money order to the department. The transfer or payment shall be made on or before the date the tax is due.

(d) If a taxpayer's financial institutions tax payment is made by electronic fund transfer, the taxpayer is not required to file a quarterly financial institutions tax return.

As added by P.L.347–1989(ss), SEC.1. Amended by P.L.68–1991, SEC.15; P.L.28–1997, SEC.21.

Historical and Statutory Notes

P.L.68–1991, Sec.15, designated the existing provisions as Subsec. (a), and added Subsecs. (b) through (d).

P.L.28–1997, Sec.21, eff. Jan. 1, 1998, amended the section by substituting "ten thousand dollars ($10,000)" for "twenty thousand dollars ($20,000)" in Subsec. (b).

Library References

Taxation ⟜366.1, 526.
WESTLAW Topic No. 371.
C.J.S. Social Security and Public Welfare §§ 203, 207 to 208.

C.J.S. Taxation §§ 431 to 432, 437, 439, 617, 1082.

6–5.5–6–4   Payment of tax

Sec. 4. When a taxpayer is required to file a tax return under this chapter, the taxpayer shall, without assessment or notice and demand from the department, pay the tax to the department at the time fixed for filing the return without regard to an extension of time for filing the return. In making an annual return and paying the tax due for a taxable year, a taxpayer is entitled to take a credit for any tax previously paid by it for the taxable year under this chapter.

As added by P.L.347–1989(ss), SEC.1.

Library References

Taxation ⟜526, 527.
WESTLAW Topic No. 371.

C.J.S. Social Security and Public Welfare §§ 203, 207 to 208.
C.J.S. Taxation §§ 617 to 618, 621, 1082.

6–5.5–6–5   Certified copy of return

Sec. 5. A taxpayer shall furnish to the department at the department's request a true and correct copy of any tax return that the taxpayer has filed with the United States Internal Revenue Service. The copy shall be certified by the taxpayer under penalties of perjury.

As added by P.L.347–1989(ss), SEC.1.

6–5.5–6–6   Alteration or modification of return; notice; form; time; penalty

Sec. 6. (a) Each taxpayer shall notify the department in writing of any alteration or modification of a federal income tax return filed with the United States Internal Revenue Service for a taxable year that begins after December 31, 1988, including any modification or alteration in the amount of tax, regardless of whether the modification or assessment results from an assessment.

(b) The taxpayer shall file the notice in the form required by the department within one hundred twenty (120) days after the alteration or modification is made by the taxpayer or finally determined, whichever occurs first.

(c) The taxpayer shall pay an additional tax or penalty due under this article upon notice or demand from the department.

As added by P.L.347–1989(ss), SEC.1.

6–5.5–6–7   Forms; certification of truth of information

Sec. 7. A return required by this chapter and other information that is reasonably requested by the department must be on the forms that are prescribed by the department. The taxpayer or other person, corporation, or entity, when required by the department, shall certify under penalties of perjury to the truth of all information on the return or other document.

As added by P.L.347–1989(ss), SEC.1.

6–5.5–6–8   Transfer of property; liability for tax

Sec. 8. In the case of a transferee of the property of a transferor, liability for an accrued tax liability of the transferor is transferred to the transferee as provided in Section 6901 of the Internal Revenue Code.

As added by P.L.347–1989(ss), SEC.1.

6–5.5–6–9   Preservation of records; examination

Sec. 9. A taxpayer subject to taxation under this article shall keep and preserve records of the taxpayer's adjusted gross income and other books or accounts necessary to determine the amount of tax for which the taxpayer is liable under this article.   Those records, books, and accounts shall be kept open for examination at any time by the department or its authorized agents. *As added by P.L.347–1989(ss), SEC.1.*

Chapter 7

Penalties

Section

6–5.5–7–1   Failure to make payment; underpayments

Sec. 1.   (a) The penalty prescribed by IC 6–8.1–10–2.1(b) shall be assessed by the department on a taxpayer who fails to make payments as required in IC 6–5.5–6.   However, no penalty shall be assessed for a quarterly payment if the payment equals or exceeds:

(1) twenty percent (20%) of the final tax liability for the taxable year; or

(2) twenty-five percent (25%) of the final tax liability for the taxpayer's previous taxable year.

(b) The penalty for an underpayment of tax on a quarterly return shall only be assessed on the difference between the actual amount paid by the taxpayer on the quarterly return and the lesser of:

(1) twenty percent (20%) of the taxpayer's final tax liability for the taxable year; or

(2) twenty-five percent (25%) of the taxpayer's final tax liability for the taxpayer's previous taxable year.

As added by P.L.347–1989(ss), SEC.1.   Amended by P.L.1–1991, SEC.55.

Historical and Statutory Notes

P.L.347–1989(ss), Sec.1, eff. Jan. 1, 1990, added this article.

P.L.1–1991, Sec.55, emerg. eff. upon passage April 23, 1991.

P.L.1–1991, Sec.55, substituted "IC 6–8.1–10–2.1(b)" for "IC 6–8.1–10–2(b)" in Subsec. (a).

Library References

Taxation ☞840.
WESTLAW Topic No. 371.
C.J.S. Taxation § 1027.

6–5.5–7–2   Violation of article; violation of preparing or filing return

Sec. 2.   A taxpayer who:

(1) violates IC 6–5.5; or

(2) fails to comply with the request of the department made under IC 6–5.5–6;

commits a Class C infraction.

As added by P.L.347–1989(ss), SEC.1.

6–5.5–7–3   **False entries in books; multiple books; failure to make return; false returns**

Sec. 3.   A taxpayer who:

(1) makes false entries in the taxpayer's books;

(2) keeps more than one (1) set of books;

(3) fails to make a return required to be made under this chapter; or

(4) makes a false return or false statement in a return;

with intent to defraud the state or to evade the payment of a tax imposed under this article commits a Class D felony.

As added by P.L.347–1989(ss), SEC.1.

6–5.5–7–4   **Failure to permit examination of books, records or property; refusal to testify or produce records**

Sec. 4.   A person who knowingly:

(1) fails to permit the examination of any book, paper, account, record, or other data by the department or its authorized agents;

(2) fails to permit the inspection or appraisal of any property by the department or its authorized agents; or

(3) refuses to offer testimony or produce a record;

required under this article commits a Class D felony.

As added by P.L.347–1989(ss), SEC.1.

6–5.5–7–5   **Concurrent jurisdiction of attorney general**

Sec. 5.   The attorney general has concurrent jurisdiction with prosecuting attorneys in instituting and prosecuting actions under sections 2 through 4 of this chapter.

As added by P.L.347–1989(ss), SEC.1.

Chapter 8

Financial Institutions Tax Fund

6–5.5–8–1 Establishment; purpose; investment of money in fund; reversion of funds

Sec. 1. (a) The financial institutions tax fund is established for the purpose of making distributions to counties and for providing revenue for state appropriations. The fund shall be administered by the treasurer of state.

(b) The treasurer of state shall invest the money in the fund not currently needed to meet the obligations of the fund in the same manner as other public funds may be invested.

(c) Money in the fund at the end of a fiscal year does not revert to the state general fund.

As added by P.L.347–1989(ss), SEC.1.

Historical and Statutory Notes

P.L.347–1989(ss), Sec.1, eff. Jan. 1, 1990, added this article.

6–5.5–8–2 Quarterly distributions to counties; amount; supplemental distributions

Sec. 2. (a) On or before February 1, May 1, August 1, and December 1 of each year the auditor of state shall transfer to each county auditor for distribution to the taxing units (as defined in IC 6–1.1–1–21) in the county, an amount equal to one-fourth (¼) of the sum of the guaranteed amounts for all the taxing units of the county. On or before August 1 of each year the auditor of state shall transfer to each county auditor the supplemental distribution for the county for the year. For purposes of determining distributions under subsection (b), the state board of tax commissioners shall determine a state welfare allocation for each county calculated as follows:

(1) For 2000 and each year thereafter, the state welfare allocation for each county equals the greater of zero (0) or the amount determined under the following formula:

STEP ONE: For 1997, 1998, and 1999, determine the result of:

(A) the amounts appropriated by the county in the year for the county's county welfare fund and county welfare administration fund; divided by

(B) the amounts appropriated by all the taxing units in the county in the year.

STEP TWO: Determine the sum of the results determined in STEP ONE.

STEP THREE: Divide the STEP TWO result by three (3).

STEP FOUR: Determine the amount that would otherwise be distributed to all the taxing units in the county under subsection (b) without regard to this subdivision.

STEP FIVE: Determine the result of:

(A) the STEP FOUR amount; multiplied by

(B) the STEP THREE result.

(2) The state welfare allocation shall be deducted from the distributions otherwise payable under subsection (b) to the taxing unit that is a county and shall be deposited in a special account within the state general fund.

(b) A taxing unit's guaranteed distribution for a year is the greater of zero (0) or an amount equal to:

(1) the amount received by the taxing unit under IC 6–5–10 and IC 6–5–11 in 1989; minus

(2) the amount to be received by the taxing unit in the year of the distribution, as determined by the state board of tax commissioners, from property taxes attributable to the personal property of banks, exclusive of the property taxes attributable to personal property leased by banks as the lessor where the possession of the personal property is transferred to the lessee; minus

(3) in the case of a taxing unit that is a county, the amount that would have been received by the taxing unit in the year of the distribution, as determined by the state board of tax commissioners, from property taxes that:

(A) were calculated for the county's county welfare fund and county welfare administration fund for 2000 but were not imposed because of the repeal of IC 12–19–3 and IC 12–19–4; and

(B) would have been attributable to the personal property of banks, exclusive of the property taxes attributable to personal property leased by banks as the lessor where the possession of the personal property is transferred to the lessee.

(c) The amount of the supplemental distribution for a county for a year shall be determined using the following formula:

STEP ONE: Determine the greater of zero (0) or the difference between:

(A) one-half (½) of the taxes that the department estimates will be paid under this article during the year; minus

(B) the sum of all the guaranteed distributions, before the subtraction of all state welfare allocations under subsection (a), for all taxing units in all counties plus the bank personal property taxes to be received by all taxing units in all counties, as determined under subsection (b)(2) for the year.

STEP TWO: Determine the quotient of:

(A) the amount received under IC 6–5–10 and IC 6–5–11 in 1989 by all taxing units in the county; divided by

(B) the sum of the amounts received under IC 6–5–10 and IC 6–5–11 in 1989 by all taxing units in all counties.

STEP THREE: Determine the product of:

(A) the amount determined in STEP ONE; multiplied by

(B) the amount determined in STEP TWO.

STEP FOUR: Determine the greater of zero (0) or the difference between:

(A) the amount of supplemental distribution determined in STEP THREE for the county; minus

(B) the amount of refunds granted under IC 6–5–10–7 that have yet to be reimbursed to the state by the county treasurer under IC 6–5–10–13.

For the supplemental distribution made on or before August 1 of each year, the department shall adjust the amount of each county's supplemental distribution to reflect the actual taxes paid under this article for the preceding year.

(d) Except as provided in subsection (f), the amount of the supplemental distribution for each taxing unit shall be determined using the following formula:

STEP ONE: Determine the quotient of:

(A) the amount received by the taxing unit under IC 6–5–10 and IC 6–5–11 in 1989; divided by

(B) the sum of the amounts used in STEP ONE (A) for all taxing units located in the county.

STEP TWO: Determine the product of:

(A) the amount determined in STEP ONE; multiplied by

(B) the supplemental distribution for the county, as determined in subsection (c), STEP FOUR.

(e) The county auditor shall distribute the guaranteed and supplemental distributions received under subsection (a) to the taxing units in the county at the same time that the county auditor makes the semiannual distribution of real property taxes to the taxing units.

(f) The amount of a supplemental distribution paid to a taxing unit that is a county shall be reduced by an amount equal to:

(1) the amount the county would receive under subsection (d) without regard to this subsection; minus

(2) an amount equal to:

(A) the amount under subdivision (1); multiplied by

(B) the result of the following:

(I [1]) Determine the amounts appropriated by the county in 1997, 1998, and 1999, from the county's county welfare fund and county welfare administration fund, divided by the total amounts appropriated by all the taxing units in the county in the year.

459

(ii) Divide the amount determined in item (I [1]) by three (3).

As added by P.L.347–1989(ss), SEC.1. Amended by P.L.21–1990, SEC.32; P.L.61–1991, SEC.5; P.L.68–1991, SEC.16; P.L.273–1999, SEC.58.

[1] So in enrolled act; probably should read "i".

Historical and Statutory Notes

P.L.21–1990, Sec.32, emerg. eff. retroactive to Jan. 1, 1990.

P.L.21–1990, Sec.32, in Subsec. (a), in the first sentence, inserted "one-fourth (¼) of", and in the second sentence, substituted "On or before August 1 of each year the auditor of state shall transfer to each county auditor" for "plus" and inserted "for the year".

P.L.61–1991, Sec.5, rewrote Subsec. (e), which formerly read:

"(e) Within ten (10) working days after a county receives a guaranteed and a supplemental distribution, the county auditor shall distribute to each taxing unit the taxing unit's guaranteed and supplemental distributions."

P.L.68–1991, Sec.16, inserted "the greater of zero (0) or" in the introductory paragraph of Subsec. (b); in Subsec. (c) inserted:

"STEP FOUR: Determine the greater of zero (0) or the difference between:

"(A) the amount of supplemental distribution determined in STEP THREE for the county; minus

"(B) the amount of refunds granted under IC 6–5–10–7 that have yet to be reimbursed to the state by the county treasurer under IC 6–5–10–13."

and in Subsec. (d), STEP TWO, (B), inserted ", as determined in subsection (c), STEP FOUR."

P.L.68–1991, Sec.20, provides:

"(a) Except as provided in subsection (b), IC 6–5.5–8–2, as amended by this act, applies to distributions to taxing units after December 31, 1990.

"(b) Before July 1, 1991, IC 6–5.5–8–2(e), as amended by this act, shall only consist of the following language:

"(e) Within ten (10) working days after a county receives a guaranteed and a supplemental distribution, the county auditor shall distribute to each taxing unit the taxing unit's guaranteed and supplemental distributions.".

"(c) This Section expires July 1, 1991."

For applicability provisions of P.L.68–1991, see Historical and Statutory Note under section 6–8–5–1.

P.L.273–1999, Sec.58, eff. Jan. 1, 2000, rewrote the section, which prior thereto read:

"Sec. 2. (a) On or before February 1, May 1, August 1, and December 1 of each year the auditor of state shall transfer to each county auditor for distribution to the taxing units (as defined in IC 6–1.1–1–21) in the county, an amount equal to one-fourth (¼) of the sum of the guaranteed amounts for all the taxing units of the county. On or before August 1 of each year the auditor of state shall transfer to each county auditor the supplemental distribution for the county for the year.

"(b) A taxing unit's guaranteed distribution for a year is the greater of zero (0) or an amount equal to:

"(1) the amount received by the taxing unit under IC 6–5–10 and IC 6–5–11 in 1989; minus

"(2) the amount to be received by the taxing unit in the year of the distribution, as determined by the state board of tax commissioners, from property taxes attributable to the personal property of banks, exclusive of the property taxes attributable to personal property leased by banks as the lessor where the possession of the personal property is transferred to the lessee.

"(c) The amount of the supplemental distribution for a county for a year shall be determined using the following formula:

"STEP ONE: Determine the greater of zero (0) or the difference between:

"(A) one-half (½) of the taxes that the department estimates will be paid under this article during the year; minus

"(B) the sum of all the guaranteed distributions for all taxing units in all counties plus the bank personal property taxes to be received by all taxing units in all counties, as determined under subsection (b)(2) for the year.

"STEP TWO: Determine the quotient of:

"(A) the amount received under IC 6–5–10 and IC 6–5–11 in 1989 by all taxing units in the county; divided by

"(B) the sum of the amounts received under IC 6–5–10 and IC 6–5–11 in 1989 by all taxing units in all counties.

"STEP THREE: Determine the product of:

"(A) the amount determined in STEP ONE; multiplied by

"(B) the amount determined in STEP TWO.

"STEP FOUR: Determine the greater of zero (0) or the difference between:

"(A) the amount of supplemental distribution determined in STEP THREE for the county; minus

"(B) the amount of refunds granted under IC 6–5–10–7 that have yet to be reimbursed to the state by the county treasurer under IC 6–5–10–13.

"For the supplemental distribution made on or before August 1 of each year, the department shall adjust the amount of each county's supplemental distribution to reflect the actual taxes paid under this article for the preceding year.

"(d) The amount of the supplemental distribution for each taxing unit shall be determined using the following formula:

"STEP ONE: Determine the quotient of:

"(A) the amount received by the taxing unit under IC 6–5–10 and IC 6–5–11 in 1989; divided by

"(B) the sum of the amounts used in STEP ONE (A) for all taxing units located in the county.

"STEP TWO: Determine the product of:

"(A) the amount determined in STEP ONE; multiplied by

"(B) the supplemental distribution for the county, as determined in subsection (c), STEP FOUR.

"(e) The county auditor shall distribute the guaranteed and supplemental distributions received under subsection (a) to the taxing units in the county at the same time that the county auditor makes the semiannual distribution of real property taxes to the taxing units."

6–5.5–8–3   Guaranteed and supplemental distributions; certified amounts

Sec. 3.   (a) Before January 15, April 15, July 15, and November 15 of each year the department shall certify to the auditor of state the amount of the next quarterly guaranteed distribution for counties. Before July 15 of each year the department shall certify to the auditor of state the amount of the August 1 supplemental distribution for counties. The certified amounts shall be based on the best information available to the department.

(b) In order to make the distributions required by this chapter, the auditor of state shall draw warrants on the financial institutions tax fund payable to the county, and the treasurer of state shall pay the warrants.

As added by P.L.347–1989(ss), SEC.1. Amended by P.L.21–1990, SEC.33.

Historical and Statutory Notes

P.L.21–1990, Sec.33, emerg. eff. retroactive to Jan. 1, 1990.

P.L.21–1990, Sec.33, in Subsec. (a), in the first sentence, inserted "next quarterly", substi-
tuted "distribution" for "and supplemental distributions", and deleted "for the next distribution" following "counties", and inserted the second sentence.

6–5.5–8–4   Appropriation

Sec. 4.   There is appropriated from the financial institutions tax fund an amount necessary to make the distributions required by this chapter.

As added by P.L.347–1989(ss), SEC.1.

Chapter 9

Miscellaneous

6–5.5–9–1   Rules

Sec. 1.   The department shall adopt rules under IC 4–22–2 to implement this article.

As added by P.L.347–1989(ss), SEC.1.

Historical and Statutory Notes

P.L.347–1989(ss), Sec.1, eff. Jan. 1, 1990, added this article.

6–5.5–9–2   Other provisions applicable to article

Sec. 2.   For purposes of administration and enforcement the provisions of IC 6–8.1 that are applicable to a listed tax and an income tax apply to the tax imposed by this article.

As added by P.L.347–1989(ss), SEC.1.

6–5.5–9–3   Effect of tax under this article held inapplicable or invalid

Sec. 3.   If the tax imposed by this article is held inapplicable or invalid with respect to a taxpayer, then notwithstanding the statute of limitations set forth in IC 6–8.1–5–2(a), the taxpayer is liable for the taxes imposed by IC 6–2.1, IC 6–3, and IC 6–5 for the taxable periods with respect to which the tax under this article is held inapplicable or invalid.   In addition, personal property is exempt from assessment and property taxation under IC 6–1.1 if:

(1) the personal property is owned by a financial institution;

(2) the financial institution is subject to the bank tax imposed under IC 6–5–10; and

(3) the property is not leased by the financial institution to a lessee under circumstances in which possession is transferred to the lessee.

As added by P.L.347–1989(ss), SEC.1.   Amended by P.L.21–1990, SEC.34.

Historical and Statutory Notes

P.L.21–1990, Sec.34, emerg. eff. retroactive to Jan. 1, 1990.

P.L.21–1990, Sec.34, in the first paragraph, in the first sentence, inserted "notwithstanding the statute of limitations set forth in IC 6–8.1–5–2(a)", deleted "and IC 6–5.1" following "IC 6–5", and made a nonsubstantive change.

6–5.5–9–4   Exemption from other taxes

Sec. 4.   (a) A taxpayer who is subject to taxation under this article for a taxable year or part of a taxable year is not, for that taxable year or part of a taxable year, subject to:

(1) the gross income tax imposed by IC 6–2.1;

(2) the income taxes imposed by IC 6–3; and

(3) the bank, savings and loan, or production credit association tax imposed by IC 6–5.

(b) the exemptions provided for the taxes listed in subsection (a)(1) through (a)(2) do not apply to a taxpayer to the extent the taxpayer is acting in a fiduciary capacity.

As added by P.L.347–1989(ss), SEC.1.   Amended by P.L.21–1990, SEC.35; P.L.1–1991, SEC.56.

Historical and Statutory Notes

P.L.21–1990, Sec.35, emerg. eff. retroactive to Jan. 1, 1990.

P.L.21–1990, Sec.35, in Subsec. (a), in the introductory sentence, inserted "or part of a taxable year"; deleted Subsec. (a)(3), which read, "the intangibles tax imposed by IC 6–5.1; and"; redesignated Subsec. (a)(4) as Subsec.

(a)(3); in Subsec. (b), substituted "(a)(2)" for "(a)(3)"; and made a nonsubstantive change.

P.L.1–1991, Sec.56, emerg. eff. upon passage April 23, 1991.

P.L.1–1991, Sec.56, inserted "or part of a taxable year" the second time that phrase appears in Subsec. (a).

United States Supreme Court

Intangibles tax imposed on corporate stock owned by state residents, deduction for corporation's exposure to state income tax, commerce

clause, compensatory tax doctrine, see Fulton Corp. v. Faulkner, 1996, 116 S.Ct. 848.

6–5.5–9–5   Depositor or owner of capital stock, share accounts, certificates of indebtedness or investment in taxpayer with principal offices in state; tax liability

Sec. 5.   A depositor or owner of capital stock, capital shares, share accounts, certificates of indebtedness or investment, or comparable investment or interest in a taxpayer with its principal offices in Indiana is not liable for taxation under this article with respect to that interest.

As added by P.L.347–1989(ss), SEC.1.   Amended by P.L.21–1990, SEC.36.

Historical and Statutory Notes

P.L.21–1990, Sec.36, emerg. eff. retroactive to Jan. 1, 1990.

P.L.21–1990, Sec.36, deleted the second sentence, which read, "Such an investment or interest may not be assessed for taxation under IC 6–5.1 for a period during which the taxpayer is subject to taxation under this article."

ARTICLE 6

MOTOR FUEL AND VEHICLE EXCISE TAXES

WESTLAW Computer Assisted Legal Research

WESTLAW supplements your legal research in many ways. WESTLAW allows you to

- update your research with the most current information
- expand your library with additional resources
- retrieve current, comprehensive history and citing references to a case with KeyCite

For more information on using WESTLAW to supplement your research, see the WESTLAW Electronic Research Guide, which follows the Preface.

Chapter 1

Motor Fuel Tax

6–6–1–1 to 6–6–1–5   Repealed

(Repealed by Acts 1979, P.L.79, SEC.2.)

Historical and Statutory Notes

Acts 1979, P.L. 79, provided in § 6, containing emergency clause, that the act takes effect April 5, 1979.

Former § 6–6–1–1 entitled the act "Motor Fuel Tax Law."

Former § 6–6–1–2 contained definitions.

Former § 6–6–1–3 related to the disposition of the license tax.

Former § 6–6–1–4 related to the rate of tax and exemptions from tax, and dedicated revenues for highway purposes.

Former § 6–6–1–5 related to distributor licenses.

DISPOSITION TABLE

The subject matter of the repealed sections of Title 6 of the Indiana Code is now covered in new sections of Title 6, West's Annotated Indiana Code as follows:

Repealed Sections	New Sections	Repealed Sections	New Sections
6–6–1–1	6–6–1.1–101		1.1–702, 6–6–1.1–801, 6–6–1.1–902, 6–6–1.1–1102 [Repealed]
6–6–1–2	6–6–1.1–103, 6–6–1.1–202 to 6–6–1.1–208		
6–6–1–3	6–6–1.1–803	6–6–1–5	6–6–1.1–401 to 6–6–1.1–406, 6–6–1.1–411 to 6–6–1.1–414, 6–6–1.1–418
6–6–1–4	6–6–1.1–201, 6–6–1.1–301, 6–6–1.1–701, 6–6–		

6–6–1–6   Repealed

(Repealed by Acts 1971, P.L.69, SEC.7; Acts 1979, P.L.79, SEC.2.)

6–6–1–7 to 6–6–1–21   Repealed

(Repealed by Acts 1979, P.L.79, SEC.2.)

Historical and Statutory Notes

Acts 1979, P.L. 79, provided in § 6, containing emergency clause, that the act takes effect April 5, 1979.

Former § 6–6–1–7 related to distributors' bonds.

Former §§ 6–6–1–8 and 6–6–1–8.5 related to distributors' monthly reports.

Former § 6–6–1–9 related to cancellation of licenses.

Former § 6–6–1–10 related to offenses and penalties for failure to pay tax.

Former § 6–6–1–11 gave the administrator power to fix the amount of delinquent taxes.

Former § 6–6–1–12 related to reports for persons other than licensed distributors.

Former § 6–6–1–13 related to the identification of fuel transportation vehicles.

Former § 6–6–1–14 related to reports by fuel transporters.

Former § 6–6–1–15 related to record keeping.

Former § 6–6–1–16 related to the administrator's investigatory powers.

Former § 6–6–1–17 related to claims by the state against distributors.

Former §§ 6–6–1–18 and 6–6–1–19 related to procedures to enforce collection of the tax.

Former § 6–6–1–20 related to notices from distributors who ceased to engage in business.

Former § 6–6–1–21 related to refunds to persons other than distributors.

Formerly:

IC 6–6–1–8.5.
IC 6–6–1–10.
IC 6–6–1–11.
IC 6–6–1–15.
IC 6–6–1–16.
IC 6–6–1–17.
IC 6–6–1–19.
Acts 1943, c. 73, ss. 11, 12, 16, 17, 18, 20.
Acts 1971, P.L.69, SEC.3.
Acts 1978, P.L.2, SEC.634.

DISPOSITION TABLE

Showing where the subject matter of the repealed sections of Title 6 of the Indiana Code is now covered in new sections of Title 6, West's Annotated Indiana Code.

Repealed Sections	New Sections	Repealed Sections	New Sections
6–6–1–7	6–6–1.1–406 to 6–6–1.1–410, 6–6–1.1–1101 [Repealed]	6–6–1–15	6–6–1.1–601 to 6–6–1.1–603 [Repealed], 6–6–1.1–605 [Repealed], 6–6–1.1–1101 [Repealed]
6–6–1–8	6–6–1.1–501, 6–6–1.1–502, 6–6–1.1–701, 6–6–1.1–705, 6–6–1.1–1201 [Repealed]	6–6–1–16	6–6–1.1–604 [Repealed], 6–6–1.1–1104 [Repealed], 6–6–1.1–1105 [Repealed], 6–6–1.1–1304 [Repealed]
6–6–1–8.5	6–6–1.1–503 [Repealed], 6–6–1.1–1302 [Repealed]	6–6–1–17	6–6–1.1–1001 to 6–6–1.1–1007 [Repealed]
6–6–1–9	6–6–1.1–415 to 6–6–1.1–417	6–6–1–18	6–6–1.1–509 to 6–6–1.1–511 [Repealed], 6–6–1.1–1001 [Repealed], 6–6–1.1–1205, 6–6–1.1–1303 [Repealed]
6–6–1–10	6–6–1.1–1301 [Repealed]		
6–6–1–11	6–6–1.1–505 [Repealed], 6–6–1.1–506 [Repealed]	6–6–1–19	6–6–1.1–507 [Repealed], 6–6–1.1–508 [Repealed]
6–6–1–12	6–6–1.1–504		
6–6–1–13	6–6–1.1–1202	6–6–1–20	6–6–1.1–512 to 6–6–1.1–514
6–6–1–14	6–6–1.1–606 to 6–6–1.1–608	6–6–1–21	6–6–1.1–901

6–6–1–22   Repealed

(Repealed by Acts 1978, P.L.47, SEC.5; Acts 1979, P.L.79, SEC.2.)

Historical and Statutory Notes

Acts 1978, P.L. 47, provided in § 6, containing emergency clause, that the act takes effect Aug. 1, 1978.

The former section related to use of motor fuel other than on highways.

See, now, IC 6–6–1.1–302 to 6–6–1.1–305, 6–6–1.1–703, 6–6–1.1–903 to 6–6–1.1–906, 6–6–1.1–1305 to 6–6–1.1–1307.

6–6–1–22.1 to 6–6–1–26   Repealed

(Repealed by Acts 1979, P.L.79, SEC.2.)

Historical and Statutory Notes

Acts 1979, P.L. 79, provided in § 6, containing emergency clause, that the act takes effect April 5, 1979.

Former § 6–6–1–22.1 related to use of motor fuel other than on highways.

Former §§ 6–6–1–23 and 6–6–1–25 related to refunds and credits for mistaken payment.

Former § 6–6–1–24 related to the deposit and disposition of revenues.

Former § 6–6–1–26 made the administrator's records public.

Formerly:

IC 6–6–1–26.
Acts 1943, c. 73, s. 27.

DISPOSITION TABLE

The subject matter of the repealed sections of Title 6 of the Indiana Code is now covered in new sections of Title 6, West's Annotated Indiana Code as follows:

Repealed Sections	New Sections	Repealed Sections	New Sections
6–6–1–22.1	6–6–1.1–302 to 6–6–1.1–305	6–6–1–23	6–6–1.1–704
			6–6–1.1–907
	6–6–1.1–703		6–6–1.1–908
	6–6–1.1–903 to 6–6–1.1–906	6–6–1–24	6–6–1.1–802
			6–6–1.1–803
	6–6–1.1–1201 [Repealed]		6–6–1.1–804 [Repealed]
	6–6–1.1–1305 to 6–6–1.1–1307		6–6–1.1–805, 6–6–1.1–909
		6–6–1–25	6–6–1.1–1206
		6–6–1–26	6–6–1.1–1102 [Repealed]

6–6–1–27   Repealed

(Repealed by Acts 1971, P.L.69, SEC.7; Acts 1979, P.L.79, SEC.2.)

6–6–1–28 to 6–6–1–35   Repealed

(Repealed by Acts 1979, P.L.79, SEC.2.)

Historical and Statutory Notes

Acts 1979, P.L. 79, provided in § 6, containing emergency clause, that the act takes effect April 5, 1979.

Former § 6–6–1–28 related to offenses and penalties.

Former § 6–6–1–29 related to the exchange of information with other states.

Former § 6–6–1–30 required the separation of fuel prices and taxes in display signs and advertising.

Former § 6–6–1–31 related to the payment of motor fuel taxes in lieu of certain other taxes.

Former § 6–6–1–32 related to rules and regulations.

Former § 6–6–1–33 enumerated duties of the attorney-general.

Former § 6–6–1–34 related to rewards for reporting tax evaders.

Former § 6–6–1–35 provided for cumulative remedies.

Formerly:

IC 6–6–1–32 to 6–6–1–35.
Acts 1943, c. 73, ss. 33 to 36.

DISPOSITION TABLE

Showing where the subject matter of the repealed sections of Title 6 of the Indiana Code is now covered in new sections of Title 6, West's Annotated Indiana Code.

Repealed Sections	New Sections	Repealed Sections	New Sections
6–6–1–28	6–6–1.1–1308 to 6–6–1.1–1313	6–6–1–31	6–6–1.1–1204
		6–6–1–32	6–6–1.1–1106 [Repealed]
6–6–1–29	6–6–1.1–1103	6–6–1–33	6–6–1.1–1107 [Repealed]
		6–6–1–34	6–6–1.1–1108 [Repealed]
6–6–1–30	6–6–1.1–1203	6–6–1–35	6–6–1.1–1109 [Repealed]

6–6–1–36 Repealed

(Repealed by Acts 1978, P.L.2, SEC.656; Acts 1979, P.L.79, SEC.2.)

Historical and Statutory Notes

Acts 1978, P.L. 2, provided in § 3602(a), containing emergency clause, that the act takes effect July 1, 1978.

The former section repealed conflicting laws.

Formerly:

Acts 1943, c. 73, s. 38.

Chapter 1.1

Gasoline Tax

Library References

Taxation ⟨⟩1293.
WESTLAW Topic No. 371.
C.J.S. Licenses §§ 30, 47, 48.

6–6–1.1–101   Short title

Sec. 101. This chapter shall be known and may be cited as the "Gasoline Tax Law."

As added by Acts 1979, P.L.79, SEC.1. Amended by Acts 1980, P.L.51, SEC.4.

Historical and Statutory Notes

Acts 1979, P.L. 79, § 1, emerg. eff. April 5, 1979, added this chapter.

The 1979 act reenacted the provisions of this chapter as part of a codification, revision and rearrangement of laws relating to the taxation of fuel.

Acts 1979, P.L. 79, provided in §§ 3 and 5:

"Section 3. (a) This act is intended to be a codification and restatement of applicable or corresponding provisions of the laws repealed by this act. If this act repeals and reenacts a law in the same form or in a restated form, the substantive operation and effect of that law shall continue uninterrupted.

"(b) This act does not affect any:

"(1) rights or liabilities accrued;

"(2) penalties incurred;

"(3) crimes committed; or

"(4) proceedings begun;

"before the effective date of this act. Those rights, liabilities, penalties, crimes, and proceedings shall continue to be imposed and enforced under prior law as if this act had not been enacted."

"Section 5. If any provision or application of this act is held invalid, the invalidity does not affect the remainder of this act unless:

"(1) the remainder is so essentially and inseparably connected with, and so dependent upon, the invalid provision or application that it cannot be presumed that the remainder would have been enacted without the invalid provision or application; or

"(2) the remainder is incomplete and incapable of being executed in accordance with the legislative intent without the invalid provision or application."

Acts 1980, P.L.51, § 4, emerg. eff. Feb. 22, 1980, substituted "Gasoline" for "Motor Fuel".

Acts 1980, P.L.51, provided in §§ 67 to 69:

"Section 67. (a) This act is intended to be a codification and restatement of applicable or corresponding provisions of the laws repealed by this act. If this act repeals and reenacts a law in the same form or in a restated form, the substantive operation and effect of that law shall continue uninterrupted.

"(b) This act does not affect any:

"(1) rights or liabilities accrued;

"(2) penalties incurred;

"(3) crimes committed; or

"(4) proceedings begun;

"before the effective date of this act. Those rights, liabilities, penalties, crimes, and proceedings shall continue to be imposed and enforced under prior law as if this act had not been enacted.

"Section 68. The general assembly may, by concurrent resolution, preserve any of the background materials related to this act.

"Section 69. If any provision or application of this act is held invalid, the invalidity does not affect the remainder of this act unless:

"(1) the remainder is so essentially and inseparably connected with and so dependent upon the invalid provision or application that it cannot be presumed that the remainder would have been enacted without the invalid provision or application; or

"(2) the remainder is incomplete and incapable of being executed in accordance with the legislative intent without the invalid provision or application."

Formerly:

IC 6–6–1–1.

Acts 1943, c. 73, s. 1.

Cross References

Administration, enforcement and collection of tax, revenue department, see IC 6–8.1–1–1 et seq.
Motor carrier fuel tax, see IC 6–6–4.1–1 et seq.
Special fuel tax, see IC 6–6–2.1–101 et seq.

Law Review and Journal Commentaries

Taxation; department of revenue: Survey of recent law. Marc S. Weinstein, 13 Ind.L.Rev. 1 (1980).

United States Code Annotated

Federal gasoline tax, see 26 U.S.C.A. 4081 et seq.

6–6–1.1–102   Application of definitions and rules of construction

Sec. 102. The definitions and rules of construction contained in sections 103 and 104 of this chapter apply throughout this chapter unless the context clearly requires otherwise.

As added by Acts 1979, P.L.79, SEC.1.

6–6–1.1–103   Definitions

Sec. 103. As used in this chapter:

(a) "Administrator" means the administrative head of the department of state revenue or the administrator's designee.

(b) "Dealer" means a person, except a distributor, engaged in the business of selling gasoline in Indiana.

(c) "Department" means the department of state revenue.

(d) "Distributor" means a person who first receives gasoline in Indiana. However, "distributor" does not include the United States or any of its agencies unless their inclusion is permitted under the Constitution and laws of the United States.

(e) "Licensed distributor" means a person holding a valid distributor's license issued by the administrator.

(f) "Marine facility" means a marina or boat livery.

(g) "Gasoline" means:

(1) all products commonly or commercially known or sold as gasoline, including casinghead and absorption or natural gasoline, regardless of their classifications or uses; and

(2) any liquid, which when subjected to distillation of gasoline, naphtha, kerosene, and similar petroleum products with American Society for Testing Materials Designation D–86, shows not less than ten percent (10%) distilled (recovered) below three hundred forty-seven degrees Fahrenheit (347 degrees F) or one hundred seventy-five degrees Centigrade (175 degrees C), and not less than ninety-five percent (95%) distilled (recovered) below four hundred sixty-four degrees Fahrenheit (464 degrees F) or two hundred forty degrees Centigrade (240 degrees C).

However, the term "gasoline" does not include liquefied gases which would not exist as liquids at a temperature of sixty degrees Fahrenheit (60 degrees F) or sixteen degrees Centigrade (16 degrees C), and a pressure of fourteen and seven-tenths (14.7) pounds per square inch absolute, or denatured, wood, or ethyl alcohol, ether, turpentine, or acetates, unless such product is used as an additive in the manufacture, compounding, or blending of a liquid within subdivision (2), in which event only the quantity so used is considered gasoline. In addition, "gasoline" does not include those liquids which meet the specifications of subdivision (2) but which are especially designated for use other than as a fuel for internal combustion engines.

(h) "Motor vehicle" means a vehicle, except a vehicle operated on rails, which is propelled by an internal combustion engine or motor and is designed to permit its mobile use on public highways.

(i) "Person" means a natural person, partnership, firm, association, corporation, limited liability company, representative appointed by a court, or the state or its political subdivisions.

(j) "Public highway" means the entire width between boundary lines of every publicly maintained way in Indiana including streets and alleys in cities and towns when any part of the way is open to public use for vehicle travel.

(k) "Taxable marine facility" means a marine facility located on an Indiana lake.

(*l*) "Taxicab" means a motor vehicle which is:

(1) designed to carry not more than seven (7) individuals, including the driver;

(2) held out to the public for hire at a fare regulated by municipal ordinance and based upon length of trips or time consumed;

(3) not operated over a definite route; and

(4) a part of a commercial enterprise in the business of providing taxicab service.

(m) "Terminal" means a marine or pipeline gasoline facility.

(n) "Metered pump" means a stationary pump having a meter that is capable of measuring the amount of gasoline dispensed through it.

(*o*) "Billed gallons" means the gallons indicated on an invoice for payment to a supplier.

(p) "Export" for gasoline and fuels taxed in the same manner as gasoline under the origin state's statutes means the sale for export and delivery out of a state by or for the seller that is:

(1) an export by the seller in the origin state; and

(2) an import by the seller in the destination state.

(q) "Import" for gasoline and fuels taxed in the same manner as gasoline under the origin state's statutes means the purchase for export and transportation out of a state by or for the purchaser that is:

(1) an export by the purchaser in the origin state; and

(2) an import by the purchaser in the destination state.

(r) "Rack" means a dock, platform, or open bay:

(1) located at a refinery or terminal; and

(2) having a system of metered pipes and hoses to load fuel into a tank wagon or tank transport.

As added by Acts 1979, P.L.79, SEC.1. Amended by Acts 1980, P.L.51, SEC.5; P.L.97–1987, SEC.1; P.L.69–1991, SEC.1; P.L.8–1993, SEC.96.

Historical and Statutory Notes

Acts 1980, P.L. 51, § 5, was made emergency effective Feb. 22, 1980.

P.L. 97–1987, Sec.1, was made effective Sept. 1, 1987.

P.L.8–1993, Sec.96, inserted "limited liability company" in the definition of "person".

Formerly:

IC 6–6–1–2.

Acts 1943, c. 73, s. 2.

Acts 1947, c. 336, s. 1.

Acts 1955, c. 111, s. 1.

Acts 1978, P.L.47, SEC.1.

Library References

Words and Phrases (Perm.Ed.)

Notes of Decisions

Gasoline 1

---

1. Gasoline

For purposes of differentiating between gasoline and other motor vehicle fuels, for purposes of former statute, fuels produced, prepared, blended or compounded for purpose of propelling motor vehicles, or suitable and practicable for propulsion of motor vehicles upon public highways, were "gasoline", and should have been so treated in application of the act [repealed; see, now, this chapter] requiring collection of tax and authorizing a refund in the case of use other than propulsion of motor vehicles upon public highways; and since state auditor was compelled by act to differentiate between two classes of fuels, he was authorized to establish appropriate engineering standards. 1937 Op.Atty.Gen. p. 511.

Dealers in industrial benzol and solvent naphtha were required to comply with the motor vehicle fuel tax act [repealed; see, now, this chapter and § 6–6–2.1–101 et seq.]. 1931–1932 Op.Atty.Gen. p. 971.

6–6–1.1–104 Rules of construction

Sec. 104. (a) Whenever a masculine gender pronoun is used in this chapter, it refers to the masculine, feminine, or neuter, whichever is appropriate.

(b) The singular form of any noun as used in this chapter includes the plural, and the plural includes the singular, where appropriate.

As added by Acts 1979, P.L.79, SEC.1.

Cross References

Construction of statutes, see IC 1–1–4–1.

Library References

Taxation ⬤1220.

WESTLAW Topic No. 371.

C.J.S. Taxation § 1232.

I.L.E. Taxation §§ 187 to 190.

6–6–1.1–105 Citation to prior law

Sec. 105. If a provision of the prior motor fuel or marine fuel tax laws (IC 6–6–1 and IC 6–6–1.5) has been replaced in the same form or in a restated form, by a provision of this chapter, then a citation to the provision of the prior law shall be construed as a citation to the corresponding provision of this chapter.

As added by Acts 1979, P.L.79, SEC.1.

6–6–1.1–201 Rate and burden of tax

Sec. 201. A license tax of fifteen cents ($0.15) per gallon is imposed on the use of all gasoline used in Indiana, except as otherwise provided by this chapter. The distributor shall initially pay the tax on the billed gallonage of all gasoline the distributor receives in this state, less any deductions authorized by this chapter. The distributor shall then add the per gallon amount of tax to the selling price of each gallon of gasoline sold in this state and collected from the purchaser so that the ultimate consumer bears the burden of the tax.

As added by Acts 1979, P.L.79, SEC.1. Amended by Acts 1980, P.L.51, SEC.6; Acts 1980, P.L.10, SEC.6; P.L.59–1985, SEC.9; P.L.68–1988, SEC.1; P.L.69–1991, SEC.2.

Historical and Statutory Notes

Acts 1980, P.L. 51, § 6, emerg. eff. Feb. 22, 1980, substituted "gasoline" for "motor fuel" throughout the section.

Acts 1980, P.L. 10, § 6, eff. July 1, 1980, substituted "at the applicable rate fixed under section 201.5 of this chapter" for "of eight cents ($.08) per gallon" in the first sentence.

P.L.59–1985, Sec.9, emerg. eff. June 1, 1985, substituted, in the first sentence, "of fourteen ($.014) per gallon" for "at the applicable rate fixed under section 201.5 of this chapter".

P.L. 68–1988, Sec.1, emerg. eff. April 1, 1988, increased the tax by 1¢ per gallon.

P.L.69–1991, Sec.2 substituted in the second sentence "billed" for "invoiced" gallonage and "the distributor" for "he".

Formerly:

IC 6–6–1–4.
IC 6–6–1.5–1.
IC 6–6–1.5–2.
Acts 1943, c. 73, s. 4.
Acts 1957, c. 48, s. 1.
Acts 1959, c. 323, s. 1.
Acts 1969, c. 319, s. 1.
Acts 1971, P.L.70, SEC.1.
Acts 1978, P.L.47, SEC.4.

Cross References

Gross retail and use tax, determination of gross retail income from gasoline sales, see IC 6–2.5–4–1. Special fuel tax rate, see IC 6–6–2.1–201.

Library References

Taxation ☞1297.
WESTLAW Topic No. 371.

C.J.S. Taxation § 1245.
I.L.E. Taxation §§ 61, 187 to 190.

WESTLAW Electronic Research

See WESTLAW Electronic Research Guide following the Preface.

United States Supreme Court

Taxation, application of motor fuels tax to fuels sold by Indian tribe, see Oklahoma Tax Com'n v. Chickasaw Nation, U.S.Okla.1995, 115

S.Ct. 2214, 515 U.S. 450, 132 L.Ed.2d 400, on remand 64 F.3d 577.

Notes of Decisions

Collection of tax   4
Conflict of laws   2
Interstate commerce   5
Power to levy tax   3
Validity of prior laws   1

---

1. Validity of prior laws

Acts 1923, c. 182 [repealed; see, now, this chapter], imposing tax upon sales of gasoline, was not violative of any express prohibition contained in Constitution of state or United

States, and the fact that tax was also paid on gasoline as property, in proportion to its assessed value did not make tax invalid. Gafill v. Bracken, 1925, 146 N.E. 109, 195 Ind. 551.

Former act imposing tax on sale of gasoline did not confer judicial power upon an administrative officer. Gafill v. Bracken, 1925, 146 N.E. 109, 195 Ind. 551.

Former act imposing gasoline tax did not violate Fourteenth Amendment [U.S.C.A.Const. Amend. 14], nor was it a "property tax," in violation of Const. Art. 10, § 1, since use of gasoline and not gasoline itself was taxed. Gafill v. Bracken, 1925, 146 N.E. 109, 195 Ind. 551.

Fact that under Act 1923, c. 182 [repealed; see, now, this chapter], part of tax receipts, paid into state treasury by residents of one county, could or would be used to build roads in other counties did not render act invalid. Gafill v. Bracken, 1925, 146 N.E. 109, 195 Ind. 551.

Title to Acts 1923 p. 532 [repealed; see, now, this chapter] which imposed a license fee upon the use of gasoline, sections of which were amended in 1925 and 1929, was accurate as to text of said acts and the acts as amended did not become invalid because the title referred to them as Acts of 1923. 1931–1932 Op.Atty.Gen. p. 48.

2. Conflict of laws

Provision in motor fuel tax act of 1943 [repealed; see, now, this chapter] to effect that motor fuel tax was in lieu of any excise, privilege, or occupational tax on manufacturing, distributing or selling motor fuel did not conflict with former sales tax act [see, now, § 6–2.5–1–1 et seq.], and sales tax could be imposed upon sale of motor fuels. Economy Oil Corp. v. Indiana Dept. of State Revenue, App. 1 Dist. 1974, 321 N.E.2d 215, 162 Ind.App. 658.

3. Power to levy tax

State may select use of gasoline for propelling vehicles on highways of state as a subject of taxation from which to raise revenue to construct, maintain, and repair highways. Gafill v. Bracken, 1924, 145 N.E. 312, 195 Ind. 551, rehearing denied 146 N.E. 109, 195 Ind. 551.

4. Collection of tax

Tax on use of gasoline, which statute requires dealer to collect from buyer and pay to state, is held by him in trust for state. Shipe v. Consumers' Service Co., D.C.Ind.1928, 28 F.2d 53.

5. Interstate commerce

Under the Indiana gasoline tax law [repealed; see, now, this chapter], tax could be exacted from motor bus and trucking companies operating busses and trucks in interstate commerce in Indiana. 1929–1930 Op.Atty.Gen. p. 229.

Where railroad companies used gasoline in motors belonging to company furnishing motive power with which they conducted their interstate business of transporting passengers, mail, freight and express, company could be compelled to pay tax on gasoline used by the Indiana tax law [repealed; see, now, this chapter]. 1929–1930 Op.Atty.Gen. p. 229.

6–6–1.1–201.5   Repealed

(Repealed by P.L.59–1985, SEC.37.)

Historical and Statutory Notes

P.L.59–1985 provided in Section 43 that Section 37 of the act takes effect June 1, 1985.

The former section related to the determination, fixing and notice of new rates.

Formerly:

Acts 1980, P.L.10, SEC.7.
Acts 1981, P.L.88, SEC.5.

6–6–1.1–202   Time considered received; in-state gasoline; withdrawal from refinery or terminal

Sec. 202. (a) For purposes of this chapter, gasoline is considered received when it is withdrawn from an in-state refinery or terminal for sale or use in this state or for transfer to a destination in this state, unless the destination is another in-state refinery or terminal.

(b) Gasoline is received by the owner of the gasoline when it is withdrawn from the refinery or terminal. However, if the gasoline is withdrawn for delivery or transportation to or for the account of the holder of a distributor license, then the gasoline is received by the distributor to whom or for whose account it is delivered or transported.

(c) Only when gasoline is withdrawn for delivery or transportation to a person who sells and distributes by tank car, tank truck, or transport is that person a distributor as defined by section 103(d) of this chapter.

As added by Acts 1979, P.L.79, SEC.1. Amended by Acts 1979, P.L.71, SEC.2; Acts 1980, P.L.51, SEC.7.

Historical and Statutory Notes

Acts 1979, P.L. 71, § 2, added Subsec. (c).

Acts 1980, P.L. 51, § 7, emerg. eff. Feb. 22, 1980, substituted "gasoline" for "motor fuel" throughout the section.

Formerly:
IC 6-6-1-2.

Acts 1943, c. 73, s. 2.
Acts 1947, c. 336, s. 1.
Acts 1955, c. 111, s. 1.
Acts 1978, P.L.47, SEC.1.

Library References

Taxation ☞1204, 1293.
WESTLAW Topic No. 371.

C.J.S. Taxation § 1231.
I.L.E. Taxation §§ 187 to 190.

6-6-1.1-203 Time considered received; imported gasoline; storage

Sec. 203. Gasoline is received by the owner at the time it is unloaded in this state if it is imported into this state and placed in storage at a place other than a refinery or terminal.

As added by Acts 1979, P.L.79, SEC.1. Amended by Acts 1980, P.L.51, SEC.8.

Historical and Statutory Notes

Acts 1980, P.L. 51, § 8, emerg. eff. Feb. 22, 1980, substituted "gasoline" for "motor fuel".

Formerly:
IC 6-6-1-2.

Acts 1943, c. 73, s. 2.
Acts 1947, c. 336, s. 1.
Acts 1955, c. 111, s. 1.
Acts 1978, P.L.47, SEC.1.

6-6-1.1-204 Time considered received; imported gasoline; use directly from transport

Sec. 204. If the gasoline referred to in section 203 of this chapter is used in this state directly from the transportation equipment by which it is transported, then it is received when it is brought into this state and by the person who uses it in this state.

As added by Acts 1979, P.L.79, SEC.1. Amended by Acts 1980, P.L.51, SEC.9.

Historical and Statutory Notes

Acts 1980, P.L. 51, § 9, emerg. eff. Feb. 22, 1980, substituted "gasoline" for "motor fuel".

Formerly:
IC 6-6-1-2.

Acts 1943, c. 73, s. 2.
Acts 1947, c. 336, s. 1.
Acts 1955, c. 111, s. 1.
Acts 1978, P.L.47, SEC.1.

6–6–1.1–205 **Time considered received; imported gasoline; transport by licensed distributor**

Sec. 205. Gasoline shipped or brought into this state by a licensed distributor which is sold and delivered in this state directly to someone other than a licensed distributor is considered received by the distributor shipping or bringing the fuel into this state.

As added by Acts 1979, P.L.79, SEC.1. Amended by Acts 1980, P.L.51, SEC.10.

Historical and Statutory Notes

Acts 1980, P.L. 51, § 10, emerg. eff. Feb. 22, 1980, substituted "gasoline" for "motor fuel".

Formerly:
IC 6–6–1–2.

Acts 1943, c. 73, s. 2.
Acts 1947, c. 336, s. 1.
Acts 1955, c. 111, s. 1.
Acts 1978, P.L.47, SEC.1.

6–6–1.1–206 **Time considered received; in-state gasoline produced or blended**

Sec. 206. Gasoline produced, compounded, or blended in this state at a place other than a refinery or terminal is considered received at the time and by the owner of the gasoline when it is produced, compounded, or blended.

As added by Acts 1979, P.L.79, SEC.1. Amended by Acts 1980, P.L.51, SEC.11.

Historical and Statutory Notes

Acts 1980, P.L. 51, § 11, emerg. eff. Feb. 22, 1980, substituted "gasoline" for "motor fuel" throughout the section.

Formerly:
IC 6–6–1–2.

Acts 1943, c. 73, s. 2.
Acts 1947, c. 336, s. 1.
Acts 1955, c. 111, s. 1.
Acts 1978, P.L.47, SEC.1.

6–6–1.1–207 **Time considered received; in-state gasoline not covered by 6–6–1.1–202 through 6–6–1.1–206**

Sec. 207. Gasoline acquired in this state by any person not covered by sections 202 through 206 of this chapter is considered received at the time of acquisition by the person acquiring it, unless the person from whom the gasoline is acquired has paid or incurred liability for, or is exempt under section 301 of this chapter from, the tax imposed on the gasoline.

As added by Acts 1979, P.L.79, SEC.1. Amended by Acts 1980, P.L.51, SEC.12.

Historical and Statutory Notes

Acts 1980, P.L. 51, § 12, emerg. eff. Feb. 22, 1980, substituted "gasoline" for "motor fuel" throughout the section.

Formerly:
IC 6–6–1–2.

Acts 1943, c. 73, s. 2.
Acts 1947, c. 336, s. 1.
Acts 1955, c. 111, s. 1.
Acts 1978, P.L.47, SEC.1.

6–6–1.1–208   Imported gasoline; motor vehicle fuel supply tanks; exemption

Sec. 208. Any person who brings gasoline into this state in the fuel supply tank directly connected to the motor of the motor vehicle is not liable for the tax imposed under this chapter.

As added by Acts 1979, P.L.79, SEC.1. Amended by Acts 1980, P.L.51, SEC.13.

Historical and Statutory Notes

Acts 1980, P.L. 51, § 13, emerg. eff. Feb. 22, 1980, substituted "gasoline" for "motor fuel".

Formerly:
  IC 6–6–1–2.

Acts 1943, c. 73, s. 2.
Acts 1947, c. 336, s. 1.
Acts 1955, c. 111, s. 1.
Acts 1978, P.L.47, SEC.1.

6–6–1.1–209   Inventory tax; imposition; computation; listed tax

Sec. 209. (a) Persons having title to gasoline in storage and held for sale on the effective date of an increase in the license tax rate imposed under section 201 of this chapter are subject to an inventory tax based upon the gallonage in storage as of the close of the business day preceding the effective date of the increased license tax rate.

(b) Persons subject to the tax imposed under this section shall:

  (1) take an inventory to determine the gallonage in storage for purposes of determining the inventory tax;

  (2) report that gallonage on forms provided by the administrator; and

  (3) pay the tax due within thirty (30) days of the prescribed inventory date.

(c) The amount of the inventory tax is equal to the inventory tax rate times the gallonage in storage as determined under subsection (a). The inventory tax rate is equal to the difference of the increased license tax rate minus the previous license tax rate.

(d) The inventory tax shall be considered a listed tax for the purposes of IC 6–8.1.

As added by P.L.59–1985, SEC.10.

Historical and Statutory Notes

P.L.59–1985, Sec.10, emerg. eff. June 1, 1985, added this section.

Library References

Gas ☞10.
WESTLAW Topic No. 190.
C.J.S. Gas § 4.

6–6–1.1–301   Exemptions

Sec. 301. The following transactions are exempt from the gasoline tax:

  (1) Gasoline exported from Indiana to another state, territory, or foreign country.

(2) Gasoline sold to the United States or an agency or instrumentality thereof.

(3) Gasoline sold to a post exchange or other concessionaire on a federal reservation within Indiana; however, the post exchange or concessionaire shall collect, report, and pay to the administrator any tax permitted by federal law on gasoline sold.

(4) Gasoline used by a licensed distributor for any purpose other than the generation of power for the propulsion of motor vehicles upon the public highways.

(5) Gasoline received by a licensed distributor and thereafter lost or destroyed, except by evaporation, shrinkage, or unknown cause, while the distributor is still the owner.

As added by Acts 1979, P.L.79, SEC.1.   Amended by Acts 1979, P.L.71, SEC.3; Acts 1980, P.L.51, SEC.14.

Historical and Statutory Notes

Acts 1979, P.L. 71, § 3, deleted "sold for export or" preceding "exported from Indiana" in Cl. (1).

Acts 1980, P.L. 51, § 14, emerg. eff. Feb. 22, 1980, substituted "gasoline" for "motor fuel" throughout the section.

Formerly:
IC 6–6–1–4.
Acts 1943, c. 73, s. 4.
Acts 1957, c. 48, s. 1.
Acts 1959, c. 323, s. 1.
Acts 1969, c. 319, s. 1.

Cross References

Deductions,
    Evaporation or shrinkage losses covered by Cl. (5) of this section not allowed, see IC 6–6–1.1–705.
    Gas exempted under this section, see IC 6–6–1.1–701.

Law Review and Journal Commentaries

State tax on storage of government-owned gasoline; Federal sovereign immunity. 39 A.B.A.J. 593 (1953).

Library References

Taxation ⬦1231.
WESTLAW Topic No. 371.

C.J.S. Taxation § 1233.
I.L.E. Taxation §§ 51, 187 to 190.

Notes of Decisions

Federal reservations 2
State agencies and instrumentalities 3
United States 1
Wholesalers 4

1. United States

Although the contractor purchases motor fuels for use in performance of the work specified in contract for which he bills the U.S. government in accordance with the terms thereof, the transaction is not tax exempt as a sale for the use of the United States, since the fuel is actually used by the contractor in his performance of the terms of the contract. 1940 Op.Atty.Gen. p. 206.

Mere fact that governor's commission on unemployment relief was a state agency did not entitle it to an exemption from state motor vehicle fuel tax on purchases made by it, but purchases of gasoline by commission with funds granted to state by federal government for use in federal emergency relief projects, in view of safeguards and rules thrown around fund to preserve its identity as federal fund, should not have been required to pay state gasoline tax. 1934 Op.Atty.Gen. p. 482.

The interest of the federal government in civil works administration projects was limited to financial support, and gasoline used by truckers employed on such a project was subject to the state gasoline tax. 1933 Op.Atty.Gen. p. 600.

Appraisers of land employed by the United States department of agriculture and paid by the United States treasury department are employees of the United States government and gasoline purchased by them for which they are reimbursed, is exempt from the Indiana gasoline tax. 1933 Op.Atty.Gen. p. 500.

2. Federal reservations
A distributor of gasoline licensed under the state law may sell gasoline direct to a post exchange tax free. 1942 Op.Atty.Gen. p. 164.

3. State agencies and instrumentalities

The Indiana toll road commission is subject to the licensing and tax provisions of the Gasoline Tax Law, [§ 6–6–1.1–1 et seq.], and the Special Fuel Tax Law, [§ 6–6–2.1–1 et seq.], with respect to gasoline and special fuel used in the commission's vehicles. 1981 Op.Atty.Gen. No. 81–14.

4. Wholesalers

Concerns which were wholesalers and jobbers of gasoline and motor vehicle fuels came under motor vehicle fuel tax law and were not exempt from payment of gasoline tax on gasoline and motor vehicle fuel stored by them in tanks notwithstanding they made purchases in large quantities to take advantage of market conditions and carried a large stock on hand. 1933 Op.Atty.Gen. p. 128.

6–6–1.1–302 Application for exemption permit; persons eligible

Sec. 302. The following persons may apply to the administrator for an exemption permit:

(1) A person who operates an airport where he sells gasoline for the exclusive purpose of propelling aircraft engines or motors.

(2) A person engaged at an airport in the business of selling gasoline for exclusive use in aircraft engines or motors.

(3) A person who operates a marine facility, except a taxable marine facility, and who sells gasoline at that facility for the exclusive purpose of propelling motorboat engines.

Such a person may apply for an exemption permit whether or not he is a licensed distributor.

As added by Acts 1979, P.L.79, SEC.1. Amended by Acts 1980, P.L.51, SEC.15.

Historical and Statutory Notes

Acts 1980, P.L. 51, § 15, emerg. eff. Feb. 22, 1980, substituted "gasoline" for "motor fuel" throughout the section.

Formerly:

IC 6–6–1–22.
IC 6–6–1–22.1.
IC 6–6–1.5–1.
Acts 1943, c. 73, s. 23a.

Acts 1963 (ss), c. 33, s. 2.
Acts 1965, c. 300, s. 1.
Acts 1971, P.L.69, SEC.5.
Acts 1971, P.L.70, SEC.1.
Acts 1973, P.L.53, SEC.1.
Acts 1975, P.L.352, SEC.2.
Acts 1978, P.L.2, SEC.635.
Acts 1978, P.L.47, SECS.2, 4.

Cross References

Deduction for sale of exempt gasoline described in this section, see IC 6–6–1.1–703.

6–6–1.1–303 Application for exemption permit; form; fee

Sec. 303. (a) A person must apply for an exemption permit on the form prescribed by the administrator. A fifteen dollar ($15) permit fee must be paid before an exemption permit may be issued.

(b) An exemption permit is conditioned on the following terms:

(1) The permit holder shall sell all gasoline purchased tax free under the exemption permit for the exclusive purpose of propelling the engines or motors of aircraft or motorboats.

(2) The permit holder shall keep for a period of three (3) years, complete records of all gasoline purchased, acquired, stored, used, or disposed of by him.

(3) The permit holder shall provide the administrator with such reports of gasoline purchased, acquired, used, or disposed of as the administrator may require.

(4) The permit holder shall permit the administrator or his authorized agent to examine during regular business hours any of the records of the applicant pertaining to the acquisition, use, and distribution of gasoline and any of the equipment of the applicant used for the receipt, storage, or use of gasoline.

(5) The permit holder shall not purchase gasoline tax free for use in motor vehicles.

(6) The permit holder shall not sell any gasoline acquired tax free under the exemption permit unless it is sold tax free and delivered directly into the fuel supply tank of an aircraft or motorboat.

As added by Acts 1979, P.L.79, SEC.1. Amended by Acts 1980, P.L.51, SEC.16; P.L.97–1987, SEC.2.

Historical and Statutory Notes

Acts 1980, P.L.51, § 16, was made emergency effective Feb. 22, 1980.

P.L.97–1987, Sec.2, was made effective Sept. 1, 1987.

Formerly:

IC 6–6–1–22.
IC 6–6–1–22.1.

Acts 1943, c. 73, s. 23a.
Acts 1963 (ss), c. 33, s. 2.
Acts 1965, c. 300, s. 1.
Acts 1971, P.L.69, SEC.5.
Acts 1973, P.L.53, SEC.1.
Acts 1975, P.L.352, SEC.2.
Acts 1978, P.L.2, SEC.635.
Acts 1978, P.L.47, SEC.2.

6–6–1.1–304 Application for exemption permit; investigation

Sec. 304. The administrator may make any investigation he considers necessary when reviewing an application for an exemption permit.

As added by Acts 1979, P.L.79, SEC.1.

Historical and Statutory Notes

Formerly:

IC 6–6–1–22.

IC 6–6–1–22.1.

Acts 1943, c. 73, s. 23a.

Acts 1963 (ss), c. 33, s. 2.

Acts 1965, c. 300, s. 1.
Acts 1971, P.L.69, SEC.5.
Acts 1973, P.L.53, SEC.1.
Acts 1975, P.L.352, SEC.2.
Acts 1978, P.L.2, SEC.635.
Acts 1978, P.L.47, SEC.2.

6–6–1.1–305   Exemption permit holders; issuance of certificate to distributors

Sec. 305. A person who holds an exemption permit may issue an executed exemption certificate to a licensed distributor. The licensed distributor may then sell gasoline to that person free of the tax imposed by this chapter. *As added by Acts 1979, P.L.79, SEC.1.*

Historical and Statutory Notes

Formerly:

IC 6–6–1–22.

IC 6–6–1–22.1.

Acts 1943, c. 73, s. 23a.

Acts 1963 (ss), c. 33, s. 2.

Acts 1965, c. 300, s. 1.
Acts 1971, P.L.69, SEC.5.
Acts 1973, P.L.538 SEC.1.
Acts 1975, P.L.352, SEC.2.
Acts 1978, P.L.2, SEC.635.
Acts 1978, P.L.47, SEC.2.

6–6–1.1–401   License to distributor; requirement

Sec. 401. A person desiring to receive gasoline within Indiana without paying gasoline tax to his supplier must hold an uncanceled license issued by the administrator to do business as a distributor. For purposes of this section and section 415 of this chapter, "supplier" means a distributor or person who sells gasoline.

As added by Acts 1979, P.L.79, SEC.1. Amended by Acts 1979, P.L.71, SEC.4; Acts 1980, P.L.51, SEC.17.

Historical and Statutory Notes

Acts 1979, P.L. 71, § 4, deleted "use, sell, or distribute" following "receive" and inserted "without paying motor fuel tax to his supplier" in the first sentence; and added the second sentence.

Acts 1980, P.L. 51, § 17, emerg. eff. Feb. 22, 1980, substituted "gasoline" for "motor fuel" throughout the section.

Formerly:

IC 6–6–1–5.

Acts 1943, c. 73, s. 5.

Acts 1971, P.L.69, SEC.1.

Cross References

Special fuel dealer's license, see IC 6–6–2.1–401 et seq.

Library References

Licenses ⚮16(.5), (9).
Taxation ⚮1293.
WESTLAW Topic Nos. 238, 371.

C.J.S. Taxation § 1231.
C.J.S. Licenses § 34.
I.L.E. Taxation §§ 187 to 190.

Notes of Decisions

Collateral actions and proceedings 2
Post exchange 1

_____

1. Post exchange

The auditor of the state could not, for purposes of simplification of administration issue a license to a post exchange as a licensed distributor of gasoline, waive the bond requirements and thereby allow the exchange the benefit of the 3% statutory allowance for collecting and reporting gasoline tax fees. 1942 Op.Atty.Gen. p. 164.

2. Collateral actions and proceedings

Action for possession of land used as filling station and for damages for unlawful detention thereof against purchaser from one who had leased land to plaintiff for use as filling station for sale of gasoline did not arise out of nor was it founded upon sale of gasoline or any commodity comprehended by prior statute [see now, this section] requiring licenses to engage in sale or storage of gasoline so as to prevent recovery by plaintiff without allegation of compliance with statute, but cause of action was merely collateral to the business of selling gasoline. Maddox v. Yocum, App.1941, 31 N.E.2d 652, 109 Ind.App. 416.

6–6–1.1–402 License to distributor; application; contents

Sec. 402. To obtain a license, every person desiring to operate as a distributor must, before commencing operations as a distributor, file with the administrator a sworn application containing the following information:

(1) The name under which the distributor will transact business in Indiana.

(2) The location, including street address, of the applicant's principal place of business.

(3) The name and complete residence address of the owner or the names and addresses of the partners, if the applicant is a partnership, the names and addresses of the managers and members, if the applicant is a limited liability company, or the names and addresses of the principal officers, if the applicant is a corporation or association.

(4) Any other information the administrator reasonably requires.

As added by Acts 1979, P.L.79, SEC.1. Amended by P.L.97–1987, SEC.3; P.L.8–1993, SEC.97.

Historical and Statutory Notes

P.L. 97–1987, Sec.3, amending this section, was made effective Sept. 1, 1987.

P.L.8–1993, Sec.97, inserted, in Subd.(3), "the names and addresses of the managers and members, if the applicant is a limited liability company,".

Formerly:

IC 6–6–1–5.
Acts 1943, c. 73, s. 5.
Acts 1971, P.L.69, SEC.1.

Library References

Taxation ☞1293.
WESTLAW Topic No. 371.

C.J.S. Taxation § 1231.
I.L.E. Taxation §§ 187 to 190.

6–6–1.1–403 License to distributor; denial; grounds; hearing

Sec. 403. (a) The administrator may refuse to issue a license to do business as a distributor in Indiana if:

(1) the application is filed by a person whose license has previously been cancelled for cause;

(2) the application is not filed in good faith, as determined by the administrator;

(3) the application is filed by some person as a subterfuge for the real person in interest whose license has previously been cancelled for cause;

(4) the applicant has an outstanding listed tax liability; or

(5) the applicant has not complied with a filing requirement of the department.

(b) Before being denied a license as a distributor, the applicant is entitled to a hearing with five (5) days written notice. At the hearing the applicant may appear in person or by counsel and present testimony.

As added by Acts 1979, P.L.79, SEC.1. Amended by P.L.96–1989, SEC.1.

Historical and Statutory Notes

P.L.96–1989, Sec.1, eff. Jan. 1, 1990.

P.L.96–1989, Sec.1, inserted Subsecs. (a)(4) and (a)(5); and made nonsubstantive changes throughout the section.

Formerly:

IC 6–6–1–5.
Acts 1943, c. 73, s. 5.
Acts 1971, P.L.69, SEC.1.

6–6–1.1–404   License to distributor; foreign corporations

Sec. 404. No license may be issued to a foreign corporation unless it is properly qualified to do business in Indiana.

As added by Acts 1979, P.L.79, SEC.1.

Historical and Statutory Notes

Formerly:
IC 6–6–1–5.

Acts 1943, c. 73, s. 5.
Acts 1971, P.L.69, SEC.1.

Library References

Taxation ⟐1270.
WESTLAW Topic No. 371.

C.J.S. Taxation § 1244.
I.L.E. Taxation §§ 187 to 190.

6–6–1.1–405   License to distributor; financial statement; fee

Sec. 405. No license may be issued unless the application is accompanied by a current financial statement and a license fee of one hundred dollars ($100). The applicant shall pay the license fee to the administrator.

As added by Acts 1979, P.L.79, SEC.1.

Historical and Statutory Notes

Formerly:
IC 6–6–1–5.

Acts 1943, c. 73, s. 5.
Acts 1971, P.L.69, SEC.1.

Notes of Decisions

_____

1. Validity of prior law

Former statute [see, now, this section] requiring payment of motor vehicle fuel license fees was not unconstitutional as embracing subject not expressed in title. Roberts v. State, 1936, 200 N.E. 699, 210 Ind. 375.

6-6-1.1-405.5   Investigations to enforce chapter

Sec. 405.5.   The administrator may make any investigation the administrator considers reasonably necessary for the enforcement of this chapter.

As added by P.L.69-1991, SEC.3.

6-6-1.1-406   License to distributor; bond, letter of credit, or cash deposit

Sec. 406.   (a) Concurrently with the filing of an application for a distributor's license, the department may require an applicant to file with the administrator a surety bond, a letter of credit, or a cash deposit:

(1) in an amount of not less than two thousand dollars ($2,000) nor more than a three (3) month tax liability for the applicant as estimated by the administrator; and

(2) conditioned upon the prompt filing of true reports and payment of all gasoline taxes levied by the state, together with any penalties and interest, and upon faithful compliance with the provisions of this chapter.

(b) The administrator shall determine the amount of the distributor's bond, cash deposit, or letter of credit.   If the applicant files a bond or a letter of credit, the bond or letter of credit must:

(1) be with a surety company or financial institution approved by the administrator;

(2) name the applicant as the principal and the state as the obligee; and

(3) be on forms prescribed by the department.

As added by Acts 1979, P.L.79, SEC.1.   Amended by Acts 1980, P.L.51, SEC.18; P.L.77-1985, SEC.1;   P.L.97-1987, SEC.4;   P.L.96-1989, SEC.2;   P.L.69-1991, SEC.4.

Historical and Statutory Notes

Acts 1980, P.L.51, Sec.18, amended this section emergency effective Feb. 22, 1980.

P.L.77-1985, Sec.1, amending this section, was made effective Sept. 1, 1985.

Section 37 of P.L.77-1985 was amended by Section 39 of P.L.59-1985 to change the effective date of the amendment of this section by P.L.77-1985 from Sept. 1, 1985 to July 1, 1985.

P.L. 97-1987, Sec.4, amending this section, was made effective Sept. 1, 1987.

P.L.96-1989, Sec.2, eff. Jan. 1, 1990.

Formerly:

IC 6-6-1-5.

IC 6-6-1-7.

Acts 1943, c. 73, ss. 5, 8.

Acts 1957, c. 228, s. 1.

Acts 1971, P.L.69, SECS.1, 2.

Cross References

Failure to file a surety bond, letter of credit, or cash deposit as required by this section, cancellation of license, see IC 6–6–1.1–415.

Notes of Decisions

Bankruptcy 1

_____

1. **Bankruptcy**
   Receiver and trustee appointed in bankruptcy proceeding to operate motor vehicle fuel busi-

ness, was required to file a bond in the sum of $10,000, the same as any other dealer, to insure payment of gasoline tax. 1936 Op.Atty.Gen. p. 144.

6–6–1.1–407 Bond or letter of credit of distributor unsatisfactory; reduction of cash deposit

Sec. 407. (a) The administrator may require a distributor to file a new bond or new letter of credit, with a satisfactory surety or financial institution in the same form and amount if:

(1) liability upon the old bond or letter of credit is discharged or reduced by judgment rendered, payment made, or otherwise; or

(2) in the opinion of the administrator any surety on the old bond or financial institution on the old letter of credit becomes unsatisfactory.

If the new bond or new letter of credit is unsatisfactory, the administrator shall cancel the license of the distributor. If the new bond or new letter of credit is satisfactorily furnished, the administrator shall release in writing the surety on the old bond or financial institution on the old letter of credit from any liability accruing after the effective date of the new bond or new letter of credit.

(b) If a distributor has a cash deposit with the administrator and the deposit is reduced by a judgment rendered, payment made, or otherwise, the administrator may require the distributor to make a new deposit equal to the amount of the reduction.

As added by Acts 1979, P.L.79, SEC.1. Amended by P.L.97–1987, SEC.5.

Historical and Statutory Notes

P.L. 97–1987, Sec.5, eff. Sept. 1, 1987, in Subsec. (a), inserted "or new letter of credit", "or financial institution" and "on the old letter of credit"; and added Subsec. (b).

Acts 1943, c. 73, s. 8.
Acts 1957, c. 228, s. 1.
Acts 1971, P.L.69, SEC.2.

Formerly:
   IC 6–6–1–7.

6–6–1.1–408 Amount of bond, letter of credit, or cash deposit insufficient; new requirements; hearing; cancellation of certificate

Sec. 408. (a) If the administrator reasonably determines that the amount of the existing bond, letter of credit, or cash deposit is insufficient to insure payment to the state of the tax and any penalty and interest for which the distributor is or may become liable, then the distributor shall upon written demand of the administrator file a new bond or letter of credit, or increase the cash deposit. The administrator shall give the distributor at least fifteen (15) days to secure the new bond or letter of credit or make the increased cash deposit.

(b) The new bond, letter of credit, or cash deposit must meet the requirements set forth in section 406 of this chapter.

(c) If the new bond, letter of credit, or cash deposit required under this section is unsatisfactory, the administrator shall cancel the distributor's license certificate.

As added by Acts 1979, P.L.79, SEC.1. Amended by P.L.77–1985, SEC.2; P.L.97–1987, SEC.6; P.L.69–1991, SEC.5.

Historical and Statutory Notes

P.L.77–1985, Sec.2, eff. Sept. 1, 1985, in Subsec. (a), substituted "fifteen (15)" for "five (5)"; and, at the end of Subsec. (b), deleted "and it must be in an amount, not to exceed fifty thousand dollars ($50,000), which the administrator determines necessary to secure at all times the payment by the distributor of all taxes, penalties, and interest due the state under this chapter".

Section 37 of P.L.77–1985 was amended by Section 39 of P.L.59–1985 to change the effective date of the amendment of this section by P.L.77–1985 from Sept. 1, 1985 to July 1, 1985.

P.L. 97–1987, Sec.6, eff. Sept. 1, 1987, inserted "letter of credit, or cash deposit" thrice, in

the first sentence of Subsec. (a), Subsec. (b), and Subsec. (c); and added "or letter of credit, or increase the cash deposit" at the end of the first sentence of Subsec. (a).

P.L.69–1991, Sec.5, amending subsec. (a), substituted "If the administrator reasonably" for "If after a hearing, the administrator" at the beginning of the first sentence, and rewrote the second sentence.

Formerly:

IC 6–6–1–7.
Acts 1943, c. 73, s. 8.
Acts 1957, c. 228, s. 1.
Acts 1971, P.L.69, SEC.2.

Library References

Taxation ☞1332.
WESTLAW Topic No. 371.

C.J.S. Taxation § 1250.
I.L.E. Taxation §§ 187 to 190.

6–6–1.1–409 Release of surety of distributor's bond or institution issuing letter of credit; retaining cash deposit; notice; cancellation of license

Sec. 409. (a) Sixty (60) days after making a written request for release to the administrator, the surety of a bond furnished by a distributor is released from any liability to the state accruing on the bond after the sixty (60) day period. The release does not affect any liability accruing before the expiration of the sixty (60) day period.

(b) One hundred eighty (180) days after making a written request for release to the administrator, the financial institution issuing the letter of credit for a distributor is released from any liability accruing on the letter of credit.

(c) The administrator shall promptly notify the distributor furnishing the bond or letter of credit that a release has been requested, and unless the distributor obtains a new bond or letter of credit which meets the requirements of section 406 of this chapter and files with the administrator:

489

(1) the new bond within the sixty (60) day period; or

(2) the new letter of credit within the one hundred eighty (180) day period;

the administrator shall cancel the distributor's license.

(d) Sixty (60) days after making a written request for release to the administrator, the cash deposit provided by a distributor is cancelled as security for any obligation accruing after the expiration of the sixty (60) day period. However, the administrator may retain all or part of the cash deposit for up to three (3) years and one (1) day as security for any obligations accruing before the effective date of the cancellation. Any part of the deposit that is not retained by the administrator shall be released to the distributor. Before the expiration of the sixty (60) day period, the distributor must provide the administrator with a bond or letter of credit that satisfies section 406 of this chapter, or the administrator shall cancel the distributor's license.

As added by Acts 1979, P.L.79, SEC.1. Amended by P.L.97–1987, SEC.7.

Historical and Statutory Notes

P.L. 97–1987, Sec.7, eff. Sept. 1, 1987, re-wrote the section, which read as added in 1979:

"(a) Sixty (60) days after making a written request for release to the administrator, the surety of a bond furnished by a distributor is released from any liability to the state accruing on the bond. The release does not affect any liability accruing before expiration of the sixty (60) day period.

"(b) The administrator shall promptly notify the distributor furnishing the bond that the surety has requested release, and unless the distributor obtains a new bond which meets the requirements of section 406 of this chapter and files the new bond with the administrator within the sixty (60) day period, the administrator shall cancel the distributor's license."

Formerly:

IC 6–6–1–7.
Acts 1943, c. 73, s. 8.
Acts 1957, c. 228, s. 1.
Acts 1971, P.L.69, SEC.2.

6–6–1.1–410   Financial statements; increased bond, letter of credit, or cash deposit amounts

Sec. 410. The administrator may in his reasonable discretion require a distributor to furnish current certified, audited financial statements. If the administrator determines that a distributor's financial condition warrants an increase in the distributor's bond, letter of credit, or cash deposit, the administrator may require the distributor to furnish an increased bond, letter of credit, or cash deposit.

As added by Acts 1979, P.L.79, SEC.1. Amended by P.L.97–1987, SEC.8.

Historical and Statutory Notes

P.L. 97–1987, Sec.8, amending this section, was made effective Sept. 1, 1987.

Formerly:
IC 6–6–1–7.

Acts 1943, c. 73, s. 8.
Acts 1957, c. 228, s. 1.
Acts 1971, P.L.69, SEC.2.

6–6–1.1–411   Temporary license; investigation; conditions and requirements

Sec. 411.   The administrator may make any investigation he considers necessary once an application has been properly filed, the license fee paid, and the bonding requirements met.   If all conditions and requirements of this chapter have been met, the administrator shall issue to the applicant a temporary license to transact business as a distributor in Indiana.   The temporary license is valid for one (1) year.

As added by Acts 1979, P.L.79, SEC.1.

Historical and Statutory Notes

Formerly:
IC 6–6–1–5.

Acts 1943, c. 73, s. 5.
Acts 1971, P.L.69, SEC.1.

6–6–1.1–412   Permanent license; minimum gallonage

Sec. 412.   If an Indiana based distributor distributes at least five hundred thousand (500,000) gallons of gasoline during the year that the temporary license is in effect and complies with all the other provisions of this chapter, the administrator shall issue a permanent license to the distributor without charge. The permanent license is effective unless canceled under this chapter.

As added by Acts 1979, P.L.79, SEC.1.   Amended by Acts 1980, P.L.51, SEC.19.

Historical and Statutory Notes

Acts 1980, P.L. 51, § 19, amended this section emergency effective Feb. 22, 1980.

Acts 1943, c. 73, s. 5.
Acts 1971, P.L.69, SEC.1.

Formerly:
IC 6–6–1–5.

6–6–1.1–413   No permanent license; insufficient gallonage

Sec. 413.   If an Indiana based distributor does not distribute at least five hundred thousand (500,000) gallons of gasoline during the year that the temporary license is in effect, the administrator may not issue a permanent license to that distributor.

As added by Acts 1979, P.L.79, SEC.1.   Amended by Acts 1980, P.L.51, SEC.20.

Historical and Statutory Notes

Acts 1980, P.L. 51, § 20, amended this section emergency effective Feb. 22, 1980.

Acts 1943, c. 73, s. 5.
Acts 1971, P.L.69, SEC.1.

Formerly:
IC 6–6–1–5.

6–6–1.1–414 License nonassignable; new license required

Sec. 414. A license issued under this chapter is not assignable and is valid only for the distributor in whose name it is issued. If there is a change in name or ownership, the distributor shall apply for a new license.
As added by Acts 1979, P.L.79, SEC.1.

Historical and Statutory Notes

Formerly: Acts 1943, c. 73, s. 5.
  IC 6–6–1–5.   Acts 1971, P.L.69, SEC.1.

6–6–1.1–415 Cancellation of distributor's license; grounds; notice; hearing

Sec. 415. (a) The administrator may, after fifteen (15) days written notice, cancel a distributor's license if the distributor:

(1) files a false monthly report of the information required by this chapter;

(2) fails or refuses to file the monthly report required by this chapter;

(3) fails or refuses to pay the full amount of the tax imposed by this chapter on the expiration of the fifteen (15) day notice period provided by this subsection;

(4) is an Indiana distributor and fails to distribute five hundred thousand (500,000) gallons or more of gasoline during a twelve (12) month period;

(5) fails to file a surety bond, letter of credit, or cash deposit as required by section 406 of this chapter;

(6) fails to honor a subpoena issued by the department under IC 6–8.1–3–12;

(7) knowingly breaks the seal on a pump sealed under section 1008 or 1110 of this chapter; or

(8) fails or refuses to comply with IC 6–8.1–5–4 or section 1314 of this chapter.

(b) The distributor may appear at the time and place given in the notice to show cause why the distributor's license should not be canceled. Notice of the hearing and of the cancellation must be sent by registered or certified mail to the distributor's last known address appearing in the administrator's files. A distributor whose license is canceled may not sell gasoline in Indiana without paying the tax imposed under this chapter to the supplier (as defined in section 401 of this chapter).

As added by Acts 1979, P.L.79, SEC.1. Amended by Acts 1979, P.L.71, SEC.5; Acts 1980, P.L.51, SEC.21; P.L.97–1987, SEC.9; P.L.96–1989, SEC.3; P.L.69–1991, SEC.6.

Historical and Statutory Notes

Acts 1979, P.L. 71, § 5, added Cl. (4) in the first sentence; inserted "or certified" following "sent by registered" in the third sentence; and added the fourth sentence.

Acts 1980, P.L. 51, § 21, emerg. eff. Feb. 22, 1980, substituted "gasoline" for "motor fuel" throughout the section.

P.L. 97–1987, Sec.9, eff. Sept. 1, 1987, in the first sentence, substituted "fifteen (15)" for "ten (10)" in the introductory clause, and added Cl. (5).

P.L.96–1989, Sec.3, eff. Jan. 1, 1990.

P.L.96–1989, Sec.3, designated the subsections; inserted Subsec. (a)(6); and made other nonsubstantive changes.

P.L.69–1991, Sec.6, inserted "on the expiration of the fifteen (15) day notice period provided by this subsection" in subsec. (a)(3), and added subsec. (a)(7) and (8).

Formerly:

IC 6–6–1–9.
Acts 1943, c. 73, s. 10.

Library References

Licenses ☞38.
Taxation ☞1222.
WESTLAW Topic Nos. 238, 371.
C.J.S. Agriculture§ 4.5.

C.J.S. Architects § 10.
C.J.S. Licenses §§ 48, 50 to 63.
C.J.S. Taxation § 1232.
I.L.E. Taxation §§ 187 to 190.

Notes of Decisions

In general 1

---

1. In general

In view of fact that cessation of operations of a motor vehicle fuel dealer was not made a ground for revocation of license under Acts 1933, c. 159, s. 7 [repealed; see, now, this section] state auditor had no authority to revoke a license for such cause alone, and when revocation was made on the statutory grounds, the revocation should have set out the specific reason therefor. 1934 Op.Atty.Gen. p. 266.

6–6–1.1–416 Cancellation of license on distributor's request; requisites

Sec. 416. A distributor may make a written request to the administrator to cancel his license, and the administrator may cancel the license effective sixty (60) days from receipt of the request if prior to cancellation the distributor has paid all tax, penalty, and interest accruing under this chapter.

As added by Acts 1979, P.L.79, SEC.1.

Historical and Statutory Notes

Formerly:

IC 6–6–1–9.
Acts 1943, c. 73, s. 10.

6–6–1.1–417 Cancellation of distributor's license for inactiveness; notice

Sec. 417. If the administrator determines that a distributor has not received, used, or sold gasoline for a period of six (6) months, and is no longer engaged as a distributor, the administrator may cancel the license by giving sixty (60) days' notice mailed to that person's last known address appearing in the administrator's files.

As added by Acts 1979, P.L.79, SEC.1. Amended by Acts 1980, P.L.51, SEC.22.

Historical and Statutory Notes

Acts 1980, P.L. 51, § 22, emerg. eff. Feb. 22,   Acts 1943, c. 73, s. 10.
1980, substituted "gasoline" for "motor fuel".

Formerly:
  IC 6–6–1–9.

6–6–1.1–418   Listing of licensed distributors;   index of applications and bonds

Sec. 418.   The administrator shall keep a file and alphabetical index of all applications and bonds, and shall keep a record of all licensed distributors. The administrator shall furnish to each licensed distributor, before August 16 of each year, a complete list of all licensed distributors as of the preceding July 1. The administrator shall also furnish to each licensed distributor monthly supplements showing any changes in the list.

As added by Acts 1979, P.L.79, SEC.1.

Historical and Statutory Notes

Formerly:
  IC 6–6–1–5.   Acts 1943, c. 73, s. 5.
                                                        Acts 1971, P.L.69, SEC.1.

6–6–1.1–501   Monthly reports to determine tax liability;   itemized contents

Sec. 501.   To determine his tax liability under this chapter, each distributor shall file a sworn report with the administrator by the twentieth day of each calendar month.   The administrator may require the following information to be included in the report:

(1) An itemized statement of the number of invoiced gallons of gasoline received by the distributor within Indiana during the preceding calendar month, as determined under sections 202 through 207 of this chapter.   The administrator may require that the statement include the date, place, and quantity of each receipt of gasoline, the point of origin, the method by which and the name of the person from whom the gasoline was received, and any other information which the administrator requires.

(2) An itemized statement showing the deductions provided by sections 701 through 705 of this chapter, together with such details to support each deduction as the administrator may require.

(3) An itemized statement showing the gallons of gasoline sold to a marine facility for which the distributor does not receive an exemption certificate authorized by section 305 of this chapter.

As added by Acts 1979, P.L.79, SEC.1.   Amended by Acts 1979, P.L.71, SEC.6; Acts 1980, P.L.51, SEC.23.

Historical and Statutory Notes

Acts 1980, P.L. 51, § 23, amended this section   **Formerly:**
emergency effective Feb. 22, 1980.   IC 6–6–1–8.

IC 6–6–1.5–2.   Acts 1969, c. 319, s. 2.
Acts 1943, c. 73, s. 9.   Acts 1971, P.L.70, SEC.1.
Acts 1959, c. 84, s. 1.

Cross References

Failure to file a report or filing of an incomplete report required by this section, civil penalty, see IC
   6–6–1.1–1315.
Special fuel tax, monthly reports, see IC 6–6–2.1–501, 6–6–2.1–503.

Library References

Taxation ☜1311, 1313.   C.J.S. Taxation § 1246.
WESTLAW Topic No. 371.   I.L.E. Taxation §§ 187 to 190.

Notes of Decisions

Post exchange   1

_____

1. Post exchange

Where a licensed distributor sells gasoline direct to a post exchange tax free the auditor of the state cannot require monthly reports from the exchange showing the total purchases and sales and remittance of the tax. 1942 Op.Atty. Gen. p. 164.

Where gasoline sold by a post exchange is purchased through the quartermaster's department the auditor of the state may demand and the officer in charge of the reservation may be required to submit monthly reports and remittances on that part of such gasoline or other motor fuel which is taxable under the Act of Congress. 1942 Op.Atty.Gen. p. 164.

6–6–1.1–502   Monthly payment of tax due; computation

Sec. 502. (a) Except as provided in subsection (b), at the time of filing each monthly report, each distributor shall pay to the administrator the full amount of tax due under this chapter for the preceding calendar month, computed as follows:

(1) Enter the total number of invoiced gallons of gasoline received during the preceding calendar month.

(2) Subtract the number of gallons for which deductions are provided by sections 701 through 705 of this chapter from the number of gallons entered under subdivision (1).

(3) Subtract the number of gallons reported under section 501(3) of this chapter.

(4) Multiply the number of invoiced gallons remaining after making the computation in subdivisions (2) and (3) by the tax rate prescribed by section 201 of this chapter to compute that part of the gasoline tax to be deposited in the highway, road, and street fund under section 802(2) of this chapter or in the motor fuel tax fund under section 802(3) of this chapter.

(5) Multiply the number of gallons subtracted under subdivision (3) by the tax rate prescribed by section 201 of this chapter to compute that part of the gasoline tax to be deposited in the fish and wildlife fund under section 802(1) of this chapter.

(b) If the department determines that a distributor's:

(1) estimated monthly gasoline tax liability for the current year; or

(2) average monthly gasoline tax liability for the preceding year;

exceeds ten thousand dollars ($10,000), the distributor shall pay the monthly gasoline taxes due by electronic fund transfer (as defined in IC 4–8.1–2–7) or by delivering in person or by overnight courier a payment by cashier's check, certified check, or money order to the department. The transfer or payment shall be made on or before the date the tax is due.

As added by Acts 1979, P.L.79, SEC.1. Amended by Acts 1980, P.L.51, SEC.24; Acts 1980, P.L.10, SEC.8; Acts 1981, P.L.93, SEC.1; P.L.59–1985, SEC.11; P.L.92–1987, SEC.5; P.L.63–1988, SEC.12; P.L.28–1997, SEC.22.

Historical and Statutory Notes

Acts 1980, P.L. 51, § 24, amended this section emergency effective Feb. 22, 1980.

Acts 1980, P.L. 10, § 8, amending this section, was made effective July 1, 1980.

Acts 1981, P.L. 93, § 1, amending this section, was made effective July 1, 1981.

P.L.59–1985, Sec.11, amended this section emergency effective June 1, 1985.

P.L.92–1987, Sec.5, amending this section, was made effective July 1, 1987.

P.L. 63–1988, Sec.12, amended this section emergency effective March 5, 1988.

P.L.28–1997, Sec.22, eff. Jan. 1, 1998, amended the section by substituting "ten thousand dollars ($10,000)" for "twenty thousand dollars ($20,000)" in Subsec. (b).

Formerly:

IC 6–6–1–8.
Acts 1943, c. 73, s. 9.
Acts 1959, c. 84, s. 1.
Acts 1969, c. 319, s. 2.

Cross References

Collection of tax, see IC 6–8.1–8–1 et seq.
Disclosure of information by department of revenue, gasoline sold by distributors, see IC 6–8.1–7–1.
Failure to file return or pay tax, liability for interest and penalties, see IC 6–8.1–10–1 et seq.
Proposed assessment of unpaid tax, see IC 6–8.1–5–1 et seq.

Library References

Taxation ⟂1331.
WESTLAW Topic No. 371.

C.J.S. Taxation § 1250.
I.L.E. Taxation §§ 187 to 190.

6–6–1.1–503   Repealed

(Repealed by Acts 1980, P.L.61, SEC.15.)

Historical and Statutory Notes

Acts 1980, P.L. 61, provided in § 16 that the act takes effect Jan. 1, 1981.

The repealed section related to filing reports regardless of tax liability.

Formerly:

Acts 1979, P.L.79, SEC.1.

6–6–1.1–504   Purchaser other than licensed distributor; same reports; payment of tax

Sec. 504. Every person other than a licensed distributor who purchases or otherwise acquires taxable gasoline and unknowingly fails to pay the gasoline tax to either a licensed Indiana distributor or Indiana dealer shall make the same reports and payment required of distributors under this chapter. Howeverer, the person is not entitled to any deductions or credits.

As added by Acts 1979, P.L.79, SEC.1. Amended by Acts 1980, P.L.51, SEC.25.

Historical and Statutory Notes

Acts 1980, P.L. 51, § 25, emerg. eff. Feb. 22, 1980, substituted "gasoline" for "motor fuel" following "acquires taxable" and "gasoline" for "motor fuel license" following "pay the" in the first sentence.

Formerly:

IC 6–6–1–12.
Acts 1943, c. 73, s. 13.

Library References

Taxation ⊜1313.
WESTLAW Topic No. 371.

C.J.S. Taxation § 1246.
I.L.E. Taxation §§ 187 to 190.

6–6–1.1–505 to 6–6–1.1–511   Repealed

(Repealed by Acts 1980, P.L.61, SEC.15.)

Historical and Statutory Notes

Acts 1980, P.L. 61, provided in § 16 that the act takes effect Jan. 1, 1981.

The repealed sections related to the investigation, assessment, and collection of unpaid motor fuel taxes.

Provisions pertaining to the assessment and collection of taxes by the department of revenue

and penalties and interest for unpaid taxes are now contained in §§ 6–8.1–5–1, 6–8.1–8–1, and 6–8.1–10–1 et seq.

Formerly:

Acts 1979, P.L.79, SEC.1.
Acts 1979, P.L.71, SEC.7.

6–6–1.1–512   Discontinuance, sale or transfer of distributor's business; notice to administrator

Sec. 512. If a distributor intends to discontinue, sell, or transfer his business, he must give written notice to the administrator at least ten (10) days prior to his ceasing business. The notice shall give the date of discontinuance or the date of sale or transfer and the name and address of the purchaser or transferee.

As added by Acts 1979, P.L.79, SEC.1.

Historical and Statutory Notes

Formerly:

IC 6–6–1–20.
Acts 1943, c. 73, s. 21.

Cross References

Failure of distributor to give notice to the administrator as required by this section, liability of purchaser or transferee, see IC 6–6–1.1–514.

6–6–1.1–513 **Discontinuance, sale or transfer of distributor's business; accrued tax liabilities due and payable**

Sec. 513. Notwithstanding any other provision of this chapter, any tax, penalty, and interest which have accrued under this chapter are due and payable at the time a distributor discontinues, sells, or transfers his business. The distributor shall file a report and pay any tax, penalty, and interest within ten (10) days after the discontinuance, sale, or transfer.

As added by Acts 1979, P.L.79, SEC.1.

Historical and Statutory Notes

Formerly:
  IC 6–6–1–20.
  Acts 1943, c. 73, s. 21.

6–6–1.1–514 **Sale or transfer of distributor's business; liability of purchaser or transferee for any accrued unpaid tax, penalty and interest**

Sec. 514. If a distributor fails to give notice to the administrator as required by section 512 of this chapter, the purchaser or transferee of his business is liable to the state for all unpaid tax, penalty, and interest accrued under this chapter against the distributor through the date of sale or transfer. However, the purchaser's or transferee's liability is limited to the value of the property and business acquired from the distributor.

As added by Acts 1979, P.L.79, SEC.1.

Historical and Statutory Notes

Formerly:
  IC 6–6–1–20.
  Acts 1943, c. 73, s. 21.

Library References

Taxation ⚿1342.
WESTLAW Topic No. 371.

C.J.S. Taxation § 1255.
I.L.E. Taxation §§ 187 to 190.

6–6–1.1–601 to 6–6–1.1–605   Repealed

(Repealed by Acts 1980, P.L.61, SEC.15.)

Historical and Statutory Notes

Acts 1980, P.L. 61, provided in § 16 that the act takes effect Jan. 1, 1981.

The repealed sections related to record-keeping requirements.

Provisions pertaining to record-keeping requirements are now contained in § 6–8.1–5–4.

Formerly:

Acts 1979, P.L.79, SEC.1.
Acts 1979, P.L.71, SECS.8, 9.

6–6–1.1–606   Monthly reports of all deliveries of gasoline in and from Indiana; forms; contents

Sec. 606.   (a) Every person, including persons engaged in for-hire interstate or intrastate commerce, who:

(1) transports gasoline by any manner from a point outside Indiana to a point in Indiana; and

(2) is not a licensed distributor;

shall report to the administrator on forms prescribed by the department all deliveries of gasoline from a point outside Indiana to a point in Indiana.

(b) The reports required by subsection (a) must cover monthly periods and must show the following:

(1) The name and address of the person to whom deliveries of gasoline have actually been made.

(2) The name and address of the originally named consignee, if gasoline has been delivered to a person other than the originally named consignee.

(3) The point of origin, point of delivery, date of delivery, number and initials of each tank car, and the number of gallons contained in each car, if the gasoline has been shipped by rail.

(4) The number of gallons contained in the boat, barge, or vessel, if the gasoline has been shipped by water.

(5) The number of gallons contained in each tank truck, if the gasoline has been shipped by motor truck.

(6) The manner in which the gasoline has been delivered if the delivery is not covered by clauses (1) through (5).

(7) Additional information relating to gasoline shipments as the administrator reasonably may require.

(c) Every person, including persons engaged in for-hire interstate or intrastate commerce who:

(1) transports gasoline from a point in Indiana to a point outside Indiana; and

(2) is not a licensed distributor in Indiana;

shall report to the administrator on forms prescribed by the department all gasoline transported from a point inside Indiana to a point outside Indiana.

(d) The report required by subsection (c) must be made under oath on a form prescribed by the administrator, must cover monthly periods, and must show the following:

(1) The name and address of the person to whom deliveries of gasoline have actually been made.

(2) The name and address of the originally named consignee, if gasoline has been delivered to a person other than the originally named consignee.

(3) The point of origin, point of delivery, date of delivery, number and initials of each tank car, and the number of gallons contained in each car if the gasoline has been shipped by rail.

(4) The name and number of gallons contained in the boat, barge, or vessel if the gasoline has been shipped by water.

(5) The registration number and number of gallons contained in each tank truck if the gasoline has been shipped by motor truck.

(6) The manner in which the gasoline has been delivered if the delivery is not covered by clauses (1) through (5).

(7) Additional information relating to gasoline shipments as the administrator reasonably may require.

As added by Acts 1979, P.L.79, SEC.1.　Amended by Acts 1980, P.L.51, SEC.30; P.L.69–1991, SEC.7.

Historical and Statutory Notes

Acts 1980, P.L. 51, § 30, amended this section emergency effective Feb. 22, 1980.

Acts 1943, c. 73, s. 15.

Formerly:
　IC 6–6–1–14.

Cross References

Failure to file a report or filing of an incomplete report required by this section, civil penalty, see IC 6–6–1.1–1315.
Waiver of filing of the report required by this section, see IC 6–6–1.1–608.

Library References

Taxation ☜1313.
WESTLAW Topic No. 371.

C.J.S. Taxation § 1246.
I.L.E. Taxation §§ 187 to 190.

6–6–1.1–606.5　Registration and licensure of persons transporting gasoline in and from Indiana; persons qualified to accept delivery of gasoline; transporter emblems; carriage of invoices or manifests

Sec. 606.5.　(a) Every person included within the terms of section 606(a) and 606(c) of this chapter shall register with the administrator before engaging in those activities.　The administrator shall issue a transportation license to a person who registers with the administrator under this section.

(b) Every person included within the terms of section 606(a) of this chapter who transports gasoline in a vehicle on the highways in Indiana for purposes other than use and consumption by that person may not make a delivery of that gasoline to any person in Indiana other than a licensed distributor except:

(1) when the tax imposed by this chapter on the receipt of the transported gasoline was charged and collected by the parties; and

(2) under the circumstances described in section 205 of this chapter.

(c) Every person included within the terms of section 606(c) of this chapter who transports gasoline in a vehicle upon the highways of Indiana for purposes other than use and consumption by that person may not, on the journey carrying that gasoline to points outside Indiana, make delivery of that fuel to any person in Indiana.

(d) Every transporter of gasoline included within the terms of section 606(a) and section 606(c) of this chapter who transports gasoline upon the highways of Indiana for purposes other than use and consumption by that person shall at the time of registration and on an annual basis list with the administrator a description of all vehicles, including the vehicles' license numbers, to be used on the highways of Indiana in transporting gasoline from:

(1) points outside Indiana to points inside Indiana; and

(2) points inside Indiana to points outside Indiana.

(e) The description that subsection (d) requires shall contain the information that is reasonably required by the administrator including the carrying capacity of the vehicle. When the vehicle is a tractor-trailer type, the trailer is the vehicle to be described. When additional vehicles are placed in service or when a vehicle previously listed is retired from service during the year, the administrator shall be notified within ten (10) days of the change so that the listing of the vehicles may be kept accurate.

(f) The department shall issue a transporter emblem for each vehicle that is listed with the administrator under this section. The department shall issue new transporter emblems at the time that the annual list is provided under subsection (d).

(g) It is unlawful for a person to transport gasoline in a vehicle with a total tank capacity of at least eight hundred fifty (850) gallons on the highways from any point in Indiana to another point in Indiana without displaying an emblem issued by the department under this section.

(h) A distributor's or an Indiana transportation license is required for a person or the person's agent acting in the person's behalf to operate a vehicle for the purpose of delivering gasoline within the boundaries of Indiana when the vehicle has a total tank capacity of at least eight hundred fifty (850) gallons.

(i) The operator of a vehicle to which this section applies shall at all times when engaged in the transporting of gasoline on the highways have with the vehicle an invoice or manifest showing the origin, quantity, nature, and destination of the gasoline that is being transported.

As added by P.L.69–1991, SEC.8.

6–6–1.1–606.6   Penalties; improper delivery of gasoline

Sec. 606.6. (a) Except as provided in subsection (c), every person included within the terms of section 606(a) of this chapter who transports gasoline in a vehicle on the highways of Indiana in a vehicle having a total tank capacity of less than eight hundred fifty (850) gallons is liable to the state for a penalty equal to the rate provided in section 201 of this chapter on all gasoline transported into Indiana and delivered to any person other than a licensed distributor.

(b) Except as provided in subsection (c), every person included within the terms of section 606(c) of this chapter who transports gasoline in a vehicle on the highways of Indiana is liable to the state for a penalty equal to the rate provided in section 201 of this chapter on all gasoline:

(1) received by the person for transportation to a point outside Indiana;

(2) not in fact transported to a point outside Indiana; and

(3) in fact delivered to a person other than a licensed distributor inside Indiana.

(c) The following are excluded when computing any liability under this section:

(1) All deliveries of gasoline when the tax imposed by law was charged or collected by the parties under the circumstances described in this section.

(2) Deliveries of gasoline used in computing the tax under section 301 of this chapter.

As added by P.L.69–1991, SEC.9.

6–6–1.1–607   Monthly accounting of all gasoline delivered to or withdrawn from refinery or terminal; lessor report of leased storage space

Sec. 607.   (a) Every person owning or operating a refinery or terminal in Indiana shall, on forms prescribed by the administrator, make a monthly accounting to the administrator of all gasoline withdrawn from a refinery or terminal, and all gasoline delivered to and withdrawn from any terminal, whether or not the fuel is owned by the owner or operator.

(b) Every person owning or operating a refinery or terminal in Indiana who leases storage space in that refinery or terminal for gasoline to another person shall on forms prescribed by the administrator make a monthly accounting to the administrator with respect to the leased storage space. The report shall show the following:

(1) The name of the lessee.

(2) The volume of storage space that is leased.

(3) The volume of gasoline existing in that storage space at the beginning and end of the month.

(4) The monthly throughput which is:

(A) the total volume of gasoline put into the storage space during the month; and

(B) the total volume of gasoline removed from the storage space during the month.

As added by Acts 1979, P.L.79, SEC.1. Amended by Acts 1980, P.L.51, SEC.31; P.L.69–1991, SEC.10.

Historical and Statutory Notes

Acts 1980, P.L. 51, § 31, amended this section   Acts 1943, c. 73, s. 15.
emergency effective Feb. 22, 1980.

Formerly:
  IC 6–6–1–14.

Cross References

Waiver of filing of the report required by this section, see IC 6–6–1.1–608.

Library References

Taxation ☞1313.   C.J.S. Taxation § 1246.
WESTLAW Topic No. 371.   I.L.E. Taxation §§ 187 to 190.

6–6–1.1–608   Waiver of reports required by 6–6–1.1–606 and 6–6–1.1–607; time limitations

Sec. 608. The reports required by sections 606 and 607 of this chapter are for information purposes only and the administrator may waive their filing if they are unnecessary for the proper administration of this chapter. Persons required to file reports under this chapter shall file them with the administrator within the time period established by section 501 of this chapter for filing distributors' reports of gasoline received.

As added by Acts 1979, P.L.79, SEC.1. Amended by Acts 1980, P.L.51, SEC.32.

Historical and Statutory Notes

Acts 1980, P.L. 51, § 32, amended this section   Acts 1943, c. 73, s. 15.
emergency effective Feb. 22, 1980.

Formerly:
  IC 6–6–1–14.

6–6–1.1–701   Deduction for exempted gasoline

Sec. 701. A licensed distributor who receives gasoline that qualifies for an exemption under section 301 of this chapter is entitled to a deduction for that gasoline after furnishing such proof as the administrator may require. The deduction must be claimed on the report covering the month of export, loss, destruction, or sale.

As added by Acts 1979, P.L.79, SEC.1. Amended by Acts 1980, P.L.51, SEC.33.

Historical and Statutory Notes

Acts 1980, P.L. 51, § 33, emerg. eff. Feb. 22,   IC 6–6–1–8.
1980, substituted "gasoline" for "motor fuel"   Acts 1943, c. 73, ss. 4, 9.
throughout the section.   Acts 1957, c. 48, s. 1.
                                                        Acts 1959, c. 84, s. 1.
                                                        Acts 1959, c. 323, s. 1.
Formerly: Acts 1969, c. 319, ss. 1, 2.

  IC 6–6–1–4.

Library References

Taxation ⚷1312.
WESTLAW Topic No. 371.

C.J.S. Taxation § 1246.
I.L.E. Taxation §§ 187 to 190.

6–6–1.1–702   Sale or exchange agreement; deduction

Sec. 702. A licensed distributor who receives gasoline in Indiana and then delivers it to or for the account of another licensed distributor in Indiana under a sale or exchange agreement is entitled to a deduction for that gasoline. The deduction must be claimed on the report covering the month of delivery.

As added by Acts 1979, P.L.79, SEC.1. Amended by Acts 1980, P.L.51, SEC.34.

Historical and Statutory Notes

Acts 1980, P.L. 51, § 34, emerg. eff. Feb. 22, 1980, substituted "gasoline" for "motor fuel" throughout the section.

Formerly:
 IC 6–6–1–4.

Acts 1943, c. 73, s. 4.
Acts 1957, c. 48, s. 1.
Acts 1959, c. 323, s. 1.
Acts 1969, c. 319, s. 1.

6–6–1.1–703   Sale of tax exempt gasoline; deduction

Sec. 703. A licensed distributor who sells tax exempt gasoline described in section 302 of this chapter is entitled to a deduction for that gasoline. The deduction must be claimed on the report covering the month of sale.

As added by Acts 1979, P.L.79, SEC.1. Amended by Acts 1980, P.L.51, SEC.35.

Historical and Statutory Notes

Acts 1980, P.L. 51, § 35, emerg. eff. Feb. 22, 1980, substituted "gasoline" for "motor fuel" throughout the section.

Formerly:
 IC 6–6–1–22.
 IC 6–6–1–22.1.
 Acts 1943, c. 73, s. 23a.

Acts 1963 (ss), c. 33, s. 2.
Acts 1965, c. 300, s. 1.
Acts 1971, P.L.69, SEC.5.
Acts 1973, P.L.53, SEC.1.
Acts 1975, P.L.352, SEC.2.
Acts 1978, P.L.2, SEC.635.
Acts 1978, P.L.47, SEC.2.

Library References

Taxation ⚷1312.
WESTLAW Topic No. 371.

C.J.S. Taxation § 1246.
I.L.E. Taxation §§ 187 to 190.

6–6–1.1–704   Refund; deduction in lieu thereof

Sec. 704. A licensed distributor who pays any gasoline tax in error, or who is entitled to a refund or credit under this chapter, may, upon authorization by the administrator, take a deduction in lieu of a refund on subsequent monthly reports for the amount of gasoline on which the tax was paid.

As added by Acts 1979, P.L.79, SEC.1. Amended by Acts 1980, P.L.51, SEC.36.

Historical and Statutory Notes

Acts 1980, P.L. 51, § 36, emerg. eff. Feb. 22, 1980, substituted "gasoline" for "motor fuel" throughout the section.

Acts 1943, c. 73, s. 24.

Formerly:
IC 6–6–1–23.

Cross References

Deduction authorized by this section in lieu of issuing warrant prescribed by IC 6–6–1.1–907(a), see IC 6–6–1.1–908.

6–6–1.1–705 Deduction for evaporation, shrinkage, losses and tax-related expenses

Sec. 705. (a) If a monthly report is filed and the amount due is remitted at or before the time required by this chapter, a distributor is entitled to a deduction equal to one and six-tenths percent (1.6%) of the remainder of:

(1) the number of invoiced gallons of gasoline he received in Indiana during the preceding calendar month; minus

(2) the deductions claimed by the distributor under sections 701 through 704 of this chapter.

This deduction is a flat allowance to cover evaporation, shrinkage, losses (except losses covered by section 301(5) of this chapter), and the distributor's expenses in collecting and timely remitting the tax imposed by this chapter.

(b) If a monthly report is filed or the amount due is remitted later than the time required under this chapter, the distributor shall pay to the administrator all of the gasoline tax the distributor received from the sale of gasoline covered by the late report, reduced by payments made under IC 6–8.1–8–1.

As added by Acts 1979, P.L.79, SEC.1. Amended by Acts 1980, P.L.51, SEC.37; P.L.77–1985, SEC.3; P.L.59–1985, SEC.12; P.L.92–1987, SEC.6.

Historical and Statutory Notes

Acts 1980, P.L. 51, § 37, emerg. eff. Feb. 22, 1980, substituted "gasoline" for "motor fuel".

P.L.77–1985, Sec.3, eff. Sept. 1, 1985, designated Subsec. (a); at the beginning of Subsec. (a), inserted "If a monthly report is filed and the amount due is remitted at or before the time required by this chapter"; in the last sentence of Subsec. (a), inserted "timely"; and added Subsec. (b).

Section 37 of P.L.77–1985 was amended by Section 39 of P.L.59–1985 to change the effective date of the amendment of this section by P.L.77–1985 from Sept. 1, 1985 to July 1, 1985.

P.L.59–1985, Sec.12, emerg. eff. July 1, 1985, substituted, in Subsec. (a), "one and six-tenths percent (1.6%)" for "two percent (2%)".

P.L.92–1987, Sec.6, eff. July 1, 1987, added at the end of Subsec. (b) "reduced by payments made under IC 6–8.1–8–1."

Formerly:

IC 6–6–1–8.
Acts 1943, c. 73, s. 9.
Acts 1959, c. 84, s. 1.
Acts 1969, c. 319, s. 2.

Library References

Taxation ☞1312.
WESTLAW Topic No. 371.

C.J.S. Taxation § 1246.
I.L.E. Taxation §§ 187 to 190.

6–6–1.1–801   Tax collected by distributor as state money in trust; liability; use restricted to authorized purposes

Sec. 801.   Until a distributor pays the license tax on gasoline he receives, the tax money he collects on the sale of gasoline is state money.   A distributor who collects such license tax money shall hold it in trust for the state and for payment to the department as provided in this chapter.   In the case of a corporate or partnership distributor, every officer, employee, or member of the employer who in that capacity is under a duty to collect the tax, is personally liable for the tax, penalty, and interest.   Taxes collected on gasoline, except those collected at a taxable marine facility, shall be used only for highway purposes and for payment of any part of the cost of traffic policing and traffic safety incurred by the state or any of its political subdivisions, as may be authorized by law.

As added by Acts 1979, P.L.79, SEC.1.   Amended by Acts 1979, P.L.71, SEC.10; Acts 1980, P.L.51, SEC.38.

Historical and Statutory Notes

Acts 1979, P.L. 71, § 10, inserted the second and third sentences; and substituted "state" for "public" in the first sentence.

Acts 1980, P.L. 51, § 38, emerg. eff. Feb. 22, 1980, substituted "gasoline" for "motor fuel" throughout the section.

Formerly:
  IC 6–6–1–4.

IC 6–6–1.5–3.

Acts 1943, c. 73, s. 4.

Acts 1957, c. 48, s. 1.

Acts 1959, c. 323, s. 1.

Acts 1969, c. 319, s. 1.

Acts 1971, P.L.70, SEC.1.

Cross References

Revenue department, tax administration, see IC 6–8.1–1–1 et seq.

Library References

Taxation ⊕1337, 1345.
WESTLAW Topic No. 371.

C.J.S. Taxation §§ 1250, 1257.
I.L.E. Taxation §§ 187 to 190.

6–6–1.1–801.5   Tax receipts; transfer to auditor; distribution

Sec. 801.5.   (a) The administrator shall transfer one-fifteenth (¹⁄₁₅) of the taxes that are collected under this chapter to the state highway road construction and improvement fund.

(b) After the transfer required by subsection (a), the administrator shall transfer the next twenty-five million dollars ($25,000,000) of the taxes that are collected under this chapter and received during a period beginning July 1 of a year and ending June 30 of the immediately succeeding year to the auditor of state for distribution in the following manner:

(1) thirty percent (30%) to each of the counties, cities, and towns eligible to receive a distribution from the local road and street account under IC 8–14–2 and in the same proportion among the counties, cities, and towns as funds are distributed under IC 8–14–2–4;

(2) thirty percent (30%) to each of the counties, cities, and towns eligible to receive a distribution from the motor vehicle highway account under IC 8–14–1 and in the same proportion among the counties, cities, and towns as funds are distributed from the motor vehicle highway account under IC 8–14–1; and

(3) forty percent (40%) to the Indiana department of transportation.

(c) The auditor of state shall hold all amounts of collections received under subsection (b) from the administrator that are made during a particular month and shall distribute all of those amounts pursuant to subsection (b) on the fifth day of the immediately succeeding month.

(d) All amounts distributed under subsection (b) may only be used for purposes that money distributed from the motor vehicle highway account may be expended under IC 8–14–1.

As added by Acts 1981, P.L.88, SEC.6. Amended by P.L.68–1988, SEC.2; P.L.18–1990, SEC.21.

Historical and Statutory Notes

Acts 1981, P.L. 88, Sec.6, eff. July 1, 1981, added this section.

P.L. 68–1988, Sec.2, emerg. eff. April 1, 1988, interpolated Subsec. (a); redesignated existing subsections accordingly; inserted at the beginning of Subsec. (b) "after the transfer required by subsection (a)" and substituted following "shall transfer the" the word "next" for "first"; and inserted in Subsec. (c) "under subsection (b)".

P.L.18–1990, Sec.21, emerg. eff. March 13, 1990.

Cross References

Special highway user tax accounts, see IC 8–14–2–1 et seq.

Library References

Taxation ⚘1344.
WESTLAW Topic No. 371.

C.J.S. Taxation § 1257.
I.L.E. Taxation §§ 187 to 190.

6–6–1.1–802   Deposits of tax receipts

Sec. 802. The administrator shall, after the transfer specified in section 801.5 of this chapter, deposit the remainder of the revenues collected under this chapter in the following manner:

(1) The taxes collected with respect to gasoline delivered to a taxable marine facility shall be deposited in the fish and wildlife fund established by IC 14–22–3–2.

(2) Twenty-five percent (25%) of the taxes collected under this chapter, except the taxes referred to in subdivision (1), shall be deposited in the highway, road and street fund established under IC 8–14–2–2.1.

(3) The remainder of the revenues collected under this chapter shall be deposited in the motor fuel tax fund of the motor vehicle highway account.

As added by Acts 1979, P.L.79, SEC.1. Amended by Acts 1980, P.L.51, SEC.39; Acts 1980, P.L.10, SEC.9; Acts 1981, P.L.93, SEC.2; Acts 1981, P.L.88, SEC.7; P.L.1–1995, SEC.50.

Historical and Statutory Notes

Acts 1980, P.L. 51, § 39, emerg. eff. Feb. 22, 1980, substituted "gasoline" for "motor fuel" in Cl. (1); and deleted "pursuant to IC 8–14–2–2.1" following "clause (1), shall" in Cl. (2).

Acts 1980, P.L. 10, § 9, emerg. eff. March 3, 1980, inserted "established under IC 8–14–2–2.1" in Cl. (2); and in the provisions of the introductory clause, substituted "The administrator shall, on a daily basis, deposit the revenues collected under this chapter in the following manner" for "The administrator shall make daily deposits with the treasurer of state of all revenues collected under this chapter. On the last day of each calendar month the auditor of state shall quietus the total receipts collected during the month as follows:"

Acts 1981, P.L. 88, § 7, eff. July 1, 1981, substituted "after the transfer specified in section 801.5 of this chapter, deposit the remainder

of the revenues" for "on a daily basis, deposit the revenues" in the introductory clause.

Acts 1981, P.L. 93, § 2, eff. July 1, 1981, substituted "fish and wildlife fund established by IC 14–3–1–16" for "marine fuel tax fund" in Cl. (1).

P.L.1–1995, Sec.50, amended the section by substituting "IC 14–22–3–2" for "IC 14–3–1–16" in Subsec. (1); and substituting "subdivision" for "clause" in Subsec. (2).

Formerly:

IC 6–6–1–24.
IC 6–6–1.5–1.
IC 6–6–1.5–3.
Acts 1943, c. 73, s. 25.
Acts 1957, c. 162, s. 1.
Acts 1971, P.L.70, SEC.1.
Acts 1978, P.L.47, SEC.4.

Cross References

Motor vehicle highway account fund, allocation, see IC 8–14–1–3.
Special highway user tax accounts, see IC 8–14–2–1 et seq.

Library References

Taxation ☞1345.
WESTLAW Topic No. 371.

C.J.S. Taxation § 1257.
I.L.E. Taxation §§ 187 to 190.

Notes of Decisions

In general 1
Investment of highway funds 2

1. In general

Legislative power to tax for constructing, maintaining, and repairing highways is unlimited, except as restricted by Constitution. Gafill v. Bracken, 1924, 145 N.E. 312, 195 Ind. 551, rehearing denied 146 N.E. 109, 195 Ind. 551.

2. Investment of highway funds

Board of county commissioners could use gasoline and motor vehicle tax funds in improv-

ing county highways by use of materials different from materials used in original construction without appropriation by county council or petition by freeholders or voters, under existing statutes. Williams v. Willett, App.1936, 1 N.E.2d 664, 102 Ind.App. 193.

There was no authority for the state finance board to invest any of the state highway funds, regardless of their sources, in short term investments. 1963 Op.Atty.Gen. No. 19.

6–6–1.1–803 Refunds and costs; payment

Sec. 803. All receipts of the motor fuel tax fund are available for payment of refunds authorized by this chapter and payment of the costs of administering and enforcing of this chapter.

As added by Acts 1979, P.L.79, SEC.1.

Historical and Statutory Notes

Formerly:
IC 6–6–1–3.

IC 6–6–1–24.

Acts 1943, c. 73, ss. 3, 25.
Acts 1957, c. 162, s. 1.

Library References

Taxation ☞1334.
WESTLAW Topic No. 371.

C.J.S. Taxation § 1252.
I.L.E. Taxation §§ 187 to 190.

6–6–1.1–804   Repealed

(Repealed by Acts 1979, P.L.71, SEC.19.)

Historical and Statutory Notes

The repealed section related to transferring
balances in the motor fuel tax fund.

Formerly:
Acts 1979, P.L.79, SEC.1.

6–6–1.1–805   Motor fuel tax fund;   transfer of residue balance to highway account

Sec. 805.   Any balance remaining in the motor fuel tax fund after making the payments required by section 803 of this chapter shall be transferred to the motor vehicle highway account for distribution as provided by law.

As added by Acts 1979, P.L.79, SEC.1.   Amended by Acts 1979, P.L.71, SEC.11.

Historical and Statutory Notes

Formerly:
IC 6–6–1–24.

Acts 1943, c. 73, s. 25.
Acts 1957, c. 162, s. 1.

Cross References

Motor vehicle highway account, see IC 8–14–1–1 et seq.

Library References

Taxation ☞1345.
WESTLAW Topic No. 371.

C.J.S. Taxation § 1257.
I.L.E. Taxation §§ 187 to 190.

6–6–1.1–806   Repealed

(Repealed by Acts 1981, P.L.93, SEC.11.)

Historical and Statutory Notes

Acts 1981, P.L. 93, provided in § 13(a) that
the act takes effect July 1, 1981.

The repealed section related to the use of the
marine fuel tax fund by the department, of
natural resources.

Formerly:
Acts 1979, P.L.79, SEC.1.

6–6–1.1–901   Refund to purchaser for gasoline lost or destroyed; limitations; requisites; distributor excepted

Sec. 901.   A person, except a distributor, who has purchased gasoline in Indiana and has paid the tax imposed on it by this chapter is entitled to a refund (without interest) of the amount of tax paid on gasoline in excess of one hundred (100) gallons which is lost or destroyed, except by evaporation, shrinkage, or unknown cause, while he owns it. To obtain the refund, the person:

(1) must, within five (5) days after the loss or destruction is discovered, notify the administrator in writing of the amount of gasoline lost or destroyed; and

(2) must, within sixty (60) days after notice is given, file with the administrator an affidavit that is sworn to by the person having custody of the gasoline at the time of loss or destruction and that sets forth in full the circumstances and amount of the loss or destruction and any other information the administrator may require.

As added by Acts 1979, P.L.79, SEC.1. Amended by Acts 1980, P.L.51, SEC.40; Acts 1981, P.L.93, SEC.3.

Historical and Statutory Notes

Acts 1980, P.L. 51, § 40, emerg. eff. Feb. 22, 1980, substituted "gasoline" for "motor fuel" throughout the section.

Acts 1981, P.L. 93, § 3, emerg. eff. April 27, 1981, inserted "(without interest)" in the first sentence.

Acts 1981, P.L. 93, provided in § 13(b):

"Because an emergency exists, the remainder of this act takes effect on passage and affects fuel tax refunds paid after the passage of this act."

Formerly:

IC 6–6–1–21.
Acts 1943, c. 73, s. 22.

Library References

Taxation ⟜1334.
WESTLAW Topic No. 371.

C.J.S. Taxation § 1252.
I.L.E. Taxation §§ 187 to 190.

Notes of Decisions

In general   1

_____

1. In general
The tax imposed by former statute [see, now, this chapter], being upon "use" of motor vehicle

fuel, refund was authorized where gasoline had been lost in flood. 1937 Op.Atty.Gen. p. 47.

6–6–1.1–902   Refund to local transit system; requisites; interest

Sec. 902. (a) A local transit system is entitled to a refund of tax paid on gasoline used:

(1) for transporting persons for compensation by means of a motor vehicle or trackless trolley; or

(2) in a maintenance or an administrative vehicle that is used by the local transit system to support the transit service.

(b) The claim for refund must contain the following:

(1) A quarterly operating statement.

(2) A current balance sheet.

(3) A schedule of all salaries in excess of ten thousand dollars ($10,000) per annum paid to any officer or employee.

(c) If a refund is not issued within ninety (90) days of filing of the verified statement and all supplemental information required by IC 6–6–1.1–904.1, the department shall pay interest at the rate established by IC 6–8.1–9 computed from the date of filing of the refund application until a date determined by the administrator that does not precede by more than thirty (30) days the date on which the refund is made.

As added by Acts 1979, P.L.79, SEC.1. Amended by Acts 1980, P.L.51, SEC.41; Acts 1981, P.L.93, SEC.4; P.L.1–1991, SEC.57; P.L.85–1995, SEC.11.

Historical and Statutory Notes

Acts 1980, P.L. 51, § 41, emerg. eff. Feb. 22, 1980, substituted "gasoline" for "motor fuel".

Acts 1981, P.L. 93, § 4, emerg. eff. April 27, 1981, designated Subsec. (a); and added Subsec. (b).

P.L.1–1991, Sec.57, emerg. eff. April 23, 1991.

P.L.1–1991, Sec.57, deleted "and" at the end of Subsec. (a)(2); and substituted "IC 6–6–1.1–904.1" for "IC 6–6–1.1–904" in Subsec. (b).

P.L.85–1995, Sec.11, emerg. eff. May 10, 1995, amended the section by designating Subsecs. (a)(1) and (2); deleting "having a seating capacity of at least twenty (20) persons. How-ever, the transporting must be done within the corporate limits of a municipality, or within the corporate limits and not more than five (5) miles beyond the corporate limits of a municipality." from Subsec. (a)(1); adding Subsec. (a)(2); designating Subsec. (b), and redesignating former Subsec. (b) as Subsec. (c).

Formerly:

IC 6–6–1–4.
Acts 1943, c. 73, s. 4.
Acts 1957, c. 48, s. 1.
Acts 1959, c. 323, s. 1.
Acts 1969, c. 319, s. 1.

Cross References

Revenue department, tax administration, refunds, see IC 6–8.1–9–1 et seq.
Verified statement, related information and procedures required to claim a refund under this section, see IC 6–6–1.1–904.

Library References

Taxation ☞1334.
WESTLAW Topic No. 371.

C.J.S. Taxation § 1252.
I.L.E. Taxation §§ 187 to 190.

6–6–1.1–902.5   Refund to rural transit system; claim; interest

Sec. 902.5. (a) A rural transit system is entitled to a refund of tax paid on gasoline used for transporting persons for compensation by means of a motor vehicle or trackless trolley. However, the transporting must be done:

(1) within a service area that is not larger than the rural transit system service area and the counties contiguous to that rural transit system service area; and

(2) under a written contract between the rural transit system and the county providers within the service area that meets the requirements prescribed by the department.

(b) The claim for refund must contain the following:

(1) A quarterly operating statement.

(2) A current balance sheet.

(3) A schedule of all salaries that exceed ten thousand dollars ($10,000) per year paid to any officer or employee.

(c) If a refund is not issued within ninety (90) days of filing of the verified statement and all supplemental information required by section 904.1 of this chapter, the department shall pay interest at the rate established by IC 6–8.1–10–1(c) computed from the date of filing of the refund application until a date determined by the administrator that does not precede by more than thirty (30) days the date on which the refund is made.

As added by P.L.45–1994, SEC.1. Amended by P.L.2–1995, SEC.34.

Historical and Statutory Notes

P.L.2–1995, Sec.34, emerg. eff. May 5, 1995, which was part of the correction bill, substituted "IC 6–8.1–10–1(c)" for "IC 6–8.1–9" in Subsec. (c).

6–6–1.1–903   Refund for tax paid on gasoline purchased or used for designated purposes; interest

Sec. 903. (a) A person is entitled to a refund of gasoline tax paid on gasoline purchased or used for the following purposes:

(1) Operating stationary gas engines.

(2) Operating equipment mounted on motor vehicles, whether or not operated by the engine propelling the motor vehicle.

(3) Operating a tractor used for agricultural purposes.

(3.1) Operating implements of husbandry (as defined in IC 9–13–2–77).

(4) Operating motorboats or aircraft.

(5) Cleaning or dyeing.

(6) Other commercial use, except propelling motor vehicles operated in whole or in part on an Indiana public highway.

(7) Operating a taxicab (as defined in section 103 of this chapter).

(b) If a refund is not issued within ninety (90) days of filing of the verified statement and all supplemental information required by IC 6–6–1.1–904.1, the department shall pay interest at the rate established by IC 6–8.1–9 computed from the date of filing of the verified statement and all supplemental information required by the department until a date determined by the administrator that does not precede by more than thirty (30) days the date on which the refund is made.

As added by Acts 1979, P.L.79, SEC.1. Amended by Acts 1979, P.L.71, SEC.12; Acts 1980, P.L.51, SEC.42; Acts 1981, P.L.93, SEC.5; P.L.97–1987, SEC.10; P.L.2–1991, SEC.40; P.L.1–1991, SEC.58.

Historical and Statutory Notes

Acts 1979, P.L. 71, § 12, added Cl. (3.1); inserted "operated in whole or in part" in Cl. (6); and substituted "103" for "102" in Cl. (7).

Acts 1980, P.L. 51, § 42, emerg. eff. Feb. 22, 1980, twice substituted "gasoline" for "motor fuel."

Acts 1981, P.L. 93, § 5, emerg. eff. April 27, 1981, designated Subsec. (a); and added Subsec. (b).

P.L.97–1987, § 10, eff. Sept. 1, 1987, in Subd. (a)(2), deleted "concrete mixing" preceding "equipment"; and in Subsec. (b), substituted "verified statement and all supplemental information required by the department" for "refund application".

P.L.60–1990, Sec.15, eff. Jan. 1, 1991, provides:

"(a) Notwithstanding IC 6–6–1.1–904, a taxpayer that:

"(1) purchased gasoline during the 1989 calendar year; and

"(2) used the gasoline for a purpose described in IC 6–6–1.1–903(1) through IC 6–6–1.1–903(6);

"may file a claim for a refund under IC 6–6–1.1–903. A refund must be filed under this section not later than December 31, 1990.

"(b) This section expires January 1, 1991."

P.L.1–1991, Sec.58, substituted "IC 6–6–1.1–904.1" for "IC 6–6–1.1–904" in Subsec. (b).

P.L.2–1991, Sec.40, in Subsec. (a)(3.1), substituted "IC 9–13–2–77" for "IC 9–1–1–2(hh)".

Formerly:
IC 6–6–1–22.
IC 6–6–1–22.1.
Acts 1943, c. 73, s. 23a.
Acts 1963 (ss), c. 33, s. 2.
Acts 1965, c. 300, s. 1.
Acts 1971, P.L.69, SEC.5.
Acts 1973, P.L.53, SEC.1.
Acts 1975, P.L.352, SEC.2.
Acts 1978, P.L.2, SEC.635.
Acts 1978, P.L.47, SEC.2.

Cross References

Revenue department, tax administration, refunds, see IC 6–8.1–9–1 et seq.
Verified statement, related information and procedures required to claim a refund under this section, see IC 6–6–1.1–904.

Library References

Taxation ⚯1334.
WESTLAW Topic No. 371.

C.J.S. Taxation § 1252.
I.L.E. Taxation §§ 187 to 190.

WESTLAW Electronic Research

See WESTLAW Electronic Research Guide following the Preface.

Notes of Decisions

In general   1
Aircraft   2
Commercial use   3, 4
   In general   3
   Motor vehicles not operated on public highways   4
Motor vehicles not operated on public highways, commercial use   4

---

1. In general

Under refund provisions of motor vehicle fuel tax law [repealed; see, now, this section], parties purchasing gasoline in large quantities, which they anticipated using for non-taxable purposes, were not entitled to refund before fuel had actually been used for non-taxable purposes. 1935 Op.Atty.Gen. p. 174.

2. Aircraft

Under former statute [See, now, this section], providing for gas tax refunds to persons operating airplanes or aircraft, the one entitled to the refund was consumer, and a flying service selling the fuel to other airplane operators could not claim a refund on such gasoline resold. 1931–1932 Op.Atty.Gen. p. 31.

3. Commercial use—In general

Gasoline purchased by a licensed dealer of Indiana for refill to ultimate consumer in sister state came within Acts 1932 (s.s.), c. 68, s. 5 [repealed; see, now, this section] providing that any person who should purchase motor vehicle fuel for any other commercial use, except for propelling motor vehicles operated in whole or in part upon public highways of state, should be reimbursed and repaid amount of license fee paid by him, and proper method of securing reimbursement from state would be by filing a necessary statement and supporting invoices and evidence required under such statute. 1933 Op.Atty.Gen. p. 17.

4. —— Motor vehicles not operated on public highways, commercial use

Under former statute [see, now, this section] providing for refund of gasoline tax to any person buying or using motor vehicle fuel for purposes of operating or propelling any motor vehicle except for propelling motor vehicles operated in whole or in part upon public highways, where vehicle was not used in whole or in part upon public highways of state, person was entitled to rebate for amount of license fee. 1935 Op.Atty.Gen. p. 365.

Under former statute [see, now, this section] which, in effect, provided for refund of gasoline

tax paid and not paid for motor vehicles which were not operated in whole or part upon any of public highways of state, when contractor was working on restricted road and within limits of particular projects and when using gasoline for purpose of completing his contract or performing duties purely connected with contract, he was entitled to rebate if project upon which he was working was closed and barricaded against all public traffic, but contractor was not entitled to rebate outside limits of barricade for transporting equipment, gravel, dirt, sand or other road materials. 1935 Op.Atty.Gen. p. 328.

Where airplane transportation company engaged in interstate and intrastate commerce in Indiana, tax could be exacted under the Indiana tax law, but where airplane transportation company and railroad company did not use highways of state, they would be entitled to refund under provisions of former statute [see, now, this section]. 1929–1930 Op.Atty.Gen. p. 229.

6–6–1.1–904   Repealed

(Repealed, as amended by P.L.35–1990, SEC.23, and as amended by P.L.48–1990, SEC.4, by P.L.1–1991, SEC.59.)

Historical and Statutory Notes

P.L.1–1991 provided in Section 224, containing emergency clause, that Section 59 of the act takes effect upon passage April 23, 1991.

Former IC 6–6–1.1–904 related to refund and procedures to claim.

See, now, IC 6–6–1.1–904.1.

6–6–1.1–904.1   Refund; required procedures to claim

Sec. 904.1. (a) To claim a refund under section 902, 902.5, or 903, of this chapter, a person must present to the administrator a statement that contains a written verification that it is made under penalties of perjury and that sets forth the total amount of gasoline purchased and used for purposes other than propelling a motor vehicle on an Indiana public highway. The statement must be filed by April 15 of the year succeeding three (3) years after the date the gasoline was purchased, and it must be accompanied by the original invoice or a certified copy of the original invoice. Such a copy must be certified by the supplier on forms prescribed by the administrator. In addition, the original invoice or certified copy must show either:

(1) that payment for the purchase has been made and the amount of tax paid on the purchase; or

(2) that the gasoline was charged to a credit card approved by the administrator under procedures designed to assure the state will not be liable for the credit card charges if the claimant does not pay for the purchases.

(b) The administrator may make any investigations the administrator considers necessary before refunding the gasoline taxes to the consumer.

As added by P.L.1–1991, SEC.60.   Amended by P.L.45–1994, SEC.2.

Historical and Statutory Notes

P.L.1–1991, Sec.60, emerg. eff. upon passage April 23, 1991.

P.L.45–1994, Sec.2, inserted ", 902.5," in Subsec. (a).

Formerly:

IC 6–6–1–22.
IC 6–6–1–22.1.
IC 6–6–1.1–904.
Acts 1943, c. 73, s. 23a.
Acts 1963 (ss), c. 33, s. 2.

Acts 1965, c. 300, s. 1.
Acts 1971, P.L.69, SEC.5.
Acts 1973, P.L.53, SEC.1.
Acts 1975, P.L.352, SEC.2.
Acts 1978, P.L.2, SEC.635.
Acts 1978, P.L.47, SEC.2.
Acts 1979, P.L.79, SEC.1.
Acts 1980, P.L.51, SEC.43.
P.L.82–1983, SEC.10.
P.L.35–1990, SEC. 23.
P.L.48–1990, SEC. 4.

Library References

Taxation ⌐1334.
WESTLAW Topic No. 371.

C.J.S. Taxation § 1252.
I.L.E. Taxation §§ 187 to 190.

Notes of Decisions

Evidence of use   1

1. Evidence of use

Where gasoline used to propel transport and gasoline delivered to filling stations were taken from common tank, state auditor could not accept meter reading for gasoline delivered as sole evidence of use of fuel for purpose of entitling user to refund under former statute [see, now, this section].   1940 Op.Atty.Gen. p. 84.

The word "original" as used in former statute [see, now, this section] to describe the invoice which could be used in application for refund of gasoline tax did not have reference to the time or method of issuing the invoice but meant that the invoice was to have been issued in the usual course of business and as part of the transaction involved in the sale and purchase and delivery of the gasoline on account of which refund was claimed.   1938 Op.Atty.Gen. p. 243.

6–6–1.1–905   Repealed

(Repealed by P.L.96–1989, SEC.25.)

Historical and Statutory Notes

P.L.96–1989 provided in Section 28 that the act takes effect January 1, 1990.

Former IC 6–6–1.1–905 related to tax credit in lieu of refund.

Formerly:

IC 6–6–1–22.
IC 6–6–1–22.1.
Acts 1943, c. 73, s. 23a.

Acts 1963 (ss), c. 33, s. 2.
Acts 1965, c. 300, s. 1.
Acts 1971, P.L.69, SEC.5.
Acts 1973, P.L.53, SEC.1.
Acts 1975, P.L.352, SEC.2.
Acts 1978, P.L.2, SEC.635.
Acts 1978, P.L.47, SEC.2.
Acts 1979, P.L.71, SEC.13.
Acts 1979, P.L.79, SEC.1.

6–6–1.1–906   Refunds or credits; rules and regulations

Sec. 906.   The department shall adopt necessary rules and regulations consistent with this chapter and IC 6–3–3–7 for the filing of refund or credit claims and for the granting of refunds or credits.

As added by Acts 1979, P.L.79, SEC.1.

Historical and Statutory Notes

Formerly:

IC 6–6–1–22.

IC 6–6–1–22.1.

Acts 1943, c. 73, s. 23a.

Acts 1963 (ss), c. 33, s. 2.

Acts 1965, c. 300, s. 1.

Acts 1971, P.L.69, SEC.5.

Acts 1973, P.L.53, SEC.1.

Acts 1975, P.L.352, SEC.2.

Acts 1978, P.L.2, SEC.635.

Acts 1978, P.L.47, SEC.2.

6–6–1.1–907   Refund or deduction; payment of tax in error; warrant; payment; requisites

Sec. 907.   (a) If the administrator determines that a licensed distributor has paid gasoline tax in error or is entitled to a refund or deduction, the administrator may issue a warrant in favor of that person.   The treasurer of state shall accept the warrant and make payment out of the revolving fund established in section 909 of this chapter.

(b) No refund shall be made under this section unless the written claim describes the reason the refund should be allowed.   The claim must be sworn to by the claimant and filed with the administrator, on forms prescribed by the administrator, within three (3) years after the end of the calendar year containing the taxable period in which the tax was erroneously collected.

As added by Acts 1979, P.L.79, SEC.1.   Amended by Acts 1980, P.L.51, SEC.44; P.L.97–1987, SEC.11.

Historical and Statutory Notes

Acts 1980, P.L. 51, Sec.44, emerg. eff. Feb. 22, 1980, substituted "gasoline" for "motor fuel" in the first sentence of Subsec. (a).

P.L.97–1987, Sec.11, eff. Sept. 1, 1987, rewrote the second sentence of Subsec. (b), which prior thereto read: "The claim must be sworn to by the claimant and filed with the administra-

tor, on forms prescribed by the administrator, within two (2) years after the date of payment of the erroneously collected taxes."

Formerly:

IC 6–6–1–23.

Acts 1943, c. 73, s. 24.

Cross References

Deduction authorized by IC 6–6–1.1–704 in lieu of issuing warrant prescribed by Subsec. (a) of this section, see IC 6–6–1.1–908.

Library References

Taxation ⟐1334.

WESTLAW Topic No. 371.

C.J.S. Taxation § 1252.

I.L.E. Taxation §§ 187 to 190.

6–6–1.1–908   Deduction in lieu of warrant for payment of refund

Sec. 908.   In lieu of issuing the warrant prescribed by section 907(a) of this chapter, the administrator may elect to permit the deduction authorized by section 704 of this chapter.

As added by Acts 1979, P.L.79, SEC.1.

Historical and Statutory Notes

Formerly:
  IC 6–6–1–23.
  Acts 1943, c. 73, s. 24.

6–6–1.1–909   Gasoline tax refund account

Sec. 909.   The administrator shall establish a revolving fund known as the gasoline tax refund account.   The amount in the fund may not exceed seventy-five thousand dollars ($75,000), and the administrator shall maintain the fund in a public depository designated by the state board of finance.   The administrator shall draw checks against the fund for each approved refund.   As the checks are returned paid by the depository, the administrator shall issue a warrant on the motor fuel tax fund in the amount of the checks returned paid, for the purpose of maintaining the depository balance at the authorized amount.

As added by Acts 1979, P.L.79, SEC.1.

Historical and Statutory Notes

Formerly: Acts 1943, c. 73, s. 25.
  IC 6–6–1–24.   Acts 1957, c. 162, s. 1.

Library References

Taxation ⌖1334.   C.J.S. Taxation § 1252.
WESTLAW Topic No. 371.   I.L.E. Taxation §§ 187 to 190.

Notes of Decisions

Appropriation of money for refund   1

---

1.   Appropriation of money for refund

Act 1923, c. 182 [repealed; see, now, this chapter] which imposed a tax on gasoline, and provided for rebate of money paid for gasoline not used in operating motor cars, itself made necessary appropriation for payment of rebates, and did not permit withdrawal of money from treasury without appropriation.   Gafill v. Bracken, 1924, 145 N.E. 312, 195 Ind. 551, rehearing denied 146 N.E. 109, 195 Ind. 551.

6–6–1.1–910   Class action for refund of tax; prerequisites

Sec. 910.   A class action for the refund of a tax subject to this chapter may not be maintained in any court, including the Indiana tax court, on behalf of any person who has not complied with the requirements of sections 901 through 908 of this chapter before the certification of a class.   A refund of taxes to a member of a class in a class action is subject to the time limits set forth in sections 901 through 908 of this chapter based on the time the class member filed the required claim for refund with the department.

As added by P.L.60–1990, SEC.1.

Historical and Statutory Notes

P.L.60–1990, Sec.1, emerg. eff. retroactive to
Jan. 1, 1990.

United States Supreme Court

Class actions, mandatory settlement class, limited fund theory, agreements of parties, see   Ortiz v. Fibreboard Corp., U.S.Tex.1999, 119 S.Ct. 2295, 144 L.Ed.2d 715.

6–6–1.1–1001 to 6–6–1.1–1007   Repealed

(Repealed by Acts 1980, P.L.61, SEC.15.)

Historical and Statutory Notes

Acts 1980, P.L. 61, provided in § 16 that the act takes effect Jan. 1, 1981.

Former § 6–6–1.1–1001 made the state a preferred creditor for unpaid motor fuel taxes in certain circumstances.

Former §§ 6–6–1.1–1002 to 6–6–1.1–1007 related to state liens on property of tax debtors.

Provisions pertaining to collection of taxes by the department of revenue are now contained in § 6–8.1–8–1 et seq.

Formerly:

Acts 1979, P.L.79, SEC.1.

6–6–1.1–1008   Sealing pumps; impoundment of vehicles or tanks; report of meter readings

Sec. 1008. (a) If any of the conditions specified in subsection (b) occur, the administrator may seal a gasoline pump, gasohol pump, aviation gasoline pump, or marina gasoline pump; impound any vehicle or tank that does not have a sealable pump; and post a sign that states that no transactions involving gasoline or gasohol, or both, can be made at the person's location.

(b) The administrator may take the actions specified in subsection (a) if:

(1) a licensed distributor becomes delinquent in the payment of any amount due under this chapter;

(2) there is evidence that the revenue of a licensed distributor is in jeopardy;

(3) a distributor is operating without the license required by this chapter;

(4) a licensed distributor is operating without the bond, letter of credit, or cash deposit required by this chapter; or

(5) a person has received gasoline in this state and the gasoline tax has not been remitted to the state as required by section 504 of this chapter.

(c) The pumps may be sealed and the sign posted until:

(1) all reports are filed and the fees, taxes, fines, and penalties imposed by this chapter are paid;

(2) the interest and penalties imposed by IC 6–8.1–10–1 and IC 6–8.1–10–2.1 are paid in full;

(3) the license required by this chapter is obtained; and

(4) the bond, letter of credit, or cash deposit required by this chapter is provided.

(d) The administrator may require any person operating under this chapter to report meter readings that show the amount of fuel dispensed or used from a metered pump.

(e) The administrator may authorize the state police department to impound any vehicle or tank under subsection (a) on behalf of the department of state revenue.

As added by P.L.97–1987, SEC.12. Amended by P.L.1–1991, SEC.61.

Historical and Statutory Notes

P.L.97–1987, Sec.12, adding this section, was made effective Sept. 1, 1987.

P.L.1–1991, Sec.61, emerg. eff. April 23, 1991.

P.L.1–1991, Sec.61, substituted "IC 6–8.1–10–2.1" for "IC 6–8.1–10–2" in Subsec. (c)(2).

Cross References

Failure or refusal to report meter readings under this section, offense, see IC 6–6–1.1–1316.

6–6–1.1–1009   Cumulative remedies

Sec. 1009. The remedies provided to the department by this chapter are cumulative, and the election to use a remedy may not be construed to exclude the use of any other remedy.

As added by P.L.97–1987, SEC.13.

Historical and Statutory Notes

P.L.97–1987, Sec.13, adding this section, was made effective Sept. 1, 1987.

6–6–1.1–1101, 6–6–1.1–1102   Repealed

(Repealed by Acts 1980, P.L.61, SEC.15.)

Historical and Statutory Notes

Acts 1980, P.L. 61, provided in § 16 that the act takes effect Jan. 1, 1981.

Former § 6–6–1.1–1101 related to forms.

Former § 6–6–1.1–1102 opened the administrator's records to public inspection.

Provisions pertaining to tax forms are now contained in § 6–8.1–3–4.

Formerly:

Acts 1979, P.L.79, SEC.1.

6–6–1.1–1103   Requests of another state for information

Sec. 1103. Upon request from an official who enforces the gasoline laws of another state, the administrator shall furnish the official with any information he has relating to the receipt, sale, use, transportation, or shipment of gasoline by any person.

As added by Acts 1979, P.L.79, SEC.1. Amended by Acts 1980, P.L.51, SEC.48.

Historical and Statutory Notes

Acts 1980, P.L. 51, § 48, emerg. eff. Feb. 22, 1980, substituted "gasoline" for "motor fuel" twice.

Formerly:

IC 6–6–1–29.

Acts 1943, c. 73, s. 30.

6-6-1.1-1104 to 6-6-1.1-1109   Repealed

(Repealed by Acts 1980, P.L.61, SEC.15.)

Historical and Statutory Notes

Acts 1980, P.L. 61, provided in § 16 that the act takes effect Jan. 1, 1981.

Former §§ 6-6-1.1-1104 to 1109 related to enforcement of chapter provisions.

Provisions pertaining to enforcement powers of the department of revenue, and the existence of cumulative remedies, are now contained in §§ 6-8.1-3-1 et seq., and 6-8.1-8-7.

Formerly:

Acts 1979, P.L.79, SEC.1.

6-6-1.1-1110   Gallonage totalizers; sealing; installation; evidence

Sec. 1110.   (a) The administrator may seal gallonage totalizers of metered pumps operated by or on behalf of a dealer or licensed distributor.

(b) If the administrator determines that a metered pump operated by or on behalf of a dealer or licensed distributor is without an effectively sealable gallonage totalizer, the dealer or licensed distributor shall at the administrator's request:

(1) adapt the pump to the administrator's specifications so that it may be effectively sealed; or

(2) replace, in whole or in part, the pump with an effectively sealable gallonage totalizer, as determined by the administrator.

(c) A dealer's or licensed distributor's failure to comply with subsection (a) or (b) is considered evidence that the revenue of the dealer or licensed distributor is in jeopardy.

As added by P.L.97-1987, SEC.14.

Historical and Statutory Notes

P.L.97-1987, Sec.14, adding this section, was made effective Sept. 1, 1987.

Cross References

Failure or refusal to report meter readings under this section, offense, see IC 6-6-1.1-1316.

6-6-1.1-1201   Repealed

(Repealed by Acts 1980, P.L.61, SEC.15.)

Historical and Statutory Notes

Acts 1980, P.L. 61, provided in § 16 that the act takes effect Jan. 1, 1981.

Former § 6-6-1.1-1201 related to filing certain tax documents.

Provisions pertaining to the filing of tax documents are now contained in §§ 6-8.1-6-1 et seq.

Formerly:

Acts 1979, P.L.79, SEC.1.
Acts 1979, P.L.71, SEC.14.

6–6–1.1–1202   Identification markings on transportation equipment

Sec. 1202.   A vehicle which transports gasoline on a public Indiana highway must have the name and address of the person, firm, limited liability company, or corporation transporting the gasoline on both sides of the driver's compartment.   The information must appear in letters at least six (6) inches high with a stroke at least three-fourths (3/4) inch wide and in a color contrasting to the background on which the letters are placed.   However, a distributor licensed in Indiana is not required to display his name and address on transportation equipment if the equipment is identified with the trade or product name or insignia generally used in identifying such equipment, and the name or insignia is well-known throughout the area in which the equipment is operated.

As added by Acts 1979, P.L.79, SEC.1.   Amended by Acts 1980, P.L.51, SEC.49; P.L.8–1993, SEC.98.

Historical and Statutory Notes

Acts 1980, P.L. 51, § 49, amended this section emergency effective Feb. 22, 1980.

P.L.8–1993, Sec.98, inserted "limited liability company" in the first sentence.

Formerly:
IC 6–6–1–13.

Acts 1943, c. 73, s. 14.
Acts 1947, c. 336, s. 2.
Acts 1949, c. 162, s. 1.
Acts 1971, P.L.69, SEC.4.

Notes of Decisions

Registration of transportation equipment   1

---

1.   Registration of transportation equipment
The corporation's failure to comply with Acts 1943, c. 73 [repealed; see, now, this section]

relative to the registration of transportation equipment resulted in the violator being subject to the general penalty provisions of that act. 1944 Op.Atty.Gen. No. 15.

6–6–1.1–1203   Separate statement of tax rate on sales or delivery slips, bills, etc.

Sec. 1203.   Distributors and all persons selling gasoline shall state the rate of the tax separately from the price of the gasoline on all sales or delivery slips, bills, and statements which indicate the price of gasoline.

As added by Acts 1979, P.L.79, SEC.1.   Amended by Acts 1979, P.L.71, SEC.15; Acts 1980, P.L.51, SEC.50.

Historical and Statutory Notes

Acts 1980, P.L. 51, § 50, amended this section emergency effective Feb. 22, 1980.

Acts 1943, c. 73, s. 31.

Formerly:
IC 6–6–1–30.

Library References

Taxation ☞1293.
WESTLAW Topic No. 371.

C.J.S. Taxation § 1231.
I.L.E. Taxation §§ 187 to 190.

6–6–1.1–1204   Political subdivisions; excise tax prohibited

Sec. 1204. (a) No city, town, county, township, or other subdivision or municipal corporation of the state may levy or collect:

(1) an excise tax on or measured by the sale, receipt, distribution, or use of gasoline; or

(2) an excise, privilege, or occupational tax on the business of manufacturing, selling, or distributing gasoline.

(b) The provisions of subsection (a) may not be construed as to relieve a distributor or dealer from payment of the state gross income tax or state store license.

As added by Acts 1979, P.L.79, SEC.1. Amended by Acts 1980, P.L.51, SEC.51.

Historical and Statutory Notes

Acts 1980, P.L. 51, § 51, amended this section emergency effective Feb. 22, 1980.

Acts 1943, c. 73, s. 32.

Formerly:
IC 6–6–1–31.

Library References

Taxation ☞1208.
WESTLAW Topic No. 371.

C.J.S. Taxation § 1231.
I.L.E. Taxation §§ 187 to 190.

6–6–1.1–1205   Criminal proceedings; precedence

Sec. 1205. All criminal proceedings arising under this chapter have precedence in court over all other cases, excepting cases in which the state or public is a moving party.

As added by Acts 1979, P.L.79, SEC.1. Amended by P.L.291–1985, SEC.8.

Historical and Statutory Notes

P.L.291–1985, Sec.8, eff. July 1, 1986, deleted "and civil" following "All criminal".

Acts 1943, c. 73, s. 19.

Formerly:
IC 6–6–1–18.

6–6–1.1–1206   Suit against state to resolve tax dispute; jurisdiction; limitation

Sec. 1206. A person who claims that any gasoline tax, penalty, or interest was erroneously or illegally collected, or that a refund was wrongfully denied may initiate a suit against the state. The tax court has original jurisdiction of the suit, which must be commenced within three (3) years from:

(1) the date of payment of the tax, penalty, or interest; or

(2) the date of final rejection by the administrator of a refund claim.

As added by Acts 1979, P.L.79, SEC.1. Amended by Acts 1979, P.L.71, SEC.16; Acts 1980, P.L.51, SEC.52; P.L.291–1985, SEC.9.

Historical and Statutory Notes

Acts 1979, P.L. 71, § 16, substituted "three (3)" for "four (4)" in the introductory clause of the second sentence.

Acts 1980, P.L. 51, § 52, emerg. eff. Feb. 22, 1980, substituted "gasoline" for "motor fuel".

P.L.291-1985, Sec.9, eff. July 1, 1986, substituted "The tax court has original jurisdiction"

for "The Marion County circuit court shall have original jurisdiction" in the introductory clause of the second sentence.

Formerly:

IC 6-6-1-25.
Acts 1943, c. 73, § 26.

Library References

Taxation ☞1336.
WESTLAW Topic No. 371.

C.J.S. Taxation § 1252.
I.L.E. Taxation §§ 187 to 190.

6-6-1.1-1301 to 6-6-1.1-1304 Repealed

(Repealed by Acts 1980, P.L.61, SEC.15.)

Historical and Statutory Notes

Acts 1980, P.L. 61, provided in § 16 that the act takes effect Jan. 1, 1981.

Former §§ 6-6-1.1-1301 and 6-6-1.1-1302 related to penalties for failure to pay taxes and file reports.

Former § 6-6-1.1-1303 prohibited the sale of fuel by tax delinquent distributors.

Former § 6-6-1.1-1304 related to the wrongful disclosure of information.

Provisions pertaining to confidentiality and penalties and interest in tax matters are now contained in §§ 6-8.1-7-1 et seq. and 6-8.1-10-1 et seq.

Formerly:

Acts 1979, P.L.71, SEC.17.
Acts 1979, P.L.79, SEC.1.
Acts 1979, P.L.321, SEC.4.
Acts 1980, P.L.51, SEC.53.

6-6-1.1-1305 Submission of false information on invoice to support refund or credit; forfeiture

Sec. 1305. A person who changes the date, name, gallonage, or other information shown on an invoice used to support a refund or a credit claim under section 904.1 of this chapter, or who submits false information on an invoice, forfeits the right to a refund or credit on that invoice. However, the administrator may approve a claim supported by an altered or changed invoice if he finds that the change or alteration was not made to improperly obtain a refund.

As added by Acts 1979, P.L.79, SEC.1. Amended by Acts 1979, P.L.71, SEC.18; P.L.1-1991, SEC.62.

Historical and Statutory Notes

Acts 1979, P.L. 71, § 18, inserted "on that invoice" in the first sentence; and added the second sentence.

P.L.1-1991, Sec.62, emerg. eff. April 23, 1991.

P.L.1-1991, Sec.62, substituted "section 904.1" for "sections 904 or 905" in the first sentence.

Formerly:

IC 6-6-1-22.
IC 6-6-1-22.1.
Acts 1943, c. 73, s. 23a.
Acts 1963 (ss), c. 33, s. 2.
Acts 1965, c. 300, s. 1.
Acts 1971, P.L.69, SEC.5.
Acts 1973, P.L.53, SEC.1.
Acts 1975, P.L.352, SEC.2.

Acts 1978, P.L.2, SEC.635.
Acts 1978, P.L.47, SEC.2.

Library References

Taxation ⟳1342.
WESTLAW Topic No. 371.

C.J.S. Taxation § 1255.
I.L.E. Taxation §§ 187 to 190.

6–6–1.1–1306 Fraudulent procurement of refund or credit; offense

Sec. 1306. A person who makes a false statement in connection with a refund or credit application under section 904.1 of this chapter, or who collects or causes to be repaid to a person money to which that person is not entitled commits a Class B infraction.

As added by Acts 1979, P.L.79, SEC.1. Amended by P.L.1–1991, SEC.63.

Historical and Statutory Notes

P.L.1–1991, Sec.63, emerg. eff. April 23, 1991.

P.L.1–1991, Sec.63, substituted "section 904.1" for "section 904 or 905".

Formerly:

IC 6–6–1–22.
IC 6–6–1–22.1.

Acts 1943, c. 73, s. 23a.
Acts 1963 (ss), c. 33, s. 2.
Acts 1965, c. 300, s. 1.
Acts 1971, P.L.69, SEC.5.
Acts 1973, P.L.53, SEC.1.
Acts 1975, P.L.352, SEC.2.
Acts 1978, P.L.2, SEC.635.
Acts 1978, P.L.47, SEC.2.

Cross References

Penalties for infractions, see IC 34–28–5–4.

Library References

Taxation ⟳1343.
WESTLAW Topic No. 371.

C.J.S. Taxation § 1256.
I.L.E. Taxation §§ 187 to 190.

6–6–1.1–1307 Submission of multiple invoices for refund; offense

Sec. 1307. A person who submits an original invoice and a certified copy of an invoice, or two (2) or more certified copies of an invoice, to the administrator under section 904.1 of this chapter for the same transaction commits a Class B misdemeanor.

As added by Acts 1979, P.L.79, SEC.1. Amended by P.L.1–1991, SEC.64.

Historical and Statutory Notes

P.L.1–1991, Sec.64, emerg. eff. April 23, 1991.

P.L.1–1991, Sec.64, substituted "section 904.1" for "section 904".

Formerly:

IC 6–6–1–22.
IC 6–6–1–22.1.

Acts 1943, c. 73, s. 23a.
Acts 1963 (ss), c. 33, s. 2.
Acts 1965, c. 300, s. 1.
Acts 1971, P.L.69, SEC.5.
Acts 1973, P.L.53, SEC.1.
Acts 1975, P.L.352, SEC.2.
Acts 1978, P.L.2, SEC.635.
Acts 1978, P.L.47, SEC.2.

6–6–1.1–1308 Failure to pay over tax collected to administrator; offense

Sec. 1308. A person who receives or collects money as tax imposed under this chapter on gasoline on which he has not paid the tax, and knowingly fails to pay the money to the administrator as required under this chapter, commits a Class D felony.

As added by Acts 1979, P.L.79, SEC.1. Amended by Acts 1980, P.L.51, SEC.54.

Historical and Statutory Notes

Acts 1980, P.L. 51, § 54, emerg. eff. Feb. 22, 1980, substituted "gasoline" for "motor fuel".

Formerly:
IC 6–6–1–28.

Acts 1943, c. 73, s. 29.
Acts 1971, P.L.69, SEC.6.
Acts 1978, P.L.2, SEC.636.

Notes of Decisions

Indictment and information 1

1. Indictment and information

In prosecution for embezzlement of motor vehicle fuel license fees, affidavit charging that accused was dealer engaged in selling motor vehicle fuel, and that he received money as license fees, was not insufficient for failure to charge that money was received in fiduciary capacity, since fees collected were property of state and accused was trustee of fees. Roberts v. State, 1936, 200 N.E. 699, 210 Ind. 375.

6–6–1.1–1309 Distributor; violations; offense

Sec. 1309. Except as otherwise provided by this chapter, a distributor who:

(1) recklessly fails to file the returns or statements and to pay the taxes as required by this chapter; or

(2) knowingly fails to keep correct records, books, and accounts required by this chapter;

commits a Class B misdemeanor.

As added by Acts 1979, P.L.79, SEC.1. Amended by Acts 1980, P.L.61, SEC.9.

Historical and Statutory Notes

Acts 1980, P.L. 61, § 9, eff. Jan. 1, 1981, deleted a former Cl. 3 which read:

"(3) knowingly fails to permit the administrator to make an examination authorized by section 604 of this chapter."

Formerly:
IC 6–6–1–28.
Acts 1943, c. 73, s. 29.
Acts 1971, P.L.69, SEC.6.
Acts 1978, P.L.2, SEC.636.

Cross References

Penalty for Class B misdemeanor, see IC 35–50–3–3.

Library References

Taxation ⚯1343.
WESTLAW Topic No. 371.

C.J.S. Taxation § 1256.
I.L.E. Taxation §§ 187 to 190.

6–6–1.1–1310   Use of untaxed gasoline; offense

Sec. 1310.   A person who knowingly uses gasoline on which the tax has not been paid commits a Class B misdemeanor.

As added by Acts 1979, P.L.79, SEC.1.   Amended by Acts 1980, P.L.51, SEC.55.

Historical and Statutory Notes

Acts 1980, P.L. 51, § 55, emerg. eff. Feb. 22, 1980, substituted "gasoline" for "motor fuel".

Formerly:
IC 6–6–1–28.

Acts 1943, c. 73, s. 29.
Acts 1971, P.L.69, SEC.6.
Acts 1978, P.L.2, SEC. 636.

Cross References

Penalty for Class B misdemeanor, see IC 35–50–3–3.

Library References

Taxation ⚯1343.
WESTLAW Topic No. 371.

C.J.S. Taxation § 1256.
I.L.E. Taxation §§ 187 to 190.

6–6–1.1–1311   Use or sale in Indiana of tax-exempt gasoline purchased for export; offense; tax liability; export sales excepted

Sec. 1311.   (a) Except as otherwise permitted by this chapter, a person who purchases tax-exempt gasoline for export and uses or sells any of the gasoline in Indiana with the intent to avoid payment of the tax imposed by this chapter commits a Class A misdemeanor.   In addition, for purposes of this chapter, such a person is considered the "distributor" with respect to all gasoline so purchased and to have "received" the gasoline as defined in this chapter, and he is liable for the full amount of the tax imposed by this chapter on the gasoline and a penalty equal to fifty percent (50%) of that tax.

(b) Subsection (a) does not apply if the gasoline is sold in Indiana for export, provided the person furnishes proof at the time and in the manner prescribed by the administrator.

As added by Acts 1979, P.L.79, SEC.1.   Amended by Acts 1980, P.L.51, SEC.56.

Historical and Statutory Notes

Acts 1980, P.L. 51, § 56, emerg. eff. Feb. 22, 1980, substituted "gasoline" for "motor fuel" throughout the section.

Acts 1943, c. 73, s. 29.
Acts 1971, P.L.69, SEC.6.
Acts 1978, P.L.2, SEC.636.

Formerly:
  IC 6–6–1–28.

Cross References

Penalty for Class A misdemeanor, see IC 35–50–3–2.

Library References

Taxation ☞1343.
WESTLAW Topic No. 371.

C.J.S. Taxation § 1256.
I.L.E. Taxation §§ 187 to 190.

6–6–1.1–1312   Reckless violations; offense

Sec. 1312.   A person who recklessly violates a provision of this chapter for which no specific penalty is provided commits a Class B misdemeanor.

As added by Acts 1979, P.L.79, SEC.1.

Historical and Statutory Notes

Formerly:
  IC 6–6–1–28.
  Acts 1943, c. 72, s. 29.

Acts 1971, P.L.69, SEC.6.
Acts 1978, P.L.2, SEC.636.

Cross References

Penalty for Class B misdemeanor, see IC 35–50–3–3.

6–6–1.1–1313   Evasion of tax; offense

Sec. 1313.   A person who violates sections 1309 through 1311 of this chapter with intent to evade the tax imposed by this chapter or to defraud the state commits a Class D felony.

As added by Acts 1979, P.L.79, SEC.1.

Historical and Statutory Notes

Formerly:
  IC 6–6–1–28.
  Acts 1943, c. 73, s. 29.

Acts 1971, P.L.69, SEC.6.
Acts 1978, P.L.2, SEC.636.

Cross References

Penalty for Class D felony, see IC 35–50–2–7.

Library References

Taxation ☞1343.
WESTLAW Topic No. 371.

C.J.S. Taxation § 1256.
I.L.E. Taxation §§ 187 to 190.

6–6–1.1–1314   Failure to keep books and records; penalty

Sec. 1314. A person subject to the tax imposed under section 201 of this chapter who fails to keep books and records as required by IC 6–8.1–5 is subject to the penalty under IC 6–8.1–10–4.

As added by P.L.97–1987, SEC.15.

Historical and Statutory Notes

P.L.97–1987, Sec.15, adding this section, was made effective Sept. 1, 1987.

6–6–1.1–1315   Failure to file reports; incomplete reports; civil penalty

Sec. 1315. A person who:

(1) is subject to the tax imposed by section 201 of this chapter; and

(2) fails to file a report or files an incomplete report required by section 501 or 606 of this chapter;

is subject to a civil penalty of one hundred dollars ($100) for each violation, as reasonably determined by the department. As used in this section, an incomplete report includes a report that does not include all schedules required by the administrator.

As added by P.L.97–1987, SEC.16.

Historical and Statutory Notes

P.L.97–1987, Sec.16, adding this section, was made effective Sept. 1, 1987.

6–6–1.1–1316   Breaking fuel pump seals; failure to report meter readings; removing post signs; failure to notify; offenses

Sec. 1316. (a) A person:

(1) who knowingly breaks a seal on a sealed fuel pump without authorization; or

(2) who knowingly fails or refuses to report meter readings under section 1008 or section 1110 of this chapter;

commits a Class D felony.

(b) A person who, without authorization:

(1) removes;

(2) alters;

(3) defaces; or

(4) covers;

a sign postéd by the department that states that no transactions involving gasoline, gasohol, aviation gasoline, or marina gasoline may be made at a location commits a Class B misdemeanor. However, the offense is a Class D felony if it is committed with the intent to evade the tax imposed by this chapter or to defraud the state.

(c) A dealer or licensed distributor shall notify the department of:

(1) a broken fuel pump seal; or

(2) a removed, altered, defaced, or covered sign that has been posted by the department.

(d) A dealer or licensed distributor that fails to notify the department, as required by subsection (c), within two (2) days after:

(1) a fuel pump seal is broken; or

(2) a sign posted by the department has been removed, altered, defaced, or covered;

commits a Class D felony.

As added by P.L.97–1987, SEC.17.

Historical and Statutory Notes

P.L.97–1987, Sec.17, adding this section, was made effective Sept. 1, 1987.

Chapter 1.5

Marine Fuel Tax

6–6–1.5–1 to 6–6–1.5–4   Repealed

(Repealed by Acts 1979, P.L.79, SEC.2.)

Historical and Statutory Notes

Acts 1979, P.L. 79, provided in § 6, containing emergency clause, that the act takes effect April 5, 1979.

The former chapter related to the marine fuel tax.

Formerly:

IC 6–6–1.5–4.

Acts 1971, P.L.70, SEC.1.

DISPOSITION TABLE

The subject matter of the repealed sections of Title 6 of the Indiana Code is now covered in new sections of Title 6, West's Annotated Indiana Code as follows:

Repealed Sections	New Sections	Repealed Sections	New Sections
6–6–1.5–1	6–6–1.1–201, 6–6–1.1–302, 6–6–1.1–802		6–6–1.1–501,
		6–6–1.5–3	6–6–1.1–801, 6–6–1.1–802
6–6–1.5–2	6–6–1.1–201,	6–6–1.5–4	6–6–1.1–806 [Repealed]

Chapter 2

Motor Fuel Use Tax

6–6–2–1 to 6–6–2–15   Repealed

(Repealed by Acts 1980, P.L.51, SEC.66.)

Historical and Statutory Notes

Acts 1980, P.L. 51, provided in § 70, containing emergency clause, that the act takes effect Feb. 22, 1980.

Former § 6–6–2–1 entitled the act the "Fuel Use Tax Act."

Former § 6–6–2–2 contained definitions.

Former § 6–6–2–3 related to the purpose of the tax.

Former § 6–6–2–4 related to the rate of the tax and to exemptions.

Former § 6–6–2–5 related to the licensing of users, and fuel oil dealers and distributors.

Former § 6–6–2–5.5 related to license fees.

Former § 6–6–2–6 related to monthly reports and payments.

Former § 6–6–2–7 related to cancellation of licenses.

Former § 6–6–2–8 related to discontinuance notices.

Former § 6–6–2–9 related to penalties for failure to pay taxes.

Former § 6–6–2–9.5 required reporting even when no tax liability existed.

Former § 6–6–2–9.6 related to sealed pumps.

Former § 6–6–2–10 related to procedures in the event of a tax deficiency.

Former § 6–6–2–11 related to record-keeping.

Former § 6–6–2–12 related to investigatory powers.

Former § 6–6–2–13 and 6–6–2–14 related to refunds of taxes erroneously collected.

Former § 6–6–2–15 related to penalties for miscellaneous violations.

Formerly:

IC 6–6–2–9, 6–6–2–9.5.
IC 6–6–2–10.
IC 6–6–2–11, 6–6–2–12.
Acts 1943, c. 74, ss. 9 to 12.
Acts 1947, c. 343, ss. 7 to 10.
Acts 1971, P.L.71, SECS.5, 7, 8.
Acts 1978, P.L.2, SEC.638.
Acts 1979, P.L.80, SECS.3, 4, 6.

DISPOSITION TABLE

Showing where the subject matter of the repealed sections of Title 6 of the Indiana Code is now covered in new sections of Title 6, West's Annotated Indiana Code.

Repealed Sections	New Sections	Repealed Sections	New Sections
6–6–2–1	6–6–2.1–101	6–6–2–5.5	6–6–2.1–411
6–6–2–2	6–6–2.1–103	6–6–2–6	6–6–2.1–501 to
6–6–2–3	6–6–2.1–702,		6–6–2.1–507,
	6–6–2.1–703,		6–6–2.1–509,
6–6–2–4(a)	6–6–2.1–201		6–6–2.1–1101 [Repealed]
6–6–2–4(b)	6–6–2.1–701(a),	6–6–2–7	6–6–2.1–415 to
	6–6–2.1–701(b),		6–6–2.1–417
6–6–2–4(c)	6–6–2.1–702	6–6–2–8	6–6–2.1–518
6–6–2–4(d)	6–6–2.1–301	6–6–2–9	6–2.1–1203 to
6–6–2–5	6–6–2.1–401 to		6–6–2.1–1205 [Repealed]
	6–6–2.1–410,	6–6–2–9.5	6–6–2.1–508 [Repealed],
	6-7-2.1-412 to		6–6–2.1–1206 [Repealed]
	6–6–2.1–414,	6–6–2–9.6(a)	6–6–2.1–1007
	6-7-2.1-418	6–6–2–9.6(b)	6–6–2.1–1207

Special Fuel Tax

6–6–2–15.5 Repealed

(Repealed by Acts 1978, P.L.2, SEC.656; Acts 1980, P.L.51, SEC.66.)

Historical and Statutory Notes

Acts 1978, P.L. 2, provided in § 3602(a), containing emergency clause, that the act takes effect July 1, 1978.

The former section related to penalties for fraudulent acts.

Formerly:

Acts 1971, P.L.71, SEC.10.

6–6–2–16 Repealed

(Repealed by Acts 1980, P.L.51, SEC.66.)

Historical and Statutory Notes

Acts 1980, P.L. 51, provided in § 70, containing emergency clause, that the act takes effect Feb. 22, 1980.

The former section related to the exchange of information among states.

See, now, IC 6–6–2.1–1009.

Chapter 2.1

Special Fuel Tax

Library References

Taxation ☞1204.
C.J.S. Licenses §§ 1 to 3.

6–6–2.1–101 to 6–6–2.1–105 Repealed

(Repealed by P.L.277–1993(ss), SEC.56.)

Historical and Statutory Notes

P.L.277–1993(ss), Sec.56, eff. October 1, 1993.

Governor's veto of H.E.A.1001(ss)(P.L.277–1993(ss)) of the 1993 Special Session was overridden by the General Assembly on June 30, 1993.

P.L.278–1993(ss), Sec.32, emerg. eff. retroactive to June 28, 1993, provides:

"(a) Notwithstanding the passage of HEA 1001ss–1993, the provisions of this act supersede the provisions of any conflicting provisions in HEA 1001ss–1993.

"(b) IC 1–1–3.1 does not apply to this act or to HEA 1001ss–1993.

"(c) Notwithstanding IC 1–1–3.1, the effective date of the Sections in this act and HEA 1001ss–1993 are as specified in this act and HEA 1001ss–1993, respectively, regardless of a veto of either act by the governor and the subsequent veto override of either or both acts."

Former IC 6–6–2.1–101 related to title of special fuel tax.

Former IC 6–6–2.1–102 related to application of definitions and rules of construction.

Former IC 6–6–2.1–103 related to definitions.

Former IC 6–6–2.1–104 related to rules of construction.

Former IC 6–6–2.1–105 related to citation to prior law.

See, now, generally, IC 6–6–2.5–1 et seq.

Formerly:
IC 6–6–2–1.
IC 6–6–2–2.
Acts 1943, c. 74, ss. 1, 2.
Acts 1947, c. 343, s. 1.
Acts 1951, c. 280, s. 1.
Acts 1971, P.L. 71, SEC.1.

Acts 1979, P.L.80, SEC.1.
Acts 1980, P.L.51, SEC.57.
Acts 1980, P.L.58, SEC.1.
Acts 1982, P.L.58, SEC.1.
P.L.77–1985, SEC.4.
P.L.73–1986, SEC.1.
P.L.97–1987, SEC.18.
P.L.96–1989, SEC.4.
P.L.2–1991, SEC.41.
P.L.8–1993, SEC.99.

6–6–2.1–201, 6–6–2.1–202   Repealed

(Repealed by P.L.277–1993(ss), SEC.56.)

Historical and Statutory Notes

P.L.277–1993(ss), Sec.56, eff. October 1, 1993.

Governor's veto of H.E.A.1001(ss)(P.L.277–1993(ss)) of the 1993 Special Session was overridden by the General Assembly on June 30, 1993.

P.L.278–1993(ss), Sec.32, emerg. eff. retroactive to June 28, 1993, provides:

"(a) Notwithstanding the passage of HEA 1001ss–1993, the provisions of this act supersede the provisions of any conflicting provisions in HEA 1001ss–1993.

"(b) IC 1–1–3.1 does not apply to this act or to HEA 1001ss–1993.

"(c) Notwithstanding IC 1–1–3.1, the effective date of the Sections in this act and HEA 1001ss–1993 are as specified in this act and HEA 1001ss–1993, respectively, regardless of a veto of either act by the governor and the subsequent veto override of either or both acts."

Former IC 6–6–2.1–201 related to imposition of tax rate.

Former IC 6–6–2.1–202 related to inventory tax on stored special fuel.

See, now, generally, IC 6–6–2.5–1 et seq.

Formerly:
IC 6–6–2–4.
Acts 1943, c. 74, s. 4.
Acts 1947, c. 343, s. 2.
Acts 1951, c. 280, s. 2.
Acts 1957, c. 51, s. 1.
Acts 1969, c. 320, s. 1.
Acts 1975, P.L.66, SEC.1.
Acts 1978, P.L.47, SEC.3.
Acts 1979, P.L.80, SEC.2.
Acts 1980, P.L.10, sec.10.
Acts 1980, P.L.51, SEC.57.
Acts 1982, P.L.58, SEC.2.
P.L.59–1985, SECS.13, 14.
P.L.8–1988, SEC.2.

6–6–2.1–203   Alternative fuel decal; annual fee; registration of alternative fuel dealers

Sec. 203.   (a) The owner of one (1) of the following motor vehicles that is registered in Indiana and that is propelled by alternative fuel shall obtain an alternative fuel decal for the motor vehicle and pay an annual fee in accordance with the following schedule:

SCHEDULE

Motor Vehicle	Annual Fee
A passenger motor vehicle, truck, or bus, the declared gross weight of which is equal to or less than 9,000 pounds, that is owned by a public or private utility.	$100
A recreational vehicle that is owned by a public or private utility.	$100

Motor Vehicle	Annual Fee
A truck or bus, the declared gross weight of which is greater than 9,000 pounds but equal to or less than 11,000 pounds, that is owned by a public or private utility	$175
An alternative fuel delivery truck powered by alternative fuel, which is a truck the declared gross weight of which is greater than 11,000 pounds	$250
A truck or bus, the declared gross weight of which is greater than 11,000 pounds, except an alternative fuel delivery truck	$300
A tractor, designed to be used with a semitrailer	$500

Only one (1) fee is required to be paid per motor vehicle per year.

(b) The annual fee may be prorated on a quarterly basis if:

(1) application is made after June 30 of a year; and

(2) the motor vehicle is newly:

(A) converted to alternative fuel;

(B) purchased; or

(C) registered in Indiana.

(c) The department may by rule adopted under IC 4–22–2 increase or decrease the fees for decals under this section. If the department increases or decreases fees, the fees must be established so that owners of motor vehicles propelled by alternative fuel pay an amount substantially comparable to license taxes paid by owners of motor vehicles propelled by special fuel.

As added by P.L.73–1986, SEC.2. Amended by P.L.277–1993(ss), SEC.43; P.L.79–1993, SEC.1; P.L.85–1995, SEC.12.

Historical and Statutory Notes

P.L.73–1986, Sec.2, eff. July 1, 1986, added this section.

P.L.79–1993, Sec.1, eff. Jan. 1, 1994, in Subsec. (a), in the introductory sentence, inserted "one (1) of the following", and substituted "vehicles" for "vehicle"; redesignated former Subsec. (d) as Subsec. (c); and deleted former Subsec. (c), which read:

"(c) The owner of a motor vehicle that is:

"(1) registered outside Indiana; and

"(2) operated on a public highway in Indiana;

"shall obtain a temporary trip permit. An alternative fuel temporary trip permit may be purchased from a licensed special fuel dealer who sells alternative fuels. A temporary trip permit is valid for seventy-two (72) hours from the time of purchase. The fee for each permit is five dollars and fifty cents ($5.50)."

P.L.79–1993, Sec.5, provides:

"(a) Notwithstanding IC 6–6–2.1–203, the annual fee for an alternative fuel decal for:

"(1) a passenger motor vehicle, truck, or bus, the declared gross weight of which is equal to or less than nine thousand (9,000) pounds; or

"(2) a recreational vehicle;

"applies only to those vehicles owned by an alternative fuel provider during 1994 and 1995.

"(b) This Section expires January 1, 1996."

P.L.277–1993(ss), Sec.43, eff. Oct. 1, 1993, inserted the first sentence of Subsec. (a); inserted the Subsec. (b) designation; redesignated former Subsecs. (b) to (d) as Subsecs. (c) to (e); in Subsec. (d), substituted "registered alternative" for "licensed special", and inserted the sentence relating to the fee for the alternative fuel temporary trip permit; and added Subsecs. (f) to (j).

Governor's veto of H.E.A.1001(ss)(P.L.277–1993(ss)) of the 1993 Special Session was overridden June 30, 1993.

Section 32 of P.L.278–1993(ss), emerg. eff. retroactive to June 28, 1993, provides:

"(a) Notwithstanding the passage of HEA 1001ss–1993, the provisions of this act supersede the provisions of any conflicting provisions in HEA 1001ss–1993.

"(b) IC 1–1–3.1 does not apply to this act or to HEA 1001ss–1993.

"(c) Notwithstanding IC 1–1–3.1, the effective date of the Sections in this act and HEA 1001ss–1993 are as specified in this act and HEA 1001ss–1993, respectively, regardless of a veto of either act by the governor and the subsequent veto override of either or both acts."

P.L.85–1995, Sec.12, eff. April 1, 1996, amended the section by adding "that is owned by a public or private utility" to Subsec. (a).

6–6–2.1–204 Alternative fuel decal; issuance; effectiveness

Sec. 204. (a) The administrator shall issue an alternative fuel decal to an owner of a motor vehicle propelled by alternative fuel who applies for a decal, pays to the administrator the fee, and provides the information that is required by the administrator.

(b) The decal is effective from April 1 of each year through March 31 of the next year. The administrator may extend the expiration date for no more than thirty (30) days. During the month of March, the owner shall display the decal valid through March 31 or the decal issued to the owner for the next twelve (12) months. If the administrator grants an extension of the expiration date, the owner shall continue to display the decal for which the extension was granted.

As added by P.L.73–1986, SEC.3.

Historical and Statutory Notes

P.L.73–1986, Sec.3, eff. July 1, 1986, added this section.

6–6–2.1–205 Display of alternative fuel decal; issuance of new decal; credit for decal for other vehicles

Sec. 205. (a) The owner of a motor vehicle propelled by alternative fuel shall affix the alternative fuel decal to the lower left side of the front windshield of the motor vehicle for which it was issued. The decal may be displayed only on the motor vehicle for which the decal was issued.

(b) Upon application of the owner and surrender of a decal, the administrator may issue a new decal or give credit toward the fee for a decal for another vehicle or for a subsequent twelve (12) months. Upon receipt of the new decal or a credit statement, the owner shall return to the administrator:

(1) the old decal; or

(2) a sworn statement indicating that the old decal has been destroyed.

(c) A credit under this section shall be computed by multiplying the fee paid for the old decal by a fraction. The denominator of the fraction is the number of whole and partial quarters for which the old decal was issued. The numerator of the fraction is the number of remaining whole quarters that the old decal would have been valid.

(d) A credit under this section may not be given during the last three (3) months before the decal expires.

(e) No refunds may be allowed under this section.

As added by P.L.73–1986, SEC.4.

Historical and Statutory Notes

P.L.73–1986, Sec.4, eff. July 1, 1986, added this section.

6–6–2.1–206 Use of alternative fuel; conditions

Sec. 206. A person may place or cause to be placed alternative fuel into the fuel supply tank of a motor vehicle only under one (1) of the following conditions:

(1) The motor vehicle has a valid alternative fuel decal affixed to the front windshield.

(2) The operator has a copy of a completed application for a decal for the motor vehicle, which application was filed with the department no more than thirty (30) days before the sale of the fuel.

As added by P.L.73–1986, SEC.5. Amended by P.L.79–1993, SEC.3.

Historical and Statutory Notes

P.L.73–1986, Sec.5, eff. July 1, 1986, added this section.

P.L.79–1993, Sec.3, deleted former Subd.(2), which read:

"The motor vehicle is registered outside Indiana, and the operator has a valid alternative fuel temporary trip permit issued for the motor vehicle."

In addition, P.L. 79–1993, Sec.3, redesignated former Subd.(3) as Subd.(2).

6–6–2.1–301 Repealed

(Repealed by P.L.277–1993(ss), SEC.56.)

Historical and Statutory Notes

P.L.277–1993(ss), Sec.56, eff. October 1, 1993.

Governor's veto of H.E.A.1001(ss)(P.L.277–1993(ss)) of the 1993 Special Session was overridden by the General Assembly on June 30, 1993.

P.L.278–1993(ss), Sec.32, emerg. eff. retroactive to June 28, 1993, provides:

"(a) Notwithstanding the passage of HEA 1001ss–1993, the provisions of this act supersede the provisions of any conflicting provisions in HEA 1001ss–1993.

"(b) IC 1–1–3.1 does not apply to this act or to HEA 1001ss–1993.

"(c) Notwithstanding IC 1–1–3.1, the effective date of the Sections in this act and HEA 1001ss–1993 are as specified in this act and HEA 1001ss–1993, respectively, regardless of a veto of either act by the governor and the subsequent veto override of either or both acts."

See, now, generally, IC 6–6–2.5–1 et seq.

Former IC 6–6–2.1–301 related to exemptions.

Formerly:

IC 6–6–2–4.
Acts 1943, c. 74, s. 4.
Acts 1947, c. 343, s. 2.
Acts 1951, c. 280, s. 2.
Acts 1957, c. 51, s. 1.

Acts 1969, c. 320, s. 1.
Acts 1975, P.L.66, SEC.1.
Acts 1978, P.L.47, SEC.3.
Acts 1979, P.L.80, SEC.2.

Acts 1980, P.L.51, SEC.57.
Acts 1980, P.L.58, SEC.2.
Acts 1981, P.L.11, SEC.34.
P.L.73–1986, SEC.6.
P.L.97–1987, SEC.19.

6–6–2.1–401 to 6–6–2.1–404   Repealed

(Repealed by P.L.277–1993(ss), SEC.56.)

Historical and Statutory Notes

P.L.277–1993(ss), Sec.56, eff. Oct. 1, 1993.

Governor's veto of H.E.A.1001(ss)(P.L.277–1993(ss)) of the 1993 Special Session was overridden by the General Assembly on June 30, 1993.

P.L.278–1993(ss), Sec.32, emerg. eff. retroactive to June 28, 1993, provides:

"(a) Notwithstanding the passage of HEA 1001ss–1993, the provisions of this act supersede the provisions of any conflicting provisions in HEA 1001ss–1993.

"(b) IC 1–1–3.1 does not apply to this act or to HEA 1001ss–1993.

"(c) Notwithstanding IC 1–1–3.1, the effective date of the Sections in this act and HEA 1001ss–1993 are as specified in this act and HEA 1001ss–1993, respectively, regardless of a veto of either act by the governor and the subsequent veto override of either or both acts."

Former IC 6–6–401 related to special fuel dealers.

Former IC 6–6–402 related to application for dealer's license.

Former IC 6–6–403 related to license.

Former IC 6–6–404 related to application for user's license.

See, now, generally, IC 6–6–2.5–1 et seq.

Formerly:
IC 6–6–2–5.
Acts 1943, c. 74, s. 5.
Acts 1947, c. 343, s. 3.
Acts 1951, c. 280, s. 3.
Acts 1959, c. 98, s. 1.
Acts 1969, c. 320, s. 3.
Acts 1971, P.L.71, SEC.2.
Acts 1980, P.L.51, SEC.57.
Acts 1982, P.L.58, SECS.3, 4.
P.L.77–1985, SEC.5.
P.L.73–1986, SEC.7.

6–6–2.1–405, 6–6–2.1–406   Repealed

(Repealed by P.L.77–1985, SEC.35.)

Historical and Statutory Notes

P.L.77–1985 provided in Section 37 that Section 35 of the act takes effect Sept. 1, 1985.

Section 37 of P.L.77–1985 was amended by Section 39 of P.L.59–1985 to change the effective date of the repeal of these sections by P.L.77–1985 from Sept. 1, 1985 to July 1, 1985.

Former section 6–6–2.1–405 required a license for fuel oil distributors.

Former section 6–6–2.1–406 related to the application for a fuel oil distributor's license.

Formerly:
IC 6–6–2–5.
Acts 1943, c. 74, s. 5.
Acts 1947, c. 343, s. 3.
Acts 1951, c. 280, s. 3.
Acts 1959, c. 98, s. 1.
Acts 1969, c. 320, s. 3.
Acts 1971, P.L.71, SEC.2.

6–6–2.1–407 to 6–6–2.1–420   Repealed

(Repealed by P.L.277–1993(ss), SEC.56.)

Historical and Statutory Notes

P.L.277–1993(ss), Sec.56, eff. Oct. 1, 1993.

Governor's veto of H.E.A.1001(ss)(P.L.277–1993(ss)) of the 1993 Special Session was overridden by the General Assembly on June 30, 1993.

P.L.278–1993(ss), Sec.32, emerg. eff. retroactive to June 28, 1993, provides:

"(a) Notwithstanding the passage of HEA 1001ss–1993, the provisions of this act supersede the provisions of any conflicting provisions in HEA 1001ss–1993.

"(b) IC 1–1–3.1 does not apply to this act or to HEA 1001ss–1993.

"(c) Notwithstanding IC 1–1–3.1, the effective date of the Sections in this act and HEA 1001ss–1993 are as specified in this act and HEA 1001ss–1993, respectively, regardless of a veto of either act by the governor and the subsequent veto override of either or both acts."

Former IC 6–6–2.1–407 to 6–6–2.1–420 related to dealer's and user's licenses.

See, now, generally, IC 6–6–2.5–1 et seq.

Formerly:

IC 6–6–2–5.
IC 6–6–2–5.5.
IC 6–6–2–7.
Acts 1943, c. 74, ss. 5, 7.
Acts 1947, c. 343, ss. 3, 5.
Acts 1951, c. 280, s. 3.
Acts 1959, c. 98, s. 1.
Acts 1969, c. 320, s. 3.
Acts 1971, P.L.71, SECS.2, 3.
Acts 1980, P.L.51, SEC.57.
Acts 1980, P.L.59, SEC.1.
Acts 1982, P.L.58, SEC.5.
P.L.77–1985, SECS.6 to 12.
P.L.73–1986, SEC.8.
P.L.97–1987, SECS.20 to 25.
P.L.96–1989, SECS.5 to 7.
P.L.79–1993, SEC.2.

6–6–2.1–501 to 6–6–2.1–507   Repealed

(Repealed by P.L.277–1993(ss), SEC.57.)

Historical and Statutory Notes

P.L.277–1993(ss), SEC.57, eff. March 1, 1994.

Governor's veto of H.E.A.1001(ss)(P.L.277–1993(ss) of the 1993 Special Session was overridden by the General Assembly on June 30, 1993.

P.L.278–1993(ss), SEC.32, emerg. eff. retroactive to June 28, 1993, provides:

"(a) Notwithstanding the passage of HEA 1001ss–1993, the provisions of this act supersede the provisions of any conflicting provisions in HEA 1001ss–1993.

"(b) IC 1–1–3.1 does not apply to this act or to HEA 1001ss–1993.

"(c) Notwithstanding IC 1–1–3.1, the effective date of the Sections in this act and HEA 1001ss–1993 are as specified in this act and HEA 1001ss–1993, respectively, regardless of a veto of either act by the governor and the subsequent veto override of either or both acts."

Former IC 6–6–2.1–501 to 6–6–2.1–507 related to monthly reports and payments.

Formerly:

IC 6–6–2–6.
Acts 1943, c. 74, s. 6.
Acts 1947, c. 343, s. 4.
Acts 1951, c. 280, s. 4.
Acts 1957, c. 314, s. 1.
Acts 1969, c. 320, s. 2.
Acts 1971, P.L.71, SEC.4.
Acts 1980, P.L.10, SEC.11.
Acts 1980, P.L.51, SEC.57.
Acts 1980, P.L.58, SECS.4 to 6.
Acts 1982, P.L.58, SECS.7 to 10.
P.L.59–1985, SEC.15.
P.L.77–1985, SECS.13 to 17.
P.L.73–1986, SEC.9.
P.L.92–1987, SECS.7, 8.
P.L.97–1987, SEC.26.
P.L.63–1988, SECS.13, 14.

6–6–2.1–508   Repealed

(Repealed by Acts 1980, P.L.61, SEC.15.)

Historical and Statutory Notes

Acts 1980, P.L. 61, provided in § 16 that the act takes effect Jan. 1, 1981.

The former section related to monthly reports required regardless of tax liability.

Formerly:

Acts 1980, P.L.51, SEC.57.

6–6–2.1–509   Repealed

(Repealed by P.L.227–1993(ss), SEC.32.)

Historical and Statutory Notes

P.L.277–1993(ss), Sec.57, eff. March 1, 1994.

Governor's veto of H.E.A.1001(ss)(P.L.277–1993(ss)) of the 1993 Special Session was overridden by the General Assembly on June 30, 1993.

P.L.278–1993(ss), Sec.32, emerg. eff. retroactive to June 28, 1993, provides:

"(a) Notwithstanding the passage of HEA 1001ss–1993, the provisions of this act supersede the provisions of any conflicting provisions in HEA 1001ss–1993.

"(b) IC 1–1–3.1 does not apply to this act or to HEA 1001ss–1993.

"(c) Notwithstanding IC 1–1–3.1, the effective date of the Sections in this act and HEA

1001ss–1993 are as specified in this act and HEA 1001ss–1993, respectively, regardless of a veto of either act by the governor and the subsequent veto override of either or both acts."

Former IC 6–6–2.1–509 related to waiver of inventory and purchase or acquisition reports.

Formerly:

IC 6–6–2–6.
Acts 1943, c. 74, s. 6.
Acts 1947, c. 343, s. 4.
Acts 1951, c. 280, s. 4.
Acts 1957, c. 314, s. 1.
Acts 1969, c. 320, s. 2.
Acts 1971, P.L.71, SEC.4.
Acts 1980, P.L.51, SEC.57.

6–6–2.1–510 to 6–6–2.1–513   Repealed

(Repealed by Acts 1980, P.L.61, SEC.15.)

Historical and Statutory Notes

Acts 1980, P.L. 61, provided in § 16 that the act takes effect Jan. 1, 1981.

Former § 6–6–2.1–510 related to fraudulent tax report filing.

Former §§ 6–6–2.1–511 and 6–6–2.1–512 related to assessments of unpaid taxes.

Former § 6–6–2.1–513 related to collection proceedings.

Provisions pertaining to the investigation, assessment and collection of taxes are now contained in §§ 6–8.1–5–1 et seq. and 6–8.1–8–1 et seq.

Formerly:

Acts 1980, P.L.51, SEC.57.

6–6–2.1–514 to 6–6–2.1–518   Repealed

(Repealed by P.L.277–1993(ss), SEC.57.)

Historical and Statutory Notes

Former IC 6–6–2.1–514 related to collection of unpaid tax or fee as debt.

Former IC 6–6–2.1–515 related to appointment of receiver.

Former IC 6–6–2.1–516 related to bond and powers of receiver.

Former IC 6–6–2.1–517 related to appeal concerning appointment of receiver.

Former IC 6–6–2.1–518 related to discontinuance of dealer's or user's business.

Formerly:

IC 6–6–2–8.
IC 6–6–2–10.5.
Acts 1943, c. 74, s. 8.

Acts 1947, c. 343, s. 6.
Acts 1979, P.L.80, SEC.5.
Acts 1980, P.L.51, SEC.57.
P.L.77–1985, SEC.18.
P.L.73–1986, SEC.10.

6–6–2.1–519 Repealed

(Repealed by P.L.79–1993, SEC.6.)

Historical and Statutory Notes

P.L.79–1993, Sec.6, became effective July 1, 1993.

P.L.277–1993(ss), Sec.56, which also repealed this section, became effective Oct. 1, 1993.

Governor's veto of H.E.A.1001(ss)(P.L.277–1993(ss)) of the 1993 Special Session was overridden by the General Assembly on June 30, 1993.

Section 32 of P.L.278–1993(ss), emerg. eff. retroactive to June 28, 1993, provides:

"(a) Notwithstanding the passage of HEA 1001ss–1993, the provisions of this act supersede the provisions of any conflicting provisions in HEA 1001ss–1993.

"(b) IC 1–1–3.1 does not apply to this act or to HEA 1001ss–1993.

"(c) Notwithstanding IC 1–1–3.1, the effective date of the Sections in this act and HEA 1001ss–1993 are as specified in this act and HEA 1001ss–1993, respectively, regardless of a veto of either act by the governor and the subsequent veto override of either or both acts."

Former IC 6–6–2.1–519 related to alternative fuel temporary trip permit fees.

See, now, generally, section 6–6–2.5–1 et seq.

Formerly:

P.L.73–1986, SEC.11.

6–6–2.1–601 to 6–6–2.1–603 Repealed

(Repealed by Acts 1980, P.L.61, SEC.15.)

Historical and Statutory Notes

Acts 1980, P.L. 61, provided in § 16 that the act takes effect Jan. 1, 1981.

The former sections related to the keeping and examination of tax records.

Provisions pertaining to tax books and records are now contained in § 6–8.1–5–4.

Formerly:

Acts 1980, P.L.51, SEC.57.
Acts 1980, P.L.58, SEC.7.

6–6–2.1–604 to 6–6–2.1–606 Repealed

(Repealed by P.L.277–1993(ss), SEC.56.)

Historical and Statutory Notes

P.L.277–1993(ss), Sec.56, eff. Oct. 1, 1993.

Governor's veto of H.E.A.1001(ss)(P.L.277–1993(ss)) of the 1993 Special Session was overridden by the General Assembly on June 30, 1993.

P.L.278–1993(ss), Sec.32, emerg. eff. retroactive to June 28, 1993, provides:

"(a) Notwithstanding the passage of HEA 1001ss–1993, the provisions of this act super-

sede the provisions of any conflicting provisions in HEA 1001ss–1993.

"(b) IC 1–1–3.1 does not apply to this act or to HEA 1001ss–1993.

"(c) Notwithstanding IC 1–1–3.1, the effective date of the Sections in this act and HEA 1001ss–1993 are as specified in this act and HEA 1001ss–1993, respectively, regardless of a veto of either act by the governor and the subsequent veto override of either or both acts."

Former IC 6–6–2.1–604 related to reporting of special fuel deliveries.

Former IC 6–6–2.1–605 related to accounting of special fuel.

Former IC 6–6–2.1–606 related to reports for informational purposes.

See, now, generally, IC 6–6–2.5–1 et seq.

Formerly:

P.L.77–1985, SEC.19.
P.L.97–1987, SECS.27, 28.

6–6–2.1–701 to 6–6–2.1–703 Repealed

(Repealed by P.L.277–1993(ss), SEC.56.)

Historical and Statutory Notes

P.L.277–1993(ss), Sec.56, eff. Oct. 1, 1993.

Governor's veto of H.E.A.1001(ss)(P.L.277–1993(ss)) of the 1993 Special Session was overridden by the General Assembly on June 30, 1993.

Former IC 6–6–2.1–701 related to alternative fuel temporary trip permit fees.

Former IC 6–6–2.1–702 related to use of tax for highway and traffic purposes.

Former IC 6–6–2.1–703 related to tax receipts.

See, now, generally, IC 6–6–2.5–1 et seq.

Formerly:

IC 6–6–2–3.

IC 6–6–2–4.
IC 6–6–2–10.5.
Acts 1943, c. 74, ss. 3, 4.
Acts 1947, c. 343, s. 2.
Acts 1951, c. 280, s. 2.
Acts 1957, c. 51, s. 1.
Acts 1969, c. 320, s. 1.
Acts 1975, P.L.66, SEC.1.
Acts 1978, P.L.47, SEC.3.
Acts 1979, P.L.80, SECS.2, 5.
Acts 1980, P.L.51, SEC.57.
Acts 1980, P.L.58, SEC.8.
Acts 1981, P.L.88, SEC.8.
P.L.77–1985, SEC.20.
P.L.73–1986, SEC.12.
P.L.79–1993, SEC.4.

6–6–2.1–801 to 6–6–2.1–807 Repealed

(Repealed by P.L.277–1993(ss), SEC.56.)

Historical and Statutory Notes

P.L.277–1993(ss), Sec.56, eff. Oct. 1, 1993.

Governor's veto of H.E.A.1001(ss)(P.L.277–1993(ss)) of the 1993 Special Session was overridden by the General Assembly on June 30, 1993.

P.L.278–1993(ss), Sec.32, emerg. eff. retroactive to June 28, 1993, provides:

"(a) Notwithstanding the passage of HEA 1001ss–1993, the provisions of this act supersede the provisions of any conflicting provisions in HEA 1001ss–1993.

"(b) IC 1–1–3.1 does not apply to this act or to HEA 1001ss–1993.

"(c) Notwithstanding IC 1–1–3.1, the effective date of the Sections in this act and HEA 1001ss–1993 are as specified in this act and HEA 1001ss–1993, respectively, regardless of a

veto of either act by the governor and the subsequent veto override of either or both acts."

Former IC 6–6–2.1–801 to 6–6–2.1–807 related to refunds.

See, now, generally, IC 6–6–2.5–1 et seq.

Formerly:

IC 6–6–2–13.
Acts 1943, c. 74, s. 13.
Acts 1947, c. 343, s. 11.
Acts 1980, P.L.51, SEC.57.
Acts 1980, P.L.58, SECS.9, 10.
Acts 1981, P.L.93, SECS.6 to 8.
Acts 1982, P.L. 58, SECS. 11, 12.
P.L.97–1987, SECS.29 to 32.
P.L.60–1990, SEC.2.
P.L.69–1991, SEC.11.
P.L.1–1992, SEC.20.

6–6–2.1–901 to 6–6–2.1–903 Repealed

(Repealed by Acts 1980, P.L.61, SEC.15.)

Historical and Statutory Notes

Acts 1980, P.L.61, eff. January 1, 1981.

The former sections related to warrants and judgment liens.

Provisions pertaining to collections by the department of state revenue are now contained in IC 6–8.1–8–1 et seq.

Formerly:

Acts 1980, P.L.51, SEC.57.

6–6–2.1–904, 6–6–2.1–905 Repealed

(Repealed by P.L.277–1993(ss), SEC.56.)

Historical and Statutory Notes

P.L.277–1993(ss), Sec.56, eff. Oct. 1, 1993.

Governor's veto of H.E.A.1001(ss)(P.L.277–1993(ss)) of the 1993 Special Session was overridden by the General Assembly on June 30, 1993.

P.L.278–1993(ss), Sec.32, emerg. eff. retroactive to June 28, 1993, provides:

"(a) Notwithstanding the passage of HEA 1001ss–1993, the provisions of this act supersede the provisions of any conflicting provisions in HEA 1001ss–1993.

"(b) IC 1–1–3.1 does not apply to this act or to HEA 1001ss–1993.

"(c) Notwithstanding IC 1–1–3.1, the effective date of the Sections in this act and HEA 1001ss–1993 are as specified in this act and HEA 1001ss–1993, respectively, regardless of a

veto of either act by the governor and the subsequent veto override of either or both acts."

Former IC 6–6–2.1–904 related to unsatisfied warrants.

Former IC 6–6–2.1–905 related to priority of lien.

See, now, generally, IC 6–6–2.5–1 et seq.

Formerly:

IC 6–6–2–10.5.

IC 6–6–3–1.

Acts 1935, c. 224, s. 1.

Acts 1979, P.L.80, SEC.5.

Acts 1980, P.L.51, SEC.57.

Acts 1980, P.L.61, SEC.10.

P.L.332–1989(ss), SEC.16.

6–6–2.1–1001 to 6–6–2.1–1005 Repealed

(Repealed by Acts 1980, P.L.61, SEC.15.)

Historical and Statutory Notes

Acts 1980, P.L. 61, provided in § 16 that the act takes effect Jan. 1, 1981.

Former § 6–6–2.1–1001 related to forms.

Former § 6–6–2.1–1002 related to rules and regulations.

Former §§ 6–6–2.1–1003 to 6–6–2.1–1005 related to enforcement powers.

Provisions pertaining to the powers and duties of the department of state revenue are now contained in § 6–8.1–3–1 et seq.

Formerly:

Acts 1980, P.L.51, SEC.57.

Acts 1980, P.L.58, SEC.13.

6–6–2.1–1006 to 6–6–2.1–1011 Repealed

(Repealed by P.L.277–1993(ss), SEC.56.)

Historical and Statutory Notes

P.L.277–1993(ss), Sec.56, eff. Oct. 1, 1993.

Governor's veto of H.E.A.1001(ss)(P.L.277–1993(ss)) of the 1993 Special Session was overridden by the General Assembly on June 30, 1993.

P.L.278–1993(ss), Sec.32, emerg. eff. retroactive to June 28, 1993, provides:

"(a) Notwithstanding the passage of HEA 1001ss–1993, the provisions of this act supersede the provisions of any conflicting provisions in HEA 1001ss–1993.

"(b) IC 1–1–3.1 does not apply to this act or to HEA 1001ss–1993.

"(c) Notwithstanding IC 1–1–3.1, the effective date of the Sections in this act and HEA 1001ss–1993 are as specified in this act and HEA 1001ss–1993, respectively, regardless of a veto of either act by the governor and the subsequent veto override of either or both acts."

Former IC 6–6–2.1–1006 to 6–6–2.1–1011 related to tax evasion report, pumps, remedies, disclosure of information, and registration of motor vehicles.

See, now, generally, IC 6–6–2.5–1 et seq.

Formerly:
IC 6–6–2–9.6.
IC 6–6–2–10.5.
IC 6–6–2–14.
IC 6–6–2–16.
Acts 1943, c. 74, ss. 14, 16.
Acts 1971, P.L.71, SEC.6.
Acts 1978, P.L.2, SEC.637.
Acts 1979, P.L.80, SEC.5.
Acts 1980, P.L.51, SEC.57.
Acts 1980, P.L.58, SEC.14.
P.L.77–1985, SECS.21, 22.
P.L.73–1986, SECS.13, 14.
P.L.97–1987, SEC.33.
P.L.1–1991, SEC.65.

6–6–2.1–1101   Repealed

(Repealed by Acts 1980, P.L.61, SEC.15.)

Historical and Statutory Notes

Acts 1980, P.L. 61, provided in § 16 that the act takes effect Jan. 1, 1981.

The former section related to the time at which documents were considered filed and received.

Provisions pertaining to filing and due dates of tax forms are now contained in § 6–8.1–6–1 et seq.

6–6–2.1–1102   Repealed

(Repealed by P.L.277–1993(ss), SEC.56.)

Historical and Statutory Notes

P.L.277–1993(ss), Sec.56, eff. Oct. 1, 1993.

Governor's veto of H.E.A.1001(ss)(P.L.277–1993(ss)) of the 1993 Special Session was overridden by the General Assembly on June 30, 1993.

P.L.278–1993(ss), Sec.32, emerg. eff. retroactive to June 28, 1993, provides:

"(a) Notwithstanding the passage of HEA 1001ss–1993, the provisions of this act supersede the provisions of any conflicting provisions in HEA 1001ss–1993.

"(b) IC 1–1–3.1 does not apply to this act or to HEA 1001ss–1993.

"(c) Notwithstanding IC 1–1–3.1, the effective date of the Sections in this act and HEA 1001ss–1993 are as specified in this act and HEA 1001ss–1993, respectively, regardless of a veto of either act by the governor and the subsequent veto override of either or both acts."

Former IC 6–6–2.1–1102 related to special counsel and collection proceedings.

See, now, generally, IC 6–6–2.5–1 et seq.

Formerly:
IC 6–6–2–10.5.
Acts 1979, P.L.80, SEC.5.
Acts 1980, P.L.51, SEC.57.

6–6–2.1–1103, 6–6–2.1–1104   Repealed

(Repealed by Acts 1980, P.L.61, SEC.15.)

Historical and Statutory Notes

Acts 1980, P.L. 61, provided in § 16 that the act takes effect Jan. 1, 1981.

Former § 6–6–2.1–1103 made liabilities of a sheriff debts due the state.

Former § 6–6–2.1–1104 made tax liabilities not subject to exemption laws.

Provisions pertaining to tax collections, penalties and interest are now contained in §§ 6–8.1–8–1 et seq. and 6–8.1–10–1 et seq.

Formerly:

Acts 1980, P.L.51, SEC.57.

6–6–2.1–1105, 6–6–2.1–1106   Repealed

(Repealed by P.L.277–1993(ss), SEC.56.)

Historical and Statutory Notes

P.L.277–1993(ss), Sec.56, eff. Oct. 1, 1993.

Governor's veto of H.E.A.1001(ss)(P.L.277–1993(ss)) of the 1993 Special Session was overridden by the General Assembly on June 30, 1993.

P.L.278–1993(ss), Sec.32, emerg. eff. retroactive to June 28, 1993, provides:

"(a) Notwithstanding the passage of HEA 1001ss–1993, the provisions of this act supersede the provisions of any conflicting provisions in HEA 1001ss–1993.

"(b) IC 1–1–3.1 does not apply to this act or to HEA 1001ss–1993.

"(c) Notwithstanding IC 1–1–3.1, the effective date of the Sections in this act and HEA 1001ss–1993 are as specified in this act and HEA 1001ss–1993, respectively, regardless of a

veto of either act by the governor and the subsequent veto override of either or both acts."

Former IC 6–6–2.1–1105 related to consent to sue.

Former IC 6–6–2.1–1106 related to storage facilities.

See, now, generally, IC 6–6–2.5–1 et seq.

Formerly:

IC 6–6–2–14.
Acts 1943, c. 74, s. 14.
Acts 1971, P.L.71, SEC.9.
Acts 1980, P.L.51, SEC.57.
Acts 1980, P.L.58, SEC.15.
Acts 1982, P.L.58, SEC.13.
P.L.291–1985, SEC.10.

6–6–2.1–1201   Repealed

(Repealed by P.L.277–1993(ss), SEC.56.)

Historical and Statutory Notes

P.L.277–1993(ss), Sec.56, eff. Oct. 1, 1993.

Governor's veto of H.E.A.1001(ss)(P.L.277–1993(ss)) of the 1993 Special Session was overridden by the General Assembly on June 30, 1993.

P.L.278–1993(ss), Sec.32, emerg. eff. retroactive to June 28, 1993, provides:

"(a) Notwithstanding the passage of HEA 1001ss–1993, the provisions of this act supersede the provisions of any conflicting provisions in HEA 1001ss–1993.

"(b) IC 1–1–3.1 does not apply to this act or to HEA 1001ss–1993.

"(c) Notwithstanding IC 1–1–3.1, the effective date of the Sections in this act and HEA 1001ss–1993 are as specified in this act and HEA 1001ss–1993, respectively, regardless of a veto of either act by the governor and the subsequent veto override of either or both acts."

Former IC 6–6–2.1–1201 related to intentional failure to pay tax.

See, now, generally, IC 6–6–2.5–1 et seq.

Formerly:

IC 6–6–2–10.5.
Acts 1979, P.L.80, SEC.5.
Acts 1980, P.L.51, SEC.57.

6–6–2.1–1202 to 6–6–2.1–1206   Repealed

(Repealed by Acts 1980, P.L.61, SEC.15.)

Historical and Statutory Notes

Acts 1980, P.L. 61, provided in § 16 that the act takes effect Jan. 1, 1981.

The former sections related to penalties and interest for tax delinquencies.

Provisions pertaining to penalties and interest are now contained in § 6–8.1–10–1 et seq.

Formerly:

Acts 1980, P.L.51, SEC.57.
Acts 1980, P.L.59, SECS.2, 3.

6–6–2.1–1207, 6–6–2.1–1208   Repealed

(Repealed by P.L.277–1993(ss), SEC.56.)

Historical and Statutory Notes

P.L.277–1993(ss), Sec.56, eff. Oct. 1, 1993.

Governor's veto of H.E.A.1001(ss)(P.L.277–1993(ss)) of the 1993 Special Session was overridden by the General Assembly on June 30, 1993.

P.L.278–1993(ss), Sec.32, emerg. eff. retroactive to June 28, 1993, provides:

"(a) Notwithstanding the passage of HEA 1001ss–1993, the provisions of this act supersede the provisions of any conflicting provisions in HEA 1001ss–1993.

"(b) IC 1–1–3.1 does not apply to this act or to HEA 1001ss–1993.

"(c) Notwithstanding IC 1–1–3.1, the effective date of the Sections in this act and HEA 1001ss–1993 are as specified in this act and HEA 1001ss–1993, respectively, regardless of a

veto of either act by the governor and the subsequent veto override of either or both acts."

Former IC 6–6–2.1–1207 related to intentional breaking of seal on pump, failure to report meter readings and removal of posted sign.

Former IC 6–6–2.1–1208 related to reckless or intentional violations.

See, now, generally, IC 6–6–2.5–1 et seq.

Formerly:

IC 6–6–2–9.6.
IC 6–6–2–15.
Acts 1943, c. 74, s. 15.
Acts 1947, c. 343, s. 12.
Acts 1971, P.L.71, SEC.6.
Acts 1978, P.L.2, SECS.637, 639.
Acts 1980, P.L.51, SEC.57.
P.L.77–1985, SEC.23.
P.L.97–1987, SEC.34.

6–6–2.1–1209 to 6–6–2.1–1211   Repealed

(Repealed by Acts 1980, P.L.61, SEC.15.)

Historical and Statutory Notes

Acts 1980, P.L. 61, provided in § 16 that the act takes effect Jan. 1, 1981.

Former §§ 6–6–2.1–1209 and 6–6–2.1–1210 related to penalties for failure to file inventories.

Former § 6–6–2.1–1211 related to penalties for sheriffs failing to make levies and sales.

Provisions pertaining to penalties and interest are now contained in § 6–8.1–10–1 et seq.

Formerly:

Acts 1980, P.L.51, SEC.57.

6–6–2.1–1212 to 6–6–2.1–1217   Repealed

(Repealed by P.L.277–1993(ss), SEC.56.)

Historical and Statutory Notes

P.L.277–1993(ss), Sec.56, eff. Oct. 1, 1993.

Governor's veto of H.E.A.1001(ss)(P.L.277–1993(ss)) of the 1993 Special Session was overridden by the General Assembly on June 30, 1993.

P.L.278–1993(ss), Sec.32, emerg. eff. retroactive to June 28, 1993, provides:

"(a) Notwithstanding the passage of HEA 1001ss–1993, the provisions of this act supersede the provisions of any conflicting provisions in HEA 1001ss–1993.

"(b) IC 1–1–3.1 does not apply to this act or to HEA 1001ss–1993.

"(c) Notwithstanding IC 1–1–3.1, the effective date of the Sections in this act and HEA 1001ss–1993 are as specified in this act and HEA 1001ss–1993, respectively, regardless of a veto of either act by the governor and the subsequent veto override of either or both acts."

Former IC 6–6–2.1–1212 to 6–6–2.1–1217 related to violations and offenses.

See, now, generally, IC 6–6–2.5–1 et seq.

Formerly:

IC 6–6–2–15.
Acts 1943, c. 74, s. 15.
Acts 1947, c. 343, s. 12.
Acts 1978, P.L.2, SEC.639.
Acts 1980, P.L.51, SEC.57.
Acts 1980, P.L.58, SEC.16.
Acts 1982, P.L.58, SEC.14.
P.L.77–1985, SECS.24, 25.
P.L.73–1986, SEC.15.
P.L.97–1987, SECS.35, 36.

Chapter 2.5

Special Fuel Tax

SPECIAL FUEL TAX

Section
6–6–2.5–66   Listed tax
6–6–2.5–67   Use of tax revenues
6–6–2.5–68   Transfer of funds to auditor; distribution
6–6–2.5–69   Class actions for refund of tax; prerequisites
6–6–2.5–70   Inspections
6–6–2.5–71   Sealing of special fuel or kerosene pump; compliance; penalty

6–6–2.5–1 "Alternative fuel" defined

Sec. 1. As used in this chapter, "alternative fuel" means a liquefied petroleum gas, compressed natural gas product, or a combination of liquefied petroleum gas and a compressed natural gas product used in an internal combustion engine or motor to propel any form of vehicle, machine, or mechanical contrivance. The term includes all forms of fuel commonly or commercially known or sold as butane, propane, or compressed natural gas.
As added by P.L.277–1993(ss), SEC.44.

Historical and Statutory Notes

P.L.277–1993(ss), Sec.44, eff. Oct. 1, 1993, added this chapter.

Governor's veto of H.E.A. 1001(ss)(P.L.277–1993(ss)) of the 1993 Special Session was overridden by General Assembly on June 30, 1993.

P.L.277–1993(ss), Secs. 58, 60 and 61, eff. Oct. 1, 1993, provide:

"Section 58. Notwithstanding any provision of this act, special fuel used for tax exempt purposes is not required to be dyed as required in IC 6–6–2.5 until January 1, 1994, or ninety (90) days after the United States Environmental Protection Agency requires high sulphur content special fuel to be dyed, whichever is later."

"Section 60. The department may waive any report requirement imposed under IC 6–6–2.5 to facilitate the phase-in of this act.

"Section 61. (a) Each person having special fuel in storage in Indiana upon which the special fuel tax has not been paid shall make a report as required by the department. The person shall include with the report a statement of gallons of special fuel on hand other than held in inventory within a refinery or terminal storage as of September 30, 1993. The report must state the portion of special fuel that is for resale or use as exempt special fuel, and the portion that is for resale or use as nonexempt special fuel.

"(b) Suppliers shall pay the tax liability when the report is filed.

"(c) If any special fuel has been declared to be held for exempt purposes or for resale for exempt use and is subsequently used for a taxable purpose, the person converting the special fuel shall report those gallons and pay the tax

due on that special fuel within thirty (30) days after the month of the converted use.

"(d) For all persons other than suppliers, the liability shown as due on the report required by subsection (a) shall be remitted in three (3) equal monthly installments. The first monthly installment shall be due on October 15, 1993.

"(e) In determining the amount of special fuel tax due in accordance with subsection (a), the person may exclude the amount of special fuel that will not be pumped out of the storage tank because the special fuel is below the mouth of the draw pipe. For this purpose, the person may deduct two hundred (200) gallons for a storage tank with a capacity of less than ten thousand (10,000) gallons, and four hundred (400) gallons for a storage tank with a capacity that exceeds ten thousand (10,000) gallons.

"(f) Instead of the determination under subsection (e), the person may compute the amount of special fuel in dead storage by using the manufacturer's conversion table for the tank and the number of inches between the bottom of the tank and the mouth of the draw pipe. If the person uses the conversion method, the distance from the bottom of the tank to the mouth of the draw pipe will be assumed to be six (6) inches until the person establishes otherwise."

Section 32 of P.L.278–1993(ss), emerg. eff. retroactive to June 28, 1993, provides:

"(a) Notwithstanding the passage of HEA 1001ss–1993, the provisions of this act supersede the provisions of any conflicting provisions in HEA 1001ss–1993.

"(b) IC 1–1–3.1 does not apply to this act or to HEA 1001ss–1993.

"(c) Notwithstanding IC 1–1–3.1, the effective date of the Sections in this act and HEA 1001ss–1993 are as specified in this act and HEA 1001ss–1993, respectively, regardless of a veto of either act by the governor and the subsequent veto override of either or both acts."

6–6–2.5–2 "Blender" defined

Sec. 2. As used in this chapter, "blender" means a person who engages in the process of blending.
As added by P.L.277–1993(ss), SEC.44.

6–6–2.5–3 "Blending" defined

Sec. 3. As used in this chapter, "blending" means the mixing of one (1) or more petroleum products, with or without another product, regardless of the original character of the product blended, if the product obtained by the blending is capable of use in the generation of power for the propulsion of a motor vehicle, an airplane, or a motorboat. The term does not include that blending that occurs in the process of refining by the original refiner of crude petroleum or the blending of a de minimis amount of products such as carburetor detergent, oxidation inhibitor, lubricating oil, and greases.
As added by P.L.277–1993(ss), SEC.44. Amended by P.L.85–1995, SEC.13.

Historical and Statutory Notes

P.L.85–1995, Sec.13, amended the section by substituting "such" for "known" and adding "a de minimis amount of" and "carburetor detergent, oxidation inhibitor."

6–6–2.5–4 "Bulk end user" defined

Sec. 4. As used in this chapter, "bulk end user" means a person who receives into the person's own storage facilities at least two hundred forty thousand (240,000) gallons annually of special fuel for the person's own consumption.
As added by P.L.277–1993(ss), SEC.44.

6–6–2.5–5 "Bulk plant" defined

Sec. 5. As used in this chapter, "bulk plant" means a gasoline or special fuel storage facility, other than a terminal, that is primarily used for redistribution of gasoline and special fuel by a motor vehicle with a capacity of not more than five thousand four hundred (5,400) gallons.
As added by P.L.277–1993(ss), SEC.44. Amended by P.L.85–1995, SEC.14.

Historical and Statutory Notes

P.L.85–1995, Sec.14, amended the section by substituting "five thousand four hundred (5,400)" for "four thousand two hundred (4,200)".

6–6–2.5–6 "Commissioner" defined

Sec. 6. As used in this chapter, "commissioner" means the administrative head of the department or that person's designee.
As added by P.L.277–1993(ss), SEC.44.

6–6–2.5–7   "Department" defined

Sec. 7. As used in this chapter, "department" means the department of state revenue.

As added by P.L.277–1993(ss), SEC.44.

6–6–2.5–8   "Destination state" defined

Sec. 8. As used in this chapter, "destination state" means the state for which a motor vehicle or barge is destined for off-loading into storage facilities for consumption or resale.

As added by P.L.277–1993(ss), SEC.44.

6–6–2.5–8.5   "Dyed fuel user" defined

Sec. 8.5. As used in this chapter, "dyed fuel user" means a person that qualifies for the federal diesel fuel tax exemption under Section 4082 of the Internal Revenue Code [1] to operate motor vehicles on the highways with dyed fuel in the fuel supply tank.

As added by P.L.61–1996, SEC.1.

[1] 26 U.S.C.A. §4082

6–6–2.5–9   "Export" defined

Sec. 9. As used in this chapter, "export" means:

(1) with respect to a seller, when special fuel is delivered out-of-state by or for the seller; and

(2) with respect to a purchaser, when special fuel is delivered out-of-state by or for the purchaser.

As added by P.L.277–1993(ss), SEC.44.

6–6–2.5–10   "Exporter" defined

Sec. 10. As used in this chapter, "exporter" means any person, other than a supplier, who purchases special fuel in Indiana for the purpose of transporting or delivering the fuel to another state or country.

As added by P.L.277–1993(ss), SEC.44.

6–6–2.5–11   "Farm machinery" defined

Sec. 11. As used in this chapter, "farm machinery" has the meaning set forth in IC 9–13–2–55.

As added by P.L.277–1993(ss), SEC.44.

6–6–2.5–12   "Heating oil" defined

Sec. 12. As used in this chapter, "heating oil" means a special fuel that is burned in a boiler, furnace, or stove for heating or industrial processing purposes.

As added by P.L.277–1993(ss), SEC.44.

6–6–2.5–13 "Import" defined

Sec. 13. As used in this chapter, "import" means:

(1) with respect to a seller, when special fuel is delivered into Indiana from out-of-state by or for the seller; and

(2) with respect to a purchaser, when special fuel is delivered into Indiana from out-of-state by or for the purchaser.

As added by P.L.277–1993(ss), SEC.44.

6–6–2.5–13.1 "Import verification number" defined

Sec. 13.1. As used in this chapter, "import verification number" means the number assigned by the department, or the department's designee or appointee, with respect to a single transport truck delivery into Indiana from another state upon request for an assigned number by a licensed importer or transporter carrying undyed or unmarked special fuel, or both, into Indiana for the account of a licensed importer.

As added by P.L.18–1994, SEC.12. Amended by P.L.85–1995, SEC.15.

Historical and Statutory Notes

P.L.85–1995, Sec.15, amended the section by adding "or unmarked" and "or both,".

6–6–2.5–14 "Invoiced gallons" defined

Sec. 14. As used in this chapter, "invoiced gallons" means the gallons accurately billed on an invoice on payment to a supplier.

As added by P.L.277–1993(ss), SEC.44. Amended by P.L.18–1994, SEC.13.

Historical and Statutory Notes

P.L.18–1994, Sec.13, inserted "accurately" following "gallons".

6–6–2.5–15 "Liquid" defined

Sec. 15. As used in this chapter, "liquid" means any substance that is liquid in excess of sixty (60) degrees fahrenheit and a pressure of fourteen and seven-tenths (14.7) pounds per square inch absolute.

As added by P.L.277–1993(ss), SEC.44.

6–6–2.5–16 "Motor vehicle" defined

Sec. 16. As used in this chapter, "motor vehicle" means a vehicle designed principally for road use and that is propelled by an internal combustion engine or motor.

As added by P.L.277–1993(ss), SEC.44. Amended by P.L.18–1994, SEC.14.

Historical and Statutory Notes

P.L.18–1994, Sec.14, rewrote the section, which formerly read:

"As used in this chapter, 'motor vehicle' means a vehicle that is propelled by an internal combustion engine or motor and is designed to permit the vehicle's mobile use on highways. The term does not include:

"(1) farm machinery; or

"(2) a vehicle operated on rails"

6–6–2.5–16.1 "Permissive supplier" defined

Sec. 16.1. As used in this chapter, "permissive supplier" means any person who does not meet the geographic jurisdictional connections to Indiana required of a supplier (as defined in section 23 of this chapter), but who holds an inventory position in a federally qualified terminal located outside of Indiana and who is registered under Section 4101 of the Internal Revenue Code[1]. *As added by P.L.18–1994, SEC.15.*

[1] 26 U.S.C.A. § 4101.

6–6–2.5–17 "Person" defined

Sec. 17. As used in this chapter, "person" means a natural person, a partnership, a firm, an association, a corporation, a representative appointed by a court, the state, a political subdivision (as defined in IC 36–1–2–13), or any other entity, group, or syndicate. *As added by P.L.277–1993(ss), SEC.44.*

6–6–2.5–18 "Public highway" defined

Sec. 18. As used in this chapter, "public highway" means the entire width between boundary lines of each publicly maintained way in Indiana, including streets and alleys in cities and towns, when any part of the way is open to the public use for motor vehicle travel. *As added by P.L.277–1993(ss), SEC.44. Amended by P.L.18–1994, SEC.16.*

Historical and Statutory Notes

P.L.18–1994, Sec.16, inserted "motor" preceding "vehicle".

6–6–2.5–19 "Rack" defined

Sec. 19. As used in this chapter, "rack" means a dock, a platform, or an open bay with a series of metered pipes and hoses for delivering special fuel from a refinery or terminal into a motor vehicle, rail car, or marine vessel. *As added by P.L.277–1993(ss), SEC.44.*

6–6–2.5–20 "Received" defined

Sec. 20. As used in this chapter, "received" means the removal from any refinery or terminal in Indiana, or the entry into Indiana of any special fuel for consumption, use, sale, or warehousing, except for transfers in bulk into or

within a terminal in Indiana between registered suppliers. The tax imposed under section 28 of this chapter with respect to special fuel removed from terminals within Indiana and with respect to special fuel which is the subject of a tax precollection agreement pursuant to section 35(j) of this chapter, shall be imposed at the same time and in the same manner as the tax imposed by Sections 4081 to 4083 of the Internal Revenue Code[1]. The definitions of the terms "removal", "entry", and "transfers in bulk" shall have the same meanings described in the Internal Revenue Code or Code of Federal Regulations.
As added by P.L.277–1993(ss), SEC.44. Amended by P.L.18–1994, SEC.17.

[1] 26 U.S.C.A. §§ 4081 to 4083.

Historical and Statutory Notes

P.L.18–1994, Sec.17, made a nonsubstantive language change in the first sentence, specified that the reference to the tax imposed under section 28 of this chapter was with respect to special fuel removed from terminals within Indiana and with respect to special fuel which was the subject of a tax precollection agreement pursuant to section 35(j) of this chapter, and deleted a reference to Section 4103 of the Internal Revenue Code in the second sentence, and deleted a specification that the Internal Revenue Code definitions referred to were as the Code existed on Jan. 1, 1992, and added a reference to the Code of Federal Regulations at the end of the third sentence.

6–6–2.5–21   "Retailer" defined

Sec. 21. As used in this chapter, "retailer" means a person that engages in the business of selling or distributing special fuel to the end user within Indiana.
As added by P.L.277–1993(ss), SEC.44.

Historical and Statutory Notes

P.L.277–1993, Sec.59, eff. Oct. 1, 1993, provides:

"Notwithstanding any provisions of this act, the exemptions set forth in IC 6–6–2.5–62(c)(1), as added by this act, are not effective until the earlier of:

"(1) October 1, 1995; or

"(2) the effective date of a waiver of 40 CFR 80.29(a) by the United States Environmental Protection Agency with respect to special fuel for use in motor vehicles that may be licensed under IC 9–29–5–13(b)."

6–6–2.5–22   "Special fuel" defined

Sec. 22. As used in this chapter, "special fuel" means all combustible gases and liquids that are:

(1) suitable for the generation of power in an internal combustion engine or motor; or

(2) used exclusively for heating, industrial, or farm purposes other than for the operation of a motor vehicle.

However, the term does not include gasoline (as defined in IC 6–6–1.1–103), ethanol produced, stored, or sold for the manufacture of or compounding or blending with gasoline, alternative fuels, kerosene, and jet fuel (if the purchaser of the jet fuel has provided to the seller proof of the purchaser's federal jet fuel registration at or before the time of sale).
As added by P.L.277–1993(ss), SEC.44. Amended by P.L.18–1994, SEC.18.

Historical and Statutory Notes

P.L.18–1994, Sec.18, in the concluding paragraph, substituted a reference to jet fuel for a reference to aviation fuel, and added the proviso relating to jet fuel at the end.

6–6–2.5–23   "Supplier" defined

Sec. 23. As used in this chapter, "supplier" means a person that imports or acquires immediately upon import into Indiana special fuel by pipeline or marine vessel from within a state, territory, or possession of the United States into a terminal or that imports special fuel into Indiana from a foreign country, or that produces, manufactures, or refines special fuel within Indiana, or that owns special fuel in the pipeline and terminal distribution system in Indiana, and is subject to the general taxing or police jurisdiction of Indiana, and in any case is also registered under Section 4101 of the Internal Revenue Code[1] for transactions in taxable motor fuels in the bulk distribution system. A terminal operator shall not be considered a supplier merely because the terminal operator handles special fuel consigned to it within a terminal.

As added by P.L.277–1993(ss), SEC.44. Amended by P.L.18–1994, SEC.19.

[1] 26 U.S.C.A. § 4101.

Historical and Statutory Notes

P.L.18–1994, Sec.19, deleted from the definition persons who import or acquire special fuel by motor vehicle from the definition, included persons who own special fuel in pipelines and terminal distribution systems in Indiana, deleted a specification that the reference to the Internal Revenue Code was to the Code as it existed on Jan. 1, 1992, and provided the registration referred to was for transactions in taxable motor fuel in the bulk distribution system, in lieu of for tax free transactions in gasoline, in the first sentence.

6–6–2.5–24   "Terminal" defined

Sec. 24. As used in this chapter, "terminal" means a fuel storage and distribution facility that is supplied by pipeline or marine vessel, and from which special fuel may be removed at a rack and that has been registered as a qualified terminal by the Internal Revenue Service for receipt of taxable motor fuels free of federal motor fuel taxes.

As added by P.L.277–1993(ss), SEC.44. Amended by P.L.18–1994, SEC.20.

Historical and Statutory Notes

P.L.18–1994, Sec.20, deleted from the definition facilities supplied by motor vehicle, and added a requirement that included facilities be registered as qualified terminals by the Internal Revenue Service for receipt of taxable motor fuels free of federal motor fuel taxes.

6–6–2.5–25   "Terminal operator" defined

Sec. 25. As used in this chapter, "terminal operator" means the person who by ownership or contractual agreement is charged with the responsibility and physical control over the operation of the terminal. However, there shall be only one (1) person charged with responsibility as operator at each terminal for purposes of this chapter.

As added by P.L.277–1993(ss), SEC.44.

6–6–2.5–25.1   "Transfer in bulk into or within a terminal" defined

Sec. 25.1.   As used in this chapter, "transfer in bulk into or within a terminal" includes the following:

(1) A marine barge movement of fuel from a refinery or terminal to a terminal.

(2) Pipeline movements of fuel from a refinery or terminal to terminal.

(3) Book transfers of product within a terminal between suppliers before completion of removal across the rack.

(4) Two (2) party exchanges between licensed suppliers and permissive suppliers.

As added by P.L.18–1994, SEC.21.

6–6–2.5–25.9   "Transporter" defined

Sec. 25.9.   As used in this chapter, "transporter" means the person and its agent, including the driver, that transports special fuel.

As added by P.L.85–1995, SEC.16.

6–6–2.5–26   "Transmix" defined

Sec. 26.   As used in this chapter, "transmix" means the buffer between two (2) different products in a pipeline shipment, or a mix of two (2) different products within a refinery or terminal that results in an off-grade mixture.

As added by P.L.277–1993(ss), SEC.44.

6–6–2.5–26.1   "Transport truck" defined

Sec. 26.1.   As used in this chapter, "transport truck" means a vehicle designed to transport motor fuel in bulk from a terminal in lots greater than five thousand four hundred (5,400) gallons.

As added by P.L.18–1994, SEC.22.   Amended by P.L.85–1995, SEC.17.

Historical and Statutory Notes

P.L.85–1995, Sec.17, amended the section by substituting "five thousand four hundred (5,400)" for "four thousand two hundred (4,200)".

6–6–2.5–26.2   "Two (2) party exchange" defined

Sec. 26.2.   As used in this chapter, "two (2) party exchange" means a transaction in which a product is transferred from one (1) licensed supplier or permissive supplier to another when:

(1) the transaction includes a transfer from the person who holds the original inventory position for special fuel in the terminal as indicated in the records of the terminal operator; and

(2) the exchange transaction is completed before removal from the terminal by the receiving exchange partner, provided that the terminal operator

in the terminal operator's books and records treats the receiving exchange party as the supplier that receives the product for purposes of reporting the events to the state of Indiana.

As added by P.L.18–1994, SEC.23.

6–6–2.5–27 "Wholesaler" defined

Sec. 27. As used in this chapter, "wholesaler" means a person that acquires special fuel from a supplier or from another wholesaler for subsequent resale to a retail establishment or bulk end user by tank cars, motor vehicles, or both.

As added by P.L.277–1993(ss), SEC.44. Amended by P.L.18–1994, SEC.24.

Historical and Statutory Notes

P.L.18–1994, Sec.24, required that the acquisitions referred to be for subsequent resale to a retail establishment or bulk end user, in lieu of for subsequent sale and distribution at wholesale.

6–6–2.5–28 License tax; presumptions; computation; liability for collection and remittance; sulfur content; penalty

Sec. 28. (a) A license tax of sixteen cents ($0.16) per gallon is imposed on all special fuel sold or used in producing or generating power for propelling motor vehicles except fuel used under section 30(a)(8) of this chapter. The tax shall be paid at those times, in the manner, and by those persons specified in this section and section 35 of this chapter.

(b) The department shall consider it a rebuttable presumption that all undyed or unmarked special fuel, or both, received in Indiana is to be sold for use in propelling motor vehicles.

(c) Except as provided in subsection (d), the tax imposed on special fuel by subsection (a) shall be measured by invoiced gallons of nonexempt special fuel received by a licensed supplier in Indiana for sale or resale in Indiana or with respect to special fuel subject to a tax precollection agreement under section 35(d) of this chapter, such special fuel removed by a licensed supplier from a terminal outside of Indiana for sale for export or for export to Indiana and in any case shall generally be determined in the same manner as the tax imposed by Section 4081 of the Internal Revenue Code[1] and Code of Federal Regulations.

(d) The tax imposed by subsection (a) on special fuel imported into Indiana, other than into a terminal, is imposed at the time the product is entered into Indiana and shall be measured by invoiced gallons received at a terminal or at a bulk plant.

(e) In computing the tax, all special fuel in process of transfer from tank steamers at boat terminal transfers and held in storage pending wholesale bulk distribution by land transportation, or in tanks and equipment used in receiving and storing special fuel from interstate pipelines pending wholesale bulk reshipment, shall not be subject to tax.

(f) The department shall consider it a rebuttable presumption that special fuel consumed in a motor vehicle plated for general highway use is subject to the tax imposed under this chapter. A person claiming exempt use of special fuel in such a vehicle must maintain adequate records as required by the department to document the vehicle's taxable and exempt use.

(g) A person that engages in blending fuel for taxable sale or use in Indiana is primarily liable for the collection and remittance of the tax imposed under subsection (a). The person shall remit the tax due in conjunction with the filing of a monthly report in the form prescribed by the department.

(h) A person that receives special fuel that has been blended for taxable sale or use in Indiana is secondarily liable to the state for the tax imposed under subsection (a).

(i) A person may not use special fuel on an Indiana public highway if the special fuel contains a sulfur content that exceeds five one-hundredths of one percent (0.05%). A person who knowingly:

(1) violates; or

(2) aids or abets another person to violate;

this subsection commits a Class A infraction. However, the violation is a Class A misdemeanor if the person has committed one (1) prior unrelated violation of this subsection, and a Class D felony if the person has committed more than one (1) unrelated violation of this subsection.

As added by P.L.277–1993(ss), SEC.44. Amended by P.L.18–1994, SEC.25; P.L.85–1995, SEC.18.

[1] 26 U.S.C.A. § 4081.

Historical and Statutory Notes

P.L.18–1994, Sec.25, rewrote Subsec. (c), which formerly read:

"(c) The tax imposed on special fuel by subsection (a) shall be measured by invoiced gallons of nonexempt special fuel received by a supplier for sale in Indiana or for export to Indiana and shall be imposed in the same manner as the tax imposed by Section 4081 of the Internal Revenue Code as in effect on January 1, 1992.";

inserted Subsec. (d), and redesignated former Subsec. (d) as Subsec. (e); and added Subsec. (f).

P.L.85–1995, Sec.18, amended the section by adding "or unmarked" and "or both," to Subsec. (b); and by adding Subsecs. (g) through (i).

Library References

Taxation ⚬⇒1294, 1316.
WESTLAW Topic No. 371.
C.J.S. Taxation §§ 1233, 1247.

Notes of Decisions

Owner, operator or supplier of special fuel   2
State agencies   3

Validity of prior laws   1

_____

1. Validity of prior laws

Prior provision requiring payment of motor vehicle fuel license fees was not unconstitution-

557

al as embracing subject not expressed in title. Roberts v. State, 1936, 200 N.E. 699, 210 Ind. 375.

2. Owner, operator or supplier of special fuel

Although taxpayer owned special fuel while it was stored in bulk tanks at service station, ownership of special fuel passed from taxpayer to station operators before it was ultimately sold to station operators' customers, for purposes of assessing special fuel tax, when special fuel flowed through meter in metered pump, where taxpayer supplied special fuel under oral metered marketing arrangements. Storm, Inc. v. Indiana Dept. of State Revenue, 1996, 663 N.E.2d 552.

Because ownership of special fuel passed from taxpayer to station operators when special fuel flowed through meter in metered pump, before it was ultimately placed into supply tanks of motor vehicles in state, there was no consignment arrangement between taxpayer and operators that could be basis for assessing special fuel

tax against taxpayer, where taxpayer supplied special fuel pursuant to oral metered marketing arrangements. Storm, Inc. v. Indiana Dept. of State Revenue, 1996, 663 N.E.2d 552.

Taxpayer remained liable for special fuel taxes incurred as operator of service station despite alleged arrangement under which supplier would remit taxes on its behalf, where taxpayer had no written agreement with supplier establishing that supplier would pay special fuel taxes and there was no evidence that supplier actually paid any such taxes. Storm, Inc. v. Indiana Dept. of State Revenue, 1996, 663 N.E.2d 552.

3. State agencies

The Indiana toll road commission is subject to the licensing and tax provisions of the Gasoline Tax Law, [§ 6–6–1.1–1 et seq.] and the Special Fuel Tax Law, [§ 6–6–2.1–1 et seq.], with respect to gasoline and special fuel used in the commission's vehicles. 1981, Op.Atty.Gen. No. 81–14.

6–6–2.5–29 Inventory tax; exclusions; amount

Sec. 29. (a) Persons having title to special fuel in storage and held for sale on the effective date of an increase in the license tax rate imposed under section 28 of this chapter are subject to an inventory tax based on the gallons in storage as of the close of the business day preceding the effective date of the increased license tax rate.

(b) Persons subject to the tax imposed under this section shall:

(1) take an inventory to determine the gallons in storage for purposes of determining the inventory tax;

(2) report the gallons listed in subdivision (1) on forms provided by the commissioner; and

(3) pay the tax due not more than thirty (30) days after the prescribed inventory date.

In determining the amount of special fuel tax due under this section, the person may exclude the amount of special fuel that will not be pumped out of the storage tank because the special fuel is below the mouth of the draw pipe. For this purpose, the person may deduct two hundred (200) gallons for a storage tank with a capacity of less than ten thousand (10,000) gallons, and four hundred (400) gallons for a storage tank with a capacity that exceeds ten thousand (10,000) gallons.

(c) The amount of the inventory tax is equal to the inventory tax rate times the gallons in storage as determined under subsection (b). The inventory tax rate is equal to the difference of the increased license tax rate minus the previous license tax rate.

(d) The inventory tax shall be considered a listed tax for the purposes of IC 6–8.1.

As added by P.L.277–1993(ss), SEC.44.

Library References

Taxation ☞197, 1331.
WESTLAW Topic No. 371.
C.J.S. Taxation §§ 222, 1250.

6–6–2.5–30 Exemptions from special fuel tax; provision of export information; refunds

Sec. 30.   (a) The following are exempt from the special fuel tax:

(1) Special fuel sold by a supplier to a licensed exporter for export from Indiana to another state or country to which the exporter is specifically licensed to export exports by a supplier, or exports for which the destination state special fuel tax has been paid to the supplier and proof of export is available in the form of a destination state bill of lading.

(2) Special fuel sold to the United States or an agency or instrumentality thereof.

(3) Special fuel sold to a post exchange or other concessionaire on a federal reservation within Indiana. However, the post exchange or concessionaire shall collect, report, and pay quarterly to the department any tax permitted by federal law on special fuel sold.

(4) Special fuel sold to a public transportation corporation established under IC 36–9–4 and used for the transportation of persons for compensation within the territory of the corporation.

(5) Special fuel sold to a public transit department of a municipality and used for the transportation of persons for compensation within a service area, no part of which is more than five (5) miles outside the corporate limits of the municipality.

(6) Special fuel sold to a common carrier of passengers, including a business operating a taxicab (as defined in IC 6–6–1.1–103(l)) and used by the carrier to transport passengers within a service area that is not larger than one (1) county, and counties contiguous to that county.

(7) The portion of special fuel determined by the commissioner to have been used to operate equipment attached to a motor vehicle, if the special fuel was placed into the fuel supply tank of a motor vehicle that has a common fuel reservoir for travel on a highway and for the operation of equipment.

(8) Special fuel used for nonhighway purposes, used as heating oil, or in trains.

(9) Special fuel sold by a supplier to an unlicensed person for export from Indiana to another state and the special fuel has been dye addityzed [1] in accordance with section 31 of this chapter.

559

(10) Sales of transmix between licensed suppliers.

(b) The exemption from tax provided under subsection (a)(4) through (a)(7) shall be applied for through the refund procedures established in section 32 of this chapter.

(c) The department shall provide information to licensed suppliers of the destination state or states to which exporters are authorized to export.

(d) Subject to gallonage limits and other conditions established by the department, the department shall provide for refund of the tax imposed by this chapter to a wholesale distributor exporting undyed special fuel out of a bulk plant in this state in a vehicle capable of carrying not more than five thousand four hundred (5,400) gallons if the destination of that vehicle does not exceed twenty-five (25) miles from the border of Indiana.

As added by P.L.277–1993(ss), SEC.44. Amended by P.L.18–1994, SEC.26; P.L. 100–1995, SEC.1.

[1]So in enrolled act.

Historical and Statutory Notes

P.L.18–1994, Sec.26, in Subsec. (a), deleted a reference to transactions in the introduction, added the second sentence, relating to passengers, in Subd. (6), and added Subds. (9) and (10); and added Subsecs. (c) and (d).

P.L.100–1995, Sec.1, emerg. eff. retroactive to July 1, 1994, amended the section by deleting the last sentence of Subsec. (a)(6) and by making other nonsubstantive changes.

Library References

Taxation ⬥1294 to 1296.
WESTLAW Topic No. 371.
C.J.S. Taxation §§ 1231, 1233, 1241 to 1242.

Notes of Decisions

Motor vehicles 5
Placing fuel into tank 7
Public highways 6
Public transportation corporation 2
Service areas 3
Special fuel dealers 1
State agencies and instrumentalities 4

---

1. Special fuel dealers

Dealers in industrial benzol and solvent naphtha were required to comply with the Motor Vehicle Fuel Tax Act, Acts 1932, p. 258 [repealed]. 1931–1932 Op.Atty.Gen. p. 971.

2. Public transportation corporation

Tax Court's use of "necessary and integral" test was appropriate for determining which activities came within "transportation of passengers for compensation," within meaning of subd. (4) of this section exempting from special fuel tax those transactions involving special fuel sold to public transportation corporation and

used for "transportation of persons for compensation". Indiana Dept. of State Revenue v. Indianapolis Public Transp. Corp., 1990, 550 N.E.2d 1277.

Exemption in subd. (4) of this section from special fuel tax of those transactions involving special fuel sold to public transportation corporation and used for "transportation of persons for compensation" within territory of corporation, exempts special fuel used in general activity of providing transportation of passengers. Indiana Dept. of State Revenue v. Indianapolis Public Transp. Corp., 1990, 550 N.E.2d 1277.

Public transportation corporation's wreckers and supervisors' automobiles were "necessary and integral" parts of transportation system, and thus fuel used in vehicles was exempt from special fuel tax under subd. (4) of this section exempting those transactions involving special fuel sold to public transportation corporation and used for "transportation of persons for compensation". Indiana Dept. of State Revenue v. Indianapolis Public Transp. Corp., 1990, 550 N.E.2d 1277.

Public transportation corporation's managers' vehicles were not "necessary and integral" parts of transportation system, and thus fuel used in vehicles was not exempt from special fuel tax under subd. (4) of this section exempting special fuel sold to public transportation corporation and used for "transportation of persons for compensation," as vehicles were used for additional response to emergency calls and personal transportation of managers. Indiana Dept. of State Revenue v. Indianapolis Public Transp. Corp., 1990, 550 N.E.2d 1277.

Department of State Revenue's regulation, which construed exemption in subd. (4) of this section from special fuel tax those transactions involving fuel sold to public transportation corporation and used for transportation for persons for compensation, was not reasonable, but instead conflicted with subd. 4 of this section, where regulation allowed exemption of fuel only so long as fuel was placed into fuel supply tank of motor vehicle operated by public transportation corporation for sole purpose of transporting persons for compensation. Indiana Dept. of State Revenue v. Indianapolis Public Transp. Corp., 1990, 550 N.E.2d 1277.

3. Service areas

For purposes of Special Fuel Tax exemption for fuel used in limited areas, term "contiguous" means touching along the boundaries for considerable distances and includes counties in adjoining states; regulation stating that "contiguous" means counties only within one state was inharmonious with plain and ordinary meaning of word "contiguous." Shoup Buses, Inc. v. Indiana Dept. of State Revenue, 1994, 635 N.E.2d 1165.

"Service area," for purposes of special fuel tax exemption for common carriers, includes all contiguous counties to base county, whether they were in Indiana or out of state, and, thus, regulation of State Taxation Department which limited counties to those within Indiana was invalid. Shoup Buses, Inc. v. Indiana Dept. of State Revenue, 1994, 635 N.E.2d 1165.

Common carrier's use of special fuel outside of service area does not render carrier ineligible for special fuel tax exemption entirely; definition of service area as one county plus contiguous counties does not restrict taxpayer from travelling outside boundaries of service areas. Shoup Buses, Inc. v. Indiana Dept. of State Revenue, 1994, 635 N.E.2d 1165.

4. State agencies and instrumentalities

The Indiana toll road commission is subject to the licensing and tax provisions of the Gasoline Tax Law, [§ 6–6–1.1–1 et seq.] and the Special

Fuel Tax Law, [§ 6–6–2.1–1 et seq.], with respect to gasoline and special fuel used in the commission's vehicles. 1981, Op.Atty.Gen. No. 81–14.

The Indiana toll road commission is subject to the licensing and tax provisions of the Gasoline Tax Law, [§ 6–6–1.1–1 et seq.] and the Special Fuel Tax Law, [§ 6–6–2.1–1 et seq.] with respect to gasoline and special fuel used in the commission's vehicles. 1981, Op.Atty.Gen. No. 81–14.

5. Motor vehicles

Operator of stone quarry and crushing plant was not exempt from payment of motor fuel use tax even if, as it contended, its vehicles were not designed primarily for use on public highways and thus were not "motor vehicles" within meaning of IC1971, 6–6–2–2(1) [repealed; see, now, Cl. (d) of this section]. Kentucky Stone Co. v. State, App. 4 Dist.1979, 396 N.E.2d 951.

6. Public highways

Operator of stone quarry and crushing plant was not exempt from paying motor fuel use tax on theory that, by agreement with county, one-mile roadway on which vehicles moved was maintained with its own funds. Kentucky Stone Co. v. State, App. 4 Dist.1979, 396 N.E.2d 951.

Whether road used by stone quarry and crushing plant was "publicly maintained" had no bearing on company's liability to pay motor fuel use tax. Kentucky Stone Co. v. State, App. 4 Dist.1979, 396 N.E.2d 951.

Motor fuel use tax is imposed for privilege of using public highways, and there is no authority for imposing it only in proportion to whatever degree of actual use is made of such public highways. Kentucky Stone Co. v. State, App. 4 Dist.1979, 396 N.E.2d 951.

7. Placing fuel into tank

All special fuel sales from gasoline station's nonhighway pump were taxable, given evidence that untaxed fuel from nonhighway pump was dispensed in taxable manner for motor vehicles, notwithstanding other evidence presented by gasoline station; facts that pump was clearly labeled to reflect its intended use and tax status, visually monitored, used primarily by customers known by employees who also knew intended uses of fuel were insufficient, since effective such reactive safeguards were not as effective or reliable in guaranteeing that special fuel was dispensed solely for nontaxable use, and since such safeguards undisputably failed to prevent improper dispensing in certain instances. Scott Oil Co., Inc. v. Indiana Dept. of State Revenue, 1992, 584 N.E.2d 1127.

Fuel oil sold from color-coded employee controlled fuel pumps to customers who did not place fuel into fuel tanks of motor vehicles was not subject to special fuel tax; taxpayer was not required to record customer names and intended uses for special fuel sold as proof of nontaxability. C & C Oil Co., Inc. v. Indiana Dept. of State Revenue, 1991, 570 N.E.2d 1376.

If special fuel is not delivered or placed into motor vehicle gas tanks, then it is beyond taxing authority of Department of State Revenue. C &

C Oil Co., Inc. v. Indiana Dept. of State Revenue, 1991, 570 N.E.2d 1376.

Taxing only special fuel delivered or placed into motor vehicle gas tanks is consistent with purpose of special fuel tax to generate funds for highway purposes, traffic safety, and policing costs. C & C Oil Co., Inc. v. Indiana Dept. of State Revenue, 1991, 570 N.E.2d 1376.

6–6–2.5–31 Exempted special fuels; dye requirements and specifications; markers

Sec. 31. (a) Special fuel exempted under section 30(a)(8) of this chapter shall have dye added to it at or before the time of withdrawal at a terminal or refinery rack. At the option of the supplier, the dye added may be either:

(1) dye required to be added pursuant to United States Environmental Protection Agency requirements; or

(2) dye with specifications and amounts as required by the department.

(b) The department may require that special fuel exempted under section 30(a)(8) of this chapter shall have a marker added to the special fuel not later than the time of withdrawal at a terminal or refinery rack. The marker must meet the specifications required by the department.

As added by P.L.277–1993(ss), SEC.44. Amended by P.L.85–1995, SEC.19.

Historical and Statutory Notes

P.L.85–1995, Sec.19, amended the section by designating Subsec. (a) and adding Subsec. (b).

6–6–2.5–32 Refunds; circumstances; claims; investigations

Sec. 32. (a) Special fuel tax that has been collected by a supplier on special fuel used for an exempt purpose, including section 30(a)(4) through 30(a)(7) of this chapter and pretaxed exempt fuel under section 30(a)(8) of this chapter, but which was not dyed or marked, or both, in accordance with section 31 of this chapter, shall be refunded by the department to the user or the user's assignee under rules adopted by the department, in accordance with subsection (c), upon presentation of proof of exempt use by the end user in the form that the department prescribes.

(b) Special fuel tax that has been collected by a supplier on special fuel that was removed from a terminal or refinery for delivery in Indiana, and was exported by a licensed exporter shall be refunded by the department to the licensed exporter in accordance with subsection (c), upon presentation of proof of export in the form that the department prescribes.

(c) Special fuel tax that has been erroneously paid by a person shall be refunded by the department in accordance with subsection (d).

(d) To claim a refund under subsection (a) through (c), a person must present to the department a statement that contains a written verification that the claim is made under penalties of perjury and lists the total amount of special fuel purchased and used for non-highway purposes. The claim must be filed not more than three (3) years after the date the special fuel was purchased. The statement must show that payment for the purchase has been made and the amount of tax paid on the purchase has been remitted.

(e) The department may make any investigations it considers necessary before refunding the special fuel tax to a person.

As added by P.L.277–1993(ss), SEC.44. Amended by P.L.85–1995, SEC.20.

Historical and Statutory Notes

P.L.85–1995, Sec.20, amended the section by adding "or marked, or both," to Subsec. (a).

Library References

Taxation ☞1334.
WESTLAW Topic No. 371.
C.J.S. Taxation § 1252.

Notes of Decisions

Burden of proof   1
Costs   3
Interest   2

———

1. Burden of proof

In case in which taxpayer seeks refund from assessment of taxes, burden of proof should rest on Department to make prima facie showing that taxpayer is subject to tax and should not be placed on taxpayer to prove nontaxability in instances which taxpayer denies taxability in first instance. Scott Oil Co., Inc. v. Indiana Dept. of State Revenue, 1992, 584 N.E.2d 1127.

2. Interest

Taxpayer's surety was entitled to an award of 8% prejudgment interest on an overpayment of motor fuel use taxes. State Dept. of Revenue v. American Motorists' Ins. Co., App. 4 Dist.1979, 396 N.E.2d 907, 182 Ind.App. 645.

Trial court was correct in fixing the period for which interest was to be paid on an overpayment of motor fuel use taxes according to terms of parties' stipulation. State Dept. of Revenue v. American Motorists' Ins. Co., App. 4 Dist. 1979, 396 N.E.2d 907, 182 Ind.App. 645.

Notwithstanding absence of specific statutory authority, taxpayer's surety was entitled to interest on overpayment of motor fuel use taxes. State Dept. of Revenue v. American Motorists' Ins. Co., App. 4 Dist.1979, 396 N.E.2d 907, 182 Ind.App. 645.

3. Costs

No costs could be assessed against state in successful action by taxpayer's surety to recover interest on a refund of motor fuel use taxes. State Dept. of Revenue v. American Motorists' Ins. Co., App. 4 Dist.1979, 396 N.E.2d 907, 182 Ind.App. 645.

6–6–2.5–32.5   Refund of special fuel tax; qualification; claim for refund

Sec. 32.5. (a) A person that pays the tax imposed by this chapter on the use of special fuel in the operation of an intercity bus (as defined in IC 9–13–2–83) is entitled to a refund of the tax without interest if the person has:

(1) consumed the special fuel outside Indiana;

(2) paid a special fuel tax or highway use tax for the special fuel in at least one (1) state or other jurisdiction outside Indiana; and

(3) complied with subsection (b).

(b) To qualify for a refund under this section, a special fuel user shall submit to the department a claim for a refund, in the form prescribed by the department, that includes the following information:

(1) Any evidence requested by the department of the following:

(A) Payment of the tax imposed by this chapter.

(B) Payment of taxes in another state or jurisdiction outside Indiana.

(2) Any other information reasonably requested by the department.

As added by P.L.85–1995, SEC.21.

Library References

Taxation ⚷1334.
WESTLAW Topic No. 371.
C.J.S. Taxation § 1252.

6–6–2.5–33 Payment of interest on refund claim

Sec. 33. If a claim for refund is not issued within ninety (90) days of the filing required by section 32 of this chapter, the department shall pay interest at the rate established by IC 6–8.1–9 from a date that is ninety (90) days after the date that the department receives the claim for refund and all necessary documentation until a date, determined by the commissioner, that does not precede by more than thirty (30) days, the date on which the refund is made.

As added by P.L.277–1993(ss), SEC.44. Amended by P.L.85–1995, SEC.22.

Historical and Statutory Notes

P.L.85–1995, Sec.22, amended the section by deleting "of filing of"; adding "that is ninety (90) days after the date that the department receives" and "and all necessary documentation,"; and by making other nonsubstantive changes.

Library References

Interest ⚷31.
WESTLAW Topic No. 219.
C.J.S. Interest and Usury; Consumer Credit § 37.

6–6–2.5–34 Supplier deduction for gallons purchased; prohibition; customer refunds; application

Sec. 34. No supplier shall claim a deduction from taxable gallons for gallons actually purchased by the customer, notwithstanding that the supplier has issued a corrective credit or rebilling to a customer adjusting the tax liability. The only remedy available to a customer to offset liability for special fuel tax paid is to apply for a refund as provided by section 32(d) of this chapter.

As added by P.L.277–1993(ss), SEC.44.

Library References

Taxation ⚷1334.
WESTLAW Topic No. 371.
C.J.S. Taxation § 1252.

6–6–2.5–35 Collection and remittance of special fuel tax; estimated tax payments

Sec. 35. (a) The tax on special fuel received by a licensed supplier in Indiana that is imposed by section 28 of this chapter shall be collected and remitted to the state by the supplier who receives taxable gallons in accordance with subsection (b).

(b) On or before the fifteenth day of each month, licensed suppliers and licensed permissive suppliers shall make an estimated payment of all taxes imposed on transactions that occurred during the previous calendar month equal to:

(1) one hundred percent (100%) of the amount remitted by the licensed supplier or licensed permissive supplier for the month preceding the previous calendar month; or

(2) ninety–five percent (95%) of the amount actually due and payable by the licensed supplier or licensed permissive supplier for the previous month.

Any remaining tax imposed on transactions occurring during a calendar month shall be due and payable on or before the twentieth day of the following month, except as provided in subsection (i). Underpayments of estimated taxes due and owing the department are not subject to a penalty under section 63(a) of this chapter.

(c) A supplier who sells special fuel shall collect from the purchaser the special fuel tax imposed under section 28 of this chapter. At the election of an eligible purchaser, the seller shall not require a payment of special fuel tax from the purchaser at a time that is earlier than the date on which the tax is required to be remitted by the supplier under subsection (b). This election shall be subject to a condition that the eligible purchaser's remittances of all amounts of tax due the seller shall be paid by electronic funds transfer on or before the due date of the remittance by the supplier to the department, and the eligible purchaser's election under this subsection may be terminated by the seller if the eligible purchaser does not make timely payments to the seller as required by this subsection.

(d) As used in this section, "eligible purchaser" means a person who has authority from the department to make the election under subsection (c) and includes every person who is licensed and in good standing as a special fuel dealer or special fuel user, as determined by the department, as of July 1, 1993, who has purchased a minimum of two hundred forty thousand (240,000) taxable gallons of special fuel each year in the preceding two (2) years, or who otherwise meets the financial responsibility and bonding requirements of subsection (e).

(e) Each purchaser that desires to make an election under subsection (c) shall present evidence of the purchaser's eligible purchaser status to the purchaser's seller. The department shall determine whether the purchaser is an eligible purchaser. The department may require a purchaser that pays the tax to a supplier to file with the department a surety bond payable to the state, upon which the purchaser is the obligor or other financial security, in an amount satisfactory to the department. The department may require that the bond indemnify the department against bad debt deductions claimed by the supplier under subsection (g).

(f) The department shall have the authority to rescind a purchaser's eligibility and election to defer special fuel tax remittances upon a showing of good cause, including failure to make timely payment under subsection (c), by sending written notice to all suppliers and eligible purchasers. The department may require further assurance of the purchaser's financial responsibility, or may increase the bond requirement for that purchaser, or any other action that the department may require to ensure remittance of the special fuel tax.

(g) In computing the amount of special fuel tax due, the supplier and permissive supplier shall be entitled to a deduction from the tax payable the amount of tax paid by the supplier that has become uncollectible from a purchaser. The department shall adopt rules establishing the evidence a supplier must provide to receive the deduction. The deduction shall be claimed on the first return following the date of the failure of the purchaser if the payment remains unpaid as of the filing date of that return or the deduction shall be disallowed. The claim shall identify the defaulting purchaser and any tax liability that remains unpaid. If a purchaser fails to make a timely payment of the amount of tax due, the supplier's deduction shall be limited to the amount due from the purchaser, plus any tax that accrues from that purchaser for a period of ten (10) days following the date of failure to pay. No additional deduction shall be allowed until the department has authorized the purchaser to make a new election under subsection (e). The department may require the deduction to be reported in the same manner as prescribed in Section 166 of the Internal Revenue Code.[1]

(h) The supplier and each reseller of special fuel is considered to be a collection agent for this state with respect to that special fuel tax, which shall be set out on all invoices and billings as a separate line item.

(i) Except as provided in subsection (e), the tax imposed by section 28 of this chapter on special fuel imported from another state shall be paid by the licensed importer who has imported the nonexempt special fuel not later than three (3) business days after the earlier of:

(1) the time that the nonexempt special fuel entered into Indiana; or

(2) the time that a valid import verification number was assigned by the department under rules and procedures adopted by the department.

However, if the importer and the importer's reseller have previously entered into a tax precollection agreement as described in subsection (j), and the agreement remains in effect, the supplier with whom the agreement has been made shall become jointly liable with the importer for the tax and shall remit the tax to the department on behalf of the importer. This subsection does not apply to an importer with respect to imports in vehicles with a capacity of not more than five thousand four hundred (5,400) gallons.

(j) The department, a licensed importer, the reseller to a licensed importer, and a licensed supplier or permissive supplier may jointly enter into an agreement for the licensed supplier or permissive supplier to precollect and remit the tax imposed by this chapter with respect to special fuel imported from a terminal outside of Indiana in the same manner and at the same time as the tax would arise and be paid under this chapter if the special fuel had been received by the licensed supplier or permissive supplier at a terminal in Indiana. If the supplier is also the importer, the agreement shall be entered into between the supplier and the department. However, any licensed supplier or permissive supplier may make an election with the department to treat all out-of-state terminal removals with an Indiana destination as shown on the terminal-issued shipping paper as if the removals were received by the supplier in Indiana pursuant to section 28 of this chapter and subsection (a), for all purposes. In this case, the election and notice of the election to a supplier's customers shall operate instead of a three (3) party precollection agreement. The department may impose requirements reasonably necessary for the enforcement of this subsection.

(k) Each licensed importer who is liable for the tax imposed by this chapter on nonexempt special fuel imported by a fuel transport truck having less than five thousand four hundred (5,400) gallons capacity, for which tax has not previously been paid to a supplier, shall remit the special fuel tax for the preceding month's import activities with the importer's monthly report of activities. A licensed importer shall be allowed to retain two-thirds (⅔) of the collection allowance provided for in section 37(a) of this chapter for the tax timely remitted by the importer directly to the state, subject to the same pass through provided for in section 37(a) of this chapter.

(*l*) A licensed importer shall be allowed to retain two-thirds (⅔) of the amount allowed in section 37(a) of this chapter of the tax timely remitted by the licensed importer directly to the state, subject to the same pass through provided for in section 37(a) of this chapter.

As added by P.L.277–1993(ss), SEC.44. Amended by P.L.18–1994, SEC.27; P.L.61–1996, SEC.2; P.L.65–1997, SEC.1.

[1] 26 U.S.C.A. 166.

Historical and Statutory Notes

P.L.18–1994, Sec.27, in Subsec. (a), specified that the special fuel be that received by a licensed supplier in Indiana; in Subsec. (b), added the reference to the Subsec. (i) exception; in Subsec. (c), deleted a limitation that the special fuel tax be on transport truck loads of at least 5,200 gallons in the second sentence; in Subsec. (d), inserted a specification that the 240,000 gallons referred to be taxable; in Subsec. (e), made a nonsubstantive language change; in Subsec. (f), required the notice to also be sent to eligible purchasers in the first sentence; in Subsec. (g), inserted a reference to permissive suppliers in the first sentence; and added Subsecs. (h) through (*l*).

P.L.61–1996, Sec.2, amended the section by adding the last sentence of Subsec. (i); substituting "section 28 of this chapter and subsection (a)," for "sections 28 and 35(a) of this chapter" in Subsec. (j); substituting "importer" for "dealer tank wagon operator importer" and "importer's" for "operator importer's" in Subsec. (k); and by deleting "dealer tank wagon" preceding "importer shall be allowed to retain two-thirds" in Subsec. (k).

P.L.65–1997, Sec.1, eff. Jan. 1, 1998, amended the section by adding the first paragraph of Subsec. (b) and Subsecs. (b)(1) and (b)(2); and substituting "Any remaining" for "All" and "twentieth" for "fifteenth" and adding the final sentence in the final paragraph in Subsec. (b).

Administrative Code References

Tax collections, see 45 IAC 1.1–3–6.

Library References

Taxation ☞1331, 1338.
WESTLAW Topic No. 371.
C.J.S. Taxation § 1250.

Notes of Decisions

Laches   1

_____

1. Laches

Delay by Department of State Revenue in resolving taxpayer's protest did not involve delay in asserting right to collect special fuel taxes from taxpayer, as was necessary for doctrine of laches to be available to taxpayer to prevent collections of tax. Storm, Inc. v. Indiana Dept. of State Revenue, 1996, 663 N.E.2d 552.

6–6–2.5–36   Remittance of tax; procedures; deadline

Sec. 36. All suppliers required to remit the special fuel tax shall remit the special fuel taxes due by electronic fund transfer (as defined in IC 4–8.1–2–7) or by delivering in person or by overnight courier a payment by cashier's check, certified check, or money order to the department. The transfer or payment shall be made on or before the date the tax is due.

As added by P.L.277–1993(ss), SEC.44.

Library References

Taxation ☞1331.
WESTLAW Topic No. 371.
C.J.S. Taxation § 1250.

6–6–2.5–37   Costs of collection, reporting, and remittance; retention of portion of remittance; amount; failure to report or remit on time

Sec. 37. (a) Every supplier and permissive supplier who properly remits tax under this chapter shall be allowed to retain one and six-tenths percent (1.6%) of the tax to cover the costs of collecting, reporting, and timely remitting the tax imposed by this chapter.

(b) The amount that the supplier is permitted to retain under subsection (a) shall be distributed by the supplier as follows:

    (1) One-third (⅓) retained by the supplier.

    (2) Two-thirds (⅔) to the wholesale distributor. If the special fuel is resold by that wholesale distributor or another wholesale distributor to an eligible

purchaser, the last wholesale distributor in the distribution process shall pass on one-half (½) of the two-thirds (⅔) to the eligible purchaser.

(3) If an eligible purchaser is the direct purchaser from a supplier, and that retail dealer or bulk end user is responsible for shipping the product, then the supplier shall pass through two-thirds (⅔) to the retail dealer or bulk end user. If the supplier is responsible for shipping the product, the supplier shall retain two-thirds (⅔) and pass through one-third (⅓) to the eligible purchaser.

(c) If a monthly report is filed or the amount due is remitted later than the time required by this chapter, the supplier shall pay to the department all of the special fuel tax the dealer collected from the sale of special fuel during the reporting period.

As added by P.L.277–1993(ss), SEC.44. Amended by P.L.18–1994, SEC.28.

Historical and Statutory Notes

P.L.18–1994, Sec.28, in Subsec. (a), substituted a reference to suppliers and permissive suppliers who properly remit tax under this chapter for a reference to suppliers required to remit tax under section 35 of this chapter.

Library References

Taxation ⟐1331.
WESTLAW Topic No. 371.
C.J.S. Taxation § 1250.

6–6–2.5–38 Duties and responsibilities of supplier in collection of tax; liability

Sec. 38. The tax the supplier collects on the sale of special fuel belongs to the state. A supplier shall hold the money in trust for the state and for payment to the department as provided in this chapter. In the case of a corporation or partnership, each officer, employee, or member of the employer who is in that capacity is under a duty to collect the tax, and is personally liable for the tax, penalty, and interest.

As added by P.L.277–1993(ss), SEC.44.

Library References

Taxation ⟐1339.
WESTLAW Topic No. 371.
C.J.S. Taxation § 1250.

6–6–2.5–39 Consumption of tax-exempt dyed or marked fuel for nonexempt purpose; remittance of tax

Sec. 39. Any person who has consumed tax-exempt dyed or marked special fuel, or both, for a nonexempt purpose, as permitted under section 62 of this chapter, shall remit the tax due by filing a monthly report and remitting the tax due on forms prescribed by the department.

As added by P.L.277–1993(ss), SEC.44. Amended by P.L.85–1995, SEC.23.

Historical and Statutory Notes

P.L.85–1995, Sec.23, amended the section by adding "or marked" and "or both"; deleting "owing with respect to the nonexempt use gal-lons the tax liability,"; and substituting "monthly" for "quarterly."

Library References

Taxation ☞1294 to 1296, 1313, 1331.
WESTLAW Topic No. 371.

C.J.S. Taxation §§ 1231, 1233, 1241 to 1242, 1246, 1250.

6–6–2.5–40   Transportation of special fuel; requirements and procedures; violations

Sec. 40.   (a) Each person operating a refinery, terminal, or bulk plant in Indiana shall prepare and provide to the driver of every vehicle receiving special fuel at the facility a shipping document setting out on its face the destination state as represented to the terminal operator by the shipper or the shipper's agent, except that an operator of a bulk plant in Indiana delivering special fuel into a vehicle with a capacity of not more than five thousand four hundred (5,400) gallons for subsequent delivery to an end consumer in Indiana is exempt from this requirement.

(b) Every person transporting special fuel in vehicles upon the Indiana public highways shall carry on board a shipping paper issued by the terminal operator or the bulk plant operator of the facility where the special fuel was obtained, which shipping paper shall set out on its face the state of destination of the special fuel transported in the vehicle, except that operators of vehicles with a capacity of not more than five thousand four hundred (5,400) gallons that have received special fuel at a bulk plant in Indiana for delivery to an end consumer in Indiana are exempt from this provision with respect to the special fuel. A person who violates this subsection commits a Class A infraction (as defined in IC 34–28–5–4).

(c) Every person transporting special fuel in vehicles upon the public highways of Indiana shall provide the original or a copy of the terminal issued shipping document accompanying the shipment to the operator of the retail outlet or bulk plant to which delivery of the shipment was made. A person who knowingly violates or knowingly aids and abets another person in violating this subsection commits a Class D felony.

(d) Each operator of a special fuel retail outlet or bulk plant shall receive, examine, and retain for a period of thirty (30) days at the delivery location the terminal issued shipping document received from the transporter for every shipment of special fuel that is delivered to that location, with record retention of the shipping paper of three (3) years required offsite. A person who knowingly violates or knowingly aids and abets another person in violating this subsection commits a Class D felony.

(e) No bulk end user, retail dealer, bulk plant operator, or wholesale distributor shall knowingly accept delivery of special fuel into storage facilities in Indiana if that delivery is not accompanied by a shipping paper issued by the terminal operator or bulk plant operator, that sets out on its face Indiana as the state of destination of the special fuel. A person who knowingly violates or knowingly aids and abets another person in violating this subsection commits a Class D felony.

(f) The department shall provide for relief in a case where a shipment of special fuel is legitimately diverted from the represented destination state after the shipping paper has been issued by the terminal operator or where the terminal operator failed to cause proper information to be printed on the shipping paper. These relief provisions shall include a provision requiring that the shipper or its agent provide notification before the diversion or correction to the department if an intended diversion or correction is to occur, and the relief provision shall be consistent with the refund provisions of this chapter.

(g) The supplier and the terminal operator shall be entitled to rely for all purposes of this chapter on the representation by the shipper or the shipper's agent as to the shipper's intended state of destination or tax exempt use. The shipper, the importer, the transporter, the shipper's agent, and any purchaser, not the supplier or terminal operator, shall be jointly liable for any tax otherwise due to the state as a result of a diversion of the special fuel from the represented destination state.

As added by P.L.277–1993(ss), SEC.44. Amended by P.L.18–1994, SEC.29; P.L.85–1995, SEC.24; P.L.1–1998, SEC.80.

Historical and Statutory Notes

P.L.18–1994, Sec.29, in Subsecs. (b) and (c), added the last sentence in each, relating to violations; in Subsec. (d), required retention of the shipping document at the delivery site for 30 days, in lieu of for 3 years, and required record retention of the shipping paper for 3 years off-site in the first sentence, and added the last sentence, relating to violations; in Subsec. (e), inserted a reference to bulk end users in the first sentence, and added the last sentence, relating to violations; in Subsec. (g), inserted references to importers and transporters, substituted a reference to purchasers for a reference to customers, required joint liability in lieu of exclusive liability, and deleted a provision for liability for misuse of special fuel as highway fuel; and made nonsubstantive language changes throughout.

P.L.85–1995, Sec.24, amended the section by substituting "five thousand four hundred (5,400)" for "four thousand two hundred (4,200)" in Subsecs. (a) and (b).

P.L.1–1998, Sec.80, amended the section by substituting "IC 34–28–5–4" for "IC 34–4–32–4" in Subsec. (b).

6–6–2.5–41 Licenses

Sec. 41. (a) Each supplier engaged in business in Indiana as a supplier shall first obtain a supplier's license. The fee for a supplier's license shall be five hundred dollars ($500).

(b) Any person who desires to collect the tax imposed by this chapter as a supplier and who meets the definition of a permissive supplier may obtain a permissive supplier's license. Application for or possession of a permissive supplier's license shall not in itself subject the applicant or licensee to the jurisdiction of Indiana for any other purpose than administration and enforcement of this chapter. The fee for a permissive supplier's license is fifty dollars ($50).

(c) Each terminal operator other than a supplier licensed under subsection (a) engaged in business in Indiana as a terminal operator shall first obtain a terminal operator's license for each terminal site. The fee for a terminal operator's license is three hundred dollars ($300).

(d) Each exporter engaged in business in Indiana as an exporter shall first obtain an exporter's license. However, in order to obtain a license to export special fuel from Indiana to another specified state, a person shall be licensed either to collect and remit special fuel taxes or be licensed to deal in tax free special fuel in that other specified state of destination. The fee for an exporter's license is two hundred dollars ($200).

(e) Each person who is not licensed as a supplier shall obtain a transporter's license before transporting special fuel by whatever manner from a point outside Indiana to a point inside Indiana, or from a point inside Indiana to a point outside Indiana, regardless of whether the person is engaged for hire in interstate commerce or for hire in intrastate commerce. The registration fee for a transporter's license is fifty dollars ($50).

(f) Each person who wishes to cause special fuel to be delivered into Indiana on the person's own behalf, for the person's own account, or for resale to an Indiana purchaser, from another state in a fuel transport vehicle having a capacity of more than five thousand four hundred (5,400) gallons, or in a pipeline or barge shipment into storage facilities other than a qualified terminal, shall first make an application for and obtain an importer's license. The fee for an importer's license is two hundred dollars ($200). This subsection does not apply to a person who imports special fuel that is exempt because the special fuel has been dyed or marked, or both, in accordance with section 31 of this chapter. This subsection does not apply to a person who imports nonexempt special fuels meeting the following conditions:

(1) The special fuel is subject to one (1) or more tax precollection agreements with suppliers as provided in section 35 of this chapter.

(2) The special fuel tax precollection by the supplier is expressly evidenced on the terminal-issued shipping paper as specifically provided in section 62(e)(2) of this chapter.

(g) A person desiring to import special fuel to an Indiana destination who does not enter into an agreement to prepay Indiana special fuel tax to a supplier or permissive supplier under section 35 of this chapter on the imports must do the following:

(1) Obtain a valid license under subsection (f).

(2) Obtain an import verification number from the department not earlier than twenty-four (24) hours before entering the state with each import, if importing in a vehicle with a capacity of more than five thousand four hundred (5,400) gallons.

(3) Display a proper import verification number on the shipping document, if importing in a vehicle with a capacity of more than five thousand four hundred (5,400) gallons.

(h) The department may require a person that wants to blend special fuel to first obtain a license from the department. The department may establish reasonable requirements for the proper enforcement of this subsection, including the following:

(1) Guidelines under which a person may be required to obtain a license.

(2) A requirement that a licensee file reports in the form and manner required by the department.

(3) A requirement that a licensee meet the bonding requirements specified by the department.

(i) The department may require a person that:

(1) is subject to the special fuel tax under this chapter;

(2) qualifies for a federal diesel fuel tax exemption under Section 4082 of the Internal Revenue Code;[1] and

(3) is purchasing red dyed low sulfur diesel fuel;

to register with the department as a dyed fuel user. The department may establish reasonable requirements for the proper enforcement of this subsection, including guidelines under which a person may be required to register and the form and manner of reports a registrant is required to file.

As added by P.L.277–1993(ss), SEC.44.   Amended by P.L.18–1994, SEC.30; P.L.85–1995, SEC.25; P.L.61–1996, SEC.3.

[1] 26 U.S.C.A. 4082.

Historical and Statutory Notes

P.L.18–1994, Sec.30, in Subsec. (b), substituted the first sentence for a former first sentence, which had read, "Each supplier that does not engage in business in Indiana but desires to collect the tax imposed by this chapter shall obtain a permissive supplier's license.", and made a nonsubstantive language change; and added Subsecs. (f) through (h).

P.L.85–1995, Sec.25, amended the section by adding "or marked, or both," and substituting "section 31" for "section 30" in Subsec. (f); and by adding Subsec. (i).

P.L.61–1996, Sec.3, amended the section by deleting former Subsec. (g); redesignating former Subsecs. (h) and (i) as (g) and (h), respectively; deleting "or (g)" from the end of (g)(1); inserting "if importing in a vehicle with a capacity of more than five thousand four hundred (5,400) gallons." at the end of Subsecs. (g)(2) and (3); and by adding Subsec. (i). Prior to its deletion, former Subsec. (g) read:

"(g) Each person who is an importer of taxable special fuel into this state by a fuel transport vehicle having a capacity of less than five thousand four hundred (5,400) gallons operating out of or controlling a bulk plant in another state shall make application for and obtain a tank wagon operator importer license from the department prior to engaging in the importation activities. However, registration as a tank wagon operator importer does not constitute authorization of the licensee to acquire nonexempt motor fuel free of the tax imposed by this chapter at a terminal either in Indiana or outside of Indiana for direct delivery to a location in Indiana. Any person who possesses a valid importer's license shall be eligible as a tank wagon operator importer without issuance of a separate license if the importer also operates at least one (1) bulk plant outside of Indiana. The fee for a tank wagon operator importer license is twenty-five dollars ($25)."

Library References

Licenses ⚷16(9).
WESTLAW Topic No. 238.
C.J.S. Taxation § 34.

6–6–2.5–42   Application for license; form and content; investigation; fingerprints

Sec. 42. (a) Each application for a license under section 41 of this chapter shall be made upon a form prepared and furnished by the department. It shall be subscribed to by the applicant and shall contain the information as the department may reasonably require for the administration of this chapter, including the applicant's federal identification number and, with respect to the applicant for an exporter's license, a copy of the applicant's license to purchase or handle special fuel tax free in the specified destination state or states for which the export license is to be issued.

(b) The department shall investigate each applicant for a license under this section. No license shall be issued if the department determines that any one (1) of the following exists:

(1) The application is not filed in good faith.

(2) The applicant is not the real party in interest.

(3) The license of the real party in interest has been revoked for cause.

(4) Other reasonable cause for non-issuance exists.

(c) Applicants, including corporate officers, partners, and individuals, for a license issued by the commissioner may be required to submit their fingerprints to the commissioner at the time of applying. Officers of publicly held corporations and their subsidiaries shall be exempt from this fingerprinting provision. Fingerprints required by this section must be submitted on forms prescribed by the commissioner. The commissioner may forward to the Federal Bureau of Investigation or any other agency for processing all fingerprints submitted by license applicants. The receiving agency shall issue its findings to the commissioner. The license application fee shall be used to pay the costs of the investigation. The commissioner may maintain a file of fingerprints.

As added by P.L.277–1993(ss), SEC.44.

Library References

Licenses ⟂22, 23.
WESTLAW Topic No. 238.

C.J.S. Architects § 9.
C.J.S. Licenses §§ 43 to 44.

6–6–2.5–43   Transporters; listing of vehicle descriptions with commissioner; contents

Sec. 43. (a) Each licensed transporter shall at the time of licensing and on an annual basis, list with the commissioner a description of all vehicles, including license numbers, to be used on the highways of Indiana in transporting special fuel from points outside Indiana to points inside Indiana and from points inside Indiana to points outside Indiana.

(b) The description required in subsection (a) must comply with what is reasonably required by the commissioner, including the carrying capacity of the vehicle. If the vehicle is a tractor-trailer type vehicle, the trailer is the vehicle

that must be described. When additional vehicles are placed in service or when a vehicle previously listed is retired from service during the year, the commissioner shall be notified not more than ten (10) days after the change so that the listing of the vehicles may be kept accurate.
As added by P.L.277–1993(ss), SEC.44.

6–6–2.5–44   Surety bond or cash deposit; filing by applicants

Sec. 44.   (a) Concurrently with the filing of an application for a license under this chapter, the department may require the applicant to file with the commissioner a surety bond or cash deposit:

(1) in an amount determined by the commissioner of not less than two thousand dollars ($2,000) or not more than a two (2) month tax liability for the applicant as estimated by the commissioner; and

(2) conditioned upon the keeping of records and the making of full and complete reports and payments as required by this chapter.

(b) If the applicant files a bond, the bond must:

(1) be with a surety company approved by the commissioner;

(2) name the applicant as the principal and the state as the obligee; and

(3) be on forms prescribed by the department.
As added by P.L.277–1993(ss), SEC.44.

Library References

Licenses ⊕26.
WESTLAW Topic No. 238.
C.J.S. Licenses § 42.

6–6–2.5–45   Disclosure of financial records; increase in bond or cash deposit

Sec. 45.   The commissioner may, at the commissioner's reasonable discretion, require a licensee to furnish current certified, audited financial statements. If the commissioner determines that a licensee's financial condition warrants an increase in the bond or cash deposit, the commissioner may require the licensee to furnish an increased bond or cash deposit.
As added by P.L.277–1993(ss), SEC.44.

6–6–2.5–46   Filing of new bond; conditions; cancellation of license; reduction of cash deposit by judgment; additional deposit

Sec. 46.   (a) The commissioner may require a licensee to file a new bond with a satisfactory surety in the same form and amount if:

(1) liability upon the previous bond is discharged or reduced by the judgment rendered, payment made, or otherwise disposed of; or

(2) in the opinion of the commissioner, any surety on the previous bond becomes unsatisfactory.

If the new bond is unsatisfactory, the commissioner shall cancel the license. If the new bond is satisfactorily furnished, the commissioner shall release in writing the surety on the previous bond from any liability accruing after the effective date of the new bond.

(b) If a licensee has a cash deposit with the commissioner and the deposit is reduced by a judgment rendered, payment made, or otherwise disposed of, the commissioner may require the licensee to make a new deposit equal to the amount of the reduction.

As added by P.L.277–1993(ss), SEC.44.

Library References

Licenses ☞26.
WESTLAW Topic No. 238.
C.J.S. Licenses § 42.

6–6–2.5–47   Deposit insufficient to ensure payment; written demand to file new bond; requirements; cancellation of license

Sec. 47. (a) If the commissioner reasonably determines that the amount of the existing bond or cash deposit is insufficient to ensure payment to the state of the tax and any penalty and interest for which the licensee is or may become liable, the licensee shall, upon written demand of the commissioner, file a new bond or increase the cash deposit. The commissioner shall allow the licensee at least thirty (30) days to secure the increased bond or cash deposit.

(b) The new bond or cash deposit must meet the requirements set forth in this chapter.

(c) If the new bond or cash deposit required under this section is unsatisfactory, the commissioner shall cancel the licensee's license certificate.

As added by P.L.277–1993(ss), SEC.44. Amended by P.L.18–1994, SEC.31.

Historical and Statutory Notes

P.L.18–1994, Sec.31, in Subsec. (a), lengthened the minimum period allowed for securing the increased bond or cash deposit from 15 to 30 days.

Library References

Licenses ☞26.
WESTLAW Topic No. 238.
C.J.S. Licenses § 42.

6–6–2.5–48   Release of surety from liability; written request; notice; cancellation

Sec. 48. (a) Sixty (60) days after making a written request for release to the commissioner, the surety of a bond furnished by a licensee is released from any liability to the state accruing on the bond after the sixty (60) day period. The release does not affect any liability accruing before the expiration of the sixty (60) day period.

(b) The commissioner shall promptly notify the licensee furnishing the bond that a release has been requested. Unless the licensee obtains a new bond that meets the requirements of this chapter and files with the commissioner the new bond within the sixty (60) day period, the commissioner shall cancel the license.

(c) Sixty (60) days after making a written request for release to the commissioner, the cash deposit provided by a licensee is canceled as security for any obligation accruing after the expiration of the sixty (60) day period. However, the commissioner may retain all or part of the cash deposit for up to three (3) years and one (1) day as security for any obligations accruing before the effective date of the cancellation. Any part of the deposit that is not retained by the commissioner shall be released to the licensee. Before the expiration of the sixty (60) day period, the licensee must provide the commissioner with a bond that satisfies the requirements of this chapter or the commissioner shall cancel the license.

As added by P.L.277–1993(ss), SEC.44.

Library References

Licenses ⚖️26.
WESTLAW Topic No. 238.
C.J.S. Licenses § 42.

6–6–2.5–49 Denial of license; hearing; notice

Sec. 49. Before being denied a license, the department shall grant the applicant a hearing of which the applicant shall be given at least five (5) days written notice.

As added by P.L.277–1993(ss), SEC.44.

6–6–2.5–50 Issuance of license

Sec. 50. If the application and bond are approved, the department shall issue a license and as many copies as the licensee has places of business for which a license is required.

As added by P.L.277–1993(ss), SEC.44.

6–6–2.5–51 Validity of license

Sec. 51. A license is valid until suspended, revoked for cause, or canceled.

As added by P.L.277–1993(ss), SEC.44.

6–6–2.5–52 Transfer of license; prohibition

Sec. 52. No license is transferable to another person or to another place of business.

As added by P.L.277–1993(ss), SEC.44.

6–6–2.5–53   Display of license at place of business

Sec. 53.   Each license shall be preserved and conspicuously displayed at the place of business for which it is issued.

As added by P.L.277–1993(ss), SEC.44.

6–6–2.5–54   Discontinuance of business; surrender of license

Sec. 54.   Upon the discontinuance of the business, the license issued for the place shall be immediately surrendered to the department.

As added by P.L.277–1993(ss), SEC.44.

6–6–2.5–55   Notice of discontinuance, sale, or transfer of business; content; liability

Sec. 55.   Whenever any person licensed to do business under this chapter discontinues, sells, or transfers the business, the licensee shall immediately notify the department in writing of the discontinuance, sale, or transfer. The notice shall give the date of discontinuance, sale, or transfer and in the event of the sale or transfer of the business, the name and address of the purchaser or transferee. The licensee shall be liable for all taxes, interest, and penalties that accrue or may be owing and any criminal liability for misuse of the license that occurs prior to issuance of the notice.

As added by P.L.277–1993(ss), SEC.44.

6–6–2.5–56   Repealed

(Repealed by P.L.61–1996, SEC.24.)

Historical and Statutory Notes

Former IC 6–6–2.5–56 related to verified statement of supplier of amount of tax due and additional reporting requirements.

Formerly:
P.L.227–1993, SEC.44.
P.L.18–1994, SEC.32.

6–6–2.5–56.5   Suppliers, permissive suppliers and licensed importers; reporting requirements; violations

Sec. 56.5.   (a) For the purpose of determining the amount of special tax due, every supplier shall file with the department on forms prescribed and furnished by the department, a verified statement by the supplier. The department may require the reporting of any information reasonably necessary to determine the amount of special fuel tax due.

(b) The reports required by this section that contain information for the preceding calendar month shall be filed before the twentieth day of each month.

(c) Each supplier and permissive supplier shall separately report:

(1) all loads of special fuel received by the supplier or permissive supplier for export to another state; and

(2) all loads of special fuel removed by the supplier or permissive supplier out of an out-of-state terminal for delivery to Indiana and sold tax free to persons for import into Indiana;

in accordance with the shipping papers issued by the terminal operator. A person who knowingly violates this subsection commits a Class D felony.

(d) Each licensed importer shall file monthly with the department a verified sworn statement of operations within Indiana and any other information with respect to the source and means of transportation of special fuel as the department may require and on forms prescribed and furnished by the department. A person who knowingly violates this subsection commits a Class D felony.

As added by P.L.65–1997, SEC.2.

Historical and Statutory Notes

P.L.65–1997, Sec.2, eff. Jan. 1, 1998.

Library References

Taxation ⚖1313.
WESTLAW Topic No. 371.
C.J.S. Taxation § 1246.

6–6–2.5–57 Terminal operators; reporting requirements; inventory records

Sec. 57.   (a) Each person operating a terminal in Indiana shall file monthly reports of operations within Indiana on forms prescribed by the department. The department may require the reporting of any information it considers reasonably necessary.

(b) For purposes of reporting and determining tax liability under this chapter, every licensee shall maintain inventory records as required by the department.

As added by P.L.277–1993(ss), SEC.44.

Library References

Taxation ⚖1313.
WESTLAW Topic No. 371.
C.J.S. Taxation § 1246.

6–6–2.5–58 **Final report upon discontinuance, sale, or transfer of business or revocation of license; payment of taxes and penalties**

Sec. 58. Every licensee shall, upon the discontinuance, sale, or transfer of the business or upon the cancellation or revocation of a license, make a report as required under this chapter marked "Final Report", and shall pay all special fuel taxes and penalties that may be due the state except as may otherwise be provided by law. The payment shall be made to the department in accordance with sections 35 and 36 of this chapter.
As added by P.L.277–1993(ss), SEC.44.

Library References

Taxation ☞1313, 1331.
WESTLAW Topic No. 371.
C.J.S. Taxation §§ 1246, 1250.

6–6–2.5–59 **Exporters; reporting requirements**

Sec. 59. Each person operating as an exporter shall file monthly reports with the department on forms prescribed and furnished by the department concerning the amount of special fuel exported from Indiana. The department may require the reporting of any information it considers reasonably necessary. However, the report shall contain the following information:

(1) The special fuel loaded in Indiana for delivery outside of Indiana.

(2) The gallons delivered to taxing jurisdictions outside Indiana.

(3) The name and federal employer identification number of the receiver of the exported special fuel.

(4) The date of the shipments.
As added by P.L.277–1993(ss), SEC.44.

Library References

Taxation ☞1313.
WESTLAW Topic No. 371.
C.J.S. Taxation § 1246.

6–6–2.5–60 **Transporters; reporting requirements; failure to report; penalty; waiver of report**

Sec. 60. (a) Each person operating as a transporter in Indiana shall file monthly reports with the department on forms prescribed and furnished by the department concerning the amount of special fuel transported in Indiana. The department may require the reporting of any information it considers reasonably necessary to track the movement of special fuel in Indiana.

(b) If a transporter fails to make the reports required by this section, the person is subject to a civil penalty of one thousand dollars ($1,000) for each violation, as reasonably determined by the department.

(c) The reports required by this section are for information purposes only and the commissioner may waive the filing of the reports if the reports are unnecessary for the proper administration of this chapter.

As added by P.L.277–1993(ss), SEC.44.

Library References

Taxation ☞1313, 1331, 1342.
WESTLAW Topic No. 371.
C.J.S. Taxation §§ 1246, 1250, 1255.

6–6–2.5–61   Composite and modified reports

Sec. 61.   The department may aggregate the information required in any of the reports required by this chapter into one (1) or more composite or modified reports in order to avoid duplicate reporting.

As added by P.L.277–1993(ss), SEC.44.

6–6–2.5–62   Special fuel restrictions; violations; exemptions

Sec. 62.   (a) No person shall import, sell, use, deliver, or store in Indiana special fuel in bulk as to which dye or a marker, or both, has not been added in accordance with section 31 of this chapter, or as to which the tax imposed by this chapter has not been paid to or accrued by a licensed supplier or licensed permissive supplier as shown by a notation on a terminal-issued shipping paper subject to the following exceptions:

(1) A supplier shall be exempt from this provision with respect to special fuel manufactured in Indiana or imported by pipeline or waterborne barge and stored within a terminal in Indiana.

(2) An end user shall be exempt from this provision with respect to special fuel in a vehicle supply tank when the fuel was placed in the vehicle supply tank outside of Indiana.

(3) A licensed importer, and transporter operating on the importer's behalf, that transports in vehicles with a capacity of more than five thousand four hundred (5,400) gallons, shall be exempt from this prohibition if the importer or the transporter has met all of the following conditions:

(A) The importer or the transporter before entering onto the highways of Indiana has obtained an import verification number from the department not earlier than twenty-four (24) hours before entering Indiana.

(B) The import verification number must be set out prominently and indelibly on the face of each copy of the terminal-issued shipping paper carried on board the transport truck.

(C) The terminal origin and the importer's name and address must be set out prominently on the face of each copy of the terminal-issued shipping paper.

(D) The terminal-issued shipping paper data otherwise required by this chapter is present.

(E) All tax imposed by this chapter with respect to previously requested import verification number activity on the account of the importer or the transporter has been timely remitted.

In every case, a transporter acting in good faith is entitled to rely upon representations made to the transporter by the fuel supplier or importer and when acting in good faith is not liable for the negligence or malfeasance of another person. A person who knowingly violates or knowingly aids and abets another person in violating this subsection commits a Class D felony.

(b) No person shall export special fuel from Indiana unless that person has obtained an exporter's license or a supplier's license or has paid the destination state special fuel tax to the supplier and can demonstrate proof of export in the form of a destination state bill of lading. A person who knowingly violates or knowingly aids and abets another person in violating this subsection commits a Class D felony.

(c) No person shall operate or maintain a motor vehicle on any public highway in Indiana with special fuel contained in the fuel supply tank for the motor vehicle that contains dye or a marker, or both, as provided under section 31 of this chapter. This provision does not apply to persons operating motor vehicles that have received fuel into their fuel tanks outside of Indiana in a jurisdiction that permits introduction of dyed or marked, or both, special fuel of that color and type into the motor fuel tank of highway vehicles or to a person that qualifies for the federal fuel tax exemption under Section 4082 of the Internal Revenue Code[1] and that is registered with the department as a dyed fuel user. A person who knowingly:

(1) violates; or

(2) aids and abets another person in violating;

this subsection commits a Class A infraction. However, the violation is a Class A misdemeanor if the person has committed one (1) prior unrelated violation of this subsection, and a Class D felony if the person has committed more than one (1) prior unrelated violation of this subsection.

(d) No person shall engage in any business activity in Indiana as to which a license is required by section 41 of this chapter unless the person shall have first obtained the license. A person who knowingly violates or knowingly aids and abets another person in violating this subsection commits a Class D felony.

(e) No person shall operate a motor vehicle with a capacity of more than five thousand four hundred (5,400) gallons that is engaged in the shipment of special fuel on the public highways of Indiana and that is destined for a delivery point in Indiana, as shown on the terminal-issued shipping papers, without having on board a terminal-issued shipping paper indicating with respect to any special fuel purchased:

(1) under claim of exempt use, a notation describing the load or the appropriate portion of the load as Indiana tax exempt special fuel;

(2) if not purchased under a claim of exempt use, a notation describing the load or the appropriate portion thereof as Indiana taxed or pretaxed special fuel; or

(3) if imported by or on behalf of a licensed importer instead of the pretaxed notation, a valid verification number provided before entry into Indiana by the department or the department's designee or appointee, and the valid verification number may be handwritten on the shipping paper by the transporter or importer.

A person is in violation of subdivision (1) or (2) (whichever applies) if the person boards the vehicle with a shipping paper that does not meet the requirements described in the applicable subdivision (1) or (2). A person in violation of this subsection commits a Class A infraction (as defined in IC 34–28–5–4).

(f) A person may not sell or purchase any product for use in the supply tank of a motor vehicle for general highway use that does not meet ASTM standards as published in the annual Book of Standards and its supplements unless amended or modified by rules adopted by the department under IC 4–22–2. The transporter and the transporter's agent and customer have the exclusive duty to dispose of any product in violation of this section in the manner provided by federal and state law. A person who knowingly:

(1) violates; or

(2) aids and abets another in violating;

this subsection commits a Class D felony.

(g) This subsection does not apply to the following:

(1) A person that:

(A) inadvertently manipulates the dye or marker concentration of special fuel or coloration of special fuel; and

(B) contacts the department within one (1) business day after the date on which the contamination occurs.

(2) A person that affects the dye or marker concentration of special fuel by engaging in the blending of the fuel, if the blender:

(A) collects or remits, or both, all tax due as provided in section 28(g) of this chapter;

(B) maintains adequate records as required by the department to account for the fuel that is blended and its status as a taxable or exempt sale or use; and

(C) is otherwise in compliance with this subsection.

A person may not manipulate the dye or marker concentration of a special fuel or the coloration of special fuel after the special fuel is removed from a terminal or refinery rack for sale or use in Indiana. A person who knowingly violates or aids and abets another person to violate this subsection commits a Class D felony.

(h) This subsection does not apply to a person that receives blended fuel from a person in compliance with subsection (g)(2). A person may not sell or consume special fuel if the special fuel dye or marker concentration or coloration has been manipulated, inadvertently or otherwise, after the special fuel has been removed from a terminal or refinery rack for sale or use in Indiana. A person who knowingly:

(1) violates; or

(2) aids and abets another to violate;

this subsection commits a Class D felony.

(i) A person may not engage in blending fuel for taxable use in Indiana without collecting and remitting the tax due on the untaxed portion of the fuel that is blended. A person who knowingly:

(1) violates; or

(2) aids and abets another to violate;

this subsection commits a Class D felony.

As added by P.L.277–1993(ss), SEC.44. Amended by P.L.18–1994, SEC.33; P.L.85–1995, SEC.26; P.L.61–1996, SEC.4; P.L.1–1998, SEC.81.

[1] 26 U.S.C.A. 4082.

Historical and Statutory Notes

P.L.18–1994, Sec.33, rewrote Subsec. (a), which formerly read:

"(a) No person shall import, sell, use, deliver, or store in Indiana special fuel as to which dye has not been added in accordance with section 31 of this chapter, or as to which the tax imposed by this chapter has not been paid. A supplier shall be exempt from this provision with respect to special fuel manufactured in Indiana or imported by pipeline or waterborne barge and stored within a terminal in Indiana.";

in Subsec. (b), added the last sentence, relating to violations; in Subsec. (c), substituted a reference to motor vehicles for a reference to vehicles in the first sentence, deleted the former subdivision designations, deleted former Subd. (1), which had read:

"(1) motor vehicles that are licensed under IC 9–29–5–13(b) where the declared gross vehicle weight is twenty-six thousand (26,000) pounds or less; and",

and added the last sentence, relating to violations; in Subsec. (d), added the last sentence, relating to violations; in Subsec. (e), substituted references to terminal-issued shipping papers for references to shipping papers in the introductory paragraph, inserted a reference to pretaxed special fuel in Subd. (2), added Subd. (3) and the concluding paragraph, and made non-substantive language changes throughout; and added Subsec. (f).

P.L.85–1995, Sec.26, amended the section by adding "or a marker, or both" to Subsecs. (a) and (c); designating Subsecs. (c)(1) and (2) and (f)(1) and (2); deleting "knowingly" from Subsecs. (c)(1) and (f)(1); adding "Class A infraction. However, the violation is a Class A misdemeanor if the person has committed one (1) prior unrelated violation of this subsection, and a" and "if the person has committed more than one (1) prior unrelated violation of this subsection" to Subsec. (c)(2); substituting "five thousand four hundred (5,400)" for "four thousand two hundred (4,200)" in Subsec. (e); and by adding Subsecs. (g) through (i).

P.L.61–1996, Sec.4, amended the section by inserting "that transports in vehicles with a capacity of more than five thousand four hundred (5,400) gallons," in Subsec. (a)(3) and by inserting "or to a person that qualifies for the federal fuel tax exemption under Section 4082 of the Internal Revenue Code and that is registered with the department as a dyed fuel user." in Subsec. (c).

P.L.1–1998, Sec.81, amended the section by substituting "IC 34–28–5–4" for "IC 34–4–32–4" in Subsec. (e).

6–6–2.5–63 Failure of suppliers, permissive suppliers, importers and blenders to collect or timely remit tax; penalties

Sec. 63. (a) A supplier, permissive supplier, importer, or blender who knowingly fails to collect or timely remit tax otherwise required to be paid to the department under section 35 of this chapter or pursuant to a tax precollection agreement under section 35 of this chapter is liable for the uncollected tax plus a penalty equal to one hundred percent (100%) of the uncollected tax.

(b) Collection of a special fuel tax arising from an out-of-state transaction does not in itself subject a supplier or permissive supplier to the jurisdiction of Indiana for any tax liability arising outside of this chapter.

(c) A person who fails or refuses to pay over to the state the tax on special fuel at the time required in this chapter or who fraudulently withholds or appropriates or otherwise uses the money or any portion thereof belonging to the state commits a Class D felony.

(d) A person who negligently disregards any provision of this chapter is subject to a civil penalty of five hundred dollars ($500) for each separate occurrence of negligent disregard as determined by the commissioner.

As added by P.L.277–1993(ss), SEC.44. Amended by P.L.18–1994, SEC.34; P.L.65–1997, SEC.3.

Historical and Statutory Notes

P.L.18–1994, Sec.34, rewrote Subsec. (a), which formerly read:

"(a) A person who knowingly violates or knowingly aids and abets another to violate any provision of section 40 or 62 of this chapter commits a Class D felony.";

inserted Subsec. (b); redesignated former Subsec. (b) as Subsec. (c); and added Subsec. (d).

P.L.65–1997, Sec.3, eff. Jan. 1, 1998, amended the section by substituting "supplier, importer, or blender" for "supplier" in Subsec. (a); and making other nonsubstantive changes.

6–6–2.5–64 Civil penalties; exemption

Sec. 64. (a) If any person liable for the tax files a false or fraudulent return, there shall be added to the tax an amount equal to the tax the person evaded or attempted to evade.

(b) The department shall impose a civil penalty of one thousand dollars ($1,000) for a person's first occurrence of transporting special fuel without adequate shipping papers as required under sections 40, 41(g), and 62(e) of this chapter, unless the person shall have complied with rules adopted under IC 4–22–2. Each subsequent occurrence described in this subsection is subject to a civil penalty of five thousand dollars ($5,000).

(c) The department shall impose a civil penalty on the operator of a vehicle of two hundred dollars ($200) for the initial occurrence, two thousand five hundred dollars ($2,500) for the second occurrence, and five thousand dollars ($5,000) for the third and each subsequent occurrence of a violation of either:

> (1) the prohibition of use of dyed or marked special fuel, or both, on the Indiana public highways, except for a person that qualifies for the federal fuel tax exemption under Section 4082 of the Internal Revenue Code [1] and that is registered with the department as a dyed fuel user; or

> (2) the use of special fuel in violation of section 28(i) of this chapter.

(d) A supplier that makes sales for export to a person:

> (1) who does not have an appropriate export license; or

> (2) without collection of the destination state tax on special fuel nonexempt in the destination state;

shall be subject to a civil penalty equal to the amount of Indiana's special fuel tax in addition to the tax due.

(e) The department may impose a civil penalty of one thousand dollars ($1,000) for each occurrence against every terminal operator that fails to meet shipping paper issuance requirements under section 40 of this chapter.

(f) Each importer or transporter who knowingly imports undyed or unmarked special fuel, or both, in a transport truck without:

> (1) a valid importer license;

> (2) a supplier license;

> (3) an import verification number, if transporting in a vehicle with a capacity of more than five thousand four hundred (5,400) gallons; or

> (4) a shipping paper showing on the paper's face as required under this chapter that Indiana special fuel tax is not due;

is subject to a civil penalty of ten thousand dollars ($10,000) for each occurrence described in this subsection.

(g) This subsection does not apply to a person if section 62(g) of this chapter does not apply to the person. A:

> (1) person that manipulates the dye or marker concentration of special fuel or the coloration of special fuel after the special fuel is removed from a terminal or refinery rack for sale or use in Indiana; and

> (2) person that receives the special fuel;

are jointly and severally liable for the special fuel tax due on the portion of untaxed fuel plus a penalty equal to the greater of one hundred percent (100%) of the tax due or one thousand dollars ($1,000).

(h) A person that engages in blending fuel for taxable sale or use in Indiana and does not collect and remit all tax due on untaxed fuel that is blended is liable for the tax due plus a penalty that is equal to the greater of one hundred percent (100%) of the tax due or one thousand dollars ($1,000).

As added by P.L.277–1993(ss), SEC.44. Amended by P.L.18–1994, SEC.35; P.L.85–1995, SEC.27; P.L.61–1996, SEC.5

[1] 26 U.S.C.A. 4082

Historical and Statutory Notes

P.L.18–1994, Sec.35, rewrote Subsecs. (b) and (c), which formerly read:

"(b) The department shall impose a civil penalty of two hundred dollars ($200) for each occurrence upon the person transporting special fuel without adequate shipping papers as required under section 40 of this chapter, unless the person shall have complied with rules adopted under IC 4–22–2.

"(c) The department shall impose a civil penalty on the operator of a vehicle of two hundred dollars ($200) for the initial two (2) occurrences in each calendar year of a violation of the prohibition of use of dyed special fuel on the Indiana public highways. Each subsequent offense in a calendar year shall be subject to a civil penalty of five thousand dollars ($5,000).";

in Subsec. (e), substituted a penalty of $1,000 for each occurrence for a penalty identical to that imposed under Subsec. (b); and added Subsec. (f).

P.L.85–1995, Sec.27, amended the section by designating Subsecs. (c)(1) and (2); adding "either:" to Subsec. (c); adding "or marked," "or both" and "or" to Subsec. (c)(1); and by adding Subsecs. (c)(2), (g), and (h).

P.L.61–1996, Sec.5, amended the section by substituting "41(g)" for "41(h)" in Subsec. (b); inserting "except for a person that qualifies for the federal fuel tax exemption under Section 4082 of the Internal Revenue Code and that is registered with the department as a dyed fuel user;" in Subsec. (c)(1); and by inserting "if transporting in a vehicle with a capacity of more than five thousand four hundred (5,400) gallons;" in Subsec. (f)(3).

Library References

Taxation ☞1342.
WESTLAW Topic No. 371.
C.J.S. Taxation § 1255.

6–6–2.5–65   Shipping documents; violations; impoundment, seizure, and sale of vehicle; evidence; release

Sec. 65.   (a) If a person is found operating a motor vehicle in violation of section 40(b), 40(c), or 62(e) of this chapter, the vehicle and its cargo is subject to impoundment, seizure, and subsequent sale, in accordance with IC 6–8.1. The failure of the operator of a motor vehicle to have on-board when loaded a terminal-issued bill of lading with a destination state machine printed on its face or which fails to meet the descriptive annotation requirements in section 40(b), 41(g)(2), 41(g)(3), or 62(e) of this chapter, whichever may apply, shall be presumptive evidence of a violation sufficient to warrant impoundment and seizure of the vehicle and its cargo.

(b) After a person:

(1) is found in violation of section 62(c) of this chapter; and

(2) pays the tax due to the state;

the department shall issue a release to the person. The release must permit the dyed or marked special fuel, or both, that is the subject of the violation to be consumed on Indiana public highways within a grace period of twenty-four (24) hours after the time that the release is issued. After the grace period expires, the person shall be considered in violation of section 62(c) of this chapter if the person or the person's agent operates or maintains the same motor vehicle on an Indiana public highway with special fuel containing dye or a marker, or both.

As added by P.L.277–1993(ss), SEC.44. Amended by P.L.18–1994, SEC.36; P.L.85–1995, SEC.28; P.L.61–1996, SEC.6.

Historical and Statutory Notes

P.L.18–1994, Sec.36, provided that failure of a bill of lading to meet the descriptive annotation requirements in sections 40(b), 41(h)(2), (41)(h)(3), or 62(e) of this chapter was also presumptive evidence of a violation.

P.L.85–1995, Sec.28, amended the section by adding Subsec. (b).

P.L.61–1996, Sec.6, amended the section by substituting "40(b), 41(g)(2), (41)(g)(3)," for "40(b), 41(h)(2), 41(h)(3)," in Subsec. (a).

6–6–2.5–66   Listed tax

Sec. 66.   The special fuel tax is a listed tax for purposes of IC 6–8.1.

As added by P.L.277–1993(ss), SEC.44.

6–6–2.5–67   Use of tax revenues

Sec. 67.   The tax collected on the use of special fuel shall be used only for highway purposes and for payment of any part of the cost of traffic policing and traffic safety incurred by the state or any of its political subdivisions, as authorized by law.

As added by P.L.277–1993(ss), SEC.44.

Library References

Taxation ⚖1345.
WESTLAW Topic No. 371.
C.J.S. Taxation § 1257.

6–6–2.5–68   Transfer of funds to auditor; distribution

Sec. 68.   (a) The administrator shall transfer the next twenty-five million dollars ($25,000,000) of the taxes that are collected under this chapter and received during a period beginning July 1 of a year and ending June 30 of the immediately succeeding year to the auditor of state for distribution in the following manner:

(1) Thirty percent (30%) to each of the counties, cities, and towns eligible to receive a distribution from the local road and street account under IC 8–14–2 and in the same proportion among the counties, cities, and towns as funds are distributed under IC 8–14–2–4.

(2) Thirty percent (30%) to each of the counties, cities, and towns eligible to receive a distribution from the motor vehicle highway account under IC 8–14–1 and in the same proportion among the counties, cities, and towns

as funds are distributed from the motor vehicle highway account under IC 8–14–1.

(3) Forty percent (40%) to the Indiana department of transportation.

(b) The auditor of state shall hold all amounts of collections received from the administrator that are made during a particular month and shall distribute all of those amounts under subsection (a) on the fifth day of the immediately succeeding month.

(c) All amounts distributed under subsection (a) may only be used for purposes that money distributed from the motor vehicle highway account may be expended under IC 8–14–1.

(d) All revenue collected under this chapter shall be used in the same manner as the revenue collected under IC 6–6–1.1. The administrator shall, after the transfers specified in subsection (a), deposit the remainder of the revenues collected under this chapter in the same manner that revenues are deposited under IC 6–6–1.1–802.

As added by P.L.277–1993(ss), SEC.44.

Library References

Taxation ☞1345.
WESTLAW Topic No. 371.
C.J.S. Taxation § 1257.

6–6–2.5–69   Class actions for refund of tax; prerequisites

Sec. 69.   A class action for the refund of a tax subject to this chapter may not be maintained in any court, including the Indiana tax court, on behalf of a person who has not complied with sections 32 and 33 of this chapter before the certification of a class.   A refund of taxes to a member of a class in a class action is subject to the time limits set forth in sections 33 and 34 of this chapter based on the time the class member filed the required claim for refund with the department.

As added by P.L.277–1993(ss), SEC.44.

Library References

Taxation ☞1334.
WESTLAW Topic No. 371.
C.J.S. Taxation § 1252.

6–6–2.5–70   Inspections

Sec. 70.   (a) The department may conduct inspections for and enforce the laws concerning coloration of diesel fuel violations, sulfur content violations, marker violations, and shipping paper violations at any place where taxable fuel is or may be loaded in transport vehicles, produced, or stored.   These places may include, but are not limited to:

(1) a terminal;

(2) a fuel storage facility that is not a terminal;

(3) a retail fuel facility; or

(4) a designated inspection site (defined as any state highway inspection station, weigh station, agricultural inspection station, mobile station, or other location designated by the commissioner).

(b) Inspections to determine violations under this chapter and enforcement of this chapter may be conducted by the state police department, agents of the department, Indiana state police motor carrier inspectors (in addition to their duties defined under IC 10–1–1–25), and any other law enforcement officer through procedures established by the department. Agents of the department have the same power and authority provided to authorized personnel under IC 16–44–2–11 and IC 16–44–2–12.

(c) The department may determine and approve all equipment used to test dyes, markers, and the chemical composition of fuel inspected under this chapter.

As added by P.L.18–1994, SEC.37. Amended by P.L.85–1995, SEC.29.

Historical and Statutory Notes

P.L.85–1995, Sec.29, amended the section by adding "and enforce the laws concerning" and "sulfur content violations, marker violations," to Subsec. (a); and by adding "and enforcement of this chapter" and "state police" to Subsec. (b).

6–6–2.5–71 Sealing of special fuel or kerosene pump; compliance; penalty

Sec. 71. (a) The department or any agent of the department may seal a special fuel or kerosene pump or impound a vehicle that does not have a sealable pump and post a sign that states that transactions involving special fuel or kerosene may not be made at the person's location if any of the following occur:

(1) A person becomes delinquent in payment of a tax due under this chapter.

(2) There is evidence that the revenue of the seller of fuel is in jeopardy.

(3) A person sells special fuel or kerosene without being licensed as required by this chapter.

(4) A person sells special fuel or kerosene without being bonded as required by the department.

(5) A person sells fuel that is taxable under this chapter without charging special fuel tax. However, this subdivision does not apply to a seller that acts in good faith and sells undyed special fuel to a person with a valid tax exemption certificate on file with the seller.

(6) A person sells dyed or marked special fuel for use in a motor vehicle operated on a public highway.

(b) A pump sealed under subsection (a) may remain sealed and a sign posted under subsection (a) may remain posted until all of the following have occurred:

(1) All reports are filed and the fees and taxes imposed under this chapter are paid in full.

(2) The interest and penalties imposed under this chapter, IC 6–8.1–10–1, and IC 6–8.1–10–2 are paid in full.

(3) The license required by this chapter is obtained.

(4) The bond, letter of credit, or cash deposit required by this chapter is provided in the amount required by the department.

(c) A person that sells special fuel or kerosene in Indiana shall allow the agents of the department to seal gallonage totalizers of metered pumps operated by or on behalf of the person selling special fuel or kerosene.

(d) If the department determines that a person is selling special fuel or kerosene from a metered pump in Indiana without an effectively sealable gallonage totalizer, the seller, at the department's request, shall:

(1) adapt the pump to the department's specifications so that the pump may be effectively sealed; or

(2) replace, in whole or in part, the pump with a pump employing an effectively sealable gallonage totalizer, as determined by the department.

(e) A person's failure to comply with subsection (c) or (d) shall be considered evidence that the revenue of the person is in jeopardy.

(f) A person that, without authorization, removes, alters, defaces, or covers a sign that:

(1) is posted by the department; and

(2) states that transactions involving special fuel or kerosene may not be made at a location;

commits a Class B misdemeanor. However, the offense is a Class D felony if the offense is committed with intent to evade the tax imposed by this chapter or defraud the state.

(h) A person that sells special fuel or kerosene shall notify the department of the following:

(1) A broken fuel pump seal.

(2) A removed, altered, defaced, or covered sign that was posted by the department.

(i) A person that sells special fuel or kerosene that fails to notify the department, as required by subsection (h), after:

(1) a fuel pump seal is broken; or

(2) a sign that was posted by the department is removed, altered, defaced, or covered;

commits a Class D felony.

As added by P.L.85–1995, SEC.30.

Chapter 3

State Lien For Motor Vehicle Fuel Superior

6–6–3–1   Repealed

(Repealed by Acts 1980, P.L.51, SEC.66.)

Historical and Statutory Notes

Acts 1980, P.L. 51, provided in § 70, containing emergency clause, that the act takes effect Feb. 22, 1980.

The former section related to state liens for motor vehicle fuel as priority liens.

See, now, IC 6–6–2.1–905.

6–6–3–9   Repealed

(Repealed by Acts 1982, P.L.6, SEC.6.)

Historical and Statutory Notes

Acts 1982, P.L.6, provided in Section 33, containing emergency clause, that the act takes effect upon passage Feb. 15, 1982.

The repeal corrected the erroneous adding of text as section 6–6–3–9 by Acts 1981, P.L.25,

Sec.6, which was intended to constitute section 6–3–3–9. For the text, see section 6–3–3–9.

Chapter 4

Motor Carrier Fuel Tax

6–6–4–1 to 6–6–4–7   Repealed

(Repealed by Acts 1982, P.L.59, SEC.7.)

Historical and Statutory Notes

Acts 1982, P.L.59, provided in Section 10, containing emergency clause, that the act takes effect Feb. 24, 1982.

Former § 6–6–4–1 provided for payment of tax on the basis of consumption.

Former § 6–6–4–2 contained definitions.

Former § 6–6–4–3 related to rate of tax.

Former § 6–6–4–4 provided for tax credits and refunds.

Former § 6–6–4–5 provided for cooperative audits of the reports of carriers.

Former § 6–6–4–6 provided for reports by carrier subject to the tax.

Former § 6–6–4–7 related to the presumption of consumption rate.

Formerly:
Acts 1969, c. 417, ss. 1 to 7.
Acts 1971, P.L.72, SECS.1, 3.
Acts 1980, P.L.51, SECS.58, 59.
Acts 1981, P.L.93, SEC.9.

DISPOSITION TABLE

Showing where the subject matter of the repealed sections of Title 6 of the Indiana Code is now covered in new sections of Title 6, West's Annotated Indiana Code.

Repealed Sections	New Sections	Repealed Sections	New Sections
6–6–4–1	6–6–4.1–4(a)	6–6–4–2(d)	6–6–4.1–1(e)
6–6–4–2(a)	6–6–4.1–1(f)	6–6–4–3	6–6–4.1–4
6–6–4–2(b)	6–6–4.1–1(b)	6–6–4–4	6–6–4.1–6
	6–6–4.1–2(a)		6–6–4.1–7
6–6–4–2(c)	6–6–4.1–1(a)	6–6–4–5	6–6–4.1–16
		6–6–4–6	6–6–4.1–10
		6–6–4–7	6–6–4.1–9

6–6–4–8   Repealed

(Repealed by Acts 1980, P.L.61, SEC.15; Acts 1982, P.L.59, SEC.7.)

Historical and Statutory Notes

Acts 1980, P.L. 61, provided in § 16 that the act takes effect Jan. 1, 1981.

The former section related to record keeping.

Provisions pertaining to bookkeeping and record requirements of the department of state revenue are now contained in §§ 6–6–4.1–20, 6–8.1–5–4.

Formerly:

Acts 1969, c. 417, s. 8.

6–6–4–9   Repealed

(Repealed by Acts 1982, P.L.59, SEC.7.)

Historical and Statutory Notes

Acts 1982, P.L.59, provided in Section 10, containing emergency clause, that the act takes effect Feb. 24, 1982.

The former section related to bond requirements of carriers entitled to refunds.

See, now, IC 6–6–4.1–7(c) and 6–6–4.1–8(a).

Formerly:

Acts 1969, c. 417, s. 9.
Acts 1971, P.L.72, SEC.4.

6–6–4–10   Repealed

(Repealed by Acts 1980, P.L.61, SEC.15; Acts 1982, P.L.59, SEC.7.)

Historical and Statutory Notes

Acts 1980, P.L. 61, provided in § 16 that the act takes effect Jan. 1, 1981.

The former section related to assessments of tax estimated to be due.

Provisions pertaining to jeopardy assessments by the department of state revenue are now contained in § 6–8.1–5–3.

Formerly:

Acts 1969, c. 417, s. 10.

6–6–4–11 to 6–6–4–14   Repealed

(Repealed by Acts 1982, P.L.59, SEC.7.)

Historical and Statutory Notes

Acts 1982, P.L.59, provided in Section 10, containing emergency clause, that the act takes effect Feb. 24, 1982.

Former § 6–6–4–11 related to carriers filing joint reports of operations.

Former § 6–6–4–12 related to commercial vehicles leased to carriers.

Former §§ 6–6–4–13 and 6–6–4–14 related to the issuance of carrier permits and authorizations.

The subject matter of the repealed sections is now covered in new sections of Title 6 as follows;

Repealed Sections	New Sections
6–6–4–11	6–6–4.1–11
6–6–4–12	6–6–4.1–3
6–6–4–13	6–6–4.1–13
6–6–4–14	6–6–4.1–12

Formerly:

Acts 1969, c. 417, ss. 11 to 14.
Acts 1971, P.L.72, SECS.5, 6.

6–6–4–15 Repealed

(Repealed by Acts 1980, P.L.61, SEC.15; Acts 1982, P.L.59, SEC.7.)

Historical and Statutory Notes

Acts 1980, P.L. 61, provided in § 16 that the act takes effect Jan. 1, 1981.

The former section required state agencies to cooperate with the department of revenue in the administration of the provisions of this act.

For similar subject matter, See, now, IC 6–8.1–3–7.

Formerly:

Acts 1969, c. 417, s. 15.

6–6–4–16 Repealed

(Repealed by Acts 1982, P.L. 59, SEC.7.)

Historical and Statutory Notes

Acts 1982, P.L.59, provided in Section 10, containing emergency clause, that the act takes effect Feb. 24, 1982.

Former § 6–6–4–16 related to tax exempt vehicles and operations.

See, now, IC 6–6–4.1–2(b).

Formerly:

Acts 1969, c. 417, s. 16.

6–6–4–17 Repealed

(Repealed by Acts 1980, P.L.61, SEC.15; Acts 1982, P.L.59, SEC.7.)

Historical and Statutory Notes

Acts 1980, P.L. 61, provided in § 16 that the act takes effect Jan. 1, 1981.

The former section related to rules and regulations.

Provisions pertaining to rules and regulations of the department of state revenue are now contained in § 6–8.1–3–3.

Formerly:

Acts 1969, c. 417, s. 17.

6–6–4–18 to 6–6–4–21 Repealed

(Repealed by Acts 1982, P.L. 59, SEC.7.)

MOTOR CARRIER FUEL TAX

Historical and Statutory Notes

Acts 1982, P.L. 59, provided in Section 10, containing emergency clause, that the act takes effect Feb. 24, 1982.

Former § 6–6–4–18 provided for reciprocal agreements with other states or jurisdictions for the waiver of taxes and for tax exemptions.

Former §§ 6–6–4–19 and 6–6–4–20 related to tax enforcement and penalties.

Former § 6–6–4–21 provided that revenues be credited to a primary highway system special account.

The subject matter of the repealed sections is now covered in new sections of Title 6 as follows:

Formerly:

Acts 1971, P.L.72, SECS.7 to 10.
Acts 1978, P.L.2, SEC.640.
Acts 1979, P.L.80, SEC.7.
Acts 1980, P.L.61, SEC.11.

Chapter 4.1

Motor Carrier Fuel Tax

MOTOR CARRIER FUEL TAX

Cross References

Records or reports maintained outside state, see IC 6–8.1–5–6.

Library References

Taxation ⚖1209.
WESTLAW Topic No. 371.
C.J.S. Indians § 131.

6–6–4.1–1   Definitions

Sec. 1.   As used in this chapter:

(a) "Carrier" means a person who operates or causes to be operated a commercial motor vehicle on any highway in Indiana.

(b) "Commercial motor vehicle" means a vehicle which is listed in section 2(a) of this chapter and which is not excluded from the application of this chapter under section 2(b) of this chapter.

(c) "Commissioner" means the commissioner of the Indiana department of state revenue.

(d) "Declared gross weight" means the weight at which a motor vehicle is registered with:

(1) the bureau of motor vehicles; or

(2) a state other than Indiana.

(e) "Department" means the Indiana department of state revenue.

(f) "Highway" means the entire width between the boundary lines of every publicly maintained way that is open in any part to the use of the public for purposes of vehicular travel.

(g) "Motor fuel" means gasoline (as defined in IC 6–6–1.1), special fuel (as defined in IC 6–6–2.5), and alternative fuel (as defined in IC 6–6–2.5).

(h) "Quarter" means calendar quarter.

(i) "Motor vehicle" has the meaning set forth in IC 6–6–1.1–103.

(j) "Recreational vehicle" means motor homes, pickup trucks with attached campers, and buses when used exclusively for personal pleasure. A vehicle is not a recreational vehicle if the vehicle is used in connection with a business.
As added by Acts 1982, P.L.59, SEC.1. Amended by P.L.73–1986, SEC.16; P.L.96–1989, SEC.8; P.L.60–1990, SEC.3; P.L.277–1993(ss), SEC.45.

Historical and Statutory Notes

Acts 1982, P.L.59, Sec.1, emerg. eff. Feb. 24, 1982, added this chapter.

Sections 8 and 9 of Acts 1982, P.L.59, provided:

"Section 8. (a) This act is intended to be a codification and restatement of applicable or corresponding provisions of the laws repealed by this act. If this act repeals and reenacts a law in the same form or in a restated form the substantive operation and effect of that law continues uninterrupted.

"(b) This act does not effect any:

"(1) rights or liabilities accrued;

"(2) penalties incurred;

"(3) offenses committed; or

"(4) proceedings begun;

"before the effective date of this act. Those rights, liabilities, penalties, offenses, and proceedings continue and shall be imposed and enforced under prior law as if this act had not been enacted.

"Section 9. The general assembly may, by concurrent resolution, preserve any of the background materials related to this act."

P.L.73–1986, Sec.16, eff. July 1, 1986, in Subd. (f), inserted "and alternative fuel as defined in IC 6–6–2.1", and deleted "and" following "IC 6–6–1.1".

P.L.96–1989, Sec.8, eff. Jan. 1, 1990.

P.L.96–1989, Sec.8, inserted the definitions of "Declared gross weight" and "Motor vehicle".

P.L.60–1990, Sec.3, eff. Jan. 1, 1991.

P.L.60–1990, Sec.3, added the definition of "Recreational vehicle".

P.L.277–1993(ss), Sec.45, eff. Oct. 1, 1993, in Subsec. (g), substituted "IC 6–6–2.5" for "6–6–2.1" in two places.

Governor's veto of H.E.A.1001(ss)(P.L.277–1993(ss)) of the 1993 Special Session was overridden by General Assembly on June 30, 1993.

Section 32 of P.L.278–1993(ss), emerg. eff. retroactive to June 28, 1993, provides:

"(a) Notwithstanding the passage of HEA 1001ss–1993, the provisions of this act supersede the provisions of any conflicting provisions in HEA 1001ss–1993.

"(b) IC 1–1–3.1 does not apply to this act or to HEA 1001ss–1993.

"(c) Notwithstanding IC 1–1–3.1, the effective date of the Sections in this act and HEA 1001ss–1993 are as specified in this act and HEA 1001ss–1993, respectively, regardless of a veto of either act by the governor and the subsequent veto override of either or both acts."

Formerly:

IC 6–6–4–2.
Acts 1969, c. 417, s. 2.
Acts 1971, P.L.72, SEC.1.
Acts 1980, P.L.51, SEC.58.

Cross References

Supplemental highway user fee, carrier defined, see IC 6–6–8–1.

Notes of Decisions

Highway 2
Validity 1

_____

1. Validity

Department of State Revenue's amendment of regulation governing motor carrier fuel tax imposed on carrier's consumption of fuel in operation on state highways to expand terms of regulation from five categories to 34 categories was not change in regulation, but was merely clarification of prior regulation. Indiana Dept. of State Revenue v. Bulkmatic Transport Co., 1995, 648 N.E.2d 1156.

Motor carrier fuel tax, as applied to consumption of fuel by motor carriers in operating on the Indiana toll road, violated neither due process nor equal protection, although toll road was not supported by the tax. Area Interstate Trucking, Inc. v. Indiana Dept. of Revenue, 1992, 605 N.E.2d 272, certiorari denied 114 S.Ct. 183, 510 U.S. 864, 126 L.Ed.2d 142.

2. Highway

Indiana toll road was "open" for public use for purposes of motor carrier fuel tax. Area Interstate Trucking, Inc. v. Indiana Dept. of Revenue, 1992, 605 N.E.2d 272, certiorari denied 114 S.Ct. 183, 510 U.S. 864, 126 L.Ed.2d 142.

Carrier that used some of its motor fuel to traverse toll roads did not come within class of carriers operating equipment having common fuel reservoir for locomotion along highway and for "another commercial purpose," in action for refund of motor carrier fuel tax attributable to other commercial purpose, given determination that toll road was "highway" within meaning of motor carrier fuel tax statutes. Area Interstate Trucking, Inc. v. Indiana State Dept. of Revenue, App. 1 Dist.1991, 574 N.E.2d 311, transfer denied.

Toll road was "highway" within meaning of motor carrier fuel tax statutes. Area Interstate Trucking, Inc. v. Indiana State Dept. of Revenue, App. 1 Dist.1991, 574 N.E.2d 311, transfer denied.

6–6–4.1–2 Applicability of chapter

Sec. 2.   (a) Except as provided in subsection (b), this chapter applies to each:

(1) passenger vehicle that has seats for more than nine (9) passengers in addition to the driver;

(2) road tractor;

(3) tractor truck;

(4) truck having more than two (2) axles;

(5) truck having a gross weight or a declared gross weight greater than twenty-six thousand (26,000) pounds; and

(6) vehicle used in combination if the gross weight or the declared gross weight of the combination is greater than twenty-six thousand (26,000) pounds;

that is propelled by motor fuel.

(b) This chapter does not apply to:

(1) a vehicle operated by:

(A) this state;

(B) a political subdivision (as defined in IC 36–1–2–13);

(C) the United States; or

(D) an agency of states and the United States, or of two (2) or more states, in which this state participates;

(2) a school bus (as defined by the laws of a state) operated by, for, or on behalf of a:

(A) state;

(B) political subdivision (as defined in IC 36–1–2–13) of a state; or

(C) private or privately operated school;

(3) a vehicle used in casual or charter bus operations;

(4) trucks, trailers, or semitrailers and tractors that are qualified to be registered and used as farm trucks, farm trailers, or farm semitrailers and tractors and that are registered as such by the bureau of motor vehicles under IC 9–18 or under a similar law of another state;

(5) an intercity bus (as defined in IC 9–13–2–83);

(6) a vehicle described in subsection (a)(2) through (a)(6) when the vehicle is displaying a dealer registration plate; or

(7) a recreational vehicle.

As added by Acts 1982, P.L.59, SEC.1. Amended by P.L.89–1983, SEC.1; P.L.77–1985, SEC.26; P.L. 97–1987, SEC.37; P.L.8–1988, SEC.3; P.L.96–1989, SEC.9; P.L.60–1990, SEC.4; P.L.2–1991, SEC.42.

Historical and Statutory Notes

P.L. 89–1983, Sec.1, eff. Jan. 1, 1984, added Subd. (5) (now, subd. (4)) to Subsec. (b).

P.L.77–1985, Sec.26, eff. Sept. 1, 1985, in Subsec. (b), Subd. (1), Cl. (B) and Subd. (2), Cl. (B), inserted "political" and inserted "(as defined in IC 36–1–2–13)"; deleted former Subd. (3) of Subsec. (b) excluding commuter van service; and redesignated former Subds. (4) and (5) of Subsec. (b) as Subds. (3) and (4).

Section 37 of P.L.77–1985 was amended by Section 39 of P.L.59–1985 to change the effective date of the amendment of this section by P.L.77–1985 from Sept. 1, 1985 to July 1, 1985.

P.L.97–1987, Sec.37, eff. April 1, 1988, in Subsec. (a), designated Subd. (4) and added Subds. (5) and (6); in Subsec. (b), added Subd. (5) (now, Subd. (6)); and made conforming nonsubstantive changes.

P.L.8–1988, Sec.3, emerg. eff. April 1, 1988, in Subsec. (b), added at the end of Subd. (4), "under a similar law of another state;", inserted Subd. (5), and renumbered former Subd. (5) as Subd. (6).

P.L. 8–1988, Sec.22, containing an emergency clause, provides that section 3 of the act amending this section takes effect April 1, 1988.

P.L.96–1989, Sec.9, eff. Jan. 1, 1990.

P.L.96–1989, Sec.9, in Subsec. (a)(5), inserted "or a declared gross weight"; in Subsec. (a)(6), inserted "or the declared gross weight"; and, in Subsec. (b)(1)(B), deleted "of this state" from the end of the subsection.

P.L.60–1990, Sec.4, eff. Jan. 1, 1991.

P.L.60–1990, Sec.4, added Subsec. (b)(7).

P.L.2–1991, Sec.42, in Subsecs. (b) (4) and (5) made Title 9 citation changes.

Formerly:

IC 6–6–4–2(b).
IC 6–6–4–16.
Acts 1969, c. 417, ss. 2, 16.
Acts 1971, P.L.72, § 1.
Acts 1977, P.L.105, SEC.4.
Acts 1980, P.L.51, SEC.58.

Library References

Taxation ☞1204.
WESTLAW Topic No. 371.
C.J.S. Taxation § 1231.

WESTLAW Electronic Research

See WESTLAW Electronic Research Guide following the Preface.

Out-of-state fuel purchases   1

---

1. Out-of-state fuel purchases

The amount of motor fuel [gasoline and/or special fuel] consumed by a carrier in its entire operations within and without the state as described in section 6–6–4.1–4(b) imposing motor carrier fuel tax includes only motor fuel [gasoline and/or special fuel] consumed by the commercial motor vehicles to which the motor carrier fuel tax law applies. 1983 Op.Atty.Gen. No. 83–2.

The tax imposed under the motor carrier fuel tax law [this chapter] on the consumption of motor fuel [gasoline and/or special fuel] by a carrier in its operations in Indiana is imposed on all carriers who operate or cause to be operated on Indiana highways a commercial vehicle; however, carriers may be exempted from the quarterly reporting requirements by rules promulgated by the Indiana department of state revenue, may purchase a five day consecutive day trip permit in lieu of paying the motor carrier fuel tax [road tax] imposed, or, under a reciprocal agreement, may be exempted or have all or any part of the motor carrier fuel tax law waived with regard to motor carriers that use in Indiana motor fuel [gasoline or special fuel] upon which gasoline and/or special fuel taxes [motor fuel tax] or road tax [motor carrier fuel tax] has been paid to the other state or jurisdiction. 1983 Op.Atty.Gen. No. 83–2.

6–6–4.1–3   Leased motor vehicles

Sec. 3. (a) Except as otherwise provided in this section, every commercial motor vehicle leased to a carrier is subject to this chapter to the same extent and in the same manner as commercial motor vehicles owned by the carrier.

(b) Except as provided in subsection (f), the department may consider a lessor of commercial motor vehicles to be a carrier with respect to the operation of the vehicles it leases to others if the lessor:

(1) supplies or pays for the motor fuel consumed by the vehicles; or

(2) makes rental or other charges calculated to include the cost of the motor fuel consumed by the vehicles.

(c) The department shall provide, by rules adopted under IC 4–22–2, for the presentation by a lessor to other carriers and to the public of evidence and identification of carrier status determined under this section.

(d) Any commercial motor vehicles leased from a lessor who is considered a carrier under subsection (b) may be excluded from the lessee's reports and liabilities under this chapter.

(e) This section governs the primary liability under this chapter of lessors and lessees of commercial motor vehicles. If a lessor or lessee who is primarily liable fails, in whole or in part, to discharge the lessor's or lessee's liability, the lessor or lessee and the other lessor or lessee who is a party to the lease transaction are responsible for compliance with this chapter and are jointly and severally liable for payment of the tax. However, the aggregate taxes collected by the department may not exceed the amount of tax that would have resulted from the operation of the leased vehicle by the owner, plus any applicable costs and penalties.

(f) This subsection does not apply if the motor vehicle is leased to the same person under two (2) or more consecutive leases. If a motor vehicle is leased for less than thirty (30) days, the holder of an annual permit issued under section 12 of this chapter for the motor vehicle is liable for the motor carrier fuel tax.

As added by Acts 1982, P.L.59, SEC.1.   Amended by P.L.96–1989, SEC.10.

Historical and Statutory Notes

P.L.96–1989, Sec.10, eff. Jan. 1, 1990.

P.L.96–1989, Sec.10, added Subsec. (f); in Subsec. (b), inserted the exception clause; and made other nonsubstantive changes.

Formerly:

IC 6–6–4–12.

Acts 1969, c. 417, s. 12.

Cross References

Supplemental highway user fee, carrier defined, see IC 6–6–8–1.

Library References

Taxation ☞1204, 1261.
WESTLAW Topic No. 371.
C.J.S. Taxation §§ 1231, 1241.

6–6–4.1–4   Imposition of tax; rates; computation of amount of fuel consumed in Indiana

Sec. 4.   (a) A tax is imposed on the consumption of motor fuel by a carrier in its operations on highways in Indiana.   The rate of this tax is the same rate per gallon as the rate per gallon at which special fuel is taxed under IC 6–6–2.5. The tax shall be paid quarterly by the carrier to the department on or before the last day of the month immediately following the quarter.

(b) The amount of motor fuel consumed by a carrier in its operations on highways in Indiana is the total amount of motor fuel consumed in its entire operations within and without Indiana, multiplied by a fraction.   The numerator of the fraction is the total number of miles traveled on highways in Indiana, and the denominator of the fraction is the total number of miles traveled within and without Indiana.

(c) The amount of tax that a carrier shall pay for a particular quarter under this section equals the product of the tax rate in effect for that quarter, multiplied by the amount of motor fuel consumed by the carrier in its operation on highways in Indiana and upon which the carrier has not paid tax imposed under IC 6–6–1.1 or IC 6–6–2.5.

(d) Subject to section 4.8 of this chapter, a carrier is entitled to a proportional use credit against the tax imposed under this section for that portion of motor fuel used to propel equipment mounted on a motor vehicle having a common reservoir for locomotion on the highway and the operation of the equipment, as determined by rule of the commissioner.   An application for a proportional use credit under this subsection shall be filed on a quarterly basis on a form prescribed by the department.

As added by Acts 1982, P.L.59, SEC.1.   Amended by P.L.90–1983, SEC.1; P.L.77–1985, SEC.27; P.L.59–1985, SEC.16; P.L.97–1987, SEC.38; P.L.69–1991, SEC.12; P.L.277–1993(ss), SEC.46; P.L.85–1995, SEC.31; P.L.222–1999, SEC.3.

Historical and Statutory Notes

P.L. 90–1983, Sec.1, emerg. eff. April 7, 1983, added Subsec. (c).

Section 3 of P.L. 90–1983 provided:

"Any action taken before the effective date of this act is legalized and validated if:

"(1) the action involved the imposition, payment, or collection of the motor carrier fuel tax imposed under IC 6–6–4 or IC 6–6–4.1; and

"(2) the action would have been valid if taken under IC 6–6–4.1–4, as amended by Section 1 of this act."

P.L.59–1985, Sec.16, emerg. eff. July 1, 1985, substituted, in the second sentence of Subsec. (a), "special fuel is taxed under IC 6–6–2.1" for "gasoline is taxed under IC 6–6–1.1, and the rate changes each time that the license tax rate for gasoline changes under IC 6–6–1.1"; and substituted "under this section" for "under this chapter" in Subsec. (c).

P.L.77–1985, Sec.27, eff. Sept. 1, 1985, added Subsec. (d).

Section 37 of P.L.77–1985 was amended by Section 39 of P.L.59–1985 to change the effective date of the amendment of this section by P.L.77–1985 from Sept. 1, 1985 to July 1, 1985.

P.L.97–1987, Sec.38, eff. Sept. 1, 1987, in Subsec. (d), substituted "equipment mounted on a motor vehicle having a common reservoir for locomotion on the highway and the operation of such equipment" for "the continuous movement apparatus of a ready mix concrete truck".

P.L.69–1991, Sec.12, inserted "in Indiana" in subsec. (d).

P.L.277–1993(ss), Sec.46, eff. Oct. 1, 1993, in Subsecs. (a) and (c), substituted "IC 6–6–2.5" for "IC 6–6–2.1"; and made a nonsubstantive change.

Governor's veto of H.E.A.1001(ss)(P.L.277–1993(ss)) of the 1993 Special Session was overridden by General Assembly on June 30, 1993.

Section 32 of P.L.278–1993(ss), emerg. eff. retroactive to June 28, 1993, provides:

"(a) Notwithstanding the passage of HEA 1001ss–1993, the provisions of this act supersede the provisions of any conflicting provisions in HEA 1001ss–1993.

"(b) IC 1–1–3.1 does not apply to this act or to HEA 1001ss–1993.

"(c) Notwithstanding IC 1–1–3.1, the effective date of the Sections in this act and HEA 1001ss–1993 are as specified in this act and HEA 1001ss–1993, respectively, regardless of a veto of either act by the governor and the subsequent veto override of either or both acts."

P.L.85–1995, Sec.31, amended the section by adding the last sentence of Subsec. (d).

P.L.222–1999, Sec.3, rewrote Subsec. (d), which prior thereto read:

"(d) The tax imposed under this section does not apply to that portion of motor fuel used in Indiana to propel equipment mounted on a motor vehicle having a common reservoir for locomotion on the highway and the operation of the equipment, as determined by rule of the commissioner. The exemption granted by this subsection shall be taken on a quarterly basis in the form of a claim for refund prescribed by the department."

P.L.222–1999, Sec.14, provides:

"(a) Notwithstanding IC 6–6–4.1–4.7(c), as added by this act, a carrier that seeks to claim a proportional use credit under IC 6–6–4.1–4(d) or IC 6–6–4.1–4.5(d) for taxes first due and payable on October 31, 1999, or January 31, 2000, must apply for certification under IC 6–6–4.1–4.7, as added by this act, before October 1, 1999.

"(b) This section expires August 1, 2000."

P.L.222–1999, Sec.15, provides:

"(a) The percentage of a carrier's fuel consumption that is eligible under IC 6–6–4.1–4 and IC 6–6–4.1–4.5 for the proportional use exemption, as determined by a rule of the department of state revenue that is in effect on January 1, 1998, shall remain in effect until July 1, 2001, as the percentage of a carrier's fuel that is eligible for a proportional use credit under IC 6–6–4.1–4(d) and IC 6–6–4.1–4.5(d), both as amended by this act.

"(b) If, after June 30, 2001, the commissioner of the department of state revenue determines on the basis of studies or other competent evidence that the percentages set forth in 45 IAC 13–4–7 do not accurately reflect actual fuel consumption that is eligible for the proportional use credit, the department may adopt rules to change those percentages or may establish by rule a different method of determining the percentage of a carrier's fuel consumption that is eligible under IC 6–6–4.1–4 or IC 6–6–4.1–4.5, both as amended by this act, for the proportional use credit. A rule adopted by the department under this section that determines eligible fuel consumption based on the type of vehicle must allow a carrier to receive a greater proportional use credit upon a showing that the carrier's actual eligible fuel consumption exceeded the amount determined under the rule.

"(c) This section expires January 1, 2003."

Formerly:
IC 6–6–4–1.

IC 6–6–4–3.
Acts 1969, c. 417, ss. 1, 3.

Cross References

Administration, enforcement and collection of tax, revenue department, see IC 6–8.1–1–1 et seq.
Gasoline tax, see IC 6–6–1.1–101 et seq.
Special fuel tax, see IC 6–6–2.1–101 et seq.

Law Review and Journal Commentaries

Taxation; department of revenue: Survey of recent law. Marc S. Weinstein, 13 Ind.L.Rev. 1 (1980).

Library References

Taxation ☞1204.
WESTLAW Topic No. 371.

C.J.S. Taxation § 1231.
I.L.E. Taxation §§ 187 to 190.

Notes of Decisions

In general   3
Commerce clause violation   2
Due process and equal protection   1
Noncommercial motor vehicles   6
Purpose   4
Regulations   5

1. Due process and equal protection

Inclusion of fuel consumed by commercial motor carrier while idling off highway in formula used to calculate motor carrier fuel tax liability did not violate equal protection clause, even though portion of fuel used by auxiliary equipment users to operate auxiliary equipment while vehicle was in motion was exempt from motor carrier fuel taxes, as commercial carrier did not operate auxiliary equipment while on highway. Roehl Transport, Inc. v. Indiana Dept. of State Revenue, 1995, 653 N.E.2d 539.

Motor carrier fuel tax, as applied to consumption of fuel by motor carriers in operating on the Indiana toll road, violated neither due process nor equal protection, although toll road was not supported by the tax. Area Interstate Trucking, Inc. v. Indiana Dept. of Revenue, 1992, 605 N.E.2d 272, certiorari denied 114 S.Ct. 183, 510 U.S. 864, 126 L.Ed.2d 142.

2. Commerce clause violation

The Indiana limitation on the proportional use exemption from the motor carrier fuel tax and motor carrier fuel surcharge tax, limiting an exemption for fuel used by equipment attached to a carrier's motor vehicle to the use of such equipment in Indiana, violated the Commerce Clause; the practical effect of the limitation was to exact a different price for the use of State roads based on the state in which a motor carrier decided to operate the attached equip-

ment. Bulkmatic Transp. Co. v. Department of State Revenue, 1999, 715 N.E.2d 26.

Exemption from motor carrier fuel tax, which applied only to motor carriers who used auxiliary or "power take off" (PTO) equipment in Indiana, impermissibly discriminated against interstate commerce in violation of commerce clause; exemption impermissibly exacted different price for use of Indiana's roads based on location of use of PTO equipment. Bulkmatic Transport Co. v. Department of State Revenue, 1998, 691 N.E.2d 1371.

Impermissible discrimination against interstate commerce through state taxation, in violation of commerce clause, is not limited to taxing companies incorporated in other states more heavily than those incorporated in taxing state, but also encompasses unequal taxation of out-of-state transactions or incidents. Bulkmatic Transport Co. v. Department of State Revenue, 1998, 691 N.E.2d 1371.

Inclusion of fuel consumed by commercial motor carrier while idling off highway in formula used to calculate motor carrier fuel tax liability does not violate Commerce Clause, as motor carriers are subject to varying tax liabilities per mile, depending on rate and manner of fuel consumption, in absence of evidence that formula discriminated against interstate carriers to advantage of intrastate carriers. Roehl Transport, Inc. v. Indiana Dept. of State Revenue, 1995, 653 N.E.2d 539.

3. In general

Tax Court reviews final determinations of Department of State Revenue de novo, and is bound neither by evidence nor issues raised at administrative level. Bulkmatic Transport Co.

v. Department of State Revenue, 1998, 691 N.E.2d 1371.

All fuel consumed by commercial motor vehicle, regardless of where and how it is consumed, is to be included in formula for purposes of calculating motor carrier fuel tax liability. Roehl Transport, Inc. v. Indiana Dept. of State Revenue, 1995, 653 N.E.2d 539.

The amount of motor fuel [gasoline and/or special fuel] consumed by a carrier in its entire operations within and without the state as described in section 6–6–4.1–4(b) imposing motor carrier fuel tax includes only motor fuel [gasoline and/or special fuel] consumed by the commercial motor vehicles to which the motor carrier fuel tax law applies. 1983 Op.Atty.Gen. No. 83–2.

4. Purpose

Legislature's manifest intent in enacting motor carrier fuel tax is to charge motor carriers for operating their commercial motor vehicles on state roads. Roehl Transport, Inc. v. Indiana Dept. of State Revenue, 1995, 653 N.E.2d 539.

5. Regulations

Motor carrier fuel tax is "use tax" and, therefore, federal constitution does not require state to establish system of motor carrier fuel taxation that reflects with exact precision every graduation in use. Roehl Transport, Inc. v. Indiana Dept. of State Revenue, 1995, 653 N.E.2d 539.

Pneumatic trucks, which had common fuel reservoir for both locomotion on highway and operation of pumping equipment, did not qualify as "tank trucks" which were given 24% exclusion from motor carrier fuel tax imposed on carrier's consumption of fuel in operation on state highways; rather, pneumatic trucks constituted "other motor vehicles" entitled to 15% exemption. West's A.I.C. 6–6–4.1–4; Ind. Indiana Dept. of State Revenue v. Bulkmatic Transport Co., 1995, 648 N.E.2d 1156.

Under regulation in effect prior to 1991 Amendment, to qualify for 24% exclusion given tank trucks from motor carrier fuel tax imposed on carrier's consumption of fuel in operation on state highways, "tank truck" was a truck with a common fuel reservoir for both locomotion on highway and operation of pumping equipment;

whether tank truck was pneumatic, single unit configuration, or tractor/trailer combination was irrelevant to determination of whether truck was tank truck. Bulkmatic Transport Co. v. Indiana Dept. of State Revenue, 1994, 629 N.E.2d 955, reversed 648 N.E.2d 1156.

Department of Revenue's amendment of regulation governing motor carrier fuel tax imposed on carrier's consumption of fuel in operation on state highways to expand terms of regulation from five categories to 34 categories was clear change in regulation, not merely clarification of prior regulation. Bulkmatic Transport Co. v. Indiana Dept. of State Revenue, 1994, 629 N.E.2d 955, reversed 648 N.E.2d 1156.

Department of Revenue's refund of proportionate share of surtax on petitioner's motor carrier fuel consumed in state highway operation for years in issue did not justify disallowance of proper exclusion for motor carrier fuel tax. Bulkmatic Transport Co. v. Indiana Dept. of State Revenue, 1994, 629 N.E.2d 955, reversed 648 N.E.2d 1156.

The tax imposed under the motor carrier fuel tax law [this chapter] on the consumption of motor fuel [gasoline and/or special fuel] by a carrier in its operations in Indiana is imposed on all carriers who operate or cause to be operated on Indiana highways a commercial vehicle; however, carriers may be exempted from the quarterly reporting requirements by rules promulgated by the Indiana department of state revenue, may purchase a five day consecutive day trip permit in lieu of paying the motor carrier fuel tax [road tax] imposed, or, under a reciprocal agreement, may be exempted or have all or any part of the motor carrier fuel tax law waived with regard to motor carriers that use in Indiana motor fuel [gasoline or special fuel] upon which gasoline and/or special fuel taxes [motor fuel tax] or road tax [motor carrier fuel tax] has been paid to the other state or jurisdiction. 1983 Op.Atty.Gen. No. 83–2.

6. Noncommercial motor vehicles

Fuel consumed to operate taxpayer's lawn mowers, generators, and company automobiles was not subject to motor carrier fuel tax, as those devices were not commercial motor vehicles. West's A.I.C. 6–6–4.1–4; Ind. Admin. Code title 45, rs. 13–1–2, 13–1–3. Roehl Transport, Inc. v. Indiana Dept. of State Revenue, 1995, 653 N.E.2d 539.

6–6–4.1–4.5 Surtax on motor fuel consumed by carrier in Indiana highway operations

Sec. 4.5. (a) A surcharge tax is imposed on the consumption of motor fuel by a carrier in its operations on highways in Indiana. The rate of this surcharge tax is eleven cents ($0.11) per gallon. The tax shall be paid quarterly by the carrier to the department on or before the last day of the month immediately following the quarter.

(b) The amount of motor fuel consumed by a carrier in its operations on highways in Indiana is the total amount of motor fuel consumed in its entire operations within and without Indiana, multiplied by a fraction. The numerator of the fraction is the total number of miles traveled on highways in Indiana, and the denominator of the fraction is the total number of miles traveled within and without Indiana.

(c) The amount of tax that a carrier shall pay for a particular quarter under this section equals the product of the tax rate in effect for that quarter, multiplied by the amount of motor fuel consumed by the carrier in its operation on highways in Indiana.

(d) Subject to section 4.8 of this chapter, a carrier is entitled to a proportional use credit against the tax imposed under this section for that portion of motor fuel used to propel equipment mounted on a motor vehicle having a common reservoir for locomotion on the highway and the operation of this equipment as determined by rule of the commissioner. An application for a proportional use credit under this subsection shall be filed on a quarterly basis on a form prescribed by the department.

As added by P.L.59–1985, SEC.17. Amended by P.L.8–1988, SEC.4; P.L.69–1991, SEC.13; P.L.85–1995, SEC.32; P.L.222–1999, SEC.4.

Historical and Statutory Notes

P.L.59–1985, Sec.17, emerg. eff. July 1, 1985, added this section.

P.L.8–1988, Sec.4, emerg. eff. April 1, 1988, raised the rate of the surcharge tax imposed by Subsec. (a) from "$0.08" to "$0.11".

P.L. 8–1988, Sec.22, containing an emergency clause, provides that section 4 of the act amending this section takes effect April 1, 1988.

P.L.69–1991, Sec.13, rewrote subsec. (d).

P.L.85–1995, Sec.32, amended the section by adding the last sentence of Subsec. (d).

P.L.222–1999, Sec.4, rewrote Subsec. (d), which prior thereto read:

"(d) The tax imposed under this section does not apply to that portion of motor fuel used in Indiana to propel equipment mounted on a motor vehicle having a common reservoir for locomotion on the highway and the operation of this equipment as determined by rule of the commissioner. The exemption granted by this subsection shall be taken on a quarterly basis in the form of a claim for refund prescribed by the department."

For related provisions of P.L.222–1999, Secs.14 and 15, see Historical and Statutory Notes under IC 6–6–4.1–4.

Library References

Taxation ⚮1294.
WESTLAW Topic No. 371.
C.J.S. Licenses § 30.

Notes of Decisions

In general 2
Noncommercial motor vehicles 4
Proportionate exclusion 5
Purpose 3
Validity 1

_____

1. Validity

The Indiana limitation on the proportional use exemption from the motor carrier fuel tax and motor carrier fuel surcharge tax, limiting an exemption for fuel used by equipment attached to a carrier's motor vehicle to the use of such equipment in Indiana, violated the Commerce Clause; the practical effect of the limitation was to exact a different price for the use of State roads based on the state in which a motor carrier decided to operate the attached equipment. Bulkmatic Transp. Co. v. Department of State Revenue, 1999, 715 N.E.2d 26.

Inclusion of fuel consumed by commercial motor carrier while idling off highway in formula used to calculate motor carrier fuel tax liability does not violate Commerce Clause, as motor carriers are subject to varying tax liabilities per mile, depending on rate and manner of fuel consumption, in absence of evidence that formula discriminated against interstate carriers to advantage of intrastate carriers. Roehl Transport, Inc. v. Indiana Dept. of State Revenue, 1995, 653 N.E.2d 539.

Inclusion of fuel consumed by commercial motor carrier while idling off highway in formula used to calculate motor carrier fuel tax liability did not violate equal protection clause, even though portion of fuel used by auxiliary equipment users to operate auxiliary equipment while vehicle was in motion was exempt from motor carrier fuel taxes, as commercial carrier did not operate auxiliary equipment while on highway. Roehl Transport, Inc. v. Indiana Dept. of State Revenue, 1995, 653 N.E.2d 539.

2. In general

All fuel consumed by commercial motor vehicle, regardless of where and how it is consumed, is to be included in formula for purposes of calculating motor carrier fuel tax

liability. Roehl Transport, Inc. v. Indiana Dept. of State Revenue, 1995, 653 N.E.2d 539.

Motor carrier fuel tax is "use tax" and, therefore, federal constitution does not require state to establish system of motor carrier fuel taxation that reflects with exact precision every graduation in use. Roehl Transport, Inc. v. Indiana Dept. of State Revenue, 1995, 653 N.E.2d 539.

3. Purpose

Legislature's manifest intent in enacting motor carrier fuel tax is to charge motor carriers for operating their commercial motor vehicles on state roads. Roehl Transport, Inc. v. Indiana Dept. of State Revenue, 1995, 653 N.E.2d 539.

4. Noncommercial motor vehicles

Fuel consumed to operate taxpayer's lawn mowers, generators, and company automobiles was not subject to motor carrier fuel tax, as those devices were not commercial motor vehicles. West's A.I.C. 6–6–4.1–4; Ind. Admin. Code title 45, rs. 13–1–2, 13–1–3. Roehl Transport, Inc. v. Indiana Dept. of State Revenue, 1995, 653 N.E.2d 539.

5. Proportionate exclusion

Motor carrier surcharge proportional tax exemption only applied to ready mix concrete trucks during years at issue and, therefore, Department of State Revenue had no authority to promulgate surcharge tax regulation because regulation created surtax exemptions that legislature did not authorize under Surcharge Tax Act during years at issue. Indiana Dept. of State Revenue v. Bulkmatic Transport Co., 1995, 648 N.E.2d 1156.

Regulation excluding portion of motor fuel used to operate equipment in or on motor vehicles from surcharge tax imposed on consumption of motor fuel by carrier provided for proportionate exclusion to surcharge tax for tank trucks. Bulkmatic Transport Co. v. Indiana Dept. of State Revenue, 1994, 629 N.E.2d 955, reversed 648 N.E.2d 1156.

6–6–4.1–4.7 Certification for proportional use credit

Sec. 4.7. (a) This section applies only to a claim for a proportional use credit under section 4(d) or 4.5(d) of this chapter for taxes first due and payable after July 31, 1999.

(b) A carrier must be certified by the department in order to qualify for a proportional use credit under section 4(d) or 4.5(d) of this chapter.

(c) A carrier must apply to the department for certification before April 1 of the first calendar year for which the proportional use credit will be claimed. An application for certification must be in writing upon forms prescribed by the department and must be signed and verified by the carrier. The department must include on all application forms suitable spaces for a listing of the following:

(1) The carrier's federal Social Security number or federal tax identification number.

(2) The address of the carrier's principal place of business.

(3) A description of each of the carrier's vehicles that has a common fuel supply reservoir for both locomotion on a public highway and a commercial purpose.

(4) The vehicle identification number for each vehicle described in subdivision (3).

(d) The department may certify that a carrier is qualified to claim a proportional use credit under section 4(d) or 4.5(d) of this chapter only upon payment by the carrier to the department of a one (1) time fee of seven dollars ($7). The carrier must pay the fee at the time the application for certification is submitted to the department. The department shall deposit the fee in the motor carrier regulation fund established by IC 8–2.1–23–1.

(e) A carrier must notify the department, on forms prescribed by the department, of any change of address by the carrier. The carrier must provide the notice not more than ten (10) days after the change of address. The department may revoke or suspend the certification of a carrier that fails to comply with this subsection.

(f) All certificates issued under this section are personal and may not be transferred.

(g) The department may require a carrier that has been issued a certificate under this section to submit additional information from time to time at reasonable intervals, as determined by the department.

(h) The department may adopt rules under IC 4–22–2 to carry out this section.

As added by P.L.222–1999, SEC.5.

Historical and Statutory Notes

For related provisions of P.L.222–1999, Sec.14, see Historical and Statutory Notes under IC 6–6–4.1–4.

P.L.222–1999, Sec.16, provides:

"(a) Notwithstanding IC 6–8.1–4–4, an owner or operator of a commercial motor vehicle may apply to the registration center established under IC 6–8.1–4–4(a) for a proportional use credit certificate (IC 6–6–4.1–4.7).

"(b) This section expires January 1, 2000."

Cross References

Application to registration center for certificate, see IC 6–8.1–4–4.

6–6–4.1–4.8   Claim for proportional use credit

Sec. 4.8.   (a) This section applies only to a claim for a proportional use credit under section 4(d) or 4.5(d) of this chapter for taxes first due and payable after July 31, 1999.

(b) In order to obtain a proportional use credit against taxes imposed under section 4 or 4.5 of this chapter, a carrier must file a claim with the department. The claim must be submitted on a form prescribed by the department and must be filed with the quarterly return for the taxable period for which the proportional use credit is claimed. A carrier is not entitled to a proportional use credit under section 4(d) or 4.5(d) of this chapter unless the carrier has paid in full the taxes to which the credit applies. A credit approved under this section shall, subject to this section, be refunded to the carrier without interest.

(c) The department shall determine the aggregate amount of proportional use credits claimed under section 4(d) or 4.5(d) of this chapter for each quarter. The department may approve the full amount of a proportional use credit claimed by a carrier if the aggregate amount of proportional use credits claimed for the quarter and for the fiscal year do not exceed the limits set forth in subsection (d). If the aggregate amount of proportional use credits claimed in a quarter exceeds the limits set forth in subsection (d), the department shall pay the claims for that quarter on a pro rata basis.

(d) The department may not approve more than three million five hundred thousand dollars ($3,500,000) of proportional use credits under this section in a state fiscal year. In addition, the amount of proportional use credits the department may approve under this section for a quarter may not exceed the following:

(1) For the quarter ending September 30 of a year, an amount equal to one million three hundred seventy-five thousand dollars ($1,375,000).

(2) For the quarter ending December 31 of a year, an amount equal to:

(A) six hundred twenty-five thousand dollars ($625,000); plus

(B) the greater of zero (0) or the result of:

(i) the limit determined for the previous quarter under this subsection; minus

(ii) the aggregate amount of claims approved for the previous quarter.

(3) For the quarter ending March 31 of a year, an amount equal to:

(A) six hundred twenty-five thousand dollars ($625,000); plus

(B) the greater of zero (0) or the result of:

(i) the limit determined for the previous quarter under this subsection; minus

(ii) the aggregate amount of claims approved for the previous quarter.

(4) For the quarter ending June 30 of a year, an amount equal to:

(A) eight hundred seventy-five thousand dollars ($875,000); plus

(B) the greater of zero (0) or the result of:

(i) the limit determined for the previous quarter under this subsection; minus

(ii) the aggregate amount of claims approved for the previous quarter.

As added by P.L.222–1999, SEC.6.

6–6–4.1–5 Disposition of tax revenue

Sec. 5.   (a) The department shall deposit revenue collected under sections 4 and 12 of this chapter in the state highway fund (IC 8–23–9–54).

(b) The department shall deposit revenue collected under section 4.5 of this chapter as follows:

(1) Forty-five and one-half percent (45.5%) in the state highway fund (IC 8–23–9–54).

(2) Forty-five and one-half percent (45.5%) in the motor vehicle highway account (IC 8–14–1).

(3) Nine percent (9%) in the motor carrier regulation fund administered by the department.

(c) The department shall deposit revenue collected under section 13 of this chapter as follows:

(1) Thirty-five percent (35%) in the motor vehicle highway account (IC 8–14–1).

(2) Sixty-five percent (65%) in the state highway fund (IC 8–23–9–54).

As added by Acts 1982, P.L.59, SEC.1.   Amended by P.L.59–1985, SEC.18; P.L.8–1988, SEC.5; P.L.18–1990, SEC.23.

Historical and Statutory Notes

P.L.59–1985, Sec.18, emerg. eff. July 1, 1985, inserted Subsec. designation (a); substituted, in Subsec. (a), "sections 4 and 12 of this chapter in the state highway fund (IC 8–13–5–19.1)" for "this chapter in the primary highway system special account established under IC 8–14–2–3"; and added Subsecs. (b) and (c).

P.L.8–1988, sec.5, emerg. eff. April 1, 1988, in Subsec. (a), decreased the revenue deposits specified in Subds. (1) and (2) from 50 percent to 45 and one-half percent, and added Subd. (3).

P.L. 8–1988, Sec.22, containing an emergency clause, provides that section 5 of the act amending this section takes effect April 1, 1988.

P.L.18–1990, Sec.23, emerg. eff. March 13, 1990.

Formerly:
IC 6–6–4–21.
Acts 1971, P.L.72, SEC.10.

Library References

Highways ☞99¼.
Taxation ☞1345.
WESTLAW Topic Nos. 200, 371.

Notes of Decisions

In general 1

1. In general

State is not required to use revenues generated by the motor carrier fuel tax from operations on the Indiana toll road for benefit of the Indiana toll road and its patrons. Area Interstate Trucking, Inc. v. Indiana Dept. of Revenue, 1992, 605 N.E.2d 272, certiorari denied 114 S.Ct. 183, 510 U.S. 864, 126 L.Ed.2d 142.

6–6–4.1–6 Credits against tax

Sec. 6. (a) A carrier is entitled to a credit against the tax imposed under section 4 of this chapter if the carrier, or a lessor operating under the carrier's annual permit, has:

(1) paid the tax imposed under IC 6–6–1.1 or IC 6–6–2.5 on motor fuel purchased in Indiana;

(2) consumed the motor fuel outside Indiana; and

(3) paid a gasoline, special fuel, or road tax with respect to the fuel in one (1) or more other states or jurisdictions.

(b) The amount of credit for a quarter is equal to the tax paid under IC 6–6–1.1 and IC 6–6–2.5 on motor fuel that:

(1) was purchased in Indiana;

(2) was consumed outside Indiana; and

(3) with respect to which the carrier paid a gasoline, special fuel, or road tax to another state or jurisdiction.

(c) To qualify for the credit, the carrier shall submit any evidence required by the department of payment of the tax imposed under IC 6–6–1.1 or IC 6–6–2.5.

(d) A credit earned by a carrier in a particular quarter shall be applied against the carrier's tax liability under this chapter for that quarter before any credit carryover is applied against that liability under section 7 of this chapter.

As added by Acts 1982, P.L.59, SEC.1. Amended by P.L.77–1985, SEC.28; P.L.277–1993(ss), SEC.47.

Historical and Statutory Notes

P.L.77–1985, Sec.28, eff. Sept. 1, 1985, in the introductory clause of Subsec. (a), inserted "or a lessor operating under the carrier's annual permit"; and, in Cl. (3) of Subsec. (a), inserted "(1)".

Section 37 of P.L.77–1985 was amended by Section 39 of P.L.59–1985 to change the effective date of the amendment of this section by P.L.77–1985 from Sept. 1, 1985 to July 1, 1985.

P.L.277–1993(ss), Sec.47, eff. Oct. 1, 1993, in Subsec. (a)(1) and Subsec. (c), substituted "IC 6–6–2.5" for "IC 6–6–2.1".

Governor's veto of H.E.A.1001(ss)(P.L.277–1993(ss)) of the 1993 Special Session was overridden by General Assembly on June 30, 1993.

Section 32 of P.L.278–1993(ss), emerg. eff. retroactive to June 28, 1993, provides:

"(a) Notwithstanding the passage of HEA 1001ss–1993, the provisions of this act supersede the provisions of any conflicting provisions in HEA 1001ss–1993.

"(b) IC 1–1–3.1 does not apply to this act or to HEA 1001ss–1993.

"(c) Notwithstanding IC 1–1–3.1, the effective date of the Sections in this act and HEA 1001ss–1993 are as specified in this act and HEA 1001ss–1993, respectively, regardless of a veto of either act by the governor and the subsequent veto override of either or both acts."

Formerly:
  IC 6–6–4–4. Acts 1969, c. 417, s. 4.
  Acts 1971, P.L.72, SEC.2.

Acts 1980, P.L.51, SEC.59.
Acts 1981, P.L.93, SEC.9.

Library References

Taxation ⚮1231.
WESTLAW Topic No. 371.

C.J.S. Taxation § 1233.
I.L.E. Taxation §§ 187 to 190.

Notes of Decisions

In general   1

_____

1. In general
  Since the 1971 amendment to IC 1971 6–6–4–4 [repealed; see, now, this section], the credit against taxes provision of the motor carrier fuel tax has been limited to the tax imposed and paid under this chapter, the motor carrier fuel tax [road tax] on travel on highways in Indiana, and then applicable only where gasoline and/or special fuel is purchased in Indiana, consumed out of state and gasoline and/or special fuel taxes [motor fuel tax] or motor carrier fuel tax [road tax] is paid to another state or jurisdiction. 1983 Op.Atty.Gen. No. 83–2.

6–6–4.1–7   Computation of credits; refunds; interest

Sec. 7.   (a) As used in this section, the credit of a carrier for any quarter is the amount by which the credit to which the carrier is entitled under section 6 of this chapter for that quarter exceeds the tax liability of the carrier under section 4 of this chapter for that quarter.

(b) The credit for any quarter shall be allowed as a credit against the tax for which the carrier would otherwise be liable in the quarter in which the credit accrued.

(c) A carrier is entitled to the refund of any credit not previously used to offset a tax liability or for any erroneously paid tax or penalty. To obtain the refund, the carrier shall submit to the department a properly completed application in accordance with rules adopted by the department under IC 4–22–2. The application must be submitted within three (3) years after the end of:

(1) the quarter in which the credit accrued; or

(2) the calendar year that contains the taxable period in which the tax or penalty was erroneously paid.

Along with the application, the carrier shall submit any evidence required by the department and any reports required by the department under this chapter.

(d) The department shall pay interest on any part of a refund that is not made within ninety (90) days after the date on which all of the following have been completed:

(1) The filing of:

(A) the properly completed application for refund; or

(B) the quarterly return on which a refund is claimed.

(2) The submission of any evidence required by the department of payment of the tax imposed under IC 6–6–1.1 or IC 6–6–2.5.

(3) The submission of reports required by the department under this chapter.

(4) The furnishing of a surety bond, letter of credit, or cash deposit under section 8 of this chapter.

(e) The department shall pay interest at the rate established under IC 6–8.1–9 from the date of:

(1) the refund application;

(2) the due date of a timely filed quarterly return on which a refund is claimed; or

(3) the filing date of a quarterly return on which a refund is claimed, if the quarterly refund is filed after the due date of the quarterly return;

to a date determined by the department that does not precede the date on which the refund is made by more than thirty (30) days.

As added by Acts 1982, P.L.59, SEC.1.   Amended by P.L.77–1985, SEC.29; P.L.97–1987, SEC.39; P.L.96–1989, SEC.11; P.L.69–1991, SEC.14; P.L.277–1993(ss), SEC.48.

Historical and Statutory Notes

P.L.77–1985, Sec.29, eff. Oct. 1, 1985, in Subsecs. (a) and (b), following "credit", deleted "balance"; in Subsec. (b), substituted "in the immediately following quarter" for "in any of the six (6) immediately following quarters"; in Subsec. (d)(1), substituted "properly completed application for refund" for "refund application"; and rewrote Subsec. (c), which formerly read:

"(c) A carrier is entitled to the refund of any credit balance not previously claimed as a credit or as a refund under this section. To obtain the refund, the carrier shall, within one (1) year after the end of the quarter in which the credit balance accrued, submit to the department a verified application in accordance with rules adopted by the department under IC 4–22–2. Along with the application, the carrier shall submit any evidence required by the department of payment of the tax imposed under IC 6–6–1.1 or IC 6–6–2.1. The department may not make a refund to the carrier until the department has audited the records of the carrier, unless:

"(1) the carrier has furnished a bond under section 8 of this chapter in an amount greater than the amount claimed as a refund; or

"(2) the department has not audited the records of the carrier within two (2) years after the date of application for the refund."

Section 37 of P.L.77–1985 was amended by Section 39 of P.L.59–1985 to change the effective date of the amendment of this section by P.L.77–1985 from Oct. 1, 1985 to July 1, 1985.

P.L.97–1987, Sec.39, eff. Sept. 1, 1987, in Subsec. (c), added "or for any erroneously paid tax or penalty" at the end of the first sentence; deleted "within one (1) year after the end of the quarter in which the credit accrued," following "shall" in the second sentence; inserted the third sentence; at the end of Subsec. (c), added "and any reports required by the department under this chapter"; and in Subd. (4) of Subsec. (d), substituted "bond, letter of credit, or cash deposit" for "bond".

P.L.96–1989, Sec.11, eff. Jan. 1, 1990.

P.L.96–1989, Sec.11, inserted Subsec. (d)(1)(B); designated Subsec. (e); and inserted Subsecs. (e)(2) and (e)(3).

P.L.69–1991, Sec.14, substituted at the end of subsec. (b) "quarter in which the credit accrued" for "immediately following quarter unless the carrier elects to claim a refund under subsection (c)".

P.L.277–1993(ss), Sec.48, eff. Oct. 1, 1993, in Subsec. (d)(2), substituted "IC 6–6–2.5" for "6–6–2.1".

Governor's veto of H.E.A.1001(ss)(P.L.277–1993(ss)) of the 1993 Special Session was overridden by General Assembly on June 30, 1993.

Section 32 of P.L.278–1993(ss), emerg. eff. retroactive to June 28, 1993, provides:

"(a) Notwithstanding the passage of HEA 1001ss–1993, the provisions of this act supersede the provisions of any conflicting provisions in HEA 1001ss–1993.

"(b) IC 1–1–3.1 does not apply to this act or to HEA 1001ss–1993.

"(c) Notwithstanding IC 1–1–3.1, the effective date of the Sections in this act and HEA 1001ss–1993 are as specified in this act and HEA 1001ss–1993, respectively, regardless of a veto of either act by the governor and the subsequent veto override of either or both acts."

Formerly:

IC 6–6–4–4.
IC 6–6–4–9.
Acts 1969, c. 417, ss. 4, 9.
Acts 1971, P.L.72, SECS.2, 4.
Acts 1980, P.L.51, SEC.59.
Acts 1981, P.L.93, SEC.9.

Library References

Taxation ☞1231.
WESTLAW Topic No. 371.
C.J.S. Taxation § 1233.

6–6–4.1–7.1   Class action for refund of tax; prerequisites

Sec. 7.1.   A class action for the refund of a tax subject to this chapter may not be maintained in any court, including the Indiana tax court, on behalf of any person who has not complied with the requirements of section 7 of this chapter before the certification of a class.   A refund of taxes to a member of a class in a class action is subject to the time limits set forth in section 7 of this chapter based on the time the class member filed the required claim for refund with the department.

As added by P.L.60–1990, SEC.5.   Amended by P.L.1–1991, SEC.66.

Historical and Statutory Notes

P.L.60–1990, Sec.5, emerg. eff. retroactive to Jan. 1, 1990.

P.L.1–1991, Sec.66, emerg. eff. upon passage April 23, 1991.

P.L.1–1991, Sec.66, substituted "section 7" for "section 76" in the second sentence.

6–6–4.1–8   Bond, letter of credit, or cash deposit; furnishing; release from liability; retaining cash deposit

Sec. 8.   (a) A carrier shall, at the request of the department and for cause, furnish a surety bond, letter of credit, or cash deposit to the department in order to ensure payment of the taxes imposed under this chapter and to permit the department to make a refund to the carrier under section 7 of this chapter. The bond, letter of credit, or cash deposit must be:

(1) in an amount of not less than two (2) times the amount of tax due or refund requested under this chapter for the reporting period applicable to the carrier, as determined by the department;

(2) payable to the state;

(3) conditioned that the carrier will pay all taxes for which the carrier is or becomes liable under this chapter from the date of the bond, letter of credit, or cash deposit to thirty (30) days after either the carrier, the surety, or the financial institution notifies the department that the bond, letter of credit, or cash deposit has been cancelled; and

(4) executed by a surety authorized under Indiana law in the case of a bond or by a financial institution approved by the commissioner in the case of a letter of credit.

(b) Sixty (60) days after making a written request for release to the commissioner, the surety of a bond furnished by a carrier is released from any liability to the state accruing on the bond after the sixty (60) day period. The release does not affect any liability accruing before the expiration of the sixty (60) day period.

(c) One hundred eighty (180) days after making a written request for release to the commissioner, the financial institution issuing the letter of credit for a carrier is released from any liability accruing on the letter of credit.

(d) The commissioner shall promptly notify the carrier furnishing the bond or letter of credit that a release has been requested. Unless the carrier furnishes a new bond within the sixty (60) day period or a new letter of credit within the one hundred eighty (180) day period, the commissioner shall cancel the carrier's annual permit.

(e) Sixty (60) days after making a written request for release to the commissioner, the cash deposit provided by a carrier is cancelled as security for any obligation accruing after the expiration of the sixty (60) day period. However, the administrator may retain all or part of the cash deposit for up to three (3) years and one (1) day as security for any obligation accruing before the effective date of the cancellation. Any part of the deposit that is not retained by the commissioner shall be released to the carrier. Before the expiration of the sixty (60) day period, the carrier must provide a bond or letter of credit or the commissioner shall cancel the carrier's annual permit.

(f) The department has cause for requiring security from a carrier under this section if:

(1) a carrier fails to file timely reports required by this chapter;

(2) a carrier fails to remit the tax imposed by this chapter; or

(3) an audit of a carrier's operations under this chapter causes the department to reasonably believe that tax collection or remittance required by this chapter is in jeopardy.

As added by Acts 1982, P.L.59, SEC.1. Amended by P.L.77–1985, SEC.30; P.L.97–1987, SEC.40; P.L.60–1990, SEC.6.

Historical and Statutory Notes

P.L.77–1985, Sec.30, eff. Sept. 1, 1985, in the first sentence, substituted "shall, at the request of the department" for "may"; following "chapter", deleted "without first auditing the carrier's records"; and, in Cl. (1), substituted "two thousand dollars ($2,000)" for "one thousand dollars ($1,000) nor more than twenty-five thousand dollars ($25,000)".

Section 37 of P.L.77–1985 was amended by Section 39 of P.L.59–1985 to change the effective date of the amendment of this section by P.L.77–1985 from Sept. 1, 1985 to July 1, 1985,

P.L.97–1987, Sec.40, eff. Sept. 1, 1987, rewrote the section, which previously read:

"(a) A carrier shall, at the request of the department, furnish a surety bond to the department in order to permit the department to make a refund to the carrier under section 7 of this chapter. The bond must be:

"(1) in an amount of not less than two thousand dollars ($2,000), as determined by the department;

"(2) payable to the state;

"(3) conditioned that the carrier will pay all taxes for which the carrier is or becomes liable under this chapter from the date of the bond to thirty (30) days after either the carrier or the surety notifies the department that the bond has been cancelled; and

"(4) executed by a surety authorized under Indiana law."

P.A.60-1990, Sec.6, eff. Jan. 1, 1991.

P.L.60-1990, Sec.6, inserted "and for cause" and "ensure payment of the taxes imposed under this chapter and to" in the first sentence of Subsec. (a); substituted "(2) times the amount

of tax due or refund requested under this chapter for the reporting period applicable to the carrier" for "thousand dollars ($2000)" in Subsec. (a)(1); and added Subsec. (f).

Formerly:

IC 6-6-4-9.

Acts 1969, c. 417, § 9.

Acts 1971, P.L.72, SEC.4.

Library References

Taxation ⊚1333 to 1336.
WESTLAW Topic No. 371.
C.J.S. Taxation § 1252.

6-6-4.1-9   Presumption of consumption rate

Sec. 9.   If there are no records showing the number of miles actually operated per gallon of motor fuel and if section 11(c) of this chapter is inapplicable, it is presumed for purposes of this chapter that one (1) gallon of motor fuel is consumed for every four (4) miles traveled.

As added by Acts 1982, P.L.59, SEC.1.

Historical and Statutory Notes

Formerly:
IC 6-6-4-7.
Acts 1969, c. 417, s. 7.

Library References

Taxation ⊚1316.
WESTLAW Topic No. 371.
C.J.S. Taxation § 1247.

6-6-4.1-10   Quarterly reports; exemptions

Sec. 10.   (a) Except as provided in section 13 of this chapter, each carrier subject to the tax imposed under this chapter shall submit to the department such quarterly reports of the operations of commercial motor vehicles giving rise to the carrier's tax liability as the department may require.   The carrier shall submit each quarterly report required under this subsection on or before the last day of the month immediately following that quarter.

(b) Subject to the restrictions of this subsection and subsection (c), the department may, by rules adopted under IC 4-22-2, exempt any carrier from the quarterly reporting requirements of this section.   The department may exempt only a carrier who submits an annual affidavit attesting that:

(1) all or substantially all of the mileage of the carrier in the previous calendar year was the result of operations in Indiana;

(2) all or substantially all of the motor fuel used in the operations of the carrier in the previous calendar year was purchased in Indiana;   or

(3) the carrier is from a state that has a reciprocity agreement with the state of Indiana relating to motor fuel taxes.

(c) The department may exempt carriers under subsection (b) only if:

(1) granting exemptions will not adversely affect the enforcement of this chapter; and

(2) the carriers that apply for exemptions purchased an equitable amount of motor fuel in Indiana.

(d) Each carrier shall submit to the department any other reports required by the department.

As added by Acts 1982, P.L.59, SEC.1.

Historical and Statutory Notes

Formerly:
IC 6–6–4–6.

Acts 1969, c. 417, s. 6.
Acts 1971, P.L.72, SEC.3.

Library References

Taxation ☞1313.
WESTLAW Topic No. 371.
C.J.S. Taxation § 1246.

Notes of Decisions

Out-of-state fuel purchases 1

_____

1. Out-of-state fuel purchases

The tax imposed under the motor carrier fuel tax law [this chapter] on the consumption of motor fuel [gasoline and/or special fuel] by a carrier in its operations in Indiana is imposed on all carriers who operate or cause to be operated on Indiana highways a commercial vehicle; however, carriers may be exempted from the quarterly reporting requirements by rules promulgated by the Indiana department of state revenue, may purchase a five day consecutive day trip permit in lieu of paying the motor carrier fuel tax [road tax] imposed, or, under a reciprocal agreement, may be exempted or have all or any part of the motor carrier fuel tax law waived with regard to motor carriers that use in Indiana motor fuel [gasoline or special fuel] upon which gasoline and/or special fuel taxes [motor fuel tax] or road tax [motor carrier fuel tax] has been paid to the other state or jurisdiction. 1983 Op.Atty.Gen. No. 83–2.

6–6–4.1–11 Pooled services; joint reports; calculation of tax; contents of reports

Sec. 11. (a) In lieu of filing individual reports under section 10 of this chapter, two (2) or more carriers regularly engaged in the transportation of passengers on through buses and through tickets in pooled service may make joint reports of their operations in Indiana. The tax imposed by this chapter shall be calculated on the basis of the joint reports as though the carriers were a single carrier. The carriers making the reports are jointly and severally liable for the tax.

(b) Joint reports made under subsection (a) must show the total number of miles traveled in Indiana and the total number of gallons of motor fuel purchased in Indiana by the reporting carriers. Credits or refunds to which the carriers making a joint return are entitled are not allowed as credits or refunds to any other carrier. Carriers filing joint reports shall permit all carriers engaged in pooled operations with them in Indiana to join them in filing joint reports.

(c) For purposes of this chapter, there is a rebuttable presumption that the vehicles of carriers filing joint reports consumed one (1) gallon of motor fuel for every six (6) miles traveled.

As added by Acts 1982, P.L.59, SEC.1.

Historical and Statutory Notes

Formerly:
    IC 6–6–4–11.
    Acts 1969, c. 417, s. 11.

Library References

Taxation ☞1313.   C.J.S. Taxation § 1246.
WESTLAW Topic No. 371.   I.L.E. Taxation §§ 187 to 190.

6–6–4.1–12   Annual permit, cab card, and emblem

Sec. 12.   (a) Except as authorized under section 13 of this chapter, a carrier may operate a commercial motor vehicle upon the highways in Indiana only if the carrier has been issued an annual permit, cab card, and emblem under this section.

(b) The department shall issue:

(1) an annual permit; and

(2) a cab card and an emblem for each commercial motor vehicle that will be operated by the carrier upon the highways in Indiana;

to a carrier who applies for an annual permit and pays to the department an annual permit fee of twenty-five dollars ($25).

(c) The annual permit, cab card, and emblem are effective from January 1 of each year through December 31 of the same year. The department may extend the expiration date of the annual permit, cab card, and emblem for no more than sixty (60) days. The annual permit, each cab card, and each emblem issued to a carrier remain the property of this state and may be suspended or revoked by the department for any violation of this chapter or of the rules concerning this chapter adopted by the department under IC 4–22–2.

(d) As evidence of compliance with this section, and for the purpose of enforcement, a carrier shall display on each commercial motor vehicle an emblem when the vehicle is being operated by the carrier in Indiana. The carrier shall affix the emblem to the vehicle in the location designated by the department. The carrier shall display in each vehicle the cab card issued by the department. The carrier shall retain the original annual permit at the address shown on the annual permit. During the month of December, the carrier shall display the cab card and emblem that are valid through December 31 or a full year cab card and emblem issued to the carrier for the ensuing twelve (12) months. If the department grants an extension of the expiration date, the carrier shall continue to display the cab card and emblem upon which the extension was granted.

(e) If a commercial motor vehicle is operated by more than one (1) carrier, as evidence of compliance with this section and for purposes of enforcement each carrier shall display in the commercial motor vehicle a reproduced copy of the carrier's annual permit when the vehicle is being operated by the carrier in Indiana.

(f) A person who fails to display an emblem required by this section on a commercial motor vehicle, does not have proof in the vehicle that the annual permit has been obtained, and operates that vehicle on an Indiana highway commits a Class C infraction. Each day of operation without an emblem constitutes a separate infraction. Notwithstanding IC 34–28–5–4, a judgment of not less than one hundred dollars ($100) shall be entered for each Class C infraction under this subsection.

(g) A person who displays an altered, false, or fictitious cab card required by this section in a commercial motor vehicle, does not have proof in the vehicle that the annual permit has been obtained, and operates that vehicle on an Indiana highway commits a Class C infraction. Each day of operation with an altered, false, or fictitious cab card constitutes a separate infraction.

As added by Acts 1982, P.L.59, SEC.1. Amended by P.L.77–1985, SEC.31; P.L.8–1988, SEC.6; P.L.60–1990, SEC.7; P.L.69–1991, SEC.15; P.L.1–1998, SEC.82.

Historical and Statutory Notes

P.L.77–1985, Sec.31, eff. Sept. 1, 1985, in Subsec. (b), increased the permit fee from $5 to $25.

Section 37 of P.L.77–1985 was amended by Section 39 of P.L.59–1985 to change the effective date of the amendment of this section by P.L.77–1985 from Sept. 1, 1985 to July 1, 1985.

P.L. 8–1988, Sec.6, eff. April 1, 1989, inserted provisions requiring carriers to possess and display cab cards and emblems; and added Subsecs. (e), (f), and (g).

P.L.60–1990, Sec.7, eff. Jan. 1, 1991, changed the dates in Subsecs. (c) and (d) from "April" to "January" and "March" to "December"; in the

first sentence of Subsec. (c), substituted "same" for "next succeeding"; and, in the third sentence of Subsec. (d), substituted "by the department" for "with the emblem for that vehicle".

P.L.69–1991, Sec.15, substituted 60 for 30 days in the second sentence of subsec. (c).

P.L.1–1998, Sec.82, amended the section by substituting "IC 34–28–5–4" for "IC 34–4–32–4" in Subsec. (f).

Formerly:

IC 6–6–4–14.
Acts 1969, c. 417, s. 14.
Acts 1971, P.L.72, SEC.6.

Library References

Licenses ⊕16(9).
WESTLAW Topic No. 238.

C.J.S. Licenses § 34.
I.L.E. Taxation §§ 187 to 190.

6-6-4.1-13 Trip permits; repair and maintenance permits; repair, maintenance, and relocation permits

Sec. 13. (a) A carrier may, in lieu of paying the tax imposed under this chapter that would otherwise result from the operation of a particular commercial motor vehicle, obtain from the department a trip permit authorizing the carrier to operate the commercial motor vehicle for a period of five (5) consecutive days. The department shall specify the beginning and ending days on the face of the permit. The fee for a trip permit for each commercial motor vehicle is fifty dollars ($50). The report otherwise required under section 10 of this chapter is not required with respect to a vehicle for which a trip permit has been issued under this subsection.

(b) The department may issue a temporary written authorization if unforeseen or uncertain circumstances require operations by a carrier of a commercial motor vehicle for which neither a trip permit described in subsection (a) nor an annual permit described in section 12 of this chapter has been obtained. A temporary authorization may be issued only if the department finds that undue hardship would result if operation under a temporary authorization were prohibited. A carrier who receives a temporary authorization shall:

    (1) pay the trip permit fee at the time the temporary authorization is issued; or

    (2) subsequently apply for and obtain an annual permit.

(c) A carrier may obtain a repair and maintenance permit to:

    (1) travel from another state into Indiana to repair or maintain any of the carrier's motor vehicles, semitrailers (as defined in IC 9–13–2–164), or trailers (as defined in IC 9–13–2–184); and

    (2) return to the same state after the repair or maintenance is completed.

The fee for the permit is forty dollars ($40). The permit is an annual permit and applies to all of the motor vehicles operated by the carrier. The permit is not transferable to another carrier. A carrier may not carry cargo or passengers under the permit. A carrier may operate a motor vehicle under the permit in lieu of paying the tax imposed under this chapter. The report otherwise required under section 10 of this chapter is not required with respect to a motor vehicle that is operated under the permit.

(d) A carrier may obtain a repair, maintenance, and relocation permit to:

    (1) move a yard tractor from a terminal or loading or spotting facility to:

        (A) a maintenance or repair facility; or

        (B) another terminal or loading or spotting facility; and

    (2) return the yard tractor to its place of origin.

The fee for the permit is forty dollars ($40). The permit is an annual permit and applies to all yard tractors operated by the carrier. The permit is not transferable to another carrier. A carrier may not carry cargo or transport or draw a semitrailer or other vehicle under the permit. A carrier may operate a yard tractor under the permit instead of paying the tax imposed under this chapter. A yard tractor that is being operated on a public highway under this subsection must display a license plate issued under IC 9–18–32. As used in this section, "yard tractor" has the meaning set forth under IC 9–13–2–201.

(e) The department shall establish procedures, by rules adopted under IC 4–22–2, for:

(1) the issuance and use of trip permits, temporary authorizations, and repair and maintenance permits; and

(2) the display in commercial motor vehicles of evidence of compliance with this chapter.

As added by Acts 1982, P.L.59, SEC.1. Amended by P.L.77–1985, SEC.32; P.L.59–1985, SEC.19; P.L.46–1994, SEC.1; P.L.88–1998, SEC.1.

Historical and Statutory Notes

P.L.59–1985, Sec.19, emerg. eff. July 1, 1985, inserted "motor" preceding "vehicle" twice in the first sentence of Subsec. (a); and substituted, in the third sentence of Subsec. (a), "for each commercial motor vehicle is fifty dollars ($50)" for "is twenty-five dollars ($25)".

P.L.77–1985, Sec.32, eff. Sept. 1, 1985, in Subsec. (a), increased the fee from $5 to $25.

Section 37 of P.L.77–1985 was amended by Section 39 of P.L.59–1985 to change the effective date of the amendment of this section by P.L.77–1985 from Sept. 1, 1985 to July 1, 1985.

P.L.46–1994, Sec.1, added a new Subsec. (c), redesignated former Subsec. (c) as Subsec. (d), and provided therein for repair and maintenance permits.

P.L.88–1998, Sec.1, amended the section by adding new Subsec. (d); and redesignating former Subsec. (d) as new Subsec. (e).

P.L.88–1998, Sec.5, emerg. eff. March 12, 1998, provides:

"(a) Notwithstanding IC 6–6–4.1–13(d), as added by this act, a yard tractor may be operated on a public highway if it displays a temporary permit issued under subsection (b).

"(b) Notwithstanding IC 9–18–32, as added by this act, the bureau of motor vehicles shall issue a temporary permit designed for display on a yard tractor that designates the yard tractor as a tractor permitted to operate on a public highway under IC 6–6–4.1–13(d).

"(c) This section expires July 1, 1999."

Formerly:

IC 6–6–4–13.

Acts 1969, c. 417, s. 13.

Acts 1971, P.L.72, SEC.5.

Cross References

Design and manufacture of license plates, see IC 9–18–32–2.
Issuance of license plate, see IC 9–18–32–1.
Yard tractor, defined, see IC 9–13–2–201.

Library References

Licenses ☞16(9).
Taxation ☞1331.
WESTLAW Topic Nos. 238, 371.

C.J.S. Licenses § 34.
C.J.S. Taxation § 1250.

Notes of Decisions

Out-of-state fuel purchases 1

------

1. Out-of-state fuel purchases

The tax imposed under the motor carrier fuel tax law [this chapter] on the consumption of motor fuel [gasoline and/or special fuel] by a carrier in its operations in Indiana is imposed on all carriers who operate or cause to be operated on Indiana highways a commercial vehicle; however, carriers may be exempted from the quarterly reporting requirements by rules promulgated by the Indiana department of state revenue, may purchase a five day consecutive day trip permit in lieu of paying the motor carrier fuel tax [road tax] imposed, or, under a reciprocal agreement, may be exempted or have all or any part of the motor carrier fuel tax law waived with regard to motor carriers that use in Indiana motor fuel [gasoline or special fuel] upon which gasoline and/or special fuel taxes [motor fuel tax] or road tax [motor carrier fuel tax] has been paid to the other state or jurisdiction. 1983 Op.Atty.Gen. No. 83–2.

6–6–4.1–14   Reciprocity

Sec. 14.   (a) The commissioner or, with his approval, the reciprocity commission created by IC 9–28–4 may enter into a reciprocal agreement with the appropriate official or officials from any other state or jurisdiction under which all or any part of the requirements of this chapter are waived with respect to motor carriers that use in Indiana motor fuel upon which tax has been paid to the other state or jurisdiction.   An agreement may be made under this subsection only with a state or jurisdiction that grants equivalent privileges with respect to motor fuel consumed in the other state or jurisdiction and on which a tax has been paid to this state.

(b) The commissioner or, with his approval, the reciprocity commission created by IC 9–28–4 may enter into a reciprocal agreement with the appropriate official or officials of any other state or jurisdiction to exempt commercial motor vehicles licensed in the other state or jurisdiction from any of the requirements that would otherwise be imposed by this chapter, including the requirements for trip permits, temporary authorizations, repair and maintenance permits, and annual permits and the payment of fees for permits and authorizations.   An agreement may be made under this subsection only with a state or jurisdiction that grants equivalent exemptions to motor vehicles licensed in Indiana.

As added by Acts 1982, P.L.59, SEC.1.   Amended by P.L.2–1991, SEC.43; P.L.46–1994, SEC.2.

Historical and Statutory Notes

P.L.2–1991, Sec.43, substituted "IC 9–28–4" for "IC 9–7–7" in two places.

P.L.46–1994, Sec.2, modified Subsec. (b) to provide for repair and maintenance permits.

Formerly:

IC 6–6–4–18.

Acts 1971, P.L.72, SEC.7.

Library References

Taxation ⚙1331.
WESTLAW Topic No. 371.
C.J.S. Taxation § 1250.

Notes of Decisions

Out-of-state fuel purchases   1

---

1.   Out-of-state fuel purchases

The tax imposed under the motor carrier fuel tax law [this chapter] on the consumption of motor fuel [gasoline and/or special fuel] by a carrier in its operations in Indiana is imposed on all carriers who operate or cause to be operated on Indiana highways a commercial vehicle; however, carriers may be exempted from the quarterly reporting requirements by rules promulgated by the Indiana department of state revenue, may purchase a five day consecutive day trip permit in lieu of paying the motor carrier fuel tax [road tax] imposed, or, under a reciprocal agreement, may be exempted or have all or any part of the motor carrier fuel tax law waived with regard to motor carriers that use in Indiana motor fuel [gasoline or special fuel] upon which gasoline and/or special fuel taxes [motor fuel tax] or road tax [motor carrier fuel tax] has been paid to the other state or jurisdiction. 1983 Op.Atty.Gen. No. 83–2.

6–6–4.1–15   Enforcement

Sec. 15. The commissioner shall enforce this chapter. The state police department shall assist the commissioner in the enforcement of this chapter. *As added by Acts 1982, P.L.59, SEC.1.*

Historical and Statutory Notes

Formerly:
  IC 6–6–4–19.
  Acts 1971, P.L.72, SEC.8.

Cross References

Revenue department, tax administration, see IC 6–8.1–1–1 et seq.
Weigh station personnel, see IC 10–1–1–25.

Library References

  I.L.E. Taxation §§ 187 to 190.

6–6–4.1–16   Agreements for cooperative audit of reports and returns

Sec. 16. The department may enter into agreements for the cooperative audit of the reports and returns of carriers with the appropriate authorities of any other state or jurisdiction that imposes a tax similar to the tax imposed under this chapter. An officer or employee of another state or jurisdiction who audits reports and returns under an agreement made under this section is considered an authorized agent of this state for the purpose of the audit. A cooperative audit conducted under an agreement made under this section has the same effect as an audit conducted by the department.
As added by Acts 1982, P.L.59, SEC.1.

Historical and Statutory Notes

Formerly:
  IC 6–6–4–5.
  Acts 1969, c. 417, s. 5.

Library References

Taxation ☞1313.
WESTLAW Topic No. 371.
C.J.S. Taxation § 1246.

6–6–4.1–17   Suspension or revocation of permit or temporary authorization; reinstatement

Sec. 17. If a carrier:

(1) fails to file a quarterly report required by this chapter;

(2) fails to pay the tax imposed under section 4 or section 4.5 of this chapter;

(3) files a report after the date established under this chapter; or

(4) with respect to a listed tax (as defined in IC 6–8.1–1–1), fails to file all tax returns or information reports or to pay all taxes, penalties, and interest;

the commissioner may suspend or revoke any annual permit, trip permit, temporary authorization, or repair and maintenance permit issued to the carrier. The commissioner may reinstate a permit or temporary authorization if a carrier files all required returns and reports and pays all outstanding liabilities.

As added by Acts 1982, P.L.59, SEC.1.   Amended by P.L.77–1985, SEC.33; P.L.59–1985, SEC.20; P.L.46–1994, SEC.3.

Historical and Statutory Notes

P.L.77–1985, Sec.33, eff. Sept. 1, 1985, inserted Cl. (4); and added the last sentence.

Section 37 of P.L.77–1985 was amended by Section 39 of P.L.59–1985 to change the effective date of the amendment of this section by P.L.77–1985 from Sept. 1, 1985 to July 1, 1985.

P.L.59–1985, Sec.20, emerg. eff. July 1, 1985, inserted, in Subd. (2), "or section 4.5".

P.L.46–1994, Sec.3, provided near the end of the section for repair and maintenance permits.

Formerly:

IC 6–6–4–20.
Acts 1971, P.L.72, SEC.9.
Acts 1978, P.L.2, SEC.640.
Acts 1979, P.L.80, SEC.7.
Acts 1980, P.L.61, SEC.11.

Cross References

Penalties for infractions, see IC 34–28–5–4.

Library References

Taxation ☞1313, 1342.
WESTLAW Topic No. 371.
C.J.S. Taxation §§ 1246, 1255.

6–6–4.1–18   Violations; penalties

Sec. 18.   (a) A person who knowingly makes a false statement or knowingly presents a fraudulent receipt for the sale of motor fuel for the purpose of:

(1) obtaining;

(2) attempting to obtain; or

(3) assisting any other person to obtain or attempt to obtain;

a credit, refund, or reduction of liability for the tax imposed under this chapter commits a Class C infraction.

(b) A carrier who knowingly violates this chapter, except for a violation covered by section 17 of this chapter, commits a Class C infraction.

As added by Acts 1982, P.L.59, SEC.1.

Historical and Statutory Notes

Formerly:

IC 6–6–4–20.
Acts 1971, P.L.72, SEC.9.

Acts 1978, P.L.2, SEC.640.
Acts 1979, P.L.80, SEC.7.
Acts 1980, P.L.61, SEC.11.

6–6–4.1–19 Impoundment of commercial motor vehicle; release of cargo

Sec. 19. (a) The department or the state police department may impound a carrier's commercial motor vehicle if:

(1) the carrier has not obtained an annual permit, a trip permit, a temporary authorization, or a repair and maintenance permit (as required under sections 12 through 13 of this chapter) and the vehicle is operating on an Indiana highway;

(2) there is not an emblem displayed on the vehicle as required by section 12 of this chapter, the driver does not have proof in the vehicle that the annual permit has been obtained, and the vehicle is operating on an Indiana highway; or

(3) the cab card required under section 12 of this chapter is altered, false, or fictitious, the driver does not have proof in the vehicle that the annual permit has been obtained, and the vehicle is operating on an Indiana highway.

(b) To obtain possession of a vehicle impounded under this section, the carrier must first obtain:

(1) the annual permit, trip permit, temporary authorization, or repair and maintenance permit;

(2) a cab card; and

(3) an emblem for the vehicle;

as required by this chapter.

(c) Any cargo in an impounded vehicle shall be released, if the cargo is to be loaded into another commercial motor vehicle that is in compliance with this chapter.

As added by P.L.97–1987, SEC.41. Amended by P.L.8–1988, SEC.7; P.L.46–1994, SEC.4.

Historical and Statutory Notes

P.L.97–1987, Sec.41, adding this section, was made effective Sept. 1, 1987.

P.L. 8–1988, Sec.7, eff. April 1, 1988, rewrote the section, which had read:

"(a) The commissioner may impound a carrier's commercial motor vehicle if the carrier:

"(1) has not obtained an annual permit, a trip permit, or a temporary authorization as required under sections 12 through 13 of this chapter; and

"(2) is operating the commercial motor vehicle on an Indiana highway.

"(b) The commissioner may authorize the state police department to impound a commercial motor vehicle under subsection (a) on behalf of the department of state revenue.

"(c) To obtain possession of a vehicle impounded under this section, the carrier must first obtain the annual permit, trip permit, or temporary authorization required by this chapter.

"(d) Any cargo in an impounded vehicle shall be released, if the cargo is to be loaded into another commercial motor vehicle that is in compliance with this chapter."

P.L.46–1994, Sec.4, inserted provision for repair and maintenance permits in Subsecs. (a)(1) and (b)(1).

6–6–4.1–20   Failure to keep books and records; penalty

Sec. 20.   A person subject to the taxes imposed under sections 4 through 4.5 of this chapter who fails to keep the books and records as required by IC 6–8.1–5 is subject to the penalty imposed under IC 6–8.1–10–4.

As added by P.L.97–1987, SEC.42.

Historical and Statutory Notes

P.L.97–1987, Sec.42, adding this section, was made effective Sept. 1, 1987.

6–6–4.1–21   Failure to file report; civil penalty

Sec. 21.   A person subject to the taxes imposed under sections 4 through 4.5 of this chapter who fails to file a quarterly report as required by section 10 of this chapter shall pay a civil penalty of three hundred dollars ($300) for each report that is not filed.

As added by P.L.97–1987, SEC.43.

Historical and Statutory Notes

P.L.97–1987, Sec.43, adding this section, was made effective Sept. 1, 1987.

Library References

Taxation ⬦1342.
WESTLAW Topic No. 371.
C.J.S. Taxation § 1255.

6–6–4.1–22   Interest on nonpayment

Sec. 22.   (a) If a person:

(1) fails to file a return for taxes due under this chapter;

(2) fails to pay the full amount of tax shown on the person's return by the due date for the return or the payment; or

(3) incurs a deficiency upon a determination by the department;

the person is subject to interest on the nonpayment.

(b) The interest for a failure described in subsection (a) is the rate of interest calculated under the interest provisions of the Base State Fuel Tax Agreement entered into by the department under IC 6–8.1–3–14.

As added by P.L.60–1990, SEC.8.

Historical and Statutory Notes
P.L.60–1990, Sec.8, eff. Jan. 1, 1991.

6–6–4.1–23 Penalty

Sec. 23. (a) If a person:

(1) fails to file a return for the tax due under this chapter on or by the due date for the return;

(2) fails to pay the full amount of tax shown on the person's return on or by the due date for the payment; or

(3) incurs, upon examination by the department, a deficiency that is due to negligence;

the person is subject to a penalty.

(b) The penalty for a failure described in subsection (a) is the penalty calculated under the penalty provisions of the Base State Fuel Tax Agreement entered into by the department under IC 6–8.1–3–14.

As added by P.L.60–1990, SEC.9. Amended by P.L.1–1991, SEC.67.

Historical and Statutory Notes
P.L.60–1990, Sec.9, eff. Jan. 1, 1991.
P.L.1–1991, Sec.67, emerg. eff. April 23, 1991.

P.L.1–1991, Sec.67, deleted "or" following "chapter" in Subsec. (a)(1).

6–6–4.1–24 Proposed assessment; protest; hearing

Sec. 24. (a) If the department believes that a person has not reported the proper amount of tax due, the department shall make a proposed assessment of the amount of the unpaid tax on the basis of the best information available to the department. The amount of the assessment is:

(1) considered a tax payment not made by the due date;

(2) subject to sections 22 and 23 of this chapter; and

(3) subject to IC 6–8.1–10 concerning the imposition of penalties and interest.

(b) The department shall issue notice and prescribe a period for payment and protest under the provisions of the Base State Fuel Tax Agreement entered into by the department pursuant to IC 6–8.1–3–14. The notice of proposed assessment is prima facie evidence that the department's claim for the unpaid tax is valid. The burden of proving that the proposed assessment is wrong rests with the person against whom the proposed assessment is made. If the person files a protest and requires a hearing on the protest, the department shall set the hearing at the department's earliest convenient time and shall notify the person by United States mail of the time, date, and location of the hearing. The department may hold the hearing at the location of the department's choice in Indiana.

As added by P.L.60–1990, SEC.10.

Historical and Statutory Notes

P.L.60–1990, Sec.10, eff. Jan. 1, 1991.

6–6–4.1–25   Registration or licensure of vehicle required to obtain annual motor carrier fuel tax permit or license; proof of issuance of permit or license

Sec. 25. This section applies whenever the owner is required by law to obtain an annual motor carrier fuel tax permit or a license under a base state fuel tax agreement under IC 6–8.1–3–14 from the department. The bureau of motor vehicles may not register or license a motor bus, truck, tractor, trailer, or semitrailer used or intended to be used by the owner for transportation of property until the owner furnishes the bureau of motor vehicles with reasonable proof that the owner has a permit or license issued by the department. *As added by P.L.69–1991, SEC.16.*

6–6–4.1–26   Issuance of excess size or weight permit; proof of registration under this chapter or Base State Fuel Tax Agreement

Sec. 26. A special permit may not be issued under IC 9–20–6 to a carrier that is required to be registered under this chapter or under a Base State Fuel Tax Agreement under IC 6–8.1–3–14 until the carrier furnishes reasonable proof of registration:

(1) under this chapter or under a Base State Fuel Tax Agreement under IC 6–8.1–3–14; and

(2) under IC 9–18–2, if applicable.

As added by P.L.69–1991, SEC.17. Amended by P.L.1–1992, SEC.21.

Historical and Statutory Notes

P.L.1–1992, Sec.21, emerg. eff. Feb. 21, 1992, made corrective changes.

6–6–4.1–27   Information sharing; confidential information

Sec. 27. (a) Notwithstanding IC 6–8.1–7 and IC 9–14–3–1, the department, the bureau of motor vehicles, and the Indiana department of transportation shall share the information regarding motor carriers and motor vehicles that is reasonably necessary for the effective administration and enforcement of IC 6–6–4.1, IC 8–2.1, and IC 9.

(b) For purposes of this section, the department may not divulge information:

(1) regarding the motor carrier fuel taxes paid by specific motor carriers; or

(2) contained on quarterly tax reports of specific motor carriers.

The department may provide statistical information that does not identify the amount of tax paid by a specific carrier.

As added by P.L.69–1991, SEC.18. Amended by P.L.1–1992, SEC.22.

Historical and Statutory Notes

P.L.1–1992, Sec.22, emerg. eff. Feb. 21, 1992,
made corrective changes.

INDEX TO TITLE 6

See volume containing end of Title

†